America Goes Green

America Goes Green

An Encyclopedia of Eco-Friendly
Culture in the United States

Volume 1: Thematic Entries

KIM KENNEDY WHITE, Editor

LESLIE A. DURAM, Contributing Editor

ABC-CLIO

Santa Barbara, California • Denver, Colorado • Oxford, England

Library of Congress Cataloging-in-Publication Data

America goes green : an encyclopedia of eco-friendly culture in the United States / Kim Kennedy White, editor.
 Contents: Volume 1: Thematic Entries; Volume 2: Thematic Entries and Primary Documents; Volume 3: The States Go Green.
 Includes bibliographical references and index.
 ISBN 978-1-59884-657-7 (hardcover : alk. paper)—ISBN 978-1-59884-658-4 (ebook)
1. Sustainable living—United States—Encyclopedias. 2. Environmentalism—United States—Encyclopedias. I. White, Kim Kennedy.
 GE197.A63 2013
 363.700973'03—dc23

                         2012030501

ISBN: 978-1-59884-657-7
EISBN: 978-1-59884-658-4

17 16 15 14 13 1 2 3 4 5

This book is also available on the World Wide Web as an eBook.
Visit www.abc-clio.com for details.

ABC-CLIO, LLC
130 Cremona Drive, P.O. Box 1911
Santa Barbara, California 93116-1911

This book is printed on acid-free paper ∞

Manufactured in the United States of America

Contents

Preface   xiii
Acknowledgments   xv
Special Note from the Editor   xvii
Introduction   xix
Social Pressures and Processes of "Going Green" in America
  Kathleen O'Halleran   xxi

Volume 1: Thematic Entries

Activism and Community Green Efforts   1
  Community Economic Development and Substantive Participation   1
  Earth Day   6
  Earth First!   9
  Ecovillage   12
  Environmental Justice   16
  Goldman Environmental Prize   23
  Green and Sustainability Fairs and Festivals   27
  Green Backlash   30
  Green Movement   31
  The Green Scare   40
  Living off the Grid   42
  Sierra Club v. Morton (1972): Greenovation Spotlight   45
  Wise-Use Movement   47
  Youth Organizations   49
Arts, Entertainment, and Media   53
  American Writers and the Environment   53
  Art, Environmental   62
  Blogs   68
  Celebrities   72
  Ecopoetics   75
  Ecorazzi   77
  Green Cinema   78
  Green Documentaries and Films   81
  Green Publishing Efforts   83
  Humor   84

Journalism and News   87
Literature, Environmental   95
Musicians, Festivals, and Radio Stations   104
Rachel Carson's *Silent Spring*: Greenovator Spotlight   109
Social Networking Sites   112
Television, Eco-Friendly Channels   115
Television, Nature and Wildlife TV   117
Video Games   124
Economics, Business, and Industry   127
Advertising   127
Agriculture   132
Airlines   139
Automobile   143
Biobased and Engineered Fibers   149
Businesses Active in Environmental Issues   153
Carbon Credits   157
Co-Ops   159
Ecotourism   162
Fair Trade   168
Farming, Conventional   171
Farming, Organic   174
Green Buildings   181
Green Cities   189
Green Entrepreneurship   192
Green Marketing   194
Greenwashing   198
Product Labeling   204
Real Estate   208
Restaurants, Adaptive Reuse in Urban Architecture   211
Socially Responsible Investments   215
Education and Employment   219
Environmental Education Act of 1970   219
Environmental and Sustainable Community State Education   220
Green Colleges and Universities   226
Green Jobs   228
Higher Education Models, Green Curriculum   231
Indigenous Entrepreneurship and Sustainability: A Case Study—
College of Menominee Nation Campus Grind Coffee Shop   236
K–12 Green Curriculum   242
Environment   249
Carbon Footprint   249
Energy   252
Energy Audits   262
Forestry and Gifford Pinchot: Greenovation Spotlight   265

Global Warming 267
Land and Habitat Reclamation and Restoration 270
National Park Service 273
Ocean Restoration and Conservation 277
Offshore Drilling 282
Permaculture 285
Pesticides 288
Population 291
Public Perceptions and Actions around Climate Change 293
Recycling 306
Rivers and Dams 308
U.S. Environmental Protection Agency 312
Water Quality and Use 314
Wildlife, Conservation and Preservation Organizations 318
Wildlife, Impact of Eco-friendly Practices and Awareness 323
Food and Drink 331
  Brewing, Eco-Friendly 331
  Corporate Food Service and Farm to Table Sustainability 334
  Diet, Vegetarian and Vegan 337
  Food and Diet 341
  Food and Entertaining 345
  Food, Drink, and Media 348
  Genetically Modified Organisms 352
  Grocers, Green 355
  Local and Sustainable Food 362
  Organic and Natural Foods 366
  Restaurants 372
  Urban Agriculture 377
Health, Home, and Garden 385
  Animal Companions 385
  Beauty, Cosmetics, and Makeup 387
  Complementary and Alternative Medicine 391
  Composting and Vericomposting 398
  Eco-therapy 402
  Garden, Home 405
  Green Funerals 408
  Home Furnishings and Interior Design 411
  Hospitals and Health Care 414
  Landscaping and Xeriscaping 418
  Lighting Design, Sustainable 422
  Population and Family 426
  Textiles for Furniture and Fashion 428
  Toys and Collectibles 431
  Travel 434

Volume 2: Thematic Entries and Primary Documents

Philosophy and Religion   437
  Biophilia   437
  Buddhist Responses to Green   440
  Christian Responses to Green   443
  Creation Care Movement   446
  Earth-Centered Religious Responses to Green   449
  Ecology and Christian Theology   452
  Environmental Pragmatism   455
  Jewish Responses to Green   458
  Muslims in America and Responses to Green   461
  Philosophical Stances on the Environment   464
  Queer Ecology   467
Politics and Law   471
  Introduction to Green Politics   471
  Joseph R. Biden Jr. (1942–): Greenovator Spotlight   476
  William O. Douglas: Greenovator Spotlight   478
  Environment as a Political Issue   479
  Albert Arnold Gore Jr.: Greenovator Spotlight   484
  The Green Party   488
  Green Political Parties   491
  Lyndon Johnson: Greenovator Spotlight   493
  Robert Kennedy Jr.: Greenovator Spotlight   497
  Law and the Environment   499
  Edmund Muskie: Greenovator Spotlight   505
  Right-to-Know Legislation   506
  Theodore Roosevelt: Greenovator Spotlight   508
Science and Technology   511
  Alternative and Renewable Energy   511
  Biofuels   520
  City and Community Planning, Eco-Friendly   524
  Coal Mining   527
  E-Waste   531
  Green Technology Companies   534
  Innovation and Invention Competitions   538
  LED Lighting   540
  Leadership in Energy and Environmental Design (LEED)   542
  Mobile Phones   547
  Frederick Law Olmsted: Greenovator Spotlight   549
  Rare Metals and Green Technologies   552
  Technology and the Impact on Green   554
  Transportation, Automobiles   556
  Transportation, Bicycles   562
  Transportation, Mass Transit   569

Waste Management   573
Water and Air Purification   579
Sports and Leisure   585
Amusement and Theme Parks   585
Blue Ribbon Coalition   591
Eco-Athletes   593
Let's Move! Outside Campaign   596
Museums   601
National Parks   604
Olympic Games   610
Outdoor Leisure: Greening within a Typical Parks System   612
Parks, State and Local   616
Sport Facilities and Event Centers   618
Trails   625
X-Games   629
Zoos and Aquariums   632

Documents

Animal Enterprise Protection Act: Public Law 102-346—August 26, 1992   635
Animal Enterprise Terrorism Act: Public Law 109-374—
    November 27, 2006   637
BioPreferred Program, United States Department of Agriculture   641
Bottled Drinking Water Standards   644
Bottled Water Report Summary from the Government
    Accountability Office   646
Brief Comparison of State Laws on Electronics Recycling   649
Childhood Obesity Facts   658
ChooseMyPlate.gov   660
Conservation Reserve Program   666
Dietary Guidelines for Americans, 2010   669
Electronics Waste Management in the United States through 2009,
    Executive Summary, Environmental Protection Agency; May, 2011   673
Electronic Waste Recycling Act of 2003, California   677
Electronic Waste Recycling Act of 2008, New Jersey   690
Environmental Tips for Earth Day   693
Executive Order on Federal Leadership in Environmental,
    Energy, and Economic Performance   697
Executive Order 12898 on Environmental Justice   700
Federal Energy Management Program Fact Sheet,
    U.S. Department of Energy   706
Federal Trade Commission (FTC) Facts for Consumers,
    EnergyGuide; Appliance Shopping with the EnergyGuide Label   709
Fight the Frost This Winter: ENERGY STAR Offers Tips to
    Keep Warm, Save Energy, and Help the Environment   711

Gas Mileage Tips, Energy Efficiency and Renewable Energy,
    U.S. Department of Energy   713
GreenFaith, Interfaith Partners for the Environment;
    Mission and Areas of Focus   717
Green Guide for New Businesses   719
Green Jobs, Bureau of Labor Statistics Jobs Initiative   721
Green Ribbon Schools Recognition Award   724
Green Your Holiday Scene   725
How a Product Earns the Energy Star Label   727
Leadership in Energy and Environmental Design (LEED)   728
Memorandum of Understanding on Environmental Justice
    and Executive Order 12898   733
Merchandising: Products/Packaging Sustainability Resources   739
Model Electronic Recycling Legislation, An Act Providing
    for the Recovery and Recycling of Used Electronic Devices   743
National Environmental Education Act of 1990   751
National Environmental Policy Act   771
Natural Resources Conservation Service Watershed
    and Easement Program   780
Organic Labeling and Marketing Information, National
    Organic Program   788
Paving the Way Toward Cleaner, More Efficient Trucks Fact Sheet,
    National Highway Traffic Safety Administration   789
President's Environmental Youth Award   791
The Presidential Green Chemistry Challenge   798
Proceedings Report from the Sustainability Education Summit   802
Questions About Your Community: What Can I Do to
    Help the Environment When I Travel for the Holidays or
    an Upcoming Meeting?   821
Reducing Holiday Waste   823
Summary of Recent Federal Agency Environmental
    Education Projects, 2011   824
Ten Tips for Hiring a Heating and Cooling Contractor   826
Tips to Save Gas and Improve Mileage, U.S. Environmental
    Protection Agency   827
Top Cities with the Most Energy Star Certified Buildings in 2010   828
Toxic 100: Top Air Polluters Index   829

Volume 3: The States Go Green

Midwest   835
    Illinois   835
    Indiana   840
    Iowa   846
    Kansas   851

Michigan	858
Minnesota	864
Missouri	873
Nebraska	880
North Dakota	887
Ohio	893
South Dakota	900
Wisconsin	906
Northeast	913
Connecticut	913
Delaware	919
Maine	926
Maryland	932
Massachusetts	939
New Hampshire	945
New Jersey	949
New York	955
Pennsylvania	962
Rhode Island	968
Vermont	975
Washington, D.C.	982
Southeast	991
Alabama	991
Arkansas	998
Florida	1003
Georgia	1009
Kentucky	1015
Louisiana	1021
Mississippi	1026
North Carolina	1033
South Carolina	1038
Tennessee	1045
Virginia	1051
West Virginia	1057
Southwest	1069
Arizona	1069
New Mexico	1075
Oklahoma	1082
Texas	1099
West	1109
Alaska	1109
California	1118
Colorado	1127
Hawaii	1132
Idaho	1140

Montana   1147
Nevada   1153
Oregon   1160
Utah   1166
Washington   1171
Wyoming   1178

Glossary   1185
Selected Bibliography   1191
Resources   1215
Primary Documents by Theme   1235
Contributors   1237
Index   1241
About the Editors   1299

Preface

Going green is a popular term that includes all the various actions we undertake to promote environmental sustainability. Typically, sustainable use of natural resources implies a long-term view that promotes ecological, economic, and social vitality. Beyond these generalizations, going green in America means something different to each person: she recycles her pop cans; he's gone vegetarian; they bought a hybrid car.

All of these actions are determined by the choices we make as individuals. We do these things because we believe they make a difference, and we think it helps the planet. But we aren't always aware of the facts behind our actions, we don't know how one action is related to other eco-activities, and we might not see the cumulative effects of all our actions. Further, we may not understand how these things vary from place to place.

This book fills these gaps by providing both specific details on hundreds of topics and the geographic context for understanding the myriad environmentally friendly activities in America. Going green is a process of information, education, beliefs, and action. It is our hope that the information provided in this book will motivate more people to take steps toward environmental sustainability.

Leslie A. Duram, Contributing Editor
Professor and Chair
Geography & Environmental Resources
Southern Illinois University

Acknowledgments

A lot of people deserve thanks and recognition for their assistance in getting this project off the ground and completed. First and foremost, I want to thank my husband and best friend, Arlo White, and my kids, Eamon and Alison. Their continued support in whatever projects I undertake is always incredible! Many thanks to my family and friends who have inspired me in multiple ways to explore what it means to "go green." Thanks to Lynn Jurgensen for believing in this project, as well as acquisitions editor, Kaitlin Ciarmello, and development editor, John Wagner, for supporting its progress along the way. Thanks also to the production coordinator, Bridget Austiguy-Preschel, the media manager, Caroline Price, and copyeditor, Mary Bearden, and the entire team at ABC-CLIO. Finally, a big thank you to the contributing editor, Leslie A. Duram, whose wisdom and insights guided this project over the course of its development. I hope this work inspires readers to make green changes in their lives.

Special Note from the Editor

Green efforts begin with individuals and organizations making changes, no matter how small. The publishing industry has its own environmental costs as books sold in the U.S. require the consumption of more than 30 million trees each year. Some publishers have increased the proportion of recycled paper they use, as well as increased the use of paper that's been certified by the Forest Stewardship Council, an organization that works for sustainable forestry. Others have increased their e-book offerings, allowing readers to access content without having to rely on printed material. But while the shift from print to e-book seems a "green" move, the industry has not come to a consensus on the issue since the creation and disposal of products designed to access e-book material, such as tablets and e-readers, come with their own environmental costs and impact.

In producing this encyclopedia, ABC-CLIO gathered information about "greening" its processes in addition to using the industry standard 20% recycled content paper and providing readers with an e-book option. They discovered that while the cost for additional "green" materials (significantly adding recycled content and FSC-certified materials) is about 15% higher than traditional printing, the increased awareness of "green" issues and the overall reduction in their carbon footprint is well worth the cost.

As ABC-CLIO employees, we make our own contributions to "greener" workplaces and lifestyles. In a recent survey of my colleagues, I found that many of us telecommute or walk, bike, and use public transportation, thus reducing the use of our cars. Some of us, including myself, have eliminated printing altogether. I read all of my manuscripts and communications on my laptop.

In our home environments, many of my co-workers plant trees, shrubs, and gardens. Some have installed solar panels on their homes, drive hybrid cars, and install energy-saving light bulbs. An overwhelming number recycle regularly, many through the convenience of curbside or recycling centers. My colleagues shared other "green" measures that include conserving water, keeping the thermostat low in the winter, turning off lights, and reading news online rather than in print. Many people use cloth bags for shopping, reuse containers for their kids' lunches, support local businesses, buy organic products, and overall, try to reduce their consumption. I found that by taking it one step at a time, we can all lead "greener" lives.

Kim Kennedy White

Introduction

We do not inherit the earth from our ancestors; we borrow it from our children.
—American Indian Proverb

Climate change, greenhouse gases, global warming, overpopulation—every day we are faced with news of humanity's role in the Earth's seemingly imminent destruction. At the same time, buzzwords like "green" and "eco-friendly" are now commonplace and permeate American culture. So what does it mean to be "green" in 21st-century America? This book considers that question by providing information about what is being done and what we can do to support the planet.

Certainly the term *green* means different things to different people. For the purposes of this book, green refers to the development of practices and behaviors that are eco-friendly or ecologically positive for both the environment and human communities. Green ideas emphasize protecting our planet, limiting and repairing our negative impact on Earth, and living in harmony with nature to prevent further damage.

Although the environmental movement in America began with a few dedicated individuals and organizations looking to conserve trees, endangered species, and natural resources, eco-friendly attitudes and practices have become pervasive throughout American culture since the last quarter of the 20th century. "Being green" is not a cohesive movement but rather a cultural shift in the way Americans think about our relationship to the environment and how this shift influences the ways in which we spend our time and resources.

This encyclopedia explores the development of green practices and eco-friendly mindfulness in contemporary American culture. Entries will present the debates, trends, viewpoints, and challenges of green living. The cross-disciplinary coverage uncovers the multilayered nature of American culture and provides readers with an understanding of eco-friendly and sustainable practices that are either useful or destructive to our planet.

This unique work presents green and eco-friendly developments within various aspects of American life. The first and second volume organizes A to Z entries into major themes:

- Activism and Community Green Efforts
- Arts, Entertainment, and Media
- Economics, Business, and Industry
- Education and Employment

- Environment
- Food and Drink
- Health, Home, and Garden
- Philosophy and Religion
- Politics and Law
- Science and Technology
- Sports and Leisure

Although the book doesn't claim to include every single instance of "green culture," it does seek to provide broad information about the influence and impact of eco-friendly ideas present in various aspects of American culture. Within the entries, readers will find sidebars with interesting tidbits on "greenovations" and "greenovators." Entries include cross-references that direct readers to other entries along with key references for further research.

The second volume of the encyclopedia also includes a variety of primary documents that demonstrate legislative, economic, and industry shifts toward green and eco-friendly practices. The material provides readers with information on legislation as well as tips and suggestions for green living.

The third volume of the encyclopedia provides state-by-state essays organized by region that give readers a broad overview of green developments and challenges in each of the 50 states. These entries don't claim to cover every aspect of green culture in each state, but instead, provide a snapshot of eco-friendly attitudes, environmental challenges, and environmental strengths. Entries provide a "jumping off point" for further research. Finally, the glossary, selected bibliography, and resources at the end of the book give readers a wealth of information for additional research.

This encyclopedia presents the work of more than 160 contributors, including college professors, environmental experts, and independent scholars from around the country. It provides 225 accessible and well-researched entries that are suitable for a range of audiences and will be an excellent addition to libraries. High school students, general readers, and academics will find a wealth of information about efforts to "go green" across American culture, quick overviews of eco-friendly developments in each of the 50 states, and guidelines, legislation, and standards for green living in the primary documents section. The book's lengthy resources section, organized by theme, provides links for additional research. It is our hope that this book will inform, educate, and inspire readers to make positive and "green" changes in their everyday lives.

Social Pressures and Processes of "Going Green" in America

Introduction

Today it may seem second nature for many Americans to consider the impact on the environment or rising energy costs when they drive their cars, run their air conditioners, heat their homes, or buy food and other commodities. Does this truly mean that America is "going green" or has the movement been hijacked by powerful political and corporatist interests? Moreover, is a more sustainable, healthy world a real possibility for all Americans and is it equally accessible for the poor and for people of all colors and ethnicities? When, why, and how did this movement emerge? To answer these questions meaningfully, it is important to consider the origins, evolution, and adaptations of this movement, as well as the various social, economic, and political tensions involved in going green in the United States.

The Development of Eco-Friendly Concepts and Growing Cultural Trends

Going green was an idea in the United States long before these two words were coined. However, even the meaning of that idea has undergone tremendous transformation and stakeholder ownership over time. "Green" thinking in the United States finds its first organized context in the conservationist movement of the mid-19th century (Worster, 1994). At the time, going green related to conservationist ecology. In fact, the term *ecology* was first coined in 1866 as part of the nation's first collective response to the deleterious effects of the philosophies and policies of Manifest Destiny. The latter was understood and practiced as the inherent mission of a civilized people to tame the country's wild and make use of the land's natural resources for the purposes of economic gain.

Early Efforts to Develop a Greener America

The most concentrated form of Manifest Destiny emerged in the course of the settlement of the American West and more specifically in the taming of its natural resources. The purpose of Manifest Destiny found shape in the transformation of the western wilderness to civilization (Deverell, 2004, 78). This era witnessed excessive and exploitive mining and logging. Large livestock operations permitted overgrazing and mass agricultural production that depleted soil nutrients. The construction of railroads cut across habitats and ecosystems and, among other things, encouraged the decimation of buffalo herds throughout the plains (Motes, 2011, 98–101). These organized activities heavily supported the nation's increasing industrialization and urbanization. As settlements grew and became more complex, they required increasing diversion of water, more building supplies, and other raw materials for domestic commerce and international trade.

Going Green through Conservationism

Conservationism emerged between the 1890s and the 1920s during the nation's progressive era in response to this runaway resource exploitation. Progressives called for government regulation of public goods to offset the excesses of market-based capitalism, including the exploitation of children, women, infirmed populations, and the environment. For progressive environmentalists such as George Perkins Marsh (1801–1882), who wrote *Man and Nature*, Gifford Pinchot (1865–1946), the first director of the U.S. Forest Service, and naturalist and author John Burroughs (1837–1921), conservationism translated into the rational and efficient utilization of nature's resources to serve the needs of American society over the long term (Worster, 1994).

Conserving water, land, natural resources, and biota through measured economic development was considered not only a social and cultural need but also a matter of national economic security. As such, Progressives argued that nature's land and its bounties were well within the government's purview to measure and manage through such technical and methodical approaches as flood control, irrigation and storage, and power generation (Hays, 1999). Such federal resource management efforts were codified through the 1902 Reclamation Act that sought sustained yield, which was defined as a balance between American society's immediate resource needs and the nation's enduring, potential resource needs. Amid the nation's social, economic, and political transformations during this era, some Americans began to resist what they interpreted as the encroachment of industrial supremacy over nature as well as over their own, everyday lives. These shared sentiments soon developed into the preservationist movement.

Preservationist Preferences for Going Green

Rising urbanization and mechanization between the 1850s and the early 1900s increasingly led to society's desire for a return to the natural world. Amid wilderness, one could escape from the rigors of city life at least for a brief, leisurely respite on the weekend, or on vacation. The idea that nature possessed intrinsic worth emerged and was perhaps best captured during this period in the writings of Henry David Thoreau. In his major work *Walden, or Life in the Woods*, Thoreau called upon members of American society to make a moral turn away from industrialization. By living in harmony with nature, Thoreau argued, people would also maintain just relationships with one another, creating a sustainable paradigm for American society (Thoreau, 2011). Essentially, rediscovering and preserving nature's wildness became the mission and passion of the preservationist movement, which also marked an early, founding conceptualization of what it meant to "go green" in America.

Beyond Thoreau's famous missive, the politicizing of the preservationist movement also took form in other larger-than-life environmentalists of this period. American naturalist and adventurist author John Muir (1838–1914) was a Scottish-born American citizen who founded the Sierra Club, still one of the nation's most influential conservation organizations. Muir was influential in passage of the 1890 National Parks Bill. In 1891, the Forest Preserve Act was also passed, which empowered the nation's presidents to convert publicly held lands into federally protected national forests.

Toward that end, Muir convinced U.S. President Theodore Roosevelt to go on a camping trip with him in 1903 to Glacier Point, one of the most scenic overlooks of Yosemite Valley. There, Muir convinced President Roosevelt to place all of Yosemite Valley and Mariposa Grove under federal park protection. This led to the creation of a unified Yosemite National Park in 1906. Called the "Father of the National Parks," Muir was also instrumental in the creation of Sequoia National Park, and he remained a forest preservation advocate author and activist throughout his lifetime. Environmental author Donald Worster, in *A Passion for Nature* wrote that Muir spent his life "saving the American soul from total surrender to materialism" (2008, 403). The preservationists' motive was to preserve nature in public spaces for the purposes of human health, rejuvenation, and enjoyment through activities such as bird watching, hiking, hunting, fishing, and camping. Muir epitomized this mission.

Mixed Motives in Early Green Movements

Early on, the preservationist movement actually coupled itself quite well to the political platform of conservationism. For example, both the utilitarian National Rifle Association and the aesthetic and scientific National Audubon Society emerged during this era, demonstrating the expansive appeal in American culture for both progressivism and conservationism. One renowned environmentalist who helped to merge the goals of conservationism with preservationist objectives was the scientific explorer John Wesley Powell (1834–1902).

Powell is perhaps best known in the American West for leading an expedition in 1869 that completed the nation's first-known passage through the Grand Canyon (Aton, 2010). An avid geologist, anthropologist, and ethnologist, Powell, who lost one of his arms in the Civil War, also commandeered several expeditions through the Rocky Mountains. Powell's published journals both informed and stirred a national, adventurous spirit for nature (Gighlieri & Bradley, 2003). As a political conduit between preservationists and conservationists, Powell successfully served from 1881 to 1894 as the second director of the U.S. Geological Survey (USGS). He also led the Smithsonian Institute's Bureau of Ethnology, where he directed sociological and linguistic research until his death in 1904.

The motive of the preservationist movement was to safeguard America's public spaces for the purposes of human health, rejuvenation, and sublime aesthetic pleasure, while the motive of the conservationist movement was to commoditize natural resources as short- and long-term economic, utilitarian benefits to be regulated and managed by the government. On the surface, both movements had in common the assumption that private industry needed to be regulated. However, their fundamental philosophical differences and policy platforms soon placed them at odds with each other.

While preservationists such as John Muir advocated policies that provided for the protection of inherently valued natural resources, especially from the nation's rapidly expanding industrial and urban sectors, conservationists such as Gifford Pinchot eyed wilderness in terms of efficient management as a current and potential resource benefit (Gottlieb, 1994, 24–27). Conservationists thus viewed preservationists as impractical, if not fundamentalist, romantics, while many preservationists viewed conservationists as industry's lap dogs.

When environmental historians consider the context of these two initial efforts at going green in the United States, they often point out that both movements actually had rather narrow appeal (Sarkar, 1999, 406). The conservationist view appealed to bureaucrats, industrial magnates, and urban planners. The preservationist perspective appealed to the country's economic elite and its middle class. Even though the preservationist approach offered a broader contextual appeal, that context was intended for only certain segments of the population. Whether promoting preservation of wilderness as commemoration of a "national treasure"; as a pastoral, spiritual retreat from materialism; as participation among nature's ecological and biodiversity; as commercial tourism and recreation; or even as an elite aesthetic experience of nature's beauty, the preservationist movement was meant "especially for those presumed to be most capable of appreciating it" (Gottlieb, 1994, 26–27).

Both of these movements therefore excluded the nation's much broader social, racial, and ethnic populations and the environmental concerns, issues, and values of these disenfranchised populations (Sarkar, 1999, 406). In essence, the clashes between these two movements have been described as "disputes among elites" that were typically white, wealthy, urban, and male (Gottlieb, 1994, 31–32). Minorities, the urban working class, and the rural and urban poor were routinely, if not purposefully, marginalized (Dowie, 1996, 2; Heinz, 2005, 47–48). It was not until the 1960s that these two opposing ecological perspectives were confronted with a third standpoint—the environmental justice movement.

The Modern Environmental Movement

According to contemporary environmental historians, the first modern context for the greening of America in the minds, hearts, and politics of its masses may have actually begun in outer space on December 24, 1968. While orbiting around the moon, America's Apollo 8 astronaut Bill Anders snapped a photo of Earth as it seemed to rise above the lunar landscape. This iconic image became known thereafter as "Earthrise," and it revealed not only the stark beauty of this vibrant blue world but also the immense vulnerability of our planet as a relatively small object suspended in space and spinning through time amid an otherwise dark void ("The Home Planet"). Also, for the first time, Earth appeared to its viewers without political or economic or cultural boundaries. It dawned on many people who viewed this image for the first time that Earth was a common home that needed to be taken care of by all.

A New Earth Rises

Before long, "Earthrise" became the poster child of a grassroots movement that aligned itself with the overarching push for civil rights in the United States during the 1960s (Bullard, 2000). This "people's" environmental movement found an emergent voice in Rachel Carson's seminal work on the devastating impact of pesticides and other toxic chemicals in her 1962 book *Silent Spring*. It was also influenced by the passage of the 1964 Civil Rights Act. It resonated deeply in the sacrifice of Dr. Martin Luther King Jr.'s 1968 fatal march to Memphis to help garbage workers who routinely confronted hazardous working conditions and unequal pay. Emerging from the heart of this grassroots movement was a dual ideal: one that limited the negative impact of human activity on the physical environment of Earth and also limited the negative impacts of this human activity on all of Earth's inhabitants.

This ideal found form first in a growing concern and increasing political momentum for preserving biodiversity and the well-being of all of Earth's species. In 1964, President Lyndon B. Johnson signed into law the Wilderness Act, which set aside 9.1 million acres of pristine national forest land for the purpose of preserving some of the nation's wildlife and its habitat. First introduced in 1956 by U.S. Senator Hubert Humphrey and U.S. Representative John Sayler, the Wilderness Act was rewritten 66 times before its successful passage. The inspiration of Wilderness Society Executive Director Howard Zahniser, the act established the National Wilderness Preservation System, which would consist of public land "untrammeled by man" and in which "man, himself is a visitor, who does not remain," and who leaves the land "unimpaired for future use and enjoyment as wilderness" ("The Wilderness Act of 1964," 1990, para. 2–4). Passage of the Endangered Species Conservation Act in 1969, which was revised and replaced in 1973 with the Endangered Species Act, was marked as a significant victory for this emergent movement in terms of providing for the protection of plant and animal species threatened with extinction as well as protection of the ecosystems these species depend on.

Reducing the human impact on the environment materialized during the 1960s and culminated in legislation passed as this tumultuous decade came to a close. The National Environmental Protection Act (NEPA) and the Clean Air Act were passed in 1970, while the federal Clean Water Act was approved in 1972. NEPA represented a significant ecological landmark for the United States, by instituting a national environmental protection policy (Phillips, 2000). The provisions of NEPA also established the Council on Environmental Quality (CEQ) that was responsible for serving as the federal government's environmental policy instrument, and it created the Environmental Protection Agency (EPA). NEPA also mandated the implementation of Environmental Impact Statements (EIS) in all cases in which proposed federal activity posed a potentially adverse environmental consequence.

Passage of the 1970 Clean Air Act also marked a profound shift in federal control over the nation's air pollution. It empowered the creation of federal and state emission limits and provided for the regulation of both fixed industrial and moveable, vehicular emission sources. The Clean Water Act was enacted in 1972 and was no less significant in its scope. The new law set forth a national pledge to "restore and maintain the chemical, physical and biological integrity of our nation's waters," and it established ambitious targets for zero pollutant discharge in the nation's fishable, swimmable, and navigable waters. This provision marked a profound reform initiative amid such common practices as habitual discharge of untreated sewage and other pollutants in open waters.

Going Green Makes a Turn to the Left

As the decade of the 1960s progressed and the civil rights movement escalated in the United States, it was not long before concerns over the environment also expanded to include the concept of environmental justice. Multiple studies had begun to emerge that demonstrated the environmental hazards that various socio-economic, racial, and ethnic groups lived in and worked among (Bullard, 2000, xii–xiii; Pellow, 2002, 15–29). As the concept of environmental racism came into sharper focus in the 1970s and 1980s, the unequal and often overlooked environmental burden shared by the nation's poor and by minorities matured as a prominent concern and a political cause of the liberal left. On the nation's first Earth Day in 1970, the popular anti-Vietnam War slogan of "Give Peace a Chance" was supplanted with chants of "Give Earth a Chance" by thousands of grassroots environmental protestors who marched on Washington, D.C. (Rome, 2003, 525).

Urban working-class, minority, and poor neighborhoods were frequently found to be where industrial and chemical factories, landfills, and hazardous waste sites were located. In acute contrast, another pattern of "white privilege" was also observed in the structure and shape of the country's relatively pristine urban and suburban landscapes. Both of these patterns seemed to demonstrate an institutionalized, structural, and spatial phenomenon of unfair disadvantage and unfair advantage (Pellow, 2002). As part of the civil rights movement, interest in environmental justice grew into a more inclusive, participatory movement throughout much of the 1960s.

Localized protests erupted frequently during this era. For example, several metropolitan "freeway revolts" broke out in the 1960s in protest of the government's planned disruption or displacement of vulnerable populations in a number of U.S. cities while the nation was building its interstate highway system. Outrage at the regional level also erupted over the 1969 Union Oil Santa Barbara Channel oil spill, the largest in the nation's history at the time. Consciousness-raising rallies were organized over Louisiana's petrochemical "cancer alley," and protests were held on behalf of American Indian reservations over the dumping of radioactive uranium waste on native lands.

In the 1960s and 1970s, many of these cases were often nationally publicized because attention was increasingly drawn to common environmental, economic, and social justice themes that often surfaced amid the multiple protests that were taking place around the country. One of the common themes was the apparent, institutionalized marginalization of poor and minority populations alongside an institutionalized neglect of the places where they lived, which were often the nation's most polluted, most hazardous places (Roberts & Toffolon-Weiss, 2001). By the 1980s, both federal reports and independent studies substantiated at least some evidence indicating just such a pattern to this phenomenon.

With considerable media coverage and the fusion of environmental justice with the civil rights movement, this bevy of localized protests soon mushroomed into a national grassroots movement. Amid these events, new power dynamics in the environmental movement were also fed by such galvanizing issues and events as nuclear nonproliferation, the 1978 toxic chemical pollution disaster at Love Canal, and the 1979 Three Mile Island nuclear accident (Evan & Manion, 2002). However, as the civil rights movement waned in the 1980s amid the nation's shift toward a more conservative, pro-industrial republican political climate, the grassroots environmental movement was all but snuffed out. In its place surfaced a sophisticated nucleus of organizers who were determined to take the movement "mainstream." This shift would last well into the 1990s.

The Positive and Negative Developments and Impacts of Mainstream Environmentalism

The nation's environmental movement into the mainstream relied less on grassroots demonstrations and localized protests and instead centered on litigation, lobbying, technical savvy, and scientific research and activism. In part, this reformation was in response to the more conservative, and often anti-environmental or environmentally lax, administrations of Presidents Ronald Reagan, George H. W. Bush, and George W. Bush. The mood of the public had also somewhat changed: The energy crisis of the 1970s had passed, and in some states, the speed limit that had been reduced to 55 miles per hour (mph) during that era was raised again to 75 mph on certain interstate highways. A pro-business political climate prevailed in Washington.

Alongside these developments, new voices emerged that significantly changed, redefined, and refined the intellectual and ethical dimensions of this reformed, mainstream environmental movement, and their messages coupled with the tenets of scientific ecology to a new breed of activists. To counter-balance President Reagan's anti-environmental deregulation policies in the 1980s, the environmental movement shifted away from its grassroots core and the bottom-up activism that characterized grassroots activism. Instead, it simultaneously created several mainstream environmental groups. The Group of 10 (G-10) consisted of a powerful board made up of the leaders of the 10 biggest environmental groups. By going mainstream and aggressively seeking new membership, the rolls of the G-10 rose to 7 million members in the 1980s (Dowie, 1996, 68–70). Many of these mainstream groups either represented or utilized specialized legislative, lobbying, scientific, and legal arms of the movement.

Out of this movement, a powerful and very unique leadership also emerged. Some had perhaps been waiting in the wings. For example, in 1968, biologist, entomologist, demographer, ecologist, and Stanford professor Paul Ehrlich renewed attention over the potential effects of exponential population expansion in his book *The Population Bomb.* This discourse, refreshed in the 1980s and 1990s, centers on the reverberating question of how many people the Earth can, in fact, support. Scientist-activist Barry Commoner became a principal spokesman for this more intellectually driven environmental movement. Commoner warned of the environmental hazards of nuclear weapons and toxic chemicals and contended that it was not population but unchecked market-based economies and pollution from technological intervention and general overconsumption that most threatened the Earth and its inhabitants. A biologist, educator, and radical activist, Commoner also ran as a third-party candidate for president of the United States in 1980 and is credited with playing an influential role in the 1963 Nuclear Test Ban Treaty (Howard & Roberts, 2010).

Another voice that lent its expertise and political clout to the growing eclectic sophistication of this movement was the Club of Rome. Founded in 1968 by a global think tank of political leaders and scientists from around the world, the Club of Rome released its first publication of *The Limits to Growth* in 1972. This treatise described simulated interactions between a world of finite resources and an exponentially expanding global population. It concluded that limited natural resources and especially depletion of oil supplies would ultimately limit economic growth (Meadows et al., 2004). The ensuing 1973 oil crisis, though sparked by international politics and their consequences, drew attention to the problems and potential long-term impact of high oil prices and disrupted supplies. *The Limits of Growth* seemed to validate these outcomes and their ensuing discomforts.

The collective refinement of the environmental movement during this period is considered to be a key point in its evolution toward a new "Age of Ecology" in America during the 1980s and early 1990s (Egan, 2010). This new movement more frequently involved the participation of a growing field of ecological scholars and experts who also envisioned themselves as activists, educators, and spokesmen and -women responsible for addressing and solving the nation's ecological challenges. This new direction appeared to be validated in 1987 with the publication of *Our Common Future,* by the United Nations World Commission on Environment and Development (WCED). Merging environmental science and economic development issues into a new concept called "sustainable development," the WCED challenged UN member-nations, including the United States, to explore and strive for a sustainable path forward (*Report of the WED,* 1987). America's ad hoc ecological think tank embraced this new directive.

While some viewed this transition as a positive event in which scientists moved out of the laboratory and toward policy formation and prescription, others saw this era as one in which the application of science actually bogged down the movement's momentum and in many ways stymied inclusive grassroots participation.

Going Green Falters Amid the Contested Sustainability Debate

By the 1990s, science was framed as the rational, mediating influence between the nation's environmental problems and the reforms that would be needed to address these issues. Borrowing heavily from the concept of sustained yield during America's earlier era of conservationism, researchers began to focus their attention on meeting the goals of sustainable development. The concept of sustainable development was briefly defined in the UN WCED's 1987 report *Our Common Future* as "development that meets the needs of the present without compromising the ability of future generations to meet their own needs" (Report of the World Commission, 1987). Contestation swiftly emerged over what sustainable development actually meant and how one might go about scientifically measuring, managing, and meeting its demands.

On one end of the spectrum were those benefiting most from a demand-driven market approach. For those corporate conservationists who view nature's resources as commodities, the ecological impacts of development can be offset elsewhere in the environment through such market mechanisms as carbon trading. Environmental costs in one location are then subtracted from the improvements or benefits to the environment made in another location. The theoretical assumption is that this formula provides a global-scale net "balance" between a corporation's negative and positive impacts on Earth's environment, as a whole (Hawkins, 1994).

On the other end of the spectrum emerged this newly vetted class of science activists, comprised of ecologists from the mainstream environmentalists groups that moved away from grassroots environmentalism in the 1980s. Rather than preserving nature for the purposes of leisure, recreation, or reflection, these ecologists seek actual sustainability in the ongoing preservation and management of natural resources for the benefit of the specific habitats involved as well as for the well-being of Earth and all of its beings. This perspective, therefore, argues for a more direct command and control relationship between economic development's negative impacts on specific environments and effective, measurable remediation to those same environments (Ropke, 2005). Regardless of these opposing approaches, both sides have often touted the accuracy and efficacy of their own scientific data in moving toward or meeting sustainable development goals (Laufer, 2003). Still, more often than not, the social and economic dimensions of sustainability are missing from these inquiries.

Environmental justice has also become a much poorer fit for the mainstream movement. The social and economic needs of low-income and minority populations for housing, land, and jobs in both rural and urban areas have often been at cross-purposes with the goals of mainstream ecological groups to condemn land, stop resource exploitation, or close down extractive polluting industries (Faber & McCarthy, 2003, 45). More often than not, however, debates in the movement continue to square off between the economic, scientific, and legal experts of these two opposing camps of corporate conservationists and science activists. These disputes are typically embedded in localized environmental issues, with efforts at reform limited to the narrow, piecemeal range of victories possible in such local venues. For the past 10 to 12 years, a primary organizing rationale for this approach appears to have been based on a model that favors incremental sectoral successes that are accompanied by equally incremental advancements in science and technology (Angel, 1998). Just as corporate clout and scientific activism have made their own assumptions and polarized their own meaning of progress or success toward sustainable development, each may also have also assumed that America's masses are following closely behind them.

Paradoxically, the public is not even near corporate's progress. The prevalence of elitist, technocratic, legal, and scientific expert speak from both camps, coupled with the narrowing, localized prioritization and framing of environmental issues has in effect decoupled the public at large from processes of participation (Backstrand, 2004). Though these reformed environmental specialists and their market-driven counterparts have more than likely conducted valid and perhaps even valuable research over the years, they appear to be no closer in agreement, particularly in defining sustainability or the ingredients of sustainable development than they were 20 years ago. Still, if recent trends are any indication, the American public appears intent to move ahead toward a "greener" America with or without them.

Conclusion: Choosing to Be Green—One at a Time, Together

Since the dawn of the millennium and particularly since the nation's economic downturn in the spring of 2008, Americans seem to have more fully embraced the prospect of going green. Alternative forms of energy are available in many locations around the country, organic foods and alternative consumer products that are eco-friendly are available for purchase, and more and more automobile makers are offering hybrid cars that improve fuel efficiency. How much are Americans partaking of these green opportunities and are they satisfied that they are doing all they can?

A Gallup poll conducted in March 2011 found that the majority of Americans believe it is important for them to take measures on their own to protect the environment, and especially to conserve energy. However, they would not favor more government regulation or intervention that would restrict their right to make their own environmentally conscious decisions. In other words, Americans are following their own lead in terms of how much and in what way they want to go green (O'Driscoll & Weise, 2011, 1A). Gallup poll responses also indicated that on their own, Americans in 2011 were disposed to do a lot more and spend a lot more to protect the environment than they were in 1991. Such willing, environmentally conscious spending decisions were identified as buying energy-efficient fluorescent light bulbs (favored by 66 percent); purchasing more gas-efficient automobiles (favored by 62 percent); investing in remodeling their homes to conserve energy and protect Earth's atmosphere (favored by 78 percent); and the careful consideration of corporate environmental track records before they make consumer purchases (favored by 80 percent).

While acknowledging that they are willing to spend more on consumer products in order to go green, Americans also indicated what they would agree to: They would not want the government to set gas mileage regulations for new domestic-made automobiles, nor would they support growth limits on suburban development. Americans also indicated they would oppose utility surcharges that penalize consumers for using more that a set amount of energy (O'Driscoll & Weiss, 2011, 1A). Many Americans also indicated that though they want to be more green, economic considerations sometimes limit their abilities to do so. Only 1 in every 10 Americans surveyed rated their effort to go green as "excellent," while 50 percent of those surveyed believed they were doing a good job of being environmentally conscious. Eco-friendly consumer products and green improvements typically cost more than conventional products and measures. Even so, some Americans believe that people are already making adjustments to consume less and to live "smarter," especially when it concerns the everyday choices they can make that save both money and energy (O'Driscoll & Weiss, 2010, 1A). Overall, these findings indicate that Americans are taking their own path toward going green. Measured and tentative though their steps may be, the footsteps of average Americans down this path seem not to be dependent on the involvement or approval of either the "science activist" ecological movement or its competing corporate conservationist contingency, both of which appear to be missing from this American go green landscape.

Recent studies indicate that despite numerous initiatives launched by environmental interests and programs undertaken by the federal government over the past 40 years, reforms have not managed to keep pace with the scale and size of the environmental problems and ecological degradation the nation has experienced. Statistics also illustrate that during this period, the overall ecological footprint of the United States had risen 270 percent, and that amid this, the capacities of both the environmental movement and the nation's institutions have been unable to do much more than react to unfavorable legislation or debilitating environmental crises (*National Footprint and Biocapacity Account*, 2004). Indeed, some even have questioned whether the environmental movement is dead, suggesting that time out for a "step back" is in order to assess reality (Shellenberg & Nordhous, 2004, 8). In the meantime, Americans one by one, en masse, are stepping forward with their own plans of action. Though time will tell whether going green will intensify or fade for the American people as the nation's economy rebounds and prospers, this emergent phenomenon epitomizes democratic civic engagement: alive, fertile, and green as its grass roots.

KATHLEEN O'HALLERAN

References

Angel, David P. 1998. "International Cooperation, Technology, and the Sustainability Challenge." In Nigel J. Rome, ed., *Sustainability Strategies for Industry: The Future of Corporate Practice*. Washington, DC: Island Press, 243–258.

Aton, James M. 2010. *John Wesley Powell: His Life and Legacy*. Salt Lake City: Bonneville Books.

Backstrand, Karin. 2004. "Precaution, Scientization or Deliberation? Prospects for Greening and Democratizing Science." In M. Wissenburg and Y. Levy, eds., *Liberal Democracy and Environmentalism: The End of Environmentalism?* New York: Routledge.

Bullard Robert. 2000. *Dumping in Dixie: Race, Class, and Environmental Quality*. Boulder, CO: Westview.

Deverell, William. 2004. *A Companion to the American West*. Madden, MA: Blackwell.

Dowie, Mark. 1996. *Losing Ground: American Environmentalism at the Close of the Twentieth Century*. Cambridge, MA: MIT Press.

Egan, Michael. 2010. "Rejoinder: Barry Commoner and the Science of Survival: The Remaking of American Environmentalism." *Book Review Perspectives* 6:1 (February 17). Retrieved January 18, 2012, from: http://sspp.proquest.com/archives/vol6iss1/book.egan.html.

Evan, William, and Mark Manion. 2002. *Minding the Machines: Preventing Technological Disasters*. Upper Saddle River, NJ: Prentice-Hall.

Faber, Daniel R., and Deborah McCarthy. 2003. "Neo-Liberalism, Globalization and the Struggle for Ecological Democracy: Linking Sustainability and Environmental Justice." In Julian Agyeman, Robert D. Bullard, and Bob Evans, eds., *Just Sustainabilities: Development in an Unequal World*. Cambridge, MA: MIT Press.

Ghiglieri, Michael P., and George Y. Bradley. 2003. *First through Grand Canyon: The Secret Journals & Letters of the 1869 Crew Who Explored the Green and Colorado Rivers*. Flagstaff, AZ: Puma.

Gottlieb, Robert. 1994. *Forcing the Spring: The Transformation of the American Environmental Movement*. Washington, DC: Island Press.

Hawkins, Paul. 1994. *The Ecology of Commerce*. New York: HarperCollins.

Hays, Samuel. 1999. *Conservation and the Gospel of Efficiency*. Pittsburgh: University of Pittsburgh Press.

Heinz, Teresa L. 2005. "From Civil Rights to Environmental Rights: Construction of Race, Community and Identity in Three African American Newspapers' of the Environmental Justice Movement." *Journal of Communication Inquiry* 29:1 (January): 47–65.

Howard, Jeff, and Jody A. Roberts. 2010. "Barry Commoner and the Science of Survival: The Remaking of American Environmentalism." *Book Review Perspectives* 6:1 (February 17). Retrieved January 18, 2012, from: http://sspp.proquest.com/archives/vol6iss1/book.egan.html.

Laufer, W. 2003. "Social Accountability and Corporate Greenwashing." *Journal of Business Ethics* 43:3: 253–261.

Lester, James P., David W. Allen, and Kelly M. Hill. *Environmental Injustice in the United States: Myths and Realities*. Boulder, CO: Westview, 2000.

Meadows, Donna, Jorgen Randers, and Dennis Meadows. 2004. *Limits to Growth: The 30 Year Update*. White River Junction, VT: Chelsea Green.

Motes, K. D. 2011. "Hosts and Horses: Envirocultural Effects of Contacts in the Amerindian West." In Gordon Morris Bakken, ed., *The World of the American West*. New York: Taylor and Francis, 81–104.

National Footprint Biocapacity Account. 2004. Global Footprint Network. Retrieved 2012 January 23, 2012, from: http://www.footprintnetwork.org/en/index.php/GFN/page/ecological_footprint_atlas_2008.

O'Driscoll, Patrick, and Elizabeth Weise. 2011. "Green Living Takes Root, but Habits Die Hard. Doing Right Thing Isn't Easy, Even for Those Who Want To." *USA Today*, March 29, 1A.

Pellow, D. N. 2002. "Social Inequalities and Environmental Conflict." *Horizontes Antropologicos* 12:25: 15–29.

Phillips, Claudia Goetz. 2000. "The Relationship of Ecosystem Management to NEPA and Its Goals." *Environmental Management* 26:1: 1–12.

Report of the World Commission on Environment and Development: Our Common Future. 1987. United Nations World Commission on Environment and Development. Geneva: UNWCED. Retrieved January 19, 2012, from: http://www.un-documents.net/wced-ocf .htm.

Roberts, J. T., and M. M. Toffolon-Weiss. 2001. *Chronicles from the Environmental Justice Frontline.* Cambridge, MA: Cambridge University Press.

Rome, Adam. 2003. "Give Earth a Chance: The Environmental Movement and the Sixties." *Journal of American History* 90:2: 525–554.

Ropke, I. 2005. "Trends in the Development of Ecological Economics from the Late 1980s to the Early 2000s." *Ecological Economics* 55: 262–290.

Sarkar, Sahotra. 1999. "Thinking of Biology: Wilderness Preservation and Biodiversity Conservation—Keeping Divergent Goals Distinct." *BioScience* 49:5: 405–412.

Shellenberger, M., and T. Nordhaus. 2004. "The Death of Environmentalism: Global Warming Politics in a Post-Environmental World." El Cerrito, CA: Breakthrough Institute. Retrieved January 25, 2012, from: http://www.thebreakthrough.org/images/ Death_of_Environmentalism.pdf.

"The Home Planet." N.d. *NASA's View of Earth.* Washington, DC: National Aeronautic Space Administration. Retrieved January 19, 2012, from: http://www.nasa.gov/externalflash/ earthday_gallery/captions.html.

Thoreau, Henry David. 2011. *Walden, or Life in the Woods.* Philadelphia: Empire Books.

"The Wilderness Act of 1964: Eight Years in the Making." 1990. *Wilderness America.* Retrieved January 29, 2012, from: http://wilderness.org/content/wilderness-act-1964.

Worster, Donald. 1994. *Nature's Economy: A History of Ecological Ideas.* New York: Cambridge University Press.

Worster, Donald. 2008. *A Passion for Nature: The Life of John Muir.* Manning, MA: Oxford University Press.

Activism and Community Green Efforts

COMMUNITY ECONOMIC DEVELOPMENT AND SUBSTANTIVE PARTICIPATION

Community economic development (CED) first gained momentum as a movement in North America in response to the economic recession of the early 1980s. Although support for CED arose from public dissatisfaction with the welfare state, it represents an optimistic and innovative attempt to alleviate urban poverty and strengthen democracy, and it serves as an apposite context for the implementation of substantive public participation in environmental decision making (Turner, 2010). CED provides an opportunity to end the historical correlation between economic growth and environmental degradation.

CED incorporates two components: that of community and economic development. It seeks to increase capital gains in such a way that benefits the entire community (i.e., housing, jobs, or business opportunities for low-income people), as well as creating nonfinancial benefits (i.e., enhanced social capital and environmental management) that enhance local quality of life (Lejano & Wessells, 2006). CED encompasses two fundamental concepts: exploring and understanding all the choices available to alter economic circumstances and engaging collaborators in building a long-term strategy that provides an overarching direction for the community. Understanding means that communities explore all available options, not just those policies that equate economic development with growth. It is critical that decision-makers recognize the importance of both short- and long-term strategies. Long-term strategies provide an overarching vision and direction for the community, while short-term projects provide tangible feedback that reinforces citizen commitment to long-term strategies. It is within this framework of a long-term vision where values of environmental, economic, and social sustainability need to be expressed. CED practitioners necessarily need to consider issues of sustainability and how specific environmentally related decisions will contribute to the long-term viability of their community.

CED implicitly assumes a democratic political system in which people have an opportunity to express their preferences; thus, citizen participation should be as inclusive and substantive as possible. Inclusive participation does not mean that every citizen must participate but rather that all groups in a community are given the access and opportunity. Substantive participation involves deep and continuous involvement from the public with regard to administrative and developmental processes, with the potential for all involved to have an impact on the decision-making process (Turner, 2010).

In a discussion of CED, it is important to distinguish between economic development and economic growth. The terms are closely related, yet fundamentally different. Growth can occur without development, and development can occur without growth (Turner, 2010). Once equated with enhanced well-being, economists now recognize economic growth as a potential source of diminished well-being. Growth seeks to increase capital, employment, and business revenues using first- and second-wave economic policies.[1] Alternatively, economic development implies change. It is a more comprehensive and innovative concept than growth. In its broadest sense, development involves social, economic, and environmental efforts to enhance quality of life. Rather than a short-term pursuit of economic gains, development seeks long-term stability through the purposeful and permanent enrichment of a community's economic situation. Thus, theories of CED reflect a holistic approach to community problem solving that combines economic and community development.

It is important for communities to consider noneconomic factors when developing CED programs. How decisions are made and how strategies are set up and implemented have a direct bearing on the outcome of any CED scheme. CED implies change. It represents a conscious and strategic intervention in community and economic development in an effort to enhance human well-being and community of life. Thus, reinterpreting the rules, or societal constraints, that dictate how resources are used, in ways that are both economically and environmentally sustainable and of benefit to the community, is an important means of achieving CED-driven change.

Substantive Participation

The role of public participation in local economic development in the United States has historically been one of ambivalence. Although the political system in the United States is designed to reflect and engender an active citizenry, it is also designed to protect political and administrative processes from a too-active citizenry and, arguably, has been biased against those with less social, political, and economic influence. It is within this context that participation in the economic arena has traditionally been framed.

In recent years, interest in public participation in local economic decision making and public administration in the United States has increased as a result of a number of factors. Championed by a citizenry with diminished trust in the government and demanding more accountability from public institutions, there is a growing recognition on the part of decision makers that decision making without public participation is ineffective (Moote et al., 1997). Paralleling this practical recognition is a more theoretical debate regarding the role of participation in administrative and economic decision making and a call for a more active accountability in which citizens are more directly involved in the administrative state (Stivers, 1990). Despite the theoretical and practical recognition that the public must be involved in public decisions, many administrators, politicians, and developers are, at best, ambivalent about public involvement or, at worst, they find it problematic.

In a qualitative study (Turner, 2010) of the role of public participation in the revitalization of the brownfields in Louisville, Kentucky, certain stakeholders (officials, business representatives, developers, and specialists) generally expressed a belief that greater citizen participation increased inefficiency because participation creates delays and increases red tape. Interview responses from these stakeholders generally exhibited an undeniable tension between the public's right to greater involvement and decision-making capacity and the prerogative of public officials and those with specialized knowledge to act as final decision makers. This "expert knows best" sentiment was explicit at times, but often implicit. Stakeholders stated that public involvement was necessary and desirable, yet they failed to connect the final decision-making process with the input generated by those in the public participation process. Alternatively, other stakeholders (predominantly residents and representatives from community organizations) reported feeling isolated from the decision-making process. Although they cared about the revitalization efforts, they did not feel as though their participation was affecting the planning process in a meaningful way. In general, there was an implicit mistrust or cynicism regarding whether or not their input would be utilized. These feelings of impotence expressed by some stakeholders, most notably residents and community organizers, dampened not only their interests in continued participation in this public process, but also in future public participation processes as well.

The stakeholders involved in this study—residents, officials, developers, and representatives from community organizations and businesses alike—agreed that participation is necessary and desirable. Certain stakeholders described participation as an opportunity to be part of something greater than them, explaining that it helped them to feel they had fulfilled a responsibility to the community. Representatives from community organizations emphasized the importance for citizens to have an opportunity to influence the decision-making process and to know that their influence has the potential to make a difference. Officials and developers also stressed the centrality of input,

---

Greenovation: Brownfield Revitalization

The U.S. Environmental Protection Agency defines brownfields as "abandoned or underutilized industrial or commercial properties where redevelopment is hindered by possible environmental contamination and potential liability under Superfund for parties that purchase or operate these sites" (EPA). Brownfields include factories, mills, and foundries and can be places such as vacant lots, gas stations, or dry cleaners. Brownfields and Superfund sites are subject to the Comprehensive Environmental Response, Compensation, and Liability Act (CERCLA), passed by Congress in 1980, grants authority to the EPA to regulate the cleanup of brownfields. The Brownfields Revitalization and Environmental Restoration Act of 2011 authorized up to $100 million per year to assess and clean up Brownfields, but it expired in 2006. The Small Business and Liability Relief and Brownfield Revitalization Act, passed in 2002 (Public Law 107-118, H.R. 2869, 6), limits the liability and costs for developers and attempts to address the environmental, economic, and environmental justice concerns associated with brownfields and their redevelopment.

Source: EPA, Office of Solid Waste and Emergency Response. "Brownfields Glossary of Terms." Available at: http://www.epa.gov/swerosps/bf/glossary.htm.

claiming that they could not make truly informed decisions without it. Stakeholders generally agreed, though, that current practices of public participation and the way they are framed do not work. They expressed the belief that finding better ways to engender participation would make it more meaningful for all involved. While officials, specialists, and developers recognized the need for participation, they could not find ways to fit the public into decision-making processes. Citizens and community organizations expressed the desire for greater participation opportunities, but admitted to harboring cynical or apathetic attitudes as a result of vacuous or false attempts to stimulate participation that asked for, yet discounted, public input.

Traditional conceptions of public participation are largely responsible for the paradoxical state reflected by those stakeholders from the Louisville case study as well as other participants in public participation processes. In order to reconcile the needs of various stakeholder groups, a more authentic and effective model of public participation, grounded in the principles of participatory democracy, is needed. Public participation processes have four major components: (1) the issue or situation; (2) the administrative structure, systems, and processes within which participation takes place; (3) the administrators; and, (4) the citizens (King et al., 1998). Traditionally, participation efforts are framed such that these components are arrayed around the issue. The citizen is placed at the greatest distance from the issue, the administrative structures and processes are the closest, and the administrator is the agent between the structure and the citizens.

In the context of conventional participation, the category into which the Louisville case study falls, the administrator controls the ability of citizens to influence the situation or the process. The administrative structure and processes are the politically and socially constructed frameworks within which the administrator must operate. These frameworks give the administrator the authority to formulate decisions only after the issue has been defined. Thus, the administrator has no real power to redefine the issue or alter administrative processes to allow for greater citizen involvement.

Also in the context of conventional participation, the administrator either plays the role of expert or recruits expert consultants within the relevant field of inquiry. Participation within this context is structured to maintain the centrality of the administrator (King et al., 1998). The citizen becomes the "client" of the professional administrator. This process establishes a practitioner-client hierarchy, reinforced by authority and expertise. In this falsely dualistic relationship, the administrator is separated from the needs and interests of the citizens, the people whom he or she is presumed to be serving.

Participation in this context is ineffective and conflictual. It happens too late in the process, that is, after the issues have been framed and most decisions have been made. Rather than cooperating to decide how best to address issues, therefore, citizens are reactive and judgmental, often refusing to support the administrators' efforts as well as the implementation of final plans. Alternatively, administrators have a tendency to be territorial and parochial; they resist sharing information and rely on their technical and professional expertise to justify their role in administrative processes. In this context, citizen participation is more symbolic than real (King et al., 1998; Moote et al., 1997). Ultimately, the power that citizens yield is aimed at blocking or redirecting administrative efforts rather than working as partners to define the issues, establish the parameters, develop methods of investigation, and select techniques for addressing problems.

Substantive participation attempts to achieve the participatory ideal of public participation, maximizing the opportunities for citizen involvement and input by (1) allowing for the direct participation of citizens or non-experts in the decision-making process; (2) giving citizens shared authority with officials in the decision; (3) encouraging face-to-face interaction between officials and the public over an extended period of time; and, (4) providing citizens with an opportunity to participate on an equal basis with officials and experts (Bachrach & Botwinick, 1992; Moote et al., 1997).

Substantive participation requires that administrators and facilitators focus on the processes as well as the outcomes of the participation process. In this context, participation is an integral part of local economic development decisions, rather than a supplement to existing practices. Substantive participation means that the public is part of the deliberation process from issue framing to decision making (Moote et al., 1997). The context of substantive participation is therefore radically different from the context of conventional or traditional participation. Substantive participation places the citizen next to the issue, with the administrative structures and

Greenovation: Smart Growth

Smart Growth is a theory of planning and transportation that seeks to balance community and neighborhood growth with sustainable practices as well as short-term goals with long-term and regional considerations. The Smart Growth Network is a network of public, private, and nongovernmental organizations that seek to improve the development practices in communities, neighborhoods, and regions in the United States. The network partners with a wide range of organizations, including historic preservation groups, environmental organizations, real estate and business developers, and government entities, to encourage balanced development that supports both communities and the environment.

According to the U.S. Environmental Protection Agency, the Smart Growth Network have developed a list of 10 basic principles:

1. Mixed land uses
2. Take advantage of compact building design
3. Create a range of housing opportunities and choices
4. Create walkable neighborhoods
5. Foster distinctive, attractive communities with a strong sense of place
6. Preserve open space, farmland, natural beauty, and critical environmental areas
7. Strengthen and direct development toward existing communities
8. Provide a variety of transportation choices
9. Make development decisions predictable, fair, and cost effective
10. Encourage community and stakeholder collaboration in development decisions

Source: Smart Growth. U.S. Environmental Protection Agency. Available at: http://www.epa.gov/smartgrowth/about_sg.htm.

processes furthest away (Turner, 2010). The administrator, however, is still the bridge between the two. Citizens are central and directly related to the issue; they have an immediate and equal opportunity to influence the process and outcomes. The administrators' influence comes from their relationship with the citizenry as well as from their expertise (and access to expertise and technical knowledge) and position. The administrative structures and processes are defined by the relationship and interactions of citizens and administrators (Turner, 2010).

ALLISON H. TURNER

See also: Ecovillage (Activism); Green Cities (Economics).

Note

1. The foundation for contemporary CED is derived from economic theories of endogenous growth (Shaffer et al., 2006). Over the past century, economic growth theory in the United States has moved through a progression that can be presented in terms of "waves" (Bradshaw & Blakely, 2002). While each wave has laid the foundation for the next, none have completely replaced that upon which it is predicated; thus, remnants of first-wave theory and policy still exist today.

References

Bachrach, P., and A. Botwinick. 1992. *Power and Empowerment: A Radical Theory of Participatory Democracy*. Philadelphia: Temple University Press.

Bradshaw, T. J., and E. J. Blakely. 2002. *Planning Local Economic Development: Theory and Practice*, 3rd ed. Thousand Oaks, CA: Sage.

King, C. S., K. M. Feltey, and B. O. Susel. 1998. "The Question of Participation: Toward Authentic Public Participation in Public Administration." *Public Administration Review* 58: 317–332.

Lejano, R. P., and A. T. Wessells. 2006. "Community and Economic Development: Seeking Common Ground in Discourse and in Practice." *Urban Studies* 43: 1469–1483.

Moote, M. A., M. P. McClaran, and D. K. Chickering. 1997. "Theory in Practice: Applying Participatory Democracy Theory to Public Land Planning." *Environmental Management* 21: 77–89.

Shaffer, R., S. Deller, and D. Marcouiller. 2006. "Rethinking Community Economic Development." *Economic Development Quarterly* 20: 59–74.

Stivers, C. 1990. "Active Citizenship and Public Administration." In G. L. Wamsley, R. N. Bacher, C. T. Goodsell, P. S. Kronenbuerg, J. A. Rohr, C. Stivers, O. F. White, and J. F. Wolf, eds., *Refounding Public Administration*. Thousand Oaks, CA: Sage, 246–273.

Turner, A. H. 2010. "Exploring the Role of Participatory Democracy in Local Economic Development Decisions: The Brownfields Institute, Louisville, Kentucky." PhD diss., University of Louisville.

EARTH DAY

Earth Day, a call for the regeneration of the earth's polluted environment, was first held on April 22, 1970. An estimated 20 million people gathered on that day to confront the earth's ecological problems. Originally organized as a day of education through environmental teach-ins on college and university campuses, Earth Day escalated to include rallies, demonstrations, and other protests (including protests against the Vietnam War). Students from 10,000 elementary and secondary schools and 2,000 colleges took part. The primary mover behind Earth Day was Gaylord Nelson, the U.S. senator from Wisconsin. Nelson had been active in environmental issues since his term as governor of Wisconsin (1958–1962). He conceived of the idea of Earth Day during the summer of 1969 while speaking at a conference on water quality in Santa Barbara, California. Nelson took note of teach-ins on the Vietnam War being conducted on college campuses and decided to promote the ideal of an environmental teach-in. The initial funding was supplied by Larry Rockefeller, an environmental lawyer at the time, and donations from Walter Reuter, president of the United Auto Workers, and George Meany, AFL-CIO president. The original coordinator of Earth Day events was Denis

Denis Hayes, head of Environment Teach-In, Inc., coordinating activities for the first Earth Day, April 22, 1970. (AP/Wide World Photos)

Hayes, a graduate student from Harvard University who had previous been involved in political organizing. The first office for Earth Day was donated by John Gardner of Common Cause. Organizers eventually spent $125,000 on the effort and reported receiving 2,000 to 3,000 letters a day.

The main thought behind Earth Day was that America must change the way it is living or smother in its own wastes. Many issues brought these concerns to the forefront: the population of the United States was expected to increase by 100 million (from 200 million to 300 million) by 2000; each year, 200 million tons of contaminants were released into the air; every second, 2 million gallons of sewage flowed into the nation's waterways; each person in the United States generated 7 pounds of solid waste a day; and chemicals, particularly DDT, remained chemically active. In anticipation of Earth Day, a group at the University of Minnesota collected 26,000 empty cams and tried to return them (unsuccessfully) to the manufacturer to be recycled. At the University of Illinois in Champaign,

Greenovator: Gaylord Nelson

Gaylord Nelson (b. 1916) was elected to two terms as Wisconsin's governor. His overhaul of the state's management of its natural resources earned him a national reputation as the "conservation governor." He was elected to the U.S. Senate in 1962 and served until 1980, when he lost his seat to Republican Robert Kasten. After leaving the Senate, Nelson was chairman of the Wilderness Society, an organization devoted to preserving the wild nature of America's public lands. In the 1990s, Nelson turned his attention to population control. Planet Earth, he warned, could not sustain an unlimited population. He received the Presidential Medal of Freedom in 1995 for his environmental work. Nelson died on July 3, 2005.

Greenovator: Denis Hayes

Denis Hayes (b. 1944) was enrolled in the Kennedy School of Government at Harvard University when Senator Gaylord Nelson tapped him to be the national coordinator of the initial Earth Day Observance on April 22, 1970. Denis Hayes served as head of the Energy Research Institute during the Jimmy Carter administration and is currently president of the Bullitt Foundation, an organization devoted to protecting the natural environment of the Pacific Northwest. He continues to coordinate Earth Day activities worldwide and has published over 100 articles and books on the environment. *Time* magazine named Denis Hayes a "Hero of the Planet" in 1999 and *Look* magazine named him one of the 100 most influential Americans of the 20th century.

students removed 6 tons of refuse from a nearby creek and lobbied local officials to adopt a beautification plan. At the University of California in Berkeley, another group planned a month-long 400-mile trek from Sacramento to Los Angeles, with a stop along with way at Delano, where Mexican American grape pickers were protesting the use of pesticides in the fields.

Television and radio observed Earth Day with special broadcasts: on NBC, *The Today Show* devoted its entire programming for the week to the environment; CBS presented the four-part *Doomsday Dilemma*, and ABC showed four special programs. The 190 stations of the Public Television Network devoted six and a half hours of programming to Earth Day concerns. Entire episodes of *Sesame Street* and *Mr. Rogers' Neighborhood* were devoted to ecology.

In New York City, the main Earth Day observances took place in Union Square, which hosted over 100 exhibits. The *New York Times* estimated that over 100,000 passed through the square during the day. Several candidates for the office of governor of New York (Nelson Rockefeller, Arthur Goldberg, Robert Morgenthau) requested to address the crowd, but organizers refused their request because they did not want to turn Earth Day into a political event. Mayor John Lindsey asked city residents to refrain from driving during the day, and municipal agencies did not use cars except in cases of emergency. For two hours, internal combustion engines were banned on Fifth Avenue between 14th and 59th streets. During the day, Lindsey rode around in an electric powered bus, provided by Con Edison.

Earth Day raised the question: Can both progress and the environment be preserved or must one be sacrificed in order to protect or further the other?

Senator Edmund Muskie of Maine, vice presidential candidate in 1968 and himself a sponsor of environmental legislation, warned that conservation could take place at the expense of the nation's economic growth. Critics also contended that Earth Day diverted the nation's attention from more pressing problems faced by minority communities. However, Earth Day's massive public support forced politicians to address the nation's environmental concerns. The first Earth Day galvanized Congress to pass landmark environmental legislation, including the Clean Air Act (1970), the Water Quality Improvement Act (1970), the Occupational Safety and Health Act (1970), the Federal Environmental Pesticide Control Act (1972), the Endangered Species Act (1973), the Safe Drinking Water Act (1974), Resource Recovery Act (1976), and the Federal Land Policy and Management Act (1976). Today, nearly every state has one or more agencies charged with protecting its environment, and 150 colleges and universities have programs in environmental studies.

Observances were held on the 20th anniversary of Earth Day (April 22, 1990), when 200 million people gathered in 140 countries (and paid particular attention to recycling efforts worldwide) and again in 2000 (when Earth Day organizers used the Internet for the first time to reach 5,000 environmental groups worldwide to draw attention to global warming and the need for clean energy). Earth Day continues to be observed internationally each year on April 22 by hundreds of millions of people. The U.S. Environmental Protection Agency encourages citizens to "make every day Earth Day" and suggests that each person commit to at least five actions to protect the environment.

WENDELL G. JOHNSON

See also: Environmental Tips for Earth Day (documents); Green and Sustainability Fairs and Festivals (Activism).

References

Cahn, Robert, and Patricia Cahn. 1990. "Did Earth Day Change the World?" *Environment* 32:7: 16–43.

Christofferson, Bill. 2004. *The Man from Clear Lake: Earth Day Founder Senator Gaylord Nelson*. Madison: University of Wisconsin Press.

Hayes, Denis. 2000. *The Official Earth Day Guide to Planet Repair*. Washington, DC: Island Press.

EARTH FIRST!

Earth First!, an environmental group, has been a leader in developing tactics to fight against what its members consider the exploitation of the environment. Environmentalism became popular in the late 1960s, and by the 1970s the environmental movement comprised a series of national and grassroots organizations that lobbied on behalf of the environment. Foremost among these organizations were the Sierra Club and the Wilderness Society. Besides having large national memberships, they had an army of lobbyists in Washington, D.C., who were working to pass environmentalist legislation. They were successful in the passage of several important pieces of legislation protecting endangered species. By the

Earth First! member and activist Darryl Cherney
plays the guitar during a rally in Arcata, California in
1996. (AP/Wide World Photos)

mid-1970s, however, many environmental activists had come to believe that these organizations had become entrenched bureaucracies more interested in compromise with the resource industry than in fighting for the environment. It was a 1977 report, the "Roadless Area Review and Evaluation II," which proposed only 15 million of the 62 million acres in the national forests be protected from resource development, that triggered a revolt by the activists in the environmentalist movement. Refusal of the national environmentalist groups to fight this review written by the Forestry Service infuriated many rank-and-file environmentalists. One of those disturbed by the growing cooperation between the environmental organizations and the resource industry was David Foreman, a Washington lobbyist for the Wilderness Society. He resigned his post as a lobbyist and moved to a new job in New Mexico.

Five political activists founded Earth First! on April 3, 1980, to fight what they deemed the exploitation of the environment. On a 10-day wilderness outing in the Pincacte Desert in Mexico, David Foreman, Ron Kezar, Bart Koehler, Mike Roselle, and Howie Wolke decided to launch a new organization to serve as a militant alternative to what they perceived to be the ineffectual policies of the Sierra Club and the Wilderness Society. They believed that these organizations had sold out to business interests. All of the founders were veterans of the environmentalist movement except Roselle, who had been active in several radical left-wing political organizations. Another shared experience was their admiration for the eco-rebels in Edward Abbey's novel *The Monkey Wrench Gang* (1975). These activists wanted a grassroots group that would take an uncompromising militant stance on the environment and be willing to use civil disobedience and guerrilla tactics. The motto for Earth First! was to be "No Compromise in the Defense of Mother Earth." They wanted to restore the wilderness to its natural state, not lobby for incremental change. Soon after its founding, Foreman started a newsletter, *Earth First!*, and leaders started making public appearances around the country spreading the new message of Earth First! By 1989, the organization had around 10,000 members and many more sympathizers.

A series of successful demonstrations initiated by Earth First! made it a force to be reckoned with in the development of wilderness areas. The first major action was a 1981 demonstration against the Glen Canyon Dam on the Colorado River. Leaders unfurled a 300-foot black polyethylene banner that resembled a crack in the dam. This symbolic attack on the dam resulted in no arrests, but it was the first step in the organization's efforts to publicize its opposition to current environmental policies.

Another demonstration followed in July 1982 over oil exploration in the Gros Ventre range of northwestern Wyoming. This action pitted Earth First! against the Getty Oil Company and the Ronald Reagan administration. Getty wanted to explore for oil in the Little Granite Creek area. A mass demonstration prevented the company from building a road to the Little Granite Creek. Earth First! supporters made their first use of sabotage of equipment as a tactic. Success on this occasion ensured that further resource development in this area would cease.

After these successful demonstrations, the leaders of Earth First! embarked on a long-range campaign of sabotage. "Ecotage" was the name given to the tactic of sabotaging road building or logging equipment. A more popular name was monkey-wrenching, which tied sabotage to Abbey's novel. In the 1980s, ecotage was estimated to have cost between $20 and $25 million a year for businesses engaged in road clearing or logging. Another popular tactic was tree spiking. A tree spike was no danger to the tree, but it destroyed tree saws and endangered loggers. Tree spiking became so widespread that Congress passed a law making it a felony. To avoid metal detectors, some monkeywrenchers resorted to tree pinning or using hardened ceramic pins. Another tactic was tree sitting. Activists occupied a tree to prevent it from being cut down.

Foreman and the rest of the original founders of Earth First! eventually found themselves displaced by new elements in the organization. As a mass movement mobilized around Earth First!, it became less a group of direct action advocates to save the environment than a political organization with a social agenda. Foreman became disillusioned by the new direction of the organization, and he resigned in 1990. New leaders, such as Judi Bari and Darryl Cherney, replaced the older leadership and transformed the group's social agenda. These leaders concentrated in fighting big business logging of California redwoods. Bari's death in 1997 has allowed another generation of leaders to transform Earth First! into more of a mainstream environmentalist organization.

Stephen E. Atkins

See also: Environmental Justice (Activism).

References

Downey, Cheryl. 1994. "Among Environmentalists It's in Earth First's Nature to Be a Little Salty." *Orange County Register* (Santa Ana, CA), March 14, p. B1.

Lee, Martha F. 1995. *Earth First!: Environmental Apocalypse.* Syracuse, NY: Syracuse University Press.

Manes, Christopher. 1990. *Green Rage: Radical Environmentalism and the Unmaking of Civilization.* Boston: Little, Brown.

Robertson, Lance. 1998. "Earth First! Splinter Group Embraces Life of Sabotage." *Register-Guard* (Eugene, OR), October 27, p. 1.

Scarce, Rik. 1990. *Eco-Warriors: Understanding the Radical Environmental Movement.* Chicago: Noble Press.

ECOVILLAGE

An ecovillage is a "human-scale, full-featured settlement in which human activities are harmlessly integrated into the natural world in a way that is supportive of healthy human development and can be successfully continued into the indefinite future" (Gilman, 1991, 10). "Human-scale" is defined as the number of members of a community where people are still "able to know and be known by the others in the community, and where each member of the community feels he or she is able to influence the community's direction" (Gilman, 1991, 10). For ecovillages, this number usually falls around 100 or fewer members. "Full-featured" communities are those where members live, work, play, relax, and grow food or manufacture goods all in one area, unlike current human settlements in industrial areas where cities are divided by functions, such as residential districts, shopping districts,

Leslie Shakespeare selects homegrown produce with son Gabriel Hicks, nine, at the neighboring produce farm at EcoVillage in Ithaca, New York, in 2004. (AP Photo/Kevin Rivoli)

manufacturing areas, agricultural areas, and financial districts. While many global communities unintentionally fit under the definition of an ecovillage (i.e., small villages in rural areas), the term *ecovillage* generally signifies a community *created with the intent to* counter current destructive environmental practices and encourage strong social bonds between members. Although every community is different, a general consensus is that each ecovillage has at least these two (ecological and social) components.

Though there are many different ways communities go about reducing their impact on the natural environment, a commitment to ecological sustainability is the key feature of all ecovillages. Some of the ways communities lessen their impact on the natural world include growing much of their own food or committing to purchasing locally grown and produced food, living in smaller homes made from local or reused or reusable materials, using renewable sources of energy, earning income from businesses that support ecological practices, and protecting biodiversity and sustainable land use through good farming practices and the protection of wilderness areas. Some communities also see themselves as places of innovation for new technologies in minimizing the use of natural resources, reducing waste and food production.

Social sustainability is equally important in the creation and maintenance of ecovillages. Ecovillage communities commit to providing members with a sense of belonging, a sense of place, a sense of self-worth, a sense of safety, and a sense of connection with nature (Kline, 1995). Ecovillages create governing structures that ensure that members have a voice in the community and are empowered to initiate change. Depending on the size of the community, this could be through consensus decision making or other participatory action. For some communities, social sustainability might also include a commitment to a shared spiritual path, sharing resources, practicing holistic health practices, encouraging ongoing education, and combating exclusionary practices such as racism or sexism.

Proponents of ecovillages claim that they provide a solution to several major problems currently plaguing industrial societies: environmental degradation, social isolation, and a lack of meaning in our lives.

The interest in ecovillages started in the early 1990s and was primarily related to growing environmental concerns. While public interest in preserving and protecting the environment grew throughout the 1980s, it became a major mainstream movement in the 1990s. By 1998, over two-thirds of the U.S. population considered themselves to be either strong or moderate environmentalists (Ridenour, 1998). Additionally, demographic changes, including the decrease of average family size, the increase in numbers of women working outside the home, single parents, and people living alone, are thought to have led to an increase in social isolation (Graber & Barrow, 2003; Hertzman, 1996). Further, increased mobility has distanced many people from their kin groups and kept others from forming close social ties in their new communities. Contemporary housing developments have generally been designed in a way that eliminates the need for any interaction with neighbors. All of these factors contribute to an increased demand for a more ecologically friendly, communal, and meaningful lifestyle, which ecovillages provide.

Greenovation: Four Key Dimensions of Ecovillage Sustainability

In ecovillages, inhabitants depend on one another and the collective community to provide sustainable environments. Four key dimensions are crucial components to the sustainability of ecovillages:

Social and Community Dimension

- Sustainable ecovillages provide supportive, safe, and empowering environments;
- Inhabitants feel they belong and are connected to their community members;
- Members share resources and provide mutual aid;
- The ecovillage community provides or creates opportunities for sustenance and meaningful work for inhabitants;
- Members are tolerant and accepting of differences;
- Ecovillages promote lifelong education and emphasize holistic and preventive health practices.

Ecological Dimension

- Ecovillages foster connections between inhabitants and the natural world;
- Members are hands-on in their interactions with the Earth and look to nature to meet their basic needs—food, shelter, and clothing;
- Inhabitants, as much as possible, grow organic food within the community and region and create homes with local materials;
- Ecovillages protect biodiversity, foster ecological business principles, and work to preserve, conserve, and protect the environment.

Cultural/Spiritual Dimension

- Ecovillages respect and support individual spiritual beliefs and practices;
- Community encourages participation and unity in shared celebrations, rituals, and cultural activities;

Although still a very small movement, the Global Ecovillage Network (GEN) estimates that there are currently "15,000 identified sustainable community experiments" (Joseph & Bates, 2003, 10) worldwide and some on every continent. The GEN is the primary organization uniting ecovillages globally, promoting the ecovillage movement, and providing educational resources to formed and forming communities. The GEN was created when Ross and Hildur Jackson, co-creators of Gaia Trust in Denmark (an association devoted to furthering the movement toward sustainability), commissioned Robert and Diane Gilman to write a report identifying the world's best examples of ecovillage models. Their report led to several international conferences, which included prominent environmentalists, social thinkers, and policy makers, and eventually led to the development of the GEN in 1994. Education is a key initiative for the GEN, and some of their current projects include curriculum development programs, the creation of a university based on the core tenet of sustainability, and a program called "Living Routes" that provides study opportunities for U.S. university students in ecovillages (Mare, 2000).

There is currently no "official" marker that designates a community as an ecovillage. While this has caused some tension within the movement because groups have differed on what "counts" as an ecovillage, the GEN has decided not to specify criteria or establish a minimum threshold of achievement for a community to identify itself as an ecovillage. Instead, it provides communities a Community Sustainability Assessment Tool that allows individual communities to self-evaluate their practices and determine areas for improvement in the three key areas: social, ecological, and spiritual (Joseph & Bates, 2003).

JADE AGUILAR

See also: Community Economic Development (Activism); Green Cities (Economics); Living off the Grid (Activism); Wise-Use Movement (Activism).

- Inhabitants share visions of an interconnectedness and interdependence with life on Earth, the community, and the community in relation to the whole;
- Ecovillagers seek to create a peaceful, sustainable, and loving world.

Economic Dimension

- Ecovillages promote a mutually beneficial economy and strive to keep money within the community;
- Inhabitants strive to earn, spend, and invest in member-owned retail and service businesses;
- Members save money in homegrown financial institutions.

KIM KENNEDY WHITE

Source: Compiled from the Global Ecovillage Network. Available at http://gen.ecovillage.org/.

References

"Dancing Rabbit Ecovillage: An Introduction." Available at: http://www.youtube.com/watch?v=iobyEjlV9AM.

Dawson, Jonathan. 2006. *Ecovillages: New Frontiers for Sustainability*. London: Green Books/Chelsea.

"Ecovillage Network of the Americas." Available at: http://ena.ecovillage.org/.

Gilman, Robert. 1991. "The Ecovillage Challenge." *In Context* 29: 10–14.

Global Ecovillage Network. Available at: http://www.gaia.org.

Graber, Robert Bates, and C. Raymond Barrow. 2003. "A General Typology of Communalism." *Communal Societies* 23: 1–28.

Hertzman, Ellen. 1996. "Cohousing: A New Type of Housing for the Way We Live." In *Communities Directory: A Guide to Cooperative Living*. Rutledge, MO: Fellowship for Intentional Community Press.

Joseph, Linda, and Albert Bates. 2003. "What Is an 'Ecovillage'?" *Communities* (Spring): 22–24.

Kline, Elizabeth. 1995. "Sustainable Community Indicators." *Community-Based Planning, and Development*. Working paper of the Global Development & Environment Institute at Tufts University, October.

Mare, Christopher. 2000. "A Concise History of the Global Ecovillage Movement." Village Design Institute Academic Papers. Available at: http://www.villagedesign.org/vdi_writings.html.

Ridenour, David. 1998. "Earth Day May No Longer Be Needed." *National Policy Analysis* (March): 191.

ENVIRONMENTAL JUSTICE

The development of green culture means the environment becomes part of the social consciousness and social institutions. Education, religion, government, and economy are social institutions that have begun to include environmental considerations. In 1970, when the U.S. Environmental Protection Agency was formed, green culture moved into the judicial, legislative, and executive branches of government. Many entities such as businesses, schools, and municipalities had to comply with some environmental oversight. With the rise of this type of green culture came greater knowledge of our past and present environmental impacts. One early report examined the controlled and uncontrolled hazardous waste sites and found that the best predictor of where one was located was the race of the people (Commission for Racial Justice, 1987). Other reports followed. These were followed in turn by court cases, legislation, and agency policies focused on environmental justice.

Environmental justice is a controversial term. Some alternative terms are environmental equity and environmental racism. Environmental justice has several components, as described in the sections that follow.

Uneven Environmental Benefits and Burdens

The first component is the uneven distribution of environmental benefits like clean air, water, and land. Pollution accumulates and can cause cancer and death via other diseases from overexposure over time. When this occurs more frequently in one demographic group than others, this is considered unjust. Often there will be other demographic groups with more environmental benefits. In the United States, some demographic groups are more exposed to toxic and hazardous waste, while other groups enjoy the benefits of clean air, land, and water. When the groups who are benefiting from environmental decisions are also a major part of the creation of waste, it heightens the sense of injustice. In the case of race in the United States, people of color generally, and African Americans in particular, suffer more so from environmental injustice. In the Southern California Air Quality District, people of color face a one-in-seven risk of cancer from the list of 148 hazardous air pollutants.

Another demographic component of environmental justice is income. Low-income people are generally more exposed to environmental burdens. There are many studies that try to disaggregate race and income data, but this is challenging. There are undercounts of population in most race data, for example. With full population counts, the imbalance of environmental benefits and burdens by race could be more disproportionate. Most U.S. studies to date indicate that race is a stronger predictive variable than income in predicting environmental burdens.

We Speak for Ourselves

The second component of environmental justice is that the affected group has no effective voice, or say, in the process. One of the themes of environmental justice all over the world is "We Speak for Ourselves." Often environmental justice communities need to increase their capacity to engage in environmental decisions, and many have. This is particularly true in decisions that affect them where they live, work, play, worship, or recreate. This theme speaks to the authenticity of voice that comes from those individuals and cultures that have been historically burdened by environmental decisions. This theme speaks to the self-empowerment that is characteristic of the environmental justice movement.

Many environmental justice communities have grown to distrust government agencies of any type, including the judicial system. They do not necessarily trust physicians or research hospitals. The use of communities of color for research dates back to the Tuskegee experiments where African American men were intentionally infected with deadly diseases without their knowledge. The black farmers were systematically stripped of any equal treatment before the law until their historic settlement in 2009. Latina/o, Asian, Asian Pacific Islander, Irish, and other recent immigrant communities fear government entanglement because it may lead to deportation, even if they are legal citizens. Indigenous peoples on reservations are self-policed by tribal law enforcement. The effect of environmental justice on the greening of U.S. culture is dampened by the distrust of large government intervention.

The first basic way communities and individuals lose the ability to meaningfully participate is through a basic lack of notice of decisions that affect them. For notice to be effective, it must be understood and must give enough time for people to prepare for whatever decision the notice requires. Often notice is in English only, late, and hard to understand. But notice is only the beginning of the problem.

Lack of Power

The third major component of environmental justice is a lack of power. Power in environmental decisions can range from advisory to controlling power. Power is exerted at various decision points in environmental decision making: local land-use controls, state-permitting regulations, and federal environmental laws. Power can also be developed in courts of law, state and federal legislature, and via the executive, or administrative, branch of government. While this power exists in theory, and sometimes as a right, it falls short of the ability to meaningfully include most environmental justice communities in the major environmental decisions of a given ecosystem or bioregion.

Even with knowledge of personal environmental stressors through the technological development of green culture and access to sources on the Internet (like scorecard.org), the lack of political power can translate into an inability to resist new environmental burdens such as waste sites and waste transfer stations. These burdens continue to grow as population and consumption increase.

For a community to resist environmental burdens and exert power it must have the capacity to do so. For the community to have the capacity to participate it must first have adequate and meaningful notice of the proposed environmental decisions. This can be a flashpoint of controversy because many environmental justice communities speak English only as a second language. Who actually gets the notice is another issue. Does every resident get a personal visit reminding him or her of the meeting? Generally, a posted notice at the site and legal ads in a local newspaper are all most communities get. Generally, a state agency will respond to most inquiries.

These decision points require days of participation, missed hours of work, and therefore lower income and intensive training (depending on the issue). Child care is seldom provided by the convening stakeholder, usually the governmental agency. Environmental justice communities are often marginalized and disenfranchised areas. Individuals struggle with racism, unemployment, crime, low income, and poor mass transit. The other two major decision makers—industry and government—both have many paid professionals who are generally very knowledgeable. The power difference is large. Proposals to pay community members for necessary training, lost wages, and child care are inadequate if ever available. Both industry and government are motivated to decrease the transaction costs that come with meaningful community involvement. Communities generally need more technical assistance and time to study the issue.

Knowledge of our past and present environmental burdens and benefits continues to grow as impacts continue to increase to global proportions. If inclusionary dialogues accompany sustainability, they may give environmental justice communities a presence in the greening of U.S. culture.

Environmental Justice as Part of Environmental Policy

Environmental justice became a significant development on environmental policy in the early 1990s. As U.S. environmental policies developed, more baseline information became available and was used to monitor changes and accumulations in pollution. It became harder to develop and implement an environmental policy without considering environmental justice distributive impacts. This information continues to allow for greater study on the impact to the environment, including to cities and to public health.

Federal Government and Environmental Justice

In February 1994 President Bill Clinton signed Executive Order 12898 on environmental justice. The essence of the order states:

> Each Federal Agency shall make achieving environmental justice part of its mission by identifying and addressing, as appropriate, disproportionately high and adverse human health or environmental effects of its programs, policies, and activities on minority populations and low income populations.

This historic executive order was preceded by years of struggle from community-based environmental justice groups. Although this did not end the community-based struggles for environmental justice, it does show how important environmental justice is to the greening of American culture by integrating it into administrative structures. In some states the federal government is a large landowner and caretaker of federal lands. Since federal agencies have to comply with Executive Order 12898 on Environmental Justice, the impact on environmental policy is far reaching, often down to the state level. The U.S. Environmental Protection Agency (EPA) went on to define environmental justice as

> the fair treatment and meaningful involvement of all people regardless of race, ethnicity, income, national origin or educational level with respect to the development, implementation, and enforcement of environmental laws, regulations, and policies. Fair treatment means that no population, due to policy or economic disempowerment, is forced to bear a disproportionate burden of the negative human health or environmental impacts of pollution or other environmental consequences resulting from industrial, municipal, and commercial operation or the execution of federal, state, local and tribal programs and policies. (EPA, 1998, 2)

State Approaches

The growing evidence of the significance of environmental justice increased the federal focus and developed a state environmental policy focus. Racial disparities persist. In 2007 the report "Toxic Wastes and Race at Twenty: 1987–2007" stated that 40 of the 44 states with hazardous waste facilities have disproportionately high percentages of people of color in host neighborhoods. On average they had about twice as many facilities.

States also incorporate environmental justice issues into their environmental policy. States are very important in environmental policy because most federal policy filters through regional federal offices and then to states. States receive substantial amounts of money and other resources from federal agencies for environmental protection. States are often in the position of enforcing sometimes controversial environmental laws.

Oregon is one example of how environmental justice grew at the state level, although each state is unique. Oregon has a history of environmental protection, primarily through state land-use planning and federal land management practices. It also has a history of racial exclusion. In this context several environmental justice advisory committees grew into what became Senate Bill 420, which was signed into Law (74th Leg. Assem., Reg. Sess. [Or 2007]).

The mission of the Oregon Environmental Justice Task Force (EJTF) is to advise the governor about environmental justice issues. Every natural resource agency is to submit an annual environmental justice report to them and the governor. Natural resource agencies are broadly defined to include public health, educational, and cultural agencies. As with most state-level environmental justice missions, the Oregon EJTF mission is to increase the public participation of individuals and communities affected by agencies' decisions. This can be challenging where many different languages are spoken and written.

Local government is the next level of environmental planning and policy making. It generally controls local land uses, but can be preempted by the state, which in turn can be preempted by the federal government. Since many environmental justice issues are community based and driven, they can appear in local land-use

Greenovation: Excerpt from Oregon Senate Bill 420

The following is an excerpt from Oregon State Senate Bill 420, which calls for establishing an Environmental Justice Task Force.

SECTION 2. (1) There is established the Environmental Justice Task Force consisting of 12 members appointed by the Governor. The members shall be persons who are well-informed on the principles of environmental justice and who, to the greatest extent practicable, represent minority communities, low-income communities, environmental interests, industry groups and geographically diverse areas of the state. Of the 12 members, the Governor shall appoint one member of the task force from each of the following commissions:

(a) The Commission on Asian Affairs;
(b) The Commission on Black Affairs;
(c) The Commission on Hispanic Affairs; and
(d) The Commission on Indian Services.

(2) The task force shall submit an annual report to the Governor setting forth its view of the progress of natural resource agencies toward achieving the goals established pursuant to section 3 of this 2007 Act and identifying any other environmental issues that the task force determines need attention.

(3) The term of office of each member is four years, but a member serves at the pleasure of the Governor. Before the expiration of the term of a member, the Governor shall appoint a successor whose term begins on January 1 of the following year. A member may be reappointed. If there is a vacancy for any cause, the Governor shall make an appointment to become immediately effective for the unexpired term.

KIM KENNEDY WHITE

Source: Senate Bill 420. 74th Oregon Legislative Assembly, 2007. Available at: http://www.leg.state.or.us/07reg/measpdf/sb0400.dir/sb0420.intro.pdf.

forums. Although some environmentalists may speak in these forums, courtrooms and legislatures are their traditional venues of choice. Traditional U.S. environmental groups include the National Resources Defense Council, the Sierra Club, and the Audubon Society. Their membership bases tend to be white people, often from middle- or higher-income groups. Environmental justice groups tend to be community based and comprise people of color or low-income people. Both generalizations are changing rapidly.

Sustainability and Environmental Justice

Sustainability is a powerful new force evidencing the greening of culture in more personal, public, and professional venues. Since the 1987 Gro Brundtland Report "Our Common Future," sustainability is generally defined as meeting the needs of the present generation without compromising the ability of future generations to meet their own needs. Most concepts of sustainability are phrased in terms of ecological health and continuity. These include all aspects of human society: businesses, governments, and communities. Through various treaties, the term sustainability grew to encompass principles of sustainability. Most of these principles aid the understanding of environmental justice.

As annunciated by the Rio Declaration and Agenda 21 (1992), a major principle is integrated decision making. Complex layers of government can often allow for fewer checks and reduced enforcement of environmental decisions, generally increasing environmental impacts. In the United States, the relationship between local land use and state and federal land-use decisions is complex. There are instances where the state is unaware of the local land-use restrictions and where the local government is unaware of the state's environmental decision-making processes. The failure of timely intergovernmental actions regarding the environment is a major omission of past and present environmental policy. Environmental justice issues have often been lost in the complex interplay of intergovernmental relations. With integrated decision making, they are observed and monitored.

Another important principle of sustainability from the Rio Declaration, Principle 15, is the "precautionary principle." The purpose of the precautionary principle is to protect the natural systems on which all life depends from irreparable damage. Essentially, the precautionary principle shifts the burden of persuasion in

Greenovator: Natural Resources Defense Council

The Natural Resources Defense Council (NRDC) is a nonprofit national environmental advocacy organization geared toward safeguarding the Earth and its inhabitants as well as restoring the quality of the Earth's land, air, and water.

Environmental awareness began taking shape in the United States during the 1960s and 1970s; the establishment of the NRDC in 1970 was timely. During the same period, additional environmental-awareness organizations formed, including Friends of the Earth (1968) and the Sierra Club Legal Defense Fund (1971). In an effort to protest the abuse of the environment and to promote awareness, 1970 marked the beginning of Earth Day.

Programs within the NRDC include a focus on air, energy, health, international issues, land, nuclear, urban, and water and oceans. Priorities within the programs include curbing global warming, moving America beyond oil dependency, saving wild land across the Americas, reviving the oceans, decreasing the use of toxic chemicals, and accelerating the greening of China.

Members of the NRDC publish various texts promoting policy solutions, such as *OnEarth* magazine and online newsletters and blogs (all available on the NRDC's Web site). NRDC staffers include attorneys, scientists, policy analysts, and educators, all of whom work toward protecting the environment and public health. Staff members present testimony before Congress in order to promote legislation geared toward the NRDC's mission.

Members of the NRDC encourage individuals to become activists by contacting decision makers and voicing support for various local, state, and federal legislation geared toward the NRDC's mission.

MICHELE LOCKHART

favor of the environment so those who create environmental impacts have the duty to mitigate them before the harm is done. They also have higher requirements to mitigate impacts. This means that when harm to the environment or to human health will result from the environmental decision (broadly defined), mitigating measures should be taken to prevent harm even if scientific evidence is inconclusive. The declining need for scientific evidence to stop environmental impacts and the increasing need for scientific evidence to demonstrate no negative environmental impacts show a heightened environmental consciousness. As a measure of the greening of U.S. culture, several municipalities now have the precautionary principle codified into their local land-use law.

Another principle of sustainability put forth by the Rio Declaration, in Principle 10, is public participation. Public participation in all its nuances and forms is a fundamental environmental justice value. This particular demand from the Environmental Justice Movement opened the door for many environmental practices and policies. This is useful for traditional U.S. environmentalists and non-environmental justice communities. Citizen monitoring of the environment helps create important ecological baselines and other indicators of sustainability. Public participation is currently considered time consuming and expensive by government and industry stakeholders. The engagement of the community most affected by a given environmental decision is often presumed. It is often the case that a community receives little or no notice of local environmentally impactful decisions. Most communities do not receive actual notice of public or private decisions that have large environmental impacts outside their local community. It is one thing to say that public participation is a right and another to make it happen for everyone. By expanding aspects of public participation, environmental justice communities will have more venues for participation. By expanding the priority that public engagement has in environmental and sustainability planning, more resources can be devoted to increasing community capacity building.

As society begins to explore ways to become more sustainable, the areas of nature that have accumulated wastes and pollution become substantial impediments. These can be environmental justice communities. It is difficult to contain the waste and pollution that can accumulate in communities to one specific location, and it tends to grow and spread to other areas of the ecosystem, such as the air and water. The equity component of U.S. sustainability is not always included in sustainability planning and programming. As environmental knowledge, population, consumption, and waste continue to increase, the environmental and ecological aspects of sustainability planning will require knowledge of the accumulation points of toxic wastes. These are often environmental justice communities.

R. WILLIAM COLLIN

See also: Executive Order 12898 on Environmental Justice (documents); Goldman Environmental Prize (Activism); Memorandum of Understanding on Environmental Justice (documents); Toxic 100: Top Air Polluters Index (documents).

References

488 Federal Supplement 2d, 889, 2007.
Adler, Jonathan H. 1997. *Environmentalism at the Crossroads: Green Activism in America.* Washington, DC: Capital Research Center.
Bullard, Robert D., ed. 1994. *Unequal Protection: Environmental Justice and Communities of Color.* San Francisco: Sierra Club.

Bullard, Robert D., Paul Mohai, Robin Saha, and Beverly Wright. 2007. *Toxic Wastes and Race at Twenty 1987-2007: A Report Prepared for the United Church of Christ Justice & Witness Ministries.* United Church of Christ.

Cole, Luke W., and Sheila R. Foster. 2001. *From the Ground Up: Environmental Racism and the Rise of the Environmental Justice Movement.* New York: New York University Press.

Collin, Robin, and Robert Collin. 2010. *The Encyclopedia of Sustainability—Economy, Environment, and Equity.* Santa Barbara, CA: ABC-CLIO.

Commission for Racial Justice. 1987. *Toxic Wastes and Race in the US.* United Church of Christ.

Environmental Protection Agency (EPA). 1998. Office of Federal Activities. *Final Guidance for Incorporating Environmental Justice Concerns in EPA's NEPA Compliance Analysis.* Washington, DC: U.S. Government Printing Office, 2.

Knight, Richard L., and Sarah F. Bates. 1995. *A New Century for Natural Resources Management.* Washington, DC: Island Press.

Natural Resources Defense Council. *OnEarth.* Available at: http://www.nrdc.org/.

Rechtschaffen, Clifford, Eileen Guana, and Catherine O'Neil, eds. 2009. *Environmental Justice: Law, Policy and Regulation,* 2nd ed. Durham, NC: Carolina Academic Press.

Rio Declaration on Environment and Development. 1992. The United Nations Conference on Environment and Development. http://www.unesco.org/education/information/nfsunesco/pdf/RIO_E.PDF.

GOLDMAN ENVIRONMENTAL PRIZE

The Goldman Environmental Prize, established in 1990 in honor of San Francisco philanthropists and civic leaders Richard N. Goldman (1920–2010) and Rhoda H. Goldman (1924–1996), annually recognizes grassroots environmental heroes—one from each of the six inhabited continents. The prize is announced each April to coincide with Earth Day, and winners receive $150,000. Additionally, six individuals are chosen each year to receive a bronze Ouroboros, a symbol of nature's power of renewal that shows a serpent biting its tail.

The prize typically goes to heroes who work to protect endangered species and ecosystems, promoting sustainability, striving for environmental justice, influencing environmental policies, and fighting against destructive environmental practices. The international jury selects "individuals for sustained and significant efforts to protect and enhance the natural environment, often at great personal risk." The following U.S. recipients of the award helped spark positive environmental change in their communities.

> **Hilton Kelley, 2011.** Hilton Kelley grew up in the Port Arthur neighborhood along the Texas Gulf Coast, which, according to the Environmental Protection Agency (EPA), has some of the highest levels of toxic air releases in the country. Port Arthur has asthma and cancer rates that are among the highest and income levels among the lowest in Texas. Hilton left the community for California and worked as a stuntman and actor, most notably on CBS's *Nash Bridges.* When he returned home for a visit in 2000, he was sickened by the crime, economic destruction, and industrial pollution. He established the Community In-power and Development Association (CIDA) to train local

residents on monitoring air quality and worked with Motiva, who runs the largest petrochemical refinery in the country located in Port Arthur, to develop a "good neighbor" agreement, which now provides health coverage for residents and implemented equipment to reduce harmful emissions. Kelley and his wife run a soul food restaurant, Kelley's Kitchen, and he continues to fight for stricter environmental regulations.

Lynn Henning, 2010. Activist and family farmer, Henning exposed the practices that pollute livestock factory farms in rural Michigan, specifically concentrated animal feeding operations (CAFOs), leading to the issuing of hundreds of citations for water quality violations in the region. She worked with other community members to form the Environmentally Concerned Citizens of South Central Michigan (ECCSCM) in 2000 and is a staff member of the Sierra Club's Michigan chapter. In 2008, a proposed CAFO facility was denied a permit by the Michigan Department of Environmental Quality largely based on Henning's research findings.

Maria Gunnoe, 2009. Lifelong Appalachian resident and member of the Cherokee tribe, Gunnoe fights against the coal industry's destructive mountaintop removal practices. She's been instrumental in enforcing stricter industry regulations and the closure of mines in the region and has created and provided trainings to neighborhood groups. In March 2007, Gunnoe, along with her partner, the Ohio Valley Environmental Coalition (OVEC), won a federal lawsuit against the Army Corps of Engineers, repealing mountaintop removal valley permits in southern West Virginia. She continues to fight, despite threats against her and her family, to organize communities and to pass the federal Clean Water Protection Act.

Craig E. Williams, 2006. A decorated Vietnam War veteran, Craig E. Williams was instrumental in convincing the Pentagon to stop plans to incinerate chemical weapons stored around the country. He founded the Chemical Weapons Working Group (CWWG), a grassroots coalition that works for the safe disposal of weapons waste. Williams continues to work to mobilize citizens living near incinerators and bringing forward whistleblowers; he was a founder of the Vietnam Veterans of America Foundation in 1980, which was one of six groups that co-founded the Nobel Peace Prize winning group (1997), the International Campaign to Ban Landmines.

Margie Eugene-Richard, 2004. The first African American recipient of the Goldman Prize, activist Eugene-Richard grew up in the Old Diamond neighborhood in Norco, Louisiana, a predominantly African American neighborhood, next to Shell Chemicals plant, also known as Cancer Alley. The 1973 Shell pipeline explosion and a 1988 industrial accident led to her decision to become an activist. She's been instrumental in a number of environmental justice victories.

Julia Bonds, 2003. Director of Coal River Mountain Watch, coal miner's daughter, activist, and community organizer, Bonds led the fight against the destructive practice of mountaintop removal in the Appalachian Mountain range. Her vigilance led to a number of victories; she passed away in 2011.

Sarah James, Norma Kassi, and Jonathon Solomon, 2002. Native Gwich'ins and lifetime members of the collective leadership voice, the Gwich'in Steering Committee, James, Kassi, and Solomon fight against the destruction of their native lands from oil exploration and drilling and campaign to protect the Arctic's porcupine caribou and their refuge.

Jane Akre and Steve Wilson, 2001. Investigative reporters and husband-wife team, Jane Akre and Steve Wilson uncovered and documented the dangers of the genetically modified growth hormone, rBGH. The hormone, which has been linked to cancer in humans and can harm cows, was approved by the government without adequate testing on the effects. Under pressure from the hormone's manufacturer and Fox News (against whom they won a lawsuit), the couple came under fire to rewrite their story and were fired in 1997. They continue to work to expose environmental and health threats.

Kory Johnson, 1998. Kory Johnson lost her older sister due to heart problems in 1989, likely the result of a contaminated well from which her mother drank when she was pregnant. Johnson, just nine years old at the time, discovered a cancer cluster in her neighborhood and formed the Children for a Safe Environment (CFSE). Now with nearly 360 members, the CFSE fights for neighborhoods that are targets for industrial waste dumps or incinerators. Johnson continues to be a tireless organizer and advocate for environmental justice.

Terri Swearingen, 1997. Swearingen co-founded the Tri-State Environmental Council to fight against Waste Technologies Industries (WTI), which built an incinerator in a low-income residential community in the Appalachian town of East Liverpool, Ohio, within 1,100 feet of an elementary school, exposing residents to toxic waste and carcinogenic heavy metals. Her protest actions got her arrested nearly a dozen times and prompted the Ohio governor to declare a moratorium on new incinerators. The Tri-State Environmental Council is credited with pushing the U.S. EPA to issue federal guidelines for siting hazardous waste management facilities.

Aurora Castillo, 1995. Aurora Castillo was a fourth-generation Mexican American who formed the Mothers of East Los Angeles (MELA) to oppose a new prison in 1984 (the eighth prison in her predominantly Latino community). The community group now fights to protect East Los Angeles from public health and environmental threats. The prison relocated in 1992, and the group continues to enjoy environmental victories; she passed away in 1998.

JoAnn Tall, 1993. JoAnn Tall, a member of the Oglala Lakota tribe and mother of eight, lives in the nation's poorest county on the Pine Ridge Reservation in South Dakota and has worked to improve environmental conditions in her community. She co-founded the Native Resource Coalition and spoke out against a proposed project to locate a landfill and incinerator on the reservation and was successful in stopping it. She now serves as a board member on the Seventh Generation Fund.

Samuel LaBudde, 1991. Biologist Sam LaBudde uncovered the capturing and slaughter of dolphins on the Mexican border by tuna fisherman by videotaping

Greenovator: Lois Gibbs

Lois Marie Gibbs is executive director of the Center for Health, Environment, and Justice (CHEJ) in Falls Church, Virginia. According to the CHEJ Web site, Gibbs and her staff advise community groups on strategic activism, scientific and technical evaluation, and public education to confront environmental health hazards. They also campaign to prevent pollution, eliminate PVC plastics, and reduce children's exposure to toxins. Gibbs founded the center in 1981 following the Love Canal crisis in her hometown of Niagara Falls, New York.

In 1978, Gibbs was 27, a high school graduate, and housewife when toxic contamination in the blue-collar Love Canal neighborhood became a national disaster. Many local workers were employed by chemical manufacturers. The *Niagara Gazette* newspaper had reported about chemicals leaching from an old landfill near the Niagara River (State University of New York). There was a pattern of residents' illnesses, particularly miscarriages and birth defects. Gibbs's ill son attended an elementary school built atop the 16-acre dump site. The Niagara Falls Board of Education had bought the land in 1953 for $1 from Hooker Chemical Company. Though more than 21,000 tons of chemical waste were disposed of there since 1942, the school board's deed included a disclaimer of liability.

The original excavation dated to the 1890s, when developer William T. Love intended to divert the river for hydroelectric power to a model industrial city, a project that failed.

Fearful for her children, Gibbs petitioned to close the school and organized families into the Love Canal Homeowners Association (Boston University School of Public Health). It was one of several advocacy groups to form as local, state, and federal authorities investigated. On August 2, 1978, the New York State Health Department declared an emergency, recommending that the school be closed and pregnant women and children younger than two be evacuated. On August 7, President Jimmy Carter approved financial aid so the state could begin buying houses to relocate families. Gibbs became a prominent spokeswoman and political activist as residents pushed for health studies to determine the extent of contamination (State University of New York at Buffalo).

the evidence and testifying before the U.S. Congress. His actions resulted in a 95 percent reduction in dolphin kills and major tuna brands processing only dolphin-safe tuna by 1990. He was also instrumental in a United Nations resolution to ban the use of damaging driftnets and used the money from his Goldman Prize to establish the Endangered Species Project (ESP).

Lois Gibbs, 1990. Executive director and founder of the Center for Health, Environment, and Justice (CHEJ), Gibbs raised her family on the infamous chemical waste site, Love Canal, and became a community activist, forming the Love Canal Homeowners Association; her efforts to clean up the site led to the creation of the U.S. Environmental Protection Agency's Superfund. CHEJ is a grassroots environmental crisis center that provides training, information, resources, and assistance for more then 8,000 community groups around the country.

KIM KENNEDY WHITE

See also: Environmental Justice (Activism).

References

Boston University School of Public Health. "Lessons from Love Canal: A Public Health Resource." Available at: http://www.bu.edu/lovecanal.

Center for Health, Environment and Justice. Available at: http://www.chej.org.

Environmental Ethics: Examining Your Connection to the Environment and Your Community. 2005. The Goldman Environmental Prize Video Project. San Francisco: Video Project.

Goldman Environmental Prize. Available at: http://www.goldmanprize.org/.

State University of New York at Buffalo. Love Canal Collections. http://library.buffalo.edu/special-collections/lovecanal.

U.S. Environmental Protection Agency. "History." Available at: http://www.epa.gov/history/topics/lovecanal.

U.S. Environmental Protection Agency. "Superfund." Available at: http://www.epa.gov/superfund/policy/cercla.

In 1979, the U.S. Justice Department and Environmental Protection Agency sued Hooker Chemical and its parent Occidental Petroleum Corporation for emergency response and cleanup costs. In 1980, Congress enacted the Comprehensive Environmental Response, Compensation, and Liability Act (CERCLA), better known as Superfund, to regulate and remediate closed waste sites (U.S. Environmental Protection Agency). In 1981, Gibbs moved to the Washington, D.C., area to create an organization to help people facing similar environmental threats. Ultimately, properties on the Love Canal site were razed, and waste remediation was undertaken.

In 1982 the television movie *Lois Gibbs and the Love Canal*, starring actress Marsha Mason, aired. Gibbs received the 1990 Goldman Environmental Prize, 1998 Heinz Award in the Environment, 1999 John W. Gardner Leadership Award, and 2004 March of Dimes Maternal and Infant Health Award. She has honorary doctorates from the State University of New York at Cortland and Haverford College and an honorary degree of humane letters from Green Mountain College.

RITA TRUSCHEL

GREEN AND SUSTAINABILITY FAIRS AND FESTIVALS

Although many traditional holidays have their roots in seasonal rituals, U.S. culture is embracing numerous environmental and sustainability fairs and festivals as it becomes more green. Fairs and festivals have historically been related to celebrations about fall harvests. Festivals tied to the seasons, such as summer solstice, are intrinsically tied to environmental conditions.

County fairs were fall celebrations of harvest. Farmers congregated to compare and compete in various agricultural categories, as well as socialize with one another. Farmers markets are growing in numbers, reaching urban dwellers. This farmer-to-consumer connection decreases the ecological impact of food production, primarily because of a decrease in trip generation by wholesalers and distributors. Rural organizations, such as the Grange, the Future Farmers of America, and 4-H, would meet at the county fairs. Today, these groups have been joined by environmental organizations. States also have state fairs that tend to celebrate the rural and agricultural heritage of the particular state.

Earth Day

One of the most well known of environmental celebrations, Earth Day represents the growing public acceptance of environmentalism. More than just an appreciation of the environment, Earth Day symbolizes an environmental activism. In 1969, U.S. Senator Gaylord Nelson announced the idea for a "national teach-in on the environment" to the national media. He collaborated with Representative Peter McCloskey, who served as his co-chair. Denis Hayes was hired as national coordinator. Hayes eventually hired a staff of 85 to promote Earth Day events. He remained the charismatic coordinator for many more Earth Days.

The first Earth Day represented a significant development in the greening of U.S. culture and public policy. It demonstrated that many different groups were concerned about pollution and environmental contamination. Shortly afterward, the U.S. Environmental Protection Agency was formed. Many significant pieces of environmental law began to be introduced shortly afterward, such as the National Environmental Policy Act, the Clean Air Act, and the Clean Water Act. Many of these laws had special provisions called "citizen suits" that let environmental activists go directly to federal court and not have to go through the U.S. Environmental Protection Agency first. If the environmental lawyer prevailed in the court case, they were paid reasonable attorneys fees. The environmental activism that Earth Day brought together year after year galvanized years of advocacy into a new generation of environmental laws and policies.

Every Earth Day allowed for greater greening of U.S. culture and public policy. It became a time to ask about environmental controversies. Earth Day was a legitimate platform for all environmental issues. In 1990 Earth Day broadened its platform to include international issues. After that celebration major international treaties to protect the environment were soon passed, showing the international power of environmental activism via Earth Day. Earth Day is now the main environmental festival in the United States.

Sustainability Day

More and more college campuses are celebrating a sustainability day. The increasing number of colleges with a sustainability day demonstrates the growth of the greening of America. It is the one day a year where the college focuses on sustainable activities and consciousness raising. It is a different day for different colleges. For example, Xavier University inaugurated its sustainability day by discussing its new sustainability efforts, convening a small conference, and examining organizational changes necessary to incorporate sustainability. Colleges can be creative in their sustainability day presentations. One example to show the amount of food wastage on campus and encourage recycling, waste reduction, and composting has the students leave their waste for one day outside in plain view. Colleges are also one of the strongest centers of environmental technology, and on their chosen sustainability day they commonly set up multicollege Web casts and Podcasts. Other sustainability day activities involve "tabling," or setting up information booths. These tables are stocked with information on the latest developments in sustainability. Sometimes they offer simple changes everyone could make in their everyday lives that would decrease environmental impacts. Some include "pledging" to implement one or more personal changes in the student's lifestyle. They generally highlight whatever sustainability programs exist at that university, and there are usually many. The concepts of living roofs, low-energy lighting, and waste reduction are presented and explained in ways students can learn to apply them to real life situations. Experimental approaches to sustainability are also presented and provide a rich backdrop for the future greening of U.S. culture.

Green Jobs Fairs

Fairs these days can take a more specialized meaning when they are applied to the greening of America. They can also refer to environmental job fairs, where prospective employers meet at a venue designed to attract prospective employees. Some colleges and high schools will sponsor an environmental job fair. Sometimes major career fairs now have an emphasis on green jobs. These job fairs highlight employment opportunities in green employment sectors such as alternative energy, green construction materials and processes, state and national park services, and waste management. These employment areas can be far ranging as environmental issues permeate U.S. culture. They include working for the local, state, or federal government, working for nonprofit organizations, and sometimes working for industry. Job fairs also offer job-seeking skills training. They will generally stress résumé writing, interviewing skills, reference letters, and research skills.

Greenovation: Green Festival

Green Festival is an annual sustainability event and project of Green America and Global Exchange. The festival's solution-based activities focus on building sustainable communities and improving social, economic, and environmental conditions. Individuals, businesses, and community leaders share and discuss strategies for protecting the planet and empowering people to make positive changes. The event features more than 300 eco-friendly businesses and more than 125 educators, leaders, and authors; workshops and films; organic and vegetarian cuisine; kid activities; and other entertainment. The Green Festival organizers strive to host a zero-waste event, encourage recycling, provide eco-friendly products (such as biodegradable food service items), and whenever possible, conserve energy use. The most recent Green Festival took place the weekend of Earth Day in New York City, April 21–22, 2012.

KIM KENNEDY WHITE

Conclusion

The greening of U.S. culture is evidenced by the greening of celebrations and their growing public policy influence. The institutionalization of Earth Day and the early and robust growth of a sustainability day provide further testament to the growth and direction of the greening of U.S. culture. The creation and focus of green job fairs, and green jobs generally, expand the idea of a celebratory day to a lifetime career.

R. WILLIAM COLLIN

See also: Earth Day (Activism); Green Movement (Activism).

References

Campus Sustainability Planning Network. Available at: http://www.campussustainability.info/.

Green Job Fairs and Environmental Careers Network. Available at: http://www.greenjobs
    .net/green-job-fairs/.
Happy Earth Day Coloring and Activities Book. Available at: http://www.epa.gov/region5/
    publications/happy/happy.htm.

GREEN BACKLASH

Green backlash is a term used to describe anti-environmental movements that often
assert property rights claims aimed at deregulation of the environment. These
movements are quite often organized around specific business interests, such as
mining, agriculture, and forestry. Although in the 1970s and 1980s these groups
were identified as part of the Wise Use movement (and later as part of the Property
Rights movement), it is probably most accurate to view them as several property
rights movements rather than one movement. This is especially true as the
movement developed through the 1990s and we began to see a proliferation of
movement activists. Similarly, while large business were (and continue to be) deeply
invested in the movement activities of property rights activists, it is also true that
local grassroots actors (farmers, ranchers, small business owners, and other private
property owners) are also involved in the movement.

One of the most organized manifestations of green backlash is a network of
lawyers that organized in the early 1970s, originally in California as the Pacific Legal
Foundation (PLF). This network, with direct ties to then Governor Ronald Reagan's
administration, is a conservative-libertarian law firm that, in its early days, spent
much of its time contesting Environmental Impact Statements in administrative
processes. As the movement grew, the number of legal foundations with lawyers
devoted to property rights cases grew, and green backlash took on a distinctively
legal characteristic. Eventually, environmentalists referred to these lawyers as the
"Takings Bar," directly referencing their use of the takings clause in the U.S.
Constitution to contest land-use regulations. Other such foundations include the
Mountain States Legal Foundation and the Washington Legal Foundation. Important think tanks also form part of this network, including the Cato Institute and the
Competitive Enterprise Institute.

The lawyers of the Takings Bar made substantial gains during the 1980s, particularly after Justice Antonin Scalia joined the U.S. Supreme Court. Several property
rights cases were heard by the federal judiciary and made their way to the Supreme
Court, where property rights activists were able to gain some victories in important
cases such as *Nollan v. California Coastal Council* and, quite importantly, *Lucas v. South
Carolina Coastal Commission*. These court cases provided precedents that the Takings
Bar believed would enable them to equate a regulatory taking (i.e., diminishment of
value of private property through a regulation) with a physical taking (i.e., a situation
where the government takes physical control of property for public use). However,
over the course of the 1990s, it became increasingly clear that the courts were not
willing to apply these precedents, preferring instead an ad hoc, case-by-case analysis
in determining whether a regulation in a particular situation required compensation
for private property owners facing diminished value of their property.

This trajectory, as Nancie G. Marzulla, a longtime property rights activists and member of the Takings Bar, has pointed out, and other important court decisions such as *Babbitt v. Sweet Home* (the spotted owl case), made clear that "courts [were] simply not curtailing the wholesale destruction of private property rights" (Marzulla, 2001, 243). Thus, the movement turned to legislation for reform, championing property rights statutes at both the state and federal levels. By the end of 1999, the Lincoln Institute of Land Policy reported that 26 states had adopted some form of property rights legislation, ranging from assessment laws, new rules around conflict resolution, or some combination thereof (Jacobs, 1999). The actual impact of these laws has yet to be fully understood, though there is some indication that the chilling effect on regulation feared by many has not been particularly strong (Brisbin et al., 2010; Botello-Samson, 2010).

Although green backlash has seen some significant gains in the form of state constitutional and statutory protection of private property, it has also been challenged by the willingness of American public opinion to support environmental protection despite a dislike of regulation (Kriz, 1995, 2076, cited in Layzer, 2006) as well as the willingness among environmental advocates to seek new strategies in the face of backlash (Layzer, 2006). As their opponents created new solutions to environmental problems, property rights activists have sought new strategies as well.

LAURA J. HATCHER

See also: Green Movement (Activism); The Green Scare (Activism).

References

Botello-Samson, Darren. 2010. "The Regulatory Response to the Legal Mobilization of Property Rights: An Institutional Analysis of Regulatory Decision-Making." In Wayne V. McIntosh and Laura J. Hatcher, eds., *Property Rights and Neoliberalism: Cultural Demands and Legal Actions*. Burlington, VT: Ashgate.

Brisbin, Richard A., Susan Hunter, and Kevin M. Leyden. 2010. "The Limits of *Kelo*: Bureaucratic Legality and Adversarial Conflict in Land Use Regulation." In Wayne V. McIntosh and Laura J. Hatcher, eds., *Property Rights and Neoliberalism: Cultural Demands and Legal Actions*. Burlington, VT: Ashgate.

Jacobs, Harvey M. 1999. *State Property Rights Laws: The Impacts of Those Laws on My Land*. Cambridge, MA: Lincoln Institute for Land Policy.

Kriz, Margaret. 1995. "Drawing a Green Line in the Sand." *National Journal* (August 12): 2076.

Layzer, Judith A. 2006. *The Environmental Case: Translating Values into Policy*, 2nd ed. Washington, DC: CQ Press.

Marzulla, Nancie. 2001. "Property Rights Movement: How It Began and Where It Is Headed." In Nicholas Blomley, David Delaney, Richard T. Ford, eds., *The Legal Geographies Reader: Law, Power and Space*. Malden, MA: Blackwell.

GREEN MOVEMENT

The green movement in America has ideological underpinnings in the teachings of indigenous peoples, Baruch Spinoza, and the enlightenment thought of

Jean-Jacques Rousseau. From them, the movement draws on the idea of sustainability over seven generations of responsibility, on the importance of individual action, and on the civic duty of good management of natural resources. Transcendentalist writers such as Henry David Thoreau, Ralph Waldo Emerson, William Wordsworth, and Amos Bronson Alcott drew on ideas of humanism and on the importance of wildlife conservation, providing an intellectual framework for respecting the natural world and influencing advocates for environmental protection, civil rights, and individual freedom.

In America today, the green movement also encompasses a value set, which emphasizes environmental considerations and costs into consumption and production choices, at levels ranging from individuals to large corporations. Social movement scholars have identified a core of values in the environmental movement, in spite of its diversity of discourses, philosophical approaches, and organizations: "human action has the potential for adversely affecting the biophysical environment, changes in the biophysical environment can harm things people care about, and steps should be taken to avoid at least some harmful actions" (Dietz et al., 1999). The environmental movement, as it became formalized into political action, was also influenced by notions of the connections between deep ecology, peace, and feminism. Ecology and conservation movements tend to emphasize the neutrality of science and a view of nature as outside of human constructions. The green movement in America is broadly based and includes social activism, cultural trends, political initiatives, design interventions, and business measures aimed at encouraging environmental sustainability.

The environmental movement in the United States coalesced in the late 19th century, as conservation activist John Muir advocated for the creation of Yellowstone National Park in 1872 and founded the Sierra Club in 1893. Gifford Pinchot and George Perkins Marsh spurred efforts in forestry and wildlife conservation, respectively, and their conservation efforts were brought into the mainstream through President Theodore Roosevelt's creation of the national parks system. During the Great Depression, presidential leadership on environmental issues continued, as Franklin Delano Roosevelt created the Civilian Conservation Corps. The program hired around 2 million citizens to work toward wilderness protection and in rural areas between 1933 and 1943. Environmental concerns again took center stage in 1949, when Aldo Leopold's work championing an ethic of land stewardship, *A Sand County Almanac*, which became a best seller. As World War II ended, nuclear technology, automobile-centric development, urbanization, and widespread air and water pollution became more problematic. The green movement responded by taking on new issues and forms of political engagement.

The modern wave of environmentalism in the United States was catalyzed by people's distress and concern with the nation's heavy reliance on nuclear weapons, pesticides, oil, and other pollutants. Rachel Carson's *Silent Spring* (1962) drew substantial concern over the human and ecological impacts of pesticide use. Worrisome events also struck a chord with the American public, bringing more people into the nascent environmental movement. Atmospheric nuclear testing during the 1950s and 1960s resulted in a public health outcry because of the

Undated image of early visitors to Yellowstone National Park. (National Park Service)

radioactive fallout from the Castle Bravo nuclear test in the Bikini Atoll in 1964. Other incidents, such as the 1968 oil spill off of the California coast and the fire on Ohio's Cuyahoga River in June 1969 from its inordinately high level of industrial pollution, caused alarm. The first photographs of the Earth from outer space, in 1968, became symbolic not only of humankind's technological capabilities, but also of the planet's fragility, uniqueness, and relative smallness in relation to the universe. Demographic concerns, most notably articulated in *The Population Bomb* (Ehrlich, 1971), highlighted issues of overpopulation and emphasized the problems of limited resources that might not meet the rising demands of human populations. An active public debate was sparked, as Barry Commoner (1971) argued in contrast with Ehrlich that Americans should look to social development and the principles of ecology in order to effectively respond to the planet's population and environmental problems. By the early 1970s, the green movement was substantial in its level of public engagement, and it gained political traction as well.

Senator Gaylord Nelson inspired the idea of Earth Day, and at the first Earth Day celebration, in 1970, 20 million people in the United States took to the streets to rally, protest, and educate others about environmental issues (Dowie, 1995). Most American environmentalists found common ground with civil rights activists and peace activists who were against the Vietnam War, and they borrowed protest frameworks from these groups (Pellow, 1999) as well as tactics such as sit-ins on college campuses and protests (Dowie, 1995). The Environmental Protection Agency (EPA) was created in 1970, and a series of environmental policies were passed so as to improve air and water quality, to regulate the use of pesticides, and to better manage coastal zones (Silveira, 2001). Globally, attention to environmental issues also grew.

By the late 1980s the idea of sustainable development gained traction, and by the time of the Rio Earth Summit in 1992, activists in the green movement worldwide were actively engaging in collaborative advocacy efforts (Keck & Sikkink, 1998). The Green Party formed in the United States in the mid-1980s, largely inspired by European peace and antinuclear activism, and worked through decentralized grassroots democratic structures in order to gain a political foothold (PBS, 2000). Still, the 1980s in the United States was a time when environmental deregulation policies were established, and large environmental organizations embraced compromises and heavily relied on lobbying, legal, and scientific exper- tise (Silveira, 2001). A wide range of approaches to being green arose during this period, at least in part as a backlash to the mainstreaming of environmentalism that had occurred.

The more radical perspectives that persist through to the present within the green movement include approaches seeking to bring about eco-friendly alternatives to modern industrial economies. Deep ecology, eco-feminism, and social ecology are among the most prominent of these approaches (Hopwood et al., 2005; Zimmer- man, 2000). Organizations such as Earth First! Greenpeace, and the Sea Shepherds embraced more extreme orientations toward environmentalism and adopted direct action and "monkeywrenching" strategies so as to raise awareness about environ- mental issues, and often, to slow down wrong-headed institutions and economic systems enough to better account for the Earth's long-term needs (Zimmerman, 2000). American green movement activists have also developed strong collaborative alliances with those in the global south, focusing on resistance to trade liberalization and World Bank and International Monetary Fund (IMF) loans that were questioned on human rights, economic justice, and environmental grounds. These broad transnational social movements developed strong ties and engaged politically, beginning in the 1980s and 1990s (Ayres, 1998; Keck & Sikkink, 1998; Rich, 1994). Most prominently, green movement activists appeared side by side with human rights and economic justice activists during the 1999 Seattle protests against the World Trade Organization.

Reformist approaches to environmentalism, in contrast, do not aim at structural or institutional changes but instead seek to work within predominant economic and political systems. Their proposals often involve individual-level changes, as well as approaching environmental problems on an issue-by-issue basis in order to address them (Bernstein, 2002). These approaches are often reliant on consumption and embrace capitalist and liberal policy orientations (Maniates, 2001).

Although much of environmentalism became mainstream and was dominated by a handful of large, well-funded organizations in the 1980s and early 1990s, new grassroots "greens" also emerged within the U.S. green movement. Often they articulated very different strategies and philosophical approaches than those of the large environmental organizations. Local and regional conservation organizations arose to respond to pressing needs for forest conservation in the United States, and some organizations, such as Friends of the Earth, the League of Conservation

Voters, and Earth Island Institute, formed as "splinter groups" off the large environmental organizations. Activists in the movement against hazardous wastes, most notably Lois Gibbs, adopted an approach to environmentalism that was based on health risks and the defense of the communities closest to environmental and public health hazards. Called "NIMBYs," signifying their "Not in My Backyard" approach, these locally oriented activists call attention to the ways in which the poor and typically underrepresented populations become victims of such harms. With a similar framework, the environmental justice movement formed out of concerns that environmental harms unduly burdened people of color. The environmental justice movement brings issues of race, class, social privilege, and political advantage to the table within the green movement (Sandler & Pezzullo, 2007; Silveira, 2001). Activists such as Van Jones and Majora Carter are outspoken proponents of green jobs and clean energy economies. Their work highlights the ways in which uniquely disadvantaged communities may offer hope to all Americans through revitalizing communities and emphasizing diversity within the green movement.

Political action through a variety of means is one of the defining features of the green movement. Although the Green Party has not had substantial national-level electoral success, it does boast over 200 local elected officials in many states. Ralph Nader, a four-time presidential candidate for the Green Party, has been outspoken on questions of consumer rights since he first began investigating automobile safety in the 1960s. Nader has helped to found dozens of nongovernmental organizations related to consumer rights, public accountability, and environmental issues and regularly lectures on the dangers of multinational corporations as they converge with government power. Moreover, city mayors across the United States have taken on pledges to reduce greenhouse gas emissions, which is especially notable given the failures of national policy to adopt meaningful targets on the issue of climate change. Former vice president Al Gore's leadership on climate change issues also helped gain traction for environmental issues at global levels, leading to his sharing the Nobel Peace Prize with the Intergovernmental Panel on Climate Change (IPCC) in 2007. These actions represent meaningful steps toward helping the green movement take hold through governmental initiatives and leadership.

Corporate greening represents a very different approach within the green movement. Corporations are taking steps toward lessening their ecological footprint through greening their supply chains, much of which entails actions outside the purview of consumers. Largely, such efforts coincide with cost-savings, although public pressure for corporate social responsibility also plays an important role in motivating adoptions of double- and triple-bottom lines. As the case of Wal-Mart shows, greening the supply chain of goods led to huge cost savings, considerable gains in terms of environmental sustainability, and fostered collaborative relationships with a range of producers, nongovernmental organizations, governmental institutions, and stakeholders (Humes, 2011; Plambeck & Denend, 2008).

Another strong wave in the green movement today encourages ecological design and systems thinking as a response to ecological problems. As new technologies have arisen, many within the green movement are looking toward ecological design, seeking to integrate ecological principles with the way in which

Greenovator: Earthjustice

With nine regional offices throughout the United States, an international agenda, and more than 30 years of legal representation, Earthjustice, formerly known as the Sierra Club Legal Defense Fund, has become one of the key nonprofit law firms in the United States. Although the group's primary function is to file lawsuits without charge for public-interest clients, it also aims to protect existing environmental statutes from being watered down or overturned. Through the two environmental law clinics it has established at the University of Denver and Stanford University, Earthjustice is also training law students and preparing them to work for other organizations. On June 1, 2000, another public-interest firm, Earthlaw, merged its legal staff with Earthjustice's attorneys in a move designed to provide more effective legal representation.

One of the most historically noteworthy actions of the group focused on a development in California's Sierra Nevada range planned by Walt Disney Productions. In one of the first citizen-enforced environmental law cases, *Sierra Club v. Morton*, the U.S. Supreme Court established in 1972 the right of citizens to sue to protect natural resources. The case served as a precedent for other citizen-based suits that have become common strategies for environmental groups.

Typical of other environmental-defense groups, Earthjustice has often sued a government agency to enforce a law. In 1968, for instance, the National Park Service was alleged to have failed to protect critical timberland adjacent to the new Redwood National Park. The lawsuit resulted in a doubling of the size of the park as nearby timberland was acquired from logging companies. On the border of Yellowstone National Park, the group successfully sued a mining company that had planned to reopen a gold and silver mine. The company was not allowed to resume mining operations and was fined millions of dollars in penalties, and the site is undergoing restoration.

In recent years, Earthjustice has become more involved in issues related to environmental justice. Citizens in a predominantly minority community in Louisiana sought help from the organization when a uranium plant was scheduled to be constructed in their area. After hearing citizens' protests, the Nuclear Regulatory Commission denied the necessary permit for the facility. The

goods, buildings, agriculture systems, and even communities might function in an eco-friendly way (Hawken et al., 1999; McDonough & Braungart, 2002; Orr, 2004). Sustainable building initiatives have also increased enormously, thanks largely to the U.S. Green Building Council's LEED (Leadership in Energy and Environmental Design) green building rating system. Permaculture, or the idea that sustainability in both culture and agriculture can come from consciously designed landscapes that mimic the patterns and relationships found in nature, has seen significantly accelerated interest in recent years (Holmgren, 2002). As systems thinking and ecological design principles have inspired significant greening, urban agriculture initiatives involving worm composting, "living machines" for water purification, aquaponic fish rearing, beekeeping, and a host of other endeavors toward making landscapes more productive and sustainable have grown in popularity. Growing Power, an organization based in Milwaukee, exemplifies many of these initiatives in action, as do many community groups that are organizing to reduce their greenhouse gas emissions, to green their neighborhoods, to make different consumption choices, and to reduce dependency on nonrenewable energy sources.

Although the political opportunities are ripe within the United States for the green movement, so too are the political challenges, with ecological stakes perhaps higher than they have ever been. In today's world, nearly every aspect of the natural world has been marked and colonized by human imprints, calling into question, effectively, if "nature" and "wilderness" even exist as something outside of human constructions (McKibben, 1989; Wapner, 2010). Environmentalism has been criticized from both outside and from within. Grassroots activists critique the big international organizations as being alienated from local people's concerns (Chapin, 2004). Moderate organizations have been criticized for setting modest goals and failing to make substantive policy change, being too friendly with corporate interests, or worse, greenwashing (Nordhaus & Shellenberger, 2007; Speth, 2004; Wapner, 2010). Radicals, meanwhile, have been critiqued for taking such extreme positions that they make themselves irrelevant or invite political backlash (Wapner, 2010). Some in the green movement today look toward energy independence and self-sufficiency as a response to ecological problems, as well as a lifestyle alternative (Rosen, 2010), while others look toward both high- and low-technology alternatives as part of their toolkits toward greater projects of "world changing" (Steffen, 2011). Such diversity, as well as this ability to be self-critical and still resilient, may help to explain why the green movement is remarkably enduring in relation to most social movements (Silveira, 2001).

organization has also expanded its agenda to a global perspective, seeking to address human rights and the environment, international trade, and support for environmental legislation in other countries.

Although legal expertise is a valuable resource, the organization also uses its own policy experts who work to prevent legislative backlash and the amending of long-standing environmental statutes. Staff members have focused on the Endangered Species Act and the Clean Air Act, two laws that have been targeted by conservative members of Congress and their supporters. After several years of attempting to develop a strategic plan, the group turned to an advertising agency. Underground Advertising surveyed potential donors, competing organizations, and prior marketing efforts and developed a new logo, brochures, and a tag line that has become synonymous with the organization's goal, "Because the earth needs a lawyer."

JACQUELINE VAUGHN SWITZER

Greenovator: Greenpeace

Greenpeace is a global independent nonprofit campaigning organization that works to protect the environment and promote peace. Its members' core values include nonviolent confrontation to increase the quality of public debate, maintaining financial independence from commercial and political interests, bearing witness to environmental destruction in a peaceful way, and seeking solutions to promote debate about society's environmental choices. While promoting environmental solutions, Greenpeace's members believe they have no permanent allies and adversaries. Greenpeace has more than 2.9 million members and a presence in 41 countries. An international board with four members and a chairman governs the organization. Its current campaigns include stopping climate change, defending the oceans, saying no to genetic engineering, fostering peace and nuclear disarmament, protecting ancient forests, promoting sustainable trade, and others.

Greenpeace began on September 15, 1971, when 12 Canadian activists sailed a chartered boat, christened Greenpeace for the trip, to Amchitka, an island off of

Alaska. Their goal was to stop a 5-megaton nuclear fusion blast by the U.S. government. The test would be the largest underground nuclear blast in U.S. history. Amchitka Island sat on a fault line of one the world's most active earthquake zones. The island had been declared a federal wildlife zone in 1913 and was home to 131 species of sea birds.

The activists were intercepted and the test went forward but they made international news. The action established the name Greenpeace in Canada. The group started as the Make a Wave Committee that spun off from the Sierra Club. In 1972, the organization officially took the name the Greenpeace Foundation. Some of the founders included Bill Darnell, who coined the name, Jim Bohlen, Paul Cote, and Irving Stowe from the Make a Wave Committee, and Patrick Moore, Robert Hunter, Ben and Dorothy Metcalfe, and Paul Watson. David McTaggart organized several groups to come together and form Greenpeace International in 1979.

In its early days, the organization was loosely organized around issues and campaigns. Parts of the group worked on nuclear disarmament, and by late 1973, other Greenpeace activists adopted the Great Whale Conspiracy as their campaign to save the whales. Greenpeace targeted Russia and Japan to change their whaling policies. After intense work, including sea actions where Greenpeace vessels tracked whaling ships, the International Whaling Commission adopted a whaling moratorium in 1982. Greenpeace helped defeat an effort by Japan and others to reintroduce commercial whaling in 2002. A few of their victories were a worldwide ban on high-seas, large-scale driftnets in 1992, a worldwide ban on the sea dumping of radioactive and industrial waste in 1993, and a major role in the adoption of the Kyoto Protocol that addresses climate change.

Six UK Greenpeace activists set an important precedent in September 2008 when they were acquitted of causing £30,000 in criminal damage for attempting to shut down a coal-fired power station in Kent, England. The activists painted the prime minister's name on smokestacks. The campaigners used the lawful excuse defense, stating that they were acting to protect property around the world from the damage caused by burning coal. The acquittal showed the public support for direct action to protect the environment from coal burning and this was the first time this defense prevailed in a climate change case.

LISA A. ENNIS

The diverse green movement of today encompasses organizations, lifestyle choices, policy shifts, and philosophical approaches to understanding the ambiguous relationship between humans and nature. The diverse tactics used by the activist—groups, institutions, businesses, and leadership of the green movement encourage all Americans to dream differently. Their suggestion is that we might enter into new social contracts that reinvent what nature, growth, materials, and "the good life" mean (Lappé, 2009; Nordhaus & Shellenberger, 2007; Speth, 2008; Wapner, 2010). The green movement in America is increasingly posing alternatives for creating a more sustainable world that involve positive responses, akin to using "silver buckshot" rather than any single "silver bullet" for solving the complexity of environmental challenges we face (Steffen, 2011). A shift away from a paradigm of deprivation and limits is under way within the green movement. It is moving toward one of overcoming environmental challenges through seeing possibilities for social, economic, and political change by adopting a worldview that is pragmatic and based on action by a disparate range of actors.

EVE Z. BRATMAN

See also: Earth First! (Activism); Environmental Justice (Activism); Goldman Environmental Prize (Activism); Green Party (Politics).

References

Ayres, Jeffrey M. 1998. *Defying Conventional Wisdom: Political Movements and Popular Contention Against North American Free Trade*. Toronto: University of Toronto Press.

Bernstein, Steven. 2002. "Liberal Environmentalism and Global Environmental Governance." *Global Environmental Politics* 2:3 (August): 1–16.

Carson, Rachel. 1962. *Silent Spring*. New York: Houghton Mifflin.

Chapin, Mac. 2004. "A Challenge to Conservationists." *World Watch Magazine* 17 (November/December): 6.

Commoner, Barry. 1971. *The Closing Circle: Nature, Man, and Technology*. New York: Knopf.

Dietz, Thomas, Troy Abel, Gregory A. Guagnano, and Linda Kalof. 1999. "A Value-Belief-Norm Theory of Support for Social Movements: The Case of Environmentalism." *Human Ecology Review* 6:2: 81–97.

Dowie, Mark. 1995. *Losing Ground: American Environmentalism at the Close of the Twentieth Century*. Cambridge: MIT Press.

Drielak, Steven C. 1998. *Environmental Crime*. Springfield, IL: Charles C. Thomas.

Earthjustice. "About Us: Major Accomplishments." Available at: http://www.earthjustice.org/about/major.

Ehrlich, Paul R. 1971. *The Population Bomb*. London: Ballantine/Friends of the Earth, in association with Pan Books.

Hawken, Paul, Amory Lovins, and L. Hunter Lovins. 1999. *Natural Capitalism: Creating the Next Industrial Revolution*. Boulder, CO: Rocky Mountain Institute Press.

Holmgren, David. 2002. *Permaculture: Principles and Pathways Beyond Sustainability*. Hepburn, Australia: Holmgren Design Services.

Hopwood, Bill, Mary Mellor, and Geoff O'Brien. 2005. "Sustainable Development: Mapping Different Approaches." *Sustainable Development* 13: 38–52.

Humes, Edward. 2011. *Force of Nature: The Unlikely Story of Wal-Mart's Green Revolution*. New York: HarperCollins.

Hunter, Robert. 1979. *Warriors of the Rainbow: A Chronicle of the Greenpeace Movement*. New York: Henry Holt.

Keck, Margaret, and Kathryn Sikkink. 1998. *Activists Beyond Borders*. Ithaca, NY: Cornell University Press.

Lappé, Francis Moore. 2009. "Liberation Ecology." *Resurgence* 252 (January/February): 18–20.

Maniates, Michael. 2001. "Individualization: Plant a Tree, Buy a Bike, Save the World?" *Global Environmental Politics* 1:3: 31–52.

McDonough, William, and Michael Braungart. 2002. *Cradle to Cradle: Remaking the Way We Make Things*. New York: North Point Press.

McKibben, Bill. 1989. *The End of Nature*. New York: Random House.

Nordhaus, Ted, and Michael Shellenberger. 2007. *Breakthrough: From the Death of Environmentalism to the Politics of Possibility*. New York: Houghton Mifflin.

Orr, David. 2004. *The Nature of Design*. New York: Oxford University Press.

Pellow, David N. 1999. "Framing Emerging Environmental Movement Tactics: Mobilizing Consensus, Demobilizing Conflict." *Sociological Forum* 14:4 (December): 659–683.

Plambeck, Erica L., and Lyn Denend. 2008. "The Greening of Wal-Mart." *Stanford Social Innovation Review* (Spring).

Public Broadcasting System (PBS). 2000. "Green Party History." Available from: http://www.pbs.org/newshour/bb/politics/jan-june00/green_history.html.

Rich, Bruce. 1994. *Mortgaging the Earth—The World Bank, Environmental Impoverishment, and the Crisis of Development*. Boston: Beacon Press.

Rosen, Nick. 2010. *Off the Grid: Inside the Movement for More Space, Less Government, and True Independence in Modern America*. New York: Penguin.

Sandler, Ronald, and Phaedra C. Pezzullo. 2007. *Environmental Justice and Environmentalism: The Social Justice Challenge to the Environmental Movement*. Cambridge: MIT Press.

Silveira, Stacy. 2001. "The American Environmental Movement: Surviving Through Diversity." *Boston College Environmental Affairs Law Review* 28:2: 497–532.

Speth, James Gustave. 2004. *Red Sky at Morning*. New Haven: Yale University Press.

Speth, James Gustave. 2008. *The Bridge at the Edge of the World*. New York: Caravan Books.

Steffen, Alex, ed. 2011. *Worldchanging: A User's Guide to the 21st Century*. New York: Abrams.

Wapner, Paul. 2010. *Living Through the End of Nature*. Boston: MIT Press.

Weyler, Rex. 2004. *Greenpeace: How a Group of Journalists, Ecologists, and Visionaries Changed the World*. Emmaus, PA: Rodale.

Weyler, Rex. 2008. "Waves of Compassion: The Founding of Greenpeace, Where Are They Now?" *Utne Reader* (October 15).

Zimmerman, Michael E. 2000. "A Strategic Direction for 21st Century Environmentalists: Free Market Environmentalism." *Strategies: Journal of Theory, Culture, and Politics* 13:1 (May): 89–110.

THE GREEN SCARE

Calling into reference the infamous Red Scare from the annals of U.S. history, the *Green Scare* is a term utilized by those who aim to chastise U.S. governmental efforts to classify radical environmentalists and animal rights activists as terrorists. During the Red Scare, ideological demonizing and xenophobia were pervasive. Governmental fear mongering ultimately resulted in what is now widely considered shameful behavior. Those who promote the term the Green Scare believe the U.S. government is making a similar misstep in its handling of the radical elements of the environmental and animal rights movements. Such individuals believe the effort to classify activists as terrorists is a politically motivated endeavor that utilizes fear of terrorism to falsely attack the environmentalist and animal rights movements. As such, environmental activists have coined the phrase "the Green Scare" in a pointed effort to draw attention to the situation through the employment of a historically loaded idiom.

In order to support their claims that the government is misclassifying radical environmentalists as terrorists, those who purport the Green Scare point to a variety of evidence. Generally, this supporting information is divided into three categories: legal, legislative, and extra-legislative. The legal evidence employed often emphasizes the fact that in the court of law the term *terrorism* is being stretched beyond traditional boundaries. This is happening, radical environmentalists claim, in order to target them and their politics. In the past, the term *terrorism* was used only in extreme cases. Offenses such as political assassinations, attacks on human life intended to instill fear, and the use of weapons of mass destruction were activities listed as terrorism. With the advent of the enhanced definition of terrorism, new yet arguably lesser crimes are now being included as acts of terrorism. Specifically, radical environmentalist actions that take precautions to not endanger human life have now been classified as terrorism. The Operation Backfire and Stop Huntington Animal Cruelty (SHAC) cases are frequently utilized to illustrate this point. In both of these examples terrorism charges were filed against activists who did not physically harm a single human being. Indeed, the latter case tried a number of individuals for simply running a Web site that encouraged people to dissent and take action against Huntington Life Sciences. By bringing terrorism charges into these cases, punishments are increasing significantly and the label of terrorist is being applied to individuals who, in the past, were considered activists.

Legislative evidence being called into use by radical environmentalists reveals that a variety of new legislation is being pushed through in order to broaden the definition of terrorism. This, promoters of the Green Scare narrative claim, is further proof of the government's oppressive actions toward activists. Indeed, many within the environmental and animal rights movements argue that such legislation specifically attacks their groups. The Animal Enterprise Terrorism Act (AETA) is one such piece of legislation. The AETA is an extension of the Animal Enterprise Protection Act (AEPA), a law already in existence at the time of the AETA's proposal. While many saw the AETA as an effort to nuance and improve a slightly flawed law, activists view it as a flagrant assault on their cause and their methods. The legislation allows for terrorism charges to be made in a wide variety of cases that involve animal rights activism. This move makes the law increasingly vague, thus opening the door for harsh punishments and unfair portrayals of activists as terrorists.

In addition to the various legal and legislative actions used as evidence to support the Green Scare narrative, environmental and animal rights activists also emphasize the significant role of extra-legislative behavior in the assault on their movements. Legal and legislative tactics are viewed as conventional methods that are being employed in order to impede these groups and portray them in a negative light. Extra-legislative actions, however, are seen as the key nontraditional component in the effort to adversely redefine the movements. Activists claim that those who attempt to portray them as terrorists employ everything from rhetoric and sophistry to media framing and subterfuge in order to achieve their desired outcome. Such tactics circumvent open discussion and established institutions by undermining the movement or appealing directly to the public. Although such efforts do not change the law, they have a significant impact on public sentiment and activist group cohesion. As such, radical environmentalists, animal rights advocates, and their supporters claim the public is unfairly turned away from their cause. Perhaps the most obvious example of such an extra-legislative move came when various news outlets devoted significant time and space to the FBI's proclamation that ecoterrorism was the number one domestic threat of 2008. Although this proclamation did not change any laws, it severely impacted these movements by widely disseminating a negative label on them. As a consequence of such maneuvers, the populous is more likely to accept legislation and rulings that are overly harsh toward environmentalists and animal rights advocates. The public is also less likely to be receptive to the movements message.

The Green Scare asserts that combined these legal, legislative, and extra-legislative efforts equal a concerted attempt to portray legitimate activists as terrorists. Although this is obviously troubling for individuals who are actively participating, those who forward the Green Scare narrative also claim that it is damaging to the populous as a whole. Concern for the natural world, they argue, has been on the rise. Environmentalism and to a lesser degree animal rights activism have been moving toward mainstream recognition. By depicting activists from these groups as terrorists, progress for the movement is being curbed. This is injurious to the population as a whole, activists claim, since it dissuades the average individual from supporting environmentalism and animal rights activism on any level. Just as the Red Scare discouraged open dialogue and peaceful action regarding communist political ideals, so too is the Green Scare deterring honest debate over concern for the natural world. Through utilization of this historically loaded phrase, those advancing the Green Scare narrative hope to draw attention to the rebranding of environmental and animal rights activism.

CALEB HUSMANN

See also: Animal Enterprise Protection Act (documents); Animal Enterprise Terrorism Act (documents); Green Movement (Activism).

References

Potter, Will. 2009. "The Green Scare." *Vermont Law Review* 33: 671–687.
Potter, Will. "Green Is the New Red." Available at: http://www.greenisthenewred.com.
Rood Justin. 2005. "Animal Rights Groups and Ecology Militants Make DHS Terror List, Right-Wing Vigilantes Omitted." *Congressional Quarterly* (March 25).
Smith, Rebecca K. 2008. "Ecoterrorism?: A Critical Analysis of the Vilification of Radical Environmental Activists as Terrorists." *Environmental Law* 38: 537–576.

LIVING OFF THE GRID

The North American power grid (the grid) is a system of interconnected high-voltage wires providing electricity to households, businesses, and public infrastructure throughout the continent. In the United States, there are three primary grid sectors: one serving the eastern half of the country, another serving the western half, and a third serving Texas (NPR). In the early part of the century, access to the electrical grid in the United States was primarily metropolitan. As the grid has expanded to cover much of the country through programs such as the Federal Rural Electrification Program initiated by President Franklin Roosevelt in the mid-1930s (Brown, 1980), people living in all but the most remote areas have gained the option of easily connecting to it. Not connecting to the grid remains a relatively common choice for those who live so far from it that the cost of bringing in a power line is prohibitive. But in most areas of the country, there is no law mandating that people must connect to the grid, and for many "living off the grid" is a matter of personal choice. Those who

Martha Maloney wipes snow off the solar panels at her home in Solon, Maine, in 2005, where she lives off the power grid. (AP Photo/Robert F. Bukaty)

make this choice either live without electrical power, or more commonly, generate their own electrical power, in which case they are often referred to as "energy independent."

People choose to live off the grid for a variety of reasons, but for many the choice is environmental. By far the most common source of electrical energy generation in the United States is coal-fired power plants. Because coal emits the most carbon dioxide of all fossil fuels, it is a primary source of the greenhouse gas emissions implicated in the phenomenon of global climate change. Nuclear energy presents the risk of catastrophic meltdowns and generates radioactive waste, which will remain toxic for millennia and must be stored somewhere. Hydroelectric dams disturb the ecosystem of waterways and threaten fish species by limiting access to their spawning grounds.

Some have become distrustful of the aging infrastructure that connects the myriad elements of the grid or fear that it is susceptible to cyber-terrorism, so they choose energy independence as a form of security. Others have chosen to purchase electric cars as a hedge against rapidly depleting oil resources, unstable prices, and supply. And they prefer to power their vehicles with energy they produce independently. Some people also believe that electrical wires produce negative health effects.

Philosophical reasons for living off the grid, whether related to environmentalism, personal autonomy, or security, have roots in the "back to the land" and homesteading movements of the 1960s and 1970s. For many young people who were dropping out and choosing lives of simplicity disconnected from mainstream society at that time, a life without reliance on modern energy sources was liberating and symbolic of their personal autonomy and independence.

Personal energy generation is typically accomplished using wind and solar power. Solar power is gathered using photovoltaic panels that collect electrical energy from the sun. Wind energy is collected by using turbines, which are the modern equivalent of windmills. In each case, harvested energy is stored in batteries that are tapped in order to generate electrical power for the home. A less common but available option is using small electrical turbines in streams.

Many off-the-grid houses also use solar water heating panels, passive solar energy via large, efficient south-facing windows, and wood burning stoves that radiate energy throughout the house through the bricks that surround them or through hot water pipes that run through the floor of the home. Most off-the-grid homes are also insulated thoroughly, which helps to retain heat in the winter and avoid collecting it in the summer.

Currently, the choice to use these technologies requires an investment that is greater than that for using grid energy. But as energy prices continue to rise and renewable energy technology continues to develop and is produced on a larger scale, this gap is slowly closing.

Living off the grid tends to make people much more aware of, and attentive to, their energy use. This is partly dependent on the size of their renewable energy collection system, but it also relates to the environmental consciousness that tends to drive their choice to begin with. As previously mentioned, the cost of renewable energy technology is significant, so many people living off the grid tend to own just enough of it to provide for their basic needs. And there are days when the sun does not shine and the wind does not blow, which also tends to make individuals living off the grid frugal in their energy use. Devices such as television sets, stereo equipment, and many other electronics use what are referred to as *phantom loads*, a term that refers to the fact that they are constantly drawing power in order to turn on quickly. These are the kinds of things off-the-grid homeowners tend to avoid. In addition they will often use more efficient and less expensive technologies, such as LED lights and small well-insulated refrigerators.

It is also important to note that the trend toward off-the-grid living that was increasing rapidly with renewable energy proponents several years ago has begun to abate. The reason for this is that in the past decade or so, utilities have begun to reimburse individuals who have renewable energy systems installed in their homes for the surplus energy they generate. In fact, utility companies will often now pay a premium for "green energy" since it is something many have begun to market to their customers. This helps to offset the cost of installing such systems. For this reason, many renewable energy advocates, such as the editors of *Home Power* magazine, have begun to advise individuals who choose to create their own renewable energy to actually hook up to the grid so that they can sell back their surplus energy when it is generated. This also eliminates the need for battery bank storage and saves home-owners the substantial cost of these storage systems. Still, many choose not to use this option since if they do, they are vulnerable to electrical service interruption when the grid goes down, which for many is related to the reason they chose to live off the grid in the first place.

TAYLOR REID

See also: Community Economic Development (Activism); Ecovillage (Activism); Wise-Use Movement (Activism).

References

Brown, D. C. 1980. *Electricity for Rural America*. Westport, CT: Greenwood.

Energy Bulletin Web site. A project of the Post-Carbon Institute. Available at: http://www.energybulletin.net/.

National Public Radio (NPR). "Visualizing the U.S. Electric Grid." Available at: http://www.npr.org/templates/story/story.php?storyId=110997398.

SIERRA CLUB v. MORTON (1972): GREENOVATION SPOTLIGHT

Sierra Club v. Morton (405 U.S. 727, 1972) is the pioneering Supreme Court case that gave conservation organizations the right to sue to enforce federal statutes and regulations. The plaintiff Sierra Club dates back to 1892, when 182 members founded it and elected John Muir as its first president. The organization exists to enjoy, explore, and protect wild places. It promotes responsible use of Earth's resources and educates and enlists people to protect and restore the environment. The Sierra Club lawsuit named Secretary of the Interior Rogers Morton and others as defendants. The case concerned the development of the Mineral King Valley, which is located in the Sierra Nevadas in Tulare, California, adjacent to Sequoia National Park. The lands are part of the Sequoia National Forest. Congress dedicated the Mineral King Valley as a special game refuge in 1926.

In January 1969, the U.S. Forest Service approved the Disney Company's plan to construct a $35 million complex that included motels, restaurants, swimming pools, parking lots, and more. The complex was designed to accommodate 14,000 visitors per day. The Sierra Club's suit alleged that the development would negatively affect the aesthetics and ecology of the area.

The case hinged on whether the plaintiff had standing to sue. The plaintiff relied on Section 10 of the Administrative Procedure Act, which permits judicial review if a person suffered a legal wrong or is adversely affected or aggrieved because of an administrative action. The lower court granted the plaintiff a preliminary injunction to stop the construction, but the Ninth Circuit Court of Appeals reversed that decision. Subsequently, the Supreme Court agreed to review the case. Supreme Court Justice Potter Stewart wrote the opinion for the majority. Stewart wrote that the plaintiff failed to assert that the organization or any of its members' activities or pastimes would be affected by Disney's development. The Sierra Club had asserted in the pleadings that it was a representative of the public with long-standing concern and expertise in matters involving natural resources.

The case is known for Justice William O. Douglas's dissenting opinion. Douglas wrote:

> The critical question of "standing" would be simplified and also put neatly in focus if we fashioned a federal rule that allowed environmental issues to be litigated before federal agencies or federal courts in the name of the inanimate object about to be despoiled, defaced, or invaded by roads and bulldozers and where injury is the subject of public outrage. Contemporary public concern for protecting nature's ecological equilibrium should lead to the conferral of standing upon environmental objects to sue for their own preservation. Inanimate objects are sometimes parties in litigation. A ship has a legal personality, a fiction found useful for maritime purposes. The corporation sole—a creature of ecclesiastical law—is an acceptable adversary, and large fortunes ride on its cases.
>
> The ordinary corporation is a "person" for purposes of the adjudicatory processes, whether it represents proprietary, spiritual, aesthetic, or charitable causes. So it should be as respects valleys, alpine meadows, rivers, lakes, estuaries, beaches, ridges, groves of trees, swampland, or even air that feels the destructive pressures of modern technology and modern life. (Opinion, 405)

The ruling affirmed the Appellate Court's decision that the Sierra Club lacked standing to maintain the action, but it did not rule on the merits of the complaint. The Court held that to have standing, the group bringing the action must plead that one of its members had suffered an injury in fact.

Second, the Court held that a mere interest in a problem is not sufficient itself to render the organization adversely affected or aggrieved. No matter how long-standing or well qualified the organization was to judge the problem, that in itself did not entitle it to legal standing in the absence of a legal wrong.

An important footnote in the case did not bar the Sierra Club from amending its complaint in the district court. When the case was returned to district court, the judge allowed the Sierra Club to amend its complaint to attempt to show it had standing. By the time the case made its way back to the lower court, Congress had passed the National Environmental Policy Act (NEPA), which required that proposed actions must consider the environmental impacts. The lower court also allowed the Sierra Club to plead violations of NEPA. During the time the case worked its way through the courts, public opinion had changed concerning the best use of Mineral King Valley. It was clear that no one had an interest in seeing the area developed. The case was dismissed for lack of prosecution in 1977, and in 1978 Congress made Mineral King Valley part of the Sequoia National Park.

The most important result of the decision was that the Court did not bar environmental groups from bringing actions to seek remedies for environmental damages. *Sierra Club v. Morton*'s legal impact was to give citizens the standing to sue to enforce environmental laws, but the case also had other important effects. The decision showed the importance of litigation in protecting and preserving public lands. Litigation blocked the process, which allowed time for alternative proposals to be formulated and offered and for the public to get its voice heard in the political process.

TIMOTHY O'BRIEN

See also: Environmental Justice (Activism); Green Movement (Activism).

References

Hoberg, George. 1992. *Pluralism by Design: Environmental Policy and the American Regulatory State*. Westport, CT: Praeger.

Knight, Richard L., and Sarah F. Bates. 1995. *A New Century for Natural Resources Management*. Washington, DC: Island Press.

Sierra Club v. Morton. 405 U.S. 727, 1972.

WISE-USE MOVEMENT

The wise-use movement is a loose coalition of right-wing interest groups tied by their opposition to environmentalists and their advocacy of unrestricted exploitation of natural resources. Founded by Ron Arnold in the late 1980s to support mining and timber matters in the western United States, wise-use advocates the removal of current environmental laws and the prevention of future measures that interfere with exploitation. The movement includes corporations and grassroots groups. The coalition continues to shift and evolve as it splinters.

Arnold's group was the model for other groups that seem to be grassroots organizations but receive their funding and direction from major corporations. The term for this sort of group is *astroturf*. The first wise-use conference in 1988 was funded by the American Freedom Coalition, associated with the Reverend Sun Myung Moon.

Ron Arnold was once an employee of the Sierra Club. His colleague Alan Gottlieb is a conservative fundraiser. When Arnold joined with Gottlieb, he got access to Gottlieb's $5 million a year direct mail and telephone fundraising apparatus. He also got Gottlieb to publish *The Wise Use Agenda* in 1988. Arnold co-authored a favorable biography of James Watt, Ronald Reagan's interior secretary, who was noted for his efforts to remove environmental laws and open federal lands to exploitation. Watt's excesses led to the revitalization of the environmental movement in the late 1980s.

Gifford Pinchot, the first head of the Forest Service, wanted wise use of trees and minerals. He and John Muir, founder of the Sierra Club, feuded because Muir wanted wilderness for its own sake, for its spiritual value. Arnold chose the name, he said in 1991, because it was ambiguous and the right size for newspaper headlines.

Wise-use groups throughout the United States engage in disinformation about environmental laws, and they are developing a true grassroots following. Wise-use groups commonly receive funding from chemical, mining, and timber companies and in return loudly claim that the hole in the ozone layer is a myth, that air and water laden with carcinogens are harmless, and that government subsidized clear-cutting promotes proper growth of trees. Wise-use advocates early on equated environmentalists with pagans and eco-Nazis and advocate using threats against environmentalists.

In the Pacific Northwest, where the group arose as People for the USA (PFUSA), it used a supposed battle between the spotted owl and the families whose livelihoods depended on exploiting the old-growth habitat. It taught loggers how to speak in sound bites and used slogans such as "jobs versus owls" to create a backlash against other environmental efforts.

When George H. W. Bush charged that environmentalists, particularly Al Gore, author of *Earth in the Balance*, were trying to lock away national resources and destroy the American way of life, it failed to save his candidacy but it did mark the high water mark of the wise-use movement.

In the early 1990s, it began developing links with anti-gay and other right-wing groups. One reason wise use declined in the 1990s was its joining with the militias, unpopular after Timothy McVeigh's bombing of Oklahoma City's Murrah Building in 1995.

When PFUSA failed in 2001, the Sierra Club and others applauded the end of a wise-use group formed in the 1988 battle against the spotted owl. It seemed then that wise use was no longer fashionable, as financing from big business and others dried up. Chevron, DuPont, and Boise Cascade were no longer funding wise-use conferences, think tanks, or public relations campaigns. The wise-use proponents were overly aggressive in rhetoric and tactics. But Sierra cautioned that the movement was not dead as the 30,000 PFUSA members shifted their allegiances to Frontiers of Freedom, the Blue Ribbon Coalition, and like-minded groups. Besides, the members were never the strength of the wise-use movement. With the George W. Bush administration, the wise-use movement was revived, more subdued than the early days when talk was of war in the woods and threats on rangers were common.

Wise users in the Bush administration included Interior Secretary Gale Norton, whose career began at the Mountain States Legal Foundation, known then as the legal arm of wise use, which was founded by James Watt. Agriculture Secretary Ann Veneman also had ties to wise use, as did several of her key staffers.

Under Bush, wise-use efforts included the push to drill for oil in the Arctic National Wildlife Refuge and the opening of the Tongass National Forest to wide-scale logging. The ideal was to sell off or fully exploit the natural resources, and Secretary Norton urged maximum exploitation of oil and gas lands.

JOHN H. BARNHILL

See also: Ecovillage (Activism); Environmental Justice (Activism); Living off the Grid (Activism).

References

Burke, William Kevin. 1993. "Right-Wing Anti-Environmentalism." *Public Eye* 7:2 (June). Available at: http://www.publiceye.org/magazine/v07n2/wiseuse.html.

Hattam, Jennifer. 2001. "Wise Use Movement, R.I.P.? Anti-Environmental Movement Promoting Big Business Initiatives." *Sierra* (May). Available at: http://findarticles.com/p/articles/mi_m1525/is_3_86/ai_74223197/.

Helvarg, David. 2004. "'Wise Use' in the White House: Yesterday's Fringe, Today's Cabinet Official." *Sierra* (September). Available at: http://www.sierraclub.org/sierra/200409/wiseuse.asp.

SourceWatch. "Wise Use Movement." 2010. Available at: http://www.sourcewatch.org/index.php?title=Wise_Use_Movement.

YOUTH ORGANIZATIONS

One of the most positive and promising signs of inspiration today is the recent proliferation of youth organizations, especially those focused on the green movement. These organizations adopt a variety of foci and some even formally register as for- and not-for-profit organizations. Some youth organizations focus exclusively on awareness and advocacy, while others focus on public policy reform. Some seek to solve a problem in their home community, while others focus on issues around the globe. Daily, youth organizations are effecting positive environmental change all around the globe. They are powerful, resourceful, and typically lack the corruption and cynicism to which many of their adult counterparts fall subject.

There exist a plethora of examples evidencing the social power youth organizations hold. Youth movements and organizations have spurred countless recycling programs and animal welfare initiatives, including the release of Keiko, the killer whale best known for his role in the *Free Willy* movies. Local, regional, and even federal legislation have been influenced by youth organizations. On October 28, 2005, the Town of Westerly, Rhode Island, passed an ordinance banning the dumping of e-waste. Following this example, on July 6, 2006, the State of Rhode

In 2004, the team from Babcock Middle School, Westerly, Rhode Island, was awarded $4,000 and captured third place at the prestigious Volvo Adventure competition in Gothenburg, Sweden. The students submitted a prize-winning E-waste solutions project dealing with the proper way of disposing used computers and other electronic equipment. (AP Photo/PRNewsFoto/Volvo Cars of North America)

Island passed a statewide bill banning the dumping of e-waste. Both of these important pieces of legislation were primarily the result of five middle school kids who in 2002 began a not-for-profit youth organization named the Westerly Innovations Network. These kids leveraged their (and their parents') social networks to set up computer component collection and recycling centers throughout the state. Additionally, they made presentations to local civic and government groups and even aided in drafting the legislation. To date, the group boasts in having helped recycle over 200,000 pounds of e-waste; refurbished enough computers to fill several media centers in Rhode Island, Kenya, Mexico, and the Philippines; and traveled the globe advocating for e-waste recycling.

Many large for- and non-for-profit corporations, foundations, and even governments have begun to support the development and efforts of youth organizations. Their efforts can be broken into two categories: developmental programs and conferences, and recognition systems (awards and prizes). Innovation Expedition, an international conference hosted by Innovation Partners International, has welcomed student team presentations at their annual meetings. The United Nations Environment Programme hosts an annual Children's Conference on the Environment averaging over 1,000 attendees (700 children and 300 chaperones) from around the globe. Past session topics have included energy, biodiversity, and water production and consumption. In May 2010, INTERPOL, the UK Environment Agency, and the U.S. and Swedish Environmental Protection Agencies hosted a global e-waste conference in Alexandria, Virginia. This unified effort brought together youth organizations, nongovernmental organizations, government officials, and individuals (spectators and reporters) from 22 countries around the globe.

Recognition systems acknowledging and rewarding the hard work and extraordinary accomplishments of youth organizations effecting positive social change have become common. MTV profiles youth and youth organizations that are working to make a sustainable environmental difference around the globe in their "MTV Agents of Change: Making the Switch" segments that air around the globe. Since 1971, the president of the United States and the Environmental Protection Agency have

---

Greenovator: Alaska Youth for Environmental Action

Alaska Youth for Environmental Action (AYEA), now a National Wildlife Federation–supported program, is an organization for Alaskan youth ages 13–18. Founded by six youth in 1998, today AYEA consists of nine student-led chapters spread throughout Alaska. Youth activists are well trained and supported by myriad AYEA-hosted activities, including activist retreats, summer training institutes, and an annual summit on civics and conservation. In 2010 one of the AYEA youth activists co-wrote an amendment to Alaskan Senate Bill 220 that allows property tax breaks for renewable energy projects. To date, AYEA youth have received over 55 national, state, and local awards, including the President's Environmental Youth Award. AYEA operates on the values of youth empowerment, sustainability, diversity, justice, healthy environments, and cross-cultural experience. A fun fact: AYEA's Web site (www.ayea.org) is 100 percent wind-powered.

partnered to promote awareness of the nation's natural resources and encourage youth and community involvement. Annually, one youth project from each region is honored with the President's Environmental Youth Award. SeaWorld and Bush Gardens annually issue Environmental Excellence Awards to outstanding youth organizations, including both a cash prize and trophy presentation by famed animal expert and advocate Jack Hanna. SocialTreps.com includes multiple award categories focused on recognizing outstanding youth organizations, including Social-Trep Student Team of the Year for students in high school or college and Jr. SocialTrep Student Team of the Year for elementary and middle school students. The list of both conference and recognition opportunities is continually growing, with the aforementioned examples representing merely a small number of the great opportunities that are available to youth organizations.

ERIC W. LIGUORI

See also: E-Waste (Science and Technology); Green Entrepreneurship (Economics); Green and Sustainability Fairs (Activism); President's Environmental Youth Award (documents).

References

Armstrong, H., and A. Dearling. 1997. *Youth Action and the Environment*. Dorset, Engl.: Russell House.

Kim, J., M. de Dios, P. Caraballo, M. Arciniegas, I. Abdul-Matin, and K. Taha. 2002. *Future 500: Youth Organizing and Activism in the United States*. New Orleans, LA: Subway & Elevated Press.

MTV. "MTV Agents of Change: Making the Switch." Available at: http://mtv-venture.org/.

SocialTreps.com. "Social Trep of the Year—Call for Nominations." Available at: http://socialtreps.com/soctrep-of-the-year/.

U.S. Environmental Protection Agency. "Presidents Environmental Youth Awards." Available at: http://www.epa.gov/enviroed/peya/index.html.

Westerly Innovations Network. "Home." Available at: http://www.w-i-n.ws/.

Arts, Entertainment, and Media

AMERICAN WRITERS AND THE ENVIRONMENT

The most prominent authors of nonfiction books on the environment are passionate about a particular cause or approach to environmentalism, and many draw on their own personal experiences with the environment in writing their books. The most popular issues include wildlife protection, wilderness protection, nuclear energy, climate change, pollution, pesticides and chemicals, environmental politics or economics, and environmentally friendly lifestyles.

One of the most influential authors in regard to wildlife protection was zoologist and primate researcher Dian Fossey (1932–1985), whose 1983 book *Gorillas in the Mist* told of her experiences studying rare mountain gorillas in Rwanda, Africa. This work brought public attention to the plight of gorillas and other species endangered by poachers, and it helped encourage the establishment of antipoaching laws and enforcement practices in various parts of the world.

Other authors who have chosen to focus on wildlife preservation include naturalist and prolific writer and poet Diane Ackerman (1948–), whose 1995 book *The Rarest of the Rare* is a collection of essays on endangered species and ecosystems; poet, essayist, and environmental activist Gary Snyder (1930–), whose works include the essay collection *The Practice of the Wild* (1990). Conservationist David Quammen (1948–) has also written about wildlife issues and animal rights in such works as *The Flight of the Iguana: A Sidelong View of Science and Nature* (1988), *Wild Thoughts from Wild Places* (1998), and *The Reluctant Mr. Darwin* (2006). Environmental activist and prolific writer and novelist Peter Matthiessen (1927–) has produced many articles on wildlife issues throughout the world, as well as books such as *Wildlife in America* (1959), *The Cloud Forest: A Chronicle of the South American Wilderness* (1961), and *African Silences* (1991).

Authors who have focused on habitat protection include environmentalist and writer Catherine Caufield, whose *In the Rainforest* (1989) provides a first-person account of Caufield's investigations into the destruction of rainforests throughout the world, and environmentalist and former oil geologist Rick Bass (1958–), who wrote *The Book of Yaak* (1997) and *Why I Came West* (2009) as a way to highlight his efforts to preserve the Yaak Valley in Montana. Also interested in habitat protection as well as wildlife preservation and biodiversity is biologist and conservationist E. O. Wilson (1929–), an expert in the study of ants and in mass extinctions. His works include *The Diversity of Life* (1992), *The Creation: An Appeal to Save Life on Earth* (2006), and *Nature Revealed: Selected Writings 1949–2006* (2006).

Aldo Leopold (1887–1948), whose influential writings of 20th-century environmentalism changed the way that many Americans viewed nature, was instrumental in the creation of Gila National Forest, the nation's first protected wilderness area. (Library of Congress)

Another prominent conservationist is Aldo Leopold (1887–1948), who was instrumental in establishing the science of wildlife management. He wrote several books on this subject, as well as *A Sand County Almanac* (1949) to share his own experiences living in the wilderness. Others concerned with wilderness conservation include U.S. Supreme Court Justice William O. Douglas (1898–1980), who wrote *A Wilderness Bill of Rights* (1965) to promote his belief that wilderness areas should be protected, and Gifford Pinchot (1865–1946), whose works *Primer of Forestry* (1899) and *The Training of a Forester* (1917) promoted the preservation and wise management of wilderness areas.

Even more prominent in terms of wilderness preservation was John Muir (1838–1914). After emigrating to America from Scotland with his family at the age of 11, he became a farmer, which he later said prepared him for life as a naturalist because working with the earth taught him to pay attention to small details in nature. After having a few other jobs as a young man, he became a guide for visitors to the Yosemite wilderness area in California, and eventually he convinced Congress to establish both the Yosemite and the Sequoia National Parks in 1890. He also founded the Sierra Club in 1892 and promoted wilderness conservation through this group and such works as *Our National Parks* (1916), one of the first books to focus public attention on problems in U.S. forestry management.

Conservation of agricultural land was the focus of farmer, poet, and essayist Wendell Berry (1934–), whose many works include *A Continuous Harmony: Essays Cultural and Agricultural* (1972), *The Unsettling of America* (1977), and *What Are People For?* (2010). Similarly, George Perkins Marsh (1801–1882) discussed ecology, resource management, and human effects on the landscape in his 1863 book

Man and Nature, or Physical Geography as Modified by Human Action. John Burroughs (1837–1921) also wrote extensively on nature conservation in such works as *Birds and Poets* (1877), *Locusts and Wild Honey* (1879), *Ways of Nature* (1905), *The Summit of the Years* (1914), *Field and Study* (1919), and *The Last Harvest* (1922).

On the issue of chemical pollution, one of the most famous authors is conservationist and scientist Rachel Louise Carson (1907–1964), who has often been credited with inspiring the U.S. environmental movement through her 1962 book *Silent Spring.* This work examines the impact of pesticide use on public health, and although it was not the first book to call attention to this issue, it was the first to combine scientific evidence on the subject with a clear, powerful, personable writing style accessible to general readers. Carson also wrote about the ecology of the ocean in *Under the Sea Wind* (1941) and *The Sea Around Us* (1951), and she was active in environmental causes, founding a nonprofit organization called the Rachel Carson Council, Inc., in 1965 to disseminate information about chemical contamination of the environment.

Long before Carson, however, another woman fought to bring attention to the dangers of pollution: U.S. physician Alice Hamilton (1869–1970), who is considered a pioneer in the field of human ecology. Her aim was

Greenovator: Wendell Berry

Wendell Berry is a writer and a farmer whose home is in Henry County, Kentucky. He is a prolific poet, novelist, and essayist whose subjects touch on virtually every aspect of American life and culture, including relationship to land, home, family, community, economies, nation, self, and God. Other Berry identifiers are expressed in terms that embody relationships expressed in his writing. These include husband, father, educator, citizen, and conservationist.

He was born Wendell Erdman Berry, in Henry County, Kentucky, on August 5, 1934. He received an AB degree from the University of Kentucky in 1956 and an MA from the University of Kentucky in 1957, the same year he married his wife, Tanya. The groundwork for his writing life continued with a Wallace Stegner Writing Fellowship at Stanford University (1958–1959). In 1960, his first novel, *Nathan Coulter*, was published.

The Berrys' Lanes Landing Farm is near the town of Port Royal; the fictional town of Port William has been a frequent setting for Berry's fiction. Berry's poetry, novels, and essays credit the land and patterns of nature and agrarian life as his most persistent teachers. His faith, he says, is a "bottom-up faith" that comes from the soil. His beliefs are rooted in a Christian theology of creation and love for one another.

Berry has been called a prophet (Goodrich, 2001). His philosophy embraces diversity, versatility, reasonableness of scale and boundaries, local adaptation, and personal thought, responsibility, and hope. He speaks out against industrial farming and other practices that reduce human beings to machines and land and animals to commodities. He blames dispassionate, geographically removed corporations for visual and emotional blight in American landscapes. He blames government for favoring "market forces" over human-scale economies.

Diversity and versatility have been hallmarks of Berry's career and have earned him a wide following. He has authored more than 30 books. From 1977 to 1979, Berry was a contributing editor for Rodale Press, publishers of *Organic Gardening and Farming* and *New Farm.* In recent years, he has been a frequent contributor to *Orion* magazine, which in 2003 printed his "A Citizen's Response to the National Security Strategy." He has held teaching positions at Georgetown College, New York

University, Stanford University, and the University of Kentucky. Berry has been a frequent conference speaker and has long been associated with the Land Institute in Salina, Kansas, founded by Wes Jackson.

In 2006, Berry was named Kentuckian of the Year and has received many other awards, including the T. S. Eliot Award, the John Hay Award, the Lyndhurst Prize, and the Aiken-Taylor Award for Poetry from *The Sewanee Review*.

CHAVAWN KELLEY

to reduce health hazards in factories, but in doing so she also called attention to the harmful industrial chemicals being released into the air and water, through such works as *Industrial Poisons in the United States* (1925) and *Industrial Toxicology* (1934).

Another author interested in protecting the water was industrial chemist David K. Bulloch (1929–2011), who wrote about ocean pollution in *The Wasted Ocean: The Ominous Crisis of Marine Pollution and How to Stop It* (1989) and *The Underwater Naturalist* (1991). Conserving water was the main issue for environmental activist Marc Reisner (1948–2000), who once worked for a group concerned with environmental politics, the National Resources Defense Council. His 1986 book *Cadillac Desert: The American West and Its Disappearing Water* offers a historical survey and in-depth discussion of water use.

For Barry Commoner (1917–), the main issue was above-ground nuclear testing, although he also wrote about how technological growth was negatively impacting the environment. Fearing that nuclear testing was threatening human health, he promoted studies on the dangers of nuclear radiation, worked for the 1963 passage of the Nuclear Test Ban Treaty, and established the Center for Biology of Natural Systems (CBNS), which studies the relationship between humans and their environment. His books include *The Closing Circle: Nature, Man, and Technology* (1971), *The Politics of Energy* (1979), and *Making Peace with the Planet* (1993).

Three other authors to bring public attention to the issue of nuclear energy are Carl Sagan (1934–1996), Amory Lovins (1947–), and Ralph Nader (1934–). A professor of astronomy and space sciences who wrote about numerous scientific and environmental issues, Sagan is credited with developing the theory of nuclear winter, which he discussed in his book *A Path Where No Man Thought: Nuclear Winter and the End of the Arms Race* (1990). Lovins is a scientist and expert on nuclear energy who worked as a professional environmentalist in the 1970s and believes that the United States should stop using nuclear power and fossil fuels and work harder to develop nonpolluting, renewable sources of power; he expressed this view most significantly in his 1979 book *Is Nuclear Power Necessary?* Nader wrote about nuclear power in *The Menace of Atomic Energy* (1977), but this lawyer, consumer activist, environmental activist, and former presidential candidate has written about many other subjects as well, including pollution in *Vanishing Air* (1970) and *Who's Poisoning America: Corporate Polluters and Their Victims in the Chemical Age* (1981).

Global warming is another popular topic for environmentalists. One of the most prominent writers on this issue is Bill McKibben (1960–), a former staff writer for the *New Yorker* magazine. His works include *The End of Nature* (1989), which warns that environmental destruction is threatening all life on Earth, *Fight Global Warming Now: The Handbook for Taking Action in Your Community* (2007), and *Eaarth* [sic]:

Making a Life on a Tough New Planet (2010), which talks about how human beings will be forced to adjust to a world where climate change has caused irreparable environmental damage. Also focusing on climate change is climatologist Stephen H. Schneider (1945–2010), whose many works include *Global Warming: Are We Entering the Greenhouse Century?* (1989), *Laboratory Earth: The Planetary Gamble We Can't Afford to Lose* (1997), and *Wildlife Responses to Climate Change* (2001), co-edited with Terry L. Root.

There are also those who write books to argue that global warming isn't a real phenomenon. For example, Ronald Bailey (1953–), an editor of *Reason* magazine, wrote *Eco-Scam: The False Prophets of Ecological Apocalypse* (1993) to accuse environmentalists of misstating the dangers of climate change. A similar work is journalist Michael Fumento's *Science Under Siege: How the Environmental Misinformation Campaign Is Affecting Our Laws, Taxes, and Our Daily Life* (1993), an indictment of the way environmentalists present environmental problems to the American public.

Human ecology, particularly related to overpopulation, is the primary issue for husband-and-wife authors and scientists Paul (1933–) and Anne (1933–) Ehrlich. They first publicized the dangers of overpopulation through their 1968 book *The Population Bomb*, which was followed in 1990 by *The Population Explosion* and in 1995 by *The Stork and the Plow*, the latter focusing on the relationship between population and food supply. The Ehrlichs also talk about endangered species in their 1981 book *Extinction: The Causes and Consequences of the Disappearance of Species*; ecology in their 1985 work *The Machinery of Nature*; and anti-environmentalism in *Betrayal of Science and Reason: How Anti-Environmental Rhetoric Threatens Our Future* (1998). Their most recent book is *The Dominant Animal: Human Evolution and the Environment* (2008). The two have also written hundreds of scientific articles related to environmentalism, and they have received numerous scientific awards.

Also interested in human ecology is Murray Bookchin (1921–2006). Credited with introducing the concept of social ecology, which in part blames capitalism and urbanization for environmental problems, he formed the Vermont-based Institute for Social Ecology to promote his views through environmental politics. Bookchin's works include *Our Synthetic Environment* (1962), *The Crisis of the Cities* (1965), *The Ecology of Freedom* (1982), *Which Way for the Ecology Movement?* (1994), and *Social Ecology and Communalism* (2007, with Eirik Eiglad).

Other authors have chosen to focus on the dangers of technology. For example, urban planner and historian Lewis Mumford (1885–1990) criticized society's belief that technology can control nature in such books as *The Condition of Man* (1944), *The Conduct of Life* (1951), and *The Myth of the Machine* (1970), the latter of which suggests that technology would ultimately destroy modern civilization. Also critical of technology is Theodore Roszak (1933–), who has written essays and books expressing his view that technology is splintering society and should be replaced with more holistic approaches to life. His works include *Person/Planet* (1978) and *The Voice of the Earth: An Exploration of Ecopsychology* (1993), which examines such issues as the Gaia hypothesis and the relationship between nature and religion.

Religion is also an aspect of environmentalism explored by Thomas Mary Berry (1914–2009), a Catholic priest who advocated deep ecology and "ecospiritualism" in such works as *Befriending the Earth: A Theology of Reconciliation between Humans and the Earth* (1991) and *Creative Energy: Bearing Witness for the Earth* (1996). Deep ecology is a philosophy that promotes the idea that an individual has a duty to limit one's affect on the planet, through such practices as living simply, minimizing waste, and reducing the number of one's children to prevent overpopulation. Authors who have chosen to focus on the subject of deep ecology include botanist Liberty Hyde Bailey (1858–1954), who expressed his environmental philosophy in *The Holy Earth* (1915), and George Sessions, who with Bill Devall wrote *Deep Ecology: Living as If Nature Mattered* (1985) to make Americans more aware of the works of Norwegian philosopher and deep ecologist Arne Naess. Sessions also edited *Deep Ecology for the Twenty-First Century*, a 1995 anthology of writings on deep ecology and environmental ethics.

One of the most significant early supporters of simple-living or back-to-nature movement in America was environmentalist Stewart Brand, the founding editor of the *Whole Earth Catalogue*. This collection of environmental products published in 1968 and at various times during the 1970s has become synonymous with communal living. Brand also wrote several books, most recently *Whole Earth Discipline: An Ecopragmatist Manifesto* (2009), in which he discusses such issues as global warming, urbanization, biotechnology, nuclear power, and genetic engineering.

In contrast to authors connected to the simple-living movement was R. Buckminster Fuller (1895–1983), who believed that expanding technological knowledge would eventually solve environmental problems. He was an inventor who decided to devote himself to creating environmentally beneficial products because of the death of his daughter, Alexandra, in 1922; the four-year-old died from a series of communicable diseases which Fuller thought arose in part from an unhealthy environment. He wrote about his views on environmental issues in his 1969 book *Utopia or Oblivion: The Prospects for Humanity*.

Other authors have been primarily interested in environmental politics. For example, Robert Gottlieb (1931–), a professor of urban environmental studies who lectures on environmental policy and conducts research on urban, industrial, and environmental issues, has authored several books on the environment, including *Environmentalism Unbound: Exploring New Pathways for Change* (2001), *Forcing the Spring: The Transformation of the American Environmental Movement* (1993), and *Reducing Toxics: A New Approach to Policy and Industrial Decision-Making* (1995). Lynton K. Caldwell (1913–2006) is also the author of books on environmental policy, including *Man and His Environment: Policy and Administration* (1975), *Biocracy: Public Policy and the Life Sciences* (1987), and *Policy for Land, Law, and Ethics* (1993); an expert in environmental politics, he was one of the architects of the National Environmental Policy Act (NEPA) signed into law in 1970. Another significant author in terms of environmental politics is political scientist and professor of sociology John Bellamy Foster (1953–) whose 1994 book *The Vulnerable Planet: A Short Economic History of the Environment* discusses environmental degradation in terms of public policy and economics.

The economy is also the focus of the environmental works of Paul Hawken (1946–), whose books include *The Next Economy* (1983) and *The Ecology of*

Commerce (1993), the latter of which outlines an ecological economic system. He is also an environmental activist who has served on boards of various environmental groups and both founded and directs the Natural Capital Institute (NCI), which maintains a database of activists and organizations focused on environmental and social justice.

In terms of activists, one of the best known in the environmentalist community is Dave Foreman (1946–), a founder of the environmental group Earth First! He talks about the tactics of this group in *Ecodefense: A Field Guide to Monkeywrenching* (1985) and about his experiences as a radical environmentalist in *Confessions of an Eco-Warrior* (1991), which involved engaging in ecotage—the sabotage or destruction of equipment such as bulldozers and chainsaws in order to stop or delay projects harmful to the environment. Another work on this subject is *Green Rage: Radical Environmentalism and the Unmaking of Civilization* (1990) by Christopher Manes, a former member of Earth First! In establishing this group, both Manes and Foreman were inspired by environmental activist Edward Abbey (1927–1989), best known for his 1975 novel *The Monkey Wrench Gang* about a band of activists who use ecotage to protest desert development in the American Southwest. Although it was a work of fiction, *The Monkey Wrench Gang* helped spread the practice of

Greenovator: Henry David Thoreau

Henry David Thoreau (1817–1862), a 19th-century author whose works have influenced a diverse audience, including poets, philosophers, ecologists, and political dissidents, is one of America's most famous naturalist writers. Despite his short life, Thoreau's publications are extensive and vary from self-meditative prose to essays and poems. However, Thoreau is best known for two works: the nonfiction book *Walden; or, Life in the Woods*, and his essay "Civil Disobedience," originally published in *Aesthetic Papers*. While interpretations of Thoreau's writing have emphasized him in polarizing roles such as recluse, anarchist, or proto-ecologist, interest in his work and character remains high.

Thoreau was born in the rural, agrarian town of Concord, Massachusetts, on July 12, 1817, to a middle-class family. Although given the name David Henry at birth for his deceased paternal uncle, Thoreau would invert the name upon adulthood. After an uneventful childhood and grammar school education, Thoreau followed his father's footsteps and enrolled in Harvard College with narrowly passing entrance exam scores. At Harvard, Thoreau's classmates noted that his demeanor was aloof and indifferent while the president of Harvard remarked his conduct was "satisfactory" and attributed any neglect in his scholarship to sickness (Harding, 1992). Primarily studying classics and theology, Thoreau completed his bachelor's degree in the summer of 1837.

During his final year at Harvard and after graduation, Thoreau became close friends with Ralph Waldo Emerson, the prominent writer and transcendentalist, who would influence Thoreau throughout his life. After numerous stints as a schoolteacher, Thoreau moved into the house he built by hand in 1845 at Walden Pond only two miles south of Concord on Emerson's property. During the two-year period in which he stayed at Walden Pond, Thoreau kept a journal that he would later edit and revise into his famous book, *Walden*. In 1846, on one of his trips to Concord, Thoreau was briefly jailed for refusal to pay a head tax on adult males in the city. His explanation for this act of defiance, motivated by his support for abolition among other issues, would be the basis for his essay "Resistance to Civil Government," which was retitled "Civil Disobedience" after his death.

In his later years, Thoreau worked as a land surveyor and made numerous trips to Maine and Cape Cod and traveled to Quebec. His writing from this period reflects his interest in natural history, and Thoreau made numerous observations in the fields of biology, botany, and zoology. Although *Walden* received critical praise, Thoreau published only one other book during his lifetime (*A Week on the Concord and Merimack Rivers* in 1849, which sold poorly) and gave lectures in the Concord area.

While living in his family's house and caring for his parents over the final decade of his life, Thoreau's long struggle with tuberculosis ended when he died on May 6, 1862, at the age of 44. Posthumously, his writings have been widely reprinted and integrated into the literary canon. However, his impact on concepts of civil liberty and environmentalism was particularly influential through the 20th century and provides the basis for his legacy.

ELIJAH MENDOZA

ecotage and had as great an impact on environmentalism as the most influential nonfiction books on the subject.

PATRICIA D. NETZLEY

See also: Christian Responses (Philosophy and Religion); Earth First! (Activism); Ecopoetics (Arts); Global Warming (Environment); Literature, Environmental (Arts); National Environmental Policy Act (documents); National Parks (Sports).

References

Abbey, Edward. 1975. *The Monkey Wrench Gang*. Philadelphia, PA: Lippincott.

Ackerman, Diane. 1995. *The Rarest of the Rare*. New York: Random House.

Bailey, Ronald. 1993. *Eco-Scam: The False Prophets of the Ecological Apocalypse*. New York: St. Martin's Press.

Bass, Rick. 1997. *The Book of Yaak*. New York: Houghton Mifflin.

Biehl, Janet. 2011. *Mumford Gutkind Bookchin: The Emergence of Eco-Decentralism*. Porsgrunn, Norway: New Compass Press.

Bonzo, J. Matthew, and Michael R. Stevens. 2008. *Wendell Berry and the Cultivation of Life, a Reader's Guide*. Grand Rapids, MI: Brazos Press.

Bowler, Peter J. 1993. *The Norton History of the Environmental Sciences*. New York and London: W. W. Norton.

Brand, Stewart. 1986. *The Essential Whole Earth Catalogue*. Garden City, NY: Doubleday.

Buell, L. 1995. *The Environmental Imagination: Thoreau, Nature Writing, and the Formation of American Culture*. Cambridge, MA: Belknap Press of Harvard University Press.

Bulloch, David K. 1989. *The Wasted Ocean: The Ominous Crisis of Marine Pollution and How to Stop It*. New York: Lyons and Burford (an American Littoral Society Book).

Cahalan, James. 2003. *Edward Abbey: A Life*. Tucson: University of Arizona Press.

Caufield, Catherine. 1989. *In the Rainforest*. New York: Knopf.

Cox, Donald W. 1971. *Pioneers of Ecology*. Maplewood, NJ: Hammond.

Dashefsky, H. Steven. 1993. *Environmental Literacy*. New York: Random House.

Davidson, Keay. 2000. *Carl Sagan: A Life*. New York: John Wiley & Sons.

Devall, Bill, and George Sessions. 1985. *Deep Ecology: Living as if Nature Mattered*. Salt Lake City, UT: Peregrine Books.

Dobson, Andrew. 1991. *The Green Reader*. San Francisco, CA: Mercury House.

Dowie, Mark. 1995. *Losing Ground: American Environmentalism at the Close of the Twentieth Century*. Cambridge, MA: MIT Press.

Drengson, Alan, and Yuichi Inoue. 1995. *The Deep Ecology Movement: An Introductory Anthology*. Berkeley, CA: North Atlantic Books.

Egan, Michael. 2009. *Barry Commoner and the Science of Survival: The Remaking of American Environmentalism.* Cambridge, MA: MIT Press.

Ehrlich, Paul R., and Anne H. Ehrlich. 1981. *Extinction: The Causes and Consequences of the Disappearance of Species.* New York: Random House.

Ehrlich, Paul R., and Anne H. Ehrlich. 1995. *The Stork and The Plow: The Equity Answer to the Human Dilemma.* New York: Grosset/Putnam.

Eller, Vernard. 1973. *The Simple Life: The Christian Stance Toward Possessions.* Grand Rapids, MI: Eerdmans.

Foreman, Dave. 1991. *Confessions of an Eco-Warrior.* New York: Harmony Books.

Fumento, Michael. 1993. *Science Under Siege: How the Environmental Misinformation Campaign Is Affecting Our Laws, Taxes, and Our Daily Life.* New York: Quill/William Morrow.

Glotfelty, Cheryll, and Harold Fromm, eds. 1996. *The Ecocriticism Reader: Landmarks in Literary Ecology.* Athens: University of Georgia Press.

Goodrich, Janet. 2001. *The Unforeseen Self in the Works of Wendell Berry.* Columbia: University of Missouri Press.

Gottlieb, Robert. 1993. *Forcing the Spring: The Transformation of the American Environmental Movement.* Washington, DC: Island Press.

Grubbs, Morris Allen, ed. 2007. *Conversations with Wendell Berry.* Jackson: University Press of Mississippi.

Hamilton, Alice. 1943. *Exploring the Dangerous Trades: The Autobiography of Alice Hamilton, M.D.* Boston: Northeastern University Press.

Harding, W. 1992. *The Days of Henry Thoreau.* Princeton, NJ: Princeton University Press.

Hatch, Alden. 1974. *Buckminster Fuller: At Home in the Universe.* New York: Crown.

Hawken, Paul. 2010. *The Ecology of Commerce Revised Edition: A Declaration of Sustainability.* New York: HarperCollins (First Harper Business edition).

Kline, Benjamin. 2011. *First Along the River: A Brief History of the U.S. Environmental Movement, 4th ed.* Lanham, MD: Rowman & Littlefield.

Lear, Linda. 2009. *Rachel Carson: Witness for Nature.* New York: Mariner Books.

Lowenthal, David. 2000. *George Perkins Marsh: Prophet of Conservation.* Seattle and London: University of Washington Press.

Manes, Christopher. 1990. *Green Rage: Radical Environmentalism and the Unmaking of Civilization.* Boston, MA: Little, Brown.

Matthiessen, Peter, and McKay Jenkins. 2000. *The Peter Matthiessen Reader.* New York: Vintage Books.

McHenry, Robert, ed. 1972. *A Documentary History of Conservationism in America.* New York: Praeger.

McKibben, Bill. 1989. *The End of Nature.* New York: Random House.

Meine, Curt D., and Wendell Berry. 1988. *Aldo Leopold: His Life and Work.* Madison: University of Wisconsin Press.

Merchant, Paul, ed. 1991. *Wendell Berry.* Lewiston: Confluence Press.

Miller, Char. 2001. *Gifford Pinchot and the Making of Modern Environmentalism.* Washington, DC: Island Press.

Mowat, Farley. 1987. *Woman in the Mists.* New York: Warner Books.

Mumford, Lewis. 1983. *Sketches from Life: The Autobiography of Lewis Mumford.* Boston: Beacon Press.

Nader, Ralph et al. 1981. *Who's Poisoning America: Corporate Polluters and Their Victims in the Chemical Age.* San Francisco: Sierra Club Books.

Netzley, Patricia D. 1999. *Environmental Literature: An Encyclopedia of Works, Authors, and Themes*. Santa Barbara, CA: ABC-CLIO.

Pepper, David. 1996. *Modern Environmentalism: An Introduction*. London and New York: Routledge.

Peters, Jason. 2007. *Wendell Berry: Life and Work*. Lexington: University of Kentucky Press.

Reich, Charles. 1970. *The Greening of America*. New York: Random House.

Reisner, Marc. 1986. *Cadillac Desert: The American West and Its Disappearing Water*. New York: Viking Penguin.

Renehan, Edward. 1992. *John Burroughs: An American Naturalist*. Hensonville, NY: Black Dome Press.

Robinson, D. M. 2004. *Natural Life: Thoreau's Worldly Transcendentalism*. Ithaca, NY: Cornell University Press.

Roszak, Theodore. 1993. *The Voice of the Earth: An Exploration of Ecopsychology*. Grand Rapids, MI: Phanes Press.

Sackman, Douglas Cazaux. 2010. *A Companion to American Environmental History*. Malden, MA, and Oxford, UK: Wiley-Blackwell.

Sale, Kirkpatrick. 1993. *The Green Revolution: The American Environmental Movement, 1962–1992*. New York: Hill and Wang.

Schneider, R. J. 2000. *Thoreau's Sense of Place: Essays in American Environmental Writing*. Iowa City: University of Iowa Press.

Schneider, Stephen Henry. 1989. *Global Warming: Are We Entering the Greenhouse Century?* San Francisco: Sierra Club Books.

Shabecoff, Philip. 1993. *A Fierce Green Fire: The American Environmental Movement*. New York: Hill and Wang.

Shi, David. 1985. *The Simple Life: Plain Living and High Thinking in American Culture*. New York: Oxford University Press.

Slovic, Scott. 1992. *Seeking Awareness in American Nature Writing: Henry Thoreau, Annie Dillard, Wendell Berry, Barry Lopez*. Salt Lake City: University of Utah Press.

Snyder, Gary. 1990. *The Practice of the Wild*. San Francisco, CA: North Point Press.

Steuding, Bob. 1976. *Gary Snyder*. Boston: Twayne.

Wolfe, Linnie Marsh. 2003. *Son of the Wilderness: The Life of John Muir*. Madison: University of Wisconsin Press.

ART, ENVIRONMENTAL

New approaches toward producing art emerged alongside environmentalism in the late 1960s and early 1970s that were influenced by this movement, but they also drew from contemporary preoccupations in art itself. These included interests in site specificity, time-based performance, the resonance of creativity within daily processes, and a general rejection of commodification. The artists recognized as innovators in "greening" art were also aligned with and active in other art and social movements, such as Fluxus, feminism, and the anti-war movement.

Overview

Environmental art calls attention to binaries of nature and culture, problems of perpetual growth, species interdependency and offers critiques of homocentrism in the political economy of the planet. This article uses two terms interchangeably—*environmental* and *ecological*, or eco-art—as a way of making distinctions, one might think of environmental as being part of a context of place and space and ecological as an approach that attends to natural systems and feedback loops. Both kinds of practice share interdisciplinary strategies, including installations, images, sculpture, performance, and media as well as an interest in time's destabilizing effect on natural processes. An early art work of Hans Haacke, "Grass Grows" (1965–1966), simply exhibited the process of grass growing. With an emphasis on research and on language, environmental art is aligned with conceptualist art. Many art practices also tended to demystify and deprofessionalize science, offering close views and do-it-yourself agency and promoting responsibility for environmental degradation and regeneration. Green art deals with specific ecological issues, as well as the larger social, historical, and political context in which an environment is imagined, constructed, and changed by human activity (Fluxus).

Site Contextual Art and Land Art

As the environment consists of real spaces, the construction of environmental meaning is key to environmental practice. Allan Kaprow was an innovator in enunciating the importance of *environment as such* through his "Environments" (ca. 1960s), which were spaces that could be inhabited and altered by visitors. Kaprow's "happenings," likewise, revealed places as processes; his 1968 happening "Fluids" involved melting ice on streets, an ecological project par excellence that offered a transformative experience. Sensitized to gallery commercialism, artists began using alternative locations in real spaces for exhibitions, including desert landscapes and trash bins (Gordon Matta-Clark). The 1970s artist Ana Mendieta created ephemeral work grounded literally in situ by making prints in the earth, mud, and sand with her naked body, calling her work earth-body art.

Social Ecological Interventions

Environmental artists take on the work of creating a social imaginary for the material and psychic detritus of contemporary society. Robert Morris advocated that artists do reclamation work after mines had outlived their industrial uses, aligning the aesthetic aims of conventional reclamation with artists' interest in raw materials and form. The prolific artist Bonnie Sherk created striking site installations in industrial waste sites that she recuperated, gardened in, and performed in ("Sitting Still," 1970). Mierle Ukeles drew her routine experiences as a female together with problems of pollution in her "Manifesto for Maintenance Art" (1969) proposal that suggested bringing containers of environmental refuse (polluted water, land, etc.) to the museum for remediation. In the 1970s, she washed public steps, making visible the necessary maintenance work of both mother and city. Her continuing work with the Sanitation Department of New York City illuminates the material waste of our consumer society. In another project addressing pollutants in the urban space, Gordon Matta-Clark and video artist Juan Downey created the Fresh Air Cart in 1972, into which people were invited to sit and inhale pure oxygen.

Time, Instability, and Performance

Living processes of growth, death, and decay are key to ecological systems. Hans Haacke's 1965 manifesto called for "time-based, dynamic, natural, indeterminate art"; reiterating the thoughts of Fluxus artists who called for "living art," as well as the influential German artist Joseph Beuys. In Haacke's "Condensation Cube" (1968), a transparent Plexiglas cube revealed the hydrological cycling of water on a diurnal rhythm. Artist Alan Sonfist invokes the biological time of forest regeneration in his "Time Landscape" (1965–ongoing), planted in New York City. Working with the annual farming cycle, in 1982 Agnes Denes planted and harvested 1,000 pounds of wheat on two acres in lower Manhattan. "Wheatfield, a Confrontation" also critiqued land use decisions placing profit over food production. In 1982, Joseph Beuys began planting 7,000 oak trees around the world. Agnes Denes, again, in 1996, planted a forest on a reclaimed mountain in Finland. "Tree Mountain—A Living Time Capsule—11,000 Trees—11,000 People—400 Years" reveals its mathematically spaced arrangement of trees, the human hand in inception to be overcome by the processes of nature.

Cultivation, Recycling, and Remediation

In the early 1970s, Helen Mayer Harrison and Newton Harrison began making earth in their studio, continuing on to combine poetry, public conversations, and intensive research and planning in collaboration with local citizens and governments to remediate massive damaged regional ecosystems. In "Revival Field" (1990), Mel Chin worked with scientist Rufus L. Chaney in cultivating plants that draw heavy metals from the soil in a land reclamation experiment. In his work on depleted and contaminated coal mining landscapes, Matthew Friday maps out the material relations between people, abandoned machinery, slag, and mines using the personal stories and memories of the people involved as part of the process of returning the landscape to other uses. With "Ocean Landmark" (1980), Betty Beaumont resourced wasted industrial materials to create a massive fish habitat off Long Island.

Environmental Pedagogy and Research Communities

Many artists and art collectives use research to produce informational projects and viable proposals. Peter Fend's research and mapping leads to solutions for international and domestic conflicts over resources; Brooke Singer and Beatriz Da Costa invited residents around New York City to participate in the mapping of city's worst air, with the intent to impact policy. Amy Balkin's "Public Smog" demystifies and critiques governmental strategies of turning carbon dioxide into a commodity. The collaborative team Future Farmers combines research with strong design and craft skills to create projects that make green technologies and concepts accessible and understandable to the public.

Other works produced through communities of researchers use new media technologies such as social media and opportunistic interventionism to call attention to environmental justice matters. Such tactical media projects involve elaborate group actions that invoke public imagination. In 2007, the Yes Men called attention to Dow Chemical Corp.'s abandonment of Bhopal disaster victims; as the Yes Lab, a larger collective pursues predominately ecological issues, frequently by targeting corporate greed.

Art and Science

Many artists have continued the impulse to explore science as amateurs, which begins with Haacke and Ukeles. Invoking interspecies interdependencies and relations, some artists work directly with animals to create habitat or develop an understanding of their experience. Lynne Hull is an artist focused on creating what she calls transspecies art and sculpture for wildlife. Brian Ballangee is trained as both a biologist and a photographer whose work bridges art and science. Natalie Jerimijenko's collaborative inductive research into environmental health has created cross-species picnics (OOZ), robot dogs that detect PCBs as well as home environmental monitors such as dust masks that indicate pollution levels.

The Critical Art Ensemble uses tactical media and performance to make science accessible; in a project about genetic engineering of food, they served homemade beer containing genetic modifications. In 2002, to address the ethics of biological manipulation, Julia Reodica and Adam Zaretsky created "Work Horse Zoo," an installation in which they lived in a simulated lab with other common lab species (e.g., frogs, *Escherichia coli* bacteria, mice). Such works expose scientific bias and expand understanding of the extent to which humans regularly intervene in domains we are conditioned to think of as "nature." Artists like Brian Collier and Mark Dion follow historically proscribed scientific and pseudo-scientific methodologies of collection, creating installations that demonstrate the degree to which human cultural habits are mixed into perceptions of the natural.

Psychogeographies

Other contemporary artists are influenced by the Situationist International, a group of 1960s writers and artists concerned with the contamination of all social relations by the commodity. Seeking forms of resistance to this enclosure, they developed strategic random walks, or "drifts," that investigated urban layers and histories. A discussion of psychogeographic space must include the descendants of precolonial natives. The work of Cherokee artist Jimmie Durham is intrinsically ecological in his use of objects, space, and narrative and addresses the tensions and contradictions of a society that has elevated the commodity as the route to pleasure.

The artist's walk is long familiar as an environmental practice, particularly as enacted by Richard Long who invokes the traditional British "ramble," by documenting the traces of his own walks through the countryside ("A Line Made by Walking," 1967). As a group activity, artists have adopted the drift or the idea of a group walk or journey as a tool for collective environmental research and restoration of conviviality (see Nick Brown, "Walking in Place"). Kanarinka's 2009 project, "It Takes 154,000 Breaths to Evacuate Boston," updates Long's embodied research in the rationalized public sphere of a post-9/11 modern city by literally graphing the energy it takes to exit in an emergency. Related is a new generation of artist maps and journeys documenting environmental injustices (in the environmental section of the 2007 exhibition "Just Spaces" at the Los Angeles Contemporary Exhibitions, artists map hunger, park access, and toxic wastes). Brooke Singer has a Web-based catalog of Superfund sites in the United States (Superfund, 365) and a map of Midwest power production made by Compass in the Midwest Radical Cultural Center.

Environmental Art and Popular Education

Although many environmental works can be understood as educational, the emergence of an art field trained on social relations, grassroots pedagogy, and participation has introduced new strategies of engagement into environmental education and environmental justice campaigns. Some of these projects bring the public together around waste upcycling; the collective Material Exchange gathers discarded materials from institutions and turns them into useful items for redistribution. Art's ability to expand environmental consciousness and nurture ecological literacy has led to the proliferation of art programs within environmental education centers. Examples include the United Nations Environment Program and the Schuylkill Center for Environmental Education. Artist Bonnie Sherk runs a pedagogical project that preserves ecological and horticultural knowledge in New York City and San Francisco.

Greenovator: Earthworks (as a precursor to Environmental Art)

Artist Robert Smithson's early earthwork projects expressed anxiety about the artifice of the gallery and were structured to address the relationship between site and nonsite. His installations used maps, photographs, and heaps of materials from a field location to address what was outside the gallery. Subsequently moving his inquiry outside to produce massive works on the Earth's surface itself, he was concerned above all with natural processes of entropy. Smithson's work sowed uncertainty as to what was manipulated by humans and what was natural. Earthworks are characterized by relatively aggressive site interventions that involve pouring, dumping, digging, building, and in other ways taking cues from industrial-scale human interventions into land, both prehistoric and contemporary; such artists include Michael Heizer, Nancy Holt, and James Turrell.

Conclusion

Ecological art sets out to show our intrinsic inclusion within the web of nature. In many of the projects and approaches above, the idea of "greening" is about the production of new subjectivities that can produce less harmful, less coercive, more web-like relationships with one another and the environments they inhabit. By forming new encounters in different kinds of spaces, environmental artists demonstrate how we emerge from and continually remake our environment.

Other Resources

The Web site Green Museum (http://greenmuseum.org/) offers many contemporary instances of environmental art. Sue Spaid's book, *Ecovention*, outlines many contemporary and historic projects (available online or for purchase). The Web site for Eco-Art Network (http://www.ecoartnetwork.org/) contains the essays of over 100 artists.

SARAH LEWISON

See also: Arts, Entertainment, and Media section entries.

References

Balkin, Amy. "Public Smog." Available at: http://www.publicsmog.org/.

Compass. Available at: http://www.midwestradicalculturecorridor.net/?cat=3.

Critical Art Ensemble. Available at: http://www.critical-art.net/.

Durham, Jimmie. "In His Own Words: The Pursuit of Happiness." *Heyoka*. Available at: http://heyokamagazine.com/HEYOKA.2.JIMMI%20DURHAM.htm.

Fluxus. Available at: http://www.fluxus.org/.

Jerimijenko, Natalie. Environmental Health Clinic Lab. Available at: http://www.environ mentalhealthclinic.net/people/natalie-jeremijenko/.

Kaprow, Allan. "How to Make a Happening." Available at: http://primaryinformation.org/ files/allan-kaprow-how-to-make-a-happening.pdf.

Kaprow, Allan. 2008. "Art as Life: Environments." Exhibition text. Geffen Museum of Contemporary Art, March 23–June 30. Available at: http://www.moca.org/kaprow/ index.php/environments/.

Krug, Don, and Jennifer Siegenthaler. "Changing Views About Art and the Earth." *Art and Ecology: Photo Essays*. Available at: http://greenmuseum.org/c/aen/Earth/Changing/ artist.php.

Material Exchange. Available at: http://material-exchange.org/home.html.

Meyer, James. 1997. "The Macabre Museum: Mark Dion." *Frieze* 32 (January–February). Available at: http://www.frieze.com/issue/article/the_macabre_museum/.

Morris, Robert. 1980. "Notes on Art as/and Land Reclamation." *October* 12 (Spring): 87–102.

Ora Sherk, Bonnie. Living Museum. Available at: http://www.alivinglibrary.org/ bonnieresume.html.

"Portable Devices Allow Tracking of Real-Time Exposure to Airborne Contaminants: Sensing a Path through Pollution." *SEED Magazine* (originally published September 27, 2006). Available at: http://seedmagazine.com/content/article/sensing_a_path_through _pollution/.

Rockman, Alexis. The Brilliant Life. Available at: http://the-brilliant-life.com/tag/ alexis-rockman/.

Singer, Brooke. Available at: http://www.superfund365.org/.

Situationist International/Guy Debord. 1958. "Theory of the Derive." Available at: http:// www.bopsecrets.org/SI/2.derive.htm.

Spaid, Sue. *Ecovention*. Available at: http://greenmuseum.org/c/ecovention.

Ukeles, Mierle Laderman. 1969. "Maintenance Art Manifesto: Proposal for an Exhibition: Care." In Alexander Alberro and Blake Stimson, eds., *Conceptual Art: A Critical Anthology*. Cambridge, MA: MIT Press.

Ulke, Christina. 2003. "Imagination Is an Instrument of Survival; On Pragmatic Multi- tudinism." *Journal of Aesthetics and Protest* 1:2 (August).

"Workhorse Zoo." Available at: http://www.emutagen.com/whzoogl.html.

Yes Men/Yes Lab. Available at: http://theyesmen.org/.

BLOGS

In popular use, a blog is a tool that allows people an online forum in which to publish journals, news, reflections, commentary, and hyperlinks directing readers to other resources. Oftentimes, blogs are frequently updated and can be created through writing, videos, art, and images. Blogs are available on practically any topic imaginable. They can be penned by one individual; they can represent a particular group, theme, or idea; and they can be associated with organizations, businesses, and government entities. The content of blogs can include personal views and commentary; company, business, and organization information; helpful hints and resources; political views, commentary, and action—basically, musings on just about anything.

With the marked increase of interest in all things "green" in the mass media and popular culture, the availability of eco/earth/environmentally friendly blogs has significantly multiplied. Green bloggers share information on everything from protecting the environment through social and political action, developing sustainable technologies, and eco-friendly products and lifestyles.

The Web site Best Green Blogs (http://www.bestgreenblogs.com) provides readers with a comprehensive directory of sustainable and green-themed blogs from around the world with a goal of empowering people to make choices that are healthier for themselves and the planet. Several other sites and news outlets provide lists of their "top" blogs; according to the green news and information site WebEcoist (http://webecoist.momtastic.com), more than 6,000 green blogs are active with more created every year. Blogs like Discovery Channel's TreeHugger (http://www.treehugger.com/), the popular The Daily Green (http://www.thedailygreen.com/), and the green news blog of the *Huffington Post* (http://www.huffingtonpost.com/green/) frequently top the list of best green blogs.

Greenovation: Green Blog—Ecorazzi

Ecorazzi (http://www.ecorazzi.com), founded by Michael d'Estries of Ithaca, New York, and Rebecca Carter of Miami, Florida, in August 2006, is an award winning blog that provides green news and the latest in green gossip. The blog covers all forms of popular entertainment (film, music, sports, Web), popular culture, lifestyle (fashion and food), and celebrity news. The site also provides information and support for a variety of causes for animals, arts and culture, environment, and people. The celebrity tab highlights green activities of popular figures such as the launch of Ellen Degeneres's vegan pet food line, Daryl Hannah's participation in the Maldives's eco-symposiums, and Leonardo DiCaprio's role in getting a California law passed banning the sale, trade, and possession of shark fins.

The Web-based blog (the founders have only met in person once) has received a number of awards:

2007: Blog of the Year from *VegNews'* Veggie Awards
2008: Most Animal Friendly Celebrity Blog from PETA's Proggy Award
2009: 70 Eco-Heroes from *Glamour Magazine*
2009: Best Celebrity Twitter Feed from Treehugger's Best of Green Award
Time magazine's Top 15 Green Websites of All Time

KIM KENNEDY WHITE

The diversity of coverage is evident in the following annotated list that provides a sampling of green blogs organized by theme.

Green Activism/Community Green Effort Blogs

Earth Activists. http://earthactivism.com/blog. Blog from an activist group "working to unite community outreach and find solutions to the climate crisis."

Earth First. http://earthfirst.com. Eco blog that covers environmental news, features, videos, and original cartoons. Not associated with EarthFirst!, the radical environmental group; this blog cuts through "the eco-fluff to get to the heart of the new green movement."

Friends of the Earth International Blog. http://www.foei.org/en/blog. Blog from the largest grassroots environmental network including some 5,000 environmental activist groups worldwide.

The Goldman Environmental Prize Blog. http://www.goldmanprize.org/blog. Blog of the annual Goldman Environmental Prize that awards $150,000 to grassroots environmental heroes across the globe.

Greenpeace Weblog—Nuclear Reaction. http://www.greenpeace.org/interna tional/en/news/Blogs/nuclear-reaction/. "Blogging the meltdown of the nuclear industry."

No Impact Man. http://noimpactman.typepad.com/. A blog from Colin Beavan (a.k.a. No Impact Man) about living off the grid in a green and sustainable lifestyle. Listed in *Time* magazine's Top 15 Green Websites.

Switchboard. http://switchboard.nrdc.org/. Staff blog from the Natural Resources Defense Council; discussions on a wide range of environmental topics, including sustainable communities, environmental justice, and nuclear energy, weapons, and waste. Listed in *Time* magazine's Top 15 Green Websites.

Green Arts, Entertainment, and Media Blogs

DH Love Life. http://www.dhlovelife.com/v2/knowdummy/. Actress and environmental activist Daryl Hannah's blog that covers green news, events, and innovations.

Ecorazzi. http://www.ecorazzi.com/. Award-winning Web site founded in 2006 that provides the latest in green gossip. Ecorazzi has won several awards including Top 15 Green Websites from *Time* magazine, *Glamour* magazine's eco-heroes and Treehugger's Best Green Award, both in 2009, among other honors.

Environmental Media Association. http://www.ema-online.org/about_us.php. An organization that mobilizes the entertainment community and industry to influence the environmental awareness of millions of people.

For the Love of Green. http://www.brittsgreenblog.blogspot.com/. Blog on eco-friendly fashion, beauty, and lifestyle.

The Green Girls. http://thegreengirls.com/. Blog for eco-friendly girls; includes celebrity news, beauty, fashion, love, food, family, and business.

Green Is Sexy. http://www.greenissexy.org/. Blog created by actress Rachel McAdams and two of her friends who share tips and tricks for reducing people's environmental impact.

Huffington Post Green. http://www.huffingtonpost.com/green/. Green news, opinions, and blogs from the Huffington Post.

TreeHugger. http://www.treehugger.com/. Produced by the Discovery Channel dedicated to "driving sustainability mainstream." Top 15 Green Websites from *Time* magazine.

Worldchanging. http://www.worldchanging.com/. Nonprofit media organization and blog dedicated to a positive planetary future. *Time* magazine's Top 15 Green Websites.

Green Economics, Business, and Industry Blogs

The Daily Green. http://www.thedailygreen.com/. Consumer's guide to green and eco-friendly living; news, features, recipes, and tips.

Earth2Tech. http://gigaom.com/cleantech/. Blog that covers breaking news and in-depth analysis on clean tech and green information technology.

EcoGeek. http://www.ecogeek.org/. Blog by Hank Green, whose work appears on Planet Green's G Word and other publications, that explores the balance of technology and protecting the planet.

Green. http://green.blogs.nytimes.com/category/business/. Blog about energy and the environment in the *New York Times*.

Inhabitat. http://inhabitat.com/. Weblog that provides information on design and innovations for sustainable architecture.

Green Education and Employment Blogs

Green Education Services. http://www.greenedu.com/about-us/. Blog for organization that provides education and LEED certification.

Planet Pals. http://earthday.ning.com/group/planetpalsenvironmentaleducation group. "Earthday Everyday Education." Blog for kids, families, educators, and groups.

Uncovered Earth. http://uncoveredearth.com/. Personal blog about education, adventure, and earth science.

Green Environment Blogs

The Clean Water Blog. http://blog.cleanwateraction.org/. Blog that supports clean water and the "zero discharge of pollution."

Climate Progress. http://thinkprogress.org/romm/issue/. Blog that explores climate change; edited by Joe Romm, fellow at American Progress and former acting assistant secretary of energy for energy efficiency and renewable energy; part of the liberal Think Progress, a project of the Center for American Progress Action Fund. One of *Time* magazine's Top 15 Green Websites.

Earth Echo International Blog. http://www.earthecho.org/news. Blog for the nonprofit organization founded by Phillipe and Alexandra Cousteau, children of Phillipe Cousteau, Sr. and grandchildren of Jacques Cousteau.

Environmental Graffiti. http://www.environmentalgraffiti.com/. All things green—nature, outdoor, travel, art and design, anthropology and history, science, environmental news, technology, and lifestyle.

The Go Green Blog. http://thegogreenblog.com/. Blog that covers eco-friendly products, energy, family, green crafts, healthy eating, recycling, politics, and environment.

Grist. http://www.grist.org/. Environmental news and commentary. On *Time* magazine's Top 15 Green Websites.

The Oil Drum. http://www.theoildrum.com/. "Discussions about energy and the our future."

Green Food and Drink Blogs

The Daily Green. http://www.thedailygreen.com/. Consumer's guide to green and eco-friendly living; news, features, recipes, and tips.

Earth Eats. http://indianapublicmedia.org/eartheats/. Weekly public radio program, podcast, and blog that brings news and recipes inspired by sustainable agriculture and local food.

The Go Green Blog. http://thegogreenblog.com/. Blog that covers eco-friendly products, energy, family, green crafts, healthy eating, recycling, politics, and environment.

The Green Gourmet. http://kimberleystakal.com/blog/. Blog from food writer, editor, and recipe developer Kimberley Stakal.

Green Options. http://www.greenoptions.com/blog/. Blog for organic living community; eco-friendly product reviews.

Organic A to Z. http://organicatoz.com/. Food blog of Chef Gregory Schaefer who focuses on farm-fresh, seasonal foods.

Green Health, Home, and Garden Blogs

The Green Guide. http://environment.nationalgeographic.com/. Green guide to living from National Geographic.

Green LA Girl. http://greenlagirl.com/. Blog by Siel about eco-friendly and sustainable living in Los Angeles.

Green Means Go. http://greenmeansgotravelshow.com/. Blog that explores green and eco-friendly travel.

Idealbite. http://idealbite.com/. Blog with information and tips on "going green."

Mother Nature Network. http://editorsblog.mnn.com/. News and information on environmental and social responsibility; editor's blog.

Natural Eco Baby's Blog. http://blog.naturalecobaby.com/. Information and education resources to parents from parents on green and eco-friendly baby products.

Green Philosophy and Religion Blogs

Dirt Worship. http://starhawksblog.org/. Blog by Starhawk, author and pagan activist, that explores earth-based spirituality, magic, permaculture, politics, and activism.

The Religion Beat. http://religionbeat.blogspot.com/. Blog that focuses on the role of "religion in the public sphere"; some coverage of environmental issues.

Green Politics and Law Blogs

Eco Politics Daily. http://nylcv.org/ecopoliticsdaily. Blog of the New York League of Conservation Voters.

Enviro Politics Blog. http://enviropoliticsblog.blogspot.com/2009/04/nj-readies-tv-computer-recycling-rules.html. Environmental and political news, issues, and opinion for New Jersey, Pennsylvania, New York, and Delaware.

Green Science and Technology Blogs

WebEcoist. http://webecoist.com/. Blog covering green design, travel, food, technology, plants and animals, and anything related to a green lifestyle.

Green Sports and Leisure Blogs

Fair Trade Sports. http://fairtradesports.com/. Blog for company that offers certified Fair Trade and green sports balls.

JH Underground. http://www.jhunderground.com/. Alternative media blog that covers sports, politics, music, and more with an eye toward the environment; based in Jackson Hole, Wyoming.

KIM KENNEDY WHITE

See also: American Writers and the Environment (Arts); Celebrities (Arts); Green Publishing Efforts (Arts); Journalism and News (Arts).

CELEBRITIES

In recent years, celebrities and their green habits have become more and more visible. Many celebrities have adopted an eco-friendly lifestyle, including wearing eco-friendly clothing, living in greener homes, and driving cars powered by electricity or alternative fuel sources. In fact, these celebrities have been featured in countless magazine and news stories in popular periodicals such as *Elle*, *Marie Claire*, *Glamour*, *Flaunt*, *Vanity Fair*, and *Surface* (Winge, 2008, 513). Notable green celebrities include Julia Roberts, Leonardo DiCaprio, Kate Hudson, Jessica Alba, Sheryl Crow, Jake Gyllenhaal, and Jamie Oliver.

Julia Roberts is noted as one of the most green celebrities around (Shea, 2010; Winge, 2008, 513). Some of Roberts's most eco-friendly habits consist of living in a solar powered home, using chlorine-free diapers, composting, and reducing water consumption (Shea, 2010). Roberts has been profiled in *Life & Style*, *Green Living*, *Vanity Fair*, and *Elle*. In addition, Roberts contributed to the 2008 book *Gorgeously*

Green: 8 Simple Steps to an Earth-Friendly Life by Sophie Uliano. Roberts wrote the foreword to the book and attests to the practices Uliano lays out for her readers.

Leonardo DiCaprio is another noted celebrity who has gone green. In 2008, DiCaprio purchased a new home: "Riverhouse, his new home overlooking the Hudson River, features a fresh filtered air system, an in-house water treatment facility, low-emission paints and finishes, and rotating solar panels" (Davis & Lomrantz, 2008). Not only does DiCaprio enjoy green living in his eco-friendly home, he is often seen riding his bike rather than driving a car or taking a subway or bus.

Sheryl Crow, Kate Hudson, and Jessica Alba can be included as celebrities on the list of green moms. Each of them contributes to a green lifestyle in a particular way. For instance, Alba lives in an eco-friendly home, with features such as "tennis ball rugs and trash cans made from potato chip wrappers" (Shea, 2010). Alba even goes as far as to use dogs beds made only of recycled fibers (Shea, 2010). Kate Hudson has contributed to eco-friendly

Leonardo DiCaprio signs a "Pledge of Allegiance to American Energy Independence" at the Global Green USA event in Los Angeles, California, Wednesday, March 24, 2004. (AP Photo/Ann Johansson)

practices in a different way: by co-creating hair-care products that avoid parabens and are not tested on animals. In fact, not only are the products organic and chemical-free, but 10 percent of the proceeds from the sales goes to help endangered species ("Gorgeous & Green," 2008, 138). Sheryl Crow not only practices green living in her home (through reducing water use, turning off lights, and washing clothes on cold), but she has also been noted for her "Stop Global Warming Tour," which took place on 11 college campuses in 2007 (Baker, 2007; Shea, 2010). The message of the tour is relatively straightforward: live a greener lifestyle—use recyclable grocery bags and longer-lasting light bulbs (which were given out on the tour), and join in as a voice for global initiatives (Baker, 2007).

Another notable celebrity with eco-friendly habits is Jake Gyllenhaal, who is known to fight for environmental causes. In fact, Gyllenhaal " not only travel[ed] to the North Pole with Salma Hayek, documenting the plight of the Inuits dealing with an increasingly warmer region, but also paid $10,000 for trees to be planted in Mozambique as a means of offsetting his carbon output" (Davis & Lomrantz, 2008). In addition to the 2005 trip with fellow celebrity Hayek, Gyllenhaal continues to do good deeds for the Earth by driving a clean fuel car, wearing green clothing, and participating in outdoor adventures, like he did on *Man vs. Wild* in 2011 ("Eco-Celeb," 2011). His involvement in shows like *Man vs. Wild* brings attention to nature and environmental issues; this type of behavior is what helped Gyllenhaal to be awarded the "Eco-Celeb of the Week" by the EcoNews Network in December 2011 ("Eco-Celeb," 2011).

Fashion designers Stella McCartney, Giorgio Armani, Todd Oldham, and many others are picking up on the green trend as well by creating designer clothing lines made of eco-friendly fabrics and produced in ways that are safer for the environment than previous practices. Several fashion shows have taken on a green slant as a result of this trend. For instance, in New Zealand, a fashion show titled *Trash to Fashion* is held each year (Winge, 2008, 516). Other major fashion shows are going this route as well, including *Ethical Fashion* in Paris, *Future Fashion* in New York City, and *Eco-Chic Fashion* in San Francisco (Winge, 2008, 516). This new trend in green fashion "allows the consumer to be both fashionable and environmentally conscious" (Winge, 2008, 518). Designers, such as those named above, entered into this trend with their designs specifically marketed toward celebrities who "understand the relationship between good taste and quality design" (Winge, 2008, 519). However, to continue to produce these quality products, the lines are now marketed to all types of consumers with an interest in eco-fashion (Winge, 2008, 519).

Organic eating is one other way celebrities get involved in the green movement. Celebrity chef Jamie Oliver has taken the lead on organic eating initiatives, particularly through his television show *Jamie Oliver's Food Revolution*. The show highlights communities in the United States overwrought with obesity; Jamie Oliver works to teach the community members (especially those involved with the school system) about eating a balanced diet filled with healthy, organic foods. His work continues as he supports the "Farm Bill" throughout 2012, which will help to provide fresh fruits and vegetables to every community ("The [Food and] Farm Bill," 2011).

Altogether, many celebrities have been working toward greener lifestyles in various ways. It can be expected that more celebrities will work to reduce their carbon footprints as the green movement continues to grow.

ELLEN SORG

See also: Ecorazzi (Arts); Food and Entertaining (Food and Drink); Green Cinema (Arts); Green Documentaries and Films (Arts); Journalism and News (Arts); Social Networking Sites (Arts); Television, Eco-Friendly Channels (Arts); Television, Nature and Wildlife TV (Arts).

References

Baker, K. C. 2007. "Inside Sheryl Crow's 'Stop Global Warming' Tour." *People*, April 7. Available at: http://www.people.com/people/article/0,,20034326,00.html.

Davis, Rebecca Willis, and Tracey Lomrantz. 2008. "Top 20 Green Celebs." *Elle*, April 28. Available at: http://www.elle.com/Fashion/Fashion-Spotlight/Top-20-Green-Celebs#mode=base;slide=0.

"Eco-Celeb of the Week: Jake Gyllenhaal." 2011. *EcoNews Network*, December 15. Available at: http://econewsnetwork.org/2011/12/eco-celeb-of-the-week-jake-gyllenhaal/.

"Gorgeous & Green." 2008. *Good Housekeeping* 247:1 (July): 136–141.

Shea, Beth. 2010. "5 Eco-Friendly Moms Who Are Doing Their Part to Save the World." *Celebrity Baby Scoop*, May 7. Available at: http://celebritybabyscoop.com/2010/04/28/top-5-eco-friendly-celebrity-moms.

"The (Food and) Farm Bill: What America Eats." 2011. *Jamie Oliver's Food Revolution*, December 19. Available at: http://www.jamieoliver.com/us/foundation/jamies-food-revolution/news-content/the-food-farm-bill-what-america-eats.

Uliano, Sophie. 2008. *Gorgeously Green: 8 Simple Steps to an Earth-Friendly Life*. New York: Collins Living.

Winge, Theresa M. 2008. "'Green Is the New Black': Celebrity Chic and the 'Green' Commodity Fetish." *Fashion Theory: The Journal of Dress, Body & Culture* 12:4 (December): 511–523.

ECOPOETICS

Although ecopoetics is a relatively new subgenre of poetry that has grown in importance and popularity over the past several decades, it may also be viewed as the inevitable manifestation of four long-standing traditions in American verse: nature writing, the poetry of place, the Jeremiad, and transcendentalism. Indeed, one need only look to the father of American poetry, Walt Whitman, and consider pieces such as "Song of Myself" to recognize that questions regarding Americans' relationship with their environment have persisted in literature for well over 150 years. As the poet and environmentalist Gary Snyder notes, though, verse that may be called ecopoetry tends to move beyond nature poetry's frequently detached, passive or merely reflective appreciation of the natural world by embarking on a "search for wildness wherever one can find it. Not just in wilderness areas, but everywhere human beings let go of the controls" (cited in Kuipers, 2010). Ecopoetry, then, explores the spiritual, physical, and social ramifications of our idea of and responses to the natural world. Poets examining these ramifications usually take the position that while human beings are a vital part of nature, their desire for dominion over the natural world is, at best, foolhardy and debilitating. At worst, this desire may be hubristic and lead to irreparable destruction. As such, much of ecopoetry can be characterized by a call for harmonious coexistence, responsible stewardship, and reform. Ecopoetry oftentimes has an implicitly ethical and even political emphasis to it, responding to an ecological crisis or advocating for an ecological cause. In this sense, it may serve to enlighten, educate, and rouse its audience both through its themes and forms.

Since Whitman, poets in every subsequent era have addressed our relationship with the environment. This concern became increasingly pointed and prominent during the modernist phase in American literature. A number of modernist poets showed a serious interest in science and wrote on themes of mechanization, social fragmentation, and alienation in the context of the environment. Poets such as William Carlos Williams, Marianne Moore, Edna St. Vincent Millay, Lorine Niedecker, and Robinson Jeffers, among others, approached these concerns from a protoenvironmentalist perspective. Millay, Niedecker, and Jeffers made particularly strong contributions to ecopoetics: Millay with her bioregional focus on New England, Niedecker with her bioregional focus on Wisconsin, and Jeffers with his bioregional focus on California. Millay's apocalyptic lyric poem "Epitaph for the Race of Man" (1934) is arguably one the most important ecopoetic statements of the age. Niedecker's deep engagement with ecology persisted into the 1960s, thereby providing an ideological and aesthetic bridge between generations of ecopoets. Jeffers's lifelong commitment to respecting and preserving the wild, both in writing and practice, has made him a well-respected figure in the environmental movement. Indeed, Jeffers's primitivist vision influenced one of ecopoetry's most respected practitioners, Gary Snyder.

With the 1950s and 1960s, the presence of ecopoetry became undeniable within counterculture circles, particularly among those Beat Generation and Black Mountain College poets who congregated on the West Coast. Some of those poets, including Snyder, Michael McClure, and Phillip Whalen, would eventually become part of the San Francisco Renaissance, a group whose members shared similar concerns with social justice and eco-consciousness. Writers such as Snyder, McClure, and Whalen meshed ecology, anthropology, Native American mythology, and their subjective personal experiences into a robust ecopoetics written from the margins of the American Dream. These poets, like their contemporary A. R. Ammons, also brought Buddhist philosophy to bear on the transcendentalist notions that had underpinned much of ecopoetry to date, thus reframing, in some respects, age-old Western notions regarding the ostensible boundaries between humankind and the natural world. Whalen and Snyder, along with the poet Lew Welch, studied and practiced Zen Buddhism, which led them to approach nature with a distinctive spiritual emphasis. Snyder's spiritual emphasis and intellectual pursuits were joined with his leanings as an activist and his devotion to the outdoors. Snyder was an avid hiker and mountain climber, and he worked as a seaman, camp counselor, and fire lookout as a young man: these activities directly informed his art. Given Snyder's interests and experiences, it is no surprise, then, that the vast majority of his writing, including the Pulitzer Prize–winning *Turtle Island* (1974), is steeped in the natural world and that he would eventually come to be regarded as one of the most vocal advocates of the deep ecology movement.

While Snyder has made some of the most definitive contributions to ecopoetics, other well-established American poets, such as Wendell Berry, Joy Harjo, W. S. Merwin, Mary Oliver, and Simon Ortiz, have also been involved in ecopoetics and environmental awareness throughout their careers. Poetry does not exist in a cultural vacuum: it has always anticipated and been responsive to social causes.

Thus, a new generation of American poets—particularly those poets with avant garde and activist associations—have fully embraced many of the ideas and practices associated with the green movement. One need only consider the large increase in the number of journals, books, conferences, and classes that directly address ecopoetics to understand that this once semiobscure subgenre has reached an unprecedented level of significance and visibility. Jonathan Skinner's freely available online journal *ecopoetics* and Amy King and Heidi Lynn Staples's anthology addressing the BP oil disaster, *Poets for Living Waters* (2010), are excellent examples of how core groups of progressive young poets are coming together to bring environmental issues to the forefront of poetry. As going green becomes a greater part of national consciousness and practice, such manifestations of ecopoetry will be more readily sought out and embraced by the general reading public.

CALEB PUCKETT

See also: American Writers and the Environment (Arts); Literature, Environmental (Arts).

References

Iijima, Brenda, ed. 2010. *Ecolanguage Reader*. Callicoon, NY: Portable Press at Yo-Yo Labs, 2010.

King, Amy, and Heidi Lynn Staples, eds. 2010. *Poets for Living Waters*. Available at: http://poetsgulfcoast.wordpress.com/.

Kuipers, Dean. 2010. "W.S. Merwin Is Green as U.S. Poet Laureate." *Los Angeles Times*, August 29. Available at: http://articles.latimes.com/2010/aug/29/entertainment/la-ca-ws-merwin-20100829.

Scigaj, Leonard M. 1999. *Sustainable Poetry: Four American Ecopoets*. Lexington, KY: University of Kentucky Press.

Skinner, Jonathan, ed. *ecopoetics*. Available at: http://ecopoetics.wordpress.com/.

ECORAZZI

There are numerous television programs, Web sites, blogs, and magazines that follow every detail of the rich and famous in the United States. The trendy, outrageous, pop singer Lady Gaga even sings about the paparazzi. In fact, some people say that television and movie stars are essentially an aristocracy for Americans to admire and emulate (with a touch of jealousy). Others question our hyperfascination with each fashion decision or style disaster, each red carpet event, and even a star's routine trip to the coffee shop. American society supports the tabloids and media, snapping thousands of such photos every day.

Recently, Americans' eco-consciousness has taken the paparazzi one step further to create ecorazzi, focusing on the stars' green trends. It's not clear if ecorazzi is consumer driven, in other words, ordinary Americans are concerned about the environment and thus the movie stars want to gain popularity, so they promote their own green activities. Or is ecorazzi actually a clever way for stars, who already have the attention of millions of Americans, to promote environmental causes they believe in? In either case, it is successful.

One Web site that specifically focuses on these topics is ecorazzi.com, which likely established the "genre of green celebrity gossip when it launched in 2006" according to Mother Nature Network (MNN.com). As noted on their Web site, ecorazzi follows green "lifestyle" aspects, such as transport, vegan, and fashion; and green causes such as animals, arts/culture, and environment. Eco Fashion World is a similar Web site that follows green "lifestyle" aspects, such as transport, vegan, and fashion; and green "causes" such as animals, arts/culture, and environment (www.ecofashionworld.com). And the Vegetarian Star (www.vegetarianstar .com) delves into celebrity vegetarian gossip and news. These Web sites and numerous others, with their corresponding Facebook pages, Twitter "tweets," and YouTube videos, all keep us up to date on the eco-activities and beliefs of the rich and famous in the United States.

LESLIE A. DURAM

See also: Blogs (Arts); Celebrities (Arts).

References

Eco Fashion World. 2012. Eco Fashion Guide. www.ecofashionworld.com.
Ecorazzi. 2012. Good Gossip. www.ecorazzi.com.
Mother Nature Network. 2012. Improve Your World. www.MNN.com.
Vegetarian Star. 2012. Celebrity Vegetarian Gossip and News. www.vegetarianstar.com.

GREEN CINEMA

Whether our orientation is toward film as business or toward film as a "narrative hook" that engages the viewer in the unfolding story of moving image as art, green cinema defies easy categorization. Green cinema is a communications practice rooted in eco-politics, the most important political discourse to emerge thus far in the 21st century. Green cinema explores how our environmental consciousness is mediated by the moving image; examines the science and technologies of audio-visual representation in the electronic age; is rooted in Aristotle's *Poetics*; narrates our search for existential authenticity in our relationship with other life forms; and assists us in coming to terms with global climate change and overpopulation. Its study and practice take into account history and ideology, art, and science. Green cinema offers countless opportunities for study and practice.

Green Cinema as Business

Almost a century ago, Hollywood writer Julian Johnson summed up the conventional wisdom regarding the movie business. He wrote that although a movie "depends for its life upon mass production," it "equally depends for its life upon mass favor." Today, that favor is expressed in the $140 billion in theater ticket sales spent by the American masses since 1995. Hollywood is an important part of the U.S.

economy. Like other U.S. industries, Hollywood has responded to the science and politics of global warming. Since 1989, the Environmental Media Association (EMA) has coordinated Hollywood's association with the environmental community through its promotion of green education and activism. In the past two decades, EMA has recognized and honored movies as diverse as *Fed Up! Genetic Engineering, Industrial Agriculture and Sustainable Alternatives* (2002), to *FernGully: the Last Rain Forest* (1992). In 2007, the Academy of Motion Picture Arts and Science announced a green initiative, embracing ecologically sustainable practices in the production and telecast of its annual awards show. Films like *The Day After Tomorrow* (2004) and *Syriana* (2005) were carbon-neutral productions, and the sets from the film *The Matrix 2* (2003) were recycled. Although Hollywood is making efforts toward sustainable business practices, some critics call for greater transparency, as well as a much more systematic approach to mitigating the environmental impact of film production. Critics who urge more green practices point out that Hollywood's environmental impact amounts to the production of 8 million metric tons of carbon dioxide. In 2006, the University of California–Los Angeles's Institute of the Environment found that Hollywood's production processes ranked second to petroleum refining in the production of air pollution in the Los Angeles region.

Green Cinema as Technology

The battle over the representation of nature informs our understanding of the importance of technology in filmic representations of ecology and environment. Hollywood loves the spectacular. It relies on technology to present the spectacular to the movie-going public. Beginning with Eadweard Muybridge's use of multiple cameras to capture the locomotion of the horse to Auguste and Louis Lumière's uses of film to advance medical science, motion picture technology was first envisioned as a tool to expand our knowledge of the physical, biological, and earth sciences. Well before the U.S. film industry found its home in Hollywood, the tastemakers and cultural leaders who saw the promise and potential of the moving image were more likely to be found in the libraries and natural history museums of Boston, Chicago, and New York, than in the thousands of nickelodeons that entertained millions of Americans throughout the country. Scholars of early film point out that the battle for the purpose and use of the moving image was a battle between those who saw film technology as a way to educate the urban and immigrant masses versus those who understood film technology as a tool of entertainment and a path to riches relying on tried-and-true formats to keep the same audiences coming back for more. In one very important sense, the conflict between education and entertainment is expressed best as a conflict between film "takers" versus film "makers" in a battle between the forces of the "real" and the "authentic" versus the nature "fakers" whose reliance on art and artifice ultimately won what is arguably one of the first culture wars over the hearts and minds of the American public. Today, technology has advanced in the movie business to satisfy a public that expects realistic and at the same time fantastic representations of the natural world.

From the three-dimensionality of *Avatar* (2009) to the story of *Pocahontas* (1995), technology is a tool to entertain and to inform while communicating messages about the environment. In green cinema, technology acts as a go-between, reconciling the competing agendas of science as knowledge, with science as entertainment, subplot, and text. Filmic representations of global warming, overpopulation, natural resource depletion, sustainable practices, wildlife biology, genetic modification, food security, nuclear war, disease epidemics, and bioterrorism owe much to technology in conveying an environmental message in American films.

Green Cinema as Art

While an up-to-date redefining of the conventional wisdom regarding the primary purpose and function of Hollywood might be expressed by the notion "if we green it, the movie-goer will come," it is important to understand that green cinema is as dependent on Aristotelian drama as it is dependent on technical artifice and public interest. Eco-criticism, film studies, and film theory all explore the practice and purpose of green cinema. At best, the results of scholarship are mixed. While the *Hollywood Reporter* identified a trend toward *cinema vert* almost a quarter century ago, the idea that green cinema is a relatively recent movement is anachronistic. Green cinema is a way of seeing. It is a green lens focusing on subtext and subplot where environmental issues, broadly defined, are both foreground and background. Green cinema cannot function with the drama left out. A documentary film like *Roger and Me* (1989) is the story of one man's quest to find out why the hubris of General Motors failed the citizens of Flint, Michigan, as much as *Who Killed the Electric Car?* (2006) is a drama about the forces of profit over those who would bring sustainable practices and renewable energies to America's failing and increasingly indefensible love affair with the internal combustion engine. A film like *Chinatown* (1974) is as much about the secrets of the human condition as it is about water as a natural resource. So too, a film like *Soylent Green* (1973) is as much about a hero's discovery of something dreadful as it is about overpopulation. Film as art depends on character development, narrative structure, and theme, and it depends on plots ranging from discovery to plots where a journey is undertaken, a secret is discovered, evil is pursued and conquered, and where escape from the forces of nature pit hero against underdog, secret agent against mad scientist, and humankind against the genetic mutations resulting from the pollution of land, sea, and sky. As art, the greening of cinema is a way of seeing that challenges us to look anew at the long history of environmental representations in American cinema in films as diverse as *Pale Rider* (1985) to *The Wizard of Oz* (1939). And just as a good witch helped a Kansas farm girl displaced by a tornado get back home, so is it important to remember that the magic of film requires the intercession of a very human wizard to give us the heart and the brain to understand how film influences our environmental consciousness.

DAVID ALAN REGO

See also: Green Documentaries and Films (Arts); Television, Eco-Friendly Channels (Arts); Television, Nature and Wildlife TV (Arts).

References

Burgess, Jacquelin A., and John Robert Gold. 1985. *Geography, the Media & Popular Culture*. New York: St. Martin's Press.

Carmichael, Deborah A. 2006. *The Landscape of Hollywood Westerns: Ecocriticism in an American Film Genre*. Salt Lake City: University of Utah Press.

Cubitt, Sean. 2005. *Eco Media*. Amsterdam: Rodopi.

Hochman, Jhan. 1998. *Green Cultural Studies: Nature in Film, Novel, and Theory*. Moscow: University of Idaho Press.

Ingram, David. 2000. *Green Screen: Environmentalism and Hollywood Cinema*. Exeter: University of Exeter Press.

Moul, Charles C. 2005. *A Concise Handbook of Movie Industry Economics*. Cambridge: Cambridge University Press.

Murray, Robin L., and Joseph K. Heumann. 2009. *Ecology and Popular Film: Cinema on the Edge*. Albany: SUNY Press.

Tobias, Ronald B. 2003. *20 Master Plots (and How to Build Them)*. Cincinnati, OH: Writer's Digest Books.

Tobias, Ronald B. 2011. *Film and the American Moral Vision of Nature: Theodore Roosevelt to Walt Disney*. East Lansing: Michigan State University Press.

Whitley, David. 2008. *The Idea of Nature in Disney Animation*. Aldershot, Engl.: Ashgate.

Wilson, Alexander. 1992. *The Culture of Nature: North American Landscape from Disney to the Exxon Valdez*. Cambridge, MA: Blackwell.

GREEN DOCUMENTARIES AND FILMS

The following is a list of suggested recent documentaries that address green issues.

Aftermath: World without Oil, 2010 (series)
Arctic Tale, 2007
At the Edge of the World, 2008
Bad Seed: The Truth about Our Foods, 2005
Bag it!, 2011
The Beautiful Truth, 2008
Blue Gold: World Water Wars, 2008
Blue Planet: Seas of Life, 2002
Blue Vinyl, 2005
Born Sweet, 2010
Burning the Future: Coal in America, 2008
Can Toads: An Unnatural History, 2000
A Chemical Reaction: The Story of a True Green Revolution, 2009
Climate Refugees, 2010
Collapse, 2009
The Cove, 2009
Crude, 2009
A Crude Awakening: The Oil Crash, 2007
The Dark Side of Chocolate, 2010
Dirt! The Movie, 2009

Greenovation: *An Inconvenient Truth*

Premiering in May 2006, *An Inconvenient Truth* is a documentary film focusing on global climate change. Directed by Davis Guggenheim, the movie follows former U.S. Vice President Albert Gore Jr. as he delivers a series of slideshow presentations designed to increase public understanding about global warming. Weaving together personal narratives from Gore's life with scientific data, *An Inconvenient Truth* quickly became an important touchstone for environmental debate as it attempted to balance scientific warnings with concrete actions audiences could take to avoid an impending global crisis.

Viewed primarily as a film dedicated to the dissemination of scientific knowledge, the documentary was well received by audiences. Critics and scientists gave the film positive reviews (Minchin, 2006). In addition to receiving critical acclaim, the film was also a commercial success. *An Inconvenient Truth* eventually went on to win an array of awards, including the 2007 Academy Award for Best Documentary Feature. Al Gore's 2006 companion book, *An Inconvenient Truth: The Planetary Emergency of Global Warming and What We Can Do About It*, met comparable success after reaching the number one spot atop the *New York Times*' best-seller list. However, the film did not go without criticism.

Shortly following the movie's release, climate skeptics attacked the film as fervently as those who praised it. Some critics speculated Gore was using the film as an opportunity to generate media attention for a future presidential run after having been defeated by George W. Bush. Gore denied these rumors and did not again run for the presidency.

Despite being challenged by climate change deniers, Al Gore's commitment to educating the public about climate change science, especially through *An Inconvenient Truth*, contributed to Gore being named a co-recipient, along with the Intergovernmental Panel on Climate Change, of the 2007 Nobel Peace Prize. To this day, *An Inconvenient Truth* remains an important part of U.S. environmental and documentary history.

RICHARD D. BESEL

Sources: Gore, Albert. 2006. *An Inconvenient Truth: The Planetary Emergency of Global Warming and What We Can Do About It*. New York: Rodale Books.

Disarm, 2005
Earth, 2009
Earth Days, 2009
Earthlings, 2005
The 11th Hour, 2007
The End of Suburbia, 2004
The End of the Line, 2010
Everything's Cool, 2007
Fed Up!, 2002
FLOW—For Love of Water, 2008
Food, Inc., 2008
Food Matters, 2008
Fresh, 2009
Fuel, 2010
The Future of Food, 2005
Garbage Warrior, 2008
The Garden, 2008
Gasland, 2010
GasHole, 2011
Global Warming: Rising Storm, 2007
Global Warming: Solutions, 2006
Go Further, 2005
The Greening of Southie, 2008
Home, 2009
An Inconvenient Truth, 2006
Ingredients, 2009
King Corn, Aaron Woolf, 2007
The Last Beekeeper, 2009
Life and Debt, 2001
Living Downstream, 2010
Manda Bala, 2007
Manufactured Landscapes, 2007
March of the Penguins, 2005
Meat the Truth, 2008
Monumental: David Brower's Fight for Wild America, 2005
National Geographic: Human Footprint, 2008
No Impact Man, 2008
Our Daily Bread, 2005
Planeat, 2011
Planet Earth: The Complete BBC Series, 2007
Planet in Peril, 2007
Plastic Planet, 2009

The Power of Community: How Cuba Survived Peak Oil, 2006

Queen of the Sun, 2010

The Real Dirt on Farmer John, 2005

Rivers and Tides, 2006

Sharkwater, 2006

Tapped, 2010

TED: The Future We Will Create, 2007

Texas Gold, 2008

Trashed, 2007

An Inconvenient Truth. 2006. DVD. Directed by Davis Guggenheim. Paramount.

Minchin, Liz. 2006. "An Inconvenient Truth or Gore's Opportunism? You Decide." *The Age* (September 9).

Trouble the Water, 2008

The Unforeseen, 2007

Up the Yangtze, 2008

Waste Land, 2010

Who Killed the Electric Car?, 2006

The World According to Monsanto, 2008

KIM KENNEDY WHITE

See also: Celebrities (Arts); Ecorazzi (Arts); Green Cinema (Arts).

GREEN PUBLISHING EFFORTS

The following list provides a sampling of the efforts made by publishers to go green.

BookSwim. http://bookswim.com. This online publisher cuts down on the paper waste by renting books online similar to the way Netflix rents movies to consumers.

Chelsea Green Publishing. http://www.chelseagreen.com/. Chelsea Green publishes books on the practice and politics of sustainable living. In addition to publishing content regarding renewable energy, organic agriculture, green building, cuisine, and business, the publisher prints 95 percent of its books on recycled paper with a minimum 30 percent postconsumer waste.

Earthscan. http://www.earthscan.co.uk/. Earthscan, part of the Taylor & Francis Publishing Group, publishes books on sustainability, climate change, and environmental technology. They are also a "carbon neutral" company and work to reduce their impact on the environment. At the 2010 Independent Publishing Awards, they received the Independent Publisher of the Year Award.

Glatfelter Paper. http://www.glatfelter.com/default.aspx. Glatfelter Paper, in business since the late 19th century, works to be environmentally responsible with their sustainable practices such as making their products with chain-of-custody forest certifications and using biomass from waste products. Through their Permanence Matters Initiative, they work to educate the literary community to choose higher-quality, long-lasting paper for books.

Green Press Initiative. http://www.greenpressinitiative.org/. According to the Green Press Initiative, 30 million trees are used to make books sold in the United States each year, and 5.7 million tons of newsprint are consumed by Americans. The nonprofit Green Press Initiative, funded primarily through grant funding, works with those in the book and newspaper industry to preserve endangered forests, conserve natural resources, minimize impacts on indigenous communities, and reduce greenhouse gas.

Ooligan Press. http://ooligan.pdx.edu/about/. Ooligan Press is a student-run teaching press affiliated with Portland State University. In 2009, they published *Rethinking Paper and Ink: The Sustainable Publishing Revolution.* Their OpenBook series focuses on sustainable publishing practices and materials.

SustainPrint. http://www.sustainprintcom/about.html. SustainPrint provides resources about green printing and publishing practices to print businesses.

KIM KENNEDY WHITE

See also: American Writers and the Environment (Arts); Blogs (Arts); Literature, Environmental (Arts).

HUMOR

Although many scientists and citizens insist that today's environmental situation is no laughing matter, there are several voices that present the problem more lightly, even if their overall message is just as adamant. Humor pervades the various media of the green movement, from add campaigns to popular television to young and adult literature. Green humor comes in various colors of comedy, including sarcasm, mockery, shock value and the grotesque, and irony, all of which share a common goal: to attract previously uninterested viewers, readers, and citizens to the importance of environmental consciousness.

For better or for worse, one of the best ways to gain the public's eye is through advertisement. T-shirts, billboards, and bumper stickers are difficult to avoid, even for uninterested viewers. Some green companies use this to their advantage, catching these casual viewers off guard. REC Solar, for example, put out the following headline in 2010: "Solar Won't Last." As one contributor to *Everyday Solar* put it, this tagline almost made him choke on his morning coffee until he read the fine print: "much longer at these prices" (for other examples of these catch lines, visit http://www.exposesolar.com/).

Though perhaps not as unavoidable as ad campaigns, television shows and movies have a similar opportunity to reach a large audience. While serious documentaries and troublesome statistics will turn some viewers off, a humorous approach may be more welcoming. A study at the University of New Mexico analyzes the use of the grotesque to present the idea of freeganism (a movement advocating less consumption and waste) in an episode of *Oprah* in February 2008 titled "Living on the Edge." The show emphasizes one aspect of the movement, that of eating trash, in order to grab audience attention more so than to suggest that viewers eat trash themselves. The author of the study explains that "Once the audience's attention is caught through the grotesque imagery of eating trash, the 'normal' consumer is repositioned as extreme, and precycling become a possible way forward" (Dickenson, n.d., 19). Shocking viewers with something gross prevents them from changing the channel, thus exposing viewers who may have otherwise flipped right by to environmental concerns.

Other shows and movies use sarcasm and mockery to attract viewers. Both the movie *No Impact Man* (2009) and the series *Living with Ed* (2008) highlight the women's supposed need for material goods and a "comfortable" life, both of whom roll their eyes at their husbands who insist on living a green lifestyle. The wife depicted in *No Impact Man* readily admits that she's "addicted" to shopping and reality television, which her husband's extreme quest demands that she gives up. Humor pervades the film, such as when the husband asks his wife, "Why is food the hardest for you?" who answers, "Because I can't eat anything that tastes good," and gives a sideways glance to the camera, suggesting to viewers that the entire idea is ridiculous. Including a character who initially views green concerns as silly or unnecessary creates a bond with like-minded viewers, creating a great chance of persuading them that environmental consciousness is actually easier and more important than they knew (the wife in *No Impact Man* eventually gets on board and excited about exchanging Prada purchases for bike rides in the park).

Grabbing the attention of uninterested readers (rather than viewers) is perhaps more challenging: nevertheless, authors use humor in similar a way to television hosts and filmmakers to get attention. The most immediate way to make a book on the environment appealing is to present your advice in a way that is understandable to the layperson. A casual tone in written texts, often bordering on silly, is found in several popular how-to-live-green books. Diane MacEachern's *Big Green Purse: Use Your Spending Power to Create a Cleaner, Greener World* (2008), for example, has a chapter titled "If It Can Happen to an Alligator, Can It Happen to Your Son? Why Your Big Green Purse Matters" (MacEachern, 2008, 1); comparing anyone's son to an alligator is surprising, unlikely, and tempting, which lures the reader to find out how this might be done. Similarly, Jamil Shariff's *50 Green Projects for the Evil Genius* (2009) reads like a conversation between friends at happy hour. Near the beginning he writes, "What else can be done, you might ask?" (2009, 3), and soon after ensures that "if you don't have an energy-efficient light bulb handy, and your bike has a flat, don't panic. You would not be the first to have faced this problem, and it only takes a little evil genius to get going, so keep reading and we'll get there together" (6). Shariff's book compiles ideas for green projects, most of which include a list of supplies. One of these lists requires "A pen and paper/A calculator, maybe" (Shariff, 2009, 9). In this way Shariff mocks complicated science projects that require long lists of obscure materials and welcomes the reader to a project in which he or she can realistically participate.

Such an informal, approachable tone is exaggerated when directed toward younger readers. A popular method in children's books depicts environmentalism as "weird" or, for slightly older readers, "lame"—stigmas that are later redeemed. Dan Gutman and Paillot's *Mr. Granite Is from Another Planet!* (2008), for example, illustrates one "Ella Mentry" school's efforts to conserve energy. One day at school the young narrator learns that if his "Ella Mentry School" is named the "greenest" school, the students will have "an all-you-can-eat chocolate cake party!" (Gutman and Paillot, 2008, 13). Each teacher designs a project that will ease the school's impact on the environment, projects that inspire the narrator to conclude that "Miss Lazar is bizarre," "Ms. Hannah is bananas," "Mrs. Cooney is loony" (Gutman and Paillot, 2008, 23), and of course, that Mr. Granite is from another planet. Indeed, the last word of the book is capped by an asterisk, which reads: "This story is supposed to be funny, but all of us should live green. To find out more, go to [a list of eight Web sites]" (Gutman and Paillot, 2008, 103). While the narrator depicts creators of green ideas as strange, in the end the projects are successful and everyone eats chocolate cake.

Jennifer Power Scott uses a strategy to reach readers who are just beyond calling teachers loony or bananas: *Green Careers: You Can Make Money and Save the Planet* (2010) uses a voice that bonds with young adults who might find environmental ideas to be impossible or just not cool. Scott compiles a list of experts in several professions who have striven to operate in environmentally friendly manners, from brewers to fashion designers to health practitioners. With a tone of camaraderie, Scott shows young readers that opportunities for conservation are everywhere. For example, she writes, "Do you think it's possible to build a $35-million empire on worm poop and garbage? Tom Szaky believed it could happen" (Scott, 2010, 16). In concluding, Scott elevates environmentalists from "hokey" dreamers to heroes: "Well, weren't they amazing? I knew you would be impressed with the green workers in this book. They have so many ideas, so much passion. For them, it's not just about making money. It's about making a difference. Sounds hokey, I guess. But it's true" (213).

Perhaps not surprisingly, writers for adults also use mockery and irony, suggesting at first that the author, too, initially perceived environmentalists as "hokey" or "weird." Greg Melville introduces his brief memoir, *Greasy Rider: Two Dudes, One Fry-Oil-Powered Car, and a Cross-Country Search for a Greener Future* (2008), by tagging (and making fun of) his wife, who inspired his idea to drive a car solely on vegetable oil across the country, as an environmentalist: "Like nearly all (of the many) kooky ideas that arise in my cozy Cape-style home near Burlington, Vermont, the one to convert a diesel car to burn grease came from my wife, Ann Marie. She is a devout saver of the earth. She feels guilty swatting a mosquito. She cleans and reuses Ziploc bags. She forces me to use organic toilet paper, which is far from cottony soft" (Melville, 2008, 1). Melville readily admits his own stereotypes against those like this wife ("Before Ann Marie and I had bought the wagon, I assumed that converting a vehicle to run on veggie oil was something that only hippies do, when they're not making their clothes out of hemp") (9) but learns to look beyond: "I simply needed to look at my reflection in the rearview mirror to realize that nearly anyone can operate and maintain a french-fry car. The terms *energy independence* and *renewable energy* were no longer abstract notions to me" (9). Melville first attaches himself to his readers—I'm like you, we're different from smelly hippies—so that by the end the reader realizes I, too, could drive a veggie car, even though I'm not a smelly hippy.

Humor is increasingly important to Western culture, as seen by the increasing success of stand-up comedians, tickets sold to comedic movies, and comedic news-sources like *The Onion* or *The Daily Show*: the literature and media cited above attest to humor's entrance into the green movement, one that, judging by humor's popularity in other issues, will help to spread environmental interest.

ALISON TURNER

See also: Green Movement (Activism); Social Networking Sites (Arts); Television, Eco-Friendly Channels (Arts); Television, Nature and Wildlife TV (Arts).

References

Cheyney, Tom. 2011. "REC Solar's New Ads—Everyday Solar." *Everyday Solar*. October 17. Available at: http://everydaysolar.wordpress.com/2010/10/17/memo-to-rec-solar-your-advertisements-may-be-sending-the-wrong-message/.

Dickinson, Elizabeth A. "Disrupting Discursive Formations: Humor as Interruption and Engagement in Case Studies of Terrorism, Race, and the Environment." Thesis. University of New Mexico. Available at: http://www.unm.edu/~edickins/Disrupting.pdf.

Gutman, Dan, and Jim Paillot. 2008 *Mr. Granite Is from Another Planet!* New York: HarperTrophy.

Living with Ed. 2008. Brentwood Communications International.

MacEachern, Diane. 2008. *Big Green Purse: Use Your Spending Power to Create a Cleaner, Greener World*. New York: Avery

Melville, Greg. 2008. *Greasy Rider: Two Dudes, One Fry-Oil-Powered Car, and a Cross-Country Search for a Greener Future*. Chapel Hill, NC: Algonquin of Chapel Hill.

No Impact Man. 2009. Oscilloscope Pictures. DVD.

Scott, Jennifer Power. 2010. *Green Careers: You Can Make Money and Save the Planet*. Montréal: Lobster.

Shariff, Jamil. 2009. *50 Green Projects for the Evil Genius*. New York: McGraw-Hill.

JOURNALISM AND NEWS

Reporters and television news anchors witnessed America going green. Environmental issues first became newsworthy in the 1960s concurrently with a string of startling environmental disasters—Centralia, Pennsylvania, in 1962, Cleveland, Ohio, in 1969, and Love Canal, New York, in 1978—and a growing awareness among Americans of damage to the world around them. In the early 1960s, people were beginning to notice environmental degradation, and naturalists and scientists began to consolidate their understanding of the effects of air and water pollution on wildlife. But scientific publications were limited and difficult for general readers to understand, that is, until Rachel Carson "translated" chemistry and biology into ecology in her best-selling book, *Silent Spring* (1962). Twentieth-century Americans hadn't thought about the effects of the new fertilizers, pesticides, and household products they used on a daily basis. But one metaphor, a springtime without birds, caught and held their attention.

Centralia Fire, 1962

The massive, underground, inextinguishable fire that ruined the town of Centralia, Pennsylvania, began quietly, out of sight. Most believe it began in May 1962 when

Mark Zanatian, one of the children endangered by the
Love Canal Chemicals under 99th Street, waves a banner
in protest during a neighborhood protest meeting in 1978.
(AP Photo/DS)

city firefighters set fire to the town
dump located in an improperly
lined pit. After days spent putting out flare-ups, they realized
that those flames had spread
into an abandoned coal mine
and stopped trying. Months later,
toxic fumes from the fire began
to rise up through the ground
and invade the homes of people
living there, causing some to fall
into unconsciousness. Gas stations emptied their tanks to keep
them from exploding. And a 12-
year-old boy could have been
burned alive when a sinkhole
opened below his feet. The people
of Centralia endured these conditions mostly alone and unaided.
Former U.S. Secretary of Interior
James Watt believed there was no
threat to health or safety. The fire
"goes down deep; the deeper it
burns the less risk there is to
safety. Eventually it will burn out."

A decade after the fire started,
when the people were at wits'
end, a Harrisburg reporter familiar with the story, David DeKok,
with the aid of a new Pennsylvania
open records act, probed the
apparent indifference of state
and federal officials in two books:
Unseen Danger (1986) and Fire Underground (2009). The first book assigned blame;
the second brought Centralia's story up to date with a surprising revelation. DeKok
found that the fire was still burning nearly 50 years later and was moving through
tunnels in the direction of a neighboring town. Most agree that the main lesson from
Centralia is about people. If it happens again, the welfare of affected people might
again be sacrificed in view of the cost of needed action. Most residents have been
relocated, but their town died (Dunkle, 2009).

Cuyahoga River Fire, 1969

This story marked a turning point in U.S. environmental protection effort and public
awareness, yet, in this case, everyone who lived and worked in the area—Cleveland,

Ohio—had seen it coming. City officials had launched a public relations campaign, citizens were onboard, and even the owners of factories and steel mills on the river were complying with calls to clean up their operations. They were poised to act, but were overtaken by events.

The idea of a river so polluted as to catch fire fascinated and appalled readers throughout the nation and around the world. The fire (one of many previous going back to 1858) took place in 1968 when Cleveland had committed itself to try, through a $100,000 bond issue, to repair the damage done by two centuries of industrial development that had wrecked the Cuyahoga.

A crew doused the fire in about half an hour, and the story "barely made the papers the next day," but everyone knew the cleanup would be long and involved. Richard Ellers, a local reporter had gone out on the river earlier with a photographer to get closeup pictures of the water. "We could see a layer of crud on the water," but they couldn't appreciate what it was like. Ellers dipped his hand into the water and withdrew "a black gooey hand . . . like a B movie swamp monster," his description of "how terrible it was" (Scott, 2009).

Media attention grew quickly, but national reporters were *in*

Greenovator: Jay Norwood "Ding" Darling

Born in 1876, J. N. "Ding" Darling was a two-time Pulitzer Prize–winning editorial cartoonist who published more than 11,000 cartoons from 1900 to 1949. He was also a dedicated conservationist and is credited with laying the groundwork for today's national wildlife refuge system (J. N. "Ding" Darling Foundation, 2010).

Darling began using the contraction "D'ing" to sign illustrations while attending Beloit College (Lendt, 1989). He published his first drawing at 23 while working for the *Sioux City Journal* (Iowa Digital Library, 2010). His nationally syndicated cartoons appeared in more than 150 newspapers nationwide and had an enormous impact on public opinion during this time before television when newspapers were the primary source of news.

In 1943, President Franklin Roosevelt appointed him part of a three-man committee to study the conservation of migratory waterfowl. Soon after, he was named chief of the Biological Survey, the forerunner of the U.S. Fish and Wildlife Service, where he implemented the Federal Duck Stamp Program, designed the first duck postage stamp, and vastly expanded the acreage of the National Wildlife Refuge system. Known for his bulldog tactics, Darling caused upheaval in the survey during the 20 months he worked there, but ultimately he built a program the nation could be proud of. He also founded the National Wildlife Federation in 1936 (Lendt 1989; U.S. Fish & Wildlife Service, 2008).

After his death in 1962, the J. N. "Ding" Darling Foundation was created to advocate for wise use of natural resources and wildlife conservation. A wildlife refuge named for Darling was created on Sanibel Island, Florida, in 1965. In 2006, the Darling Foundation assigned its copyrights and trademarks to a nonprofit corporation, the "Ding" Darling Wildlife Society, in order to support the National Wildlife Refuge system (J. N. "Ding" Darling Foundation, 2010).

KATHERINE MCLAUGHLIN

Cleveland on the day of the fire, invited by Mayor Carl Stokes to showcase the city's plans to improve its environment. Naturally, when news of the fire reached them, the visitors wanted to know what he was going to do about the situation. All he could do was show them. The mayor in Cleveland and his brother, the newly

Earthrise

One of the more famous images of the Earth from the Apollo program, taken by the *Apollo 8* astronauts as they became the first humans to circumnavigate the Moon. (NASA)

On December 24, 1968, when the crew of *Apollo 8* came from behind the Moon after the lunar orbit insertion burn, they beheld planet Earth, lit by the sun, rising above the moon's horizon. What better Christmas gift "for all the people of Earth"? With their movie camera at the window, lunar module Commander William Anders began to read a Christmas message:

> In the beginning God created the heaven and the earth,
> And the earth was without form, and void; and darkness
> was upon the face of the deep,
> And the Spirit of God moved upon the face of the waters,
> And God said, Let there be light; and there was light,
> And God saw the light, that it was good; and God divided
> the light from the darkness.

Each of the three astronauts, in turn, read the ancient creation story from the book of Genesis.

appointed Congressman Louis Stokes in Washington, assembled the funding and support needed to launch a very successful cleanup.

A *Time* magazine story pointed out a pollution source often overlooked by the media; they could see the steel mills and slaughterhouses, but the city's many outdated sewage treatment plants were up river and out of sight. In one month, in 1969, they released 25 million gallons of untreated sewage into the river. Cleveland had plans and funding lined up for that project as well. The article cited one federal report that said the Cuyahoga "has no visible life, not even low forms such as leeches and sludge worms that thrive on wastes."

In 1972, Congress passed the Clean Water Act that called for the monitoring of water quality and created the Environmental Protection Agency (EPA) to administer the law. In 1974, President Gerald Ford created the Cuyahoga Valley Recreation Area (which attained National Park status in 2000), and in 1984, scientists began to see the river coming back to life, with 60 species of clean-water fish, blue herons, and bald eagles.

Love Canal, 1978

Love Canal was a residential area of Niagara Falls, New York, a heavily industrialized city also dependent on tourist trade. The *EPA Journal* published one of the most poignant stories about

A fire tug fights flames on the Cuyahoga River near downtown Cleveland, Ohio, where oil and other industrial wastes caught fire on June 25, 1952. (AP/Wide World Photos)

the Love Canal disaster in its January 1979 edition. Eckardt C. Beck, EPA Region 2 administrator from 1977 through 1979, simply described what he saw: "Corroding metal drums could be seen in backyards. Trees and gardens were turning black and dying . . . a swimming pool raised up floating on a small sea of chemicals. Chemical puddles in basements, on school grounds, . . . the smell." Townspeople suspected that repeated soakings from record rainfalls had rusted out oil drums containing chemical waste that had been buried by a factory in what was left of the two ends of an unfinished canal. William T. Love, a turn-of-the-century entrepreneur, had started digging there in a failed attempt

The estimated 1 billion viewers/listeners of this live broadcast saw the planet Earth as it is in the heavens, a synoptic, all-in-one eyefull, on a day of rest and peace in most of the world. That image of Earth as vulnerable, yet awesome, came at a time when Americans were taking notice of environmental pollution for the first time. But "Earthrise" lives on for us as an inspiration. We have viewed many more such images of Earth since 1968, the technology to do so is at our fingertips, but that first experience was a turning point. The Christmas Eve broadcast can be viewed online at NASA's Web site and the "Earthrise" image is widely available in poster form, a symbol of peace, hope, and inspiration.

Source: Williams, David R. "The Apollo 8 Christmas Broadcast." Available at: http://www.nasa.gov/vision/livinginspace/christmas.

to harness electric power from the Niagara River for a proposed housing development. The Hooker Chemical Company bought the property from Love in the early 1920s and sold the land and its waste site to the Niagara Falls school board in the mid-1950s with a hold harmless clause that informed them of the potential danger (Beck, 1979).

On August 2, 1978, the New York Health Department declared the site dangerous. The following day, the department released findings and recommendations from its months' long study. Epidemiologists found a "very high" rate of miscarriages and warned of "great and imminent peril"; they advised women and infants to leave the area immediately and warned the school board not to reopen the elementary school—ground zero for Love Canal toxins—in the fall.

The city manager, having coped with citizen questions and complaints for some time, told reporters that the city had spent $40,000 getting ready to build a tile drainage system for the elementary school property. A spokesperson for the Hooker Company, now Hooker/Occidental, said the company was paying for testing of the waste site under way at the time. He also wanted people to know that his company had informed the board of education about the buried chemicals and that the board had acknowledged that fact before the sale was completed.

In 1976, two *Niagara Falls Gazette* reporters had tested water from sump pumps in the area and found chemicals, but nothing came of it. In 1978, another *Gazette* reporter, Michael Brown, investigated and wrote extensively about the neighborhood around the waste site. Again, the story wasn't taken seriously. The people who lived there, affected by miscarriages, birth defects, and other rare conditions, were seriously concerned and running out of patience. Brown advised them to organize. Lois Gibbs, the mother of a young son with many serious ailments, surveyed the area's property owners and found that 56 percent of the families with children born between 1974 and 1978 had at least one child with at least one birth defect. Getting help and advice was difficult.

Gibbs's campaign took place simultaneously with efforts of scientists to untangle the chemicals and substances involved and the causation of more than one physical ailment. Researchers were able to pinpoint how the chemicals affected the residents by exposure to groundwater (not tap water) seeping into the soil of basements, evaporating into the air, and being inhaled by people inside their homes (Brown, 1983; Whalen, 1978). As a result of Love Canal, Congress passed what we now know as the Superfund Act to compensate people and clean up toxic spills. The EPA sued Hooker/Occidental in 1995 and a judge found it negligent but not reckless and imposed a $129 million judgment.

Three Mile Island, March 28, 1979

This nuclear accident burst onto the front pages of U.S. newspapers at a time when people were still reading about Love Canal and, importantly, at a time when the oversight of nuclear power plant safety was a top concern for activists and members of Congress alike. The Nuclear Regulatory Commission (NRC) described Three Mile Island (TMI) as the worst nuclear accident in the history of the operation of commercial nuclear power plants.

For the first day of this incident, plant operators, owners, state and local officials, and NRC experts were in the dark about the true situation inside the nuclear portion of the plant. At first, when little information was available, the situation was downplayed, then false and conflicting information confused plant operators; the NRC ordered an evacuation, but found that it was not needed; the reactor cooled, but then experts feared it would explode, but they had overestimated the radiation danger. Then when everyone had fled the area, the whole picture could be seen accurately, and the drama ended.

The partial meltdown of reactor 2 began at 4:00 a.m. on March 28 when a water pump stopped running in that reactor; this prevented steam generators from removing heat from the nuclear core. As a result, the reactor shut down automatically and pressure began to rise in the inner chamber, and, according to the system's design, a valve opened to release the steam. The meltdown began when that valve failed to close, allowing the crucial cooling water to flow out. Unfortunately, the indicator signal for this problem also malfunctioned, giving operators at the control panel false and contradictory information. Operators, believing the chamber was full, reduced the flow of water. The temperature of the reactor's core quickly rose to around 5,000°F and melted the exposed zirconium casings of the nuclear tubes, thus initiating a classic nuclear meltdown (NRC, 2011). They call it "the China syndrome" because, unless the rods can be cooled quickly, they will continue to melt, deeper and deeper, into the ground, supposedly all the way to China.

Through the morning, plant officials notified local and state officials and company executives. Aware by early morning that the control room—normally sealed off from the threat of radiation—was contaminated, operators quickly put on full hazardous materials protective suits, including gas masks with oxygen tanks, and ordered all nonessential employees off the property. Operators worked frantically with nuclear safety experts and scientists to understand what was happening and, simultaneously, to keep authorities informed. But with only two working phones on the property and operators' mouths covered by thick masks, communication was extremely frustrating. After hours of fumbling, a Babcock and Wilcox (manufacturer of the reactor) employee managed to scream advice to operators: "Get water moving through the core!" (Gazit, 2000). It must have been a scene as suspenseful as some in the movie *The China Syndrome*, which had opened to large audiences 12 days earlier.

In this early phase of the response, Pennsylvania Governor Dick Thornburgh relied on the owner-operator of the plant, Metropolitan Edison (Met Ed), for information. But Met Ed's media representative, an engineer with no press experience, reported to a throng of reporters the same statement he had made to Governor Thornburgh, that there was "no problem, the plant is functioning properly, and we expect soon to be in shut-down condition." Few believed him, neither reporters nor local officials, and the crisis deepened (Gazit, 2000).

Later that morning a significant amount of radioactive steam came out of the damaged reactor. The governor needed to make an informed decision about whether or not to evacuate but could not rely on Met Ed for information. He called on President Jimmy Carter, himself a nuclear engineer, for help. Carter dispatched NRC official Harold Denton, someone Carter knew and trusted, to help Thornburgh verify information and advise residents of the area. While anxiously waiting for Denton, Pennsylvania emergency staff reviewed emergency evacuation plans for the two nearby towns and found them unworkable. In the meantime, without consulting Pennsylvania officials, another NRC official in Washington issued an evacuation order. Much later, they realized their calculations were in error and the amount of radiation was not dangerous.

Some charged the media with exaggeration in reporting the TMI incident. A Carter administration presidential investigation report considered "The Public's Right to Information" and found that only "a few" (of about 50) U.S. newspapers had exaggerated the danger or published misleading information, and that most reporters fully and adequately informed the public, despite the obstacles of doubtful information and their own unfamiliarity with the science of nuclear power plants (Kemeny, 1979, 57–59).

Reactor 2 stabilized, was safely shut down, and was never restarted. The cleanup ended in December 1993. After years of medical monitoring of people in the area, a court decision found insufficient evidence of health effects from their exposure to radiation to warrant compensation. A greater effect of the TMI accident was psychological: the fear of nuclear power. Since TMI, not one new nuclear power plant has been licensed and put into operation. But many new plants are in the planning stages around the country, even after the disaster at Fukushima, Japan, following a massive earthquake/tsunami in March 2011. Perhaps that reminder will engender caution. One factor that led to the TMI accident was the Organization of Petroleum Exporting Countries (OPEC) oil embargo and the recession that followed, causing the need for less expensive electricity to take precedence over safety.

Conclusion

America stumbled onto the path of environmental protection as it dealt with the unexpected. Front-page disasters continued: Bhopal, India, in 1984, Chernobyl in 1986, Exxon *Valdez* in 1989, the Gulf oil spill in 2010, and Fukushima in 2011. All of these stories have all of the elements that make any story interesting and profitable: drama, danger, and human interest. The presence of reporters and the stories they wrote—ever more informed—educated citizens and held polluters accountable in a way that rules could not. And as a result of this sustained coverage, journalism has a new subfield—environmental journalism—requiring science courses in degree programs around the country since 1990.

KATHY HARRIS

See also: Ecorazzi (Arts); Goldman Environmental Prize (Activism); Green Publishing Efforts (Arts); Rachel Carson's *Silent Spring* (Arts); Social Networking Sites (Arts).

References

Beck, Eckardt C. 1979. "The Love Canal Tragedy." *EPA Journal* (January). Available at: http://www.epa.gov/history/topics/lovecanal

Brown, Michael. 1983. *Laying Waste: The Poisoning of America by Toxic Chemicals*. New York: Pocket Books.

Carson, Rachel. 1962. *Silent Spring*. New York: Houghton-Mifflin.

DeKok, David. 1986. *Unseen Danger: A Tragedy of People, Government, and the Centralia Mine Fire*. State College: University of Pennsylvania Press.

DeKok, David. 2009. *Fire Underground: The Ongoing Tragedy of the Centralia Mine Fire*. Guilford, CT: Globe-Pequot Press.

Dunkle, David N. 2009. "Centralia's Coal-Fueled Fire Could Reach Mount Carmel, Newly Released Maps Indicate." *Patriot News*. Available at: http://blog.pennlive.com/midstate _impact/print.html?entry.

Gazit, Ghana. 2000. "Meltdown at Three Mile Island." Stewart-Gazit Productions, Inc. Film and interview transcripts for PBS *American Experience* series, WGBH Education Foundation, 1999.

Iowa Digital Library. 2010. "The Editorial Cartoons of J. N. 'Ding' Darling." Available at: http://digital.lib.uiowa.edu/ding/.

J. N. "Ding" Darling Foundation. 2010. "About the Man." Available at: http://www .dingdarling.org/about.html.

Kemeny, John G. 1979. "Report of the President's Commission on the Accident at Three Mile Island." October. Available at: http://www.threemileisland.org/downloads//188.pdf.

Lendt, David L. 1989. *Ding: The Life of J. Norwood Darling*. Ames: Iowa State University Press. Available at: http://www.dingdarling.org/darling.pdf.

NRC. 2011. "Three Mile Island Backgrounder." Available at: http://www.nrc.gov/reading-rm/doc-collections.

Scott, Michael. 2009. "Cuyahoga Fire 40 Years Ago Ignited Ongoing Cleanup." *Cleveland Plain Dealer*. Available at: http://www.time.com/time/magazine/article.

U.S. Fish & Wildlife Service. 2008. "Jay Norwood 'Ding' Darling." Available at: http:// www.fws.gov/dingdarling/About/DingDarling.html

Whalen, Robert P. 1978. "Love Canal Public Health Time Bomb: A Special Report to the Governor and Legislature." September. Available at: http://www.health.ny.gov/ environmental/investigations/love-canal/timbmb.htm.

LITERATURE, ENVIRONMENTAL

A survey of environmental literature shows that people's relationship with and concern for the Earth have changed dramatically over time. The earliest American writings on the natural world were the works of explorers describing their travels, naturalists seeking to describe and categorize the plants and animals of the New World, and farmers seeking to harvest agricultural resources. During the 19th century, however, worries about resource depletion led many writers to advocate a wiser use of the land. For example, Gifford Pinchot's *Primer of Forestry* (1899) emphasized good forest management, while George Perkins Marsh's *Man and Nature, or Physical Geography as Modified by Human Action* (1863) examined the ways in which humans were adversely altering the landscape.

Still, the common view at the beginning of the 20th century was that nature could not be permanently damaged. This is expressed, for example, in the work of botanist Frederic E. Clements, who in 1905 published the first textbook on ecology as a science, *Research Methods in Ecology*. Although Clements argued that farming was a destructive activity that interfered with the health of the land, he also stated that this health could quickly be restored simply by leaving the land alone so that nature could reclaim it.

Nonetheless, as population growth and the spread of urbanization reduced wilderness areas, individuals who had enjoyed these areas recognized the need to preserve them. Many of the early conservationists in America were hunters who wanted certain forests set aside for future enjoyment. This was the case, for example, with naturalist John Burroughs, whose books include *Ways of Nature* (1905) and *Field and Study* (1919). But the most influential person in terms of forest preservation was not a hunter but someone who simply enjoyed hiking through wilderness areas: John Muir, whose works include *The Mountains of California* (1896), *My First Summer in the Sierra* (1911), and *Our National Parks* (1916). In 1892 Muir founded the Sierra Club, a conservation group devoted to promoting wilderness concerns and activities, and his conservation efforts were instrumental in convincing Congress to establish the national park system in 1916.

At this point, most people believed that the wilderness was something separate from humankind. During the 1930s and 1940s, however, they increasingly embraced the idea that humans and nature are interconnected. A study of the works of wildlife scientist Aldo Leopold serves as an example of this shift in viewpoint. From 1915 to 1933, he wrote several books on how to manage game, fish, and wildlife, but in the late 1930s he began writing *A Sand County Almanac* (published posthumously in 1949), which condemns the exploitation of natural resources and argues that such exploitation will ultimately harm humankind.

Naturalist and author John Muir, ca. 1902. (Library of Congress)

A more dire warning appeared in the form of *Our Plundered Planet* by Fairfield Osborn, published in 1948. This work typifies the earliest apocalyptic environmental literature, in which human beings are seen as destroyers of the natural world. It argues that overpopulation, deforestation, soil erosion, and poor agricultural practices will lead humankind to run out of habitable, farmable land, which means that if environmental problems are left unsolved, then all civilization will end.

By the early 1960s, the belief that damaging the wilderness will ultimately damage humans had taken hold in the general public, thanks not only to apocalyptic writing but to well-reasoned books focusing on the ways in which environmental practices were leading to health problems like cancer. One of the most influential of these books is Rachel Carson's *Silent Spring* (1962), considered by many environmentalists to have been instrumental in encouraging the conservation movement to transform into the environmental movement (the former being primarily concerned with an individual's enjoyment of nature, and the latter with the environment's impact on humankind). Appearing first in serial form in the *New Yorker* magazine, *Silent Spring* focused on the ways in which pesticides were harming the environment and threatening human health. Murray Bookchin's *Our Synthetic Environment* (1962) also talked about the hazards of pesticide use, while his book *The Crisis of the Cities* (1965) addressed the dangers of pollution.

During the first three decades of the environmental movement, environmentalists published hundreds of books on environmental issues, and the subjects of these books reflected factions within the movement that arose out of differing opinions regarding how best to lessen damage to the Earth. Members of one faction argued that the only way to protect the Earth was to fight for it, via radical activism that might involve illegal and perhaps violent activities. An opposing faction condemned radical activism while proposing various ways to work legally with governments to effect changes to environmental laws and practices. Still another faction focused on individual actions and personal responsibility for stewardship of the Earth, promoting the simple living or back-to-nature movement, whereby people abandoned modern conveniences to live off the land.

One of the most famous books of the environmental movement was written by a member of the radical faction, environmental activist Edward Abbey. Titled *The Monkey Wrench Gang*, this 1975 novel concerns a gang of activists who use guerrilla tactics and environmental sabotage, or ecotage, to protest desert development in the American Southwest. In 1981 Abbey's book inspired the creation of a radical environmental group called Earth First!, whose members engaged in activities that became known as monkeywrenching. Such activities included chaining themselves to trees slated for destruction, destroying logging equipment, and booby-trapping trees so that loggers attempting to cut them down would get hurt.

One of the founders of Earth First!, Dave Foreman, wrote a book promoting monkeywrenching, *Ecodefense: A Field Guild to Monkeywrenching* (1985), as well as *Confessions of an Eco-Warrior* (1991) and a guide to roadless areas titled *The Big Outside* (1989). Another founder of Earth First!, Christopher Manes, wrote *Green Rage: Radical Environmentalism and the Unmaking of Civilization* (1990) to defend the philosophy and practices of radical environmentalism; this work also advocates civil disobedience and questions the right of humans to control nature. In contrast, the 1970 book *Ecotactics: The Sierra Club Handbook for Environmental Activists*, published by the environmental group the Sierra Club and edited by

Greenovator: Edward Abbey

Edward Abbey's works and ideas influenced the fledgling environmental movement during the 1960s and continue to remain important in environmental thought today. Abbey was born on January 29, 1927, in Indiana, Pennsylvania, a town in northern Appalachia. In the summer of 1944, 17-year-old Abbey hitchhiked across the country and for the first time encountered the Southwest, the region that subsequently became the central focus of his life and career. From 1945 to 1946, Abbey served with the U.S. army in Alabama, New Jersey, and Italy. On the G.I. Bill, he studied English and philosophy at the University of New Mexico from 1947 to 1951. After receiving the Fulbright Fellowship, Abbey took courses at the University of Edinburgh, Scotland, and in 1954 returned to the University of New Mexico to pursue a graduate degree in philosophy. His master's thesis on anarchism and the morality of violence signaled the interests he would continue to explore in his later work. In the years 1956–1971, Abbey worked as a firefighter and park ranger in what is now Arches National Park, Utah. Later in life, Abbey taught writing at the University of Arizona, Tucson. Abbey died on March 14, 1989. Following his wishes, his body was buried in an undisclosed location in the Cabeza Prieta Desert, Arizona.

Although in his work Abbey described the natural beauty of the Southwestern landscape and warned of the threats that industrialization and urbanization posed to this terrain, he resisted the labels of nature and environmental writer. *Desert Solitaire* (1968), his musings on the Southwestern wilderness he got to know while working as a park ranger and *The Monkey Wrench Gang* (1975), a novel about a group of ecoteurs, are Abbey's best-known works. Abbey's nonconformist ideas, especially his views on environmentally motivated resistance and sabotage, have influenced the radical environmental movement, most notably the group known as Earth First!

MARTA BLADEK

John G. Mitchell and Constance L. Stallings, discusses legal tactics that environmentalists can use to protect the planet.

Another work supported by a major environmental group is *The Challenge of Global Warming* (1989), published by the National Resources Defense Council (NRDC) and edited by scientist Dean Edwin Abrahamson. This work presents the views of leading experts in global warming, with each chapter written by a different expert on the Earth's climate. Similarly, the 1982 book *Down to Earth* by environmentalist Erik P. Eckholm was funded by the United Nations to commemorate the 10th anniversary of its 1972 conference on the human environment, the Stockholm Conference. This book advocates the establishment of an international environmental agency dedicated to monitoring environmental problems and having the authority to develop global solutions to those problems.

More typically, however, the works of mainstream environmentalists have been issue specific, focusing on such subjects as climate change, habitat protection, wildlife conservation, biodiversity, nuclear energy, pollution, and environmental politics. For example, Diane Ackerman's *The Rarest of the Rare* (1997) concerns endangered species and the importance of biodiversity; David Bulloch's *The Wasted Ocean* (1991) addresses the health of oceans worldwide; and William Rathje and Cullen Murphy's 1992 book *Rubbish!* focuses on recycling and other issues related to waste disposal. Also notable is former vice president Al Gore's *Earth in the Balance* (1992), which discusses environmental policy in terms of economics. Two years after its publication, anti-environmentalist Wallace Kaufman attacked *Earth in the Balance* in his book *No Turning Back: Dismantling the Fantasies of Environmental Thinking*, arguing that Gore was exaggerating the seriousness of environmental problems.

Although such specific attacks are rare, anti-environmentalists have written many books arguing that particular environmental issues are not actually the problem that environmentalists claim them to be. For example, Dixy Lee Ray's 1993 book with Lou Guzzo, *Environmental Overkill: Whatever Happened to Common Sense?*, argues that environmentalists' claims about threats and damage to the Earth are often an exaggeration and says that government policy decisions related to environmental issues such as global warming are typically not based on scientific facts. Other anti-environmentalists' works focusing on global warming include *Climategate: A Veteran Meteorologist Exposes the Global Warming Scam* (2010) by Brian Sussman and *Climate of Corruption: Politics and Power Behind the Global Warming Hoax* (2011) by Larry Bell. An example of a broader anti-environmentalist attack is *Green Hell: How Environmentalists Plan to Control Your Life and What You Can Do to Stop Them* (2009) by Steven Milloy.

Environmentalists have examined the anti-environmentalism movement in such books as David Helvarg's *The War Against the Greens* (1994), but they have also written their own books critical of the environmental movement. These include *Living Through the End of Nature: The Future of American Environmentalism* (2010) by Paul Wapner, *The Rebirth of Environmentalism: Grassroots Activism from the Spotted Owl to the Polar Bear* (2009) by Douglas Bevington, and *Break Through: From the Death of Environmentalism to the Politics of Possibility* (2007) by Michael Shellenberger and Ted Norhaus, all of which suggest that the environmentalism of the 1960s through 1990s is outdated. Also critical of the environmentalism is *Playing God in Yellowstone: The Destruction of America's First National Park* (1986), which accuses environmentalists of taking the wrong approach to wilderness issues.

Another work by an environmentalist critical of environmentalism is Gregg Easterbrook's 1995 book *A Moment on the Earth*, which bemoans the amount of pessimism in the environmental movement and argues that both environmentalists and anti-environmentalists need to practice "ecorealism," the unbiased evaluation of environmental facts. This position was in large part a reaction to a rash of environmental apocalypse literature that appeared in the 1980s. One of the foremost examples of apocalyptic writing from this period is *Extinction: The Causes and Consequences of the Disappearance of Species* (1981) by Paul and Anne Ehrlich, which suggests that animal extinctions will lead to the destruction of the Earth's ecosystem and, therefore, the end of all life on the planet. Other examples include *The End of Nature* (1989) by Bill McKibben, which predicts a series of global disasters due to environmental destruction, particularly because of global warming; and *Our Angry Earth* (1991) by Isaac Asimov and Frederik Pohl, which argues that if human beings become too destructive to the Earth, then the Earth will be forced to get rid of humans in order to protect itself.

The view that the Earth will defend itself is part of a concept called the Gaia hypothesis, first developed by scientist James Lovelock during the early 1970s.

He wrote about his belief that the Earth is a living entity that seeks to survive and protect itself in *Gaia: A New Look at Life on Earth* (1979), and this position has gained so many supporters over the years that three large international conferences have been held on the subject, most recently in 2006. In addition, books continue to be written on the subject, including *The Symbiotic Planet* (1999) by Lynn Margulis, and *The Revenge of Gaia* (2006) and *The Vanishing Face of Gaia: A Final Warning* (2009), both by James Lovelock.

Most apocalyptic environmental literature is intended as a call to action, and the action envisioned by its authors typically involves aggressive global cooperative efforts. This is in contrast to the branch of environmentalism that emphasizes individual actions and personal responsibility for environmental stewardship. Members of mainstream environmentalist groups typically practice individual activism as well, and some of them have written books integrating the two forms of environmentalism; for example *Ethics: Choices for Concerned Citizens* (1980) by the Science Action Committee with Albert J. Fritsch discusses environmental issues in terms of individual ethics and morals but says that if individuals refuse to change their behavior then governments must mandate them to do so. However, many proponents of the simple living or back-to-nature movement—or the related deep ecology movement, which combines simple living with practices related to broader environmental concerns such as a couple limiting the number of children to prevent overpopulation—dislike or even shun government intrusion into their lives, and their written works reflect this.

Among the best-known books to focus on simple living and deep ecology are *Ecology, Community, and Lifestyle* (1976) by Norwegian philosopher Arne Naess, one of the founders of the deep ecology movement; *Deep Ecology: Living as If Nature Mattered* (1985) by sociologist Bill Devall and ecophilosopher George Sessions; *A Continuous Harmony* (1972) by farmer and ecologist Wendell Berry; *The Simple Life* (1973) by Vernard Eller, who provides a religious perspective on the subject; and *Small Is Beautiful* (1974) by Fritz Schumacher, who eschewed materialism after serving as economic adviser to the British National Coal Board from 1950 to 1970. More recent works include *The Self-Sufficiency Handbook: The Complete Guide to Greener Living* (2007) by Alan Bridgewater and Gill Bridgewater and *Confessions of an Eco-Sinner: Tracking Down the Sources of My Stuff* (2009) by Fred Pearce, which condemns materialism. Also popular today are books on green living, which involves creating a simple-living, environmentally friendly lifestyle without going back to nature; such works include *Green Living* (2007) by the editors of *E/The Environmental Magazine*, *Voluntary Simplicity* (2010) by Duane Elgin, and *The EcoFriendly Home: Living the Natural Life* (2011) by Dan Phillips.

One of the main inspirations for the simple living movement was *Walden* (1854) by naturalist Henry David Thoreau. This book describes Thoreau's experiences in living off the land for two years in a self-made retreat near Walden Pond in Concord, Massachusetts. *Walden* also discusses nature and the environment in terms of modern lifestyles and human spirituality. However, it was not appreciated in Thoreau's time; only 2,000 copies of the work sold during its first five years of print, whereas by the 1950s—thanks to the growing conservation movement—there had been 133 editions of the book.

Personal narratives like *Walden* remain extremely popular today. These include *The Road Washes Out in Spring: A Poet's Memoir of Living off the Grid* (2008) by Baron Wormser and *Twelve by Twelve: A One-Room Cabin Off the Grid and Beyond the American Dream* (2010) by William Powers, as well as numerous books that focus on short-term wilderness experiences as opposed to long-term living off the land. Some of these personal narratives have a spiritual aspect, and in recent years there has been an increase in other types of environmental books with a spiritual aspect as well. Two prominent examples of this are *A Greener Faith: Religious Environmentalism and Our Planet's Future* (2006) by Roger S. Gottlieb, who argues that religious people and organizations are among the most active environmentalists today, and *A New Climate for Theology: God, the World, and Global Warming* (2008) by Sallie McFague.

Businesspeople have also expressed their interest in environmentalism, through such books as *Green to Gold: How Smart Companies Use Environmental Strategy to Innovate, Create Value, and Build Competitive Advantage* (2009) by Daniel Esty and Andrew Winston and *Guerrilla Marketing Goes Green: Winning Strategies to Improve Your Profits and Your Planet* (2010) by Jay Conrad Levinson and Shel Horowitz. These works show just how dramatically attitudes toward environmentalism have changed since the 19th century. Whereas business owners were once at odds with conservationists and environmentalists, today many corporations embrace environmentalism as a sound business practice, in large part because public opinion regarding environmentalism has been affected by the efforts and written works of those arguing that humankind needs to rethink its relationship with the Earth.

PATRICIA D. NETZLEY

See also: American Writers and the Environment (Arts); Earth First! (Activism); National Parks (Sports); Rachel Carson's *Silent Spring* (Arts).

References

Abbey, Edward. 1975. *The Monkey Wrench Gang*. Philadelphia, PA: Lippincott.

Abrahamson, Dean Edwin, ed. 1989. *The Challenge of Global Warming*. Washington, DC: Island Press.

Ackerman, Diane. 1997. *The Rarest of the Rare*. New York: Random House.

Allaby, Michael. 1989. *A Guide to Gaia: A Survey of the New Science of Our Living Earth*. New York: E. P. Dutton.

Asimov, Isaac, and Frederik Pohl. 1991. *Our Angry Earth*. New York: Tor.

Bailes, Kendall E., ed. 1985. *Environmental History: Critical Issues in Comparative Perspective*. Lanham, New York, and London: University Press of America and American Society for Environmental History.

Bailey, Ronald. 1993. *Eco-Scam: The False Prophets of Ecological Apocalypse*. New York: St. Martin's Press.

Bell, Larry. 2011. *Climate of Corruption: Politics and Power Behind the Global Warming Hoax*. Austin, TX: Greenleaf Book Group.

Berry, Wendell. 1972. *A Continuous Harmony: Essays Cultural and Agricultural.* New York: Harcourt Brace Jovanovich.

Bevington, Douglas. 2009. *The Rebirth of Environmentalism: Grassroots Activism from the Spotted Owl to the Polar Bear.* Washington, DC: Island Press.

Biehl, Janet. 1999. *Murray Bookchin Reader.* Montreal: Black Rose Books.

Bilsky, Lester J., ed. 1980. *Historical Ecology.* Port Washington, NY, and London: Kennikat Press.

Bowler, Peter J. 1993. *The Norton History of the Environmental Sciences.* New York and London: W. W. Norton.

Bulloch, David K. 1991. *The Wasted Ocean.* New York: Lyons and Burford (an American Littoral Society Book).

Cahalan, James A. 2000. *Edward Abbey: A Life.* Tucson: University of Arizona Press.

Callicott, J. Baird. 1987. *Companion to a Sand County Almanac: Interpretive and Critical Essays.* Madison: University of Wisconsin Press.

Carson, Rachel L. 1962. *Silent Spring.* Boston: Houghton Mifflin.

Chase, Alston. 1987. *Playing God in Yellowstone: The Destruction of America's First National Park.* San Diego, CA, New York, and London: Harcourt Brace Jovanovich.

Dashefsky, H. Steven. 1993. *Environmental Literacy.* New York: Random House.

Devall, Bill, and George Sessions. 1985. *Deep Ecology: Living as if Nature Mattered.* Salt Lake City, UT: Peregrine Books.

Dobson, Andrew. 1991. *The Green Reader.* San Francisco: Mercury House.

Dowie, Mark. 1995. *Losing Ground: American Environmentalism at the Close of the Twentieth Century.* Cambridge, MA: MIT Press.

Easterbrook, Gregg. 1995. *A Moment on the Earth.* New York: Viking Penguin.

Eckholm, Erik P. 1982. *Down to Earth.* New York: W. W. Norton.

Ehrlich, Paul R., and Anne H. Ehrlich. 1981. *Extinction: The Causes and Consequences of the Disappearance of Species.* New York: Random House.

Eller, Vernard. 1973. *The Simple Life: The Christian Stance Toward Possessions.* Grand Rapids, MI: Eerdmans.

Esty, Daniel, and Andrew Winston. 2009. *Green to Gold: How Smart Companies Use Environmental Strategy to Innovate, Create Value, and Build Competitive Advantage.* Hoboken, NJ: John Wiley & Sons.

Fenimore, David. 1975. "Edward Abbey, The Monkey Wrench Gang." In George Hart and Scott Slovic, eds., *Literature and the Environment.* Westport, CT: Greenwood, 95–109.

Finch, Robert, and John Elder. 1990. *The Norton Anthology of Nature Writing.* New York: W. W. Norton.

Foreman, Dave. 1991. *Confessions of an Eco-Warrior.* New York: Harmony Books.

Glotfelty, Cheryll, and Harold Fromm, eds. 1996. *The Ecocriticism Reader: Landmarks in Literary Ecology.* Athens: University of Georgia Press.

Gore, Al. 1992. *Earth in the Balance: Ecology and the Human Spirit.* Boston and New York: Houghton Mifflin.

Gottlieb. 1993. *Forcing the Spring: The Transformation of the American Environmental Movement.* Washington, DC: Island Press.

Gottlieb, Roger S. 2006. *A Greener Faith: Religious Environmentalism and Our Planet's Future.* New York: Oxford University Press.

Helvarg, David. 1994. *The War Against the Greens: The "Wise Use" Movement, the New Right, and Anti-Environmental Violence.* San Francisco: Sierra Club Books.

Kaufman, Wallace. 1994. *No Turning Back: Dismantling the Fantasies of Environmental Thinking.* New York: Basic Books.

Kline, Benjamin. 2011. *First Along the River: A Brief History of the U.S. Environmental Movement*, 4th ed. Lanham, MD: Rowman & Littlefield.

Kroeber, Karl. 1994. *Ecological Literary Criticism.* New York: Columbia University Press.

Leopald, Aldo. 1966. *A Sand County Almanac.* New York: Oxford University Press.

Levinson, Jay Conrad, and Shel Horowitz. 2010. *Guerrilla Marketing Goes Green: Winning Strategies to Improve Your Profits and Your Planet.* Hoboken, NJ: John Wiley & Sons.

Lovelock, James. 1979. *Gaia: A New Look at Life on Earth.* New York: Oxford University Press.

Luke, Timothy W. 2008. "In Defense of the American West: Edward Abbey's *Desert Solitaire: A Season in the Wilderness.*" *Organization & Environment* 21.2: 171–181.

Manes, Christopher. 1990. *Green Rage: Radical Environmentalism and the Unmaking of Civilization.* Boston: Little, Brown.

McFague, Sallie. 2008. *A New Climate for Theology: God, the World, and Global Warming.* Minneapolis: Fortress Press.

McHenry, Robert, ed. 1972. *A Documentary History of Conservationism in America.* New York: Praeger.

McKibben, Bill. 1989. *The End of Nature.* New York: Random House.

Milloy, Steven. 2009. *Green Hell: How Environmentalists Plan to Control Your Life and What You Can Do to Stop Them.* Washington, DC: Regnery Publishing.

Mitchell, John G., ed., with Constance Stallings. 1970. *Ecotactics: The Sierra Club Handbook for Environmental Activists.* New York: Pocket Books.

Nash, Roderick Frederick. 1976. *The American Environment: Readings in the History of Conservation.* Reading, MA: Addison-Wesley.

Nash, Roderick Frederick. 1989. *The Rights of Nature: A History of Environmental Ethics.* Madison: University of Wisconsin Press.

Netzley, Patricia D. 1999. *Environmental Literature: An Encyclopedia of Works, Authors, and Themes.* Santa Barbara, CA: ABC-CLIO.

Osborn, Fairfield. 1948. *Our Plundered Planet.* Boston: Little, Brown.

Pearce, Fred. 2009. *Confessions of an Eco-Sinner: Tracking Down the Sources of My Stuff.* Boston: Beacon Press.

Pepper, David. 1996. *Modern Environmentalism: An Introduction.* London and New York: Routledge.

Philippon, Daniel J. 2004. *Conserving Words: How American Nature Writers Shaped the Environmental Movement.* Athens and London: University of Georgia Press, 219–265.

Rathje, William, and Cullen Murphy. 1992. *Rubbish! The Archaeology of Garbage.* New York: HarperCollins.

Ray, Dixy Lee, with Lou Guzzo. 1993. *Environmental Overkill: Whatever Happened to Common Sense?* New York: HarperPerennial.

Richardson Jr., Robert D., and Barry Moser. 1988. *Henry Thoreau: A Life of the Mind.* Berkeley, CA: University of California Press.

Sackman, Douglas Cazaux. 2010. *A Companion to American Environmental History.* Malden, MA, and Oxford, UK: Wiley-Blackwell.

Sale, Kirkpatrick. 1993. *The Green Revolution: The American Environmental Movement, 1962–1992.* New York: Hill and Wang.

Schumacher, E. F. 1974. *Small Is Beautiful.* London: Abacus.

Shabecoff, Philip. 1993. *A Fierce Green Fire: The American Environmental Movement.* New York: Hill and Wang.

Shellenberger, Michael, and Ted Norhaus. 2007. *Break Through: From the Death of Environmentalism to the Politics of Possibility.* New York: Houghton Mifflin.

Shi, David. 1985. *The Simple Life: Plain Living and High Thinking in American Culture*. New York: Oxford University Press.

Sussman, Brian. 2010. *Climategate: A Veteran Meteorologist Exposes the Global Warming Scam*. Washington, DC: WND Books.

Thoreau, Henry David. 1965. *Walden, or Life in the Woods and On the Duty of Civil Disobedience*. New York: Harper & Row.

Wapner, Paul. 2010. *Living Through the End of Nature: The Future of American Environmentalism*. Cambridge, MA: MIT Press.

Wolfe, Linnie Marsh. 2003. *Son of the Wilderness: The Life of John Muir*. Madison: University of Wisconsin Press.

MUSICIANS, FESTIVALS, AND RADIO STATIONS

Green musicians, festivals, and radio stations have, in many ways, blended environmentalism with entertainment. These musicians, festivals, and radio stations have hailed from areas across the United States, and they've embraced the green cause.

As a whole, these musicians have been diverse in nature, encompassing bands, groups, orchestras, duos, and solo artists. They've represented various types of music ranging from pop, rock, and rhythm and blues music to country, classical, and gospel music. These musicians have diligently prepared and delivered performances to admiring audiences, and they've played instruments, performed on stages, and

Melissa Etheridge performs at the Dow Live Earth Run For Water event in Los Angeles California, on Sunday, April 18, 2010. (AP Photo/Donald Traill)

toured nationally and internationally all in the name of music. While getting their musical acts together, these environmentally minded musicians have taken steps to ensure their work and music activities do not hurt the environment.

Green festivals have given attendees opportunities to take in music and entertainment in outdoor settings. Environmentalism has been emphasized throughout these festivals with hopes that attendees get the message about caring for Earth. Festival organizers and performers have kept Mother Nature in mind as they set up festival events. Going green has been a priority when considering options such as festival concessions or transportation to and from the festivals.

Green radio stations not only have provided music and news to listeners but they also have made sure their work is in tune with the environment. Much of radio stations' activities have been carried out in studios and at times out of the radio station's vehicles. Stations have fortunately been able to grab the attention of wide audiences of listeners who have tuned into their radio programs via radios and the Internet wherever they may be.

Eco-Minded Musicians

In their quest to be eco-friendly, green musicians have been resourceful with the types of music instruments they play. Musicians such as the Giving Tree Band of Illinois have tried using instruments made from materials that are far less disruptive to the environment. For example, rather than using wood from trees that had been cut down, members of the Giving Tree Band have used wood from trees that fell on their own in order to make guitars for the band. Similarly, another band, the Garbage-Men of Florida, had some eco-friendly ideas for their instruments. This band, interestingly, found treasures in the trash. Their instruments have been made from materials that would have been thrown away, such as clothes pegs, PVC pipes, and other unusual items.

Green musicians have made other moves on behalf of Mother Nature. They've joined forces with eco-minded organizations and companies, and together, the two forces have been able to strengthen one other's environmental efforts. In support of these organizations, musicians have been able to use their status to give the green cause greater visibility. Likewise, these organizations and companies have helped musicians to better carry out their musical activities in eco-friendly manners. Examples of musicians teaming up with green organizations and companies include Sheryl Crow and Tom's of Maine, John Legend and Reverb, Green Day and the Natural Resources Defense Council, Jack Johnson and 1% for the Planet, and lastly, the Roots band and both People for the Ethical Treatment of Animals (PETA) and Global Inheritance.

Another environmentally friendly option musicians have been exploring is telecommuting for performances. As opposed to performing in person or touring in distant locations, telecommuting musicians may perform in one spot, record their performances, and share their archived or live shows with viewers online or through television. Telecommute performances may require less overhead and, in particular, may eliminate the need to travel extensively in gas-guzzling tour buses, which could be less harmful to the environment. Moreover, musicians have tried to ease environmental problems associated with transportation by using eco-friendly tour buses. Musicians, including singers Jack Johnson and Sheryl Crow, have toured on buses running on biodiesel fuel, which is said to be less dangerous for Earth. Additionally, vegetable oil has been used in the vehicles of members of the Florida band Look Mexico.

Several musicians have taken up either vegetarianism or veganism, moves that are considered to be more eco-friendly. Vegetarians eat meat-free meals, whereas veganists eat both meat-free and dairy-free foods. Considering all that goes into producing meat and the cruel slaughter of animals, vegetarianism and veganism are thought to be gentler on the environment. The list of musicians who have called themselves vegetarians or vegans is long and includes Carrie Underwood, India Arie, Fiona Apple, Erykah Badu, Kevin Eubanks, Lenny Kravitz, Kesha Sebert (better known as Ke$ha), the Giving Tree Band, and the Roots band, to name just a few.

Instead of using tons of paper for ticketing at music events, musicians such as singers Miley Cyrus and Bruce Springsteen have gravitated toward paperless ticketing and mobile ticketing, which do not require a great deal of paper. With paperless ticketing, ticket transactions may be done online and handled through a company such as TicketMaster. Paperless ticketing eliminates the need to print tickets for the hundreds or thousands of people attending music events. Instead, attendees using TicketMaster simply need to bring identification and a credit card for admission and verification purposes. Mobile ticketing is another paperless option whereby people obtain tickets through their cell phones or other wireless gadgets. Tickets are conveniently delivered through text messaging. This mobile ticketing option was used for a 2011 concert featuring music group LMFAO and music celebrity Swizz Beatz. Everyone attending this concert received tickets by mobile means, and the mobile ticketing process was facilitated through a company called ShowClix.

Green Efforts at Music Festivals

It has been common for festival organizers to collaborate with companies, sponsors, and partners to further their eco-friendly efforts at festivals. These companies have contributed brainpower, manpower, and resources, which have helped to strengthen festivals' green efforts. For example, Colorado's Eco Music Festival (EMU) welcomed support from the Neenan Company, which helped them create and set up a one-of-a-kind, earth-friendly tent for the festival. Another festival, California's High Sierra Music Festival, teamed with Clean Vibes, LLC to handle the festival's waste. Similarly, Texas's Free Press Summer Fest music festival linked up with both Greenie Recycling Company and Little Joy Recycling to deal with recycling efforts at the festival. Festivals have indeed been putting much energy into recycling and composting in order to deal with festival waste. Recycling gives materials another life and keeps the materials from completely going to waste, whereas composting refers to putting all waste together and letting it disintegrate over time. Once the waste in compost crumbles down, all that is left is grainy material that can be used for other purposes such as fertilizer.

Purchasing carbon offsets has become popular among those involved in music festivals, such as the Free Press Summer Fest in Texas. For every carbon emission, a carbon offset certificate has been bought to make up for the carbon emission. The money gained from the sale of carbon offset certificates has gone toward furthering environmental efforts elsewhere.

Festivals such as Milwaukee's Rock the Green festival have aimed to include green vendors who offer environmentally friendly products and who are locally based. This has been a way to connect local vendors with festival goers, who could potentially become the vendors' regular customers—another plus for the environment.

Also noteworthy, festivals have been putting a fun spin on environmentalism through the use of incentives. Rewards and incentives have been ways to catch festival goers' attention and get them excited about going green. A good example is the Illinois Lollapalooza festival's raffle, which offered attendees the chance to win an earth-friendly vehicle if they performed a green act such as bicycling their way to and from the event.

Indeed, more eco-friendly forms of transportation including bicycles and public transportation have been used to transport participants and attendees to and from festivals. Carpooling has also been encouraged. Additionally, biodiesel fuel has been used in participants' vehicles at events such as the Seattle, Washington, Bumbershoot Festival.

Greenovation: The X Tent

The Neenan Company, based in Colorado, has been devoted to pursuing environmentally friendly projects. Neenan Company staff members deserve much credit for embarking on a 2011 tent-making contest in which they had to generate unique ideas on how to create a festival tent that conforms to green standards. The winning tent idea, the X Tent, was the vision of Ben Shepard. This tent ended up being used at Colorado's Eco Music Festival (EMU) in the summer of 2011. What helped make the X Tent so earth friendly was its good transportability and the green materials it was made from, such as bamboo.

Environmentally Friendly Radio Stations

Radio stations have been turning to alternate sources for power and electricity, such as the sun and wind. Compared to other power sources, such as oil and gas, solar power and wind power have an environmental edge. They are both pollutant free and they are in sufficient supply. In other words, there's enough to use over and over again since the supply of solar and wind power does not dwindle. The list of radio stations tapping into solar power goes on: Hoopa, California's KIDE-FM station, Taos, New Mexico's KTAO-FM station, and Fairfield, Iowa's KRUU-FM station have all used it. Wind power has been used by the WARW radio station of Washington, D.C., among others.

Interestingly, radio stations have been taking steps to make sure the very buildings housing their studios are made from eco-friendly materials. They have focused on making everything earth friendly from top to bottom in their buildings in efforts to go green. Pittsburgh's WYEP radio station did just that, reusing materials for the station's ceilings and floors.

Additionally, radio stations have directed attention to their vehicles, taking steps to make their modes of transportation more environmentally friendly. Since much activity takes place out of radio station vehicles, such as at local events and outside broadcasts, radio stations haven't ignored green vehicle options. Washington, D.C.'s WARW station, for example, has gravitated toward more use of eco-friendly hybrid vehicles.

Also noteworthy, radio stations have been featuring news programs and segments broadcasting earth-friendly content. They've delved into environmental topics, stimulating listeners' interest and encouraging them to go green. Several radio stations, including Iowa's KRUU radio station, have put together these types of enlightening radio programs.

Impact

Since musicians, festivals, and radio stations have been able to reach out to large numbers of people, they have been in good positions to set positive examples. Their exposure to wide audiences of viewers and listeners has given them opportunities to influence the masses. There has been strong evidence that musicians, festivals, and radio stations have been effective in getting the public to take an active rather than a passive stance toward the environment. The following examples show how musicians, festivals, and radio stations have motivated the public to play a hands-on role in taking care of Mother Nature. Moreover, these examples reveal how receptive the public has been in response to the eco-friendly ideas of musicians, festivals, and radio stations, showing a willingness to take part in green efforts. When the LMFAO/Swizz Beatz concert wanted to encourage attendees to use mobile ticketing for their concert, the concert organizers were remarkably able to garner participation from everyone who attended the concert. Similarly, New Mexico's green radio station KTAO-FM station opened its green facilities for rent to the public, and local music acts have indeed taken advantage of this station's Solar Center for music events.

BROOKE POSLEY

See also: Celebrities (Arts); Green and Sustainability Fairs and Festivals (Activism).

References

Carty, Daniel. "For Miley Cyrus Tour, TicketMaster Goes Paperless." Available at: http://www.cbsnews.com/8301-503983_162-5071747-503983.html.

"Greenest Event Tent at EMU Music Festival." *Design Inspiration Magazine*. Available at: http://www.oamahou.com/2011/07/11/greenest-event-tent-at-emu-music-festival/?lang=en.

Industrial Fabrics Association International. "Sustainable Festival Tent has 'X' Appeal." Available at: http://specialtyfabricsreview.com/articles/0911_sw3_sustainable_tent.html.

Rupal, Reetu. "Concert Experiments with All-Mobile Ticketing." Available at: http://abcnews.go.com/Entertainment/wireStory?id=14308828.

Union of Concerned Scientists. "UCS Partners with Musicians to Green the Music Industry." Available at: http://www.ucsusa.org/news/press_release/ucs-partners-with-musicians-to-green-music-industry-0342.html.

Waddell, Ray. 2007. "Smells Like Green Spirit." *Billboard* (June): 32.

RACHEL CARSON'S *SILENT SPRING*: GREENOVATOR SPOTLIGHT

It is difficult to overestimate the impact of Rachel Carson's best-selling exposé, *Silent Spring* (1962), on the American environmental movement. Originally serialized in the *New Yorker*'s three June 1962 editions, *Silent Spring*'s controversial critique of the widespread use of synthetically derived pesticides gave way, as one reviewer quipped, to a "noisy summer" of public outcry (Lee, 1962). The book's premise is relatively simple: citing numerous studies, books, and anecdotal evidence, Carson argues that highly toxic new insecticides such as DDT (dichloro-diphenyl-trichloroethane) had been marketed in the years since World War II for municipal, agricultural, and commercial use without due consideration for these substances' effects on the ecosystem. Far more enduring, however, is the book's philosophical case against this new technology and its makers' attempts at "the 'control of nature'"— "a phrase conceived in arrogance, born of the Neanderthal age of biology and philosophy when it was supposed that nature exists for the convenience of man" (Carson, 1962, 297). Advocating instead a precautionary principle whereby new technologies would not be broadly applied until their risk to living systems had been proven minimal, *Silent Spring* sparked a debate about the role of science in society that continues to resonate in contemporary environmentalism.

Much of the public interest in *Silent Spring* can be attributed to Carson's previous success as a nature writer. Her three previous books—*Under the Sea-Wind* (1941); *The Sea Around Us* (1952); and *The Edge of the Sea* (1955)—were noted for their ability to communicate ecological science in an artful and awe-inspiring fashion, and similarly, *Silent Spring* began as an attempt to create a general-interest account of how new technologies such as the atom bomb and the hundreds of newly created industrial chemicals (including pesticides) flooding American markets were quickly altering, in Carson's words, "life and the relations of life to the physical environment" (Carson & Freeman, 1994, 249). Carson became interested in the specific problem of pesticides in the wake of a 1957 lawsuit waged by residents of Long Island against the U.S. Department of Agriculture, whose attempts to eradicate the gypsy moth through the aerial spraying of DDT, residents claimed, needlessly killed birds and fish, poisoned garden crops, and tainted locally produced milk. In her subsequent research, Carson corresponded with dozens of research biologists, conservationists, government agencies, and doctors, discovering similar cases throughout the United States. Through an agonizing five-year process—during which she also struggled with the cancer that eventually claimed her life—Carson synthesized a small mountain of sources into a shocking 279-page account of

Rachel Louise Carson, wildlife biologist, wrote *Silent Spring*, a book that has drawn public attention to health problems caused by unregulated use of agricultural pesticides, inspired the DDT ban in 1972. (AP/Wide World Photos)

just how serious America's pesticide problem had become, and what its long-term implications might be.

Silent Spring's disturbing trajectory traces pesticides from their creation in laboratories, up through the food chain, and into human cells. Opening chapters describe the chemical processes by which synthetic pesticides are created and these substances' ability to permeate soil, groundwater, and the tissues of plants. Carson then describes the process of bioaccumulation whereby pesticides become highly concentrated in the bodies of birds, fish, and other species feeding on contaminated insects and plants, often resulting in death and reproductive defects for effected animals. The book's second half treats the surprising prevalence of synthetic pesticides not only in insect eradication campaigns and agricultural use, but in bug sprays, treated linens and shelf liners, and other products designed for home use. *Silent Spring* then turns to the grim implications of humans' continuous exposure to these chemicals, noting the prevalence of cancer in the postwar years and connecting pesticide-related fertility problems in other species with the possibility of such symptoms in human beings. The book's final chapters delve into the moral implications behind "the current vogue for poisons" and levy a powerful case for caution:

> As crude a weapon as a cave man's club, the chemical barrage has been hurled against the fabric of life—a fabric on the one hand delicate and destructible, on the other miraculously tough and resilient, and capable of striking back in unexpected ways.

These extraordinary capacities of life have been ignored by the practitioners of chemical control who have brought to their task no "high-minded orientation," no humility before the vast forces with which they tamper. (Carson, 1962, 297)

Interestingly, the well-known "Fable for Tomorrow" that opens the book—imagining a peaceful town poisoned by pesticides—would draw the most attention and criticism. The Monsanto Corporation's parody ("The Desolate Year"), describing the tide of insect destruction that would sweep the globe if pesticides were never employed, was typical of attacks that valorized the technology of pesticides without addressing Carson's premise that these substances were overused. Many critics questioned Carson's scientific credentials or berated the "feminine" emotional appeals her text employed. However, the general public was largely receptive: *Silent Spring* sold half a million copies in its first year, inspired hundreds of discussion groups, and brought Carson dozens of speaking engagements, including an invitation to appear on the popular television program *CBS Reports* in April 1963. When Carson testified before President John F. Kennedy's specially appointed Science Advisory Committee in June 1963, Senator Abraham Ribicoff wryly compared *Silent Spring* to another landmark book, *Uncle Tom's Cabin*, referring to Carson (as President Abraham

Greenovator: Lynton Caldwell

Lynton Caldwell was Arthur F. Bentley professor emeritus of political science at Indiana University in Bloomington. He held that rank from 1984, the year of his retirement, until his death in 2006. The author of hundreds of articles and dozens of books, Caldwell is most notable for his work as a founder of the field of environmental policy studies and as an architect of the National Environmental Policy Act (NEPA).

Lynton Keith Caldwell was born November 21, 1913, in Montezuma, Iowa. He completed his undergraduate degree at the University of Chicago in 1934 and his PhD at the same institution in 1943. In the 1950s, Caldwell was attached to UN missions to Colombia, the Philippines, and Japan and was appointed co-director of the United Nations Public Administration Institute for Turkey and the Middle East. He had appointments at Syracuse University and the University of California–Berkeley. In 1956, he was appointed professor of government at Indiana University, Bloomington, where he remained until his retirement in 1984.

Besides his voluminous academic achievements, Caldwell is most notable for his work on the National Environmental Policy Act of 1970. NEPA's most significant contribution to the enhancement of the environment was first to formalize the procedure by which government agencies prepare environmental assessments, and second to create the Environmental Impact Statement (EIS). The existence of the EIS has been attributed to Caldwell's testimony before the U.S. Senate. NEPA's influence can be seen in similar acts in many states as well as in many foreign countries.

Caldwell was honored by many organizations, including the American Political Science Association, the American Society for Public Administration, the United Nations Environmental Program, and others. An avid outdoorsman and lover of nature, he was a founding member of the Audubon Society's South Bend, Indiana, chapter, and the Nature Conservancy's New York and Indiana chapters. The Caldwell Center for Culture and Ecology was established in his name in 2006. Caldwell died August 15, 2006, in Bloomington, Indiana.

ROBERT C. ROBINSON

Lincoln had once done to Harriet Beecher Stowe) as "the lady who started all this" (Lear, 1997, 3).

Silent Spring is credited with inspiring significant environmental legislation such as the National Environmental Policy Act (1970), the establishment the Environmental Protection Agency (1970), as well as the banning of general DDT use in the United States (1972). Yet its enduring significance also lies in the development of Americans' environmental consciences. In a September 1962 letter to Carson, a reader described the transformational effect of *Silent Spring* on her community: "We homemakers who are aware simply of the risks our families are subjected to because of thoughtless use of dangerous farm poisons and mass spraying programs are so very grateful for your wonderful book which has awakened so many complacent people into present (and we hope continued) action" (Rachel Carson Papers, 1962).

CHARLOTTE AMANDA HAGOOD

See also: American Writers and the Environment (Arts); Literature, Environmental (Arts).

References

Carson, Rachel. 1962. *Silent Spring*. Boston: Houghton Mifflin.
Carson, Rachel, and Dorothy Freeman. 1994. *Always, Rachel: The Letters of Rachel Carson and Dorothy Freeman, 1952–1964*. Boston: Beacon Press.
Lear, Linda. 1997. *Rachel Carson: Witness for Nature*. New York: Henry Holt.
Lee, John M. 1962. "'Silent Spring' Is Now Noisy Summer." *New York Times*, July 22.
The Nature Conservancy. "Lynton Keith Caldwell, Indiana's Conservation Giant." Available at: http://www.nature.org/wherewework/northamerica/states/indiana/misc/art24490.html.
Rachel Carson Papers. 1962. Ruth Desmund Ruth to Rachel Carson. September 29. Beinecke Rare Book and Manuscript Library, Yale University.

SOCIAL NETWORKING SITES

The Internet and social networking have become a part of everyday American life. Within the past 10 years, the social networking boon of Web sites such as Facebook, Twitter, and YouTube has initiated a viral phenomenon that has grown worldwide. Uniquely, the Internet has been found to act as a socialization agent, and from this powerful role, the green movement, environmentalism, and eco-friendly individuals have benefited immensely. Generally, socialization refers to the learning process in which individuals absorb information and selectively add it to their knowledge and understanding of the world. Thus, as the Internet and social networking have revolutionized the manner in which individuals communicate and interact with one another, the green movement and environmentalism have become socialized components of the overarching American conscience and behavior. Essentially, as a popular and encompassing medium of instantaneous communication, and thus information and education dissemination, social networking Web sites facilitated by Internet technology are motivating change, change that is tinted a distinct shade of green.

Currently, the Internet reaches hundreds of millions of individuals throughout the world. The standard social networking Web site Facebook alone has over 350 million users. Internet penetration within the specific U.S. populace is reported at 73 percent, with social networking Web sites accounting for a large number of such use. Moreover, to address the population who is using the Internet, it is reported that primary users tend to be of a younger cohort and members of a more affluent socioeconomic status. The most extreme level of Internet penetration, however, is found among the American middle class, with use reaching over 90 percent. Thus, the evidence of the Internet acting as an agent of socialization is compelling as the use of the Internet and social networking Web sites is immensely pervasive within American contemporary culture. Such use of the Internet in general and social networking Web sites in particular provides a medium of access to a population spanning a broad range of American individuals. Middle-aged business professionals, young teenagers, and the typical American middle-class family alike are able to employ the informative, communicative, and connective capacities provided by the Internet and social networking. Indeed, for the cause of environmentalism and the green movement, the utilization of such ubiquitous tools as the Internet and social networking is beneficial.

The use of social networking Web sites specifically has definitive advantages to the green movement and environmentalism. An important study has demonstrated the many capabilities provided by social networking. Principally, members of social networking Web sites are exposed to other individuals who have similar interests and values, perhaps environmentally or ecologically oriented. As such, connecting with like-minded individuals while consistently seeking a larger population to join the environmental cause allows for the immediate, inexpensive, and paperless distribution of environmental information and education. Reaching both an involved base population and a continually growing interested population, social networking Web sites offer an outlet for members of the green movement to meet, connect, organize, and mobilize for the environmental cause. Fundamentally, within modern American society, social networking provides the imperative element required for the success of the green movement and environmentalism, bringing individuals together to make a positive change toward an ecologically friendly American culture. Such a positive change, however, requires mobilization. Mobilization within the U.S. green movement and environmentalism occurs through information spread between and among formal organizations, institutional structures, and informal networks; in other words, information spread through the modern medium of the Internet and its social networking Web sites. Essentially, social networking presents individuals the structural prospective connection to participate within the green movement, socialization toward positive change, and a forum of available information from which to make environmentally and ecologically conscious decisions. In sum, the effect that the Internet and social networking Web sites have had on the green movement and environmentalism is impressive. Through the power of connecting environmentally and ecologically aware individuals, social networking has created a structural sphere by which involved members can reach interested members. Offering an arena of environmental information and education diffusion, social networking Web sites increase individual participation within the green movement and facilitate mobilization toward positive change. In short, the Internet and social networking Web sites provide the opportunity to connect with others and, importantly, act as socialization agents by shaping pro-environmental and pro-ecological beliefs and behavior. For the U.S. green movement and environmentalism, the Internet and social networking Web sites are critical.

One way that social networking is working toward the socialization of pro-environmental beliefs and behaviors is through the particular action of Facebook, arguably the most widely employed social networking Web site. Recently, Facebook offered ecologically conscious users a new page to "like": Green on Facebook. Outlining the environmental measures that this specific company engages in to promote sustainability, Green on Facebook not only acts as a virtual resource circulating information on what Facebook is doing to go green, but it also shares green information and news from around the Internet. Openly advocating the ideals of the green movement, clean energy, and environmentally friendly behavior, Green on Facebook enables hundreds of millions of individuals from diverse backgrounds and diverse locations to easily meet, connect, organize, and mobilize for the cause. Acting as an agent of socialization, Green on Facebook allows an entire population of involved members of the Green Movement to reach, inform, and educate interested members; by overtly discussing and explaining the ecologically conscious actions of the company, Facebook acts as a role model and an entity encouraging positive change toward the environment. Through such social networking conduit, Green on Facebook conveys a pro-environmental message by revealing its own green performance. As a company, Facebook has reduced water consumption and energy use, increased green transportation service, and implemented an overall more efficient computer and software programming. This demonstrates the ability of social networking to influence the green movement through example and information advocacy. Thus, as a social network, Green on Facebook holds the capacity to reach hundreds of millions of users and to subsequently influence individual beliefs and behavior. In sum, Facebook, the ever-popular social networking Web site, is an encouraging advocate of the green movement and environmentalism. The spread of ecologically conscious information and education certainly impacts the overall state of the environment in positive ways.

ELIZABETH KUSKO

See also: Green Movement (Activism).

References

Coleman, John, Kenneth Goldstein, and William Howell. 2011. *Understanding American Politics and Government*. New York: Pearson Education.

"Facebook 'Friends' the Green Movement." 2010. *Forbes*. Available at: http://blogs.forbes.com/eco-nomics/2010/11/10/facebook-friends-the-greenmovement/?utm_source=all activity&utm_medium=rss&utm_campaign=20101111.

Mankoff, Jennifer et al. 2007. "Leveraging Social Networks to Motivate Individuals to Reduce Their Ecological Footprints." HICSS 2007 Proceedings of the 40th Annual Hawaii International Conference on System Science.

TELEVISION, ECO-FRIENDLY CHANNELS

Television has been the primary method of communication in the United States since the early part of the 20th century. In 1928, Americans sat and watched an experimental telecast of a statue of Felix the Cat, and later huddled in front of their television sets to watch news reports of the Korean War and a few years later reports on the Vietnam War. The television added proximity to important events in the world both at home and in other countries and gave its audience a visual representation of the news. Television in American culture has come to mean public awareness of what eco-friendly, green, and environmentalism mean. It gives children and adults important information on how to help protect and restore the environment, and it also launches channels that look at new projects that are being developed across the United States that will have an impact on making earth a healthier place. Television will influence future generations of Americans into leading a more eco-friendly lifestyle and help create a culture that places great importance on the environment's health.

The Disney Channel

The Disney Channel defines corporate social responsibility as corporations conducting business in a way that is intended to have a holistic positive impact. Disney's intention is to look at the environment's overall situation and devise messages that educate and encourage Americans to live an eco-friendly or green lifestyle. Living green in American culture means that Americans live in a way that helps protect and restore the environment for current and future generations. The best way to protect the environment for the future is to educate children to recycle and protect the planet by convincing viewers that they should help protect the one planet they live on.

Disney Channel launched its "Friends for Change: Project Green" campaign in 2008. The campaign's goal is to make television more eco-friendly by encouraging Americans to lead greener lifestyles. The materials and methodology of the project are said to be eco- friendly. This is an element of Disney Channel's corporate social responsibility initiatives that promote environmentally friendly lifestyles. Disney Corporation's other projects include recycling and waste reduction projects. Together these initiatives have given Disney the public image of a corporation that truly cares about the environment and the health of human beings.

In the "Friends for Change: Project Green" press release, Disney called these corporate social responsibility initiatives "a multiplatform environmental initiative that will help kids help the planet" (http://www.corporate.disney.go.com/citizenship/environment.html). Disney has assembled a group of 29 of its most popular stars, including Miley Cyrus, Selena Gomez, the Jonas Brothers, and Demi Lovato, to participate in outreach plans that are going to be broadcast on Disney Channel, Disney XD, Radio Disney, and Disney.com. Disney hopes these stars will influence Americans into leading an eco-friendly lifestyle. As children are typically prone to advertising, Disney is bringing together this concept and its most popular stars to strengthen the notion of environmental awareness.

Disney's "Friends for Change: Project Green" encourages adolescents to work in unison and help the environment by drawing awareness to climate, water, waste, and habitats. Young Americans will learn useful methods to safeguard the planet and help them follow the impact they have made together. Moreover, they have the chance to vote on how over $1 million donated by Disney will be distributed and allocated in a variety of ecological causes over one year. Disney believes that it will influence Americans to live greener lifestyles by using their biggest stars from its widely popular network to appeal to its target demographic.

The Disney advertisements are centered on empowering children and teenagers to work together to make a difference and participate in preserving the environment. On May 14, 2009, Kids Turn Central reported that "if 500,000 kids participate in Disney Friends for Change: Project Green events, together they can: Prevent approximately 100,000 tons of CO_2 per year from polluting the air by adjusting their home thermostats. Save 5 million gallons of water in a single day by reducing shower times. Prevent 1 million pounds of waste from entering landfills by bringing trash-free lunches for a week. Create new habitats for local animals by planting 500,000 trees" (Kids Turn Central, n.d.). The objective is to make sure children understand the importance living a green lifestyle and have them convince their families to do the same.

Planet Green

In 2008, Discovery Home Channel invested over $50 million on an eco-friendly initiative and announced its Planet Green channel. Discovery's intention was to turn itself into a network concerned on how to live an eco-friendly lifestyle, so it changed its Home channel into a new cable network about living green. The presentation was delivered to advertisers in New York. They announced that the new programming would reach over 50 million households and provide online resources where people could network and view videos on how to live green. The online resources are educational tools that are updated regularly. Eileen O'Neill was named as the head of the new network.

Discovery built the Planet Green channel on its miniseries, *Planet Earth*, which drew close to 4 million viewers for weekly premiere episodes and attracted

Greenovator: The Green on the Sundance Channel

The Sundance Channel, named after Robert Redford's character in *Butch Cassidy and the Sundance Kid*, is a network formed in partnership with Robert Redford and Showtime Networks to air independent television programming and films as an extension of Redford's nonprofit film organization, the Sundance Institute. The Sundance Channel hosts *The Green*, now in its third season, that provides innovative television shows focusing on the environment as well as eco-friendly films, a green blog, greenzine, the action-oriented Eco-mmunity, and green series, including *Big Ideas for a Small Planet*, *The Lazy Environmentalist*, *It's Not Easy Being Green*, *Eco Trip*, *Eco Heroes*, *Carbon Cops*, and *Green Porno*.

KIM KENNEDY WHITE

supporters like Bank of America. Planet Green entered Discovery's plans after it drew double-digit yearly ratings when it returned to science and nature-oriented programming. The network had wandered away from that type of programming in favor of reality-based television. Like other major media corporations, Discovery's goal is to increase its ratings. Discovery achieves this goal partly by informing the public on environmental con-

Greenovator: Green on Current TV

The television and online network Current TV was founded in 2005 by former Vice President Al Gore and Joel Hyatt. The channel features award-winning shows (including the Emmy, Peabody, Webby, and other awards) that provide political and social analysis and commentary. Green on Current TV posts videos and news and hosts discussions on all things green and the environment.

KIM KENNEDY WHITE

cerns like global warming. Discovery used ecological shows like *10 Ways to Save the Planet* to find potential solutions to environmental threats. Planet Green has made a significant contribution to American culture by emphasizing how Americans must live an eco-friendly lifestyle to ensure both they and Earth remain healthy.

GERARDO DEL GUERCIO

See also: Celebrities (Arts); Ecorazzi (Arts); Television, Nature and Wildlife TV (Arts).

References

Carlson, Kim. 2009. "The Green Revolution." In *Green Your Work: Boost Your Bottom Line While Reducing Your Carbon Footprint*. Avon: Adams Business, 19–32.
Kids Turn Central. N.d. "The Walt Disney Company Launches Disney's Friends for Change." Available at: http://www.kidsturncentral.com/topics/news/news051409.htm.
Walt Disney Company. N.d. "Environment and Conservation." Available at: http://corporate.disney.go.com/citizenship/environment.html

TELEVISION, NATURE AND WILDLIFE TV

Since its origins in the late 19th century, cinematic technology has provided Americans an important medium through which to expand their knowledge about nature and, in particular, the animal species that inhabit natural environments. Indeed, one of the earliest experiments in videography, photographer Eadweard Muybridge's 1882 *The Horse in Motion*, was conducted to determine whether horses lift all four feet in gallop—a physiological question that could not be settled by human vision alone. With the popularization of such cinematic forms as television and the ever-increasing sophistication of motion picture technology, however, the moving image has become more than a method of discovering and recording facts about the natural world. As William Beinart and Katie McKeown (2009) remind us, "Filming [is] not a simple act of witnessing: camera technology [has] to be manipulated to achieve particular sequences; shots [are] staged for the camera—even when the aim [is] to represent nature accurately; and time [is] concertinaed" (436). Critical viewers of nature television should thus understand that this medium does not simply document nature, but can also express deeply embedded ideas about human relationships to the environment, and even influence how new understandings of nature develop in other cultural realms.

By the time television began to appear in American households in the late 1940s, the extraordinarily popular wildlife films of earlier decades had established a set of conventions upon which television programs would build. Blending travelogue, action sequences, and documentary, films such as Martin and Osa Johnson's *Simba: King of the Beasts* (1928) portrayed intrepid Americans on safari in locations such as the African savanna, encountering native peoples, ensnaring exotic wildlife, and introducing distant locales and cultures to U.S. audiences. However, such films tread uneasily between the scientific accuracy they boasted and the heart-pounding spectacle they delivered, often staging violent confrontations between animals and even killing animals on screen to create sensational dramatic effects. This tension between science and entertainment—and, in later years, between the conservation and exploitation of nature—would continue to develop as wildlife film reached the small screen.

One of the earliest television programs, *Zoo Parade* with Marlin Perkins (1950–1957, NBC) broadcasted live from the Lincoln Park Zoo in Chicago, Illinois. Perkins, lifelong animal lover and the zoo's director from 1944 to 1962, co-hosted with down-to-earth sidekick, Jim Hurlbut, introducing television audiences to such zoo celebrities as 550-pound gorilla Bushman and a host of other creatures great and small. The program's wholesome, family-oriented approach, which often cast the zoo's specimens as something more like family pets and drew situational elements from game shows and sitcoms, coincided with the optimistic vision of "educators, psychologists, and sociologists" that the rising medium of television "would not only bring the family together, but also offer educational enrichment in the lives of children" (Mitman, 1999, 135). *Zoo Parade* also pioneered another important element in wildlife television programming: sponsorship. Partnering with other animal-related enterprises such as pet supply company Ken-L-Ration, the show created an important cultural link between appreciation of wild animals and affection for domestic ones (Mitman, 1999, 140).

Disney's *True-Life Adventures* (1948–1960) also made new species and ecosystems familiar to American audiences, but through an innovative documentary format. Originally produced for cinema, shorts such as *Seal Island* (1948), *Nature's Half Acre* (1951), and *Mysteries of the Deep* (1959), as well as feature-length films such as *The Living Desert* (1953), were broadcast on television as of 1954, and many were successfully repackaged as educational films for use in schools. Through its newly created distributor (Buena Vista, founded in 1953), Disney hired skilled wildlife photographers from among scientists, outdoor enthusiasts, and educators to capture what one such photographer, Lois Crisler, referred to as "nuggets"— fleeting moments of action or expression that distinguished each animal's individuality (Mitman, 1999, 119). After filming, plot lines and script would be developed from collected footage, which would then be set to a tasteful soundtrack of classical

Jim Hurlbut, left, announcer for Chicago's NBC-TV *Zoo Parade*, holds Ling Wong, an orangutan, as Marlin Perkins, director of the Lincoln Park Zoo and kingpin of the parade, gingerly holds Sweet William, the skunk in 1951. (AP Photo/Edward Kitch)

pieces and original scores—thus supporting Disney's claim that "nature wrote the screenplay; the eloquence, the emotion, and drama were nature's own" (Mitman, 1999, 110). The alleged objectivity of the *True-Life Adventures* has been questioned by both midcentury and contemporary critics. The former found some of the films' creature-characters too much like "scampish little animals right out of *Bambi*." The latter noted that the series deals unrealistically with animal reproductive behavior (particularly birth) and makes no mention of evolutionary theory, arguing that the films "focus on animals whose activities can be seen as analogous to, or sentimentally reminiscent of, the activities of the largely middle-class families who were their primary audience" (Mitman, 1999, 121; McDonald, 2006, 10). Even so, *True-Life Adventures* set a formal precedent of an off-camera, documentary-style narrator and cinematography that brought the viewer intimate and highly focused access to the activities of animal subjects. This formula would be further developed by programs such as *The Undersea World of Jacques Cousteau* (1966–1976, David L. Wolper Productions), *The Wild, Wild World of Animals* (1973–1978, Time-Life Films), and *National Geographic*'s television specials.

Beyond documentaries, wildlife television continued to evolve in two new, though somewhat divergent, directions, satisfying a growing market. First, recalling the safari-themed films of the 1920s and 1930s, *Mutual of Omaha's Wild Kingdom*

(1963–1971, Don Meier Productions), hosted by *Zoo Parade*'s Marlin Perkins, featured on-location action adventures with wild animals. Much like a news broadcast, the program alternated between "Animal Central"—its "anchor room" located in the St. Louis Zoological Garden—and segments filmed in exotic locales throughout the world with "correspondents" including Jim Fowler and Peter Gros. The show was known for its suspenseful narratives and sensational animal stunts (often involving Fowler or other "correspondents"), an aspect that, producers believed, kept the program engaging, despite its substantial use of prefilmed footage. *Wild Kingdom* also marked a new era in program-sponsor relations: its sponsor, the venerable insurance company, was personally endorsed by Perkins as part of the program's advertising segments, with Perkins often comparing animals' instincts to protect their young with human beings' desire to protect their families—with a good insurance policy. *Wild Kingdom* was revived on the Animal Planet channel in 2002.

Another important wildlife genre that emerged during the mid-1950s was the "pet" adventure series, with two programs concerning the exploits of a boy and his dog—*Lassie* (1954–1974, Lassie Television) and *The Adventures of Rin-Tin-Tin* (1954–1959, Screen Gems Television)—serving as prominent examples. The programs' focus on the intimate relationship between human and animal subjects, as well as between the pair and the wild animals they would often encounter, did much to reinforce popular opinions about the value of certain animal species. In this regard, perhaps the most interesting example of this genre is *Flipper* (1964–1967, Metro-Goldwyn-Mayer), which portrayed a park warden's family (Porter, Sandy, and Bud Ricks) and their friendly bottlenose dolphin "pet" Flipper, as they worked to protect wildlife and stop crime in the fictional Coral Key Park and Marine Preserve. The series' popularity was partly based on the hit movie (*Flipper*, 1963) that preceded it, but as Gregg Mitman has shown, dolphins had already generated an extraordinary combination of scientific and entertainment interest by the time of the movie's premier. Since the 1938 opening of Marine Studios near St. Augustine, Florida—a laboratory-cum-theme park designed to afford ordinary citizens the chance to view marine animals in a naturalistic context—dolphins had been frequently used in aquatic entertainment acts, and their reputation for playful, affectionate, and bright behavior had inspired serious scientific inquiry into dolphin intelligence. Dolphins' status as a "glamour species"—perceived as similar in intelligence and sociability to human beings, and therefore singled out for protection—helped spur worldwide interest in marine conservation, and many Americans continue to cite *Flipper* as an important influence on their environmentalist beliefs (Mitman, 1999, 157–179). Interestingly, however, in the 2009 documentary *The Cove* (Oceanic Preservation Society), one of the show's dolphin trainers, Rick O'Barry, would decry the role that the franchise had played in popularizing dolphins and creating theme parks, which kept them as captive entertainers.

As the example of *Flipper* attests, ecological conservation was becoming an increasingly important idea in many wildlife programs by the beginning of the 1970s. As the United States held its first nationally recognized Earth Day, launching a new era of public awareness, television producers followed suit. A new generation of wildlife programs, such Marty Stouffer's *Wild America* (1982–1994, Marty Stouffer

Productions) and *Nature* (1982–present, Thirteen/WNET New York)—both of which originally aired on Public Broadcasting stations—returned to the documentary format, taking a less sensational, more focused look at various animal species within their habitats, often with an emphasis on the danger that factors such as poaching, habitat degradation, and other anthropogenic factors posed to animal species. As its name implies, Stouffer's 30-minute program featured North American ecology, with species- or habitat-centered episodes such as "Amazing Armadillo" (1992) and "The Controversial Coyote" (1986), each part of Stouffer's aim to raise awareness about indigenous species. *Nature*, on the other hand, was (and remains) global in its range and audience, with one-hour episodes treating a wide variety of plants, animals, and fungi, and multipart series on everything from the "Nature of Australia" (1988) to "The Realms of the Russian Bear" (1992), to the sexual behaviors across the animal kingdom ("The Nature of Sex," 1993). Both programs relied on the tried-and-true format of voice-over narration paired with stunning photography, though in 1996, Stouffer's success was compromised by charges that he had illegally built an access trail into an elk migration route in Colorado ("Marty Stouffer," 2011). Though Stouffer continues to produce wildlife films, the scandal illustrates the ongoing paradox of wildlife filmmaking: in order to create the eyewitness aesthetic that has come to characterize the best wildlife films, it is often necessary to intrude upon, or even artificially create, the very spaces and situations that constitute the "wild."

This tension has serious implications for the message of conservation that many wildlife films attempt to impart. Writer and filmmaker Derek Bousé boldly claims that wildlife films are "primarily narrative entertainments that usually steer clear of real social and environmental issues" (Bousé, 2001, xiv). Karla Armbruster (1998) suggests that in "constructing a monolithic, inaccurate representation of non-human nature that focuses on one aspect of the natural world," wildlife documentaries tend to overlook the biological and behavioral interdependencies that actually make ecosystems function. They also run the risk of "constructing [nature] as a place without room for human beings, ultimately distancing humans from the non-human nature with which they are biologically and perceptually interconnected, and reinforcing the dominant cultural ideologies responsible for environmental degradation" (221). Similarly, other critics have argued that wildlife television frustrates its own conservationist ends by changing audience expectations for what nature "should" actually look like: Charles Siebert contrasts the "non-specific, un-narrated, and ongoing anonymity" of actual field study with the misleadingly "rapid, focused, and framed" character of nature documentaries, which he characterizes as "a potent distillation of someone else's waiting designed just for me" (cited in Armbruster, 1998, 223).

Such criticisms seem relevant in light of the latest chapter of wildlife television history. Beginning in 1985, the Discovery Channel (Discovery Communications) has brought wildlife films to cable television audiences with such widely anticipated programming as their yearly *Shark Week* (1987–present), a full week of celebrity-hosted programming on sharks, and *Deadliest Catch* (2005–present), which portrays the extremely dangerous work of Alaskan king crab fishermen. In 1996, Discovery launched the Animal Planet channel, which offers round-the-clock programming treating many dimensions of human-animal experience: *Dogs 101* and *Cats 101* (2008–present) describe the history and characteristics of cat breeds for current and future pet owners; *River Monsters* (2009–present, Icon Films), features "extreme angler" Jeremy Wade tracking ferocious fish the world over; and *Whale Wars* (2008–present, RIVR Media), a reality television program, follows the Sea Shepherd Society's attempts to protest and harass illegal whaling operations. The ferocity captured in many of these programs' themes (and animal "actors") partly reflects Animal Planet's 2008 relaunch, which included a bold new logo, a new tagline ("Surprisingly Human"), and more aggressive program offerings designed for a more mature audience. Eschewing older wildlife film conventions, and its once family-oriented tone, Animal Planet introduced reality television-style melodrama, including a new emphasis on visceral sights, sounds, and feelings over the presentation of facts. As President and General Manager of Animal Planet Media Marjorie Kaplan, explained, "We're being more aggressive and tapping into the instinctual nature of compelling animal content" (cited in Becker, 2008).

One of Animal Planet's most popular programs (predating the relaunch) puts such questions of wildlife film aesthetics in an intriguing perspective: *The Crocodile Hunter* (1997–2004), starring charismatic Australian wildlife expert Steve Irwin and his wife, Terri. Together, Steve and Terri owned and operated Australia Zoo (in Queensland), a reptile preserve and rehabilitation facility that Irwin had inherited from his parents, and Irwin also became involved in numerous conservation initiatives, including the Steve Irwin Conservation Foundation (since renamed Wildlife Warriors) and the International Crocodile Rescue, before his death in 2006. His celebrity extended beyond the television series, with multiple appearances on *The Tonight Show with Jay Leno*, a starring role in a

Steve and Terri Irwin of the TV show *The Crocodile Hunter* in 1999. Irwin was killed on Sept. 4, 2006, by a stingray barb during a diving expedition. (AP Photo/ Russell McPhedran)

2002 FedEx ad campaign, several ventures into film, including *Dr. Doolittle II* (2001), *Happy Feet* (2006), and *The Crocodile Hunter: Collision Course* (2002), and the naming of a newly discovered species of turtle (*Elseya irwini*) to his credit—making him a ubiquitous voice for conservation. *The Crocodile Hunter* is chiefly remembered for Irwin's hands-on, occasionally violent encounters with his animal subjects, accompanied by his enthused narration. Irwin's knowledge of the animals he showcased came from lifelong experience (which included some youthful crocodile wrestling) rather than formal training, and his environmentalist agenda was always in evidence, aligning him with a new trend in wildlife programming that Mark Berettini identifies as "adventure activism." This new form paradoxically mixes conservation messages with "dangerous, exciting, and sometimes violent human-interactions." Berettini quotes Irwin in explaining how this seemingly "uneasy" combination can potentially motivate viewers:

> I have to get right, fair smack into the action because this day has come where the audience, you, need to come with me and be there with that animal because if we can touch people with wildlife then they want to save it. Gone are the days of sitting back on the long lens tripod and looking at wildlife way over there. (cited in Berettini, 2005)

The urgency of our ecological crisis, according to this logic, calls for an equally urgent form of filmmaking: one that is fast-paced, action-packed, and emotionally engaging. While winning new audiences to the cause of environmental conservation through more appealing filmmaking seems a worthy goal, the history of wildlife television suggests that the journey from film viewer to committed environmentalist is slightly more complicated. The nature that we see portrayed in wildlife films is best understood as a cultural artifact, a product of cinematography, editing, script, music, and all the other human-directed processes that produce any other kind of film; it can reveal as much, if not more, about its makers and its viewers as it can about nature itself.

CHARLOTTE AMANDA HAGOOD

See also: Celebrities (Arts); Green Cinema (Arts); Green Documentaries and Films (Arts); Television, Eco-Friendly Channels (Arts).

References

Armbruster, Karla. 1998. "Creating the World We Must Save: The Paradox of Television Nature Documentaries." In Richard Kerridge and Neil Sammells, eds., *Writing the Environment: Ecocritism and Literature*. London: Zed Books.

Becker, Anne. 2008. "Animal Planet Changes Its Stripes." *Broadcasting and Cable*. January 13. Available at: http://www.broadcastingcable.com/article/111964-Animal_Planet_Changes_Its_Stripes.php.

Beinart, William, and Katie McKeown. 2009. "Wildlife Media and Representation of Africa, 1950s to the 1970s." *Environmental History* 14:3 (July): 429–452.

Berettini, Mark L. 2005. "'Danger! Danger! Danger!' or When Animals Might Attack: Adventure Activism and Wildlife Film and Television." *Scope* 1 (February). Available at: http://www.scope.nottingham.ac.uk/issue.php?issue=1.

Bousé, Derek. 2001. *Wildlife Films*. Philadelphia: University of Pennsylvania Press.

"Marty Stouffer." 2011. *The Encyclopedia of Arkansas History and Culture.* Central Arkansas Library System. Available at: http://www.encyclopediaofarkansas.net/encyclopedia/entry-detail.aspx?entryID=4427.

McDonald, Scott. 2006. "Up Close and Political: Three Short Ruminations on Ideology in the Nature Film." *Film Quarterly* 59:3 (Spring): 4–21.

Mitman, Gregg. 1999. *Reel Nature: America's Romance with Wildlife on Film.* Cambridge, MA: Harvard University Press.

VIDEO GAMES

Video games arose during the late 1960s and 1970s at about the same time as the growth of environmentalism, but their technological basis and digital and virtual nature did not make them likely candidates for involvement in the green movement, so it was some time before the two found a connection. Today, however, they can be connected to the green movement in two ways: through their form (since they consume energy) and through their content (which can be designed to teach and encourage green ideas and practices).

As electronic devices that consume energy, home video game console systems should be turned off when not in use. A 2008 report from the Natural Resources Defense Council reported that many game consoles are left on continuously, and that over 11 billion kilowatt hours a year of wasted energy, costing consumers over $1 billion, could be saved by turning them off (Horowitz, 2008). According to the report, of the three seventh-generation consoles, the Nintendo uses the least energy at 16 watts, while the Microsoft Xbox 360 uses 119 watts, and the Sony PlayStation 3 uses 150 watts. Sony does feature an online update that helps power management in the system, and both the Xbox 360 and the PlayStation 3 have auto-shutdown modes, but these have to be enabled by the user.

Some companies have designed their systems to be energy efficient. San Diego–based Zeebo Inc. has produced the Zeebo console, which is aimed at consumers in emerging markets in Brazil, India, China, and Mexico, and which uses only 1 watt of power, making it by far the most power-efficient contemporary system (Aslinger, 2010). Packaging is another area where costs to the environment can be reduced. Like the music industry, some game companies have reduced the amount of packaging surrounding their products, and online distribution of games has eliminated the need for packaging altogether.

Games also can encourage the green movement by teaching and embodying environmentalist ideas in an interactive, educational format. Some of the earliest games that could be arguably connected to the green movement would include *SimCity* (1989) and *SimEarth* (1990), which simulated environments and required players to manage resources to keep their cities and planets healthy. The design of *SimEarth* was even assisted by James Lovelock, author of the *Gaia Hypothesis*, which looks at a planet's organic and inorganic elements as one big self-regulating system. Since then, a number of games have contained green themes, like *Awesome Possum . . . Kicks Dr. Machino's Butt* (1993), in which players collect recyclable bottles and answer questions about the environment, or *Oddworld: Abe's Oddysee* (1997), about environmental destruction. More recently, one can find green games ranging from casual games, like Nintendo's *Chibi-Robo Park Patrol* (2007) or National Geographic's *Plan It Green* (2009), to serious games likes the urban-planning simulator *IBM CityOne* (2010) or Red Redemption's *Climate Challenge* (2006) and *Fate of the World* (2011). Other games, like the experimental game *Flower* (2009), also can evoke green themes in more subtle ways, causing players to consider the natural world and our effects on it.

Mark J. P. Wolf

See also: Green Movement (Activism).

References

Aslinger, Ben. 2010. "Video Games for the 'Next Billion'?: The Launch of the Zeebo Console." *Velvet Light Trap* 66 (Fall): 15–25.

Horowitz, Noah. 2008. "Lowering the Cost of Play: Improving Energy Efficiency of Video Game Consoles." November. Available at: http://www.nrdc.org/energy/consoles/contents.asp.

Economics, Business, and Industry

ADVERTISING

Advertising is most commonly defined as a type of mass communication designed to increase the sale of goods and services. It is a technique of marketing practice—a channel through which goods and services travel from producer to purchaser. Advertising is also a method of influence, as evinced by public relations and political advertising. Whether it is employed to sell automobiles, used to portray a positive image of an oil company in response to public outrage at an environmental disaster, or engaged so as to obfuscate the ties to special interest of an unctuous candidate for public office, advertising is the art and science of influence and persuasion. Advertising is not a phenomenon restricted to the American experience. But as the world's first and oldest postindustrial, consumer-driven, service economy, advertising occupies a prominent place in the political, social, and economic life of the United States. Advertising's important role in our national life is evident in the $131.1 billion spent by advertisers in 2010 to influence the purchasing behavior of U.S. consumers. Advertising is the language of the marketplace. The persuasiveness of its rhetoric is measured in brand loyalty and market share. Advertising's purpose is to increase consumption. It is a business, and profit is its bottom line. As a form of mass communication, advertising is the logical result of the ascent of mass production in the late 19th and early 20th centuries.

Advertising reflects American cultural values. Depending on one's point of view, these values are either worthy of emulation or woefully deficient. In a country where consumer spending accounts for 70 percent of the gross domestic product, it is easy to defend advertising's important and necessary role in the U.S. economy. But with less than 5 percent of the world's population, the United States uses 21 percent of the world's energy. This fact alone is a sufficient critique of U.S. consumption. By extension, a critique of consumption is a critique of advertising. Certainly, criticism of U.S. consumption and U.S. advertising is warranted. When reduced to its lowest common denominator, consumption is not so much about the consumption of goods as it is about the consumption of raw materials. By this measure, a child born in the United States today will use 3.6 million pounds of minerals, fuels, and metals in his or her lifetime. This same child will be exposed to 6 to 10 hours of television advertisements each week. At adulthood, this child—now grown up—will be exposed to 600 to 625 advertisements each day. Television and radio, newspapers and magazines, billboards and direct mail, personal computers and smart phones—these are the media where advertising will deliver its principal message—consumption. From their first disposable diaper to their first must-have brand-name pharmaceutical quick-fix for adult diseases of aging linked to a lifetime of overconsumption of fat and sugar, an American child born today can expect to live 78.37 years—or depending on how you look at—can expect to consume 125.85 pounds of raw materials daily in the journey from cradle to grave. Just as raw materials are refined and produced into consumer goods, so too does advertising refine consumption from basic biological necessity into a complex finished product of idea and image. Advertising transforms consumption from biological necessity into the social act of consumption as consumerism.

In recent decades, a growing awareness of the human impact on the environment has increased the number of goods and services advertised as being green—advertisements that focus on the relationship between goods and services and their impact on the biophysical environment; advertisements that convey a positive image of the consumer's environmental awareness, concern, and stewardship; or advertisements that communicate a corporate image of social responsibility and commitment to sustainability in manufacturing processes, labor and community relations, corporate earnings, and corporate growth. But is what makes an advertisement green the same thing as the qualities and processes that make a product or service or business model green? When we say something is green or environmentally or eco-friendly, what is implied by these labels? When a claim is made that something is good for the environment, what is the definition of "environment" that informs our assessment? Irrespective of whether or not an advertisement truly touts a product with little to no impact on the biophysical environment, or if the advertisement makes false claims of greenness to sell goods—a practice known as greenwashing—advertising must be understood as a communication practice rooted in the episteme of environmentalism, a centuries-long narrative grounded in the ideas of European enlightenment science and philosophy. As a product of the enlightenment, environmentalism privileges humankind's preeminence in, and domination of, the natural world. Environmentalism sustains liberal capitalism and its faith in science, technology, bureaucratic management, and legislative regulatory solutions in the management of natural resources and raw materials.

Today, with the scientific community itself recognizing that the products of science and technology are contributing to global warming and worldwide depletion of natural resources, our enlightenment-based faith in cornucopian progress is now in question. Advertising's experience in promulgating the green attributes of products and services has mostly failed, resulting in consumer distrust and the subsequent governmental regulation of environmental claims in advertising. Centuries-old thinking based on misguided assumptions about limitless resources now forces new ways of thinking about the purpose and habits of consumption, forcing advertisers to think ecologically—even while it has yet to master its environmental voice. The great challenge for advertising is to remain relevant as a method of marketing communications, as consumer consciousness begins a shift from environmentalism's anthropocentric assumptions to ecologism's holistic and synergistic view of humankind's place in the world. Advertising as a technique of mass communication illustrates that the impact of global warming extends to our use of language as a means of exchange, forcing us to search for new ways to express ourselves within the rubric of enlightenment-based presumptions about the primacy of acquisition and consumption in the face of ecological imperatives for the redistribution of wealth.

An obstacle in the transformation of advertising from an environ-centric to an eco-centric discourse is that the dearth of quality scholarship addressing the historical origins of green advertising suffers doubly from anachronistic analyses that privilege false watersheds in the emergence of the so-called green consumer. Indeed, the almost ritual identification of Rachel Carson's *Silent Spring* (1962) and the first celebration of Earth Day (1970) in much of marketing literature as *the* seminal events in the emergence of green advertising and the green consumer fails to consider the impact of many other publications of which Vance Packard's critique of planned obsolescence in *The Waste Makers* (1961) and the Club of Rome's critique of environmentalism in *The Limits of Growth* (1972) are but two examples. Where Carson's book is given preeminence, no mention is made of her public relations work as an employee of the U.S. Bureau of Fisheries in the 1930s, thus neglecting the role of government in the growth of environmental consciousness. Where the Club of Rome's important book is mentioned in passing, little to no reference is made to the role of this international think tank's impact on monetary policy or the far-reaching consequences of its research on the unabated effort at identifying new green consumers. Where scholarship attends to identifying and modeling consumer behavior, no attention is paid to the impact of filmmaker Frank Capra's 1958 educational film on air pollution and global warming, *Unchained Goddess*, thus leaving unexplored the impact of Earth science education on the emergence of environmental and ecological consciousness in the first generation of green consumers.

Also unexamined is the post–World War II growth of higher education—a phenomenon itself of the postindustrial service economy—and the impact of marketing departments in schools and colleges across the United States in the epistemology of advertising theory and practice. Although the Vietnam War, the Arab oil embargo, and the mid-20th-century constitutional crisis known as Watergate are also mentioned as important events in the emergence of green consumers and green advertising, no mention is made of the thousands of men and women who received their PhDs in marketing in the 1960s and 1970s and in which ways these events impacted them as teachers, scholars, and consumers. Scant attention is paid to the Ad Council's now iconic public service announcements on air and water pollution in the 1970s, nor does the literature explore the Ad Council's origins in the U.S. Office for War Information and its World War II advertising campaigns encouraging recycling and carpooling in ad campaigns steeped in racist portrayals of the enemy as competitor for natural resources.

Today, environmentalists' presumptions about humankind's ability to find a technological fix to global warming has reached an almost quasi-religious ludicrousness in extreme utopian visions and dollars-and-cents calculations on the science of terra-forming a life sustaining atmosphere on Mars. If in the lifetime of a child born today an extraterrestrial solution to the present ecological crisis comes into view, advertising need not question its relevancy. But because it is more likely that starting anew on Mars is not in the offing, the child born today will live in an Earth-based world where restraints on consumption are the new paradigm, and advertising will need to change if it is to remain relevant. As the enlightenment moved humankind beyond the constraints of the village, so too the enlightenment has brought humankind full circle in a revolution in communications that has brought us back to a global village. And like the village of old, that which is false or foolish in the global village of today can earn the derision and sanction of inhabitants. Advertising today—while trying to reconcile technological solutions to ecological degradation by selling the green attributes of products that are by their very nature unecological—still has a way to go if is to avoid offending a new generation of taste makers and opinion leaders whose criticisms of "conspicuous conservationists" can now go viral at the click of a button.

Advertisements for the hybrid passenger car illustrate the nature of advertising as a phenomenon of environmentalism, rather than as evidence of environmentalism's antithesis—ecologism. Hybrids are advertised as "environmentally friendly"—their owners are often portrayed in advertisements as harmoniously temperate consumers in a nation of fuel-guzzling, earth-unfriendly excessiveness. When we drive a hybrid (so one notable advertisement shows us), nature is anthropomorphized; each and every flower petal, blade of grass, and drop of water greets us with open arms in an expression of love and admiration for our environmental stewardship. Off message is the fact that hybrid batteries still rely on fossil fuel and still emit carbon dioxide. The difference in fossil fuel consumption between two consumers who drive 12,000 miles in one year in an energy-efficient passenger car at 38 highway miles per gallon versus a brand new hybrid at 50 highway miles per gallon is a mere 76 gallons of gasoline—a difference in carbon dioxide emissions easily counterbalanced by purchasing $30 in carbon offsets to cover the used car's lifetime emissions. A 30-second television commercial designed to sell a car cannot be expected to discuss environmentally preferable purchase decisions or to delve into other mundane details of ecological and political importance, such as the fact that a vital component of hybrid batteries is the rare earth metal dysprosium, with China mining over 95 percent of the world's known supply. Competition for dysprosium increases competition for alternatives to coal and fossil fuel. Dysprosium is an important component in nuclear reactor cooling systems and a key ingredient in emerging clean energy technologies. The world's biggest hybrid manufacturer's plan to bring 2 million vehicles per year to market will soon exhaust the world's known supply of dysprosium, with even the most conservative estimates asserting that by year 2015, a shortfall of dysprosium will impact America's vital national interests in much the same way Mideast oil has. Finite natural resources, competition for raw materials, and a worldwide population expected to exceed 9 billion people by 2050 do not make for good advertising copy or advertising image.

Commonsense and critical thinking are anathema to advertising because the power of advertising rests in advertisings' understanding of the power of emotional appeal. And no other product has been advertised with as much all-encompassing emotional appeal in America as has the automobile. Even in the face of inconvenient truths that bring questions of national security to the fore, advertisings' arsenal of influence still calibrates the utility of appeal to American cultural values like self-sufficiency, freedom, and independence. As manufacturing processes and fuel systems for passenger cars are arguably made greener through hybrids and other alternative fuels, the fact remains that today the average vehicle occupancy of a city bus is 26.6 passengers compared to 1.58 for a passenger car. But with America's axiomatic love affair with the automobile, riding the bus is not how one is supposed to define—much less live—the American Dream. While mass transit is logically the environmentally friendliest alternative, convenience trumps common sense. Common sense is anathema to advertising because the power of advertising is in its understanding of the power of the emotional appeal as a way to sell goods. Advertising knows how to use emotional appeal and knows when and where such appeals can increase sales. Recognizing that political ideology is emotionally laden, American cultural values are merely tools employed by advertising to achieve the bottom line.

Advertising in America reflects a national ideology steeped in a theology of perfectibility and a rejection of fixedness of class and status. But even beyond the uses of advertising's appeals to ideas and values of American culture, what does the future hold for advertising in America in light of climate change? By ever-consuming, ever-upgrading, and ever-trading in the old model for the new, one troublesome element of our cultural ethos is the notion that success is measured by the number and quality of our possessions. In order for advertising to remain relevant, it will need to come to terms with the unsustainable dominance of our unchecked consumption. Our present understanding of advertising and its role in the future obliges us to fully grasp the role it has come to play so as to determine its future usefulness in the face of enormous ecological challenges not only for the United States but for all humans and all forms of life around the world.

DAVID ALAN REGO

See also: Green Entrepreneurship (Economics); Green Marketing (Economics); Product Labeling (Economics).

References

Cialdini, Robert B. 1984. *Influence: How and Why People Agree to Things*. New York: Morrow.
Dobson, Andrew. 2007. *Green Political Thought*. Milton Park, Abingdon, Oxon: Routledge.
Federal Trade Commission. 2011. "Guides for the Use of Environmental Marketing Claims." Available at: http://ftc.gov/bcp/grnrule/guides980427.htm.
Fisk, George. 1974. *Marketing and the Ecological Crisis*. New York: Harper & Row.
Iyer, Easwar, and Bobby Banerjee. 1993. "Anatomy of Green Advertising." *Advances in Consumer Research* 20: 494–501.
Kangun, Norman, Les Carlson, and Steven Grove. 1991. "Environmental Advertising Claims: A Preliminary Investigation." *Journal of Public Policy and Marketing* 12 (Fall): 47–58.
Kilbourne, William E. 1995. "Green Advertising: Salvation or Oxymoron?" *Journal of Advertising* 24:2: 7–19.

Maslow, Abraham H. 1943. "A Theory of Human Motivation." *Psychological Review* 50: 370–396.

Meadows, Donella H., Jorgen Randers, and Dennis L. Meadows. 2004. *The Limits to Growth: The Thirty Year Update.* White River Junction, VT: Chelsea Green.

TerraChoice. 2011. "The Sins of Greenwashing, Home and Family Edition, 2010." Available at: http://sinsofgreenwashing.org/findings/greenwashing-report-2010/.

Wells, William, John Burnett, and Sandra E. Moriarty. 2006. *Advertising: Principles and Practice.* Upper Saddle River, NJ: Pearson/Prentice-Hall.

White, Lynn. 1967. "The Historical Roots of Our Ecological Crisis." *Science* 155: 1203–1207.

AGRICULTURE

There are more than 900 million acres of cropland in the United States and over 400 million acres of pasture for grazing livestock. That adds up to a lot of land, equipment, and money invested in providing food, fuel, and other products through agriculture. Today's agricultural landscape is much different from that of our ancestors who first domesticated plants and animals. Technology makes large-scale agriculture more efficient, increases yields, fights pests, and gives us the tools to expand operations into places once inaccessible.

As we expand our agricultural operations, the natural order is forever changed. Some of these changes are detrimental to plant and animal species, including humans. There is a growing movement to change the direction of U.S. agriculture away from industrialized production toward sustainable agriculture. Also, within modern industrialized agriculture there is an increase in conservation and efficiency practice implementation. Ecological considerations are becoming more important as available land is increasingly populated.

Industrial Agriculture

This is a broad categorization, but it describes today's agricultural practices. Technology is the backbone of modern agriculture. From the tractors, to the combines, and the seeds, everything is becoming increasingly sophisticated. Technology has harnessed rivers and aquifers to irrigate plants and plowed under millions of acres of native prairie and woodlands. It has also increased yields worldwide. The scientific advances in agriculture have the option of making genetic alterations to nature.

Genetically modified (GM) foods are those that have had genes from a different organism combined with their own. This process is known as recombinant DNA technology. Genetic traits are selected for a variety of reasons, such as improving crop yield, adding vitamins, drought tolerance, and repelling insects. In the future, food could be engineered to produce medicines and plastics. Immunity to specific herbicides is standard in crops today, and herbicide rotation is usually part of the program, as is crop rotation. This is an important debate, because any changes could be irreversible.

The potential problems associated with GM crops are big concerns. This is cutting-edge research, and we are pioneers in this world of genetic manipulation.

It is unknown if there are any negative impacts on human health or the nutrition of our food. Further, these genes could spread to non-GM varieties, thus polluting the natural pool of genes and forever changing the course of evolution for a species. This is an entirely new kind of concern for humanity. Technology continues to explore the boundaries of ethics. Seed banks have been established around the world to provide genetic libraries of non-GM varieties. One extreme example is the Norwegian island of Svalbard. North of Norway in the arctic, the Svalbard Global Seed Vault is designed to offer protection against loss of crop diversity. It is a huge underground freezer created out of international concern, and the seed reserve will stay frozen without electricity. Universities in the United States have smaller-scale seed banks serving the same function.

From an environmental perspective, there are some reasons to like GM organisms (GMOs). Crops with built-in pest resistance are designed for specific threats to the crop, thus reducing the killing of species that happen to be in the vicinity when pesticides are applied. This is also positive for soil, water, and air quality. The chemicals needed to combat the same organisms are applied broadly and get into the soil, runoff into water supplies, or volatilize into the atmosphere. Crops can also be tailored to reduce their impact on the environment through decreased water consumption and increased yields on fewer acres. This would leave more room for restoration and protection of natural ecosystems.

GMOs are a recent arrival to the world stage, and they have been adopted in many of the world's largest agriculture producing countries, including the United States. The crops will experience their largest growth in developing countries in the coming years. New genetic advances will be made, making the early generation's products look primitive. Technology is at work in the seeds, but DNA combination is not the only type of technology utilized.

Precision agriculture is a growing part of industrial agriculture. Here, space age technology is used to tailor crop management to individual fields. Tractors and combines can be equipped with global positioning systems (GPS), which are combined with yield monitors. Maps are produced showing intrafield variations in yield and compared to soil quality data to allow for variable fertilizer application. This reduces the amount of chemicals applied to fields, which equates to fewer chemicals in our air, water, soil, and ultimately us. Autodrive technology for tractors is also being developed to allow for speed and power variations that can only be achieved by a computer. This allows for adjustments to be made based on topography while the tractor is in motion.

Precision agriculture has been shown to reduce fuel consumption and increase yields of some crops. However, some of these technologies are too cost-prohibitive, given the difficulty of predicting yield based on interconnected complex variables. This too is new science and involves advanced geographic information systems (GIS) and robotics.

Irrigation efficiency is another field that technology has improved. The center pivot sprinkler system is a common water-saving technology. Water pivots around a center point, and crops grow in the circular pattern of the sprinkler's path. Water is more efficiently applied than furrow, or ditch, irrigation. An even more efficient

Center pivot irrigation system on a Delaware farm in 2008. This system is using Low Elevation Spray Application (LESA), which uses less water and reduces evaporation. (U.S. Department of Agriculture)

system is the subsurface drip system. Soaking hoses are buried in the field, and water is applied directly to the root zone. This reduces water loss to evaporation. Finally, furrow irrigation also has conservation methods available. Surge valves, which increase water-use efficiency by limiting runoff, are commonly used, as are reuse pits, which capture irrigation runoff in order to reuse it.

These technologies ultimately help to increase profitability of farming operations, but they also provide an environmental benefit. Field mapping provides detailed information about the type of land being farmed. The maps produced allow for unprofitable lands to be retired or entered into conservation programs.

Today, nearly 40 million acres of agricultural land are enrolled in a federal conservation program. The Conservation Reserve Program (CRP) and Wetlands Reserve Program (WRP) are the two main sources of funds for farmers. The goal is to take marginal farm ground that is subject to erosion, or what was once a wetland, and restore it to a state similar to what it had been before it was plowed. Land owners receive cost-sharing rent payments to establish the natural plants on their land, if it qualifies. Both programs are voluntary, and they create long-term contracts to preserve natural ecosystems. In parts of the country, there are more applications than funds available for these incentive programs.

There are also programs available to help farmers reduce soil erosion. This natural process can be exacerbated by agricultural processes, such as tilling the soil and leaving the soil without ground cover. When runoff encounters poorly managed soil, it can create large washouts and gullies. In order to counter this, land owners plant highly susceptible slopes, and other settings conducive to erosion, to native vegetation buffer strips, sometimes in alternative sections with crops. Wind erosion is another concern, and it is reduced by planting trees for wind breaks. Permanent native vegetation cover can also limit the wind's ability to carry off the topsoil. Farmers can also employ low-till or no-till techniques to reduce soil erosion; however, this can sometimes lead to an increase in the use of synthetic pesticides.

Sustainable Agriculture

Sustainable agriculture seeks to meet present-day needs without putting future generations' needs at risk of not being met. While industrial agriculture shapes nature to suit humans' needs, sustainable agriculture is based on limiting human impact on nature. Profitability is still a concern, but it is grounded in eco-centric principles.

Greenovator: Alternative Farming Systems Information Center, USDA

The U.S. Department of Agriculture's (USDA) Alternative Farming Systems Information Center (AFSIC) provides resources and information about sustainable food production systems and concepts. It offers support for several sustainable food initiatives, including Community Supported Agriculture (CSA) and "Know Your Farmer, Know Your Food." AFSIC is part of the USDA's National Agricultural Library (NAL).

AFSIC was founded in 1985 by Jayne Maclean as part of the NAL. Its initial funding came from the USDA's Low-Input Sustainable Agriculture (LISA) program, which later became the Sustainable Agriculture Research and Education (SARE) program. While the center's primary method of communication has been the Internet, in the late 1980s and early 1990s, it produced the "AFSIC Oral History Interview" series, which includes 11 videotaped interviews with leaders in sustainable agriculture.

Currently, AFSIC is part of three USDA programs that offer services to support sustainable agriculture. The other two are SARE, which offers funding resources for farmers, and the National Sustainable Agriculture Information Service (ATTRA), which answers questions about sustainable agriculture. AFSIC is staffed by librarians under the NAL. The AFSIC Web site lists a large number of publications and resources on sustainable agriculture, broken into the following categories: sustainability in agriculture (in general); alternative crops and plants; education and research; farm energy options; farms and community; grazing systems and alternative livestock breeds; alternative marketing and business practices; organic production; and soil and water management.

TREVOR L. DRAKE

Organic farming is probably the most recognized form of sustainable agriculture in the nation. Americans see the term at the grocery store, which is why federal standards were enacted. Before the legislation became the law of the land, there were differing sets of standards and requirements, which caused confusion among consumers and producers. Today, all organic operations must comply with these federal standards. Commercial operations that make more than $5,000 annually must go through a certification process, which takes a few years to complete. Some of the key standards include bans on certain chemicals, synthetic pesticides and fertilizers, and genetically modified organisms. This is completely the opposite of industrialized agriculture.

The central focus of organic farming is the use of natural management techniques in the production of crops. Natural methods are the primary defenses against pests. Crop rotation and plant diversity are important proactive strategies for keeping unwanted insects and funguses away. Fertilizer is also a naturally produced input in organic farming, primarily animal manure. This method of production is increasingly demanded by consumers, which is changing the composition of grocery store inventories.

In 2012, there are more than 4 million acres of organic agriculture land in the United States, nearly 54 percent of which is cropland. There are more than 125,000 additional acres currently being transitioned to organic. The transition period allows for any banned chemicals to filter out of the soil. As the demand for organically produced food increases, more land will be converted from industrialized agricultural land. The average organic farm size is 285 acres, less than half of a one-by-one-mile section of land. These are generally not large operations and often have local distribution channels.

The "locally produced" movement seeks to reduce the amount of pollution generated by our food production by limiting the amount of miles the food is transported to get to your table. There are an increasing number of vegetable cooperatives being started, especially near urban areas. Some of these farms operate on yearly subscription fees, which buys the subscriber vegetables on a regular basis. Urban agriculture is an expanding enterprise, as people seek to incorporate more nature into their concrete-filled environments.

Land is at a premium in metropolitan areas, so urban agriculturists have to use limited space creatively. Vacant lots are being cleaned and converted into community gardens, providing produce to those who help with the operation. Roof-top gardening is another form of urban agriculture that is becoming more common. Systems can be installed to allow soil to be placed directly on the roofs of buildings. Not only do these two examples provide locally produced food in cities, but they also increase green space in a place where it is often severely lacking. This improves

Greenovation: Sustainable Beef Production

On the high plains of Colorado, sustainable beef production is centered on coexisting with nature. The Lasater Ranch developed the Beefmaster cattle breed as part of a project to raise them as part of the natural ecosystem. No hormones or antibiotics are given to calves, nor are predators removed from the equation. Rotational grazing is used to allow the cattle to harvest grasses, till soil, and provide fertilizer in a manner similar to the bison herds that once roamed the plains. Lasater cattle are not fed grains and are not confined, which reduces demand for industrially produced corn. Operations like this have the potential to make our food supply more ecologically sustainable.

aesthetics of neighborhoods, reduces storm water run-off, and perhaps most importantly, reduces the urban heat island effect. This effect is so named because it describes the higher temperatures that occur in cities as compared to the rural lands in close proximity to them. Green spaces decrease the amount of heat stored in concrete and asphalt.

Finally, as with industrialized agriculture, soil is essential to sustainable farming. It provides substrate in which the roots will grow and anchor, which in turn prevents erosion. Sustainable agriculture incorporates perennial plants and year-round ground cover, when possible, in order to help maintain the integrity of the local soil ecology.

Summary

There are multiple environmental movements occurring within the field of agriculture. Industrialized production is the largest agricultural sector, and implementing small conservation techniques across the country has a big multiplier effect on the nation's ecosystems. Whether it is fertilizer application or irrigation timing, resources are invested to get the most return on the dollar. This is a win-win situation for producers and environmental advocates, as often improving the bottom line removes potential pollutants from the ecosystem or reduces the amount of land or water required for production, ultimately reducing the ecological footprint of our food production. There are many programs available for farmers, providing them with incentives to take marginal land out of production and return it to a more natural state. Here again, the benefits are both economic and environmental. While these examples have little impact on the use of GMOs and synthetic chemicals in general, there is a growing movement to address these concerns.

Sustainable agriculture, spearheaded by organic farming, is antithetical to modern industrial agriculture. Working symbiotically with nature is the focus of this movement. Soil, water, and air quality are improved when natural farming practices are used. Further, ecosystem health is not as threatened by synthetic chemical pollution or any potential negative consequences that might result from the use of GMOs. Converting a farm to certified organic is a big commitment; it is labor intensive and requires time. When the produce is sold locally, the amount of fuel used to transport crops decreases, thus reducing pollution.

As our population increases, more consideration needs to be given to the ecological footprint of our agricultural systems. Nature provides ecosystem services, without which we could not survive. Working more symbiotically with natural process in all forms of agriculture helps these ecological processes to function as they are supposed to. If symbiosis is not of primary concern, natural ecosystems might be thrown out of balance, the effects of which could even negatively impact the productivity of the agriculture that helped to create the problem in the first place. This is not a cycle that is conducive to the sustainability of our society. Instead, working with natural cycles and tailoring agriculture to local conditions offer the potential to sustainably feed ourselves for generations to come.

NATHAN EIDEM

See also: Conservation Reserve Program (documents); Farming, Conventional (Economics); Farming, Organic (Economics); Garden, Home (Health); Land and Habitat Reclamation and Restoration (Environment); Natural Resources Conservation Service Watershed and Easement Programs (documents); Urban Agriculture (Food).

References

"Agriculture." Available at: http://www.trimble.com/agriculture/.

Crop Trust. "Svalbard Global Seed Vault." Available at: http://www.croptrust.org/main/arcticseedvault.php?itemid=211.

Duram, L. A. 2006. *Good Growing: Why Organic Farming Works*. Lincoln: University of Nebraska Press.

Environmental Protection Agency (EPA). "Organic Farming." Available at: http://www.epa.gov/agriculture/torg.html#Organic%20Foods%20Production%20Act.

Human Genome Project. "Genetically Modified Foods and Organisms." Available at: http://www.ornl.gov/sci/techresources/Human_Genome/elsi/gmfood.shtml.

National Aeronautics Space Administration (NASA). "Precision Agriculture." Available at: http://www.ghcc.msfc.nasa.gov/precisionag/.

Pollan, M. 2006. *The Omnivore's Dilemma: A Natural History of Four Meals*. New York: Penguin.

Schimmelpfennig, D., and R. Ebel. 2011. "On the Doorstep of the Information Age: Recent Adoption of Precision Agriculture." *Economic Information Bulletin* 80. Available at: http://www.ers.usda.gov/Publications/EIB80/EIB80.pdf.

Thompson, S. A. 1999. *Water Use, Management, and Planning in the United States*. San Diego: Academic.

UC Davis. "What Is Sustainable Agriculture?" Available at: http://www.sarep.ucdavis.edu/concept.htm.

University of Wyoming. "Lasater Grasslands Beef: A Case Study on Natural and Sustainable Meats." WEMC FS#10-08. Available at: http://ag.arizona.edu/arec/wemc/nichemarkets/10grasslandsbeef.pdf.

UNL Water. "Agricultural Irrigation." Available at: http://water.unl.edu/web/cropswater/centerpivot.

U.S. Department of Agriculture (USDA). "Alternative Farming Systems Information Center." Available at: http://afsic.nal.usda.gov/nal_display/index.php?tax_level=1&info_center=2.

U.S. Department of Agriculture (USDA). "2007 Census of Agriculture." Available at: http://www.agcensus.usda.gov/Publications/2007/Full_Report/Volume_1,_Chapter_1_US/index.asp.

U.S. Department of Agriculture (USDA). "Conservation Reserve Program," Available at: http://www.nrcs.usda.gov/programs/CRP.

U.S. Department of Agriculture (USDA). "2008 Organic Survey." Available at: http://www.agcensus.usda.gov/Publications/2007/Online_Highlights/Organics/.

U.S. Department of Agriculture (USDA). "Precision, Geospatial & Sensor Technologies." Available at: http://www.csrees.usda.gov/precisiongeospatialsensortechnologies.cfm.

U.S. Department of Agriculture (USDA). "Urban Agriculture." Available at: http://afsic.nal.usda.gov/nal_display/index.php?info_center=2&tax_level=2&tax_subject=301&level3_id=0&level4_id=0&level5_id=0&topic_id=2719&&placement_default=0.

U.S. Department of Agriculture (USDA). "Wetlands Reserve Program." Available at: http://www.nrcs.usda.gov/programs/WRP.

AIRLINES

Flying travelers between points on the globe creates certain undesirable, though to some extent unavoidable, consequences, some of which may be harmful to the environment. More serious among these are the production of polluting emissions (e.g., carbon monoxide, oxides of nitrogen, smoke, and unburned hydrocarbons), the creation of excessive noise, particularly around urban airports, and the introduction of greenhouse gases (GHG) into the atmosphere. In terms of environmental effects, perhaps less significant (though certainly not insignificant) would be the application of deicing fluids, which may contaminate surface and groundwater, and the creation of contrails, which some speculate trap heat to raise night temperatures and reduce diurnal thermal averages (Travis et al., 2002) while contributing to the Earth's changing climate (Lee et al., 2009). Further, the heavy consumption of hydrocarbon fuels (primarily kerosine hydrocarbon fractions) in aircraft engines (gas turbines, a.k.a. powerplants) raises questions of sustainability. Interrelated forces and factors acting over multiple decades have both compelled and provided incentives for domestic airlines to become more eco-friendly by mitigating many of these problems. Moreover, because aviation is an international endeavor, these same influences have globally reduced the environmental impacts attributable to the operation of transport category aircraft (airliners).

Beginning with the Wright brothers' first flight, the development of aircraft and the advancement of aviation was largely an American endeavor. Initially, the driving force of this evolutionary process was improving aircraft performance (i.e., flying higher and faster), with little regard for fuel efficiency or environmental impacts. In the decade of the 1970s, several forces converged, acting in concert to largely alter aircraft manufacturers' design goals and the needs of the airlines. Much of the impetus for change was social and political as governments and regulatory agencies, responding to public pressure, instituted pollution control and noise abatement mandates. Congress enacted the Clean Air Act in 1970, and, shortly thereafter, the Los Angeles County Air Pollution Control District and the San Diego Air Pollution Control District became the first regulatory agencies to establish limits for oxides of nitrogen (NOx) emitted by gas turbines (NETL, 2011). Subsequently, multiple regulatory agencies (e.g., the Environmental Protection Agency, Federal Aviation Administration, the Civil Aviation Authorities of several countries, the International Civil Aviation Organization, and the Joint Aviation Authorities, which later morphed into the European Aviation Safety Agency) developed guidelines and regulations for the development of cleaner operating aircraft power plants. About the same time, Congress authorized the Federal Aviation Administration (FAA) to implement a plan (in several stages) to regulate aircraft design and equipment for the purpose of reducing noise emissions. A 1969 FAA regulation established noise standards for turbojet aircraft of new design; an amendment in 1973 extended the same standards to all new aircraft of older design. Defined in 1977, still more stringent Stage III regulations took effect on December 31, 1999. (Aircraft are currently manufactured according to Stage IV standards. The criteria for these most recently enacted regulations were largely developed by the international aviation community under the auspices of the International Civil Aviation Organization, or ICAO.)

During the early 1970s, fuel prices increased dramatically. Between 1973 and 1975, the cost of aircraft fuel tripled (Dawson, 1991) as a result of the oil quotas and price-fixing strategies of an international cartel, the Organization of Petroleum Exporting Countries (OPEC). Compared to the 1950s, the cost of aircraft fuel had increased by 1,000 percent (Dawson, 1991) at a time when the U.S. fleet of commercial aircraft consumed approximately 10 billion gallons of jet fuel each year. Therefore, events of the 1970s provided the impetus to abandon the traditional goal of going higher and faster to solve the increasingly pressing problems of reducing specific fuel consumption, as well as the environmental problems of noise and pollutant emissions.

In 1970, the world's first commercial high-bypass fan, the CF6-6, installed on the McDonnell Douglas DC-10-10, entered service. Because, in comparison to a turbojet engine or low bypass fan powerplant, a high-bypass fan accelerates a larger mass of air to a lesser velocity (for a given level of thrust), design advantages inhere to the use of a higher bypass ratio. (The bypass ratio is the amount of air discharged by the fan around the powerplant compared to that entering the core engine.) One advantage is attributable to the fact that, as a rough rule of thumb, the amount of energy required to accelerate a mass of air varies as the square of change in velocity. Thus, because a turbofan accelerates a larger mass of air to a lower velocity than a turbojet, the fan engine is inherently more fuel efficient—that is, generally speaking, for a given level of propulsive force, the higher the bypass ratio, the more fuel efficient the powerplant. A second advantage is that the air discharged by the fan contains higher-frequency, lower-energy air disturbances, making turbofans much quieter than turbojets. Further, turbofan powerplants, in comparison to the older turbojet engines, produced less emissions, particularly smoke and particles of unburned hydrocarbons.

For the preceding reasons, due to the introduction of the CF6-6 and other early high bypass fan engines (e.g., Pratt & Whitney's JT9-D and the Rolls-Royce RB211), the airlines were able to meet the new noise and emission standards that began taking effect in the 1970s. However, despite the improved fuel efficiency afforded by the new high-bypass engines, the reduction in the airline industry's fuel consumption was not enough to offset the dramatic increases in fuel prices that were then occurring. Consequently, Congress attempted to resolve the problem of skyrocketing fuel costs by funding the Energy Efficient Engine, or 3-E, program. Under the congressional mandate, the National Aeronautics and Space Administration (NASA) was to work with powerplant and component manufacturers (e.g., Pratt & Whitney, General Electric, Hamilton Standard, Dowty Rotol) to develop enhanced technologies that would produce more fuel-efficient aircraft powerplants. A happy bit of serendipity is that, often, reducing fuel consumption produces major reductions in pollutant emissions and also in noise levels associated with a given powerplant. For example, the two-stage or dual-zone combustors, improved fuel nozzles, and clearance control strategies that engineers developed during the 3-E program not only decreased fuel consumption, but also greatly reduced both carbon monoxide and NOx emissions, while improved airfoil aerodynamics and more efficient fan designs further reduced the noise signature of existing aircraft powerplants. Moreover because both NOx, a precursor to certain greenhouse gases, and CO_2, itself a GHG, are both reduced in more efficient combustor designs, these improvements also reduced the airlines' contribution of gases suspected of, in part, inducing global climate change. Thus, much of the advanced technology intended to make currently produced aircraft engines more environmentally friendly evolved from concepts developed several decades ago, during a turbulent period of change.

More recently, computers have contributed to the advancement of powerplant technology in ways that have made air travel more eco-friendly. Current technology powerplants use computers to precisely meter fuel as a function of various operating parameters. Such engines are said to have Full Authority Digital Engine Control (FADEC) systems. FADEC-managed fuel delivery systems have made aircraft gas turbines not only more fuel efficient, but, also, by producing less emissions, less harmful to the environment. Further, digital design techniques have greatly improved engine performance while reducing the environmental impacts attributable to commercial aviation. As an example, computers running computational fluid dynamics programs have provided the

Greenovation: Aircraft Emissions Carbon Trading Scheme

Most, if not all, environmental issues have an economic component, and the reduction of aircraft emissions is no exception. One approach to the reduction of greenhouse gas (GHG) emissions, the course of action favored by the countries comprising European Union (EU), is the implementation of a carbon trading scheme. According to the European Commission's Climate Action Web site (http://ec.europa.eu/clima/policies/ets/index_en.htm), "The EU Emissions Trading System (ETS) is a cornerstone of the EU's policy to combat climate change and its key tool for reducing industrial greenhouse gas emissions cost-effectively." The regulatory structure is basically a "cap-and-trade" framework in which airlines will pay for CO_2 emissions exceeding an established goal (or cap). More efficient operators may sell unused EU ETS credits to those airlines producing carbon dioxide in excess of their allotment, thus encouraging those producing greater amounts of pollutants to reduce their emissions.

But not everyone agrees that the inclusion of airlines in the EU ETS is cost-effective. Industry representatives have estimated that compliance through 2020 would cost U.S. airlines $3.1 billion USD while adding $57 to the cost of flying between New York and London (Rosenthal, 2011). Indian Environment Minister Jayanthi Natarajan was quoted as saying, "The EU's 'unilateral' imposition of a 'carbon tax' on aviation was 'disguised trade action taken in the name of the climate'" (Blaine, 2011). Canadian and Asian airlines have publically objected (EUbusiness, 2011), and China has reportedly canceled, in protest of the pending regulations, an order worth billions to the European aerospace company, Airbus (Der Spiegel, 2011). Even the United Nations and International Civil Aviation Organization have notified the EU that the proposed regulations violate state sovereignty and, further, will place an economic burden on airlines already struggling under heavy fuel costs (EUbusiness, 2011).

However, no entity has more vigorously objected to the pending ETS than the United States. Wendell Albright, director of the Barack Obama administration's Office of Aviation Negotiations at the State Department, has been quoted as saying, "The European Union is imposing this [EU ETS] on U.S. carriers without our agreement. . . . It is for the U.S. to decide on targets or appropriate action for U.S. airlines with respect to greenhouse gas emissions" (Rosenthal, 2011). Vice President for Environmental Affairs at the Air Transport Association of America (ATA) Nancy Young was quoted as saying, "the EU is 'attempting to regulate the airlines of the world . . . . The plan violates international law'" (Der Spiegel, 2011). Late in October 2011, the U.S. House passed a resolution, the European Union Emissions Trading Scheme Prohibition Act (H.R. 2594), making it illegal for U.S. airlines to participate in the EU's ETS. In December of that same year, John Thune (R-S.Dak.) introduced a similar bill in the Senate. American, United, and Continental Airlines and the ATA filed a law suit in the European Court of Justice, claiming that the unilateral imposition of ETS rules on U.S. airlines violates international aviation agreements.

As the Obama administration threatens the EU with an impeding trade war (GREENAIRonline.com, 2011), "European climate action commissioner Connie Hedegaard [said] there is 'no way' the European Union will budge on its decision to include aviation in its Emissions Trading Scheme" (Blaine, 2011). The EU's ETS regulations are scheduled to become effective early in 2012. As of this writing, resolution of the debate remains uncertain. However this issue is resolved, the debate over the economics, efficacy, and jurisdictional authority of the proposed ETS regulations, as applied to the airlines and air travel, represents a microcosm of what are often larger, more rancorous, and more widely publicized environmental debates.

means for engineers to further evolve more efficient fans, compressors, combustors, and turbines to the benefit of the environment. Most recently, powerplant manufacturers and the airlines (e.g., Lufthansa, KLM, Iberia, Air France, United, and Alaska Airlines), hoping to make the rapid transport of travelers more sustainable, have begun to experiment with renewable biofuels (Wall, 2011). The International Air Transport Association, an airline industry advocacy group, has established the goal of replacing, by 2017, at least 10 percent of the airlines' conventionally obtained (fractionated) kerosene with aviation-specific biofuels (Wall, 2009). Thus, in these many ways, attributable to a variety of influences and factors, air travel has become, over the preceding four to five decades, much more eco-friendly.

MICHAEL MOST

See also: Transportation, Automobile (Science); Transportation, Bicycle (Science); Transportation, Mass Transit (Science).

References

Blaine, S. 2011. "COP–17: EU Adamant on Aviation Emissions." Business Day. Available at: http://www.businessday.co.za/articles/Content.aspx?id=160655.

Dawson, V. P. 1991. *Engines and Innovation: Lewis Laboratory and American Propulsion Technology*. Washington, DC: National Aeronautics and Space Administration.

Der Spiegel. 2011. Spiegel Online International. "Emissions Trading Schemes." Available at: http://www.spiegel.de/international/europe/0,1518,777169,00.html.

EUbusiness. 2011. "EU Sticks to Airline Carbon Rules Despite UN Opposition." Available at: http://www.eubusiness.com/news–eu/us–airline–court–un.dbt/.

GREENAIRonline.com. 2011. "US DOT official warns of damaging trade war between US and EU over EU ETS." Available at: http://www.greenaironline.com/news.php?viewStory=1381.

Lee, D. S., D. W. Faheyb, P. M. Forsterc, P. J. Newtond, R. C. N. Wite, L. L. Lima, B. Owena, and R. Sausenf. 2009. "Aviation and Global Climate Change in the 21st Century." *Atmospheric Environment* 43: 3520–3537.

Mattingly, J. 1996. *Elements of Gas Turbine Propulsion.* Reston, VA: American Institute of Aeronautics and Astronautics/McGraw-Hill.

National Energy Technology Laboratory (NETL). 2011. Department of Energy, "Lean Pre-mixed Combustion," Available at: http://www.netl.doe.gov/technologies/coalpower/turbines/refshelf/handbook/3.2.1.2.pdf.

Rosenthal, E. 2011. "US and Europe Battle Over Carbon Fees for Airlines." *New York Times.* Available at: http://www.nytimes.com/2011/07/28/business/energy–environ ment/us–air–carriers–brace–for–emissions–fees–in–europe.html?pagewanted=all.

Timnat, Y. M. 1996. *Advanced Airbreathing Propulsion.* Malabar, FL: Krieger Publishing.

Travis, T. J., A. M. Carleton, and R. G. Lauritson. 2002. "Climatology: Contrails Reduce Daily Temperature Range." *Nature* 418: 601.

Wall, R. 2009. "Carbon-Trading Moves to Center Stage in Fight over Airline Emissions Standards." *Aviation Week & Space Technology* 171 (2009): 43–44.

Wall, R. 2011. "Fueling Debate." *Aviation Week & Space Technology* 173: 28.

AUTOMOBILE

Almost from its inception, the automobile has been eagerly accepted by the American populace, but a number of environmental problems have accompanied the benefits that it has conferred. In the 1950s, the United States had the world's highest ratio of cars per person, and U.S. automobile manufacturing was the wealthiest and most powerful industry on earth. But most U.S. drivers didn't give much thought to environmental issues, and the industry's leaders were slow to accept responsibility for the environmental damage caused by their products. This indifference was evident when air pollution became a severe problem in several parts of the United States during the 1950s. Automobile manufacturers denied that the combustion products of automobile engines were a major source of smog, and they resisted the efforts of state and federal governments to require the development and use of technologies that promised cleaner skies. That attitude is much less evident today. Through a combination of governmental mandates, public pressure, and self-interest, the U.S. automobile industry has made impressive strides in reducing automotive emissions. It has also made significant progress in improving environmental quality through the design, manufacture, and even the recycling of its products. Despite these efforts, however, the automobile still exists in an uneasy relationship with the natural environment.

Air Pollution

In the 1950s some regions of the country, most notably Southern California, often lay under a grayish-brown blanket of smog that afflicted the region's residents with watering eyes, burning lungs, and shortness of breath. By then the chemistry of this form of air pollution was well understood. Southern California's infamous

Smog obscures the view of the Chrysler Building from the Empire State Building, New York City, 1953. (Library of Congress)

smog was caused by a photochemical reaction that converted unburned hydrocarbons, volatile organic compounds, and atmospheric nitrogen and oxygen into carbon monoxide, oxides of nitrogen, and ozone. In the early 1950s, Arie Haagen-Smit of the California Institute of Technology identified automobile exhaust as a major contributor to smog formation. His results were disputed by the automobile industry for a number of years, but in late 1953 the industry's trade group, the Automobile Manufacturers Association, established a committee to study the problem and come up with some possible solutions. The most promising was a catalytic converter invented by Eugene Houdry.

In the years that followed, the catalytic converter developed into the key technology for the reduction of automotive emissions, but it was not a simple technological fix. Catalytic converters were permanently damaged by the presence of lead in gasoline, which, in the form of tetraethyl lead, had been used since the 1920s to boost octane and increase the compression ratio of engines. Successful deployment of catalytic converters therefore required the removal of lead from gasoline and some redesign of automobile engines. Pressured by impending mandates from the U.S. Environmental Protection Agency, gasoline companies began to offer 91-octane unleaded gasoline in 1970, and by 1996 lead had been banned as a gasoline additive. This had the additional benefit of significantly diminishing the amount of lead, a dangerous toxin, in the environment.

The adoption of several complementary technologies was also essential. Catalytic converters are most effective when an engine's air-to-fuel ratio stays close to 14.6 to 1. This was beyond the capability of conventional carburetors. Instead, the induction of fuel and air had to be done by a computer-controlled fuel injection system that constantly received information from an oxygen sensor in the exhaust manifold. The onboard computer also precisely regulated ignition timing in order to further limit emissions. Along with these changes to automobile engines, the fuel they used was reformulated and seasonally adjusted to burn more cleanly and produce lower emissions.

Legislation for Cleaner Air

New technologies made cleaner vehicles a possibility, but these technologies would never have emerged from the laboratory if state and federal agencies had not heavily leaned on the industry. Government action was needed because air pollution is a classic example of a "negative market externality," the consequence of transaction in the marketplace that harms parties not involved in the transaction. Car manufacturers and their customers both benefit from the sales of new automobiles, but every car sold means more tail-pipe emissions and more smog. A few environmentally minded customers might choose to pay a higher price for a cleaner car, but there really is no point in doing so when few other purchasers are willing to do the same. Under these circumstances, the government has to intervene with laws and regulations that require manufacturers to produce cleaner cars and prevent customers from buying dirty ones.

This was no easy task. Getting the manufacturers to produce

Greenovation: The Catalytic Converter

A catalytic converter is a component of an automobile's exhaust system that uses metals such as palladium, iridium, and platinum to promote a catalytic process that converts exhaust products into nonpolluting compounds. The first practical catalytic converter was developed in the early 1950s by Eugene Houdry, a French inventor who had developed the process of catalytic cracking to more efficiently refine crude oil into gasoline and other petroleum products. The first catalytic converters eliminated 80 percent of hydrocarbon emissions by converting their constituents into water and carbon dioxide. Further development led to converters that turned carbon monoxide into carbon dioxide, followed by the three-way converter, which performed the difficult chemical task of turning oxides of nitrogen into free oxygen and nitrogen. After a considerable amount of political wrangling, automobile manufacturers bowed to the inevitable and began to install two-way converters on 1975 model year cars. By 1977, some new cars were equipped with three-way catalysts, although they did not become universal until the 1980 model year.

Today's catalytic converters, which are about the size of a large soda bottle, are installed in a car's exhaust pipe between the engine and the muffler. They have an inner structure lined with a catalyst-coated ceramic honeycomb that provides a total surface area about the size of a football field. Because they need heat to work efficiently, most of a car's polluting emissions occur during the first minutes after a cold engine is started, and electric preheating eventually may have to be added for more complete emission control.

RUDI VOLTI

cleaner cars took many years and a great deal of legislative action, far too much to even be summarized here. It can only be noted that from the 1960s onward, the federal government took many legislative actions to reduce air pollution by mandating regional air quality standards and regulating automobile emissions. California, a state with some of the nation's most polluted air, passed regulations that were more stringent than those of the federal government, and they were eventually adopted at the national level.

In addition to lowering acceptable levels of emissions, government regulations reduced air pollution and at the same time eased pressures on petroleum supplies by

Greenovation: *California v. General Motors Corp.* (2006)

California sued six automakers in September 2006, alleging that the vehicles of General Moters, Ford, Toyota, Honda, Nissan, and DaimlerChrysler introduced into the atmosphere 289 million metric tons of carbon dioxide and other greenhouse gases. California regarded this pollution as a public nuisance under state and federal common law. Vehicle pollution reduced the snowpack, raised sea levels, increased ozone, and added to risks of wildfire and flooding. It harmed the elderly, children, fish, and wildlife. California wanted monetary damages to compensate for the millions it spent correcting the problems caused by the automakers.

The case was consistent with *Massachusetts v. Environmental Protection Agency* (2007) in that the court found that the public-nuisance argument was inappropriate in seeking redress for climate damage from industry. After a district court ruled, as the manufacturers contended, that the matter was political and not appropriate for judicial resolution, California dropped the case in 2009. The automakers also contended that the Clean Air Act and Energy Policy and Conservation Act made the California case inappropriate.

California's withdrawal of its appeal came with a statement that the Barack Obama administration was showing signs of progress on related issues such as fuel economy and emission standards and a finding by the Environmental Protection Agency that greenhouse gases are a public health hazard as defined under the Clean Air Act.

Related litigation still in the circuit courts in 2009 included *Connecticut v. American Electric Power* and *Comer v. Murphy Oil. Kivalina v. ExxonMobil Corp.*, filed in 2008, dealt with a barrier reef Eskimo village endangered by rising water levels due to oil company negligence. The case was dismissed in October 2009 at the same time that *Comer v. Murphy*, a Katrina-related case, was reinstated on appeal.

JOHN H. BARNHILL

mandating fuel economy standards for automobiles and light trucks. Under these regulations, a manufacturer's fleet of cars had to meet certain mileage standards defined by its Corporate Average Fuel Economy (CAFE). The standard first applied to 1978 passenger cars only and was pegged at 18.5 miles per gallon. For the 1985 model year, the standard rose to 27.5 miles per gallon for cars and 19.5 for light trucks, which represented a doubling of the mileage achieved by cars manufactured in the late 1970s. In 2007 a more stringent CAFE standard of 35 miles per gallon for cars and light trucks alike is scheduled to take effect in 2020. Depending on the political winds, this figure may increase substantially in the years to come.

Cars and Climate Change

The combination of technological advances and government mandates have resulted in air that is far cleaner than it had been a few decades ago, despite the addition of millions of more cars. But present emission controls do nothing to reduce the inevitable byproduct of gasoline combustion, carbon dioxide. Although CO_2 does not contribute to visible air pollution, its long-term effects may be far more damaging than smog. Carbon dioxide, along with other gases, has been implicated for its contribution to the greenhouse effect, which may bring disastrous changes to the earth's climate.

An automobile uses nearly 15 kilograms of air for every kilogram of gasoline. As a result, more than 2.3 kilograms of CO_2 are formed for every liter of gasoline burned.

This means that on an annual basis, a typical passenger vehicle produces 5.1 metric tons of CO_2. When other gases implicated in global warming, such as methane and nitrous oxide tailpipe emissions, along with air conditioner leaks are taken into account, the figure rises to 5.5 metric tons of carbon dioxide equivalent. Collectively, cars and light trucks account for nearly 18 percent of the greenhouse gases emitted in the United States.

Since CO_2 production is an inevitable accompaniment of fossil fuel combustion, some environmentalists look to the replacement of internal combustion engines by electric motors as a key means of reducing CO_2 emissions. Although it is true that electric cars are virtually emission free, the electricity to recharge their batteries has to come from somewhere. If the source is a coal-fired plant, more greenhouse gases may be released than occurs through the operation of automobiles powered by internal combustion engines. Electricity generated in nuclear plants would obviate this problem, but at the cost of other environmental hazards. Wind and solar power are promising alternatives, but their present state of development prevents them from being a major source of electricity generation for many years to come.

Making Cars

Although air pollution is usually noted as the automobile's greatest negative environmental impact, the manufacture of cars also has had unfortunate consequences for the environment. Before the practice was banned or regulated, many automobile manufacturers dumped their effluents into nearby rivers, while their smokestack emissions befouled the air for many miles around. Strict environmental laws now prohibit these practices. Some automobile firms have even surpassed legal requirements by making a conscious effort to protect the environment while building cars. One such manufacturer is Ford, which has applied a number of environmentally friendly technologies to its mammoth River Rouge factory in Dearborn, Michigan. The factory features a 10-acre "living roof" where plants keep the building warm in the winter and cool in the summer. The complex also includes solar collectors to heat water for several buildings, and features parking lots with porous surfaces that allow water to be stored and recycled in underground reservoirs.

Recycling

Environmentalists are fond of noting that everything has to go somewhere, even when it is no longer a useful commodity. Automobiles are big, bulky items containing a diversity of materials, and their disposal is not easily accomplished. For decades, many wrecked and worn-out cars were used as feedstock for steel manufacture, but changes in steel production technology reduced the demand for scrap metal in the 1960s, resulting in large accumulations of defunct cars piling up in roadside junkyards or simply being abandoned. The highway beautification movement of the 1960s put the automobiles that had been consigned to junkyards out of immediate view in fenced enclosures, but this only hid the problem and did not solve it.

The rise of mini-mills for steelmaking allowed the use of more scrapped cars. Large numbers of automobile carcasses are now recycled, but quite a lot of preparation is required. After being stripped of useful components, automobile bodies are shredded and compressed in huge recycling facilities prior to being fed into the mini-mills. The environmental costs of automobile disposal also have been reduced by laws in some European countries, which require the use of recyclable and biodegradable materials and place limits on the amount of toxic materials they can contain.

Effects on the Built Environment

Air pollution, resource depletion, and the environmental costs of producing new cars and disposing of old ones have had the most direct effects on the ecosystem. It is also important to take into account the less direct, but highly significant environmental consequences of an automobile-based transportation system. Although the historical trend of suburbanization cannot be attributed solely to the automobile, this way of life would have been impossible without widespread automobile ownership. In turn, the spread-out living and commercial patterns of most suburban communities results in higher energy costs than an urban community with the same size population.

Automobiles have also contributed to sound and visual pollution. Being constantly exposed to the noise of a freeway or busy highway can be most unpleasant and may even pose long-term health hazards. Also, a great amount of visual pollution in the form of billboards and other signs can be attributed to the need to catch the attention of drivers and passengers as they speed by.

In surveying the current scene, it is apparent that the automobile's impact on the environment is less severe than it was a few decades ago. But with steady increases in both the human and the automobile populations, continued efforts to develop and apply new technologies, encouraged and at times mandated by evolving government policies, will be necessary if the automobile and the many benefits it brings are to be reconciled with a greener planet.

RUDI VOLTI

See also: Gas Mileage Tips (document); Paving the Way toward Cleaner, More Efficient Trucks (documents); Tips to Save Gas and Improve Mileage (documents); Transportation, Automobile (Science); Transportation, Bicycle (Science); Transportation, Mass Transit (Science).

References

Bryner, Gary C. 1995. *Blue Skies, Green Politics: The Clean Air Act of 1990 and Its Implementation*. Washington, DC: CQ Press.

Endangeredlaws.Org. *California v. General Motors Corp*. Available at: http://www .endangeredlaws.org/case_california.htm.

Lichtman, Joanne. 2009. "*California v. General Motors*: State Moves to Voluntarily Dismiss Climate Change Lawsuit against Major Automakers." Global Climate Law Blog. June

23. Available at: http://www.globalclimatelaw.com/2009/06/articles/climate change litigation/california-v-general-motors-state-moves-to-voluntarily-dismiss-climate-change-lawsuit-against-major-automakers/.

McCarthy, Tom. 2007. *Auto Mania: Cars, Consumers, and the Environment.* New Haven, CT, and London: Yale University Press.

McCrea, Hannah. 2009. "A Victory for Katrina Victims; A Defeat for Alaskan Villagers. Climate Law Update." October 20. Available at: http://www.grist.org/article/2009-10-19-a-victory-for-katrina-victims-a-defeat-for-alaskan-villagers/.

Pew Center on Global Climate Change. 2007. *California v. General Motors, et al.* Available at: http://www.pewclimate.org/federal/analysis/judicial/california-v-general-motors-et-al-2007.

Theusconstitution.org. 2009. "Update: California Drops Its 'Nuisance' Suit Against Carmakers; Other Tort-Based Climate Change Lawsuits Await Decisions in Federal Courts." *Warming Law.* July 24. Available at: http://theusconstitution.org/blog.warming/?p=664.

U.S. Department of Transportation. "Transportation and Greenhouse Gas Emissions." Available at: http://climate.dot.gov/about/transportations-role/overview.html.

U.S. Environmental Protection Agency. "Emission Facts: Greenhouse Gas Emissions from a Typical Passenger Vehicle." Available at: http://www.epa.gov/oms/climate/420f05004.htm.

Volti, Rudi. 2003. "Reducing Automobile Emissions in Southern California: The Dance of Public Policies and Technological Fixes." In Arthur Molella and Joyce Bedi, eds., *Inventing for the Environment.* Cambridge, MA, and London: MIT Press.

BIOBASED AND ENGINEERED FIBERS

Biobased and engineered fiber is any manmade or manufactured fiber that uses renewable natural resources as raw materials. The U.S. Department of Agriculture National Institute of Food and Agriculture (USDA-NIFA) defines the term *biobased product* as "(1) an industrial product (including chemicals, materials, and polymers) produced from biomass; or (2) a commercial or industrial product (including animal feed and electric power) derived in connection with the conversion of biomass to fuel" (7 CFR 3430). Natural fiber, such as cotton, flax, ramie, wool, and silk, which are well known to consumers, is a biobased product because it is directly produced from plants, animals, or insects. However, natural fiber is not engineered fiber, considering the fact that the fiber is formed in a specific biological way with a large variance in physical shape and property. In contrast, synthetic fiber, like polyester, nylon, and polypropylene, is engineered fiber but not biobased fiber, because it is made of synthesized polymers and is formed by an engineering approach combining thermal, mechanical, and chemical processes.

Inventions of manmade fiber are mainly tied with the development of the petroleum industry, which is not only a base for fuel and energy production, but also a supplier for the manufacturing of plastics and chemicals. Since the availability of different synthetic fibers, end-use demands for synthetic fibers keep substantially increasing. During the past 30 years, global production of manmade fiber has tripled, reaching over 42 million metric tons per year, which accounts for approximately 63 percent of the world textile fiber market (AFMA, 2011; Blagoev et al.,

2011), compared to cotton production—about 24 million metric tons per annum (USDA, 2011) and wool production (about 1.3 million metric tons per annum). With this production capacity, manmade fiber has firmly dominated today's textile end-use market from apparel to diverse industrial applications. Checking manmade fiber inventory currently available on market, there are few products of biobased and engineered fiber. Only regenerated cellulose fiber and polylactic acid or polylactide (PLA) fiber fall into this category.

Regenerated cellulose fiber, mostly indicating rayon fiber, is the first manmade fiber invented for textile applications. Regenerated cellulose fiber is made from raw cellulose, mainly in the form of wood pulp. Wood cellulose is an abundant natural resource that supplies renewable feedstock for production of consumer and industrial products. For the production of rayon fiber, raw cellulose first needs to be converted into sodium cellulose xanthate by alkalization and xanthation. The formed cellulose xanthate is then dissolved in a weak caustic soda to form a spin solution called viscose. By extruding the viscose solution through a spinnerette in a sulfuric bath, cellulose polymer is regenerated and cellulose fiber is formed after further process of drawing, washing, and drying. Because rayon fiber is produced in such an engineering approach, its end-use properties are changed accordingly. Overall, these changes benefit the enhancement of fiber properties. Its fiber-like appearance has a smooth and lustrous look much like silk. Its shape is uniform in both longitudinal and lateral directions. The fiber's physical aspects make it stronger and more absorbent than cotton. As a result, rayon fiber becomes a very attractive fiber material for apparel applications, because it is not only comfortable, it is also easily draped, dyed, and tailored. Currently, the world production capacity of regenerated cellulose fiber (including rayon and acetate fibers) is around 3 million metric tons, sharing about 5 percent of the world manmade fiber market. It is envisaged that the rayon production and demand will keep growing worldwide at an increasing rate of 3.8 percent per year from 2009 to 2014 (Blagoev et al., 2011).

Although rayon fiber is a type of biobased and engineered fiber with attractive properties and a competitive price, the manufacturing method of rayon fiber is not environmentally friendly due to heavy use of strong acid and alkaline chemicals that cause harsh working conditions and severe environment impact. For this reason, a new technology has been developed to produce the new generation of rayon fiber, called lyocell fiber (U.S. brand name Tencel®). Lyocell fiber is also made from raw cellulose, but the whole process of fiber spinning is eco-friendly, without chemical reactions and effluents. The lyocell technology uses the organic solvent N-methylmorpholine-N-oxide (NMMO) to directly dissolve cellulose pulp. The formed cellulose solution is extruded into a water spin bath where cellulose fiber is regenerated as the NMMO solvent is washed away in the spin bath. By recycling the spin bath, the dilute NMMO solvent is recovered for dissolving new cellulose pulp. Because of this closed-loop approach for cellulose dissolution and regeneration, the lyocell technology bears a vision of green technology. Lyocell fiber produced in this method is different from viscose rayon in fiber shape and appearance. In general, lyocell fiber has a higher dry and wet tensile strength, better fabric hand and drape, enhanced fabric dimensional stability, and improved dye uptake and colorfastness. It certainly represents the future of rayon fiber. Current global capacity of producing lyocell fiber is very limited, only contributing about 5 percent to the rayon fiber market. The Austria-based company Lenzing is today's largest lyocell fiber manufacturer in the world, capable of supplying about 0.13 million metric tons of lyocell fiber annually for the global rayon market.

PLA fiber is a new type of biobased and engineered fiber developed for textile and apparel applications. In contrast to petro-based synthetic fibers, such as polyester and nylon, PLA fiber is made of PLA polymer, a polymer synthesized using natural sugars. The Federal Trade Commission defines PLA fiber as: "A manufactured fiber in which the fiber-forming substance is composed of at least 85% by weight of lactic acid ester units derived from naturally occurring sugars." To produce PLA polymer, the first step is a biochemical fermentation of various sources of natural sugars to produce lactic acid. These sugars can be obtained from renewable agricultural crops such as corn or sugar beets. Using these naturally produced sugars as chemical feedstock, a synthesizing process, called the ring-opening approach, is carried out to polymerize lactide monomer into PLA polymer by using a specific catalyst (Farrington et al., 2005). Melt spinning is a commonly used method for PLA fiber production in order to take advantage of PLA's low melting temperature.

The U.S. company Cargill Dow LLC first commercialized the production of PLA polymer in 2002, with the brand name NatureWorks® (Gruber, 2004). In early 2003, Cargill Dow LLC initiated the manufacture of PLA fiber, the world's first synthetic fiber made from bio-polymer, under the trademark of Ingeo™ (Vink et al., 2004). Cargill Dow LLC currently produces over 0.14 million metric tons of PLA polymer per year. PLA fiber has a specific gravity of 1.25 g/cm^3, lower than that of natural fibers, regenerated cellulose fiber, and polyester. This enables PLA fiber to make lightweight fabrics for comfort fashion apparel applications. PLA fiber is also high wicking and flame retardant, with low moisture retention and UV resistance, making it ideal for diverse end-use applications in sportswear, performance apparel, and outdoor furniture.

Although PLA fiber has become an icon for renewable synthetic fiber, its campaign for a completely sustainable material is still facing some challenges. Sustainability of an industrial product implies economic viability of production and lifecycle impact on the environment (carbon neutral, water and soil conservation, noncompetition with food supply, and recyclability). To achieve this ultimate goal, other researchers are dedicated to a biological approach for producing biopolymer polyhydroxyalkanoate (PHA). PHA naturally exists in a variety of microorganisms of which the bacterium *Bacillus megaterium* was the first found in 1926 by Maurice Lemoigne. This means that renewable agricultural feedstock can be used as raw material to produce PHA through a biofermentation process. In this process, also called biosynthesis, the raw material (medium) is sugars extracted either from food crops or from lignocellulose energy crops, and microorganisms play a role of biocatalyst to complete a PHA synthesis. Metabolix, an MIT spin-off company, is pioneering a genetic engineering method to produce PHA in plant cells. Researchers in Metabolix have been working on tobacco and switchgrass plants to develop a transgenic pathway of expressing PHA synthesis that can result in the formation of

PHA as energy storage in plant tissues. Meanwhile, Metabolix has partnered with Archer Daniels Midland Co. (ADM) and established a commercial-scale facility capable of producing 50,000 tons of PHA annually in Clinton, Iowa, using an industrial fermentation approach. This new business development marks a milestone for a significant growth of bioplastic industry.

Similar to petro-based polymers, PHA polymers are thermoplastic material suitable for processing with conventional plastic technologies such as injection molding and film blowing. PHA polymers are also renewable and biodegradable. This feature makes PHA a stronger competitor in today's plastic market. End-use applications of PHA are diverse, ranging from industrial molding parts and consumer packing materials to surgical mesh. However, because PHA plasticity tends to be brittle and stiff, it is not readily applicable for spinning textile fiber. Much research is needed to develop new grades of PHA polymers or co-polymers, so that manmade fiber manufacturers can use them to produce truly sustainable synthetic fibers from renewable resources.

In summary, the research and development for biobased and engineered fiber has made remarkable progress in the past 20 years. The technologies of PLA and PHA biopolymers demonstrated by the industry are transformative for a broader biobased industry, including agriculture, energy, plastics, and textile manufacture. The iconic brands of lyocell and PLA fiber are illustrative of the future green fiber market attracting textile designers, producers, and consumers. It can be envisaged that sustainable fiber and its derived textiles will be increasingly used in fashion design, apparel design, and various textile end uses, as consumers are more and more concerned with the nation's energy security, environment improvement, and sustainable economic growth. However, there is still a long way to go if today's fiber king polyester could be totally replaced by biobased and engineered fibers and the whole textile market could be filled with many choices of renewable and biodegradable manufactured fiber. Economic performance of producing these new types of sustainable fiber remains a big challenge for the entire manufacture community.

JONATHAN Y. CHEN

See also: Home Furnishings and Interior Design (Health); Textiles for Furniture and Fashion (Health).

References

7 CFR 3430. 2011. U.S. Code of Federal Regulations Title 7, Part 3430. Competitive and Noncompetitive Non-Formula Federal Assistance Programs—General Award Administrative Provisions. Available at: http://www.federalregister.gov/articles/2010/06/14/2010-14159/competitive-and-noncompetitive-nonformula-federal-assistance-programs-administrative-provisions-for.

AFMA. 2011. "Fiberfacts." Available at: http://www.fibersource.com/f-info/fiber%20production.htm.

Blagoev, M., S. Bizzari, and Y. Inoguchi. 2011. "Rayon and Lyocell Fibers." Available at: http://www.sriconsulting.com/CEH/Public/Reports/541.3000/.

Farrington, D. W., J. Lunt, S. Davies, and R. S. Blackburn. 2005. "Poly(lactic acid) fibres." In R. S. Blackburn, ed., *Biodegradable and Sustainable Fibres*. Cambridge, Engl.: Woodhead, 191–220.

Gruber, P. R. 2004. "Cargill Dow LLC." *Journal of Industrial Ecology* 7:3/4: 209–213.

U.S. Department of Agriculture (USDA). 2011. "Cotton and Wool Outlook." Available at: http://usda.mannlib.cornell.edu/MannUsda/viewDocumentInfo.do?documentID=1281.

Vink, E. T. H., K. R. Rabago, D. A. Glassner, B. Springs, R. P. O'Conner, J. Kolstad, and P. R. Gruber. 2004. "The Sustainability of NatureWorks Polylactide Polymers and Ingeo Polylactide Fibers: An Update of the Future." *Macromolecular Bioscience* 4: 551–562.

BUSINESSES ACTIVE IN ENVIRONMENTAL ISSUES

Known as green or sustainable businesses, companies active in environmental issues engage in environmental practices that do not harm the local or global environment. They also typically donate money to environmental organizations or sponsor fundraisers that benefit environmental causes. In addition, some companies dedicated to environmentalism have policies that encourage employees to participate in environmentally friendly activities on company time.

For example, an outdoor-apparel company called Patagonia allows its employees to take a leave of absence from work, with full pay and benefits for up to two months, in order to volunteer for nonprofit environmental organizations of their choice. Another example of a company that encourages employee volunteerism is Clif Bar, which makes health and energy food bars. Its Project 2080 program is committed to donating a minimum of 2,080 hours—the amount of time one full-time employee works in a year—in collective "worker sweat" to environmental organizations. In addition, Clif Bar's "In Good Company" program joins companies

Greenovation: Green Guide for New Businesses

The following is from the U.S. Small Business Administration:

Adopting environmentally friendly and energy efficient business practices provides numerous benefits to new business owners looking to control costs, attract customers and become socially responsible.

The following 10 steps will help you develop an environmental strategy for your business, and get you on your way to becoming energy efficient, compliant with environmental regulations and a recognized "green business."

Step 1: Comply with Environmental Regulations
Compliance not only protects the environment, it protects your business from fines and legal action that could be imposed by the government.

Step 2: Develop an Environmental Management Plan
Help minimize your company's **eco-footprint** and encourage green business practices throughout your organization.

Step 3: Build Green
If you are opening a business in a new or remodeled building, make sure you build green by installing

energy efficient heating and air conditioning systems, appliances, equipment and lighting.

Step 4: Buy Green Products

Consider buying environmentally-friendly products that are made from post-consumer, recycled, bio-base, non-toxic materials.

Step 5: Adopt Energy Efficient Practices

The prudent and conservative use of energy is one of the easiest and most cost-effective steps you can take to cut costs, increase profitability and create shareholder value.

Step 6: Reduce, Reuse, Recycle Wastes

In addition to lower removal costs, waste reduction measures help **cut costs** on raw materials, office supplies and equipment.

Step 7: Conserve Water

By implementing a water efficiency program, not only can you help conserve this precious resource, but also cut the costs associated with buying, heating, treating and disposing of water.

Step 8: Prevent Pollution

Other businesses may generate hazardous or toxic wastes that require special handling and disposal.

Step 9: Create a Green Marketing Strategy

If you are starting a green business, you need to market yourself as one.

Step 10: Join Industry Partnership and Stewardship Programs

The EPA sponsors a wide variety of industry partnership and stewardship programs that aim to reduce the impact of industrial activities on the environment. These partnerships will help you build relationships with other green business owners in your industry and a brand that's credible with your customers.

KIM KENNEDY WHITE

Source: Adapted from the U.S. Small Business Administration. Available at: http://www.sba.gov/content/green-guide-new-businesses.

together to participate in hands-on environmental volunteerism at the local level. Among these companies are Annie's Homegrown, an organic food company; Numi Tea, an organic tea company; Seventh Generation, which makes natural cleaning products; and Timberland, which makes hiking boots and outdoor clothing and gear.

Patagonia is also known for having donated millions of dollars to environmental causes over the past two decades. In addition, in 2002 the company co-founded an alliance of businesses committed to donating 1 percent of their total sales to environmental causes. This alliance, called 1% for the Planet, currently comprises over 1,400 companies that continue to donate money to nearly 2,500 environmental organizations. (Information on and links to these companies can be found at the alliance's Web site, www.onepercentfortheplanet.org.) Another alliance founded in 1989 by Patagonia and three other outdoor companies (the North Face, REI, and Kelty) is the Conservation Alliance (www.conservationalliance.com), which encourages companies to contribute money directly to organizations that protect the wilderness; this organization now has over 175 member companies and has contributed nearly $10 million to North American dam removal and wilderness preservation efforts. Similarly, Patagonia-sponsored Freedom to Roam (www.freedomtoroam.org) is a coalition of people in business, government, and conservation committed to wildlife corridor conservation.

Another example of a company establishing ways for green businesses to contribute money to environmental causes is CBS Corporation, a media conglomerate best known for television broadcasting, CBS established EcoMedia in 2002 to direct advertising dollars into environmental efforts like urban refor-estation projects, the clean-up of urban waterways, and the installation of solar panels on school buildings. In 2011, the company expanded EcoMedia to include the EcoAd, which puts a symbol on an ad that designates the advertiser as being directly linked to environmental efforts related to local renewable-energy and energy-efficiency projects.

Many green businesses are also dedicated to minimizing their footprint on the earth, which means that they engage in practices that reduce waste and use resources wisely. For example, Timberland uses renewable energy in its facilities, plants trees throughout the world to combat deforestation and fight global warming, and supports the creation of environmentally friendly technological advances like Green Rubber^{TM}, a compound that allows it to make 42 percent recycled rubber outsoles for its boots. Similarly, Patagonia has a recycling program for the clothing it manufactures; started in 2005, the Common Threads Recycling Program encourages customers to return certain items of used clothing to its stores so these items can be used to make new clothing.

One of the pioneers of this approach to business was auto-mobile manufacturer Henry Ford. In shipping his Model A trucks to customers, he used crates whose boards became the trucks' floorboards upon arrival. (Using a disposable item in this way is now known as upcycling.) Ford also experimen-ted with more environmentally friendly materials for his prod-ucts, including soy. Today the Ford Motor Company uses renewable soy foam seat bases in its vehicles, and it uses and is developing other practices and policies related to sustainability and environmentalism as well.

Another company known for its recycling and upcycling efforts is Stonyfield Organic, an organic dairy that produces not only milk but also smoothies and yogurt. In addition to enga-ging in its own green business practices, Stonyfield has part-nered with TerraCycle, a com-pany that makes a variety of

In 1993, Stonyfield Farm was the first dairy maker in the United States to pay farmers NOT to use milk from cows treated with artificial bovine growth hormone (rBST/ rBGH). The organic yogurt maker also ran ads like this one touting its stance against the artificial hormone. (PRNewsFoto/Stonyfield Farm)

Greenovator: Green Business Network

The Green Business Network (GBN) is made up of more than 5,000 businesses concerned with social and eco-enterprises and green business. The network provides businesses with the information, tools, and consumer base to build successful eco-friendly and sustainable businesses. According the Green Business Network, green businesses are those that adopt practices, principles, and policies that have a positive impact on the environment. Environmental sustainability, economic and social justice, and community success are key goals for GBN member businesses who provide products and services in support of sustainable agriculture, education, affordable housing, and clean energy. Joining the GBN allows members access to a number of programs and Webinars among other benefits. Learn more at http://greenbusinessnetwork.org/.

KIM KENNEDY WHITE

eco-friendly products, to collect used yogurt cups from schools and nonprofit organizations throughout America so these cups can be remade into planters and vegetable-growing kits. Stonyfield has also partnered with Preserve^R, which manufacturers 100 percent recycled household products, in order to turn its used yogurt cups into spoons, razors, tongue cleaners, and toothbrushes.

Author Richard Seireeni discusses Stonyfield's approach to environmentalism in his 2009 book *The Gort Cloud*, which examines 12 green businesses. He also discusses the ways in which an invisible "green community" supports green businesses and provide insights into consumer preferences. This social network, which Seireeni calls the Gort Cloud, includes environmentally conscious consumers, environmentalists, environmental organizations, business alliances, bloggers, environmental reporters, and others dedicated to sustainability who exchange information on green products and services. (The name Gort Cloud is derived from Oort Cloud, a vast cloud of stellar debris orbiting the solar system that is invisible to the human eye.)

Not only does the Gort Cloud provide a market for green products, but it supports companies that engage in eco-friendly business practices. Consequently, such businesses often find that going green increases profits—a realization that is the foundation of market-based environmentalism, whereby companies are drawn to environmentalism through economic incentives. For most green companies, however, environmentalism is not about economics but rather about ethics, values, and accountability.

PATRICIA D. NETZLEY

See also: Green Entrepreneurship (Economics); Green Guide for New Businesses (documents); Green Jobs (Education); Green Jobs (documents); How a Product Earns the Energy Star Label (documents); Merchandising (documents).

References

"Henry Ford's Eco-Friendly Automobile." Available at: http://www.harbay.net/henry ford.html.

Kenny, Brad. "Ford Mustang to Feature Soy Foam." Available at: http://www.industryweek.com/articles/ford_mustang_to_feature_soy_foam_14625.aspx.

CARBON CREDITS

Carbon credits are a key component in the effort to combat greenhouse gas emissions (GHG). Although a wide variety of strategies have been proposed or utilized to reduce GHGs, one in particular has risen to prominence. Specifically, an economic market-based approach is now employed widely around the world. Carbon credits find their integral role as a fundamental component of this approach. Indeed, carbon credits are a direct product of this market-based system. Every economic-based strategy relies on common units of account. These units typically reflect a standard of quantity for a commodity that can then be bought, traded, and sold on a larger scale. Carbon credits are this type of unit of accounting for the carbon marketplace. Each credit is equivalent to 1 ton of carbon dioxide or a carbon dioxide equivalent GHG. Thus, the possession of a carbon credit allows for the emission of 1 ton of carbon dioxide. Through this approach, carbon emissions become a tangible cost that entities can see on their balance sheets. As a result of carbon credits, the price of GHGs is commodified, allowing them to rest alongside more traditional business expenses.

The creation of carbon credits as well as the entire effort to reduce GHG emissions is largely a reaction to increasing worries over global climate change. Since GHGs are viewed as the primary cause of climate change, they have naturally become the dominate gauge for evaluating the impact that particular countries or businesses are having on the atmosphere. By standardizing GHGs through the creation of carbon credits, emissions are tracked more easily and various entities are held more accountable. Due to the fact that carbon credits and the market for them are artificial man-made creations, binding agreements must exist in order for them to establish legitimacy. The Kyoto Protocol is the most significant and widespread effort to instill such a system. This international agreement, as well as other similar climate change policies, establishes a cap-and-trade system. Such systems regulate the amount of emissions entities can produce and allows them to sell any surplus they possess. Through utilization of this approach, the fundamentals of the capitalist market are called into use by those concerned for the future of the environment. Under the agreement, entities that are efficient and clean benefit; these entities are able to capitalize on their surplus by selling to others in need of additional carbon credits. Similarly, those in need of additional credits are penalized by having to purchase extra from more efficient groups. Thus, responsible, environmentally friendly behavior is encouraged in a pragmatic and efficient manner. By utilizing basic incentives, the desired result is achieved without the implementation of strict, draconian measures.

Although the Kyoto Protocol has found widespread support, the United States has refused to sign on to the legally binding agreement and as such is not responsible for meeting any of the demands it outlines. Consequently, carbon credits are less significant in the United States than they are in many other areas of the world. Without the repercussions that result from signing on to the agreement, the United States is free to exceed the recommended GHG levels and, as a result, the value of carbon credits is greatly diminished in the United States. Yet, this does not mean that carbon credits are irrelevant in the United States. Many within the United States still utilize the units in order to offset GHG emissions. Individuals, groups, and corporations can choose to voluntarily engage in carbon credit management, but the decision to make such a purchase is ethically motivated rather than legally commanded, as it is elsewhere in the world. The State of California is the one notable exception to the United States' anti-cap-and-trade sentiment. While efforts to establish a national carbon market have been unable to gain traction in Washington, D.C., California's state-based efforts have shown promise. Utilizing this federalist-driven approach, California may enter the worldwide carbon market on its own.

In order to reduce GHG emissions and stay within the bounds of their allotted carbon credits, many entities have begun to utilize cleaner practices and install more carbon friendly machinery. Others meet their demands through the purchase of credits. While some of these credits are put on the market by entities with a surplus, others make it onto the market as the result of carbon sinks. Various types of carbon sinks exist; some natural (forests and oceans), some artificial (landfills). Their commonality, however, rests in the fact that they all remove carbon dioxide from the atmosphere. Through this process of carbon sequestration, GHG emissions are offset. The Kyoto Protocol emphasizes the importance of carbon sinks in the effort to reduce GHG emissions worldwide. Likewise, scientific studies have demonstrated the value of carbon sinks. Biological carbon sinks that develop in mature ecosystems have been found to be particularly useful in the effort to reduce GHGs. Unfortunately, for promoters of carbon emission reduction, the establishment of new carbon sinks is largely offset by deforestation elsewhere in the world, a reality that is not properly addressed by the Kyoto Protocol.

The vast majority of individuals concerned with reducing GHGs in the atmosphere have lauded carbon credits and the market-driven approach that accompanies them. The absence of the United States in the worldwide carbon market is a notable problem, and the Kyoto Protocol is not flawless. Yet, the general sentiment toward a cap-and-trade system on carbon emissions is still favorable. The carbon credit approach is certain to face adjustments. Price changes, alterations to carbon offsetting procedures, and membership modification are but a few of the changes that are likely to take place over the coming years. While all of these adjustments will likely impact carbon credits, it is unlikely that this fundamental unit of account will change.

CALEB HUSMANN

See also: Businesses Active in Environmental Issues (Economics); Green Marketing (Economics).

References

Bissa, Sharrad, and A. Bohra. 2010. "Carbon Credits: Today's New Currency Mantra." *Current Science* 99:4: 411–412.

Grace, John. 2004. "Presidential Address: Understanding and Managing the Global Climate Cycle." *Journal of Ecology* 92:2: 189–202.

Nordhaus, William. 2008. *A Question of Balance: Weighing the Options on Global Warming Policies*. New Haven, CT: Yale University Press.

Victor, David F., and Joshua C. House. 2004. "A New Currency: Climate Change and Carbon Credits." *Harvard International Review* 26:2: 56–59.

CO-OPS

With a rich and inspiring history, cooperatives have come to be an important facet of the American experience; in fact, cooperatives are perhaps the single largest expression of U.S. environmentalism and eco-friendly living today. The word *cooperative*, sometimes spelled co-operative and often shortened to co-op, comes from the Latin *cooperat*, meaning "work together." The idea of working together continues to be embodied in contemporary co-ops, though the idea has been broadened from its social roots to incorporate working with the environment toward a sustainable lifestyle across social, natural, and economic facets of experience. Simply put, a co-op is an organizational format where members own and manage the enterprise to benefit members. Purpose, ownership, and management styles reflect the diversity in co-ops: some aim to benefit just their members, while others endeavor to support the community writ large; some are owned with all members holding equal equity, while others permit more concentrated ownership or allow patrons to become owners; and some aim to allow for economic bulk purchases, while others intend to be a community gathering space. Though not comprehensive, a list of the type of co-ops would include communal housing arrangements; food, grocery, and other consumption-based organizations; financial organizations, such as savings and loans firms; not-for-profit organizations; a multitude of businesses, for instance, manufacturing facilities; and many others. This entry provides an abridged history on the origin of co-ops before moving on to co-ops in the contemporary U.S. environmental movement.

According to the International Co-operative Alliance, a co-op is "an autonomous association of persons united voluntarily to meet their common economic, social, and cultural needs and aspirations through a jointly-owned and democratically-controlled enterprise" (ICA, 2010a). Co-ops, broadly defined as seen in the ICA's definition, have their historical roots with the Industrial Revolution in England. If one person could be described as the figurehead of the earliest co-ops, it would be the cotton industrialist, Robert Owen, and they would be situated in New Lanark, Scotland. Followers of Owen, or Owenites as they became known, created villages of co-operation in Scotland and stateside in Indiana. These communities were to be autonomous groups of individuals working together in every manner. Though these early Owenite communities did not last, co-operatively run stores, trade unions, and other organizations lived on. One of the earliest successful co-ops was the Rochdale Society of Equitable Pioneers formed in Rochdale, England, in 1844. Members funded, organized, and ran a store selling a small number of grocery items and providing their patrons a dividend of the proceeds. The Rochdale Principles, a set of principles that provide the basis for many co-ops today, were created by this early consumer co-op.

Co-ops in America History to Present

The earliest forms of co-operation in America did not arrive with the establishment of the United States of America or the arrival of the colonists, but rather, with the many millions of Native Americans. Mirroring the famous French philosopher Proudhoun's idea that "property is theft," most Native American tribes did not recognize ownership of land or resources (for an example of Native American society see Eggan, 1950). The early English colonists functioned largely as a commune, with farmers depositing their produce into a common storehouse and acquiring goods through the common store. However, with an increasing number of highly capitalized and chartered companies, profit-driven enterprises with indentured servitude and slavery came to dominate the colonies. Other co-operative enterprises developed largely out of necessity. For example, Ben Franklin helped organize a firefighting company that would come to members' aid.

Cooperatives in the agricultural sector took hold across America in the 19th century. Farmers organized to combat the low prices they often received for their crops and realize the discounts of collective transportation and purchase. One example of an early agricultural cooperative was the Order of the Patrons of Husbandry, known as the Grange. The Grange worked to bring producers and consumers into direct contact, eliminating the middle man and providing savings on both ends. Retail cooperatives formed in increasing numbers alongside producer and manufacturing cooperatives. In 1916, the Cooperative League of the United States of America (CLUSA) formed to promote cooperatives broadly. With the onset of the Great Depression, cooperatives gained a stronger presence, aided in many ways by the federal government through New Deal legislation. For example, the Rural Electrification Act of 1937 helped form rural electric cooperatives that would bring power to millions of rural Americans for the first time. Utility cooperatives now include telephone and water, in addition to electricity, and serve vast swaths of rural America.

Cooperatives continued to play an increasing role in the U.S. economy, while they built on long-standing support for social issues such as reduced working hours. Cooperatives and umbrella organizations such as the Federation of Southern Cooperatives supported the Civil Rights Movement in the 1960s. Consumer food cooperatives enjoyed rapid expansion with an increasing consumer interest in organic and natural foods. The food cooperatives that grew quickly over the 1960s and 1970s were not unique in one important aspect of cooperatives: broadly speaking, cooperatives have formed when individuals come together to address their own needs, be that selling commodities, purchasing goods, or pooling resources for individual and community benefit.

Since the advent of the environmental movement, many cooperatives have taken on a green agenda. Arguably the most visible form, for Americans, is the cooperative grocery store and food buying club. Individuals become members, typically through payment of a lifetime or annual fee, and can then shop at the cooperative. Cooperative grocers continue to provide natural and organic foods, though many now partake in local and regional food distribution, education and cooking classes, food storage, and other innovative areas. According to research conducted by the University of Wisconsin Center for Cooperatives, there are nearly 30,000[1] cooperatives operating in the United States, with 73,000 establishments owning more than $3 trillion in assets and generating over $500 billion in revenue (Deller et al., 2009). However, out of some 73,000 establishments, fewer than 1,000 are grocery and retail cooperatives. Other cooperative categories have higher numbers of establishments, for example, farm supply and marketing (approximately 4,500) or housing (approximately 9,500), though all categories are dwarfed by credit unions (approximately 29,000) and mutual insurance (approximately 20,000) cooperative organizations. The simple difference between cooperative financial services like credit unions relative to other institutions is that cooperatives return revenues to their membership as opposed to investors in the stock ownership corporate model.

Many cooperatives are at the forefront of ecological living, though there is the persistent challenge of meeting their members' needs while reducing their footprint. For instance, electricity cooperatives provide power for customers more geographically disbursed than investor-owned utilities. The electricity industry uses revenue per mile as a standard measure for the money generated from transmission and distribution lines. Electric cooperatives earn slightly more than $10,000 per mile, while investor-owned utilities and municipally owned utilities both earn above $60,000 per mile (NRECA, 2011). Even while providing electricity to less profitable customers, electric cooperatives received 11 percent of their power from renewable sources, relative to 9 percent for other utilities (2008 data from NRECA); furthermore, they have increased their renewable portfolio by 60 to 70 percent in recent years relative to national growth at less than 25 percent (NRECA, 2011).

The International Co-operative Alliance has established seven cooperative principles: voluntary and open membership; democratic member control; member economic participation; autonomy and independence; provision of education, training, and information; cooperation among cooperatives; and concern for the community (ICA, 2010b). The last principle, concern for the community, is especially important regarding the environment. "Community" historically referred to geographically or interest-specific groups of stakeholders (e.g., a neighborhood co-op). However, stakeholders within the community might now include workers thousands of miles away in another country. Importantly, the community for many cooperatives now frequently encompasses future generations through sustainable development and environmental protection.

Additional Resources

The University of Wisconsin–Madison Center for Cooperatives is an accessible Web site that

2012 United Nations' International Year of Co-Operatives

The 2012 UN's International Year of Co-operatives theme is "cooperative enterprises build a better world." The resolution adopted by the UN General Assembly states, "cooperatives, in their various forms, promote the fullest possible participation in the economic and social development of all people, including women, youth, older persons, persons with disabilities and indigenous peoples, are becoming a major factor of economic and social development and contribute to the eradication of poverty." For more see http://www.ncba.coop/ncba/what-we-do/co-op-marketing-a-promotion/international-year-of-cooperatives/839-materials-for-cooperatives-iyc.

provides wide-ranging information as well as contemporary research projects (http://www.uwcc.wisc.edu/index.aspx).

For a sector-specific, though somewhat dated, collection of essays by leading authorities see David W. Cobia, ed., *Cooperatives in Agriculture* (Upper Saddle River, NJ: Prentice-Hall, 1989). For an excellent examination of worker cooperatives see Robert Jackal and Henry M. Levin, eds., *Worker Cooperatives in America* (Berkeley: University of California Press, 1984).

For an international perspective see Johnston Birchall, *The International Co-operative Movement* (Manchester and New York: Manchester University Press, 1997).

For a simple and easy to read overview see Stefano Zamagni and Vera Zamagni, *Cooperative Enterprise: Facing the Challenge of Globalization* (Northampton, MA: Edward Elgar Publishing, 2010).

ROBERT J. WENGRONOWITZ

See also: Community Economic Development and Substantive Participation (Activism); Ecovillage (Activism); Living off the Grid (Activism); Wise-Use Movement (Activism).

Note

1. The Center for Cooperatives' research explicitly provides a conservative figure. According to John Curl (2009), in 2008 there were more than 120 million Americans belonging to nearly 50,000 cooperatives. The U.S. National Cooperative Business Association puts the figure at 48,000 cooperatives serving 120 million Americans.

References

Curl, John. 2009. *For All the People: Uncovering the Hidden History of Cooperation, Cooperative Movements, and Communalism in America*. Oakland, CA: PM Press.

Deller, Steven, Ann Hoyt, Brent Hueth, and Reka Sundaram-Stukel. 2009. *Research on the Economic Impact of Cooperatives*. Madison: University of Wisconsin Center for Cooperatives. Available at: http://reic.uwcc.wisc.edu/sites/all/REIC_FINAL.pdf.

Eggan, Fred. 1950. *Social Organization of the Western Pueblos*. Chicago: University of Chicago Press.

International Co-Operative Alliance (ICA). 2010a. "Statement on the Co-operative Identity." Available at: http://www.ica.coop/coop/principles.html.

International Co-Operative Alliance (ICA). 2010b. "What Is a Co-Operative?" Available at: http://www.ica.coop/coop/index.html.

National Rural Electric Cooperative Association (NRECA). 2011. "Co-op Facts & Figures." Available at: http://www.nreca.org/members/Co-opFacts/Pages/default.aspx.

ECOTOURISM

Ecotourism, also known as sustainable tourism or nature-based tourism, takes into consideration the environmental and cultural conditions of a tourist destination, the means of travel to the tourist destination, and the behaviors of tourists

Colorado Trail marker on a tree along the trail. The Colorado Trail runs 500 miles from Denver to Durango through the stunning vistas of the Rocky Mountains. The not-for-profit Colorado Trail Foundation, which maintains the trail, exemplifies the notion of eco-tourism. For a nominal fee, the foundation supplies food and campsites to teams of volunteers who act as maintenance crews for weekend or weeklong stints. (Patrick Poendl/Shutterstock.com)

themselves. There are many competing definitions, so it is best to think of ecotourism as a set of loosely defined principles. First, it is characterized by travel that minimizes environmental and cultural impact. Second, it incorporates an educational component about the cultural and environmental conditions of a region or destination. Finally, it should provide financial support for local conservation efforts and local communities. Some also suggest that it should empower local communities, encourage democratic movements, and support human rights.

A way to differentiate ecotourism or ecotourists from other nature-based or adventure tourism is the inherent interest in the well-being and integrity of the locale in which the tourists are visiting. Ecotourists are generally from well-educated families, active, and have a genuine interest in cultures and nature. They often belong to conservation associations or have a strong interest in environmental protection. Their motivation for choosing ecotourism-based vacations over other types of vacations includes their preference for nature experiences, educational components of tourism, and a concern for the environment. They often travel for longer periods of time and opt out of the mainstream travel industry. Others have countered this argument by suggesting that it is only preference for the type of experiences tourists prefer and not a desire to protect the environment that drives the ecotourism industry. Regardless of whether a tourist is motivated by experiences desired or inherent concern for the environment, ecotourists seek a recreational and pleasurable experience while demonstrating a responsibility toward the environment through their choices and behaviors.

Some of the biggest impacts that tourism can have on the environment is through the development of permanent structures such as hotels, restaurants, transportation networks, recreational structures, and other facilities that can alter the landscape, change habitat, degrade the soil, vegetation, and aesthetic appeal. Another major impact is the production of waste and pollution. This can be anything from an increase in solid waste and wastewater effluent to increased air pollution from transportation emissions and noise pollution. Tourist activities are another large source of environmental degradation. Many recreational activities interfere with the flora and fauna of a location, causing soil or water degradation and changes in species habitats and populations. Finally, tourism attracts further development of a region, and the subsequent increase in population exacerbates the impacts on the environment and increases demand on the region's resources. Altogether, these pressures damage global ecosystems and deplete natural aesthetics.

Part of the problem is that ecotourism generally brings people to locales that have been previously undisturbed, so the effects on the environment are worse than in an area that has already been developed. If a destination is well planned with sustainable ecotourism practices, then much of the degradation can be avoided or minimized. Although, no matter how deliberate the development is, there are almost always unintended consequences, such as wildlife disruption or accidental introduction of invasive species. These are the consequences that are most difficult to plan for, monitor, and mitigate.

The groundwork for the development of ecotourism is found in four distinct sources: nongovernmental organizations focused on conservation and scientific research, developing countries looking for ways to encourage economic development, aid institutions that are also looking for economic development opportunities, and finally the travel industry (both travel businesses and consumers). Often the shift to ecotourism took place when many countries began privatizing popular tourist destinations beginning in the 1990s. For developing countries, ecotourism provided an opportunity to bring in foreign money without resorting to destructive resources extraction (such as logging, mining, and food production). Some researchers have suggested that ecotourism can bring in more money than the resource extraction alone because it brings in more job opportunities and long-term viability to a region. In the case of wildlife, species that were once valuable for skins or food are now more profitable as a sightseeing feature. More recently, ecotourism can be found in some form in both developing and developed countries.

In the past decade, ecotourism has started to influence even the mainstream travel industry. The UN General Assembly deemed 2002 the Year of Ecotourism in order to promote the concept and successful frameworks, share resources about planning and managing ecotourism activities, and plan for the future. The World Ecotourism Summit was held in Quebec City, Canada, with participants from 133 different countries. The result was a Quebec Declaration on Ecotourism that was supposed to be a framework for further developing ecotourism and reducing poverty in tourist destinations. Another result was a large network of regional organizations dedicated to increasing ecotourism activities. With the international attention turned to the environmental and cultural impacts of travel, many tour operators and travel organizations were working hard to create ecotourism options. Certification programs, labeling systems, and "eco" awards gained prominence as a way for consumers to identify authentic ecotourism and for businesses to gain accountability in the marketplace. In addition, ecotourism was no longer considered an issue only for developing countries.

In the United States, tourism is a major economic driver. It follows only France and Spain in the number of visitors each year and has an extraordinarily large amount of domestic tourism, contributing to the largest earnings and employment sector in the United States. In 2009, more was spent by international travelers visiting the United States than by U.S. travelers abroad. This supports businesses, creates employment opportunities, and generates a large amount of tax revenue for local, state, and federal governments. The national parks system, which makes up the largest amount of legally protected land in the world, constitutes the most popular recreation destination in the United States. Much of the trend toward green travel in the United States has occurred on the state level, as organizations and state-level governments work directly with industry to create their own eco-labels.

Another area of growth is with outbound ecotour operators who are starting to develop trips in the United States in addition to their overseas offerings. Hotels and other accommodations are seeing the largest push from consumers on environmental issues. Hotel chains in the United States have been participating in energy- and water-saving measures for about two decades now, but there is even more push for recycling programs, beachfront protection, and locally sourced food. Several of these programs have encouraged hotel chains to create their own environmental policies, especially when those policies are also cost-saving measures. In developing countries, consumers want hotels to go beyond improving environmental conditions to help alleviate poverty in the immediate vicinity by hiring locals to work in the hotels or by using their services.

Unlike many other countries, the United States does not have a comprehensive policy that supports, develops, or regulates ecotourism. Instead, aspects of ecotourism are managed by individual departments of the federal government. Most of the federal recreation lands are managed by the U.S. Parks and Recreation Department or the Bureau of Land Management (BLM). In addition to managing the land and creating educational programs, these departments work with local businesses to provide approved ecotourism services. Another department working on ecotourism is the Environmental Protection Agency (EPA). They have created ways of calculating the environmental impact of various tourism activities and provide guidelines on how to minimize the impacts.

In the early stages of the ecotourism model, parks, governments, and scientists were focused on limiting the number of visitors to a particular location in order to prevent environmental degradation. They soon discovered that the number of visitors was not as important as the types and timing of activities allowed. Providing education to visitors and limiting activities that are particularly destructive (such as all-terrain vehicles or hiking off trails) are more protective in the long term. In the early 1970s and 1980s, the U.S. Forest Service developed several educational programs, including the "Leave No Trace" and "Tread Lightly" campaigns, to encourage visitors to minimize their impact on natural lands. The parks do face a number of challenges though. There is pressure from a variety of stakeholders over how the land is managed, who has what kind of access, developing enough proper infrastructure, and the cost of operation and maintenance. Although visitors are charged an entrance fee to the parks, the parks are underfunded and fees only cover a small portion of the budget. At the heart of all these challenges is the ongoing debate between preservation and recreation, which goes back to the purpose and origins of the U.S. national parks system.

Challenges

Although the main principles of ecotourism are widely recognized, there is no single clear definition that is accepted by all in the tourism industry, or even by certifying organizations. A serious problem in the industry is "greenwashing," where ecotourism is used as a marketing tool rather than as guiding principles. Occasionally, a business may have some token environmentally friendly practices, but in reality has not shifted its overall impact. More often, greenwashing occurs where no effort is put into the principles of ecotourism. Consumers in search of genuine ecotourism must take some responsibility to investigate the legitimacy of eco-marketing claims. Unfortunately, this is not easy to do because certification is not well developed.

The evolution of labeling and certification of ecotourism started with nongovernmental organizations calling for tourism practices that conform to the principles of ecotourism. This was followed quickly by industry co-opting the term as a marketing scheme, while only a few companies actually followed through on the practices. Several certifying bodies then came into existence in order to recognize those who were in fact complying with the original principles until this approach too became co-opted by industry organizations. The next step would be to develop an international certification body to oversee and enforce the certification and labeling process. So far, this development has been hampered by industry players who stand to lose out when the certification gains more teeth and lack of consumer interest. A further concern for certification organizations is making the application process equitable, affordable, and efficient. This can be difficult to do in an international context, so there are many organizations working to certify in single countries or regions. In order for ecotourism to make progress, it needs to become a standard part of making travel plans.

Interestingly, studies have indicated that most consumers pay little attention to eco-certification when choosing a tour operator. While many consumers say they are interested in supporting ecotourism and even go as far as suggesting they would pay more for ecotourism, very few do the work involved in finding those options. Most tourists are paying for all-in-one style travel to agencies based in the global north. This money doesn't stay in the host country, which decreases the economic and environmental benefits for the local community. It also challenges the main principles behind ecotourism. Involving the communities around the eco-destination is a good way to ensure that local communities benefit from the industry, but it also encourages the local community members to invest in the conservation and sustainability of their local resources.

Travel to ecotourist destinations is potentially a major contributor to environmental degradation since most of that travel will be long-haul flights overseas. Some of the impacts of long-haul travel can be mitigated through carbon off-setting programs or through better fuel efficiency. The implications of climate change and travel by air or car are fairly significant. On the other hand, bringing wealthy visitors to a developing country helps local communities stabilize their economy without depleting their natural resources. Like many of the other debates around ecotourism, there is no clear-cut solution. One way countries can work with this issue and prepare for volatile markets dependent of fossil fuels is to develop more domestic travel and tourism. This already occurs to a significant extent in developed nations such as the United States, but as developing countries begin to prosper, more people will have the funds to make travel a part of their routine.

Another major debate about the impacts and influence of ecotourism is around scale and the mainstream tourism industry. Many proponents of ecotourism believe that small-scale operations are much better at maintaining and adhering to ecotourism principles, and that once you begin to scale up you lose the integrity of the practice. Others argue that some degree of greening throughout the mainstream tourism industry has more impact, even if they are only superficial changes. This debate about scale is unlikely to have any clear answers, although some research has indicated that many of the smaller-scale operations that have managed to be successful and maintain their commitment to ecotourism principles have expanded in location and size without losing the integrity of their operation. In the end, ecotourism must remain sustainable in the long term to remain effective. Therefore, while eliminating all impact may be desired, it may not be realistic.

SHAUNA M. BLOOM

See also: Travel (Health).

References

"Global Sustainable Tourism Alliance." Available at: http://www.gstalliance.net/.

Higham, James, ed. 2007. *Critical Issues in Ecotourism: Understanding a Complex Tourism Phenomenon*. Oxford: Elsevier.

Hill, Jennifer, and Tim Gale, eds. 2009. *Ecotourism and Environmental Sustainability: Principles and Practice*. Burlington: Ashgate.

Honey, Martha. 2008. *Ecotourism and Sustainable Development: Who Owns Paradise?* 2nd ed. Washington, DC: Island Press.

"The International Ecotourism Society." Available at: http://www.ecotourism.org/.

"Responsible Travel." Available at: http://www.responsibletravel.org/.

FAIR TRADE

Fair trade can refer to a social movement that attempts to address deficiencies in the traditional global trade system or as a certification and labeling scheme designed to improve transparency in the supply chain. Both the social movement and the certification systems working within the movement argue that free trade takes advantage of marginalized producers in the global south who lack access to information, infrastructure, and capital that would allow them to participate in the global economy as equal trading partners. Fair trade, on the other hand, is based on transparency in the supply chain so that profits are distributed more fairly among the retailers, processors, distributors, and producers.

Transfair USA logo. Transfair USA is the fair trade certifier in the United States. Fair-trade-labeled coffee, tea, and cocoa certify that fair prices were paid for the product. (Transfair USA)

Fair trade started in the 1940s as a social movement geared toward providing an income for impoverished communities from the global south. The original fair trade organizations, called alternative trade networks, were primarily faith-based organizations that worked with refugee communities and communities from South America, helping them sell handicrafts directly to consumers. In the 1980s, fair trade took on several new developments. The first fair trade cooperative in North America (Equal Exchange) was established in order to facilitate the importation of fair trade coffee. In 1998, a third-party certification system (TransFair USA) was established in the United States.

The central tenets of fair trade ensure that producers have control of production either through land ownership, labor associations, or cooperative structures. Certification programs include standards for safe working conditions and strict rules about child labor and access to education. There are environmental standards and sustainability goals geared to be appropriate for each country of origin and production method. All of this is accomplished by setting minimum price guarantees and adding social premiums that pay for community infrastructure, improvements in working conditions or production practices, continuing education, child care, and health care. Buyers of fair trade products are encouraged to develop long-term relationships with producers that encourage consistency in product quality for the buyer and income for the producers. One of the most important benefits of fair trade for the producers is a stable income during times of drastic price fluctuations.

Many fair trade cooperatives use some of the social premium payments to invest in better environmental practices, such as organic certification or new equipment and training. Although there are specific environmental standards for each product, they all must comply with some basic standards. These standards encourage sustainable land conservation, emphasize practices that improve soil fertility and minimize soil erosion, conserve water sources and protect against water pollution, protect species diversity and virgin habitats, use organic practices and minimize agrochemicals as much as possible, and avoid genetically modified species. For nonfood commodities, the standards emphasize the use of recycled, sustainably and locally sourced raw materials, and manufacturing processes that minimize energy use and pollution. Distribution is generally by boat rather than by airplane to reduce fuel usage, and packaging is required to be recyclable or biodegradable.

Organic coffee is currently the best-selling fair trade product in the United States, with bananas coming in at a close second. In recent years, there has been huge growth in the fair trade industry as consumers become more familiar with fair trade labels and issues. Alternative trade gained mainstream popularity because consumers were motivated by ecological and health issues, but consumers have yet to become more aware of the social justice issues involved. Therefore, products labeled as certified organic, shade grown, and other ecological labels tend to fare better than the fair trade label. Many cooperatives that choose to become fair trade certified also become certified organic in order to appeal to eco-minded consumers. Almost half of the fair trade products sold in the United States are also certified organic. Producers often prefer to become certified organic because it provides an additional price premium, and it often means better working conditions, less input costs, and longer-term viability.

Challenges and Environmental Impacts

In some instances, the standards desired by northern consumers and fair trade organizations are not suitable or feasible for local social or ecological conditions.

Requiring a strict removal of agrochemicals may increase labor needs to a level that is not feasible for the community to manage. In many cases, cooperatives make recommendations to certification bodies to adjust for local conditions, but this does not always resolve the issue. One of the many challenges in creating transparency for the consumer is determining how to create and set standards that are appropriate and fair for different regions of the world and types of products. Another aspect of having one system of certification (method of transparency) is that not all producers who would benefit from fair trade are able to participate. Having stringent regulations is important, but many producers cannot participate because of their remote locations, because they live on ecologically marginal land, or because they do not have the resources to provide the proper working conditions for laborers and meet environmental standards. For example, coffee growers who live on marginal landscapes may not have the resources to plant shade cover for the coffee plants.

A second challenge is related to the growth of the fair trade market place, one where supply has increased faster than demand. Frequently, producers are able to sell only a portion of their premium product to a fair trade buyer. The rest is sold on the open market where the price often doesn't cover the cost of production, let alone improvements in the local community. A related but separate issue is the cost of multiple environmental labels, such as bird friendly and shade grown, in addition to organic and fair trade. Several studies have indicated that having just one label for environmental issues would decrease costs to producers and make labeling efforts more straightforward for consumers, but others claim that one label for fair trade and environmental concerns would degrade the environmental standards as larger corporations become involved in fair trade.

Overall, the biggest green impact of fair trade has been the investment of social premiums into environmental programs and long-term sustainability projects. Producers are able to access training and education to learn about soil and water quality and have the capacity to choose lower yielding, but more environmentally friendly, production practices.

SHAUNA M. BLOOM

See also: Organic and Natural Foods (Food).

References

DeCarlo, Jacqueline. 2007. *Fair Trade: A Beginner's Guide*. Oxford: Oneworld Publications.

"Fair Trade Resource Network." Available at: http://www.fairtraderesource.org/.

"Fair Trade USA." Available at: http://www.transfairusa.org/.

Fairtrade Labelling Organizations International. "Fairtrade International." Available at: http://www.fairtrade.net/.

Nelson, Valerie, and Barry Pound. 2009. *The Last Ten Years: A Comprehensive Review of the Literature on the Impact of Fair Trade*. Greenwich: University of Greenwich, Natural Resources Institute.

FARMING, CONVENTIONAL

Conventional farming can be generally defined as the high-input, high-output agrichemical petroleum-based agricultural paradigm under which most food in the United States is produced today. Typically, conventional farming is focused on yield optimization (producing as much of a given crop or commodity as possible) and has embraced genetically modified technologies in order to maximize both output and the ease of production, both of which directly impact the short-term profitability of the agricultural operation. It is this short-term profit-maximization focus and its downstream impacts that have angered environmentalists, health advocates, as well as those involved in the burgeoning organic and local food movements. Despite these criticisms, advocates of the current food production system continue to argue that this system is the only way to continue to feed the burgeoning world population in a cost-effective manner and that consumer choice is driving or demanding the food options that only their industrialized system can produce.

While this debate is wide ranging in scope and the opinions held, this entry focuses specifically on two aspects within the milieu of issues flowing around conventional farming as an industry to provide a starting point for engaging in the greater debate regarding the environmental impacts associated with conventional farming. This entry focuses exclusively on crop production (rather than animal agriculture), although perhaps even more controversy surrounds this aspect of the industry. First, this entry focuses on the debate regarding the merits of conventional farming as a system for producing most of the food that Americans eat on a daily basis. Second, this entry goes beyond the debate and looks at a few ways that some conventional farmers are working to minimize their impacts. These issues are addressed in turn.

The Debate

Over the past decade in particular, conventional farming has come under fire from environmental and health groups. Environmental, local food, and health advocates routinely criticize conventional farming for its heavy dependence on petroleum products, reliance on genetically modified crops, as well as for the condition of the crops that it ultimately markets and the health impacts they argue flow from this system. To this end, these groups have waged strong campaigns to alter the federal subsidies that flow or reinforce conventional farming operations, campaigns that continue to bring issues associated with conventional farming to the foreground.

Petroleum Based and Dependent

The first critique focuses on the fact that synthetic fertilizers, designed to boost crop yields, are created with petroleum inputs shipped in from vast distances, which generally serve to further feed into the carbon issues faced by U.S. society at large, particularly when the fuel utilized to produce the crops and transport the products to their end destination is also factored into this equation. This argument has been heightened in recent years as the proportion of grain crops converted back into ethanol or other alternative fuel sources has increased along with demand. Some have focused on the relatively low conversion factor between the amount of petroleum utilized to actually grow the crops versus the fuel equivalent that comes out as an end product as a negative externality flowing out of conventional farming.

Reliance on Genetically Modified Organisms

The second critique relates to conventional farming's increasing reliance on genetically modified organisms (GMOs) to increase both yields and efficiency, with regard to both weeds and insect threats to growing crops. Over the past decade and a half, agricultural seed companies have developed new varieties of seeds that either maximize production or control for certain weed or pest varieties. Notable among these products are Monsanto's Roundup Ready™ seeds (and similar products from competitors), which have been developed to be resistant to Roundup™ (or generic glyphosate), an effective form of synthetic herbicide. The value of these GMOs is that glyphosate can be applied to kill off competing vegetation (weeds) while leaving the commercial crop unimpacted. This serves to effectively provide strong weed control, often without the necessity of repeated applications of herbicide. Environmentalists, however, criticize the increased usage of this technology as potentially leading to unintended consequences, such the drift of these genetic variants into non-GMO crops, and as allowing for the potential for resistance to the commercial herbicides and pesticides to build up within the range of weeds and insects being addressed.

Health Impacts

The last principal critique relates to the impact of these products on the consumers who actually eat the end products of the current food system. Conventional farming, in the view of these groups, leads to the production of foodstuffs that are not as nutritious or are less desirable from a health standpoint and have led or contributed to a variety of health epidemics, including the obesity issues currently facing Americans.

Conventional farmers, however, counter these arguments by pointing to their ability to maximize or concentrate their production of foodstuffs on a relatively small amount of working land, which allows for the conservation of other land and allows the ever-increasing world population to be supported and generally have sufficient food and nutrition. Absent such techniques, the proponents of conventional farming argue that either more land would be required to produce food (which would likely be more subject to erosion than those lands already devoted to agricultural production) or vast percentages of the population would face food insecurity. The current system also allows for the production of relatively cheap (as far as fixed costs) food for the U.S. consumer, which any shift away from, it is argued, will result in higher priced food and less choice for consumers in making their purchasing decisions.

Improvements within Conventional Agriculture

In recent years, however, even farmers within the conventional farming sector have begun seeking ways to minimize the impacts of their production, and certain farmers within this sector have implemented a variety of reforms to their production methods in an effort to both increase efficiency and minimize the environmental impacts of their farming operations. One of these improvements or efforts to green these operations is the use of improved tillage methods. Tillage refers to the disruption of soil in order to prepare for the planting of crops. In the United States, this is commonly performed by mechanized means and prior to the 1980s was done almost exclusively through plowing. Plowing, in this traditional sense, left the soil exposed and, with the disruption of any crop residue on the surface layer, was highly conducive to soil erosion.

Within the past few decades, many conventional farmers have realized the environmental impacts of conventional tillage methods and have worked to implement alternative tillage methods in order to minimize soil erosion to ensure the long-term viability of their working lands and also to minimize input costs (i.e., relating to the highly disruptive conventional tillage methods). No-till or reduced-till methods center on the farmer leaving all or a large percentage of the prior year's crop residue on the surface. This residue creates a protective or buffer layer between the elements and the soil, which has the direct environmental benefit of preventing or limiting soil erosion, and has been widely adopted and accepted within the conventional agricultural paradigm as a conservation success. Additional improvements, including the development of more precise targeting for the application of agrichemicals, continue to lessen the environmental impacts of conventional farming and will likely continue to do so going forward.

Conclusion

In sum, conventional farming, reliant on a wide array of petroleum-based inputs and genetically modified organisms, is the way that an overwhelming majority of food within the U.S. food supply chain is currently produced. Many conventional farmers are cognizant of their impacts and have worked to minimize these impacts when possible. To this end, some have diligently worked to implement some conservation efforts (both voluntarily and through governmental mandates), particularly when such efforts have also been economically beneficial. Despite these efforts, criticism of this sector remains widespread and will continue to be so as the debate continues over the future direction of the U.S. food supply and farming generally, particularly within the debate over whether federal subsidies should continue to flow into this sector. As is always the case, however, this direction will likely be largely driven by consumer demand and individual customer decisions at the checkout aisle.

JESS R. PHELPS

See also: Agriculture (Economics); Conservation Reserve Program (documents); Farming, Organic (Economics); Garden, Home (Health); Natural Resources Conservation Service Watershed and Easement Program (documents).

References

Baker, C. J., K. E. Saxton, W. R. Ritchie, W. C. T. Chamen, D. C. Reicosky, M. F. S. Ribeiro, S E. Justice, and P. R. Hobbs. 2007. *No Till Seeding in Conservation Agriculture*. Cambridge, MA: Cabi.

Baram, Michael, and Mathilde Bourier, eds. 2011. *Governing Risk in GM Agriculture*. New York: Cambridge University Press.

Howard, Albert. 2006. *The Soil and Health: A Study of Organic Agriculture*. Lexington: University of Kentucky Press.

Kay, Ronald, William M. Edwards, and Patricia A. Duffy. 2012. *Farm Management*. New York: McGraw-Hill.

FARMING, ORGANIC

The word *organic* applies to both plants and livestock. It is the process, not the product. Organic farmers grow their crops using natural fertilizers and no chemical pesticides or herbicides; they use strategies such as arranging crops in ways that

A sign announces an organic farm in English and Spanish and warns against spraying pesticides. (Elswarro/Dreamstime.com)

discourage the growth of unwanted plants, rotating crops to avoid stripping the soil of a given nutrient, and avoiding deep plowing with heavy equipment to prevent erosion. Organic farmers raise animals and birds without antibiotics or growth hormones. Despite some added burdens in organic farming, its cost-benefit ratio is advantageous beyond the farmer, extending into the environment. Technically, before World War II, all farming was organic farming because synthetic fertilizers and pesticides were not available for use. But some farmers were more conscientious than others. Agriculture has always been a risky business, and it is useful for us to begin by looking back at how farmers have tried, with only natural means available, to increase their odds in the love-hate interactions of man with nature.

Origins

The effort to reduce the risk and raise the productivity of farming in America goes back to the founding fathers themselves. Thomas Jefferson, a gentleman farmer and prolific letter writer throughout his time in public life, used and advocated the advantages of enlightened farming methods, most of them found today in organic farming literature. Jefferson was idealistic, his vision of America was one of productive, profitable small landholdings managed by a healthy and growing citizenry. In his time, simply sowing seeds in rows was an innovation. Free-thinking Jefferson never stopped wondering:

> Why could we not have a moveable airy cow house to be set up in the middle of the field which is to be dunged, and [keep] our cattle in that thro' the summer as well as the winter? (Peterson, 1984, 1021)

Jefferson's obsessive interest in and practice of agriculture was not unequalled. British farmers, notably King George III, preceded him in an "agrarian revolution" that was ignited by Britain's Industrial Revolution in the 1700s. By the early 1800s, new farm machines spurred dramatic increases in crop yields and new farming laws produced a boom in agriculture that was sorely needed to feed a booming population.

Throughout the 19th and the first decades of the 20th centuries, American farmers mechanized and enlarged their operations as quickly as they could afford, always increasing their yield, to stay ahead of declining market prices, in an uphill battle against the laws of nature and economics. They never thought about the effects of their actions on the future productivity of the land. It wasn't until the combined catastrophes of the Great Depression and the Great Dustbowl that agricultural reform reemerged. When faced with ruin, people began to recognize the effects of intensive cash crop farming on the land and the importance of a more natural agriculture to the health of the soil and the people it fed. But it wasn't until howling Midwestern dust storms engulfed Washington, D.C., in the winter of 1934–1935 that Congress realized that government aid to agriculture was necessary and appropriate.

Also in the 1930s, agricultural innovation and development came (again) from Britain, now facing the threat of hostilities from Nazi forces, poised to cut off food

Greenovator: Lady Evelyn Barbara Balfour

"How is it that we have made such a mess of things?" After a university agriculture degree and decades of farming, Lady Eve Balfour (1899–1990) had attained success, but was worried about "the disappearance of [our] soil" and "famine [that] overruns a whole continent." She called for a new way of farming that would enrich the soil, and arranged her farm as a scientific laboratory to compare the effects of conventional farming to organic farming. This was the Haughley Experiment. In 1943, Lady Eve published her findings in a book, *The Living Soil*, that struck a blow at the old 19th-century British conservatism or social Darwinism. "Factory farming," she believed, would have to be replaced because "the soil is very much alive and reacts violently against any treatment which weakens its vitality."

The heart of *Living Soil* was the Haughley Experiment. Its long-term testing and comparisons of prevailing theories and methods vindicated organics. Lady Eve's vision of postwar England (New Britain) made her a revolutionary. Among other things, she demanded strict government control of every aspect of land use and food production, including such 21st-century notions as recycling of what we call gray water (rainwater and bathwater) and the belief that food must be produced domestically and as near as possible to the point of consumption.

Source: Balfour, E. B. 1947. *The Living Soil*, rev. ed. London: Faber and Faber.

imports at any moment. Renewed interest in organic farming there and in America began in a big way with a young noblewoman, Lady Eve Balfour. One of the first women to study agriculture, she began farming in Suffolk soon after graduating from the University of Reading in 1920. In 1939 she established the Haughley Experiment, the world's first scientific comparison of organic and chemical-based farming ever undertaken. Her book, *The Living Soil*, published in 1943, presented both the principles of organic farming and early findings from Haughley (IFOAM, 2011).

Lady Balfour and other British reformers inspired American J. I. Rodale to leave New York City in the 1930s to farm in Pennsylvania. Rodale aimed to find practical methods of protecting and rebuilding the soil of U.S. farmland. Two immediate effects of the outbreak of World War II accelerated his efforts: (1) the sudden shortage of chemical nitrogen fertilizer (nitrogen being the main ingredient in explosives), and (2) the sudden shortage of food due to rationing, which led American families to the backyard "victory garden" to grow their own. To build on wartime momentum and further organic gardening, Rodale established *Organic Gardening* magazine and, soon afterward, the Rodale Institute. These two entities were vitally important at a time before U.S. government support for anything organic or environmental. The Rodale farm would demonstrate the value of organic methods and the Rodale magazine would be an information clearinghouse for the public (Rodale Institute, 2011).

When wartime deprivation ended, farmers returned to the easier, "modern" way of producing food, and gardening became a hobby. The pesticide DDT (dichloro-diphenyl-trichloroethane) had been discovered in 1939 and chemists had produced other substances useful in agriculture. These were put to use on a grand scale in the 1950s, and they produced spectacular increases in yield per acre of a few staple crops. They called it a green revolution. All over the world, farmers clamored for more of the miracle seeds and the chemicals they needed, and U.S. agrobusinesses, funded by the Ford Foundation and other wealthy investors, fertilized and fumigated much of the developing world to improve life in poor countries once under British rule. Synthetic fertilizers, pesticides, and super seeds would buy the time needed by the fledgling governments of those new countries to pursue political and economic development, before the hungry masses revolted and turned to communism. But in many cases, this approach ruined the land.

In 1971, J. I. Rodale, by then a guru of organics and health, died, but his work continues. His son Robert expanded the Rodale farming and publishing enterprise, and his children took control when Robert died in 1990. Today, a surge in public awareness fostered by advocates like

Greenovator: Jerome Irving (J. I.) Rodale

Many Americans revere J. I. Rodale (1898–1971) as a pioneer in organic agriculture and healthy living, but they may not know of his years in Manhattan as a writer, theatrical personality, and manufacturer/purveyor of electrical parts. His love of nature and healthy living led Rodale to leave New York and go to Emmaus, Pennsylvania, to live the life he wrote about. There he bought a farm and quickly established *Organic Gardening* magazine in 1942, the Rodale Institute in 1947, and *Prevention* magazine in 1950. Rodale soon had a devoted following. At the height of his fame, in 1964, the Federal Trade Commission filed charges against him, claiming that some of his remedies were quackery. Rodale fought the charges and won.

Though not a farmer by training, Rodale ordered his world in Emmaus as an ecological system: the farm, the magazines, the publishing house, and the institute each nourishing the other. The farm grew organic produce and functioned as a proving ground for crops and methods, the institute published findings, and the magazines made them available to the public. Rodale died of a heart attack in the midst of an appearance on the *Dick Cavett Show* in 1971. His work lives on in Emmaus, first by the hand of his son, Robert, and now under the guidance of Robert's children.

the Rodales brought on a second wave of scientific inquiry, growing demand for safer, more nutritious food, and government support for organic farming.

Organic Farming Methods

To enrich soil and fertilize crops, organic farmers apply on-farm nutrients such as manures and a variety of plant materials, and they use cover crops whose roots transfer nutrients into the soil around them. They rotate crops that draw certain nutrients from the soil. They often reject deep tilling with heavy equipment. If done correctly, the results are integrated and self-reinforcing. Naturally feeding the soil reduces water use and protects water quality. Rotating crops and growing a variety of crops (diversity) make the crops resilient to diseases, pests, and extreme weather. Avoiding deep tilling prevents soil erosion and conserves biological life. The farm becomes an integrated system that minimizes inputs, maximizes outputs, and enriches the environment.

A glance at one of Robert Rodale's charts reveals the many substances commonly available on farms that can be used instead of commercial fertilizers. These plants and substances provide any farmer's trinity of nutrients: nitrogen, phosphorous, and potash (or the "N-P-K" formula found on every commercial fertilizer package). Alfalfa is rich in nitrogen and potash; bat guano is rich in both nitrogen and phosphorous; seaweed is very high in potash, tobacco stems are even higher; and chicken manure is rich in all three. Organic farms with livestock or poultry can use a rotational grazing system that keeps animals moving from pasture to pasture to provide them high-quality forage, reduce feed costs, and, as an added benefit, apply and distribute manure across the fields.

Organic farmers don't need to depend on pesticides and herbicides the way most conventional farmers do. A variety of nontoxic commercial products will work as well because organically grown plants are healthier and more resistant to insects. Large-scale remedies include "trap crops" to shield main crops and arranging crops to smother or shade out weeds and create a habitat for beneficial insects. Weeding and physical removal of insects can't be avoided, but are not great concerns.

Biodiversity (maintaining many plant species on a piece of land) is a key principle of organic agriculture. Farmers have known for generations that stripping away all but one form of plant life on a farm or in a region (called monoculture) depletes the soil and leaves one species open to attack by a variety of predators, whereas a diverse culture encourages a balance of beneficial plants and insects. In recent years, soil scientists have found a link between biodiversity and carbon sequestration—the removal of carbon from the atmosphere. Carbon in the atmosphere may be the cause of rises in global average temperatures, but carbon in the soil is definitely the cause of healthy plants and is the natural effect of organic soil improvement. At a conference in 2009, a soil scientist from the Czech Republic presented findings that, for the first time, established a direct relationship between biodiversity and the carbon content of soil. In this case, the greater the number of plant species in a pasture, the higher the carbon content of the soil. This means that Czech farmers are "improving biodiversity [with all of the benefits of that] while producing organic food [that] also sequesters carbon," a welcome triple play (Grantham, 2009).

Many organic farmers spend years of experimentation with crop and animal rotations, trying different cover crops and food crops, and methods and strategies for pest and weed control before finding an optimal mix for productivity and profit. Sustainability is the overarching goal. Sustainability is the creation of an organic system that efficiently and effectively feeds the earth, the plants, the animals, and the people within (and outside) its borders, and one that works economically so it can live on year after year. To thrive in this way, in addition to sustained effort on the farm, farmers must become a part of their community (SARE, 2011).

Community-Supported Agriculture

Community-supported agriculture (CSA) answers the needs of farmers as well as consumers. Shoppers sign up (usually online) to buy directly from the CSA farmer. The farmer offers a number of "shares" to the public; shareholders—CSA members—receive a certain quantity of fresh food every week delivered to a central location in town for pick up. This arrangement is a win-win partnership. Farmers can market ahead of time, before the long days in the field, and receive payment early. Consumers, seeking the flavor, nutritional value, and safety of carefully grown food, can get it conveniently, at a good price, on a regular basis. But CSAs go beyond the usual impersonal business transaction. Farmers invite members to visit the farm once a season to see the operation firsthand and get acquainted.

There are other types of organic farming organizations even more directly connected to communities. Georgia Organics is a good example. This group is a member-supported nonprofit organization whose mission is statewide: "to integrate healthy sustainable locally grown food into the lives of all Georgians." Lately, Georgia Organics is best known for its school gardening program that reaches 350 Georgia public schools.

Other activities include legislative advocacy, farmer services, and consumer education. The Farm to School program caught the eye of First Lady Michelle Obama who visited Burgess-Peterson Academy in Atlanta in February 2011. Mrs. Obama—an organic gardener herself at the White House—saw this as an opportunity to talk about exercise and good nutrition through gardening as the key to preventing childhood obesity, the aim of her "Let's Move" campaign (*Georgia Organics*, 2011).

Economics of Organic Farming

Government involvement in farming began in the 1930s with the creation of the U.S. Department of Agriculture (USDA), but this federal agency took no interest in organic farming until the 1980s. As a result of the revival of public interest in organic farming in the 1970s, several groups successfully lobbied the U.S. Congress to recognize, support, and regulate organic farming. Most Washington lobbyists decry federal regulation, but organic farmers need regulation as a way to define, protect, and promote their produce, if only to distinguish it from perhaps better looking fruits and vegetables that cost about 20 percent less.

Organic food is not cheap for consumers, and organic farming is not the easy way for farmers. The farmer's first challenge is the USDA's long certification process. The application centers on the Organic System Plan (OSP). The OSP describes practices and substances (some banned, some mandated), monitoring to verify correct implementation of the plan, a record-keeping system, and prevention of commingling of organic and nonorganic products. Following three years of annual onsite inspections by qualified inspectors, a farm is certified "organic" and its produce can be labeled "USDA Organic".

Natural food stores and farmers' markets are no longer the sole outlets for organic foods. Consumer demand for organically grown foods, mainly fruits and vegetables, has brought them into supermarkets. Today, surveys conducted by the Organic Trade Association show that more organic produce is sold in supermarkets than in specialty stores; only 7 percent of organic produce is sold in farmers' markets. Recent USDA estimates show an increase in sales of organics from $5.2 billion in 2000 to $2.5 billion in 2010. Surveys show that consumers of organic foods are increasingly mainstream; a clear majority of all shoppers say they buy organic foods, and respondents explain that they buy organic food for a number of reasons: nutrition and health, food safety, environmental protection, and animal welfare. When they can, people enjoy shopping for fresh fruits and vegetables in the open air. The number of farmers markets grew from 1,755 in 1994 to 4,685 in 2008 as farmers responded to growing demand and took advantage of government marketing assistance. According to a USDA survey, market managers in many states say more organic farmers are needed to meet the demand.

For all the growth in organic farms, farming, and markets, the adoption of organic farm systems (i.e., the shift from conventional to organic farming) has remained low—0.5 percent of all U.S. cropland and 0.5 percent of all pastureland in 2005. Obstacles to organic farming include higher operating costs, risks of shifting to a new way of farming, and inability to capture marketing economies. Still, organic farming has lower inputs (chemical fertilizers and pesticides), conserves nonrenewable resources, captures high-value markets, and boosts farm income. Worldwide, adoption of organic systems is highest in European Union countries.

Growth in organic farming and spread of markets has been aided by targeted U.S. organic agriculture policies that were passed by the U.S. Congress and implemented by federal agencies in the early 1990s and into the 21st century. The USDA first provided its "USDA-organic" label in 2002. The agency also provides financial aid to farmers to defray costs of certification and for crop insurance, but it is not enough to interest conventional farmers in going organic or reduce the price differential.

Conclusions

Organic farming is a small enterprise. It represents only 0.5 percent of U.S. cropland and pastureland, and it produces only about 3 percent of total food purchases. Yet it is a fast-growing enterprise and an important one. Americans today are concerned about food safety, environmental protection, and animal welfare. Organic farming answers these needs, in a small way. It also helps small farmers stay in business in an age of agrobusiness super farms and economic challenges. Though lasting change usually begins when people adapt to challenges, it is heartening to believe that government agencies and food producers are getting more serious about agricultural and environmental problems. Over time, if present circumstances and attitudes prevail, all farming may become more like organic farming.

KATHY HARRIS

See also: Agriculture (Economics); Composting and Vericomposting (Health); Conservation Reserve Program (documents); Farming, Organic (Economics); Garden, Home (Health); Natural Resources Conservation Service Watershed and Easement Program (documents).

References

Balfour, E. B. 1947. *The Living Soil*, rev. ed. London: Faber and Faber.
"First Lady Tours Georgia Organics Farm to School Garden." 2011. *Georgia Organics* (February).
Grantham, Alison. 2009. "Soil Carbon Research Insights Show Co-Solutions." Rodale Institute. Available at: http://www.rodaleinstitute.org.

International Federation of Organic Agriculture Movements (IFOAM). 2011. "Growing Organic: Lady Eve Balfour." Available at: http://www.ifoam.org/growing_organic.

Peterson, Merrill D., ed. 1984. *The Writings of Thomas Jefferson*. Jefferson to John Taylor, December 29, 1794. Library of America by Penguin Putnam.

Rodale Institute. 2011. "Our Mission." Available at: http://www.rodaleinstitute.org.

Sustainable Agriculture Research and Education (SARE). 2011. "What Is Sustainable Agriculture?" SARE booklet.

U.S. Department of Agriculture, Economic Research Service (USDA). 2009a. "Organic Agriculture: Organic Certification." Available at: http://www.ers.usda.gov.

U.S. Department of Agriculture, Economic Research Service (USDA). 2009b. "Organic Agriculture: Market Overview." Available at: http://www.ers.usda.gov.

U.S. Department of Agriculture, Economic Research Service (USDA). 2009c. "Organic Agriculture: Organic Production and Costs." Available at: http://www.ers.usda.gov.

U.S. Department of Agriculture, Economic Research Service (USDA). 2009d. "Organic Agriculture: Organic Policy." Available at: http://www.ers.usda.gov.

GREEN BUILDINGS

Chevron's Northpark building, located just outside of New Orleans, is one example of the growing green movement in construction. This 300,000-square-foot office is the first gold-certified Leadership in Energy and Environmental Design (LEED) building in the State of Louisiana. (To see a video of the green building, visit http://www.willyoujoinus.com/commitment/whatweredoing/wwd3/?autoplay=True.)

What Is a Green Building?

Simply stated, a *green building* is a structure that is planned and designed to use energy, water, natural resources, and materials efficiently and to reduce wastes and pollution. The basic principles of green building apply to all types of new construction and renovation, from remodeling a kitchen to constructing a gymnasium or a four-story building.

Some of the components of green buildings should include:

- conserving natural resources
- increasing energy and water efficiency
- reducing wastes an toxic materials
- improving indoor air quality.

The Impact of Buildings on the Natural Environment

Most people think of vehicle exhausts and factory emissions when they consider the impact of humans on the natural environment. However, according to the Environmental Protection Agency, each year buildings are responsible for

- 65 percent of all energy consumption
- 39 percent of what is classified as greenhouse gas emissions
- 36 percent of all energy consumption
- 30 percent of all raw materials usage

- 12 percent of potable (drinking-quality) water usage
- 30 percent of waste output.

Based on these facts, many communities, cities, and municipalities have drafted green building guidelines.

LEED Leads the Way

A U.S. effort to set standards for design and construction practices is exemplified by the LEED program. As per the LEED standards, factors such as sustainable sites, water efficiency, energy and atmosphere, material, resources, and indoor environmental quality are given different weighted points. Based on these weighted points, certification levels are calculated and graded as certified, silver, gold, and platinum. The highest certification level offered by LEED is platinum. The U.S. LEED standards are being used by Canada, India, and Israel for some of their green architecture projects. Other countries use their own standards for green architecture. Some of these nations include Australia, France, Germany, Japan, Malaysia, Mexico, New Zealand, and the United Kingdom, to name a few.

Criteria for Residential Green Buildings Products

According to green builders and architects, there are four key decisions to be made when choosing and installing sustainable construction materials into a green building. These include indoor air quality, energy efficiency, resource efficiency, and water conservation.

- *Indoor air quality:* All air conditioning units and heating units must be efficient at filtering indoor air pollutants.
- *Energy efficiency:* Install energy-efficient appliances such as Energy Star refrigerators, central air conditioners, and other appliances that will reduce the home's carbon footprint.
- *Resource efficiency:* Use recycled building material when possible, such as paneling, hardwood flooring, doors, and staircase material. Use locally available material goods and renewable materials.
- *Water conservation:* Install showerheads and low-flow toilets to conserve water. The current standard for toilets in the United States is 1.6 gallons per flush.

Green Roof Architecture

Green roofs are living plants installed on top of conventional roofs. A green roof can keep buildings cooler, save energy, extend the useful life of the roof, and add beauty and usable space.

Around the World with Green Roofs

If you travel to most cities in the world, you will find green-roof buildings. In Europe, you would see one of the oldest green roofs created. In 1914 a green roof was installed at the Moos Lake water-treatment plant. The more than 90-year-old plant near Zurich, Switzerland, has a huge nine-acre roof that looks like a meadow.

Germany is well known for its thousands and thousands of homes with green roofs. In fact, it has been estimated that 10 percent of the buildings in this country have green roofs.

The city of Linz, Austria, has been installing green roofs since the 1980s. In France, a huge green roof of roughly 86,000 square feet has been incorporated into the new museum L'Historial de la Vendée that opened in June 2006 at Les Lucs-sur-Boulogne.

Back in the United States, the Gap Headquarters in San Bruno, California, includes a 69,000-square-foot green roof. The new California Academy of Sciences building in San Francisco's Golden Gate Park has a green roof that provides 2.5 acres of native vegetation designed as a habitat for indigenous species, including the threatened bay checkerspot butterfly. Going south to Atlanta, Georgia, the green roof on Atlanta's city hall became the first municipal green roof in the Southeast.

Green Roofs Are Effective

The Environmental Protection Agency states that green roofs can be effectively used to reduce storm water runoff from com-

Greenovation: A Rating System for Go-Green Sustainable Buildings

The organization Leadership in Energy and Environmental Design (LEED) is a leader in sustainable construction. It has developed LEED for Homes, which is a rating system for dwellings that have been built with a plan toward lower utility bills, minimized greenhouse gas emissions, and reduced indoor toxin levels.

According to LEED, once a home or building has been inspected and is LEED certified, the owner will be reassured that the home is not only environmentally friendly but also more attractive to potential buyers in the future. The LEED checklist for certification is very detailed and includes such areas as:

- project planning
- building site selection (above the floodplain defined by the U.S. Federal Emergency Management Association, no endangered species, etc.)
- proximity to mass transit systems
- landscaping methods (drought tolerance, mulch, reduced irrigation demand, etc.)
- nontoxic pest control
- water reuse
- indoor water use (low-flow toilets and shower heads, etc.)
- Energy Star performance appliances
- heating, ventilation, and air conditioning refrigerants
- construction materials
- interior heating methods
- radon protection.

(To learn about the Empire State Building going green and, in doing so, becoming 40 percent more energy efficient, go to http://greenlivingideas.com/topics/green-building/empire-state-building-green (2:22 minutes) or http://www.youtube.com/watch?v=17i7Q5Dr3PA&NR=1 (5:48 minutes). For a story on a rooftop farm in New York, go to http://www.cbsnews.com/stories/2009/10/02/eveningnews/main5361333.shtml?tag=contentBody;featuredPost-PE.)

mercial, industrial, and residential buildings. In contrast to asphalt or metal roofing, green roofs absorb and store large quantities of precipitation. Thereby, the green

A living, green roof planted atop the gymnasium at the Tarkington Elementary school in Chicago, 2005. (AP Photo/Nam Y. Huh)

roofs act as a storm water management system that reduces the volume of storm water entering waterways and sewer systems. This is important because during periods of heavy rainfall and snow melt, storm water systems and sewer systems can become overwhelmed by the volume of water and can overflow into nearby water bodies. This can cause a large discharge of millions of gallons of sewage into local waterways. Green roofs offer additional benefits, too. The green roof provides more thermal and acoustic insulation when compared to the insulation found in conventional roofs. Many residential, commercial, and industrial buildings are suitable for green roof programs.

What Is a Green Roof Made of?

Let's start at the top of a green roof. Here you will find a layer of rows and rows of plants. These plants have shallow rooting systems, grow low to the ground, and are drought tolerant. Plants found on many green roofs include delosperma, chives, talinum, and the popular sedum. The variety of coloration of these plants provides a colorful mosaic on any rooftop. The plants can be grown in a mixture of lightweight soils, crushed shale, vermiculite, and other material.

The shallow depth of the soil helps in keeping weeds from establishing themselves on the roof. Most gardeners know that most weeds cannot survive in the arid and shallow soil conditions found on a vegetated green roof.

Now let's look at what is underneath the garden roof. Here you find either a membrane of rubberized asphalt or a layer of synthetic rubber. These are root-repellant materials that function to stop the moisture of the growing plant roots from damaging the roof.

A layer of pebbles or special drain matting that acts as a drainage layer is placed on the membrane. The drainage layer allows excess water to move freely and prevents the soil from lifting up and flowing off the roof.

Maintenance

Keeping up with an extensive green roof is not difficult because it is low maintenance. The drought-resistant plants used on these green roofs do not need additional watering after they get established, except in extreme conditions. In many green roofs, weeding tasks for gardeners take place only once or twice a year.

Greenovator: A Green Roof in Dearborn, Michigan

One of the largest green roofs to be found in the United States and in the world is located at the Ford Motor Company's River Rouge plant. The plant in Dearborn, Michigan, has 450,000 square feet of green roof covered with sedum, a succulent groundcover, and other plants. The roof reduces storm water runoff by holding an inch of rainfall. The roof also provides a habitat for some local wildlife.

The River Rouge plant won the 2004 Green Roofs for Healthy Cities Award of Excellence in the Extensive Industrial Commercial category. William McDonough designed the green roof.

Benefits of Green Roofs

As mentioned previously, green roofs have many benefits. Green roofs can save homeowners on cooling and heating costs. The leafy cover of a green roof helps cool the air through evaporation, by providing shade and by forming a more lightly colored surface than the dark roof underneath. The insulation provided by the green roof can also help lower heating costs during the winter months and keep the home cooler during the hot weather. A green roof can help to reduce noise level in a home.

What kind of savings does a green roof provide? Savings on heating and cooling costs depend on the size of the building, the local climate, and the type of green roof installed. "Using a simulation model, Environment Canada found that a typical one-story building with a grass roof and 3.9 inches of growing medium would result in a 25% reduction in summer cooling needs."

Some Issues with Green Roofs

Before planning and constructing a garden roof, experts agree that the underlying roof system must be able to accommodate increased maintenance traffic and be designed to meet or exceed expected garden service life. They all agree that leak detection is difficult and that roof repair and maintenance may be more complicated than originally planned.

University and College Courses in Green Architecture

The interest in going green and the creation of green jobs has resulted in the growth of green degree programs at universities near and far.

As one example, the University of Texas, Austin, offers a number of environmental engineering programs. Cornell University offers a range of green programs in biological and environment engineering as well as design and environmental analysis. There are many other colleges that offer green degree programs, too. To get a suggested list, including the top 10 colleges that offer go-green degrees, check the following Web site: http://www.campuscorner.com/articles/top-ten/top-colleges-green-degrees.htm.

Technical School Courses

U.S. technical high schools and community colleges provide hands-on opportunities and experience for students in green building programs as well. In classes and in workshops, students learn how to make buildings less wasteful and more energy efficient.

Some of the energy-efficient construction courses include everything from how to seal walls against energy leaks to how to install and insulate drywall for soundproofing. Students in one technical high school in Rhode Island partnered with a local community organization to build an energy-efficient home for a low-income family. Establishing an energy-savvy, highly trained workforce in the construction trades is vital to increase green building projects.

U.S. Green Cities

The Natural Resources Defense Council recently announced on a new Web site called Smarter Cities its list of the greenest cities in the United States. The survey includes all cities in the United States with populations larger than 50,000. Smarter Cities is considered to be one of the nation's most comprehensive databases of U.S. cities working toward sustainability. The cities are grouped into three size categories to enable comparison between those with similar environmental challenges and constraints on social and financial resources.

Of 67 cities with a population greater than 250,000 that were ranked in the survey, Seattle is America's greenest and most sustainable large city. Seattle is followed by two other western cities, San Francisco and Portland. Among the 176 medium-sized cities evaluated in the survey, Madison, Wisconsin, placed first, and Santa Rosa, California, came in second.

The following criteria were used to rank the cities: air quality, energy production and conservation, environmental standards and participation, green building, green space, recycling, transportation, standard of living, and water quality and conservation.

How Do the Rankings Work?

The data for the rankings came from the U.S. Census Bureau and the National Geographic Society's *Green Guide*. The data included government statistics for U.S. cities with over 100,000 people in more than 30 categories. As noted, the listing includes areas such as air quality, electricity use, and transportation habits. The data were divided into four broad categories. Each was scored with either 5 or 10 possible points. The sum of these four scores determined a city's place in the rankings. The four categories were:

- *Electricity* (10 points): Cities scored points for drawing their energy from renewable sources such as wind, solar, biomass, and hydroelectric power, as well as for offering incentives for residents to invest in their own power sources, such as roof-mounted solar panels.
- *Transportation* (10 points): High scores went to cities whose commuters take public transportation or carpool. Air quality also plays a role.
- *Green living* (5 points): Cities earn points for the number of buildings certified by the U.S. Green Building Council, as well as for devoting areas to green space, such as public parks and nature preserves.
- *Recycling and green perspective* (5 points): This evaluates a city's recycling program and how important its citizens consider environmental issues.

If you are interested in more information and advice, contact the U.S. Green Building Council's Green Home Guide at http://greenhomeguide.com.

A Snapshot of Some Cities Going Green

San Jose, California: The city has a green city plan called the Green Vision program. The 15-year goal is the creation of 25,000 clean technology jobs and a reduction in nonrenewable energy use by 50 percent by using a larger percentage of its electrical power from renewable resources. The city's public transportation vehicles will run on alternative fuels.

Portland, Maine: Portland was among the first communities to sign the U.S. Conference of Mayors Climate Protection Agreement. The city plans to take steps to reduce carbon dioxide (CO_2) emissions by 7 percent over five years. All city-owned diesel vehicles run on a mix of 20 percent vegetable-based biodiesel fuel and 80 percent regular diesel.

Little Rock, Arkansas: The city hosts the headquarters building for Heifer International, a nonprofit organization dedicated to combating hunger. The structure was named one of the 10 greenest buildings in the United States by the American Institute of Architects. The building is designed to use up to 55 percent less energy than a standard building of its size.

Billings, Montana: In Billings, the Trash into Trees program has diverted 3.9 million pounds of newspaper and 68 tons of aluminum cans from landfills. The program earned enough money to purchase and plant 2,152 trees in Billings.

Austin, Texas: Austin has pledged to meet 30 percent of its energy needs with renewable sources by 2020. Its plan is to install more efficient wind generators.

Boulder, Colorado: Boulder imposed the country's first electricity tax to pay for greenhouse-gas emission reductions.

Boston, Massachusetts: In Boston there is a special power plant that can convert 50,000 tons of grass and leaves into power and fertilizer. In the plant, anaerobic bacteria feeding on the grass can make enough methane to power several electrical generators. The heat in the machine can break down leaves, twigs, and grasses into compost.

Green Cities in Other Countries

Masdar City, United Arab Emirates: Masdar City in the United Arab Emirates will be the world's first zero-carbon and zero-waste city. The new city will be powered entirely by renewable energy sources. Masdar City will be built on the outskirts of the city of Abu Dhabi over seven years. The Masdar headquarters building will receive much of its power from a large photovoltaic array on its roof.

The surrounding communities will be linked to Masdar City by a network of existing roads and new railways and public transport routes. The city will be car free and pedestrian friendly. Utility services in the city will include energy, district cooling, water, wastewater, reuse water, storm water, and telecommunications and waste management.

In 2008 Masdar developed a CO_2 capture network system. The network is capable of creating a large reduction in Abu Dhabi's carbon footprint. The first phase of the network will capture and store around 6.5 million tons of CO_2 from power plants and industrial facilities in Abu Dhabi by 2013. Once the CO_2 is captured and stored, it will be transported and injected in oil reservoirs for enhanced oil recovery. Under this type of system, gas injected into the reservoir expands, pushing additional oil to the production site. As it dissolves, the injected gas also lowers the oil's viscosity, thus improving the flow rate.

London, England: There are plans in London to establish future green communities in some of the city's boroughs. One of the areas is Gallions Park at the Royal Albert Dock. When completed, the neighborhood will have 200 or more apartments surrounded by greenhouses, as well as roof-mounted solar panels and some wind turbines. The heat and power plant will use biomass for fuel.

Dongtan, China: In China, the government has started constructing a city on a small island off the coast of Shanghai. Plans for the city include using renewable resources such as wind and solar and zero-emission vehicles. They also will be installing green roofs to collect and filter rainwater to be used as irrigation for local farmers. One of the most ambitious plans is to design the city to consume 40 percent less water than a conventional city. After completion, the goal is to have 500,000 people living in the green city by 2050.

Something to Do

A sustainable or green building is the result of planning techniques that increase the efficiency of resources and reduce the building's impact on human health and the environment.

Research practices and techniques can reduce or eliminate the negative impacts of buildings on the environment and human health. In your research, include efforts to take advantage of renewable resources, environmentally friendly building materials, harmony of the building with the surrounding natural features, measures to reduce energy use, on-site generation of renewable energy, and recycling methods that reduce waste of energy, water, and building materials. Consult the following Web sites: www.epa.gov/greenbuilding, www.energystar.gov, and www.en.wikipedia.org.

JOHN F. MONGILLO

See also: City and Community Planning, Eco-Friendly (Science); Green Cities (Economics); Leadership in Energy and Environmental Design (LEED) (documents); Top Cities with the Most Energy Star Certified Buildings in 2010 (documents).

References

Bauer, Seth, ed. 2008. *Green Guide*. Washington, DC: National Geographic.

Casey Trees Endowment Fund and Limno-Tech, Inc. "Re-greening Washington DC: A Green Roof Vision Based on Quantifying Stormwater and Air Quality Benefits." Available at: http://www.caseytrees.org.

"Green Roofs for Healthy Cities." Available at: http://www.greenroofs.org.

"Jerry Yudelson: Top Ten Green Building Trends for 2009." 2009. Island Press blog, January 28. Available at: http://blog.islandpress.org/296/jerry-yudelson-top-ten-green-building-trends-for-2009.

Jones, R. C., and C. C. Clark. 1987. "Impact of Watershed Urbanization on Stream Insect Communities." *Water Resources Bulletin* 23:6: 1047–1055.

Osmundson, Theodore. 1999. *Roof Gardens: History, Design, and Construction*. New York: Norton.

Riley, Trish. 2007. *Guide to Green Living*. New York: Alpha-Penguin.

Scholz-Barth, K. 2001. "Green Roofs, Stormwater Management from the Top Down." *Environmental Design and Construction*. Available at: http://www.edcmag.com.

U.S. Department of Energy. 2005. *A Place in the Sun: Solar Buildings*. Merryfield, VA: EERE Clearing House.

Van Metre, P. C., and B. J. Mahler. "The Contribution of Particles Washed from Rooftops to Contaminant Loading to Urban Streams." *Chemosphere* 52 (2003): 1727–1741.

GREEN CITIES

As there is a continuous rise of population shifting to cities, there are also exponentially increasing harmful impacts to the ecosystem, including massive amounts of pollution, colossal amounts of land usage, and immense consumption of natural resources. As a result of this influx of urban migration, economic growth, and industrial progress, there is a rapid rate of consumption of energy and nonrenewable resources. Urban design since the late 20th century has explored various ways in which cities can be redesigned in order to reduce the negative consequences of urban sprawl, such as dependency on automobile traffic, excessive land and water consumption, and a lack of pedestrian environment. A true green city involves several variables of sustainability, environmental science, urbanism, and architecture. Sustainable urbanism is a growing field of study that integrates knowledge from these disciplines in an attempt to establish standards and seek new ways of restructuring development of infrastructure, architecture, and

Electric street car in Seattle, Washington. Seattle was rated America's greenest city in 2010 by the National Resources Defense Council. (iStockphoto.com)

community in today's cities in order to foster a progressive, environmentally sensitive way of life.

The green cities movement has roots in the emergent desires of the late 20th century to return to the small-town lifestyle. During the postwar 1900s, there was an urge to revisit the garden city ideals pioneered by the English architect and planner Ebenezer Howard in the 1890s. His approach to urban design was the maximization of the qualitative aspects of the traditional agricultural town, while adapting to the needs of the modern city. This garden city movement not only brought about new ideas on land usage, but also attempted to reorganize society and its impact on urban migration. Urban design of the later 1900s was also significantly impacted by works of other prominent designers, including the book *Design with Nature* by Ian McHarg. This work by the Scottish landscape architect was influential in questioning the progress of human society within the ecosystem. Through his critique of such urban conditions as pollution, overcrowding of buildings, and the absence of open space, he encouraged a harmonious cityscape that merged human living with the natural environment.

In the 1930s, a seminal group of European modernist architects at the International Congresses of Modern Architecture proposed ideas that enforced a vertical growth of density. The central premise behind these studies was that the high-rise building type could accommodate urban population, allowing the potential to create the desired open public green space. Inspired by such ideas of restructuring the density of cities, the Congress for New Urbanism supported the creation of pedestrian walkways and narrow streets and the preservation of farmland and open space as solutions to the growing problems of urban sprawl of the 1990s. In addition, they promoted mixed-use communities, pedestrian networks, and a diversity of architectural styles to define the cityscape.

Contemporary approaches toward sustainable urban design since the 1950s share the same underlying goals of the earlier models while placing priorities on the redesign of infrastructure, the zoning of open green space, and reducing the impact on the environment. Urban designers are rejecting the effects of autodependent suburban sprawl and are beginning to seek ways of integrating modern human ways of life with "natural systems." As explored by the historic models of the early 1900s, the control of urban density is crucial to the success of a community. Although the ideal size of a neighborhood is variable according to local regional contexts, a community prospers with diversity in land use. The creation of compact, high-density, mixed-use developments reduces the overall demands of infrastructure for automobile traffic and other utilities.

Therefore, density limits can not only address communal and environmental needs, but can also create a more engaging pedestrian environment for residents. However, designing these dense neighborhoods in isolation will only encourage the return of dependency on automobile transportation. Infrastructure, therefore, should be thought of as a collective public system, consisting of a coherent dialogue between mass transit and traffic for pedestrians and automobiles. Mass transit systems should utilize the capacity to connect these concentrated establishments to enable a convenient urban lifestyle for residents. In addition to maximizing accessibility and efficiency, infrastructure should also be supported accordingly, with zoning codes for other utilities, such as sewer, gas, electrical, and gray water systems.

Through the overcrowded center cities and isolated private lots of today's suburbs, humans have become detached from the outdoor environment. Furthering concepts by Howard, McHarg, and other leading visionaries, urbanists of the present century have studied ways in which the modern city can incorporate proportionate zones of public green space. Park spaces, greenways, and other such open green public spaces have numerous energy-efficient and experiential benefits in urban neighborhoods. In addition to providing opportunities for gray water recycling systems, these zones of open space also promote healthy lifestyles for residents. For example, the smart-growth movement views the design of green field development as another integral layer of urban infrastructure. This integration within the land uses of the city allows access for all residents and strengthens the natural biodiversity of the region.

Although there are numerous projects and developments that exemplify strategies of sustainable urbanism in cities throughout the country, the movements have yet to dynamically influence codes of practice. Specific legislative regulation is essential to the management of such redevelopment strategies. Some of the most successful groups that have stimulated enforcement in America's large cities include the active leadership of architects and urban designers at different levels of legislation, along with elected officials and local citizens. It allows the potential to share their knowledge and design skills to educate the public about the rapid environmental decline and urge the steps of change. The Neighborhood Conservation Program in some states is one such influential body that has encouraged planning councils that urge policies for implementation into the existing urban fabric before designing new communities.

Following the lessons learned from various models from the 19th and 20th centuries, architects and urban designers of this decade are shifting their focus toward progressive visions of cities for the 21st century. The goals for green cities of the future include establishing the balance between efficient living for all citizens, economic and industrial vitality, and environmentally conscious lifestyles. The ultimate challenge lies in that these designs must allow the city to constantly readapt to needs of changing society while highlighting conservation and enhancing the quality of life.

MOHAMMAD GHARIPOUR

See also: Community Economic Development and Substantive Participation (Activism); Green Buildings (Economics); Leadership in Energy and Environmental Design (LEED) (documents); Top Cities with the Most Energy Star Certified Buildings in 2010 (documents).

References

Brown, David E., ed. 2005. *Sustainable Architecture: White Papers*. New York: Earth Pledge.

Buder, Stanley. 1990. *Visionaries and Planners: The Garden City Movement and the Modern Community*. New York: Oxford University Press.

Farr, Douglas. 2008. *Sustainable Urbanism: Urban Design with Nature*. Somerset, NJ: Wiley & Sons.

Kahn, Matthew E. 2006. *Green Cities: Urban Growth and the Environment*. Washington, DC: Brookings Institutional Press.

Ward, Stephen Victor. 1992. *The Garden City: Past, Present, and Future*. New York: Routledge.

GREEN ENTREPRENEURSHIP

Green entrepreneurship, also known as eco-preneurship or enviro-preneurship, is entrepreneurial behavior that has an environmental benefit. Green entrepreneurship arises when individuals recognize an unmet (or unsolved) environmental need (or problem) and proceed to satisfy it. To be considered green entrepreneurship, the focus must be on providing a green solution to the problem of interest. That is, a firm that is merely using sustainable processes to produce a product (a widget, for example) is not necessarily practicing green entrepreneurship; whereas a firm producing a widget that has an environmental benefit is.

The green entrepreneurship movement dates back to the 1970s, though it really did not gain momentum until the mid-1990s. The main driving force behind the movement is individual recognition that prior business models and practices were not environmentally conscious. Fueled by mass media's coverage of the climate change debates, some have termed the sudden explosion of green entrepreneurship as the "cleantech boom." Arguably, the underlying notion of the movement is that green perspectives can provide the foundation necessary for the creation, growth, and success of new business ventures. These ventures can be for-profit or nonprofit; and the past 20 years has evidenced that there is room for both forms to succeed in the market. It has been argued that some industries or sectors are friendlier to green entrepreneurship than others (tourism or greenhouse gas emissions are more viable segments than banking, for example). Likewise, it is widely recognized that green entrepreneurship can be fostered by legislation and regulation given they both help to shape how businesses behave.

The terms *green entrepreneurship*, *enviro-preneurship*, *eco-preneurship* and the like are sometimes used synonymously and yet sometimes argued to be distinct. Regardless of the specific terminology used, broadly speaking green entrepreneurship is said to possess three common themes or characteristics (Schaper, 2010): (1) it involves risk including the potential of failure; (2) it aims to have an overall positive effect on the environment; and (3) it is typically pursued by individuals sharing a common set of beliefs (environmental protection, sustainability, conscientiousness, humility, passion), though no complete characteristic or trait profile has become widely accepted.

Likewise, green entrepreneurs (individuals practicing green entrepreneurship) have been classified into four types (Taylor & Walley, 2004): (1) visionary champions, (2) innovative opportunists, (3) ethical mavericks, and (4) accidental enviropreneurs. Visionary champions are the most well known or common type. These individuals embrace a transformative sustainability orientation; they set out to change the world, regardless of how difficult it may be to do. Innovative opportunists are more financially oriented; these individuals identify a green opportunity (like a change in regulation or legislation) and exploit it. Ethical mavericks are primarily influenced by their social networks and past experiences; they are not focused on changing the world and have a tendency to set up boutique-style businesses on the fringes of the market. Accidental enviropreneurs are largely financially motivated; these individuals focus less on the values behind what they are doing and more on generating a profit. These individuals are most heavily influenced by their social networks rather than regulatory or legislative changes.

Greenovation: Project Turning Grease into Fuel (Project T.G.I.F.)

The Project Turning Grease into Fuel (Project T.G.I.F.) developed by the Westerly Innovations Network, is a great example of an greenovative solution to multiple societal problems. Project T.G.I.F. recognized that (1) many restaurants use and must regularly pay to dispose of cooking oil, (2) local shelters were in need of fuel to provide heat to residents during the winter season, and (3) the use of traditional petroleum-based fuels produced emissions that were detrimental to the environment. Project T.G.I.F. developed an innovative solution to these three problems. Restaurants donate their used cooking oil (at no cost) and the oil gets recycled and refined into biodiesel fuel. A portion of the fuel gets donated by the refinery to the shelter, helping to heat the homes of the less fortunate while also greatly reducing the traditional environmental footprint. Currently, Project T.G.I.F. is operating in three states, with several others having expressed interest in replicating the program. It has won numerous local, regional, and national awards. To date over 7,000 gallons of fuel have been donated to local shelters. Project T.G.I.F. represents just one of the Westerly Innovation Network's award-winning innovative solutions. More information on the project and the organization can be found at http://www.w-i-n.ws.

Of course, no typology is perfect, and it can sometimes be difficult to place a given individual or business perfectly within the typology. That being said, the above framework does provide a user-friendly way to think about the differences in motivations (legislation vs. social networks) and orientations (sustainability vs. profit) of individuals as they pursue green entrepreneurship.

Though the overall impact of the green entrepreneurship movement is almost impossible to quantify, it is arguably quite large. The U.S. Green Building Council (the organization responsible for Leadership in Energy and Environmental Design [LEED] building certifications) estimates that some basic climate and energy policy changes could save the U.S. economy over $130 billion annually, create 300,000 new jobs, and reduce emissions by over a gigaton annually. More specifically, they advocate for retrofitting some existing buildings, improved building codes, full disclosure of energy performance, and improved water efficiency. The incorporation of any of these recommended policy changes would spur numerous opportunities for green entrepreneurship, ultimately resulting in a more green way of life for us all.

Eric W. Liguori

See also: Businesses Active in Environmental Issues (Economics); Executive Order on Federal Leadership in Environmental, Energy, and Economic Performance (documents); Green Marketing (Economics).

References

Berchicci, L. 2009. *Innovating for Sustainability: Green Entrepreneurship in Personal Mobility*. New York: Routledge.

Koester, E. 2010. *Green Entrepreneur Handbook: The Guide to Building and Growing a Green and Clean Business*. Boca Raton, FL: CRC Press.

Schaper, M., ed. 2010. *Making Ecopreneurs: Developing Sustainable Entrepreneurship*, 2nd ed. Burlington, VT: Ashgate.

Taylor, D. W., and E. E. Walley. 2004. "The Green Entrepreneur: Opportunist, Maverick, or Visionary." *International Journal of Entrepreneurship and Small Business* 1: 56–69.

U.S. Green Building Council. "Buildings & Climate Change." Available at: http://www.usgbc.org/.

GREEN MARKETING

Marketing is defined as "the activity, set of institutions, and processes for creating, communicating, delivering, and exchanging offerings that have value for customers, clients, partners, and society at large" (Lotti & Lehmann, 2007). Marketing incorporates processes that concentrate on selling goods, services, or ideas, as well as processes that provide value and benefits to customers. Marketing applies communication, distribution, and pricing strategies to deliver desirable goods, services, ideas, values, and benefits to customers and stakeholders. Marketing aims to deliver these items at a time and place where customers want or need them.

Growing trends in marketing, such as green marketing, focus on establishing long-term, mutually beneficial relationships with customers. When this type of relationship is attained, both parties, which typically refers to the buyer and the seller, receive benefits in some manner. By building relationships with customers, marketing concentrates on retaining customers, which is often more profitable than solely focusing on gaining new customers.

The American Marketing Association defines green marketing as the production and marketing of products intended to enhance the physical environment or intended to reduce the negative effects on the physical environment. Green products often have useful and recognizable benefits for consumers. For instance, energy-efficient appliances reduce electric costs, heat-reflective windows reduce air conditioning costs, and organic foods eliminate pesticides from contaminating the food or earth.

Current trends suggest that consumers have growing concerns about the environment, and that more consumers plan to purchase environmentally friendly products and adhere to environmentally friendly companies. Consumers who are concerned about the environment typically have higher levels of income and are willing to pay higher prices for green products. Research indicates that an emerging segment of consumers, called LOHAS (an acronym for lifestyles of health and sustainability), is fueling the demand for green products. This segment includes individuals who are concerned about the environment and desire products to be manufactured in a sustainable way. The Natural Marketing Institute, an organization that follows the LOHAS segment, predicts that these individuals will constitute roughly 16 percent of the adults in the United States, or 35 million people. In addition, this organization values the market for socially conscious products at over $200 billion (Conscious Wave).

Companies are responding to consumer concerns as they develop new green formulations or partner with other organizations to promote environmentally friendly behavior. For instance, Clorox partnered with Sierra Club to promote a new line of eco-friendly, nontoxic cleaners called Green Works. The cleaners are made from natural ingredients such as coconuts and lemon oil, contain no phosphorus or bleach, are biodegradable in compost conditions, and are not animal tested. Green Works products are packaged in bottles that are recyclable and display the Sierra Club's name and logo—a giant sequoia tree framed by mountain peaks.

In agreement with growing consumer concern, firms following green marketing practices often receive financial benefits by showing increases to their bottom line (Lamb et al., 2011). However, as companies realize the increasing demand for green products, more companies are claiming their products are biodegradable, recyclable, or made with renewable resources—whether or not the product truly has these characteristics. This practice is referred to as greenwashing, defined as inflated statements regarding a product's environmental benefits (Solomon, 2011).

In an effort to reduce greenwashing, the Federal Trade Commission (FTC) provides *Green Guides* that offer clarity to the use of specific terms and delineate

Greenovations: Coca-Cola

Coca-Cola established the campaign "Live Positively" to reflect the company's dedication to making a positive difference in the world. The campaign focuses on seven areas critical to the company's sustainability: beverage benefits, active healthy living, community, energy and climate, sustainable packaging, water stewardship, and workplace. Coca-Cola strives to be the industry leader in energy efficiency and climate protection and aims to reduce the company's impact on the environment by decreasing carbon emissions. Coca-Cola is dedicated to developing sustainable packaging by creating more value with less material, using more recycled and renewable materials, and by increasing community recycling. Lastly, part of the campaign includes water stewardship, in which Coca-Cola aims to improve the company's water efficiency, recycle the water used in company operations, and replenish it by way of community water access and watershed restoration and protection. (More information on Coca-Cola's "Live Positively" campaign can be found at http://www.thecoca-colacompany.com/citizenship/index.html.)

Greenovator: U.S. Small Business Administration of Green Marketing

The following is from the U.S. Small Business Administration of Green Marketing:

> If you are already competitive in terms of price, quality and performance, adding "green" claims and eco-labels to your marketing strategy may enhance your brand image and secure your market share among the growing number of environmentally concerned consumers.
>
> Start your green marketing campaign by ensuring your green claims are credible. Do this by having your product certified that it was produced in an environmentally sound manner. Once certified, use the eco-labels from the certifying organizations to help consumers make educated choices. The links below can help you learn how to get certified!

general principles applicable to all environmental marketing claims. The current guides state that marketers should: (1) clearly qualify claims; (2) clearly indicate whether the environmental attribute or benefit being proclaimed applies to the product, the product's packaging, a service or to a part of the product, package, or service; (3) not overstate claims regarding environmental attributes; (4) clearly describe comparison claims; (5) not assert unqualified general claims of environmental benefits; and (6) clearly articulate claims regarding whether a product or package is biodegradable, compostable, refillable, recyclable, made of recycled content, and ozone safe.

The FTC continually reviews the guides, and on October, 6, 2010, the FTC proposed revised guidelines that are currently under review. The proposed new guides caution marketers from using broad terms, including "environmentally friendly" or "eco-friendly" because consumers tend to interpret these terms as having widespread benefits with few weaknesses. The proposed guides also caution marketers against using unqualified certifications or seals of approval that do not clearly describe certification requirements. To be labeled biodegradable, a product must completely break down within one year. Marketers would also be prohibited from labeling products bound for landfills or recycling centers "biodegradable" or compostable" because they will not break down in these locations. The proposed guides also provide guidance on terms such as "made with renewable materials," "made with renewable energy," and "carbon offsets." In order to declare a material as renewable, marketers would need to list specific information, including what the material is, how it is sourced, and why it is renewable. Renewable energy claims would have to identify the renewable energy source (wind, solar, etc.), and claims would not be permitted if fossil fuels were used to produce any part of the product. Additionally, the revised guides plan to recommend marketers to have scientific evidence supporting any carbon offset assertions and recommend marketers to proclaim if the offset will not occur for two years or more. Lastly, carbon offset assertions would be considered invalid if the offsets were mandatory by law.

The *Green Guides* are not enforceable on their own. Nonetheless, if a marketer makes claims conflicting with the guides, the FTC can intervene under Section 5 of the FTC Act, which forbids unfair or deceptive acts. (More information about the prosed revised guides can be found at http://www.ftc.gov/bcp/edu/microsites/energy/about_guides.shtml.)

Substantiating the *Green Guides'* objectives, research is indicating consumer skepticism regarding green products. One study found that nearly 25

Green Your Products

- Read the Environmental Protection Agency's (EPA) guide "Greening Your Products" (http://www.epa.gov/epp/pubs/jwod_product.pdf) which describes how to introduce new and improved green products.
- Certify your offerings as being "green" products.
- Evaluate your product packaging (http://www.epa.gov/retailindustry/products/sustainability.html#packaging) to reduce waste.

Advertising and Eco-Labeling

- Regulations for green marketing and advertising (http://www.ftc.gov/bcp/grnrule/guides980427.htm).
- Add "green" claims and eco-labels (http://www.ecolabelindex.com/) to your marketing strategy.
- Learn the top six e-marketing tips (http://www.greenbiz.com/research/report/2004/02/13/top-6-emarketing-tips-reaching-green-consumers) for marketing to green consumers over the Internet.

Market Research

The following resources will help you get started researching consumer attitudes and behaviors toward green products.

- Environmental E-Market Express (http://export.gov/): Provides current environmental market research data, international trade leads and events.
- Talk the Walk (http://www.talkthewalk.net/): Offers research and statistics on consumers' attitudes and behaviors in the context of successful green products and sustainable lifestyle marketing strategies.
- Green Consumers: A Growing Market for Local Businesses (http://www.uwex.edu/CES/cced/downtowns/ltb/lets/LTB1106.pdf): Explains how local businesses can better serve green consumers.
- Green Food Claims (http://planetgreen.discovery.com/food-health/common-misleading-food-claims.html): Reports on how self-declared environmental claims have mislead consumers about a food's green credentials.

- Understanding Environmental Literacy in America (http://www.resourcesaver.org/file/tool manager/CustomO16C45F53366.pdf): Provides information on consumers' understanding of environmental issues and the need for further environmental education.
- Consumer Reports: Greener Choices (http://www.eco-labels.org/home.cfm): Supplies information on buying greener products that have minimal environmental impact and meet personal needs.

KIM KENNEDY WHITE

Source: Green Marketing. U.S. Small Business Administration. Available at: http://www.sba.gov/content/green-marketing.

percent of U.S. consumers state they have "no way of knowing" if a product is green or truly performs as it claims. In the same study, participants were asked to name companies they considered to be socially and ethically responsible; remarkably 41 percent of the participants could not name a single company (Loechner, 2009).

DORA SCHMIT

See also: Businesses Active in Environmental Issues (Economics); Green Entrepreneurship (Economics); Green Guide for New Businesses (documents); How a Product Earns the Energy Star Label (documents); Merchandising (documents); Product Labeling (Economics).

References

American Marketing Association. "Green Marketing." Available at: http://www.marketing power.com/_layouts/Dictionary.aspx?dLetter=G.

Conscious Wave. "LOHAS Background." Available at: http://www.lohas.com/about.

Federal Trade Commission. "Proposed Revisions to the Green Guides." Available at: http://www.ftc.gov/os/fedreg/2010/october/101006greenguidesfrn.pdf.

Lamb, Charles W., Joseph F. Hair Jr., and Carl McDaniel. 2011. *MKTG 4*. Mason, OH: South-Western.

Loechner, Jack. 2009. "Consumers Want Proof It's Green." *Media Post*, April 9. Available at: http://www.mediapost.com/publications/?fa=Articles.showArticle&art_aid=103504.

Lotti, Mike, and Don Lehmann. 2007. American Marketing Association. "AMA Definition of Marketing." December 17. Available at: http://www.marketingpower.com/About AMA/Pages/DefinitionofMarketing.aspx.

Sierra Club. "Green Works." Available at: http://www.sierraclub.org/greenworks/.

Solomon, Michael R. 2011. *Consumer Behavior: Buying, Having, and Being*, 9th ed. Upper Saddle River, NJ: Prentice-Hall.

GREENWASHING

Although the term *greenwash* officially entered the English lexicon in 1999 when it first appeared in the *Oxford English Dictionary*, its first use is generally attributed to a 1989 essay written by New York environmental activist Jay Westerveld. The essay was in reaction to a plastic sign in his hotel room encouraging patrons to conserve water by reusing their towels instead of having the hotel wash the towels daily. The irony was that the hotel was spending significant sums of money encouraging a token behavior that would do more to save the hotel money than it would to help the earth. The money spent asking customers to reuse their towels, Westerveld argued, could have been better used to change the hotel's laundry detergent to a less polluting, more ecologically benign formula. The hotel, thought Westerveld, seemed more interested in cultivating an image of sustainability than in actually being green. "Wash my towels please," he pleaded "just don't 'greenwash' me" (Sullivan, 2009).

In the intervening decades the term greenwash, literally a blending of the words "green" and "white wash," has come to describe public relations or marketing efforts designed to create the misleading perception that a person, a product, or a company is environmentally friendly when it is not. Examples of greenwashing include the 1989 introduction by Mobil Chemical Corporation of Hefty brand trash bags that they billed as biodegradable. The bags, however, only degraded if exposed to direct sunlight. If the bags were buried, as they usually are in the landfills that are the final destination for most trash bags, they would not break down. Even worse, the bags were not actually biodegradable. Biodegradation is the chemical dissolution of materials by bacteria or other biological means. For example, it's the process that turns a piece of paper into soil. The Hefty bags did not biodegrade; they simply broke down into smaller pieces of plastic akin to simply cutting the aforementioned piece of paper into smaller pieces. A Mobil Chemical spokesman later admitted that "degradability is just a marketing tool. We're talking out of both sides of our mouth because we want to sell our bags" (Whiteley, 1997).

Similarly, in 1989 the energy company Chevron launched its "People Do" campaign featuring a television commercial carefully designed to align the company with an eco-friendly image. The commercial opens with the image of a grizzly bear nestling in its den as a large winter gale complete with blindingly thick snowfall swirls outside. The narrator intones, "in a den high in Montana's Blackfeet country a grizzly settles for a long winter's nap unaware that down below people with motors and machinery will explore for oil through deep winter." The image then fades from a gray, dark winter, to lush, sunny grassland as the narrator continues, "But before she wakes the people will be gone. The explored land will be replanted so it will soon look as if no one had ever been there." Continues the narrator in soothing dulcet tones as the grizzly bear emerges onto a lush landscape, "The people sometimes work through the winter, so that nature can have spring all to itself. People do." Not only was the ad visually inaccurate as to what occurs with mineral extraction (and note, the heavy machinery was never pictured in the commercial), in 1993 Greenpeace Chevron found that Chevron was a major contributor to political groups working to roll back environmental regulations (Bruno, 2001).

Although greenwashing has gotten more attention in recent years, it has existed for almost as long as the modern environmental movement. For nearly as long as there have been activists demanding that business and government act in accordance with environmental sustainability there have been those who try to cloak themselves in the mantle of green without doing the work. The 1970 book *The Environmental Handbook* featured a chapter titled "Ecopornography, or How to Spot an Ecological Phony," discussing how oil, chemical, and timber companies were spending money on advertising to tout their questionable credentials as good environmental citizens (Turner, 2009). What has changed, according to the environmental marketing agency TerraChoice, is the pace of that greenwashing. In 2009, the company surveyed some 2,219 consumer products making green claims—a 79 percent increase over the company's first report two years prior—and found that over 98 percent had committed some form of greenwashing (Dahl, 2010).

TerraChoice is not alone in focusing its work on highlighting the issue of and working toward getting companies to stop the practice of greenwashing. BSR, a consulting and research firm focused on sustainable business strategies and solutions, released in 2009 *Understanding and Preventing Greenwash: A Business Guide* to help businesses better understand what greenwashing is and how they can avoid engaging in the practice (Horiuchi et al., 2009). EnviroMedia, a public relations and advertising agency focused on improving public health and the environment, has, in conjunction with the University of Oregon, created the *Greenwashing Index*, an online tool designed to help consumers become savvy at evaluating environmental marketing claims while also holding businesses accountable to their environmental marketing claims (EnviroMedia Social Marketing, 2011). OgilvyEarth, the sustainability focused arm of New York City–based advertising, marketing, and public relations firm Ogilvy & Mather, released *From Greenwash to Great: A Practical Guide to Great Green Marketing (without the Greenwash)* in 2010.

What these guides share in common is an attempt to quantify and qualify the practice of greenwashing. TerraChoice in particular breaks down the act of greenwashing into seven categories or "sins," which strongly correlate with the broad categories laid out by the other organizations. These categories include:

1. *Hidden trade-off.* This form of greenwashing occurs when a product is labeled "green" based on an unreasonably narrow set of characteristics. For example, in the paper versus plastic bag debate, paper bag manufacturers may label their product green because it's harvested from a sustainable forest and is biodegradable. Plastic manufacturers may argue that their product is green because it uses less energy in production than a paper bag. The reality, however, is that neither is green and we're all better off toting our own bags to the store or going bag less.

2. *No proof.* This occurs when a company or product makes an environmental claim that cannot be easily substantiated.

3. *Vague claims.* Is a claim that is so poorly defined that its real meaning is likely to be misunderstood by the consumer. A classic example is the term *all-natural*, which may evoke the notion of green for many people, but has no environmental basis and may include many natural toxic materials (such as arsenic, mercury, and formaldehyde).

4. *Irrelevant.* These claims are technically true but not particularly helpful for customers seeking environmentally preferable products.

5. *Distraction.* A company will distract consumers by calling attention to its improved emissions record, or energy-efficient factories or other "green"

credentials, allowing the customer to forget that its core product is inherently unsustainable. Examples of this include organic cigarettes, which still cause lung cancer, or oil companies that brag about solar power stations that still sell gas.

6. *Lying*. Occurs when a product or company makes environmental claims that are patently untrue, for example, stating that a product doesn't contain a chemical when it actually does.

7. *Claiming false certification*. When a product gives the impression of having some form of third-party sustainability certification when the third-party endorsement does not actually exist. (TerraChoice Environmental Marketing, 2009).

A decade before TerraChoice came out with its list of greenwashing sins, the environmental nonprofit Greenpeace came out with its own four-point checklist to help ascertain when companies were engaging in the practice of greenwashing. Titled CARE, where, **C** stands for the company's core business. If the company's core or main business is based primarily on an activity that significantly contributes to environmental degradation, then the company is likely engaging in greenwashing. **A** stands for the company's advertising practice. Is the company spending large sums of money to highlight their one or two "sustainable" practices while the rest of the company continues on as business as usual? **R** stands for research and development funding. Since companies expend significant sums of money bringing into production new products and manufacturing processes, there is opportunity for them to expend their resources creating newer, more ecologically friendly products and technologies. Are they using their research and development budgets to do so? Finally, **E** stands for environmental lobbying. Are businesses lobbying for policies that usher in environmental sustainability or for policies that limit environmental legislation?

These frameworks, though helpful in analyzing on a deeper level whether or not a product or a company is engaging in greenwashing, fall short of helping consumers to select a product while at the store or otherwise in the moment. When faced with two near identical products, which product, based on its environmental sustainability, should a consumer choose? The concept of the sustainability certification grew out of this need for a tool to help consumers easily identify green consumer products. Issued by companies and nonprofit organizations, these labels offer a promise of environmentally friendly qualities covering nearly every consumer category imaginable—from clothes to coffee, trees to tea, food to energy. These labels inform us that our coffee is Fair Trade (grown with equitable labor practices with farmers guaranteed a reasonable rate of income), bird friendly (which means tropical bird habitats were not destroyed), shade grown (which lets purchasers know that the forest was left intact, as opposed to chopped down, to grow the coffee), and certified organic (grown without artificial pesticides or fertilizers). Some, such as the government sponsored Energy Star, are applied to products that significantly contribute to the reduction of energy use nationwide (Energy Star, n.d.). Similarly, Forest Stewardship Council (FSC) certification signals to consumers that products bearing their logo contain wood products that have been harvested from a well-managed and sustainable forest (Forest Stewardship Council, n.d.). Others such as the 1% for the Planet states that companies whose products bear that logo donate at least 1 percent of their annual revenues to environmental organizations worldwide. Additional certifications include U.S. Department of Agriculture Certified Organic, Rainforest Alliance Certification, Fair Trade Certification, and more than 500 certification labels (Epstein, 2010).

Although originally conceived with the goal of clarifying the sustainability landscape, the sheer quantity of eco-labels has in recent years begun to do more to cloud than to clarify the green consumer landscape (Dahl, 2010). Some certifications, for example, are of dubious origin, requiring absolutely no oversight or verification of a company's claims and seemingly more intent on financing the certifiers' operations than in ushering in true sustainability. Others, while in earnest, rely heavily on voluntary, nonaudited measures that allow companies to claim the certification while not engaging in the practice. Still others are rigorous programs with strict requirements and excellent mechanisms in place to ensure compliance. However, without significant personal research, it's often difficult for consumers to tell one certification apart from the other, placing many companies and products in an untenable situation. The heavy analysis and awareness of greenwashing practices has led many customers to be dubious of *all* environmental claims except for those from the most well-known certifications, such as the governmentally regulated certified organic certification. A company, or an industry, with a vested interest in sustainability may resist adopting a specific certification unless it can be ensured that the certification will be both highly recognized and regarded by consumers. This, however, creates a bottleneck effect, as certification standards with similar goals but different certifying bodies find themselves pitted against each other with limited room for adoption until one reaches a tipping point of field domination (Epstein, 2010). The FSC and the Sustainable Forestry Initiative (SFI) are both working toward reducing the negative environmental impact associated with harvesting wood, but some prefer the former's focus on the rights of indigenous peoples and ban on genetically modified trees, while others find the SFI standards easier to comply with. Yet because both systems have their pros and cons the U.S. Green Building Council, which oversees the Leadership in Energy and Environmental Design (LEED) standards of green building, has not been able to come to a decision as to which certification it should use if green builders want to earn points toward meeting the council's environmental requirements.

With the hope of clarifying some of the landscape, the Federal Trade Commission's *Green Guides* seek to give marketers clear guidance to aid them in refraining from making misleading environmental claims (FTC, 2010). First created in 1992, updated in 1998, and published under Title 16 of the Federal Code of Regulations, the goal of the *Green Guide* is to protect consumers from unsubstantiated or unscrupulous environmental marketing and advertising. The problem with the guide, however, is that in the intervening years from its conception to its update, there's been a proliferation of green claims in the marketplace that are not addressed in the *Green Guides* (Dahl, 2010). The next edition, now under review, is expected to deal with some of the problems not addressed in prior versions such as giving strict definitions to terms such as *carbon neutral* and standardizing the certification process so that it's not simply organizations or people self-certifying.

In the interim, however, we have an environmentally savvy populace who is aware of the problem of greenwashing but for all but the most motivated feels powerless to do much about it. Therein lays the problem with greenwashing. It misleads consumers into purchases that don't deliver on their environmental promise, leading to misplaced consumer trust and increased cynicism and doubt about all environmental claims. It also slows the spread of real environmental innovation by taking away market share from products that offer legitimate benefits, resulting in an overall deceleration in the movement toward true sustainability. In much the way whitewash can mask a rotted floorboard until it collapses, green-washing can mask dirty industries until it is far too late.

KENDRA PIERRE-LOUIS

See also: Green Marketing (Economics); Product Labeling (Economics).

References

Bruno, Kenny. 2001. "Greenwash, Inc." *Sierra* (May/June): 82–83.

Dahl, Richard. 2010. "Green Washing: Do You Know What You're Buying?" *Environmental Health Perspectives* (June): A247–A252.

Energy Star. "How a Product Earns the Energy Star Label." Available at: http://www.energy star.gov/index.cfm?c=products.pr_how_earn.

EnviroMedia Social Marketing. 2011. "The EnviroMedia Greenwashing Index." Available at: http://www.greenwashingindex.com/.

Epstein, Julia. 2010. "Environmental Certification Becoming Increasingly Crowded and Contested Field." *Washington Post*, May 3.

Federal Trade Commission (FTC). 2010. "Federal Trade Commission Proposes Revised 'Green Guides': Seeks Public Comment on Changes that Would Update Guides and Make Them Easier to Use." October 6. Available at: http://www.ftc.gov/opa/2010/10/greenguide.shtm.

Forest Stewardship Council (FSC). "The Forest Stewardship Council: Principles & Criteria." Available at: http://www.fscus.org/standards_criteria/.

Horiuchi, Rina, Ryan Schuchard, Lucy Shea, and Solitaire Townsend. 2009. "Understanding and Preventing Greenwash: A Business Guide." White Paper, BSR and Futerra Sustainability Communications.

Sullivan, John. 2009. "'Greenwashing' Gets His Goat: Environmental Activist Coined Famous Term." *Times Herald-Record*, August 1.

TerraChoice Environmental Marketing. 2009. "The Seven Sins of Greenwashing—Environmental Claims in Consumer Markets Summary Report: North America." White Paper, TerraChoice Environmental Marketing.

Turner, Tom. 2009. "Ecopornography Revisited." Earth Justice Blog. April 21. Available at: http://earthjustice.org/blog/2009-april/tom-turner/ecopornography-revisited.

Whiteley, Nigel. 1997. *Design for Society*. London: Reaktion Books.

PRODUCT LABELING

Product labels appear on products or their packaging to provide information that informs and information that sells. There is a wide variety of information that can be useful or even necessary to consumers in order to use or dispose of a product properly. In addition, product appearance plays a role in whether consumers will be willing to make a purchase. Product labels are considered a form of advertising under the Fair Packaging and Labeling Act (FPLA, 1966) and are regulated by the U.S. Federal Trade Commission (FTC). Many other federal agencies are involved in regulating product labels, including the U.S. Food and Drug Administration (FDA), the U.S. Environmental Protection Agency (EPA), the U.S. Department of Energy (DOE), and the U.S. Department of Agriculture (USDA). Labels such as Nutrition Facts and Energy Star are two familiar forms of labels regulated by federal agencies. Of increasing interest today are eco-labels, labels that give information about the sustainability of a product. The Energy Star label is one example of an eco-label. Product labels in general may give information about any number of things that are important to the consumer or mandated by law. Materials, ingredients, prices, size, volume, and instructions are some common components of product labels. Eco-labels provide information about aspects of the product that will be good for the health of the environment or the consumer. Many eco-labels are regulated by federal agencies through certification processes or legislation. Some represent voluntary compliance on the part of businesses. As a result, consumers may be frustrated by the myriad claims made on product labels, and regulations will continue to evolve.

In many ways, labels have become a way for consumers to know they can trust the products they use and make better choices as consumers for their health and ethical interests. As consumers' demand for sustainable

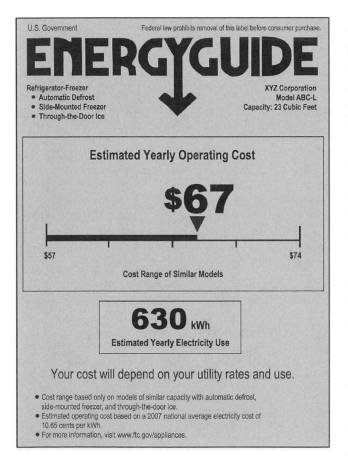

The bright yellow EnergyGuide label appears on Energy Star-qualified appliances and shows the estimated yearly operating cost of the appliance in dollars per year. (Federal Trade Commission)

products has increased, so too have claims of environmentally friendly ingredients, packaging, and manufacturing. Consumers are increasingly willing to pay a premium price for products that are safer or produced according to a higher ethical standard. Words that sound "green" are a way for companies to benefit from this profitable shift in consumer trends toward valuing more sustainable products. Companies cannot, however, make just any claim about being environmentally friendly. In response to exaggerated and false marketing claims, the FTC administers *Green Guides*, marketing guidelines for avoiding unjustifiable environmental claims. First issued in 1992, the guides have been updated several times. In the most recent update, the words *sustainable*, *natural*, and *organic* were not addressed. Instead, guidelines cover many of the other potential loopholes whose parameters are easier to establish. They address the necessary specificity of claims, ask for supporting evidence, and require the accessibility of facilities such as recycling plants in order to substantiate environmental claims and not be deceptive to consumers (FTC, 1999). Though the *Green Guides* are not laws themselves, the FTC has the authority to challenge deceptive marketing claims.

Consumers interested in purchasing organic products can rely on organic certification schemes. Certification is an increasingly popular way for producers to provide consumers with assurance about product claims. The USDA administers the federal program for organic certification and was one of the first governmental agencies in the world to implement organic labeling. There are several levels of USDA organic certification, based on the percentage of organic ingredients in the product. Products that are made with at least 95 percent organic ingredients earn the right to feature the USDA Certified Organic seal, but only products that are 100 percent organic can bear the seal and print "100 percent organic" on the label. Products with ingredients that are 70 percent or more organic can list their organic ingredients on their product label but do not receive the seal. There are extensive requirements to obtain organic certification. Smaller organic farms some-times have trouble meeting the standards applied to larger farm operations in the certification process because they are expensive and sometimes have legal require-ments that do not apply to smaller operations or are too difficult to meet. There is an alternate labeling program tailored to small-scale farmers with different require-ments and a separate labeling system. The Certified Naturally Grown label signifies products that have met the requirements of being grown using organic methods on a small farm operation, but avoids using the word organic because of the legal implications of using the central word in the federal organic certification process.

Fair trade is another example of a well-known certification process. Fair trade labels combine environmental and social justice concerns and, like organics, also use third-party certification (certification that is not done by the producer or the consumer). The certification process is intended to ensure farmers receive a fair price, above market value for their products. Often, fair trade products are also grown organically because consumers interested in the welfare of farmers also care about the benefits of organic farming practices. Farmers supplying fair trade products likewise want to provide a premium product that will command a premium price. Coffee, chocolate, flowers, and tea are just a few examples of products for which a portion of the global market is certified fair trade.

There are existing and evolving eco-labeling systems for a number of products, including automobiles, appliances, cleaning products, beauty products, clothing, seafood, timber, and the list is always growing. USDA organic certification frequently serves as a model for other certification schemes. Certifications, while able to provide many assurances about the final product, do not capture the grander vision many have of more comprehensively transparent conditions of production. "While the focus of organic certification is on the ecological conditions of production, negative social ramifications can undermine the integrity of the system" (Getz & Shreck, 2006, 500). Certification and even voluntary labeling schemes place a lot of power to encourage or discourage sustainable practices in the hands of the consumer, who is not always well informed about what takes place in production. Many products, even those that are organic, are increasingly produced globally rather than locally so that it is not just a matter of geographic distance from production, but production processes are becoming increasingly foreign to the workforce in developed countries (Eden, 2011, 171). Even when labels list the name of the place of product origin, consumers do not have the full story about the impact of

---

Greenovation: Green Certification and Eco-Labeling

The U.S. Small Business Administration offers links and information on a variety of eco-labeling certification programs.

To differentiate your product or service as environmentally sound, you may want to obtain certification from an independent third-party so that you can include their logo or "ecolabel" on your product's label and other marketing materials. Ecolabeling is an important way to market your product to green consumers.

Domestic Certification

- Green Seal sets product standards and awards its label to a wide variety of products: http://www.greenseal.org/
- Agriculture, Manufacturing, and Electricity: Certified by Scientific Certification Systems: http://www.scscertified.com/
- Buildings: The U.S. Green Building Council LEED [Leadership in Energy and Environmental Design] Green Building Rating System: http://www.usgbc.org/
- Chlorine-Free Products: Certified by the Chlorine Free Products Association: http://www.chlorinefreeproducts.org/
- Energy Efficient Products: Certified by the U.S. Government's ENERGY STAR Program: http://www.energystar.gov/index.cfm
- Organic Produce: Certified by the USDA National Organic Program: http://www.ams.usda.gov/AMSv1.0/nop
- Renewable Energy: Certified by the Green-e Certification Program: http://www.green-e.org/
- Wood Products: Criteria set by Forest Stewardship Council; Certified by Scientific Certification Systems and Smartwood: http://www.fscus.org/; http://www.scscertified.com/; http://www.smartwood.org/

their product. Food miles labels have been suggested as a way to inform consumers how far their food travels before reaching the kitchen. This captures distance and part of the carbon emissions involved but is also an incomplete way to measure the impact of externalities on the environment and on people. These increasingly global concerns are sure to continue impacting product labels and the trend of eco-labels in the future.

JENNIFER BJERKE

See also: Businesses Active in Environmental Issues (Economics); Green Entrepreneurship (Economics); Green Guide for Businesses (documents); Green Marketing (Economics); How a Product Earns the Energy Star Label (documents); Merchandising (documents).

References

Eden, Sally. 2011. "The politics of certification: consumer knowledge, power, and global governance in ecolabeling." In Michael Watts and Paul Robbins, eds., *Global Political Ecology*. New York: Routledge, 169–184.

Federal Trade Commission (FTC). 1999. "Sorting Out 'Green' Advertising Claims." Facts for Consumers Fact Sheet. Available at: http://www.ftc.gov/bcp/edu/pubs/consumer/general/gen02.pdf

Getz, Christy, and Aimee Shreck. 2006. "What Organic and Fair Trade Labels Do Not Tell Us: Towards a Place-Based Understanding of Certification." *International Journal of Cultural Studies* 30:5: 490–501.

International Certification

- The European Union Eco-Label Program is a voluntary scheme designed to encourage businesses to market products and services that are kinder to the environment and for European consumers: http://ec.europa.eu/environment/ecolabel/index_htm
- Canada's EcoLogo Label program certifies products from the United States and Canada in over 120 categories: http://www.ecologo.org/
- Germany's Blue Angel program provides ecolabeling for a wide variety products: http://www.blauer-engel.de/en/index.php
- Scandinavia's Nordic Swan allows companies to apply for an ecolabel in over 66 product categories: http://www.svanen.nu/Default.aspx?tabName=StartPage
- Japan's EcoMark Program provides product certification and ecolabeling for several product types: http://www.ecomark.jp/english/
- Taiwan's Green Mark and Energy Label programs provide certification and ecolabeling for green and energy efficient products: http://greenliving.epa.gov.tw/GreenLife/greenlife-v2/E_GreenMark_systems.aspx; http://www.energylabel.org.tw/index_en.asp

Resources

- The Global EcoLabeling Network is a non-profit association of third-party, environmental performance labeling organizations to improve, promote, and develop the "ecolabelling" of products and service: http://www.globalecolabeling.net/
- Collaborative Labeling and Appliance Standards Program (CLASP) is a an international organization that helps broker national policies for energy efficiency standards and labeling for appliances, equipment, and lighting products: http://www.claspronline.org

KIM KENNEDY WHITE

Source: Green Certification and Ecolabeling. U.S. Small Business Administration. Available at http://www.sba.gov/content/green-certification-and-ecolabeling.

REAL ESTATE

Real Estate and Private Property

Real estate refers to ownership of interests in the land. These interests in the land may include buildings and natural resources located on the land. Ownership of land is holding "title" to it. The evidence of that title is the deed. The rights of individuals to hold land as private property is a strongly held value, embodied in many important governmental documents. Private property itself is a bundle of rights and has changed over time. Generally, this bundle of legal rights included the right to possession, the right to control use of the land within the laws, the right to exclude others from using or entering the land, the right to enjoy the land in any legal manner, and the right to dispose of the land by selling, renting, or other legal manner.

But these rights are not absolute. The government may take away private property for a legitimate public purpose, and when it does so, it must pay for it. This is called the power of eminent domain, and it has its roots in the Fifth Amendment to the U.S. Constitution.

Real Estate and Environmental Conflict

Private property interests can conflict with environmental public policy. The expectation of complete freedom to do whatever the owner wants to do with the land is limited by the needs of ecosystems and communities. For example, water quality laws may require land owners to refrain from some of the activities private property owners come to expect. Water use is a common example of this and is the subject of intense local controversies in times of drought and expanding water usage through population growth and industrial agriculture. Air quality laws can require industrial owners to refrain from emitting or discharging pollutants into the air.

The Greening of U.S. Real Estate

Real estate also refers to the buying and selling of land. The value of the land is subject to market trends, government subsidies, and other public policies. As environmental policies evolve, they become part of value considerations in land transactions through zoning requirements, home owner association requirements, and building codes. Selling land that is, or could be, contaminated also affects real estate values.

Zoning requirements, home owner association requirements, and building codes can help "green" real estate because they often require, or strongly encourage, energy efficient designs, use of sustainable building materials, and planning to lessen environmental impacts. For example, many environmentally sensitive codes force greater population density to decrease overall environmental impacts. Low-density, spread out suburban and exurban real estate development has high environmental impacts, primarily because of increased vehicle usage and energy consumption.

Some building codes require that new residential construction have built in recycling areas, solar power ability, and green roof potential. For a structure to hold a green roof it is helpful if it is built specifically for that kind of roof because of weight and drainage concerns. These requirements differ greatly from state to state and from locality to locality. Enforcement of these codes may be controversial especially if the environmental protection is expensive or decreases market attractiveness.

Contaminated Sites and Real Estate Value Redefined

U.S. urban areas contain many contaminated sites. Other areas of past contamination include military bases, old dumps (now landfills), and petrochemical refinery, storage, and transport locations. Pollution of these sites continues and the number of sites continues to increase. The fundamental environmental laws are first passed by Congress, then developed into regulations, litigated, and finally enforced. The U.S. Environmental Protection Agency (EPA) was formed in 1970 and did not begin stronger enforcement until the 1980s. Federal environmental laws, like Superfund, require the owner to clean up these sites. An owner of a contaminated site has a strong incentive to sell the land because if the owner does not clean it up and the EPA does, they will charge the owner for it. The EPA can also place a lien on the property so that the owner may not profit from the suddenly increased value of the property cleaned up by the government. Any excess profit, or windfall, to the owner for the sale of a cleaned site goes to the EPA to pay for the cleanup.

One unique characteristic of real estate is that there is a limited supply. As the U.S. population and industrialization grow, so too do both the economic demand of for this land and the intensification of its use. The long-term environmental impacts, including years of pollution, now affect more and more of the available real estate supply, and the issue of owner liability for cleanup is a hotly contested issue. Basic Superfund law requires the creator, a shipper, or a storer of the toxic or hazardous material to pay for the clean up, and if they cannot be found, the owner of the property must clean it up. The owner of the property can also be in one of the other classes of potentially liable parties. The EPA sues all potentially liable parties, recovering all its costs from the party with the most assets without concern for degree of liability. Then, these parties can sue one another for liability based on culpability. Cleanup litigation is lengthy and expensive. Win, lose, or draw, this type of real estate litigation seriously limits land value.

The greening of America has changed some fundamental mechanisms for doing business in real estate. The cost of the cleanup of a piece of contaminated real estate has changed the value determination. Value is often defined as what a willing purchaser pays a willing seller for a good or service. This definition assumes that the purchaser is aware of all the liabilities of owning a particular piece of real estate. Both seller and buyer have some responsibility to exercise due diligence to determine if there is contamination. However, it remains a controversial area. Traditionally, real estate value was partially determined by an appraisal. Now lending institutions are requiring more than this in their commercial and large residential land transactions to evidence due diligence. Banks, mortgage brokers, and other lenders do not want to be responsible for the costly contingent liabilities of a cleanup. They are requiring an environmental valuation. Environmental evaluations can come in phases or levels, often depending on the size of the real estate transaction and the degree of financial risk.

There are many differences between a traditional real estate appraisal and an environmental evaluation of value. Both appraisals and environmental valuations must conform to Uniform Standards of Professional Practice. The traditional appraisal is the beginning of the environmental valuation. Under appraisals, most environmental issues are assumed away as a finding of no comparables in the market. Traditional appraisals determine value by using sales of comparable properties nearby.

Environmental evaluations actually examine the real-time condition of the property. Traditional appraisals rely heavily on comparable market data, which can often be obtained from commercial data sources. Environmental valuations require cross-referencing agency databases with public records. Key market participants are interviewed regarding the dynamics of comparable commercial properties. Traditional appraisals usually do not consider environmental agency research, remediation costs, impacts on land use, environmental risks, consideration of mitigation of environmental impacts, or an "as is" valuation. Environmental valuations consider all these factors. They require extensive agency research, research into the cost of professional consultants and contractors to perform any work, and knowledge of zoning and other land use controls.

Engineers are often engaged to consider the most cost-effective remediation strategies. However, the least cost alternative for cleanup may only restore the land to an industrial level of cleanup, not one that is safe for residential uses. For some communities, cleanup options may be limited to industrial standards or not all. All impacts on land use are considered in an environmental evaluation of value, including loss of use during environmental assessments or remediation activity. Mitigation is closely considered because offsets, potentially responsible parties, and legal claims greatly affect the value of the property. This is a very complicated, often controversial, and costly process. Finally, in environmental valuations, the actual environmental conditions are included. Generally, better environmental evaluations will examine the current condition of ecosystems that could be affected beyond the property boundaries.

Supply and Demand of Land

As the demand for land continues to increase and the supply of urban and suburban land remains stable, the value of land will increase. If the land is contaminated and the owner must pay for the cleanup, much of the profit incentive is diminished. The greening of America forced a modern-day recognition of past environmental impacts and the need to clean them up.

R. WILLIAM COLLIN

See also: Green Buildings (Economics); Green Cities (Economics).

References

Collin, Robert W. 2006. *The Environmental Protection Agency: Cleaning Up America's Act.* Westport, CT: Greenwood.

Collin, Robert W. 2008. *Battleground: Environment.* Westport, CT: Greenwood.

Freyfogle, Eric T. 2007. *On Private Property: Finding Common Ground on the Ownership of the Land.* Waltham, MA: Beacon Press.

Keeping, Miles, and David Shiers. 2004. *Sustainable Property Development: A Guide to Real Estate and the Environment.* Oxford: Blackwell Science Publishing.

Moskowitz, Joel S. 1995. *Environmental Liability and Real Property Transactions: Law and Practice, 2nd ed.* New York: Aspen Law and Business.

RESTAURANTS, ADAPTIVE REUSE IN URBAN ARCHITECTURE

Since the 1970s, restaurants in the United States have steadily gained importance in economic, cultural, and environmental spheres. Economically, Americans spent roughly $325 billion on food away from home in 2008. Dual-earning households also steadily increased from the 1970s to the present, accounting for roughly 44 percent of all U.S. restaurant spending. Culturally, restaurants in the United

Site of the former Paramount Theater, this landmark Hard Rock Cafe sits in the heart of Times Square in New York City. Locating restaurants in vacant and often historical buildings is an example of the trend of adaptive reuse of architecture. (SeanPavonePhoto/Shutterstock.com)

Greenovation: Adaptive Reuse

Adaptive reuse is the practice through which historic, vacant, or obsolete structures are rehabilitated to function in a capacity not originally intended. The practice has its modern origin in 19th-century Europe, with France and Britain at the headwaters. It was not until the mid-20th century that U.S. states and cities were persuaded to follow suit. Adaptive reuse projects are most numerous in eastern and midwestern U.S. cities, which contain large numbers of shuttered factories, prewar office towers, riverfront structures, and other buildings that have outlived their original uses.

States serve as markers of social identity and measurements of consumer taste. This dynamic has also increased substantially since the 1970s as various industry trends, such as ethnic restaurants, themed eateries, fusion cooking, the slow food movement, and the emergence of celebrity chefs, gave rise to sharper restaurant sensibilities in terms of what people ate, where, and why. Within environmental spheres, restaurant growth in the United States since the 1970s has placed higher pressures on ecosystems. To minimize these pressures, restaurants adopted eco-friendly practices regarding both the human and nonhuman worlds. These included the use of local ingredients to reduce the energy required to transport meats and vegetables from farm to store, incorporating healthier menu selections and publishing caloric content, and greater usage of outdoor space (where permissible) for seating, which lessened the use of electricity and climate-control systems.

When considering the built environment, a growing practice among U.S. restaurants addresses the obsolescence of urban architecture. Following the energy crises of the 1970s, an ecological sensibility developed in the United States that insisted structural demolition equaled waste. In large cities, such as Philadelphia, New York, Baltimore, and Detroit, and smaller cities such as Franklin, Tennessee, and Danville, Kentucky, restaurants became vehicles for the adaptive reuse of buildings whose original tenants no longer held occupancy. Philadelphia's South Broad Street, New York's Meatpacking District, Baltimore's Inner Harbor, and Detroit's Corktown all benefited from this type of restaurant development. In Danville and Franklin, municipal associations banded together to revitalize their downtown storefronts with retail shops and restaurants. Inspired by tenets of modern planning such as new urbanism,

New Urbanism

New urbanism is a form of urban planning (though it originated in suburban locales) that gained popularity in the 1990s. It eschews metropolitan sprawl and the traditional suburban forms of cul de sacs, large home lots, long driveways, and a general sense of disconnection. Instead, it focuses on density, social integration, walkability, familiarity with neighbors, mixed-use projects of residence and retail, and nostalgic interpretations of Main Street U.S.A. While its creators and supporters hail the movement as successful, its detractors lament the process as inequitable, exclusively expensive, and devoid of true socioeconomic diversity.

transit villages, rehabilitation tax credits, and other initiatives to regenerate urban density, restaurants through adaptive reuse preserved historic architecture, enlivened neighborhoods, encouraged investment, reduced sprawl, and provided cities with new amenities to attract residents and visitors.

As historic preservation laws in the United States were strengthened over the past three decades and cities provided rehabilitation tax credits, restaurateurs and developers recognized the benefits of adaptive reuse. The practice required less demolition and removal of materials while upholding the historic integrity of neighborhoods. In Philadelphia's South Broad Street corridor, building exteriors were required to remain unaltered, while interiors were refitted for new uses. Restaurant companies such as Morton's of Chicago, the Darden Group, Del Frisco's Double Eagle, Ruth's Chris, and the Starr Restaurant Organization opened upscale steakhouses in spaces formerly occupied by the banks, stock exchanges, and brokerages once vital to that city's economic strength. After a series of mergers and consolidations in the 1980s, many of these institutions disappeared, leaving their grand buildings empty. At the same time, suburbs were growing larger and spreading outward, making portions of the city's built environment obsolete. Questions then surfaced regarding what types of businesses could occupy buildings whose original purposes were outmoded. In many cases, cities redeveloped neighborhoods with restaurants, retail stores, convention centers, hotels, and condominiums. In New York's meatpacking district, once a forbidding industrial zone, the former National Biscuit Company building now contains the Craftsteak and Del Posto restaurants. Adjacent to Baltimore's Inner Harbor, a retail and restaurant area with more than two dozen dining options, the former Pratt Street Power Plant now houses the Hard Rock Café. The independently owned Slow's BBQ and Le Petit Zinc bistro helped attract residents and visitors to Detroit's Corktown, long a blighted neighborhood. In Franklin and Danville, whose downtown businesses suffered due to the suburban growth of nearby Nashville and Lexington, respectively, popular restaurants such as Franklin's Red Pony and those along Danville's Main Street have helped bring those areas new vitality.

Although restaurants are vital agents in resuscitating unused portions of the built environment, their continual spread has been questioned. Restaurants rely heavily on discretionary spending, making economic downturns a threat to their longevity and success. In dense urban areas, several restaurants in close proximity can create a glut of

Transit Villages

Transit villages, also known as transit-oriented developments (TODs), typically feature mixed-use developments configured around or adjacent to light- or regional railway stations. They also incorporate pedestrian features such as sidewalks, footbridges, and other connectors between transit hubs and mixed-use developments. Designed to create vitality and direct both public and private investment into struggling cities and towns, the amenities of transit villages appeal to growing numbers of Americans, such as young professionals, Gen-Xers, and empty-nesters.

competition and increase the rate of occupant turnover. For the health of cities, restaurants, which require frequent deliveries and parking spaces for customers, can contribute to increased congestion and pollution. As sociologists and geographers have argued, the continual up-scaling of urban centers with restaurants and retail stores can erode notions of authenticity, community, and history within the built environment. In the early 21st century, urban economies in the United States relied more on the consumption of experiences rather than the production of goods. Urban planners point to sustainability issues with this reliance; in order to remain economically vibrant, cities must offer more than opportunities for dining and shopping.

Despite these challenges, restaurant development remains an aesthetically appealing and less-destructive way to reintegrate spatial vacancies of the built environment. As Americans increasingly patronize restaurants and formulate their consumer identities based on their dining experiences, mayors, city councils, realtors, urban planners, and business improvement associations continually encourage the opening of restaurants to enliven neighborhoods, preserve history, and encourage investment and growth.

STEPHEN NEPA

See also: Corporate Food Service (Food); Fair Trade (Economics); Food and Entertaining (Food).

References

Allison, Eric, and Lauren Peters. 2011. *Historic Preservation and the Livable City*. Hoboken, NJ: John Wiley and Sons.

Flint, Anthony. 2006. *This Land: The Battle Over Sprawl and the Future of America*. Baltimore: Johns Hopkins University Press.

Haas, Tigran, ed. 2008. *New Urbanism and Beyond: Designing Cities for the Future*. New York: Rizzoli.

Harris, Neil. 1999. *Building Lives: Constructing Rites and Passages*. New Haven, CT: Yale University Press.

Hauck-Lawson, Annie, and Jonathan Deutsch, eds. 2009. *Gastropolis: Food and New York City*. New York: Columbia University Press.

Johnston, Josee, and Shyon Baumann. 2009. *Foodies: Democracy and Distinction in the Gourmet Foodscape*. New York: Routledge.

Mintel Market Research Reports. 2010. "American Families and Dining Out—US—February, 2010." Available at: http://academic.mintel.com/sinatra/oxygen_academic/search_results/show&/display/id=543099/display/id=482468/display/id=507570?select_section=507573.

Powell, Kenneth. 1999. *Architecture Reborn: Converting Old Buildings for New Uses*. New York: Rizzoli.

Smith, Andrew F., ed. 2007. *The Oxford Companion to American Food and Drink*. New York: Oxford University Press.

Zukin, Sharon. 2010. *Naked City: The Death and Life of Authentic Urban Places*. New York: Oxford University Press.

SOCIALLY RESPONSIBLE INVESTMENTS

Socially responsible investing, also referred to as responsible investing, sustainable investing, environmental, social, and governance (ESG) investing, mission-related investing, and ethical investing, encompasses many investment practices and goals that incorporate social and environmental concerns into the evaluation and selection of financial products and firms (Forum for Sustainable and Responsible Investment [US SIF] 2009, 2010).

Socially responsible investing includes several different practices. Individuals or fund managers may screen stocks or mutual funds based on social or environmental criteria (for example, a corporation's carbon footprint or contribution to the local community), excluding or including those products that meet or do not meet the set standards (Schueth, 2002, 117; US SIF, 2011a).

Shareholder advocacy is another approach in which owners of company stock initiate and maintain dialogue with company leaders about social and environmental issues; shareholders may also file resolutions on issues such as worker rights, pollution, corporate governance, or discrimination, which are presented to all owners of a corporation for a vote (Schueth, 2002, 117–118; US SIF, 2011a). From 2008 to 2010, over 200 public and labor funds, religious investors, foundations, and endowments filed or co-filed proposals on such issues (US SIF, 2010). Shareholder advocacy can be national and international in scope as well. For instance, the Carbon Disclosure Project, which pushes for increased reporting of greenhouse gas emissions by corporations, including the S&P 500, grew from 35 institutions with $4.5 trillion in assets in 2000 to 551 institutions with $71 trillion in assets in 2011 (Carbon Disclosure Project, 2011).

Another increasingly popular practice is community investing in which financial resources, ranging from low-interest loans to basic banking services, are directed to traditionally underserved communities. These resources allow local community banks and organizations to offer money to low-income residents for education, health care, and small business creation, among other uses. Acumen Fund, for example, employs what they call "patient capital," which is investment characterized by long-term thinking, risk tolerance, and a goal of maximizing social rather than financial returns, to fund small business loans to individuals and communities in Africa and Asia to solve key problems such as access to health care or clean water (Acumen Fund, 2011). Similar community investment occurs throughout the United States. Community investing is the fastest growing area of socially responsible investment, having increased more than 60 percent between 2007 and 2010 from $25 billion to $41.7 billion (US SIF, 2011a). Community investments often have smaller returns than other investments; nonetheless, many investors prefer the high social impact of these strategies (Camejo, 2002, 113).

Concern over the social impacts of money use can be traced back to the prohibition of charging interest on loans in Jewish law and, in the United States, to the recognition of money as a moral and religious issue by Methodists and the Society of Friends (Quakers) in the 1700s. Quakers and other religious people refused to be involved in the slave trade and munitions purchases, and John Wesley, founder of the Methodist Church, applied the biblical principle of being a good neighbor to business practices. Modern interest in socially responsible investing originated in the social unrest of the 1960s and events that sparked increased sensitivity to social and moral responsibility. Key issues during this time included the Vietnam War and civil rights and gender equality, and these expanded during the 1970s to include labor and nuclear issues. In the 1980s, many sectors of society focused investment strategies on ending apartheid in South Africa by putting financial pressure on the white minority government. Environmental disasters, such as the Exxon-Valdez oil spill and the Chernobyl nuclear explosion, and increasing information on global warming and ozone depletion brought environmental concerns to the forefront of socially responsible investing. More recently, concerns over workers' rights and human rights abuses by foreign governments (for example, in Darfur, Africa) have garnered investor attention (Schueth, 2002, 115–116).

In the United States, professionally managed assets that adhere to socially responsible principles rose 380 percent from 1995 to 2010 (from $639 billion to $3.07 trillion), while overall market assets rose only 260 percent during this time period, from $7 trillion to $25.2 trillion. In addition, while managed assets overall have remained flat during the recent economic recession (2007–2010), assets following socially responsible standards have shown substantial growth. In 2010, institutional investors made up the largest share of these assets with $2.3 trillion. Registered investment firms, of which mutual funds are the largest group, made up $316.1 billion of the total investments that incorporated socially responsible investing factors (US SIF, 2010).

Despite growing interest and capital in socially responsible investments, a 2009 survey found that fund managers are still cautious about bringing up this type of investing unless the clients themselves broach the subject. Although a large percentage of respondents (38–49 percent) thought that socially responsible investments had a positive impact on portfolios, a quarter to a third said they were unsure of the practice's impact (US SIF, 2009). A recent review of academic studies, though, found that in 20 of 36 studies there was a positive relationship between socially responsible investment practices and fund performance, and only three showed an outright negative relationship (Mercer Consulting, 2009). Socially responsible indexes, which compare performance of these investments to a regular market index (such as the S&P 500), have kept pace or outperformed traditional indexes: from 1990 to 2009, the socially responsible index (called the FTSE KLD 400) had returns of 9.51 percent compared to 8.66 percent returns from the S&P 500 (US SIF, 2011b). The weight of evidence seems to be that socially responsible investments perform at least on the same level as other investments and may outperform these, especially over the long term (US SIF, 2009, 2011b). The growing investment in socially responsible funds by state pensions and university endowments is further testament to this, as these groups are legally obligated to seek only investments with competitive returns (US SIF, 2011b).

With the increasing demand for socially responsible investment products and the recognition of their competitive performance, the investment practice has become mainstream. Most traditional investment companies like TIAA-CREF, Merrill Lynch, and Charles Schwabb offer their own socially responsible mutual funds or include funds from socially responsible companies in their offerings (Camejo, 2002, 111). One of the earliest modern socially responsible funds was started by Pax World Investments in 1971. Other well-established companies focusing solely on socially responsible investing include Domini Social Investments, Calvert Investments, and Green Century Funds. A more complete list is provided by US SIF (2011b).

Micah G. Bennett

See also: Businesses Active in Environmental Issues (Economics).

References

Acumen Fund. 2011. "What Is Patient Capital?" Available at: http://www.acumenfund.org/about-us/what-is-patient-capital.html.

Camejo, Peter. 2002. "SRI for the Individual Investor." In Peter Camejo, ed., *The SRI Advantage*. Gabriola Island, BC, Canada: New Society Publishers, 97–114.

Carbon Disclosure Project. 2011. "What We Do: Overview." Available at: https://www.cdproject.net/en-US/WhatWeDo/Pages/overview.aspx.

Forum for Sustainable and Responsible Investment (US SIF). 2009. *Investment Consultants and Responsible Investing: Current Practice and Outlook in the United States*. Washington, DC: US SIF.

Forum for Sustainable and Responsible Investment (US SIF). 2010. *Report on Socially Responsible Investing Trends in the United States*. Washington, DC: US SIF.

Forum for Sustainable and Responsible Investment (US SIF). 2011a. "Socially Responsible Investing Facts." Available at: http://www.ussif.org/resources/sriguide/srifacts.htm.

Forum for Sustainable and Responsible Investment (US SIF). 2011b. "Performance and Socially Responsible Investments." http://www.ussif.org/resources/performance.cfm.

Logue, A. C. 2009. *Socially Responsible Investing for Dummies*. Hoboken, NJ: Wiley.

Mercer Consulting. 2009. *Shedding Light on Responsible Investment: Approaches, Returns and Impacts*. London: Mercer Consulting.

Schueth, Steven J. 2002. "Socially Responsible Investing in the United States." In Peter Camejo, ed., *The SRI Advantage*. Gabriola Island, BC, Canada: New Society Publishers, 115–122.

Education and Employment

ENVIRONMENTAL EDUCATION ACT OF 1970

The National Environmental Education Act of 1970 (NEEA, also known as the Environmental Quality Education Act of 1970 or Public Law 91-516) was signed into law by President Richard Nixon on October 30, 1970. The act was one of many environmentally related laws passed during the 1970s (e.g., the Clean Air Act, the Clean Water Act, the Endangered Species Act, the Safe Drinking Water Act, and the Resource Conservation and Recovery Act), as this was a time of high environmental consciousness in the United States. Senator Gaylord Nelson (D.-Wis.) is credited with writing the act, which had the expressed purpose of protecting the environment and enhancing environmental quality through education.

Considered the impetus of environmental education in the United States, the NEEA's mandate was to incorporate environmental education into the larger fabric of both formal and informal U.S. education, especially K–12 schools. Specifically, it called for an enhancement of environmental appreciation and management through broadly diffused education (Marcus, 1984). The NEEA authorized the creation of an Office of Environmental Education (OEE) in the U.S. Department of Health, Education, and Welfare (HEW); the establishment of a National Advisory Council for environmental education; and the establishment of a domestic grants program to provide professional development for teachers and develop environmental-education curricula. The act also provides a definition of environmental education. For the purposes of the NEEA, environmental education was defined as the educational process dealing with man's relationship with his natural and human-made surroundings, and including the relation of population, pollution, resource allocation and depletion, conservation, transportation, technology, and urban and rural planning to the total human environment (Public Law 91-516).

Though the intent of the NEEA was to incorporate learning about the environment into the U.S. school system, it was controversial and unpopular with many school officials, especially those at the elementary and secondary levels (Marcus, 1984).

Officials claimed overload: that environmental education could not be incorporated into the existing curriculum without giving up something else. In addition, although the NEEA and its amendments (PL 93-278, PL 94-273, and PL 95-561) authorized significant annual budgets to the OEE, congressional allocations to support the OEE's work were minimal. Allocations maintained the office but limited the number of grants that the OEE could provide. By 1981, funding issues, problems with implementation, and an eventual shifting of focus toward economic issues brought about the NEEA's demise. The passage of the Omnibus Budget Reconciliation Act of 1981 repealed the NEEA and eliminated the OEE and the programs it managed.

The federal government's commitment to environmental education was restored, however, on November 16, 1990, with the passage of the National Environmental Education Act of 1990 (Public Law 101-619). The 1990 act again established an Office of Environmental Education, placing it within the Environmental Protection Agency to develop and administer. The 1990 act also authorized an environmental education and training program, environmental education grants, student fellowships, the President's Environmental Youth Awards Program, the Federal Task Force and National Advisory Council, the National Environmental Education and Training Foundation, and the Council for Environmental Education.

BRIGETTE BUSH-GIBSON

See also: National Environmental Education Act of 1990 (documents).

References

Brezina, Dennis W. 1974. *Congress in Action: The Environmental Education Act*. New York: Free Press.

Marcus, Melvin G. 1984. "The Environmental Education Act: Success or Failure?" *Transition: A Quarterly Journal of the Socially and Ecologically Responsible Geographers* 14:4: 2–8.

Palmer, Joy A. 1998. *Environmental Education in the 21st Century: Theory, Practice, Progress, and Promise*. New York: Routledge.

ENVIRONMENTAL AND SUSTAINABLE COMMUNITY STATE EDUCATION

The development of green culture means the environment becomes part of the major social institutions. Education, religion, government, and economy all begin to include environmental considerations. In 1970, when the U.S. Environmental Protection Agency (EPA) was formed, green culture moved into the judicial, legislative, and executive branches of government. All sorts of entities like businesses, schools, and municipalities had to comply with some form of environmental oversight. Primary and elementary schools were a major concern for lead pollution because of the potential impacts of lead on children. They needed workers who understood the new environmental rules. Federal and state agencies needed workers with enough of an environmental understanding to actually write the first clean air and clean water rules. The explosion of environmental law that followed the greening of U.S. culture created a green labor force demand that was not met by higher education at the time. Education responded to these needs and in this manner contributed to the institutionalization of environmental education that formed one of the bases for the greening of the United States.

Center High students help with water monitoring and river cleanup at Indian Creek in Kansas City, Missouri in 2011. (Environmental Protection Agency)

In 1990, the National Environmental Education Act was passed into law. This legislation moved environmental education forward. The law responded to rising environmental concerns and focused directly on education. It became a pioneering model for environmental education in the United States at the state and local levels. Among the legislative findings in the National Environmental Education Act are that environmental problems are becoming more complex, global in scale, and are a threat to both urban and rural areas. The act further found that effective responses to complex environmental problems required a workforce with training and education of the natural and built environment, awareness of environmental issues and controversies, and problem-solving skills. The passage of the National Environmental Education Act laid the foundation for environmental education. It made environmental education a national priority and thus helped ease its passage into resistant school districts.

Environmental Education

Education is one of the fundamental institutions in our society. A well-educated citizenry is a valuable human resource for a nation. Public education is state supported and legally mandated. State-supported education at the primary and secondary levels tends to shy away from controversial issues. When U.S. environmentalism became an important national issue, it was fraught with many controversies. Today, it is still fraught with controversies, but the environmental movement grew to include law, public policy, and public health. Environmental issues even became part of children's television programming. In order to keep up with the needs of society for more accurate, accessible, and timely environmental information, public education began to incorporate more environmental experiences in the schools. Although still a matter of local political controversy, public education's curriculum then began to expand with more specialized courses and expansion of current subjects to include environmental considerations. Advanced placement courses in environmental sciences and environmental studies now exist at the secondary level in some locations. Environmental education is expected to grow into a lifelong learning experience.

Basic Goals of Environmental Education

As an emerging and dynamic field, environmental education changes rapidly. The growth of knowledge is almost as fast as the incorporation of technology in this area. As a result of rapid changes and controversial issues, there is often great uncertainty around environmental issues. However, the goals of environmental education remain generally the same. Environmental education can take a holistic, or ecological, perspective of the environment. This perspective can include many categories, including cultural, social, economic, political, biological, ecological, or literary views. Many educators take this opportunity to teach earth sciences, sometimes combining real-life outdoor activity. The educational goal would be an understanding of the total environment around the student.

Other common goals in environmental education include developing an understanding of global problems. This includes a subset of goals such as the ability to understand information from different sources, technological skills to access real-time data, and an awareness of the political, social, and economic interdependence of world systems. The rise in social concern around "sustainability" has also provided an impetus for this goal. Also part of the goal of understanding global problems is the ability to think in more ecologically based timeframes, instead of short-term timeframes. Many short-term timeframes can irreparably damage natural resources such as forests and freshwater. They can also lower species diversity and increase desertification. Timeframes that are based on the local ecosystem are considered more sustainable. The overall goal of increasing the understanding of global environmental problems challenges current models of short-term natural resource exploitation.

Another basic goal of environmental education is one of citizen empowerment. This set of goals emphasizes active and effective citizen involvement; understanding the values, ethics, and morals that determine policy decisions; and developing a lifelong learning model inclusive of adult education. For environmental education in particular, understanding the rights, responsibilities, and legal mechanisms of civic environmental engagement is important. Short-term decision-making processes are often tied to the electoral cycles of public officials because of political aspects of U.S. environmentalism. Short-term decision making is characterized by a lack of enforcement of environmental agreements, a lack of useful ecological monitoring of actual environmental conditions, and a failure to plan for future uncertainty. An example of an unplanned future uncertainty is a natural disaster like Hurricane Katrina. Short-term decision making used now in land use and environmental policy development may have to be replaced with longer-term processes that monitor the environment and determine usage from that information. This is currently done with air monitors in London. If the air is too polluted, then traffic is restricted. The role of citizen monitoring of the environment may be essential for some communities to broach sustainable practices. In this way, environmental education becomes a lifelong learning experience.

Challenges and Controversies

Environmental education represents the growth of the greening of our culture. Because U.S. public education is conflict averse, environmental education generally does not advocate a particular point of view. Ultimately, its goal is to prepare society to understand and solve complex environmental problems. The environmental challenges are large, such as climate change, and cumulative, such as pollution. There is much uncertainty and greater urgency in most large-scale environmental decisions.

Education is very important to meet these unavoidable challenges. As environmental education grows into new areas, like sustainability, these challenges will be larger. There are challenges in environmental education as curriculum changes to meet the needs of society. The demographic mix of U.S. society is rapidly changing. The United States, like the world, is now mostly an urban population and becoming more so. In the United States, cities have been ignored by traditional U.S. environmental organizations until recently. Cities are points of immigration and pollution. Cities are now where most of the people live, where most of the pollution is, and where most of the people of color live. Where cities were once considered unsustainable, they may now be more sustainable than suburban areas because of smaller ecological footprint achieved through density. Environmental education often challenges cultural norms and values.

Education always touches on cultural issues. The definition of the word *environment* can range from national parks to all ancestors (in some indigenous cultures). Lack of access to resources for environmental education, and for technology, is a budgetary reality in many U.S. urban educational districts. This is sometimes referred to as the digital divide. Students with access to the Internet and to computers perform better in school than those without access. Environmental education can be resource intensive because of the use of computers and the Internet to monitor environmental conditions. Cultural and income differences affect environmental education. However, social concern for sustainability is increasing. To the extent that inclusion is a sustainable value, cultural and income differences will require more opportunities for collaboration. Multicultural environmental education, whether planned or not, is a growing reality.

Sustainability Education

Sustainability education is relatively new in the United States. It is beginning to find its way into primary and secondary public education curriculum. Many educational institutions have pursued sustainable practices in their physical plant. They seek to reduce waste and exposure to dangerous chemicals in grounds maintenance, housekeeping, and food services. They prioritize recycling efforts, provide invaluable onsite baseline scientific observations in student projects, and pursue energy efficiencies. They encourage mass transit use and bicycle commuting. Many college campuses now have a sustainable village or eco-dormitories that pursue similar sustainable practices. Colleges are seeking some type of sustainability certification metric and are currently in the process of developing some test models. These models examine the practices of the physical plant, the curriculum, the faculty and other resources.

More and more colleges now offer some type of sustainability course, minor, concentration, or major. The first law school course in sustainability was offered in 1993 at the University of Oregon School of Law and taught by Professor Robin Morris Collin. Arizona State University offered one of the first sustainability degrees in 2007. Colleges now celebrate Sustainability Day, where sustainable practices and experimental results are highlighted.

The 1992 Earth Summit was a foundational event for sustainability education worldwide. This summit created a blueprint for sustainability known as *Agenda 21*. (Chapter 36 is called "Promoting Education, Public Awareness and Training.") It is a detailed list of actions designed to meet this goal. It stresses that education is critical for sustainability and increasing community capacity to engage in environmental decisions. It underscored the need for a multidisciplinary approach to environmental issues. Its specific recommendations included preservice education for future teachers of environmental issues, enhanced program development and education research in environmental education, and collaboration with nongovernmental organizations (NGOs). *Agenda 21* increased the development and agenda of other organizations focused on sustainability education. Various scientific organizations advocated for more environmental and sustainability education. Other education advocacy groups issued reports and lobbied for environmental education.

One of the major challenges of incorporating sustainability into college curriculum is the rigidness of disciplines at the college and postgraduate levels of education. The natural and social sciences and the humanities contain disciplines that self-identify their boundaries. Publication in narrow traditional journals matters to college rankings, faculty tenure, and promotion. Faculties that do not follow narrow disciplinary boundaries tend to be bypassed for tenure or promotion. Environmental education still faces these same challenges, but sustainability education is just beginning to engage them. These fields transcend current disciplinary boundaries of higher education. However, new journals in sustainability are starting to meet some of the requirements for universities.

Summary

Environmental education helped institutionalize the greening of American culture by increasing ecological literacy. Pushed by a green labor demand and a strong national act, environmental education has taken a giant step forward. In the United States, environmental education has not yet reached the lower primary grades in most places. Most colleges, and many high schools, offer some type of environmental education. Sustainability is just beginning to find its way into the laws and public policies. Sustainability education is just starting to create a labor demand, and higher levels of education have begun to respond in both their physical plant and in their curriculum.

R. WILLIAM COLLIN

See also: Community Economic Development and Substantive Participation (Activism); Environmental Education Act of 1970 (Education); Indigenous Entrepreneurship and Sustainability: A Case Study— College of Menominee Nation Campus Grind Coffee Shop (Education); K–12 Green Curriculum (Education); National Environmental Education Act of 1990 (documents); Proceedings Report from the Sustainability Education Summit (documents); Summary of Recent Federal Agency Environmental Education Projects (documents).

Greenovation: President's Environmental Youth Award

The following describes the President's Environmental Youth Award (PEYA) program from the U.S. Environmental Protection Agency:

> The PEYA program promotes awareness of our nation's natural resources and encourages positive community involvement. Since 1971, the President of the United States has joined with EPA to recognize young people across the U.S. for protecting our nation's air, water, land, and ecology. It is one of the most important ways EPA and the Administration demonstrate commitment to environmental stewardship efforts created and conducted by our nation's young people.
>
> One outstanding project from each region is selected for national recognition. Projects are developed by young individuals, school classes (K–12), summer camps, and youth organizations to promote environmental stewardship. Thousands of young people from all 50 states and the U.S. territories have submitted projects to EPA for consideration. Winning projects in the past have covered a wide range of subject areas, including:
>
> • environmental science projects
> • recycling programs in schools and communities
> • construction of nature preserves
> • major tree planting programs
> • videos, skits, and newsletters that focused on environmental issues
>
> Evaluation results consistently demonstrate that the experience is frequently a life-changing event for many of the young people and sponsors who attend.

KIM KENNEDY WHITE

Source: U.S. Environmental Protection Agency. President's Environmental Youth Awards (PEYA). Available at: http://www.epa.gov/peya/.

References

Collin, Robin, and Robert Collin. 2010. *Encyclopedia of Sustainability*. Santa Barbara, CA: Greenwood Press an Imprint of ABC-CLIO.

Corcoran, Peter Blaze, and Arjen E. J. Wals. 2007. *Higher Education and the Challenge of Sustainability: Problematics, Promise, and Practice*. New York: Springer.

Huckle, Jonathan, and Stephen Sterling, eds. 1996. *Education for a Sustainable Future.* London: Earthscan Publications.

Johnson, Edward A., and Michael J. Mappin, eds. 2009. *Environmental Education and Advocacy: Changing Perspective of Ecology and Education.* London: Cambridge University Press.

Orr, David W. 2004. *Earth in Mind: On Education, Environment, and the Human Prospect.* Washington, DC: Island Press.

Orr, David W., Michael K. Stone, Zenobia Barlow, and Fritjof Capra. 2005. *Ecological Literacy: Educating Our Children for a Sustainable World.* San Francisco, CA: Sierra Club Books.

Rappaport, Ann, and Sarah Creighton. 2007. *Degrees that Matter: Climate Change and the University.* Cambridge, MA: MIT Press.

GREEN COLLEGES AND UNIVERSITIES

Since 2006, the number of colleges and universities reporting green initiatives has grown exponentially. When the first "College Sustainability Report Card" was published, "less than one quarter of institutions had a green building policy" (Ezarik, 2011, 66). However, when the 2011 report card was released, 79 percent of colleges and universities had such a policy (Ezarik, 2011, 66). In addition, over 600 colleges in the United States have signed on as part of the American College and University Presidents Climate Commitment (Dunkel, 2009, 12). Colleges and universities seem to be prioritizing the green movement, and they are doing so through building policies and many other energy-saving initiatives.

Universities such as Harvard, Williams, and Cornell are leaders in the green movement, but so are many other smaller institutions, such as Lakeland Community College and Owens Community College, both in Ohio. At Lakeland, a plan for energy conservation was put in place in 2006; over the next 20 years, the plan aims to reduce "direct and indirect creation of greenhouse gases—by 60%" (Mayher, 2010, 875). The energy saving plan maps out three stages for green improvements: gaining control of the campus's energy consumption in stage one, repairing and improving buildings in stage two, and looking for and implementing alternative energy sources in stage three (Mayher, 2010, 876).

At Owens Community College, several strategies have been put in place that have helped the college reduce energy consumption by over 20 percent (Owens, 2012). The college has installed wind turbines and photovoltaic arrays in addition to putting many other green practices into place. For instance, the college has replaced nearly 12,000 lighting fixtures with high-efficiency products, installed 354 water-saving fixtures, and added 75,000 square feet of insulated roofing materials (Owens, 2012). Students can also be a part of the green movement at Owens: the college offers a degree in "Alternative Energy and Sustainability Systems Technology" (Owens, 2012).

Other schools have gotten involved as well. Specifically, Yale has started the Yale Sustainable Food Project, which has helped to provide organic food for the campus from local farmers. In fact, 40 percent of the food on campus comes from these local farmers (Underwood, 2007, 63). By using local foods, Connecticut's farm land losses are reduced and students consume food that is fresher and healthier (Underwood, 2007, 63). Arizona State has also become part of the green movement: in 2008, the college began a School of Sustainability. Many researchers believe sustainability is the key in the green movement, as it reduces energy consumption, pollution, and health care costs and has the potential to create jobs (Underwood, 2007, 63).

Some colleges see the green movement as way to promote new curricular goals. At some colleges, green housing is offered to students interested in "sustainability education" (Dunkel, 2009, 18). The green residences offered on campus provide a "sustainability-themed living-learning community" (Dunkel, 2009, 18). Programs like these help students to focus on green living while increasing their environmental awareness. A number of researchers suggest that connecting green living to college curriculum is the best way to promote green initiatives on college campuses: doing so "helps turn the entire campus into a living laboratory" (Ezarik, 2011, 67). Colleges, such as Lakeland Community College, Owens Community College, and universities, such as Yale, Harvard, Arizona State, are making these curricular changes throughout their campuses in an effort to provide support for their green practices. Even without specific curricular changes, "university presidents hope that even students who don't pursue increasingly popular majors in environmental studies will learn simply from being on a green campus, living in green buildings, eating sustainable food and absorbing everyday messages of conservation" (Underwood, 2007, 61).

Not only does the environment benefit from the implementation of green initiatives on college campuses, the college benefits as well, in many ways. Colleges embracing the green movement have the potential to save nearly 20 percent of their energy costs, which can amount to over $300,000 per year (Bradley, 2009, 6). Saving money is certainly a benefit, but equally important is the desire for colleges to be able to continue operations now and into the future. Data centers require a significant amount of power; as a result, colleges and universities must find new energy supplies in order to keep those data centers up and running (Bradley, 2009, 7). Reducing current energy consumption and looking for alternative energies will help colleges remedy this situation. Some colleges are already working with alternative energy sources such as wind and solar power.

The Barack Obama administration is on board with green initiatives on college campuses. In fact, the administration "pledged to spend $150 billion over five years in green technology" (Bradley, 2009, 7). The hope of the administration is that colleges will be "carbon-neutral" by 2030. In order for this to be a possibility, new laws and legislation are in the works (Bradley, 2009, 7). As noted, over 600 colleges and universities in the United States are already part of a green movement for sustainable and energy-efficient campuses. That number will continue to grow as leaders in the green movement share their successes and provide pathways for energy improvements.

ELLEN SORG

See also: Higher Education Models, Green Curriculum (Education).

References

Bradley, Paul. 2009. "Saving Green by Going Green." *Community College Week* 22:4 (October 5): 6–8.

Dunkel, Norbert W. 2009. "Green Residence Halls Are Here: Current Trends in Sustainable Campus Housing." *Journal of College & University Student Housing* 36:1 (April): 10–23.

Ezarik, Melissa. 2011. "Growing Green Building Policies." *University Business* 14:6 (June): 66–67.

Mayher, Michael E. 2010. "Going Green Doesn't Have to be Sexy: Lakeland Community College's Practical Approach to Addressing Energy Conservation and Sustainability." *Community College Journal of Research & Practice* 34:11 (November): 874–877. *Academic Search Premier*, EBSCOhost (accessed January 1, 2012).

Owens Community College. 2012. "Project Green." Available at: https://www.owens.edu/green/index.html.

Underwood, Anne. 2007. "The Green Campus." *Newsweek* 150:8/9 (August 27): 60–66.

GREEN JOBS

Going green is no longer exclusively about being environmentally conscious. Green is green. Being sustainable is now as much about reducing operating costs for businesses and expanding the market. It's becoming a market-driven endeavor, populated by public money and policies from the government coupled with private investment and entrepreneurs looking for upstart companies with the latest green technologies, from renewable energy to electric cars to green data centers.

In the past few years, the emergence of a true green market sector has pushed environmental careers into new and intriguing sectors. Companies are falling over themselves to be as green as they can be, enhancing environmental stewardship in order to minimize costs and maximize profits. The mantra of green jobs has pervaded not only the usual environmental-leaning organizations and publications, but has also become a real part of the economic picture in the United States, as well as globally. Like many burgeoning career paths, there are some ups and down, failures and successes. But the push to a more sustainable future and the resulting economic impact of jobs that involve sustainability are on an upward trajectory.

One of the biggest challenges for green jobs has been the country's economic recovery from the recession that began in 2007. There were a lot of hopes pinned on green jobs as the savior of the country's jobless. But the growth of green jobs has followed a more traditional upward move, as opposed to some predictions of green jobs taking over a big portion of the country's job picture. That being said, green jobs have emerged as a relative bright spot in the employment picture.

The public perception of green jobs has been driven by renewable energy, more specifically solar and wind power. Though the myriad of green jobs span from corporate sustainability consultants to eco-tourism, alternative energy has become the bellwether for green employment. And the numbers have been on the upswing. Solar power is making news daily, whether through new companies and new technological breakthroughs, or new business deals and training programs for workers looking to transition into the sector. And the numbers are bearing it out. In

Solar panels are installed at Littlestown Veterinary Hospital in Littlestown, Pennsylvania, in September 2010. (U.S. Department of Agriculture)

2010, over 96,000 Americans worked in the solar industry. The trade organization Solar Foundation's job census of 2010 predicted a 26 percent increase in solar jobs across the country in 2011 ("Renewable Energy," 2011).

Wind energy enjoyed a banner year in 2008, but it was hit by the economic downturn and had a less than stellar growth rate in 2009 through early 2010. However, the installations of wind turbines have increased, and the power generated by them, while still a small portion of the overall energy picture, is growing (American Wind Energy, 2010).

Another, often under-the-radar renewable energy, geothermal, has also experienced growth in employment. The Geothermal Engineering Association, the leading trade group in the sector, predicts a growth of 3,800 direct and ancillary jobs (Jennejohn, 2010).

Much of the growth in geothermal will be relegated to Nevada and California, which points to another truth regarding the availability of green jobs. Many of these jobs are regional in scope, and some states are far in front of others in sustainability-related employment. For example, Colorado has seen a 32 percent increase in employment in the clean tech sector between 2005 and 2010 (PR Newswire). By 2010, the sector employed over 19,000 workers at 1,600 companies. In Iowa, over 2,700 people work in wind turbine manufacturing and technician positions (Piller, 2010). The numbers vary across the country, but it needs to be

Greenovator: Employment and Training Administration News Release, June 22, 2011

The following news release from the U.S. Department of Labor describes the green jobs grant program.

US. Department of Labor announces $38 million in grants awarded through Green Jobs Innovation Fund
WASHINGTON—The U.S. Department of Labor has awarded six organizations a total of $38 million in Green Jobs Innovation Fund grants to serve workers in 19 states and the District of Columbia.

"This grant program is an important part of the administration's efforts to equip workers with the necessary knowledge, skills and abilities to succeed in green industry jobs," said Secretary of Labor Hilda L. Solis. "These are smart investments in the green energy jobs of today and the green energy economy of the future."

The Green Jobs Innovation Fund was authorized under the Workforce Investment Act to help workers receive job training in green industry sectors. These funds will help organizations with existing career training programs leverage Registered Apprenticeships, pre-apprenticeship programs and community-based partnerships to build sustainable green career pathways.

The grants will help employers, as well, by providing participants with the training they need for the industry-recognized credentials on which employers rely.

For more information on the range of Department of Labor employment and training programs, visit http://www.doleta.gov.

Release Number: 11-0949-NAT

KIM KENNEDY WHITE

Source: Employment and Training Administration. U.S. Department of Labor. Green Jobs Innovation Fund. Available at http://www.doleta.gov/ETA_News_Releases/20110949.cfm.

noted that certain areas are more conducive to green jobs, whether through the nature of the job (e.g., geothermal in the west) or from government support for sustainability. If you want to be a corporate sustainability consultant, a location in a major metropolitan area would be advantageous. If you wanted to start an eco-tourism company, you might want a place close to natural areas.

One career path that really took a hit from the current recession was the construction industry. But even there, green has become a bigger piece of the pie as construction starts to come back, albeit at a much slower pace than in the early 2000s.

Green building starts have increased from $42 billion in 2008 to over $71 billion in 2010, and account for over 25 percent of all new construction activity (McGraw Hill Construction). Green building drives ancillary businesses producing products for Leadership in Energy and Environmental Design (LEED) certifications and general green-conscious consumers. The rise of LEED accreditation has been one of the major factors that brought green building practices to the forefront of the industry. LEED has also become part of the vernacular, though it is not the only green building accreditation available.

Traditional environmental sciences also went through a challenging few years during the recession as declining government budgets and a saturated market led to a less-than-desirable job climate. Consulting companies were laying off workers and engineering firms struggled as the private construction market tumbled. But after some stabilizing and shifting of market sector, the growth outlook looks promising.

There are some green career paths that may be more promising if only for the nature of the current workforce. Engineers are retiring at a rapid rate, as are wastewater system operators and public works employees. These careers are at the cutting edge of low-impact development, green building, water resources, and green technology. However, there is a dearth of younger workers to take their place. If a person is interested in a green path outside of renewable energy or sustainability, the wastewater/water system path might be a good opportunity.

Green jobs may not be the be-all and end-all to future employment, but to ignore the growth of the sector and the massive increase in private capital and funding, as well as the emergence of hundreds of small businesses and major corporations embracing sustainability, is simply foolish. Green jobs, in one form or another, are here to stay as part of the American economic landscape.

SCOTT M. DEITCHE

See also: Green Jobs, Bureau of Labor Statistics Jobs Initiative (documents).

References

American Wind Energy Association. 2010. *20% Wind Energy by 2030–2009 Report Card*.
Jennejohn, Dan. 2010. *Green Jobs Through Geothermal Energy*. Report for the Geothermal Energy Association. Washington, DC.
McGraw Hill Construction. "Green Building Market Grows 50% in Two Years Despite Recession, Says McGraw-Hill Construction Report." Available at: http://construction .com/AboutUs/2010/1112pr.asp.
Piller, Dan. 2010. "Green Jobs Take Wind Technicians to Dizzying Heights." Available at: http://www.desmoinesregister.com/article/20110519/BUSINESS/105190354/-1/ GETPUBLISHED03wp-content/Green-job-takes-wind-technicians-dizzying-heights.
PR Newswire. "Colorado Is the Hub of National Green Jobs Creation." Available at: http:// www.prnewswire.com/news-releases/colorado-is-the-hub-of-national-green-job-creation -122437923.html.
"Renewable Energy Will See Breakout Job Growth in 2011 with Solar Leading Charge." Available at: http://www.solar-products-blog.com/?p=1673.

HIGHER EDUCATION MODELS, GREEN CURRICULUM

Ecological literacy has become a mandate in many higher education institutions and is evident in a wide spectrum of disciplines that include sustainable-centric courses or programs in agriculture, business and communications, education and liberal arts, engineering and sciences, fine and applied arts, health and medicine, and law and legal studies. Many curricula have integrated approaches, both philosophical and pedagogical in structure, that share parallel perspectives in developing an environmentally protected, energy-efficient, and healthier world. Initiating change and committing to responsible green decisions are anchored on four Ps, namely: practice, principle, perspective, and process. Scholars also refer to

Colorado State University students do a trash audit as part of Recyclemania, March 2, 2011. In September 2011 CSU was one of the top universities participating in the STARS program of the Association for the Advancement of Sustainability in Higher Education (AASHE). (Colorado State University)

these as the 4Ps in crafting knowledge-based change (Walker, 2006). Other programs have extended their sustainable endeavors with additional Ps, noted as policy and performance assessments of initiatives.

The Association for the Advancement of Sustainability in Higher Education (AASHE) has listed a total of 237 U.S. institutions that are active participants in the Sustainability Tracking Assessment and Rating System (STARS) program since its inception in 2009 (AASHE, 2011). Over 600 institutions also catalog their various sustainability-related activities in response to the growing environmental awareness. Activities are spread out into three main areas: education and research; campus-wide planning and operations; and administration and finance matters, human resource, and policy engagement (AASHE, 2009). A brief review of university and college initiatives under this report will link us to diverse green and ecological models in higher education. They range from specific topics within subjects to immersive learning field studies, from a three-credit course instruction to full program development initiatives, and from a core elective shared across departments to new program disciplines offered as a major or minor.

The compendium of sustainable endeavors in higher education was also equally reflected in several publications promoted by the U.S. Green Building Council

(USGBC). The USGBC is considered the nation's leading coalition uniting all building industries "to promote buildings that are environmentally responsible, profitable, and healthy places to live and work" (Winchip, 2007, 63). Every year, the USGBC sponsors international conferences with topics on "thought leadership and research track" (USGBC, 2011). Since its inception in 2002, the USGBC promotes green building education and research disseminating initiatives in new data analyses relevant to green building market trends, business case studies, cost-effective approaches, as well as health and productivity assessments.

Parallel to these initiatives, 11 institutions in Europe and Latin America have collaborated in restructuring their curricula. They created a working model known as the ACES network that defines their collective mission toward an education for sustainability. (ACES is a Spanish acronym for Curriculum Greening of Higher Education.) Their joint effort generated a model of 10 distinct characteristics, which has significant value in multiple university structures, diverse disciplines and programs, and at several levels in the educational strata. It seeks to reorient university studies and create a curriculum toward sustainability with the following characteristics:

Greenovator: Sierra Club's Ranking of the Greenest Colleges in 2011

The following is from the Fifth Annual Sierra Club green college rankings:

For the past five years, the Sierra Club has ranked the top 100 "Coolest Schools." Institutions considered for the list are four-year colleges and universities in the United States. Each of the 940 eligible schools complete a questionnaire that assesses ten areas of sustainability efforts: efficiency, energy supply, waste management, purchasing, academics, food, transportation, administration, financial investments, and other initiatives. Sierra Club's top ten greenest colleges and universities for 2011 were:

1. University of Washington, Seattle, Washington
2. Green Mountain College, Poultney, Vermont
3. University of California, San Diego, California
4. Warren Wilson College, Asheville, North Carolina
5. Stanford University, Stanford, California
6. University of California, Irvine, California
7. University of California, Santa Cruz, California
8. University of California, Davis, California
9. Evergreen State College, Olympia, Washington
10. Middlebury College, Middlebury, Vermont

KIM KENNEDY WHITE

Source: Sierra Club's Coolest Schools. Available at: http://sierraclub.org/sierra/201109/coolschools/.

- integrating the paradigm of complexity into the curriculum
- introducing flexibility and permeability in disciplines
- contextualizing the curricular project
- taking the subject into account in the construction of knowledge
- considering the cognitive, affective, and action aspects of people
- a consistent relationship between theory and practice
- working within a prospective orientation of alternative scenarios

- methodological adaptation, which includes new teaching and learning strategies
- creating space for reflection and democratic participation, and
- reinforcing the commitment to transforming relations between society and nature. (Junyent & de Ciurana, 2008, 768–770)

The literature search for sustainable strategies in higher education programs elucidated one inspiring model, introduced in 1971, which is related to human ecology and social change. Victor Papanek (1995) states that designing toward ecology and environmental equilibrium is fundamental to the relationship of human life with earth. He introduced a six-sided functional matrix in view of the designer's ethical obligation to create a safer environment and a better future. The matrix calls for a balanced integration of method, association, aesthetics, need, consequences, and use (Papanek, 1995, 34). This model has been proven to inspire and guide multiple versions of ecological postulations and has been cited in various publications.

In sustainable architecture, Simon Guy and Graham Framer also promote a six-typology approach in building design: eco-technic, eco-centric, eco-aesthetic, eco-cultural, eco-medical, and eco-social (Tucker, 2009, 83). Briefly, eco-technic is associated with integrated technology, eco-centric focuses on harmony with nature and its system, eco-aesthetic pertains to ecological sensitivity and knowledge, eco-cultural considers local traditions, eco-medical qualifies what is harmful to humans' health and well-being, and eco-social denotes collective and community participation. These eco-ethos significantly parallel the model developed by Papanek, who associated method with tools, materials, and processes; association with family, education, and culture; aesthetics characterized by visual perception and social givens; need distinguishing survival, identity, and goal formation; consequences alluding to ecological-environmental aspects, social-societal patterns, and material and energy use; and use with tools as communication or as symbol (Papanek, 1984, 7). Another model used in landscape architecture developed by Volkman (2009) looks at the intersections of human need, environmental sustainability, and aesthetics. Volkman explains that good design can be generated by looking into the broad spectrum of practical and social needs;

Greenovator: The U.S. Environmental Protection Agency's Green Power Partnership Top 20 Colleges and Universities for 2011

The following is the EPA's 2011 Top 20 College and University's purchasing green power:

The Top 20 College & University list represents the largest purchasers among higher education institutions within the Green Power Partnership. The combined green power purchases of these organizations amounts to more than 1.4 billion kilowatt hours of green power annually, which is the equivalent amount of electricity needed to power more than 121,000 average American homes annually.

The Green Power Partnership works with a wide variety of leading organizations—from Fortune 500 understanding the natural environment as natural systems; and the regulating value of aesthetics. He concludes that his paradigm can be applied in many disciplinary subfields, including housing.

The expanded program reviews of specific disciplines construe distinct commonalities that point to a holistic and integrated education. Holistic education is about educating the whole person—body, mind and soul (Clarken, 2009) and one's development into a responsible citizen of society and the environment. Integrated approach is an educational model that prepares one to sensitively consider all factors that clearly connect human needs, culture, and ecology (Papanek, 1984).

Keniry states that curriculum is one of the 12 benchmarks of success in evaluating campus stewardship programs (1995, 187). His idea of weaving environmental responsibility into the curriculum was to essentially make it an intrinsic part of academic life. His idea proposed that all faculty engage in teaching environmental issues from either their disciplinary fields or from an interdisciplinary perspective, link the classroom activities to campus-wide operations, create field studies related to resources consumption or environmental assessment, and seek for joint research efforts among faculty, staff, and students within an environmental education that harmonizes content with process (1995, 194–195).

THELMA LAZO-FLORES

companies to local, state and federal governments, and a growing number of colleges and universities.

1. University of Pennsylvania, Pennsylvania
2. Carnegie Mellon University, Pennsylvania
3. University of Utah, Utah
4. Oregon State University, Oregon
5. Drexel University, Pennsylvania
6. Pennsylvania State University, Pennsylvania
7. Northwestern University, Illinois
8. Apollo Group, Inc./University of Phoenix, Arizona
9. University of Oklahoma, Oklahoma
10. University of Maryland, Maryland
11. The City University of New York, New York
12. American University, Washington, D.C.
13. The Ohio State University, Ohio
14. Texas A&M University System, Texas
15. The Catholic University of America, Washington, D.C.
16. Auraria Higher Education Center, Denver
17. Western Washington University, Washington
18. University of Wisconsin, Wisconsin
19. Quinnipiac University, Connecticut
20. Georgetown University, Washington, D.C.

KIM KENNEDY WHITE

Source: Top 20 College & University. U.S. Environmental Protection Agency's Green Power Partnership. Available at: http://www.epa.gov/greenpower/toplists/top20ed.htm.

See also: Green Colleges and Universities (Education); Green Ribbon Schools Recognition Award (documents); K–12 Green Curriculum (Education).

References

Association for the Advancement of Sustainability in Higher Education (AASHE). 2009. "A Review of Campus Sustainability News." Available at: http://www.aashe.org/files/documents/resources/AASHEdigest2009.pdf.

Association for the Advancement of Sustainability in Higher Education (AASHE). 2011. "Sustainability Tracking Assessment and Rating System (STARS) Dashboard." Available at: https://stars.aashe.org/institutions/data-displays/dashboard/.

Beringer, Almut, and Maik AdomBent. 2008. "Sustainable University Research and Development: Inspecting Sustainability in Higher Education Research." *Environmental Education Research* 14:6: 607–623.

Clarken, Rodney H. 2009. "Holistic Education." In E. F. Provenzo, Jr., ed., *Encyclopedia of the Social and Cultural Foundations of Education*. Thousand Oaks, CA: Sage, 416–417.

Junyent, Merce, and Anna M. Geli de Ciurana. 2008. "Education for Sustainability in University Studies: A Model for Reorienting the Curriculum." *British Educational Research Journal* 34:6: 763–782.

Keniry, Julian. 1995. *Ecodemia: Campus Environmental Stewardship at the Turn of the 21st Century*. Washington, DC: National Wildlife Federation.

Papanek, Victor. 1984. *Design for the Real World: Human Ecology and Social Change*. London: Thames and Hudson.

Papanek, Victor. 1995. *The Green Imperative: Natural Design for the Real World*. New York: Thames and Hudson.

Shrivastava, Paul. 2010. "Pedagogy of Passion for Sustainability." *Academy of Management Learning and Education* 9:3: 443–455.

Stegall, Nathan. 2006. "Designing for Sustainability: A Philosophy for Ecologically Intentional Design." *Design Issues* 22:2: 56–63.

Tucker, Lisa. 2009. "Sustainability and Information Gathering." In Joan Dickinson and John P. Marsden, eds., *Informing Design*. New York: Fairchild Books, 79–106.

U.S. Green Building Council (USGBC). 2011. http://www.usgbc.org/News/Press Releases.aspx?PageID=257&CMSPageID=163.

Volkman, Nancy. 2009. "Landscape Architecture, Design, and Preservation." In J. B. Callicott and R. Frodeman, ed., *Encyclopedia of Environmental Ethics and Philosophy*. Detroit: Macmillan Reference USA, 2:26–33.

Walker, Stuart. 2006. *Sustainable by Design: Explorations in Theory and Practice*. London: Earthscan.

Winchip, Susan. 2007. *Sustainable Design for Interior Environments*. New York: Fairchild Books.

INDIGENOUS ENTREPRENEURSHIP AND SUSTAINABILITY: A CASE STUDY — COLLEGE OF MENOMINEE NATION CAMPUS GRIND COFFEE SHOP

The Campus Grind Coffee Shop is located at the College of Menominee Nation (CMN), a tribal college on the Menominee Reservation in northern Wisconsin. The Campus Grind is an indigenously owned, student-run coffee shop selling fair-trade, organic, shade-grown coffee blends developed by two student organizations at CMN: Strategies for Environmental Education, Development and Sustainability (SEEDS) and the American Indian Business Leaders (AIBL). The SEEDS/AIBL campus coffee shop is an excellent example of an eco-friendly indigenous business that is mutually beneficial to both the environment and human communities. Although eco-friendly mindfulness is not new to indigenous cultures, the practice of sustainability within this entrepreneurial context is unique.

Development of the Campus Grind Coffee Shop

The SEEDS student organization created a portable coffee cart in 2007 to sell fair-trade, organic, shade-grown coffee blends on campus and in the community. The coffee gained a respectable following, and SEEDS used part of the profits from the coffee sales to finance a trip of seven students and an advisor for a week-long trip to Chiapas, Mexico, to visit the communities where the coffee is grown. The trip was an extremely powerful experience for the students, opening their eyes to the linkages between consumer behavior, environmental degradation, poverty, human rights, and global economies.

In 2008, the chapter developed its own coffee blend called Campus Grind: CMN-SEEDS. By 2009 the SEEDS coffee was being sold at the CMN campus bookstore, local Earth Day festivals, tribal pow-wows, regional police officer training seminars, and many other campus events. Word was getting out around the community and people began to request the coffee and come to campus to buy it. Nationally, too, the efforts were being recognized; in 2009 the chapter received the designation of runner-up in the national SEEDS Chapter of the Year competition. It was soon obvious to SEEDS members that with such rapid growth and demand, the coffee project was growing beyond the limited business skills possessed by the group. Discussion began about integrating the project with the AIBL student group.

Responding to SEEDS request to assist with the coffee project, the AIBL students wrote a business plan to open a permanent coffee shop on the CMN campus. The business plan contained detailed sections on management, marketing, and finances for a small, student-owned and operated campus coffee shop. The students entered and presented the plan in the 2008 American Indian Higher Education Consortium (AIHEC) business plan competition, earning first place. The winning plan was then submitted to the CMN development office for consideration of a microloan for startup funds. A microloan was secured and construction of a permanent coffee shop began six months later.

The new Campus Grind Coffee Shop opened for business during the 2009 fall semester and is still open today. The AIBL and SEEDS students work in the coffee shop as baristas and are paid through the federal work study program. Students, faculty, and staff members assist with strategic planning, marketing, promotion, and distribution of the coffee. The campus, community, and indigenous cultures are definitely reflected in how the business operations are conducted.

Cultural Influences on Entrepreneurship

The use of national cultural dimensions (Hofstede, 1980) provides a common ground for discussion of shared cultural values and their impact on entrepreneurship in indigenous communities. The general consensus among researchers is highly individualistic, and masculine societies value entrepreneurial activities (Foley, 2008; Redpath & Nielsen, 1997). The indigenous tribes of North America are overwhelmingly collectivistic societies with concern for the community over

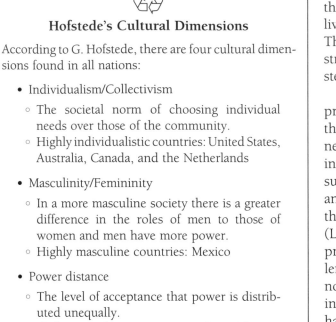

Hofstede's Cultural Dimensions

According to G. Hofstede, there are four cultural dimensions found in all nations:

- Individualism/Collectivism
  - The societal norm of choosing individual needs over those of the community.
  - Highly individualistic countries: United States, Australia, Canada, and the Netherlands

- Masculinity/Femininity
  - In a more masculine society there is a greater difference in the roles of men to those of women and men have more power.
  - Highly masculine countries: Mexico

- Power distance
  - The level of acceptance that power is distributed unequally.
  - High power distance countries: Iran, Pakistan, and Malaysia

- Uncertainty avoidance
  - A society's level of tolerance for uncertainty minimized through strict rules, laws, and policies.
  - High uncertainty avoidance countries: Guatemala, El Salvador, and Colombia

Source: Hofstede, G. 2009. Geert-Hofstede-itim.

concern for self, and are less oriented toward masculinity than the dominant one in which they live (Redpath & Nielsen, 1997). This is the opposite of the mainstream U.S. population (Hofstede, 1980).

The Western sense of entrepreneurship is shaped around the individual who finds businesses that lead to rapid growth, increased net assets, and money, supporting the individualistic and masculine dimensions of the mainstream Western culture (Lindsay, 2005). This type of approach to business poses problems for societies with social norms that do not readily support individualistic or masculine behaviors. Oftentimes, in fact, the social norms will deter indigenous people from having entrepreneurial intentions at all; however, with the inclusion of culture and family into the business setting, indigenous people can be successful entrepreneurs (Lindsay, 2005).

Model of Indigenous Entrepreneurship

The foundation of indigenous entrepreneurship is the inclusion of culture and family in the business setting (Foley, 2008), as reflected in Lindsey's indigenous business model (Lindsey, 2005). The model includes the owner, board of directors, and a management team as typical, but it also incorporates the cultural and family values of the indigenous business owner. By including culture and family, Lindsey's model embraces and supports the opinion that culture and family influence the indigenous business owner. Indigenous people in North America have cultural dimensions that may clash with traditional entrepreneurial values, making the indigenous entrepreneur of special interest. Acknowledging, understanding, and incorporating the family, community, and culture in the indigenous business is reflected in the Campus Grind coffee shop's daily and strategic operations and intertwined with the Menominee philosophy of sustainability.

Foundations of Sustainability

The origin of the discourse on sustainable development is often attributed to the idea that the Earth has limits, and to meet the needs of the present, people must not compromise the ability of future generations (World Commission on Environment and Development, 1987). For indigenous people, the concept of sustainability is woven into the very tapestry of life, with the "way of living" based on the concepts of sustainability. This worldview is supported by two fundamental beliefs: (1) all life is sacred and should be respected, and (2) nature will supply all our needs, but not all our wants.

Blanchett (2008) stated no other Native American people understand sustainability more than the Menominee Tribe of Wisconsin, exemplified in the management of the famed Menominee forest. The Menominee have practiced a deliberate, sustained yield practice on their reservation. Paul Hawken stated: "The preservation of the forest has not only benefited wildlife, streams, and biodiversity, but also has provided a steady income for many of the tribe's members, allowing them to maintain their lives in the ten small towns dotting the reservation" (1993, 142–143).

The Menominee approach to sustainable development is an integration of tribal wisdom, knowledge, values, understandings, and practices viewing sustainability as a continual process by which Menominees' affinity to place balances with the six dimensions of community life. The CMN's Sustainable Development Institute logo serves as the framework to illustrate the inextricable linkage among the historical, social, cultural, and spiritual foundations of Menominee life. Each of the dimensions can be demonstrated in the daily operations of the Campus Grind.

Land and Sovereignty

Sovereignty is defined as "the legal underpinning for American Indian/Alaska Native rights to self-determination, including self-governance, cultural preservation and revitalization, and education" (Lomawaima & McCarty, 2002). The philosophy of inclusion of community and family clearly depicts the definition of sovereignty. The Campus Grind business model includes typical aspects of a business such as a board and management team, yet it also includes indigenous aspects of community and family in the business model. The owners of the Campus Grind are the students in the SEEDS and AIBL organizations at CMN. The board consists of the advisers for the SEEDS and AIBL clubs. The management team members fluctuate each semester, but they include federal work study students and business and sustainable development interns.

The Campus Grind business model also includes the "family" members. While the family members may be directly related to anyone on the board or management team, the majority of the "family" is the campus community. Students, faculty, and staff help guide the business decisions made at the Campus Grind. Although this process takes longer than the typical business, it builds community support for the business. By only purchasing fair-trade coffee, the Campus Grind owners, board members, community, and family enable farmers in southern Mexico to maintain ownership of their land by earning a higher income and move toward the ultimate goal of building a more autonomous and sovereign society for themselves.

Technology

The Campus Grind incorporates technology through a variety of means, involving sustainable practices. Sustainability practices in technology are portrayed in the Campus Grind coffee shop building, machines purchased, and social media. The coffee shop is located in a building designed and built based on the college's commitment to sustainability, using sustainable building practices. It is considered the equivalent of a U.S. Green Building Council's Leadership in Energy and Environmental Design (LEED) Silver rating, designed to be 29 percent more efficient than the state minimum standards. Earth-friendly features include 36 geothermal wells to heat and cool the main and upper floors of the building; natural daylight throughout the building; daylight and occupancy sensors; heat recovery ventilation; and low volatile organic compounds and locally produced building materials, including white pine paneling from the Menominee Tribe's sustainably managed forests.

The equipment used in the coffee shop is very high quality, commercial coffee equipment found in other shops; however, the equipment was purchased used. It was not only less expensive to buy the used equipment, but it fit well with the sustainability value of reusing a piece of equipment rather than buying new. Technology is also intertwined through the social media use of Facebook. The Campus Grind Facebook page promotes the weekly specials, upcoming events, and other announcements. Students who access the page are especially interested in the barista's updated song list, as Facebook friends are able to request what songs they want to hear on the Campus Grind iPod playlist.

Natural Environment

The concept of natural environment is engrained in Menominee culture, and the Campus Grind epitomizes this cultural value. The coffee sold is grown organically under the shade of tropical forests. This leads to a healthy habitat for plant and animal species, intact forests that are crucial in our fight to stabilize climate change, a cleaner watershed, and less exposure to toxins for the coffee farmers (Ingebretsen, 2008). These types of practices limit high production and sales, but ultimately contribute to a healthier environment for producer and consumer. The coffee shop composts all coffee filters and grounds in a nearby vermiculture compost bin. The compost is then applied to the flower and vegetable gardens that dot the campus environs. Additionally, the Campus Grind promotes sustainability through promotion of reusable coffee mugs made of compostable materials.

Institution

Since the College of Menominee Nation is an institution of higher learning developed by Menominee people, sustainability has strong support from the leadership team of the college, the members of which have all received training on triple bottom line accounts management. In addition, President Verna Fowler is a signatory to the American College and University Presidents Climate Commitment. Fowler often says CMN is about moving whole heart, mind, body, soul, and actions into sustainability. This commitment was manifested in three tangible actions the college undertook in support of the coffee shop: (1) the college administration provided space in the lobby of the new college library for the coffee shop; (2) AIBL/SEEDS secured a microloan from the college development office for $5,000 to help pay for equipment purchases; and (3) every student who intends to graduate from the college is required to take an the Introduction to Sustainable Development class.

Economics

The Campus Grind coffee shop provides economic vitality to the campus community through real-life job exposure, introduction to fair-trade concepts, loan processes, and social responsibility. Students from the SEEDS and AIBL clubs gain hands-on work experience as they work as baristas, help with marketing, and assist with the financial and accounting responsibilities. The student baristas can articulate the idea that farmers in other regions of the world are being paid more fairly for their crops as a result of this designation, increasing the awareness of fair trade and encouraging students and community members to not only purchase CMN coffee, but also other products that carry a fair trade certification. The microloan for startup expenses was secured through the college's development office. The payoff for the loan will take two to four years, but even after the loan is repaid, the students plan to continue paying toward the fund to assist other student activities.

Human Culture and Behavior

The indigenous culture is clearly reflected in the coffee menu and marketing materials, as well as in the daily operations. The Campus Grind menu offers the normal espresso drinks of mochas and cappuccinos, but there are other drinks more expressive of the indigenous culture. The menu has a Native Americano (espresso and coffee) and Sovereign Teas (organic teas). Also, the Campus Grind coffee club is referred to as Kapeh Club, with *kapeh* being the Menominee word for coffee. The eco-friendly mugs sold are imprinted with a Kapeh logo. The culture is also depicted in the collaborative decision making of the students, advisors, and student workers. Making the schedule, purchasing the equipment, choosing the coffee blends, deciding on the hours of operation, and selecting menu items are all decisions made together.

As a result of opening the coffee shop, changes in human behavior are shown in increased global awareness of the campus community. The coffee blends sold come from Mexico, Bolivia, and Peru, but the students were also exposed to other beans from other regions in the world on their visit to the coffee roaster, Just Coffee Cooperative. The partnership with Just Coffee Cooperative led to increased knowledge of cooperatives around the world, how they work, and who they benefit. Students like the idea of helping families similar to them all over the world earn a living.

Conclusion

Although the Campus Grind Coffee Shop was established to provide CMN business and sustainable development students with real-world experiences and to promote the concepts of sustainable practices, it has evolved into something much more. It is a small business on a reservation run by indigenous people whose cultural makeup personifies sustainability, not necessarily mainstream entrepreneurial traits, yet it is successful. The success of the Campus Grind coffee shop is in large part a result of operating under an indigenous business model wrapped within the strong cultural influence of the tribe's philosophy toward sustainability.

WILLIAM VAN LOPIK AND STEPHANIE J. ERDMANN

See also: Community Economic Development and Substantive Participation (Activism); Environmental Education Act of 1970 (Education); K–12 Green Curriculum (Education); National Environmental Education Act of 1990 (documents); Proceedings Report from the Sustainability Education Summit (documents); Summary of Recent Federal Agency Environmental Education Projects (documents).

References

Blanchett, K. 2008. "Sustainability Program Profile: College of Menominee Nation Carries on a Sustainable Tradition." *Sustainability: The Journal of Record* 1:6: 377–380.

Foley, D. 2008. "Does Culture and Social Capital Impact on the Networking Attributes of Indigenous Entrepreneurs?" *Journal of Enterprising Communities: People and Places in the Global Economy* 2:3: 204–224.

Hawken, P. 1993. *The Ecology of Commerce.* New York: Harper Business, 1993.

Hofstede, G. 1980. *Culture's Consequences: International Differences in Work-Related Values.* Beverly Hills, CA: Sage.

Ingebretsen, M. 2008. *Conservation International.* March 19. Available at: http://www .conservation.org/FMG/Articles/Pages/starbucks_shadegrown_coffee.aspx.

Lindsay, N. J. 2005. "Toward a Cultural Model of Indigenous Entrepreneurial Attitude." *Academy of Marketing Science Review* 5: 1–15.

Lomawaima, K., and T. McCarty. 2002. "When Tribal Sovereignty Challenges Democracy: American Indian Education and the Democratic Ideal." *American Educational Research Journal* 39:2: 279–305.

Redpath, L., and M. Nielsen. 1997. "A Comparison of Native Culture, Non-Native Culture and New Management Ideology." *Canadian Journal of Administrative Sciences* 14:3: 327–339.

World Commission on Environment and Development. 1987. *Our Common Future.* Geneva: Oxford University Press.

K–12 GREEN CURRICULUM

The terms *green curriculum* and *environmental education* encompass a wide variety of topics, teaching methods, and resources. Since the advent of the modern environmental movement in the 1960s, there have been numerous efforts to develop "green curriculums" for the schools. Many environmental and educational organizations offer a broad array of lesson plans, books, videos, and other materials for use in K–12 classrooms. The U.S. Environmental Protection Agency (EPA) offers a wealth of resources for teachers and students on its Web site, as do such national organizations as the North American Association for Environmental Education (NAAEE), the National Resources Defense Council (NRDC), and the Sierra Club. Some environmental organizations, both on the national and regional levels, offer seminars and workshops for teachers. Articles published in *Green Teacher*, a prominent national magazine, are also collected and published in anthologies that are part of a "Teaching Green" series.

Despite the plethora of readily available resources, there is no national K–12 green curriculum. To a great extent, school curriculum varies from state to state, even from district to district or school to school. Some states like New York and Vermont have defined science curriculum programs that tie some themes of environmental education into their standards, but other states do not. In an era of Internet access, teachers throughout the country have instant access to an impressive variety of resources, but it is difficult to gauge with precision which themes and materials are most commonly incorporated into North American classrooms. According to the authors of a recent and well-publicized academic study, *The Failure of Environmental Education*, the current educational climate with its emphasis on testing, has made it

Greenovation: Teacher Award

The following describes the U.S. EPA and White House Council on Environmental Quality's Teacher Award:

The White House Council on Environmental Quality (CEQ), in partnership with the U.S. Environmental Protection Agency (EPA), is proud to announce the 2011–2012 Presidential Innovation Award for Environmental Educators. As discussed in the "America's Great Outdoors: A Promise to Future Generations" report, in order to make environmental stewardship and conservation relevant to young Americans, environmental and place-based, experiential learning must be integrated into school curricula and school facility management across the country. This program recognizes outstanding kindergarten through grade 12 teachers who employ innovative approaches to environmental education and use the environment as a context for learning for their students. Two teachers from each of EPA's 10 regional offices will be selected to receive this award.

Monetary Awards

The awardee teacher will receive an award of $2,000, to be used to further the awardee's professional development in environmental education, as well as a commemorative plaque.

An award of $2,000 will be given to the awardee's local education agency to fund environmental educational activities and programs that support the awardee teacher (but not for construction costs, general expenses, salaries, bonuses, or other administrative expenses).

As a condition of their awards, the awardee and the awardee's local education agency shall separately submit a one-page report summarizing the utilization and distribution of the funds each received. These reports will be due within 10 months of receipt of the award.

Awards Ceremony

Awardees and applicants selected for Honorable Mentions will be acknowledged at a recognition ceremony.

Disclaimer

EPA reserves the right to reject all applications in one or more of the EPA regions and to make no awards in those region(s) under this announcement. In addition, EPA reserves the right to make fewer than two awards in one or more regions. If EPA decides to make fewer than two awards in one or more regions, it will do so in a manner that does not prejudice any applicant or affect the basis upon which the applicants were evaluated or selected for award and maintains the integrity of the competition and the evaluation and selection process.

KIM KENNEDY WHITE

Source: "Teacher Award." Environmental Education. U.S. Environmental Protection Agency. Available at: http://www.epa.gov/enviroed/teacheraward/index.html.

Greenovation: Green Ribbon Schools Recognition Award

Green Ribbon Schools is an awards program, beginning the fall of 2011, which recognizes schools that are working to be sustainable and promote healthy communities and environmental literacy. Currently, more than 400 schools nationwide are participating in the program. The following factsheet provides information on the Green Ribbon Schools Recognition Award that honors the nation's highest performing green schools:

On September 29, 2011, the U.S. Secretary of Education opened the pilot year of the Green Ribbon Schools award to recognize the highest performing green schools in the nation. The recognition award recognizes exemplary achievement in environmental impact, health and education. The standards and resources that the award relates advance the complementary aims of cutting schools' costs, saving jobs; fostering health, wellness and productivity; providing a well-rounded education, increasing STEM skills, and ensuring students' college and career preparedness.

Green schools are critical to schools' fiscal health and our nation's economy. Much needed

more difficult for teachers to give priority to environmental issues (Saylan & Blumstein, 2011).

There is also the ongoing phenomenon of ideological polarization around such issues as climate change and the question of how this polarization affects teachers' presentations of environmental topics. With so many ideologically driven controversies currently raging—on matters that range from the regulation of pollutants, to whether to drill in protected habitats, to strip-top mining, to policies regarding energy efficient light bulbs—it would seem that broad-scale political tensions may reach into some classrooms. Though many American students are exposed to positive views of the green and environmental movements, it would appear that other students receive mixed and negative messages.

Despite these complicating factors, "green curriculum" does exist, and it can take many forms within the K–12 curriculum. One of its most common forms is as a component of the natural sciences. Nature-themed units introduce children to the concept of ecosystems, the interconnection of various life forms, and the importance of preserving forests, lakes, wetlands, and other habitats. Many lesson plans spotlight the challenges facing the world's oceans, rainforests, and coral reefs. Also popular is the theme of animals—their diversity, their roles in ecosystems, and the dangers they face at a time of dwindling habitats. Some green-themed materials feature the achievements of environmental heroes, such as conservationist John Muir. Most green-themed resources encourage students to be conscientious citizens—to write letters to legislators, to start and support recycling programs, and to consider future careers in such fields as marine biology, clean energy, and green architecture. Even if the problems discussed are dire, the message tends to be phrased in positive and uplifting terms. Students are urged to explore the natural world, to see connections between all life forms, and to take positive steps to protect ecosystems, to conserve energy, assist animals, and work toward a sustainable future.

Some history and social studies textbooks also introduce students to the history of the modern environmental movement of the 1960s and 1970s. Typical topics include the work of Rachel Carson, author of *Silent Spring* (1962), who warned about the danger of industrial poisons like DDT (dichloro-diphenyl-trichloroethane); the history of Earth Day; and the passage during the 1970s of the Clean Air, Clean Water, and Endangered Species acts. Even if there are few history textbooks that dedicate extensive coverage to the environmental perspective, many books do touch on topics that range from the pollution crises of the Industrial Revolution of the 1800s, to President Theodore

improvements to school facilities create new jobs and save schools money. They prepare students to participate in the green economy, reduce chances of losing American jobs to other countries, strengthen the nation's energy security and conserve precious natural resources.

Healthy behaviors, environmental education and green facilities are as vital to individual students as they are to the nation. High standards of nutrition, fitness and facility conditions improve student and staff health, attendance and productivity, and enhance achievement and engagement, particularly in science, technology, engineering and mathematics (STEM).

As with the Blue Ribbon Schools recognition award, schools do not apply to the Department of Education but to state education departments. ED encourages state departments of education to use the following dates to guide their state nomination process:

> *By November 22nd*: Notify ED of participation
> *By March 22nd*: Submit nominees to ED

Schools should contact state departments of education for information on nomination selection.

While the award confers no federal funds, winners of the Green Ribbon, like Blue Ribbon Schools, may experience national and local press coverage, re-energized staff and parents, enhanced community support, increased application rates, and new private financial assistance. Winners will be invited to participate in national and local recognition ceremonies.

Each state may nominate up to four schools. If a state wishes to nominate more than one public school, at least one must be a school with at least 40 percent of their students from a disadvantaged background. If a state wishes to nominate a fourth school, one must be a private school. ED will select approximately 50 award winners in the pilot year.

KIM KENNEDY WHITE

Source: Green Ribbon Schools Factsheet. U.S. Department of Education. Available at: http://www2.ed.gov/programs/green-ribbon-schools/factsheet.pdf.

Greenovator: The U.S. Environmental Protection Agency's Green Power Partnership Top 20 K–12 Schools for 2011

The following is the EPA's Top 20 K–12 schools that purchased green power in 2011:

The Top 20 K–12 Schools list represents the largest purchasers among K–12 school partners within the Green Power Partnership. The combined green power purchases of these organizations amounts to more than 220 million kilowatt hours of green power annually, which is the equivalent amount of electricity needed to power nearly 19,000 average American homes each year.

1. Chicago Public Schools, Illinois
2. Austin Independent School District, Texas
3. Round Rock Independent School District, Texas
4. Bullis School, Maryland
5. The Chapin School, New York
6. Norwood School, Maryland
7. Hotchkiss School, Connecticut
8. Greenwich Academy, Connecticut
9. The Dalton School, New York
10. Lake Travis Independent School District, Texas
11. Lycee Francais of New York, New York
12. Sidwell Friends School, Washington, D.C.
13. Spence School, New York
14. Spirit Lake Community Schools, Iowa
15. Maret School, Washington, D.C.
16. Kentfield School District, California
17. Kent Place School, New Jersey
18. The Nightingale-Bamford School, New York
19. Pflugerville Independent School District, Texas
20. Grace Church School, New York

KIM KENNEDY WHITE

Source: "Top 20 K–12 Schools." U.S. Environmental Protection Agency Green Power Partnership. Available at: http://www.epa.gov/greenpower/toplists/top20k-12 schools.htm.

Roosevelt's expansion of national parks in the early 1900s, to the broad ecological challenges facing us in the 21st century.

In sum, American students may be exposed to a variety of green topics in classes that range from science to social studies, and there exists a wealth of creatively designed, informative lesson plans that are available to teachers and their students. But the level of student exposure varies from state to state, from school to school, even from classroom to classroom, depending on the interests, training, and perspectives of individual teachers. There is no national curriculum, even though national organizations have produced teaching resources that are well designed and digitally accessible.

CHRISTINA M. STERN

See also: Environmental Education Act of 1970 (Education); Green Ribbon Schools Recognition Award (documents); Indigenous Entrepreneurship and Sustainability (Education); National Environmental Education Act of 1990 (documents); Proceedings Report from the Sustainability Education Summit (documents); Summary of Recent Federal Agency Environmental Education Projects (documents).

References

Foner, Eric. 2006. *Give Me Liberty! An American History*, Vol. 2. New York and London: Norton.

Grant, Tim, and Gail Littlejohn, eds. 2004. *Teaching Green—The*

Middle Years. Portland, ME: Stenhouse Publishers.

Grant, Tim, and Gail Littlejohn, eds. 2005. *Teaching Green—The Elementary Years*. Portland, ME: Stenhouse Publishers.

Grant, Tim, and Gail Littlejohn, eds. 2009. *Teaching Green—The High School Years*. Portland, ME: Stenhouse Publishers.

Green Teacher. "Education for Planet Earth." Available at: http://greenteacher.com/.

National Resources Defense Council. "Environmental References/Links." Available at: http://www.nrdc.org/reference/kids.asp.

New York State Learning Standards and Core Curriculum. "The Living Environment: Core Curriculum." Available at: http://www.p12.nysed.gov/ciai/mst/pub/livingen.pdf.

Great Green Web Sites

Check out the following links to explore creative green-themed resources:

American Museum of Natural History: http://www.amnh.org/ology/marinebiology. This colorful Web site offers a wealth of information about the world's oceans.

Field Trip Earth: http://fieldtripearth.org/. Discover wildlife conservation projects around the world. This is a useful resource for middle and high school students.

University of Illinois Extension: http://urbanext.illinois.edu/woods/. Visitors of any age can take a walk in the woods via this Web site.

North American Association for Environmental Education (NAAEE). "Environmental Education." Available at: http://www.naaee.net/.

Saylan, Charles, and Daniel T. Blumstein. 2011. *The Failure of Environmental Education (And How We Can Fix It)*. Berkeley: University of California Press.

Sierra Club. "Environmental Education." Available at: http://www.sierraclub.org/education/.

State of Vermont Department of Education. "Common Core State Standards." Available at: http://education.vermont.gov/new/html/pubs/framework.html.

U.S. Environmental Protection Agency. "Students for the Environment." Available at: http://www.epa.gov/students/.

Environment

CARBON FOOTPRINT

A *carbon footprint* is the total amount of carbon dioxide (CO_2) emitted by an individual, industrial process, or entity (corporation, country, etc.) usually on an annual basis. However, there is disagreement over more specific definitions, units of measurement, and other aspects of the term. The carbon footprint has also been referred to as embodied carbon, carbon content, embedded carbon, carbon flows, virtual carbon, greenhouse gas (GHG) footprint, and climate footprint by various authors (citations in Pandey et al., 2011).

Roots of the concept can be traced back to the idea of the "ecological footprint" proposed by Rees and colleagues (Rees, 1992; Wackernagel & Rees, 1996), which evaluates the area of land and sea required to support a given human population (expressed in global hectares). Under this concept, carbon footprint would refer to the area of land and sea required to store the CO_2 emitted by a population or process (mainly through photosynthesis by plants) and would form one component of the total ecological footprint (Kitzes & Wackernagel, 2009). Carbon footprints have been measured in a different context for decades as part of lifecycle assessment (an examination of the environmental impacts of a process or product through all stages of production) of different processes in business and industry (Finkbeiner, 2009). There is disagreement over whether the carbon footprint should be reported or measured straightforwardly as the amount of CO_2 produced by the process/entity (metric tons of CO_2) or in terms of area required for storage, in keeping with the ideas of the ecological footprint. Proponents of the ecological footprint argue that a land-based measurement allows those not familiar with climate science to more easily visualize and understand the impacts of different entities/processes on carbon emissions and thus climate. This utility is seen in the World Wildlife Fund's "One Planet Living Index" (WWF, 2011), which uses the ecological footprint to focus on the unsustainable use of the world's resources. Also, expressing the carbon footprint in terms of area allows for easier comparison to footprints of other uses of land, which have been calculated for two decades, and may reveal scenarios in which decreasing impacts in one area may increase impacts in another (Kitzes & Wackernagel, 2009). On the other hand, conversion of the carbon footprint from mass-based units (metric tons of CO_2) into the area-based units of the ecological footprint relies on assumptions about the amount of CO_2 absorbed by a given area of land, which can be highly variable (depending, among other things, on vegetation type and cover) and difficult to determine. Proponents of mass-based units for the carbon footprint do not prefer the area-based units of ecological footprinting because of the additional uncertainty and error introduced by converting mass of CO_2 into required land area for CO_2 storage (Wiedmann & Minx, 2008).

Another point of discussion in calculating carbon footprints is the use of CO_2 equivalents. A CO_2 equivalent expresses the amounts of other greenhouse gases (e.g., methane) in terms of CO_2. For instance, methane gas is 25 times more powerful than CO_2 at trapping heat (in a 100-year period), and thus the mass of methane would be multiplied by 25 to obtain the equivalent mass of CO_2 (Climate Change Connection, 2011). Although this method of reporting is widely used by the U.S. Environmental Protection Agency (EPA) and other groups and governments worldwide, some question the usefulness of the conversion, and the equivalency values for different gases are continuing to be refined; however, an aggregate measure of greenhouse gas emissions, such as a comprehensive "climate footprint," would obviously be a useful and more complete way to assess climate impacts (Wiedmann & Minx, 2008).

Although there is much disagreement over the terminology and measurement of carbon footprints, determining a standard methodology for carbon footprinting is essential for comparing the climate impacts of different countries and industrial processes and for identifying components and stages of processes that should be targeted to reduce CO_2 emissions. Consistent measurement procedures are also necessary for any climate change legislation attempting to reduce CO_2 emissions through carbon trading (Pandey et al., 2011).

In the United States, some companies are required to track emissions under the Consolidated Appropriations Act of 2008, although there are still no federal emissions standards for CO_2. Some city and state governments such as the city of Seattle and the State of California have made efforts to quantify and reduce their carbon footprints, and a national standard for defining and measuring the carbon footprint is probably inevitable but needs more attention (Pandey et al., 2011).

Carbon footprinting has been applied to such entities as different diets (vegetarian versus others), households, universities (e.g., University of Pennsylvania, University of British Columbia), individual industrial plants, conferences (e.g., 2008 United Nations Climate Change Conference), industrial processes, fuel production (e.g., biofuels; Holzman, 2008), sporting events (e.g., FIFA World Cup, 2006), major cities (e.g., Seattle, Vancouver), countries, natural disasters (e.g., wildfires; Wiedinmyer & Neff, 2007; hurricanes; Chambers et al., 2007), and the world (citations in Pandey et al., 2011).

Although carbon footprinting has a long history, the practice has received increased attention from the media and the public recently. Carbon footprint calculator applications are now a popular addition to the Web sites of many nonprofit conservation organizations (e.g., The Nature Conservancy, World Wildlife Fund), corporations (e.g., Hewlett-Packard, BP), and government entities (e.g., EPA, Grand Rapids Area Chamber of Commerce), allowing individuals to estimate their carbon footprint based on average daily or weekly activities (e.g., number of miles driven per week, kilowatt hours of electricity used per month). The widespread use of carbon footprinting indicates interest in the practice; however, it is difficult to evaluate the impact of carbon footprinting on public sentiment and action on climate change.

National polling by the Sacred Heart University Polling Institute in 2009 indicated that only about 7 percent of the 800 respondents had attempted to measure their carbon footprint. Almost 32 percent of those surveyed were aware of the term *carbon calculator*, and about 43 percent of these thought they understood how it works. More people (65 percent) were aware of the term *carbon footprint*, and over 69 percent indicated that they understood the term (Sacred Heart University, 2009). These findings are similar to a national poll conducted in 2008 by Harris Interactive that found that about 11 percent of Americans had determined their personal or household carbon footprint.

Greenovations: Carbon Footprint Calculator

Several institutions and nonprofit organizations offer online calculators that help determine an individual's impact on the climate and measure things such as the impact of driving a car, traveling by airplane, and using energy in homes and at work. The following includes a sampling of resources:

CoolClimate Calculators from the University of Berkeley's Renewable and Appropriate Energy Laboratory. http://coolclimate.berkeley.edu/tools.

Ecological Footprint Quiz. http://www.myfootprint.org/

Footprint Calculator from the Global Footprint Network. http://www.footprintnetwork.org/en/index.php/GFN/page/calculators/

Free Carbon Footprint Calculator from the Nature Conservancy. http://www.nature.org/greenliving/carboncalculator/index.htm

Household Emissions Calculator from the U.S. Environmental Protection Agency. http://www.epa.gov/climatechange/emissions/ind_calculator.html

Zero Footprint Youth Calculator. http://calc.zerofootprint.net/youth/

KIM KENNEDY WHITE

Younger people were more likely to have calculated their carbon footprint, with 18 percent of 18- to 31-year-olds and 11 percent of 32- to 43-year-olds having done so, compared to 9 percent of 44- to 62-year-olds and 6 percent of those 63 and older (Harris Interactive, 2008). Although more recent polling indicates that Americans view global warming as less of a threat, these polls have not included further questions on the carbon footprint (Harris Interactive, 2009; Gallup, 2012); therefore, it is difficult to assess whether public use and awareness of the carbon footprint is increasing or impacting personal or policy action on climate issues. Regardless, the carbon footprint and the ideas surrounding its measurement will continue to play a major role in climate change policy and action.

MICAH G. BENNETT

See also: Alternative and Renewable Energy (Science); Biofuels (Science); E-Waste (Science); Global Warming (Environment); Local and Sustainable Food (Food); Recycling (Environment).

References

Chambers, Jeffrey Q., Jeremy I. Fisher, Hongcheng Zeng, Elise L. Chapman, David B. Baker, and George C. Hurtt. 2007. "Hurricane Katrina's Carbon Footprint on U.S. Gulf Coast Forests." *Science* 318: 1107.

Climate Change Connection. 2011. "CO₂ Equivalents." Available at: http://www.climate changeconnection.org/Emissions/CO2_equivalents.htm.

Finkbeiner, Matthias. 2009. "Carbon Footprinting—Opportunities and Threats." *International Journal of Life Cycle Assessment* 14: 91–94.

Gallup Poll. 2012. "Fewer Americans, Europeans View Global Warming as a Threat." Available at: http://www.gallup.com/poll/147203/Fewer-Americans-Europeans-View-Global-Warming-Threat.aspx.

Harris Interactive. 2008. *For Earth Day: Two-Thirds of Americans Believe Humans Are Contributing to Increased Temperatures.* Rochester, NY: Harris Interactive.

Harris Interactive. 2009. *Big Drop in Those Who Believe that Global Warming Is Coming.* New York: Harris Interactive.

Holzman, David C. 2008. "The Carbon Footprint of Biofuels—Can We Shrink It Down to Size in Time?" *Environmental Health Perspectives* 116: A246–A252.

Kitzes, Justin, and Mathis Wackernagel. 2009. "Answers to Common Questions in Ecological Footprint Accounting." *Ecological Indicators* 9: 812–817.

Pandey, Divya, Madhoolika Agrawal, and Jai Shanker Pandey. 2011. "Carbon Footprint: Current Methods of Estimation." *Environmental Monitoring and Assessment* 178: 135–160.

Rees, William E. 1992. "Ecological Footprints and Appropriated Carrying Capacity: What Urban Economics Leaves Out." *Environment and Urbanisation* 4: 121–130.

Sacred Heart University. 2009. "National Poll—Carbon Footprints? Environmentally Conscious Americans Not Measuring Up." Available at: http://www.sacredheart.edu/pages/29054_national_poll_carbon_footprints_environmentally_conscious_americans_not_measuring_up.cfm.

Wackernagel, Mathis, and William E. Rees. 1996. *Our Ecological Footprint: Reducing Human Impact on the Earth.* Gabriola Island, BC, Canada: New Society Publishers.

Wiedinmyer, Christine, and Jason C. Neff. 2007. "Estimates of CO₂ from Fires in the United States: Implications for Carbon Management." *Carbon Balance Management* 2: 10.

Wiedmann, Thomas, and Jan Minx. 2008. "A Definition of 'Carbon Footprint'." In C. C. Pertsova, ed., *Ecological Economics Research Trends*. Hauppauge, NY: Nova Science Publishers, 1–11.

World Wildlife Fund. 2011. "About One Planet Living." Available at: http://www.wwf.panda.org/what_we_do/how_we_work/conservation/one_planet_living/about_opl.

ENERGY

Energy is a component of everything the modern world requires. It is part of food, housing, and transportation. Energy affects the supply and demand of goods, services, and our economic security. Cheap, reliable sources of energy fuel the transportation of raw materials, finished products, food, wastes, livestock, and people. In the United States, wood, coal, and oil fueled railroad expansion that eventually laid the infrastructure for modern day settlement patterns, especially in the western United States. Energy is intrinsically tied to the transportation and urban development settlement patterns today. The development of the car led to a rapid increase in demand for gas and oil. The United States leads most other nations in the amount of energy devoted to transportation because of the reliance on cars and trucks in the transportation system. Energy is also an increasingly larger part of construction and structure maintenance, which comes with development. Buildings, both commercial and residential, consume more than one-third of our total energy use. Appliances and computer equipment are part of this. The size of structures continues to increase, increasing the need for energy to heat and cool them. Industrial processes can be very energy intensive. Overall, the United States uses about one-third of its energy on manufacturing processes. The rapid rate of technological advancement, combined with the growing world population of energy consumers, has increased demand for energy, with its increasing impacts on the environment. By 2035, world energy use is projected to increase by as much as 53 percent from 2011 energy use.

As global concern for climate change rises, so too does the focus on emissions from energy sources. For example, about 947 pounds of carbon dioxide (CO_2) are produced from a barrel of conventional crude oil. CO_2 threatens to erode the ozone layer of the Earth's atmosphere. The ozone layer protects Earth from harmful solar radiation. Many international agreements now seek to reduce these hydrocarbon-based petrochemical emissions to reduce global warming. Reduction of emissions could reduce profit for oil industries, although many U.S. oil companies recently experienced very high profit margins.

Current Energy Use Patterns in the United States

The end consumer uses electricity distributed through various grid systems. Energy to make electricity can come from many sources, which differ greatly in their economic and environmental costs. Traditional U.S. sources of energy are wood, coal, natural gas, and oil. They are characterized by the combustion of hydrocarbons (e.g., burning wood). These sources vary in energy efficiency, and they also emit byproducts of combustion (e.g., carcinogens and metals) depending on the processes. These emissions can have negative impacts on the environment and nearby communities.

The development of grid systems of electrical power lines generally followed the lines of the U.S. railroad expansion. The distribution of electricity to the end consumer was facilitated by the expansion of the grid system and transformers that reduced voltage loads and gave instant on-and-off usage. The U.S. electrical grid system is a complex web of about 500 independently owned and operated power plants and about 300,000 kilometers of transmission lines. Much of the infrastructure is aging and needs repair, all as demand increases. The U.S. electrical grid system is a three-part system. The eastern, western, and Texas sectors make up the majority of the U.S. electrical grid system. There are problems in the interconnections because some of the electricity is direct current and the rest is alternating current. The Energy Policy Act of 2005 and the Energy Independence and Security

A Tennessee Valley Authority towboat heads off after pushing a barge load of coal in place to be unloaded in Cumberland City, Tennessee in 2008. (AP Photo/The Leaf-Chronicle, Greg Williamson)

Act of 2007 were designed to deal with some of the problems of the aging electrical grid infrastructure and interconnectedness.

Several major issues confront the obsolescing U.S. electrical grid system. Some basic ones include interconnectedness and net metering. It is still difficult for most end consumers to plug into, or interconnect with, the electrical grid system. Right now most people are not able to access the grid, although some experimental programs are under way. The current grid systems were not designed for this potential input, but for more controllable, steady-state systems. Supply and demand of electricity must be closely timed for its effective use. Altering demand or supply is traditionally timed for steady input systems where increasing supply rapidly is difficult. The United States is now reliant on a 24-hour, seven-days-a-week supply of electricity. When the grid supply of electricity is over capacity, it can shut down in what are called brownouts, where the supply of electricity in one or more parts of the grid is reduced. Giving end consumers the ability to input energy and energy information is a way to decrease demand from the grid. Local, state, and federal government agencies have rules and regulations about interconnectedness and net metering that often confuse both industry and community.

Another grid systems' challenge is net metering. This occurs when the power you produce is sold back to the power company or your produced power is subtracted from your overall demand. The primary environmental reason for doing this is for energy conservation. Environmental impacts are further reduced if the power production method itself has fewer environmental impacts. If the home energy producer is using solar, wind, or some combination of off-the-grid power source, then the overall environmental impact is smaller. If, on the other hand, the home energy producer is using low-grade diesel fuel to power generators, then the environmental impacts could be greater. Allowing public grid access may provide an economic incentive for private homeowners to develop end-user and onsite alternative energy sources. As the greening of America advances, use of lower impact, onsite energy sources is evidence of environmentally sensitive behavior changes.

Traditional Sources

Traditional sources for the production of energy for electricity include hydropower from dams, steam from coal-burning power plants, steam from oil-burning power plants, and nuclear energy.

Environmental issues with traditional sources all relate to their large and destructive impacts on the environment. Coal-burning power plants emit the byproducts of combustion into the air. This can include particulate matter, metals, sulfur, carbon dioxide, and other chemicals. (See scorecard.org for the Toxics Release Listing near you.)

Oil

U.S. consumption of oil is about 20 million gallons of petroleum per day. The United States meets almost one-half of the demand with domestic production. The rest of the oil comes from about 90 other countries, with oil from

Greenovator: The U.S. Environmental Protection Agency's Green Power Partnership Top 20 Retail Stores for 2011

The following is the EPA's list of Top 20 Retail Stores who purchased green power in 2011:

The Top 20 Retail list represents the largest purchasers among retail partners within the Green Power Partnership. The combined green power purchases of these organizations amounts to nearly 4 billion kilowatt-hours of green power annually, which is the equivalent amount of electricity needed to power more than 335,000 average American homes each year.

1. Kohl's Department Stores
2. Whole Foods Market
3. Starbucks
4. Staples
5. Wal-Mart Stores, Inc./California and Texas Facilities
6. Lowe's
7. Best Buy
8. Safeway, Inc.
9. H-E-B Grocery Company
10. REI
11. Estée Lauder Companies, Inc./Operations
12. FedEx Office
13. Gander Mountain
14. Giant Eagle, Inc.
15. The North Face
16. Office Depot
17. prAna
18. Price Chopper Supermarkets
19. Panera Bread/Maryland Locations
20. Half Price Books/Texas Facilities

KIM KENNEDY WHITE

Source: Top 20 Retail. U.S. Environmental Protection Agency Green Power Partnership. Available at: http://www.epa.gov/greenpower/toplists/top20retail.htm.

The Trans-Alaska Pipeline snakes across a vast expanse of land and can move two million barrels of oil each day. (Corel)

Canada, Mexico, and Venezuela dominating the U.S. oil imports. Oil imports from the Middle East make up about 17 percent of U.S. imported oil. Currently, oil from the Middle East has the highest return of energy invested for any energy source in the world. Energy investments include roads, wells, refineries, and pipelines. Currently, there is much discussion of an oil pipeline from Alberta, Canada, to Cushing, Oklahoma, and from there to Port Arthur, Texas, and the refineries around the U.S. Gulf Coast. These pipelines would also have feeder pipelines to various U.S. locations. Pipelines present a host of environmental impacts. As opposed to how the oil is now moved, use of a pipeline may have fewer fugitive emissions as long as there are no leaks, breaks, or human attacks. The oil is now stored in Canada and then imported to the United States via railroad and trucks. Both these transportation systems consume large amounts of energy and produce emissions that can affect the environment in negative ways. The Valdez oil pipeline in Alaska is strongly associated with a continuing controversy on whether that pipeline hurts migratory animals such as the caribou.

Environmental Impacts

Energy use, research, transportation, and storage can have large environmental impacts. The greening of the United States often engages controversial energy issues, such as drilling for oil in the Arctic Wilderness Refuge. The combustion of petrochemicals by the end user leaves emissions in the air. These chemical emissions can be hazardous air pollutants. They can move through the water and land and can accumulate over time, sometimes creating toxic hot spots. Oil-drilling processes can differ, but they often burn excess natural gas into the atmosphere and spill oil either directly or through volatilization in the transportation, refining, and distribution processes. These emissions are known as fugitive emissions. Very few environmental rules were developed or are enforced enough to prevent these. These emissions can include chemicals that persist in the environment and can accumulate over time. The cost of capturing these fugitive emissions decreased the profit of oil corporations so they did not capture fugitive emissions from natural gas "flaring" in the drilling, refining, and storage of oil. The low pressure gas that escapes from crude oil storage tanks is more than twice as energy efficient than piped natural gas. Energy demand overall, and for natural gas, is strong and growing. Currently, better technology is being rapidly developed to capture these types of fugitive natural gas emissions.

Drilling for oil or natural gas requires the development of infrastructure such as roads, landing strips, ports, and depots. The true cost to develop oil includes costs of accidents, with widespread consequences to the environment and communities. All the vehicles required to drill, transport, refine, and distribute oil products also produce a set of environmental emissions. The degree of environmental impact is related to the resiliency of the ecosystem to rebound from the development and any spills. Sensitive environmental areas are those that are the breeding grounds for endangered or species threatened with extinction. They can also be places of very slow flora and fauna recovery, such the desert sands of northern Alberta, Canada, and the oil drilling there. Oil drilling and refining also produce wastewater and sludge. How the particular refinery handles these byproducts often determines their ecological impact. The wastewater can often contain polycyclic aromatic hydrocarbons, which can persist in aquatic and land ecosystems. They also can affect the biological health of mammals, including humans, depending on the exposure.

Natural Gas

Many countries rely on natural gas for energy. Unlike oil, it moves primarily through pipelines. As the supply and demand of oil fluctuates, many nations are reexamining natural gas as a source of energy. Liquefied natural gas lines and ports are being developed in the United States. At first, natural gas in the United States was burned off in the refining processes of oil. Less than 10 percent of the United States relied on natural gas before 1940. In 2010, U.S. natural gas provided for about 25 percent of the energy needs. It is estimated that the United States has 2,552 trillion cubic feet of natural gas. Natural gas has lower emissions than oil, impacting the environment less.

Natural gas is often found at oil sites, as well as in shale. Hydraulic fracturing (or fracking) is the process used to get the natural gas or oil out of the shale. Generally, very high pressure steam is driven into the shale through boreholes into assessed gas

Natural gas rig in the Gulf of Mexico off the coast of Alabama. (iStockPhoto.com)

or oil fields, and the natural gas is then removed from the newly created cracks and fissures. Fracking raises some controversy and is outlawed in some countries. Many communities are concerned with the chemical in the "steam" used to develop the cracks, wells, and fissures. Sometimes radioactive tracer chemicals are used to facilitate monitoring the injection. The actual chemical component of the "steam" may change from site to site and from different stages of a given injection well. There is also environmental concern with how the wastewater from the injection is treated, as these often contain toxic chemicals.

Hydropower

Hydropower is one of the oldest forms of energy. Hydropower uses the energy of flowing water to spin turbines to create electricity. It was not until an electrical grid system was established that this electricity could be distributed. The water flow is captured by the creation of a dam that usually directs the flow of water to the turbines. Most dams in the United States are used to control flooding, provide drinking water, and assist irrigation, not provide energy. Hydropower creates about 6 percent of U.S. electricity, and currently about 60 percent of the energy from all renewable sources in the United States. Most of the dams that create energy are located in Oregon, Washington, and California. The dams used for hydropower destroyed salmon runs, because salmon return to their birthplace to spawn. If they cannot return, they cannot spawn, and the species dies. Dams also affect the turbidity, temperature, and sedimentation of the rivers, which can in turn affect other species. Indigenous people culturally tied to the river and the fish, sport fishers, and commercial fishers are particularly impacted.

Nuclear Energy

About one-fifth of the U.S. electricity supply comes from nuclear power. Generally, atoms are split in a process called fission. Elements such as uranium 235 are split into radioactive elements. Some of these elements have very long half-lives, or periods of time in which they remain unstable. There are currently 104 reactors in use in the United States and about 22 outstanding applications to the Nuclear Regulatory Commission (NRC) to license reactors. Generally, the NRC licenses the nuclear reactors for 40 years. But it has already extended the licenses for 63 reactors. There are about 19 more renewal applications pending before the NRC. Very few new licenses have been approved by the NRC until recently. It is anticipated that the rate of reactor approval for licensure will increase.

The most widely used form of renewable energy, hydroelectric generation produces no waste or carbon dioxide. (Shutterstock.com)

There are major concerns with nuclear power. Leaking or exploding radioactive material is a concern in many communities. A fundamental environmental issue is the treatment of radioactive waste, which lasts for a very long time and is very harmful to life. Safety concerns increase community resistance, which increases the difficulty in new license approval. Many of the current reactors are old but still in production because of license renewals from the NRC. The front-end costs of building a nuclear reactor are very expensive relative to oil, gas, and coal. Nuclear energy proponents point out that there are new design features in the new reactors that enhance safety. Some of the new reactors have passive safety features that do not require power or human action, but these are still untested.

Safety is also important in the context of the impact on the environment and is often compared to other sources of power. Compared to coal, for example,

The cooling tower of a nuclear power plant turns steam back into water that can be used again and again. (PhotoDisc, Inc.)

coal-burning power plants emit 80 percent of the CO_2 emissions in the United States and provide about 50 percent of the electricity. Nuclear power produces one-fifth of the power with no emissions. The type of emissions of coal-burning plants can be directly hazardous to human health and may have long-term ecological impacts. When nuclear waste is included in the safety discussion, the focus can change to monitored storage and retrieval of nuclear wastes. How the waste is transported, where it travels, and where it is stored are all controversial safety issues.

National Security Energy Issues

The relationship of energy-dependent nations to energy-provider nation can raise serious national security issues. In most nations, national security issues revolve around subordinate environmental considerations. Security issues focus on oil and natural gas supplies and reserves. For example, because drilling for oil can have large and long-lasting environmental impacts, depending on the particular ecosystem, drilling is usually constrained unless there is a threat to national security. A provider nation's decision to stop shipping oil can be deemed a threat to national security. This allows the energy reserve supplies, in the form of oil and gas, to be accessed, including oil and gas reserves in environmentally sensitive areas. Most of the United States' 727-million-barrel Strategic Petroleum Reserve is stored underground in Texas and Louisiana. The most oil allowed out per day is 4.4 million barrels. However, there are untapped oil deposits on federal lands, most of which are currently protected by law. It is estimated that 800 billion barrels of oil exists in Colorado, Utah, and Wyoming.

A question of national security and nuclear energy safety is whether plants are designed to save costs at the expense of safety. After the terrorist attacks of September 11, 2001, the Nuclear Regulatory Commission ruled that all nuclear power plants had to be able to withstand an airplane impact. This requires new designs that can be very expensive with little safety result. The question of how much the power plant owner should spend on containment safety systems is often a focus of the debate. Another question is what environmental risks should be incorporated in the safety design. Legally, the NRC requires nuclear power plant owners and operators to build their plants to withstand the largest flood, earthquake, or tsunami based on all available information in the past 10,000 years.

Subsidies for Energy

Because energy is so important for economic development, and because economic development is often a primary goal of government, government provides subsidies to energy producers and users. One main example is the Foreign Tax Credit. This allows oil companies to deduct leases for drilling for oil. Alternative energy sources and consumers can sometimes claim tax credits or other subsidies on their local, state, and federal income taxes. Billions of dollars have been spent to subsidize traditional energy sources, which environmentalists argue underwrites pollution. Subsidies come from the government in the form of tax relief, direct assistance, and technical assistance. Other public policy reasons for governmental energy subsidies include job creation, increased energy supply, and faster technological development.

Conclusion

The U.S. and world demand for more energy is an undeniable part of every environmental decision. Because of rapid world population growth and even faster rising industrialization, much attention is given to newer more environmentally sensitive approaches in all our environmental impacts. Energy, from production to end use, is no exception. Conservation programs, demand-response electrical grid timing efficiencies, and alternative energy development all help harness the environmental impacts the large increase in demand for energy will require.

R. WILLIAM COLLIN AND ROBIN MORRIS COLLIN

See also: Alternative and Renewable Energy (Science); Energy Audits (Environment); Executive Order on Federal Leadership in Environmental, Energy, and Economic Performance (documents); Federal Energy Management Program Fact Sheet (documents); Federal Trade Commission (documents); Fight the Frost This Winter (documents); Leadership in Energy and Environmental Design (LEED) (documents); Ten Tips for Hiring a Heating and Cooling Contractor (documents).

References

Collin, Robin, and Robert Collin. 2010. *The Encyclopedia of Sustainability*. Santa Barbara, CA: ABC-CLIO.

Geri, Lawrence R. 2011. *Energy Policy in the US: Politics, Challenges, and Prospects for Change*. Boca Raton, FL: CRC Press.

Gronlund, Lisbeth, et al. 2007. "Nuclear Power in a Warming World." Union of Concerned Scientists. December. Available at: www.ucsusa.org.

Tomain, Jonathan P. 2011. *Ending Dirty Energy Policy: A Prelude to Climate Change*. London: Cambridge University Press.

ENERGY AUDITS

Energy comes from many different sources, but traditionally it comes from wood, gas, oil, and nuclear power. As the traditional supplies decrease, conservation measures are developed to save losses of energy. One way to begin an energy conservation program is to measure and monitor energy use. In response to the 1973 oil embargo, the United States adopted many stringent energy conservation measures, including energy audits. Concerns about rising greenhouse gas emissions have caused the practice of energy auditing to regain popularity and become more professionalized. Professional energy auditors are certified by the Building Performance Institute or the Residential Energy Services Network. Increased public awareness about sustainability and some newly emerging sustainability policies also focus on energy's environmental impacts.

Energy audits are used to evaluate the efficiency of energy use. They are becoming an increasing part of the greening of U.S. public policy. For example, in January 2011, Nevada became the first state to require energy audits for the resale of a house. Not only do energy leaks cost money, but they can pollute the environment. In large oil drilling and refining operations, there can be 50,000 to 100,000 potential valves and connections, in addition to basic cracks in the pipes that may leak. While many U.S. government regulators call these types of emissions "de minimus" or "fugitive," failure of safety valves in the British Petroleum (BP) Deep Water Horizon well resulted in 12 lost lives and hundreds of thousands of barrels of oil blasting its way into the hot and shallow Gulf of Mexico. Environmental impacts from the explosion and

Greenovation: Tips for Energy Efficiency Energy Saving Tips: Heating and Air Conditioning

The following list of green heating and air conditioning is from the U.S. Small Business Administration:

- "Tune-up" your heating, ventilating and air-conditioning (HVAC) system with an annual maintenance contract. Even a new ENERGY STAR qualified HVAC system (http://www.energystar.gov/index.cfm?c=heat_cool.pr_hvac), like a new car, will decline in performance without regular maintenance. A contract automatically ensures that your HVAC contractor will provide "pre-season" tune-ups before each cooling and heating season. You save energy and money, and your system may last years longer with minimal costs for yearly maintenance fees.
- Regularly change (or clean if reusable) HVAC filters every month during peak cooling or heating seasons. New filters usually only cost a few dollars. Dirty filters cost more to use, overwork the equipment and result in lower indoor air quality.
- Install an ENERGY STAR qualified programmable thermostat (http://www.energystar.gov/index.cfm?fuseaction=find_a_product.show ProductGroup&pgw_code=TH) to automate your HVAC system. This solid-state, electronic device optimizes HVAC operation "24/7" based on your schedule and can be "overridden" as needed for unscheduled events. This "smart thermostat" can also turn on the HVAC system one hour before staff arrival, instead of heating or cooling unoccupied space to ensure the facility is comfortable *and* saving energy.
- Control direct sun through windows, depending on the season and local climate. During

subsequent raging fire were large, affecting the shrimp fishing communities, native and migratory birds, and fish. Longer-term ecological effects are still being studied as the oil works its way through wetlands and mammalian populations. Energy audits on large industrial operations may reveal safety as well as environmental issues and prevent this type of disaster.

Energy audits can be building specific, organizationally focused, or based on true cost principles of ecological impact assessment. Home energy audits examine the building envelop for leaks using blowers attached to a door and measuring pressure differences. Heat detecting infrared equipment can also be used to detect heat leaks. Building-specific energy audits examine how the energy is actually used in the structure. The usual goal is the most efficient use of energy for the least cost while maintaining the levels of comfort for the people who work there. Often changing to LED lights with motion detectors can save money, which is an example of what these types of energy audits are designed to do. Audits of heating and cooling systems often target the cost of the energy, regardless of the source of that energy.

cooling season, block direct heat gain from the sun shining through glass on the East and especially West sides of the facility. Depending on your facility, options such as "solar screens," "solar films," awnings, and vegetation can help keep facilities more cool. Over time, trees can attractively shade the facility and help clean the air. Interior curtains or drapes can help, but it's best to prevent the summer heat from getting past the glass and inside. During heating season, with the sun low in the South, unobstructed southern windows can contribute solar heat gained during the day.

- Use fans to maintain comfortable temperature, humidity and air movement, and save energy year round. Moving air can make a somewhat higher temperature and/or humidity feel comfortable. Fans can help delay or reduce the need for air conditioning, and a temperature setting of only three to five degrees higher can feel as comfortable with fans. Each degree of higher temperature can save about 3 percent on cooling costs. When the temperature outside is more comfortable than inside, a "box fan" in the window, or large "whole facility" fan in the attic can push air out and pull in comfortable air from the outside.

- Plug leaks with weather stripping and caulking. Caulking and weather stripping let you manage your ventilation, which is the deliberate controlled exchange of stuffy inside air for fresher outdoor air. To learn more about indoor air quality in your facility visit the Environmental Protection Agency's EPA Indoor Air Quality (http://www.epa.gov/iaq/).

KIM KENNEDY WHITE

Source: "Tips for Energy Efficiency." U.S. Small Business Administration. Available at: http://www.sba.gov/content/energy-efficiency.

Some energy audits take a more comprehensive approach. In addition to a simple building energy audit, these examine the organizational practices, procedures, and policies that affect energy usage. They may or may not consider the impact on the environment of the source of energy they get. For example, some organizations, like cities or companies, that want to become more green may require a procurement policy that all paper items they purchase must be recyclable.

Greenovation: Tips for Energy Efficiency
Energy Saving Tips: Office Equipment

The following green tips for office equipment come from the U.S. Small Business Administration:

- Always buy ENERGY STAR qualified products for your small business. The ENERGY STAR mark indicates the most efficient computers, printers, copiers, refrigerators, televisions, windows, thermostats, ceiling fans, and other appliances and equipment.
- Turning off machines when they are not in use can result in enormous energy savings. There is a common misconception that screen savers reduce energy use by monitors; they do not. Automatic switching to sleep mode or manually turning monitors off is always the better energy-saving strategy.
- To maximize savings with a laptop, put the AC adapter on a power strip that can be turned off (or will turn off automatically); the transformer in the AC adapter draws power continuously, even when the laptop is not plugged into the adapter.
- Common misconceptions sometimes account for the failure to turn off equipment. Many people believe that equipment lasts longer if it is never turned off. This incorrect perception carries over from the days of older mainframe computers.
- Consider buying a laptop for your next computer upgrade; they use much less energy than desktop computers, resulting in long-term savings.
- Many appliances continue to draw a small amount of power when they are switched off. These "phantom" loads occur in most appliances that use electricity, such as VCRs, televisions, stereos, computers, and kitchen appliances. In the average home, 75 percent of the electricity used to power home electronics is consumed while the products are turned off. This can be avoided by unplugging the appliance, or using a power strip and the strip's on/off switch to cut all power to the appliance.

Energy audits in this general category are often considered "investment grade," meaning that the return on the investment (ROI) in energy infrastructure is considered along with other capital expenditures of the business or government entity.

In pursuit of sustainability, a more comprehensive energy audit is emerging that examines the long-term ecological impacts of the energy source. In the model, it often makes more sense to adopt a clean, alternative source of energy. This model will often consider solar, wind, geothermal, or biofuel on site energy sources. It may also consider the energy expended to handle waste flows. Building materials, site design, landscaping, and interior design could be evaluated for energy conservation in an energy audit working toward sustainability.

The Future

Energy audits for residential, commercial, and industrial sites lay the groundwork for a more efficient energy policy that measures and monitors use and environmental impacts. Off-grid energy systems such as solar, wind, biofuels, and geothermal energy sources regularly incorporate energy audits to adjust their various systems. Large energy consumers at commercial and industrial sites could calibrate their energy usage to when it is necessary.

R. WILLIAM COLLIN AND ROBIN
MORRIS COLLIN

See also: Alternative and Renewable Energy (Science), Energy (Environmental); Federal Energy Management Program Fact Sheet (documents), Federal Trade Commission (documents); Ten Tips for Hiring a Heating and Cooling Contractor (documents).

References

Krarti, M. 2000. *Energy Audit of Building Systems: An Engineering Approach*. Boca Raton, FL: CRC Press.

Wulfinghoff, Donald. 2000. *Energy Efficiency Manual*. Wheaton, MD: Energy Institute Press.

- Unplug battery chargers when the batteries are fully charged or the chargers are not in use.
- Studies have shown that using rechargeable batteries for products like cordless phones and PDAs is more cost effective than throwaway batteries. If you must use throwaways, check with your trash removal company about safe disposal options.

KIM KENNEDY WHITE

Source: Tips for Energy Efficiency. U.S. Small Business Administration. Available at: http://www.sba.gov/content/energy-efficiency.

FORESTRY AND GIFFORD PINCHOT: GREENOVATION SPOTLIGHT

Gifford Pinchot (1865–1946) was an American conservationist and forester best known as the first chief of the U.S. Forest Service. Pinchot was the fourth chief of the Division of Forestry from 1895–1905 and served two terms as Pennsylvania governor (1923–1927; 1931–1935). He is widely considered to be the father of American conservationism because of his great impact on U.S. environmental issues and legislation.

Pinchot was born on August 11, 1865, in Simsbury, Massachusetts. The child of James and Mary Eno Pinchot, he was raised as part of an elite family of American mercantilists. James Pinchot encouraged his son to study forestry in order to rectify the environmental damage caused by the Pinchot family enterprises. When Pinchot began his studies at Yale, there were no American forestry education programs. Pinchot went to Europe to study forestry as a result, enrolling at L'Ecole Nationale Forestiere in Nancy, France. While there, he met eminent European foresters William Schlich and Dietrich Brandis and developed an understanding of the forest as a crop rather than a strictly recreational resource.

Upon returning to the United States, Pinchot worked as a resident forester for the Vanderbilts' Biltmore Forest Estate for three years. Shortly thereafter, he became involved with the National Forest Commission, traveling throughout the west during the summer of 1896 to scout areas for potential forest reserves. He was named the fourth chief of the Division of Forestry shortly afterward. The Division (later Bureau) of Forestry was founded as part of the Department of Agriculture in reaction to public concerns that American national resources were rapidly disappearing. This agency answered citizens' questions and gathered statistics but did

Gifford Pinchot, photographed at his desk ca. 1945. (Library of Congress)

not formulate policy as public forestlands fell under the jurisdiction of the Department of the Interior.

In 1905, the Transfer Act transferred forest reserve management to the newly created U.S. Forest Service. Pinchot acted as the primary advocate for this legislation, with support from his friend President Theodore Roosevelt. Pinchot was selected as the U.S. Forest Service's first chief, serving in this capacity from 1905 to 1910. During this period, this agency focused on providing public recreation, protecting lands against exploitation, controlling and combating wildfires, and mapping national forests.

Pinchot also recognized the need for collaboration with the private sector. He created the Division of State and Private Forestry in 1908 to address issues of forest taxation and assist private forest owners with practical forestry problems. Arguments over coal leasing in Alaska brought Pinchot into conflict with Secretary of the Interior Richard A. Ballinger. Pinchot believed that Ballinger sought to halt the U.S. conservation movement and accused him of siding with private trusts. These arguments, which turned into a national debate, resulted in Pinchot's dismissal in 1910 by President William Howard Taft for "insubordination."

Following his departure from the Forest Service, Pinchot went on to become a two-term governor of the State of Pennsylvania. He continued conservation efforts, founding the National Conservation Association and working for progressive causes for the rest of his life. He died on October 4, 1946, of leukemia. The Gifford Pinchot National Forest in southern Washington is named in his honor, as is Gifford Pinchot State Park in York County, Pennsylvania.

GWEN PERKINS

See also: National Park Service (Environment); National Parks (Sports and Leisure).

References

Miller, Char. 2001. *Gifford Pinchot and the Making of Modern Environmentalism*. Washington, DC: Island Press.
Nash, Roderick. 2001. *Wilderness and the American Mind*. New Haven, CT: Yale University Press.
Pinchot, Gifford. 1998. *Breaking New Ground*. Washington, DC: Island Press.
Pinchot, Gifford. 2001. *The Conservation Diaries of Gifford Pinchot*. Harold K. Steen, ed. Durham, NC: Forest History Society.

GLOBAL WARMING

Global warming, or climate change as it is often described, refers to the long-term heating of the planet due to greenhouse gases. It pertains not only to human effects but also to natural processes. The idea that human, or anthropogenic, effects result in the majority of global warming has been largely responsible for the controversy associated with global warming. Greenhouse gases are those that remain in the atmosphere, becoming concentrated and affecting the outgoing movement of solar radiation. Any change in the Earth's energy balance due to this phenomenon is known as radiative forcing. According to the most recent report by the International Panel on Climate Change (IPCC), global emissions of greenhouse gases by humans have increased 70 percent from 1970 to 2004. The most common greenhouse gases resulting from humans are carbon dioxide, methane, nitrous oxide, and halocarbons (IPCC Synthesis Report, 2007).

As of 2008, the United States was responsible for the annual emission of about 5,839 million metric tons of carbon dioxide. This number represented a 3 percent decrease in emissions from 2007. Though 3 percent may seem like a marginal amount, this decrease was the largest decrease in the 18 years between 1990 and 2008 (U.S. Emissions Report, 2008). Among developed countries, the United States will be responsible for the largest output of carbon dioxide emissions until at least 2035. Nonetheless, the majority of *growth* in emissions tonnage is directly attributable to developing countries, which continue to use relatively abundant and cheap fossil fuels such as coal, oil, and natural gas (U.S. Energy Information Administration, 2011).

Policy measures ("mechanisms") used to control greenhouse gas emissions include command-and-control, taxation, and cap-and-trade. Though command-and-control and taxation each has its merits, it is cap-and-trade—dealing mostly with carbon dioxide emissions—that is currently of the greatest interest in the United States. Cap-and-trade involves the trade or transfer of carbon allocations (one allocation is generally equal to one ton of carbon emitted) among polluters, usually heavy industry. Polluters can freely trade allocations among themselves or purchase additional allocations if they plan to emit more carbon dioxide than the "cap" allows for (Perdan & Azapagic, 2011).

Perhaps the most recent and interesting developments in the United States concerning cap-and-trade is taking place in California. The California cap-and-trade program is part of California's Global Warming Solutions Act (Assembly Bill 32), signed in 2006 by former Governor Arnold Schwarzenegger. This measure is the first mandatory cap-and-trade policy set forth and implemented by a single state. The program began on January 1, 2012 (California Environmental Protection Agency Air Resources Board). Overall, this program will contribute heavily to California's economy. Another cap-and- trade system under way in the United States is the Regional Greenhouse Gas Initiative (RGGI). This program is the first mandatory emissions trading scheme to be implemented in the United States. Though it began in 2005, it did not go into effect until 2009. It deals solely with the power sector in 10 eastern states, encompassing a total of 209 power plants with outputs of at least 25 megawatts (Perdan & Azapagic, 2011).

Smoke rises out of an oil refinery in Carson California. California became the first state to impose a cap on all greenhouse gas emissions in a bold deal made by Governor Arnold Schwarzenegger and legislative Democrats in 2006. (AP/Wide World Photos)

There are a number of U.S. scientists and intellectuals who are vocal in advocating emissions reductions, just as there are still those who remain skeptical of the connection between human activities and global warming. Among the most well-known scientific proponents of global warming is James Hansen of the NASA Goddard Institute for Space Studies (http://www.giss.nasa.gov/staff/jhansen.html). Hansen was one of the first scientists to speak about global warming, bringing it into the public sphere. As of late, he has become involved as an activist against the effects of global warming. Although certain individuals have achieved some fame in the global warming dialogue, there are many grassroots organizations fighting to slow global warming. Four such organizations include the Sierra Club, the National Resources Defense Council, the Center for Biological Diversity, and 350.org, co-founded by author and environmental activist Bill McKibben. According to this organization, the number 350 represents the maximum amount of atmospheric carbon dioxide that can exist (in parts per million) to effectively reduce the effects of global warming (http://www.350.org/mission).

CHRISTOPHER PETERS

See also: Alternative and Renewable Energy (Science); Biofuels (Science); Carbon Footprint (Environment); Energy (Environment); Energy Audits (Environment); Recycling (Environment).

References

Betsill, Michele, and Matthew J. Hoffmann. 2011. "The Contours of 'Cap and Trade': The Evolution of Emissions Trading Systems for Greenhouse Gases." *Review of Policy Research* 28:1 (January): 83–106.

California Environmental Protection Agency Air Resources Board. Available at: http://arb.ca.gov/cc/capandtrade/capandtrade.htm.

Cart, Julie. 2011. "California Becomes First State to Adopt Cap-and-Trade Program." *Los Angeles Times* October 21. Available at: http://www.latimes.com/news/local/la-me-cap-trade-20111021%2C0%2C1125437.story?track=rss.

Center for Biological Diversity. Available at: http://www.biologicaldiversity.org/programs/climate_law_institute/index.html.

International Panel on Climate Change (IPCC). 2007. "Synthesis Report." R. K. Pachauri and A. Reisinger, eds.

Klein, Ezra. 2011. "Will California's Cap-and-Trade Experiment Catch On?" *Washington Post*, October 25. Available at: http://www.washingtonpost.com/blogs/ezra-klein/post/will-californias-cap-and-trade-experiment-catch-on/2011/10/25/gIQAZDyZGM_blog.html.

Perdan, Slobodan, and Adisa Azapagic. 2011. "Carbon Trading: Current Schemes and Future Developments." *Energy Policy* 39:10 (October): 6040–6054.

U.S. Energy Information Administration. 2008. "U.S. Emissions of Greenhouse Gases Report," Report No. DOE/EIA-0573. Available at: http://www.eia.gov/oiaf/1605/ggrpt/carbon.html.

U.S. Energy Information Administration. 2011. "International Energy Outlook 2011," Report No. DOE/EIA-0484. (September). Available at: http://205.254.135.24/forecasts/ieo/emissions.cfm.

LAND AND HABITAT RECLAMATION AND RESTORATION

Since European settlement, human activity has rapidly and profoundly transformed the terrestrial and aquatic ecosystems of North America. Increasingly, scientists, policy makers, and citizens are attempting to reverse environmental degradation through positive forms of human intervention. *Restoration* is broadly defined as the process of helping ecosystems recover from human-induced degradation or disturbance (Society for Ecological Restoration International Science and Policy Working Group, 2004). It implies an attempt to return a habitat to a former natural or seminatural state. Although restoration aims to reverse environmental degradation and restore habitat, land *reclamation* refers to the process of making an area suitable for cultivation (van Andel & Aronson, 2006). Reclamation transforms a system into a state that is in some way useful, either for agriculture, habitat conservation, development, or other priorities. Another distinction is that restoration often focuses on biodiversity conservation and the construction of habitat, while reclamation projects are mainly concerned with modifying aspects of the physical abiotic system, such as soils and drainage patterns. In the United States, reclamation is commonly used to refer to the irrigation of farmland or the improvement of mined lands.

Although restoration projects generally attempt to mitigate or reverse human-induced environmental change, there are no universal techniques that all projects entail. Both restoration and reclamation can include a wide variety of practices, from

Greenovator: Center for Biological Diversity

The Center for Biological Diversity is an organization that uses biological data, legal experts, and the citizen petition provision of the Endangered Species Act to force officials to protect animals, plants, and ecosystems in the United States. They have gone to court and obtained judgments forcing the government to set aside habitats and to protect hundreds of species. The center has a 93 percent success rate in its lawsuits and has become a major stakeholder in environmental protection in the United States.

The center was founded in 1989 after three men doing an owl survey in New Mexico's Gila Wilderness found a rare Mexican spotted owl. The area was due to be clear-cut, and the Forest Service did not want to block that. Kierán Suckling, Peter Galvin, and Todd Schulke went to the media about the problem, and the area was spared. Robin Silver joined the three in forming the group that would eventually become the Center for Biological Diversity. First the group focused on New Mexico, then widened the focus to the southwestern United States, and now works on causes throughout the country. They also do some international work.

The lawsuits the center brings can block development, restrict the right to use water from rivers, and force landowners to restore habitat. As such, the center often stirs bitter opposition. Cook (2007) discusses the impact of forcing the Environmental Protection Agency to consult with the U.S. Fish and Wildlife Service before licensing a new pesticide. As a pest-control professional, Cook claims that is unreasonable and will result in increased costs and possibly the removal of some pesticides already on the market. Other groups object to the loss of jobs and restrictions on land and water use that result from the center's actions.

STEPHANIE SUESAN SMITH

dredging stream channels to planting native vegetation to the reintroduction of predators such as wolves. Goals and priorities also differ from project to project. While some projects aim to reintroduce particular species, others focus on increasing overall biodiversity. Still other projects do not prioritize biodiversity but instead attempt to restore certain ecosystem functions or services, such as nutrient cycling or the provision of wildlife habitat. Restoration and reclamation projects also vary in scale. The reintroduction of wolves, for example, requires large expanses of land and is thus performed on a regional scale and requires interaction between states, federal agencies, and local stakeholders. The reclamation of abandoned mine lands, conversely, is often done on a more local scale, with projects that focus on one or more particular mines.

Proponents of restoration claim that it is the future of environmental conservation, because of widespread recognition of ecological degradation caused by human processes such as urbanization, mineral extraction, and deforestation, coupled with the decline in the amount of natural habitat that remains unaltered by humans (van Andel & Aronson, 2006). In the United States, restoration projects became prevalent during the zenith of the environmental movement of the 1960s and 1970s. The passage of the Clean Air Act (CAA) (1963), Clean Water Act (CWA) (1972), National Environmental Policy Act (NEPA) (1970), and the Surface Mining Control and Reclamation Act (SMCRA) (1977) brought greater attention to environmental concerns and explicitly involved government and commercial interests in various restoration and reclamation projects. For example, under SMCRA, mine operators are required to reclaim mined land to "former or better use" (Wali et al., 2002, 18), and one of the principal aims of CWA is to restore and maintain aquatic ecosystems. Although these regulations have encouraged restoration and reclamation, the *type* of transformation is at times contested. Following SMCRA, coal mine operators transformed many Appalachian surface mines into grass- or shrub lands on which forest cannot grow because of extreme soil compaction. In response, the federal Office of Surface Mining (OSM) established a citizen, industry, and government partnership called the Appalachian Regional Reforestation Initiative (ARRI) in 2004. This partnership advocates for a new reclamation technique that aims to create forests rather than grasslands on reclaimed coal mines in the Appalachian region.

Conflict over reclamation and restoration reflects the social and political nature of such projects. Successful restoration efforts need to incorporate not only scientific knowledge but also the cultural, political, and economic milieu (Higgs, 1997). Because restoration may pit different visions of the landscape against one another, the process can be contentious. The Chicago Wilderness is a network of hundreds of organizations that works to restore native habitats in the Chicago area. Since it was launched in 1996, its restoration projects have triggered tremendous public conflict. In particular, members of the public have criticized the movement for cutting down trees, culling deer populations, and setting fire to ecosystems in the name of restoration (Helford, 2000). A heated political battle ensued and a moratorium was temporarily placed on all restoration activities in the Chicago area in the late 1990s. Such conflicts occur in part because restoration projects are planned and carried out in relation to social norms and values. Restoration can pit economic values versus environmental values, but it can also pit environmentalists against one another, as it did in the Chicago Wilderness case.

Proponents of the Chicago Wilderness and other restoration efforts, however, emphasize that restoration and reclamation offer opportunities for social cohesion as well as conflict. Unlike the preservation of wilderness, restoration explicitly includes humans in ecosystems and thus, some argue, paves the way for a new relationship between humans and the natural world (Jordan, 2003). While assisting in the recovery of ecosystems, "place-based values" and a sense of responsibility for the environment can be cultivated (Center for Humans and Nature, 2011). Most restoration projects require a great deal of labor and rely heavily on volunteers to monitor ecosystems, remove invasive species, plant trees, and create habitat. Successful restoration, therefore, is often a collective endeavor and requires not only labor, resources, and planning, but also support from local communities. Some consider volunteer-based restoration projects as opportunities to take ownership of the environment, remedy degradation and devastation, and create new cultures of conservation that emphasize the integration of nature and society (Jordan, 2003; Center for Humans and Nature, 2011). Efforts such as the Chicago Wilderness also aim to educate both volunteers and the broader public about local ecosystems and to foster greater environmental consciousness through habitat restoration projects.

CHRISTINE BIERMANN

See also: Forestry and Gifford Pinchot (Environment); National Park Service (Environment); Ocean Restoration and Conservation (Environment); Water and Air Purification (Science); Wildlife, Conservation and Preservation Organizations (Environment).

References

Center for Biological Diversity. "Our Story." Available at: http://www.biologicaldiversity.org/about/story/index.html.

Center for Humans and Nature. 2011. Available at: http://www.humansandnature.org.

Cook, A. 2007. "Lawsuits against EPA Threaten Pesticide Use Nationwide." *Pest Management Profession* (November): 44–47.

Helford, Reid M. 2000. "Constructing Nature as Constructing Science: Expertise, Activist Science, and Public Conflict in the Chicago Wilderness." In Paul H. Gobster and R. Bruce Hull, eds., *Restoring Nature: Perspectives from the Social Sciences and Humanities*. Washington, DC: Island Press, 119–142.

Higgs, Eric S. 1997. "What Is Good Ecological Restoration?" *Conservation Biology* 11:2: 338–348.

Jordan, William R. 2003. *The Sunflower Forest: Ecological Restoration and the New Communion with Nature*. Berkeley: University of California Press.

Society for Ecological Restoration International Science and Policy Working Group. 2004. *The SER International Primer on Ecological Restoration*. Tucson: Society for Ecological Restoration International.

Van Andel, Jelte, and James Aronson, ed. 2006. *Restoration Ecology: The New Frontier*. Oxford: Blackwell.

Wali, Mohan K., Nirander M. Safaya, and Fatih Evrendilek. 2002. "The Americas: With Specific Reference to the United States of America." In Martin R. Perrow and Anthony J. Davy, eds., *Handbook of Ecological Restoration*, Vol. 2. Cambridge: Cambridge University Press, 3–31.

NATIONAL PARK SERVICE

The United States was the first nation to create a system of national parks, the National Park Service (NPS). Yellowstone National Park, the world's first such park, was created in 1872. In 1916, Congress passed the Organic Act of the National Park Service, creating the National Park Service to administer the nation's national parks. This system now administers more than 83 million acres of parkland, wilderness, recreation areas, and historic sites.

Congress first acted to protect important natural areas at Hot Springs, Arkansas, and Yosemite Valley in California. In 1832, the Hot Springs Reservation was set aside to preserve its thermal springs. In 1864, Congress granted federal land to the State of California to protect Yosemite Valley (in 1906, it was reincorporated into the new Yosemite National Park). When Congress authorized Yellowstone National Park in 1872, it set a precedent for the establishment of modern national parks by the federal government. Congress added 14 new national parks between 1872 and 1916, including Sequoia, Yosemite, Crater Lake, Glacier, and Zion.

Saint Mary Lake in the Waterton-Glacier International Peace Park in Glacier National Park, Montana. Glacier was officially designated a national park in 1910. (Wellych/Dreamstime.com)

These initial parks were created for various reasons. The establishment of Yellowstone was supported by individuals who wanted to protect the natural beauty from private encroachment as well as from the Northern Pacific Railroad, which saw the park as a tourist destination. The creation of individual national parks is often the result of conservation efforts coupled with local political and economic influences. Several early national parks and monuments were later deemed inappropriate for this designation and removed from the system. These included Mackinac National Park, which became a Michigan state park, and Sullys Hill National Park, which became a national wildlife refuge.

In 1906, Congress passed the Antiquities Act, which gave the president the authority to create national monuments to protect important areas from private development and removal of artifacts. The act gave the president broad powers to establish monuments and has been most frequently used to prevent exploitation of mineral or natural resources for commercial purposes. National monuments can be administered by the National Park Service, the Forest Service, the Fish and Wildlife Service, or the Bureau of Land Management. This new power was used 18 times by President Theodore Roosevelt to create such monuments as the Petrified Forest, Chaco Canyon, and Grand Canyon (later a national park). Since the creation of national monuments does not require congressional approval, this power has generated controversy when used to remove lands from potential development.

By 1916, a diverse collection of national parks, monuments, and other sites was administered by a number of federal agencies, including the Army, Department of Agriculture, Department of the Interior, and other offices in Washington, D.C. Soldiers remained in Yellowstone until 1918. With so many agencies and their different missions operating parks, there was no consistent national policy on the management or use of these resources.

Stephen T. Mather, a business leader from Chicago, and Frederick Law Olmsted, a renowned landscape architect, were among the key advocates of establishing a national park system. The Department of the Interior sponsored three conferences on national parks between 1911 and 1916. In addition to scientists, park managers, and government officials, these conferences were attended by representatives of railroads, the automobile industry, and other businesses seeking to benefit from the economic impact of an expanding network of parks.

Efforts by Mather, Olmsted, and others led to the passage of the Organic Act in 1916. This act established the National Park Service and laid out a general mission for the agency. The mission focused on two primary purposes: (1) "to conserve the scenery and the natural and historic objects and the wild life therein" and (2) "to provide for the enjoyment of the same in such manner and by such means as will leave them unimpaired for the enjoyment of future generations" (National Park Service). The act also allowed for the development of accommodations and the leasing of concessions within parks. Despite its focus on conservation, the general language of the Organic Act established a tension between recreation and conservation that continues within the NPS.

The park service was created as an agency within the Department of the Interior. The agency's director is appointed by the secretary of the interior and reports to the assistant secretary for fish and wildlife. In addition to a headquarters in Washington, D.C., parks within the NPS are under the jurisdiction of seven regional offices. Under a decentralization plan from the 1950s, superintendents of national parks operate with a relatively high level of autonomy.

The NPS is one of several federal agencies within the Department of the Interior charged with managing public land. Other agencies such as the Bureau of Land Management, the Fish and Wildlife Service, and the Bureau of Reclamation have missions that occasionally place them in conflict with the NPS. The proposed Echo Park Dam in Dinosaur National Monument highlighted policy differences with the secretary of interior and Bureau of Reclamation and led to the ouster of NPS Director Newton Drury in 1951. At various times in its history, the NPS also has displayed a strong bureaucratic rivalry with the U.S. Forest Service (part of the Department of Agriculture).

Following the creation of the National Park Service, Mather was named the agency's first director. He and his assistant Horace Albright replaced politically appointed park superintendents and hired staff to fill the void left in some parks by the departure of troops who had acted as rangers. They set standards of operation for parks and organized the collection of existing parks into a system based on a utilitarian interpretation of the Organic Act.

Although the Great Depression of the 1930s was a challenging period for the park service, New Deal economic recovery projects, including the Civilian Conservation Corps (CCC), resulted in development of many infrastructure projects, including roads, trails, campgrounds, and visitor facilities in parks throughout the NPS.

Beginning with the start of World War II, the park service entered a period of neglect and decline that continued through the mid-1950s. Prior to the start of the war, in 1940, many scientific staff transferred to the Fish and Wildlife Service. In 1942, the CCC was eliminated as resources were shifted to the war effort. With the end of major public works projects, a huge drop in park visits and major cuts in staffing, the park service was reduced to a caretaker role during the war.

Following the end of World War II, there were dramatic increases in the number of park visitors. Although parks experienced increased demands for facilities and services, there were few resources in postwar federal budgets. The strain placed by the growth in park visits, from 17 million in 1940 to 56 million by 1955, combined with a lack of adequate funding from Congress resulted in controversy about the decline of conditions in national parks. During this period, there were even calls for the closure of some parks to protect them from further deterioration (Sellars, 1997).

When Conrad Wirth became director of the NPS in 1951, he inherited a system that was experiencing an enormous pressure to accommodate more visitors while struggling to operate with budgets that were stuck at approximately prewar levels. To counter this pattern of decline, in 1951, Wirth introduced Mission 66, a plan to expand park facilities, strengthen and increase NPS services, and accommodate significant increases in park visitors by the 50th anniversary of the park system in 1966. This ambitious effort resulted in additional funding and the construction of roads and facilities that allowed the NPS to accommodate more than 124 million visitors by 1966 (Carr, 2007). Because it involved significant construction in areas that were previously undeveloped, Mission 66 highlighted the conflict within the park service mission between preserving pristine parkland and providing access to the public for recreational activities.

Controversies over development activities within parks during the Mission 66 era raised questions about the direction of the NPS. The Sierra Club and other conservation groups began to take active roles opposing development in national parks. There was concern that the NPS had focused on promoting recreation at the expense of preserving wilderness. The NPS did not actively support passage of the Wilderness Act of 1964. This act expressly prohibited development of park facilities in wilderness areas and was seen, in part, as a reaction to Mission 66. In 1963, concerns about NPS policies led to the Leopold Report (and a second report by the National Academy of Sciences) calling for changes in NPS management policies with greater emphasis on ecological systems and the use of scientific information in management decisions. The Leopold Report, commissioned by Secretary of Interior Stewart Udall to examine wildlife-management practices, recommended that the NPS attempt to preserve or restore wilderness in the parks. Resistance in the NPS to implement recommendations from both reports highlighted tensions within the agency over the dual elements in its mission of conservation and recreation.

George B. Hartzog, who became director in 1963, sought to maintain the funding and growth momentum created by Mission 66. Many of Hartzog's initiatives were included in a program, known as Parkscape U.S.A., which sought to continue the growth of the NPS. During his tenure as director, several new types of park units were created. These included national scenic river ways, national lakeshores, and national trails. These were followed and enhanced by passage of the National Trails System Act of 1968 and the Wild and Scenic Rivers Act of 1968. During this period, there was significant expansion in the number and size of national recreation areas within the NPS. Hartzog also sought to expand political support for the NPS within Congress by consciously seeking to place park units in every possible congressional district.

In the late 1970s, there was dramatic expansion of national park acreage. An important piece of legislation authored by Phil Burton (D.-Calif.) was the National Parks and Recreation Act of 1978. The act included $1.8 billion in spending for 150 park-related projects in more than 200 congressional districts and 44 states. It was called the "park barrel" bill since it was the first time park authorizations had been packaged in the same way as omnibus bills for road or water projects. A second landmark piece of conservation legislation during this period was the Alaska National Interest Lands Conservation Act (ANILCA). This act was intended to resolve conflicts over federal lands that originated at Alaska's statehood. When Congress failed to act in a timely manner, President Jimmy Carter created 15 new national monuments in Alaska under the Antiquities Act. When it finally passed, ANILCA included more than 43 million acres of national parkland.

The 1980s marked the end of rapid expansion of the NPS. Budgets for land acquisition were drastically reduced, and the agency faced challenges over its management of lands, particularly in western states. The number of new national parks slowed dramatically after the passage of ANILCA, with just two new national parks created during Ronald Reagan's presidency, none under George H. W. Bush, four under Bill Clinton, and two under George W. Bush. Of the parks created since 1980, all except the National Park of American Samoa either incorporated national monuments into new larger parks or redesignated national monuments to park status. During the Clinton presidency, the Antiquities Act was utilized to create more national monuments than under any other president; however, only three of those are administered by the NPS. In 1997, Robert Stanton became the first African American to serve as director of the NPS; he was succeeded as director in 2001 by Fran Mainella, the agency's first female director.

The National Park Service is frequently cited as one of the most popular and publicly respected federal agencies. As of 2009, the NPS oversees 391 areas of natural, historic, or recreational significance, 58 of which are designated as national parks by acts of Congress. Today the NPS faces challenges posed by a multibillion dollar backlog of maintenance needs, lagging staff morale, and encroaching development activities on the borders of some parks.

DAN WAKELEE

See also: Forestry and Gifford Pinchot (Environment); National Parks (Sports); Parks, State and Local (Sports).

References

Carr, Ethan. 2007. *Mission 66: Modernism and the National Park Dilemma*. Amherst: University of Massachusetts Press.

Lowry, William R. 1994. *The Capacity for Wonder: Preserving National Parks*. Washington, DC: Brookings Institution.

Mackintosh, Barry. "The National Park Service: A Brief History." Available at: http://www.nps.gov/history/history/hisnps/NPSHistory/briefhistory.htm.

National Park Service. "The National Park Service Organic Act." Available at: http://www.nps.gov/legacy/organic-act.htm.

Rettie, Dwight F. 1995. *Our National Park System*. Urbana and Chicago: University of Illinois Press.

Ridenour, James M. 1994. *The National Parks Compromised: Pork Barrel Politics and America's Treasures*. Merrillville, IN: ICS Books.

Rothman, Hal. 1989. *America's National Monuments: The Politics of Preservation*. Lawrence: University of Kansas Press.

Sellars, R. W. 1997. *Preserving Nature in the National Parks: A History*. New Haven, CT: Yale University Press.

Wirth, Conrad L. 1980. *Parks, Politics, and the People*. Norman: University of Oklahoma Press.

OCEAN RESTORATION AND CONSERVATION

The World Conservation Union has marked the issues of pollution, habitat destruction, overfishing/exploitation, and climate change as the greatest emerging threats to the world's ocean. The "blue revolution" refers to the massive growth in industrial aquaculture over the past half century comparable to that of the "green revolution" in industrial agriculture following World War II. The fish catch grew from less than 5,000 metric tons in 1970 to over 30,000 in 2006 (FAO, 2009). Instrumental in the depletion of ocean fish reserves are the standard practices used in aquaculture or industrial fish farming.

The Food and Agriculture Organization (FAO) estimated that 2010 was the first year that fish farms provided more seafood than wild fisheries combined. Each pound of farm-raised fish requires 2 to 5 pounds of wild fish, resulting in a net loss of food produced by fish farming (FAO, 2009). In addition to depleting ocean fish reserves, factory fish farming is criticized for its destructive environmental practices similar to that of livestock feedlots on land. Because the water from the fish farms exchanges freely with the surrounding water, aquaculture threatens widespread pollution, endangerment to marine habitats, wild populations, and watersheds.

In a 2011 report on aquaculture, the Ocean Conservancy identified the greatest environmental impact to be from pollution, escaped fish, disease/parasites/chemicals, and predator impacts. Pollution released from aquaculture operations include fish, food, and chemical waste that causes habitat destruction, eutrophication, and dissolved oxygen depletion. In addition to their waste, millions of fish escape from fish farms thereby bringing disease, parasites, and loss of genetic fitness to native populations through interbreeding. Finally, predator impacts include the loss of predator animals such as sea lions that are naturally drawn to fish cages and then killed to prevent loss of fish crops.

The widespread practice of trawling by the fish industry has been instrumental in the depletion of ocean fish. Trawling is a method of towing large nets behind commercial fishing boats to catch fish from the water surface down to the sea floor. Trawling is an environmentally destructive practice because of its lack of selectivity. Trawling does not distinguish between fish desirable and undesirable for market nor between those legal and illegal to catch. "By-catch" refers to any species that are inadvertently caught by fishing boats. These species are often killed during the trawling process and include dolphins, sea turtles, and sharks. According to the International Union for Conservation of Nature, approximately one-third or 64 species of ocean sharks and rays are endangered (2009). An Australian study of the Clarence River found that in one year alone, 177 tons of by-catch were discarded (Liggins & Kennelly, 1996). Though fishermen also consider by-catch unfavorable because it is inconvenient to sort these species, the incentives to profit from market fish outweigh the perceived disincentives of losing marine life. Trawling also kills coral reefs by breaking them up and burying them in sediments that are stirred up by the trawling process.

The building of dams for hydroelectric power has also resulted in massive declines in fish populations around the world because of less inorganic nutrient runoff and nutrient availability from ocean depths. Dams restrict the flow of fertile silt and sediments, resulting in coastal erosion and lower nutrient availability to primary producers and fish species. In Egypt, the construction of the Aswan High Dam on the Nile River in 1964 sharply reduced fish catch in the Levantine Basin of the Mediterranean. Before this construction, approximately 5,500 tons of phosphate and 280,000 tons of silicate flowed into the Mediterranean. The restriction of nutrient flow by the dam led to a quartering of the fish catch over a period of six years (El-Sayed & van Dijken, 1995).

Anadromous species such as salmon are highly sensitive to restricted nutrient flow and sediment distribution caused by dams. In addition to impacting their food source, dams impact fish directly by blocking migration patterns in upstream and downstream directions, a migratory pattern critical to the lifecycle and reproduction of anadromous species. Fish survival is also threatened when they pass through dam discharge structures.

Sediment restriction by dams is a problem that extends down the entire marine food web. Pelagic fish such as herring, sardines, tuna, and sharks live near the surface of water in oceans and lakes and compose 11 percent of known fish species. Pelagic fish rely on nutrients from land runoff and upwelling. Upwelling describes the movement of cool, nutrient-rich waters from the ocean depths that replace warmer, nutrient-deplete water on the surface. Runoff and upwelling provide inorganic nutrients used by phytoplankton and other microscopic organisms during photosynthesis to produce organic nutrients, used in turn by organisms higher on the food chain. The restriction of sediment by dams compromises the nutrient flow upon which all organisms directly or indirectly depend. Restoration of waterways and

Greenovation: Marine Protection, Research, and Sanctuaries Act of 1972

The Marine Protection, Research, and Sanctuaries Act of 1972 (also known as the Ocean Dumping Act) is an act passed by the U.S. Congress to "regulate the transportation for dumping, and the dumping, of material into ocean waters." Titles I and II of the act address ocean dumping specifically and call for further research on the topic in order to safeguard the health of humans living near ocean waters and to preserve the overall ecological integrity of these waters in the face of dumping by both domestic and foreign agents. Anyone wishing to dump sewage sludge or industrial waste in the ocean is required to obtain a permit, which would be granted only after studies had been done on how the dumping would impact human health and the environment. Perhaps the most influential part of this act is Title III, which empowers the Secretary of Commerce to establish National Marine Sanctuaries to preserve marine environments "of special national significance" in coastal and ocean waters, the Great Lakes, and submerged lands under U.S. jurisdiction (MPRSA, 1972). When Title III, which became known as the National Marine Sanctuaries Act (NMSA) was reauthorized by Congress in 2002, it was expanded to create a single system of national marine sanctuaries covering nearly 150,000 square miles; it was dubbed the National Marine Sanctuary System (Dunnigan, 2008). Title IV establishes Regional Marine Research Programs in nine maritime regions of the United States. Title V, the National Coastal Monitoring Act, focuses on the welfare of coastal ecosystems specifically (MPRSA, 1972).

The federal government has struggled with ocean dumping since the turn of the 20th century. In 1899, it passed the Rivers and Harbors Act to regulate the pollution of the ocean, but this act did not stop cities from emitting raw sewage into coastal waters. Despite passage of the Marine Protection, Research, and Sanctuaries Act in 1972, the coasts of New Jersey and Long Island saw an unusual amount of sewage debris on their shores in 1976 and 1977. When the act came up for reauthorization in 1977, Congress attached an amendment to forbid the dumping of sewage sludge altogether after December 31, 1981 (Payton, 1985), but a series of lawsuits brought by New York City meant that the dumping of municipal sludge was not permanently banned until 1988, when Congress passed the Ocean Dumping Ban Act (P.L. 100-688), which made such dumping illegal after August 14, 1989. Congress also banned the dumping of medical waste in 1988 (P.L. 100-688).

In 1983, Public Law 97-424 was passed, banning the dumping of radioactive waste, and any dumping was made illegal after December 31, 1991, as part of P.L. 100-688 (EPA, 1991). Since the 1991 ban on dumping, Title I has been referred to most often regarding the removal of dredged matter from the ocean floor (FWS, 2010). Title III, or the National Marine Sanctuaries Act, stems from 11 different bills brought before the House of Representatives in 1968 that were spurred by the dumping of nerve gas and oil off the Florida coast and an oil spill off Santa Barbara, California, in 1968. Presidential interest varied. Only two sanctuaries were named during the Richard Nixon and Gerald Ford administrations: the site of the wreckage of the USS *Monitor* off of Cape Hatteras, North Carolina, and the shore of Key Largo, Florida. President Jimmy Carter revived the NMSA with the naming of an additional five sanctuaries, including the Channel Islands off the coast of California. President Ronald Reagan designated only one sanctuary during his time in office, but the George H. W. Bush and Clinton administrations enthusiastically designated numerous sanctuaries. The National Oceanic and Atmospheric Administration (NOAA) established a Maritime Heritage Program to preserve underwater cultural artifacts as part of George W. Bush's Preserve America Initiative. In 2002, NOAA and the U.S. Navy raised the armored turret from the wreck of the USS *Monitor*, and in 2004, a Maritime Archaeology Center was opened in Newport News, Virginia, as a means of supporting this initiative. In 2006, President Bush established the largest region of natural conservation in the United States and the largest marine sanctuary in the world when he designated the Papahānaumokuākea Marine National Monument, covering 140,000 square miles off the Hawaiian Islands. Looking to the future, some commentators have emphasized that the NMSA, which is the most active part of the Marine Protection, Research, and Sanctuaries Act, needs to have its mission better defined and guidelines for naming national marine sanctuaries need to be clarified to ease the process of designating sites.

PHILIP SWAN

removal of dams are critical in reviving the fish habitat and nutrient availability that have been impacted by dams.

Industrial pollution and climate change also contribute to the anthropogenic damage imposed on the world's aquatic environment. This damage consists of acidification of Earth's water, air, and soils due to emissions from combustion of fossil fuels and smelting of ores, mining of coal and metal ores, and application of nitrogen fertilizer to soils (Rice & Herman, 2012). According to a recent report by the U.S. Geological Survey, ocean acidification results from increased carbon dioxide concentration in the atmosphere, acidic atmospheric deposition that acidifies soils and bodies of freshwater, acid mine drainage that acidifies bodies of freshwater and ground waters, and nitrification that acidifies soils. Acidification destroys aquatic habitats and has food web consequences such as increasing the conversion rate of mercury to methyl-mercury, leading to greater bioaccumulation of methyl-mercury in fish, a neuro-developmental environmental contaminants highly toxic to humans.

Fossil fuel waste in the form of plastic has also contributed greatly to the pollution of the ocean. The estimated mass of plastic found in what is called the "Great Pacific Garbage Patch" is 100 million tons and it spreads across hundreds of thousands of square miles in the North Pacific

Gyre (Moore et al., 2001). An estimated 0.4 to 8.0 percent of the Pacific Ocean now contains high concentration of dissolved or partially dissolved plastic in the upper water column, and fish tested there have higher concentrations of plastic than plankton in their tissues.

This description of ocean health indicates that disposable materials, industrial waste, and excess fish consumption are the driving factors in the destruction of the ocean environment. Ocean conservation and restoration efforts range in approach and target topics including ocean cleanup, dam removal, reducing plastic waste and industrial pollution, modifying fisheries practices, and decreasing demand on threatened fish species.

RAINBOW VOGT

See also: Rivers and Dams (Environment); Water and Air Purification (Science); Water Quality and Use (Environment); Wildlife, Conservation and Preservation Organizations (Environment); Wildlife, Impact of Eco-Friendly Practices and Awareness (Environment).

References

El-Sayed, S., and G. L. van Dijken. 1995. "The Southeastern Mediterranean Ecosystem Revisited: Thirty Years after the Construction of the Aswan High Dam." Available at: http://ocean.tamu.edu/Quarterdeck/QD3.1/Elsayed/elsayed.html.

Food and Agriculture Organization (FAO). 2009. "Aquaculture Production Database (Quantities and Values): 1950–2007" FAO Fisheries and Aquaculture Department, Fishery Information, Data and Statistics Unit. FishStat Plus version 2.32. Universal software for fishery statistics time series. Rome. Available at: www.fao.org/fishery/statistics/software/fishstat/en.

International Union for Conservation of Nature. 2009. "Third of Open Ocean Sharks Threatened with Extinction." Available at: http://www.iucn.org/?3362/Third-of-open-ocean-sharks-threatened-with-extinction.

Liggins, G. W., and S. J. Kennelly. 1996. "By-catch from Prawn Trawling in the Clarence River Estuary, New South Wales, Australia." *Fish* 25: 347–367.

Moore, C., S. L. Moore, M. K. Leecaster, and S. B. Weisberg. 2001. "A Comparison of Plastic and Plankton in the North Pacific Central Gyre." *Marine Pollution Bulletin* 42:12: 1297–1300.

Payton, B. M. 1985. "Ocean Dumping in the New York Bight." *Environment* 27:9: 26–42.

Rice, K. C., and J. S. Herman. 2012. "Acidification of Earth: An Assessment Across Mechanisms and Scales." *Applied Geochemistry* 27:1 (January): 1–14.

U.S. Congress. Marine Protection, Research and Sanctuaries Act of 1972 (MPRSA). (Public Law 92-532; October 23, 1972; 86 Stat. 1052 and 1061. Titles I and II are codified at 33 U.S.C. 1401–1445. Title III is codified at 16 U.S.C. 1431–1445.) Amendments to Titles I (ocean dumping permit program) and II (ocean dumping research) include: P.L. 93-254; March 22, 1974; 88 Stat. 50; P.L. 93-472; October 26, 1954; 88 Stat. 1430; P.L. 94-62; July 25, 1975; 89 Stat. 303; P.L. 94-326; June 30, 1976; 90 Stat. 725; P.L. 95–153; November 4, 1977; 91 Stat. 1255; P.L. 96-381; October 6, 1980; 94 Stat. 2242; P.L. 96-470; October 19, 1980; 94 Stat. 2245; P.L. 96-572; December 22, 1980; 94 Stat. 3344; P.L. 97-16; June 23, 1981; 95 Stat. 100; P.L. 97-424; January 6, 1983; 96 Stat. 2165; P.L. 99-272; April 7, 1986; 100 Stat. 131; P.L. 99-499; October 17, 1986; 100 Stat. 79; P.L. 99-662; November 17, 1986; 100 Stat. 4259; P.L. 100-4; February 4, 1987; 101 Stat. 79;

P.L. 100-17; April 2, 1987; 101 Stat. 172; P.L. 100-536; October 28, 1988; 102 Stat. 2710; P.L. 100-627; November 7, 1988; 102 Stat. 3213; P.L. 100-688; November 18, 1988; 102 Stat. 4153; P.L. 102-580, title V, October 31, 1992, 106 Stat. 4870 and P.L. 104-303, October 12, 1996, 110 Stat. 3791.

U.S. Environmental Protection Agency (EPA). 1991. Office of Water (WH-556F). Report to Congress on Ocean Dumping 1987–1990 (EPA 503/9/90-007). Washington, DC: Government Printing Office. Available at: http://www.epa.gov/history/topics/mprsa/Annual%20Report%20to%20Congress%201987-1990.pdf

U.S. Fish and Wildlife Service (FWS). 2010. "Digest of Federal Resource Laws of Interest to the U.S. Fish and Wildlife Service: Marine Protection, Research, and Sanctuaries Act." Available at: http://www.fws.gov/laws/lawsdigest/marprot.html.

OFFSHORE DRILLING

Offshore oil exploration—the locating and drilling of oil in the earth's crust below the water's surface in lakes, oceans, or other large bodies of water—in the United States began as early as the mid-1890s. It was during this time oil companies were walking just barely offshore and drilling into the sand right below the water. Staying relatively close to shore allowed oilmen to utilize technology they were already familiar with by drilling through piers into shallow water or placing the oil derrick into the sand to drill. This either produced very little oil or no oil at all. However, going farther out into deeper waters posed a set of unique challenges: a stable platform needed to be constructed to support rigorous drilling in deep waters; knowledge of weather conditions including tides, wind, and possible storms was

Oil wells set off the coast of Summerland, California in the late 1800s. (National Oceanic and Atmospheric Administration)

essential for keeping workers safe; and overall, the expense of such exploration was immense as it required oil companies to investigate different drilling techniques that would make drilling feasible with no guarantee of success.

In 1933, the semisubmersible barge was utilized for offshore exploration. The barge was towed to the drilling site and then sunk, where it provided a stable base for the drilling platform. Once drilling was complete, the barge could be raised and moved to another location. This technology made drilling offshore more efficient and cost effective for oil companies. In October 1947, Oklahoma-based Kerr-McGee drilled a successful well 10 and a half miles off of the Louisiana coast.

In 1953 two separate pieces of legislation were passed that would shape and impact offshore drilling. The first was the Submerged Lands Act, which allowed states to hold the title to lands within three miles of the shore. The second was the Outer Continental Shelf Lands Act, which authorized the secretary of the interior to lease the Outer Continental Shelf in the Gulf of Mexico for mineral exploration and exploitation. These two acts allowed states to choose the extent to which oil companies could be involved in their local economies and affect their lands. The amount of drilling done off various U.S. coastlines is a direct reflection on the culture of each state and the value residents place on conservation/protection of land and resources and the lure of economic growth. For example, the states that line the Gulf of Mexico are more inclined to back the oil companies that boost their economy and are less supportive of green initiatives that might take a source of income away from residents.

Environmental Concerns

Oil spills and leaks are two of the many reasons Americans often oppose offshore drilling. The history of oil spills off of the U.S. coastline has Americans worried about future spills. The spills are devastating for coastal marine, plant, and animal life. A spill on January 28, 1969, in the Santa Barbara Canal helped to shape California's strict drilling regulations and the attitudes of its residents toward offshore drilling, and it passed the National Environmental Policy Act in late 1969. This incident was also directly related to Wisconsin Senator Gaylord Nelson's establishment of Earth Day in 1970.

Of particular environmental concern for Americans are the coastal ecosystems that thrive on or near the U.S. coast. Many of them house either endangered species or protected species, and offshore drilling poses a risk to these ecosystems even if there is no spillage. The location of drilling platforms can disrupt the migratory patterns of birds and affect the marine mammals that live off the coast. Fishing off the U.S. coast can also be damaged by offshore drilling, which can impact the fishing grounds and, in turn, affect state economies.

Despite the spill in the Santa Barbara Canal in the early 1970s, the Arab Oil Embargo helped to increase offshore drilling. The embargo restricted the flow of Arab oil into the United States, causing a shortage of oil for Americans. As a result, President Richard Nixon announced a project to help the United States become independent of foreign oil. Nixon's plan included offering support for oil exploration in America, which included the Alaska pipeline and increased leases off the Outer Continental Shelf (submerged land belonging to the United States).

In sharp contrast to the technological developments that allow for offshore drilling in ever-deeper waters and carry oil to the surface for Americans to consume, the technology to clean up after oil spills has not been able to keep up. The use of skimming, dispersables (chemicals used to disperse oil in water after it's spilled), and collecting oil after it has washed up on the beach are insufficient when compared with the technological advances that make it possible for companies to drill miles below the water's surface into the gulf. This disparity between technological advances validates the concerns of environmental groups especially in the wake of the 2010 BP gulf spill.

During the summer of 2010, Americans were glued to their televisions watching coverage of the BP oil spill from the oil platform the Deepwater Horizon in the Gulf of Mexico. Despite being the "top of the line" in terms of technological advancements, the Deepwater Horizon platform exploded and sunk to the bottom of the gulf. Americans' worst fears were realized when the BP well began to leak and spill oil into the gulf. Unlike oil spills such as that from the Exon *Valdez* spill, the Deepwater Horizon leak was not from oil transportation but rather a leak from the well itself. The only other significant leak of this kind was the 1969 Santa Barbara Canal spill.

Fire boat response crews battle the blazing remnants of the off shore oil rig Deepwater Horizon on April 21, 2010. (U.S. Coast Guard)

The BP leak occurred in a very vulnerable location. Very close to the loop current in the gulf, which turns into the gulf stream, the current could have potentially carried oil far from the site of the spill. The gulf also plays a major role in the migration of many birds, which are often casualties of oil spills. The spill occurred off the Louisiana coast, home to roughly 40 percent of America's wetlands. It will be years before we know the full impact of the spill on the gulf's ecosystems.

By the time BP had capped and closed the well, it was estimated that some 200 million barrels of oil had been spilled directly into the Gulf of Mexico. Unfortunately, the BP spill of 2010 will continue to be studied by environmentalists for decades to come. Hopefully, it will be the catalyst that pushes technological advancements in the direction of environmental protection.

CRYSTAL TODD WRIGHT

See also: Ocean Restoration and Conservation (Environment); Technology and the Impact on Green (Science).

References

Cockerill, Alan. 2005. *Drilling Ahead: The Quest for Oil in the Deep South 1945–2005.* Jackson: University Press of Mississippi.

Freudenburg, William R. 2011. *Blowout in the Gulf: The BP Oil Spill Disaster and the Future of Energy in America.* Cambridge, MA: MIT University Press.

Freudenburg, William R., and Robert Gramling. 1994. *Oil in Troubled Waters: Perceptions, Politics, and the Battle Over Offshore Drilling.* Albany: State University of New York Press.

Gramling, Robert. 1996. *Oil on the Edge: Offshore Development, Conflict, and Gridlock.* Albany: State University of New York Press.

Holing, Dwight. 1990. *Coastal Alert: Ecosystems, Energy, and Offshore Oil Drilling.* Washington, DC: Island Press.

Yergin, Daniel. 1991. *The Prize: The Epic Quest for Oil, Money, and Power.* New York: Free Press.

PERMACULTURE

The concept of permaculture was developed in the early 1970s by Australian scientists Bill Mollison and David Holmgren and introduced to the world through their 1978 publication *Permaculture One*. Permaculture, as explained by Mollison, is a combined form of the words *permanent* and *culture*, with emphasis on the Latin root of the latter—*cultura*, referring to cultivation of the land or of the intellect. The original permaculture idea focused on integrated, evolving, and self-perpetuating plant and animal systems useful to humans. In the years since, it has expanded to encompass more than just agriculture. The concept of permaculture has been defined in many different ways, yet there remains a high level of commonality among these definitions. In its most basic sense, permaculture is a system for designing sustainable human environments. The original permaculture concept focused on the idea that agricultural systems should use the patterns and relationships found in nature as their basis for development. The term *permaculture design* refers to the application of permaculture principles (see below) to the assembly of patterned

Located two miles west of Alamosa, Colorado, this fish farm utilizes three geothermal wells. They are 2000 feet deep with 105 degree Fahrenheit, 85 degree Fahrenheit, and 70 degree Fahrenheit water respectively, all with artesian flow. (National Renewable Energy Laboratory)

systems consciously arranged and implemented in a way that sustains both human and nonhuman life.

In 2002, Holmgren articulated a theoretical and conceptual basis for permaculture that includes three ethical principles and 12 design principles. The ethical principles include care for the Earth, care for people, and distributing surplus while setting limits on consumption. The design principles are: (1) observe and interact; (2) catch and store energy; (3) obtain a yield; (4) apply self-regulation and accept feedback; (5) use and value renewable resources and services; (6) produce no waste; (7) design from patterns to details; (8) integrate rather than segregate; (9) use small and slow solutions; (10) use and value diversity; (11) use edges and value the marginal; and (12) use and respond to change creatively. They are often depicted in the nonhierarchical form of a flower, with the design principles surrounding the ethical principles. Holmgren emphasizes that permaculture should be understood as holistic and that its philosophical basis is in systems theory. Embedded in the permaculture concept are the ideals of sustainability, multifunctionality, diversity, resilience, efficiency, stability, and coexistence.

Holmgren also suggests that in the practice of permaculture, the ethics and principles should be applied to seven domains necessary to sustain humanity in a progressive and evolving way, thereby expanding the concept beyond agriculture. These are: (1) land and nature stewardship; (2) the built environment; (3) tools and technology; (4) culture and education; (5) health and spiritual well-being; (6) economics and finances; and (7) land tenure and community. Like the ethics and principles, these domains are meant to be integrated rather than hierarchical.

Agricultural applications of permaculture design involve ecological practices such as companion planting (plants that benefit when grown next to each other) and intercropping (growing two or more crops in close proximity) to make use of plant diversity and beneficial interactions. Maximizing productivity of available space is also considered important and includes the use of efficient designs such as spirals and tiers and practices such as succession planting and alley cropping. There is also a strong emphasis on the use of perennial crops and the practice of agroforestry (an integrated approach of combining crops, trees, and shrubs for mutual benefits). The concept of diversity extends to the incorporation of animals, as well as to the importance of soil microorganisms, birds, insects, and other wildlife. Also essential is the practice of resource conservation through the reuse and recycling of plant materials and water, taking advantage of natural means of nutrient cycling, and biological nutrient fixation. Permaculture emphasizes site specificity, favoring the use of native plants, and focusing on local resource use and limitations. Reliance on natural means of pest control and on design and diversity rather than input use are important as well. Permaculture systems are often organic, though the two terms are not synonymous. Another important issue is the promotion of labor efficiency through the use of observation as a primary tool, the idea being that by first seeing and analyzing the system one can make more effective and informed decisions about when and how to apply physical work.

The concepts inherent in permaculture design are no longer applied solely to agricultural systems. They are also used in development of renewable energy sources such as biofuels and the efficient use of solar and wind power. They are being used in the practice of green building through the incorporation of living roofs and walls, water catchment and recycling systems, and passive means for heating and cooling structures. Permaculture concepts are now used in urban planning, in the development of local economies, in the use participatory systems of community problem solving, in the development of intentional financial and business plans, in the practice of education, and even in politics and law. An emphasis on the inherent interconnection between various aspects of human endeavor is central to the integration of permaculture practice as applied to all of these issues.

Permaculture is not simply a theoretical model for thinking about the world, nor is it just a set of specific practices. Instead it is conceived by many as a way of life—a reflective and self-conscious way of interacting with the world on a daily basis. And beyond simply limiting the environmental impacts of human activity, it seeks to be regenerative. In his book *The Permaculture Way* (2005) Bell suggests that its practice involves a kind of selflessness that when fully realized manifests as understanding the self as "one with the universe." In this sense, permaculture practice can be understood to have a spiritual (though not religious) dimension. This is not a new formulation of the permaculture concept, but rather an extension of it. Central to Mollison and Holmgren's thinking in developing the ideas that became permaculture was the observation of patterns in nature and a conscious recognition of the individual's place within them.

Although many books, Web sites, workshops, and other educational materials now proliferate, permaculture practice is often taught through a permaculture design course. This educational form was developed by Bill Mollison in 1981, and its concepts have since been published in book form, as in *Introduction to Permaculture* (1994). The book presents a comprehensive overview of the practice of permaculture systems design in a variety of different temporal, spatial, and ecological settings. The design course is taught in different ways by different educators, and it is focused on practices appropriate to local conditions and the specific needs and abilities of learners.

Permaculture has come to exhibit some of the qualities of a social movement. From the start it has been cast as an alternative to conventional farming, and many of its advocates are united in a radical critique of both modern agriculture and social systems. Networks of practitioners exist across the globe in both formal and informal organizations. And permaculture ideas and techniques are actively debated and developed in discussion forums, educational programs, journals, and meetings.

Permaculturists emphasize that its practice can take place anywhere, including urban and rural settings. And while it is typically practiced in discrete spaces, its intent and ideology involve sustainability and improvement on a macro level. Thus, while emphasizing the local, permaculture seeks to affect the global. By promoting shared space, shared resources, and shared responsibility, permaculture practices aspire to improve both human interactions and interactions between human and nonhuman elements of the world.

TAYLOR REID

See also: City and Community Planning, Eco-Friendly (Science); Innovation and Invention Competitions (Science); Wise-Use Movement (Activism).

References

Bell, G. 2005. *The Permaculture Way: Practical Steps to Create a Self-Sustaining World.* White River Junction, VT: Chelsea Green.

Holmgren, D. 2002. *Permaculture: Principles and Pathways Beyond Sustainability.* Tasmania, Australia: Holmgren Design Services.

Mollison, B. C., and D. Holmgren. 1978. *Permaculture One.* Melbourne, Australia: Transworld Publishers.

Mollison, B. C., with R. M. Slay. 1994. *Introduction to Permaculture*, 2nd ed. NSW, Australia: Tagari Publications.

PESTICIDES

Pesticides are substances or mixtures used to control organisms that may pose a threat to the food supply, the health of humans or animals, or quality of life (Environmental Protection Agency). A pesticide is usually chemical in nature, although the U.S. Environmental Protection Agency (EPA) recognizes an increasing number of biological pesticides in use today. The term *pesticide* refers to a range of

Sign indicating no use of pesticides at a farmer's market in Sonoma, California. (U.S. Department of Agriculture)

products, including insecticides, herbicides, fungicides, and other pest control agents. Pests may be insects, plants, animals, fungi, microorganisms, and prions (Environmental Protection Agency). Pesticides are useful in controlling disease and pest outbreaks, but can be harmful when they reach unintended targets. Many transformations of food and fiber production have occurred in the United States over the past several decades in order to reduce or eliminate the unwanted effects of pesticides.

Although pesticide use goes back many centuries, the most well-known pesticides are the synthetic chemical pesticides developed in the years leading up to and during World War II. DDT (dichloro-diphenyl-trichloroethane) is the most famous of the synthetic chemical pesticides. Pesticide use increased significantly after World War II, and food production increased in kind. Most pesticides are used in agriculture to maintain or increase the value of crops. Most pesticides are used in agricultural applications (Grube et al., 2011). There are still many nonagricultural uses for pesticides. They are sometimes applied to lawns, forests, golf courses, and swimming pools. About three-quarters of U.S. households use some type of pesticide (Grube et al., 2011). The costs and benefits of pesticides have been questioned, measured, and debated in numerous ways. An economic cost-benefit analysis of pesticide use in agriculture demonstrates that pesticides are valuable to farmers. There is a higher return for money invested from the value of crops that might have otherwise been damaged by pests. Still, the economic benefit of pesticide use may not outweigh other factors. Many pesticides are toxic and can cause harm to individuals coming in contact with them in high concentrations, or even in small concentrations over a period of time. Some pesticides persist in the environment and become hard to control after they are applied to the intended target.

One of the most famous disputes over the use of pesticides comes from Rachel Carson's 1962 book *Silent Spring*, a meticulous work chronicling the effects of the pesticide DDT on birds and other species. Largely because of her efforts, DDT has been banned in the United States with few exceptions. At first DDT was considered a panacea, or cure-all, because it was an affordable broad-spectrum pesticide that did not appear to harm mammals. It was applied liberally for years without much cause for concern. Carson's book demonstrates that the danger of many synthetic chemicals comes from harm caused to nontarget organisms and from its persistence in the environment. Persistent chemicals like DDT are insoluble in the environment because they do not break down in water. Instead, they break down and accumulate in fatty tissues. This leads to biomagnification, an increase in concentration moving up the food chain. *Silent Spring* triggered widespread changes in public opinion and inspired some of the regulations governing pesticide development and application today. DDT was banned in the United States in 1972, although it is still approved for use in special cases.

In the United States, the EPA is responsible for regulating pesticides. The agency was given this control by a revision of the Fungicide, Insecticide, and Rodenticide Act (FIFRA) in 1972. This legislation provided new safeguards against harm to humans and the environment by controlling the sale and use of pesticides. It established strict registration requirements and use guidelines. Other agencies and laws are involved in making sure pesticides do not reach consumers in unsafe quantities. The Food and Drug Administration and the U.S. Department of Agriculture help protect food from harmful pesticide residues, monitoring and enforcing safe allowable levels. At the federal level, the Food Quality Protection Act (FQPA, 1996) and the Federal Food, Drug and Cosmetic Act (FFDCA, 1996) establish restrictions and tolerances for pesticide levels in foods. States also have their own laws regulating pesticides and setting tolerance levels in foods. These laws are usually similar to the federal laws.

Pesticide residue on food and the potential health consequences of pesticide exposure in the home have contributed to the success of the organic movement. Among consumers interested in purchasing organic products, there are different ideas about what should be considered organic food in addition to the common desire for foods produced without pesticides. Some organic products, such as packaged lettuce, have transitioned into mass production, and while this makes organic food available to more people, it is farther from the broader meaning the organic movement holds for some (Guthman, 2003). Smaller producers of organics tend to grow products that are still considered by consumers to be worth a higher price than mass-produced products. Organic food may be pock-marked by the insects that are naturally attracted to it, but the benefits of a safer, healthier product reinforces that the standard consumers hold of a piece of fruit looking the same every time is not natural, but rather a social construction of what we want food to be.

Farmers have also altered cultivation practices to reduce pesticide applications. Farmers' concerns stem from the expense of pesticide applications, pesticide toxicity, and increasing pesticide resistance among unwanted insects. Before people knew that pesticides such as DDT could cause significant harm to nontarget species, they were applied liberally, ensuring that a crop would be resistant to pest damage. Today the high financial, environmental, and health-related costs of pesticides work against this environmentally risky behavior. It is often more profitable in agriculture to reduce pesticide use. Integrated pest management (IPM) is one popular approach to pesticide use, which incorporates knowledge about the pest, the environment in which it is applied, and the pesticide's effectiveness in past management actions. IPM can include a spectrum of possibilities for the amount of pesticides used on a crop. The more that is known about crops, the more IPM reduces reliance on pesticides to a minimum and leads to more sustainable land use.

JENNIFER BJERKE

See also: Agriculture (Economics); Farming, Conventional (Economics); Farming, Organic (Economics); Garden, Home (Health); Rachel Carson's *Silent Spring* (Arts); Water and Air Purification (Science); Water Quality and Use (Environment).

References

Carson, Rachel. 1962. *Silent Spring*. Boston: Houghton Mifflin.

Grube, Arthur, David Donaldson, Timothy Kiely, and La Wu. 2011. *Pesticides Industry Sales and Usage: 2006 and 2007 Market Estimates*. Washington, DC: GPO.

Guthman, Julie. 2003. "Fast Food/Organic Food: Reflexive Tastes and the Making of 'Yuppie Chow'." *Social and Cultural Geography* 4: 45–58.

Robbins, Paul. 2007. *Lawn People*. Philadelphia: Temple University Press.

U.S. Environmental Protection Agency. "About Pesticides." Available at: http://www.epa.gov/pesticides/about/index.htm.

POPULATION

The United States is the third most populous country in the world (Christenson et al., 2004). At the time of the 2010 Census, there were 308.7 million people living within its borders (Mackun & Wilson, 2011). It is considered a developed country and has a high population growth rate compared to other developed countries. The population is sustained by long life expectancies, high rates of migration into the country, and relatively high fertility (the average number of children a woman will have in her lifetime). Currently, developed countries tend to have low fertility rates, which leads to shrinking populations. U.S. population growth in the 20th century was similar to world population growth, with both populations increasing by more than three times their 1900 levels by the end of the century. The U.S. Census Bureau projects that population growth in the United States through 2050 will continue at a steady pace, perhaps reaching 450 million in the middle of the 21st century and remaining the third most populous country (Christenson et al., 2004, 13).

For many decades, the Malthusian model has dominated ideas about environmental limits on population growth. Thomas Malthus was a scholar who in 1798 wrote an influential pamphlet on the "natural" limits to population growth (Malthus, 1992). He believed populations would continue to grow geometrically (exponentially) and food production would continue to increase arithmetically (in a linear fashion), so that people would always outgrow their ability to produce adequate food. By Malthus's model, if other problems such as war and disease did not keep population numbers low, famine would be the final limiting factor. Since then, population has indeed grown rapidly. In many places around the world, mortality rates have fallen dramatically followed by declining birth rates (these rates are measures of the number of births or deaths per 1,000 people per year). Generally, populations have experienced a drop in mortality with people living longer, healthier lives before families begin to decrease in size. The lag time between these two changes is part of what produced exponential population growth. According to the Malthusian model, this exponential growth is not sustainable.

The relationship between population and environment is a complex one. Technological developments in the United States beginning in the 1940s helped increase food production significantly by the 1960s, challenging concerns about population growth limits. It appeared food production could increase and keep pace with population in ways Malthus never imagined. This increase in agricultural productivity became known as the Green Revolution and temporarily allayed population-related fears. One explanation for this unexpected increase is found in the idea that more people lead to more innovation. As more people crowd onto the same piece of land, people may find creative solutions to use less land area or fewer resources. This does not mean that the Earth can support an unlimited population, but it challenges the simplicity of Malthusian thinking. By the 1970s, increasing environmental degradation and resource depletion helped renew those fears of overpopulation.

Humans do not all have equal impact on the planet's resources. While today many concerns about overpopulation are focused on high fertility rates in developing countries, scholars have suggested that resource consumption, technology, and economics also play a large role in the environmental impact of populations rather than simply the total number of people (Ehrlich & Holdren, 1971; Wackernagel & Rees, 1996). In many cases, U.S. citizens use the most resources or are among the world's leading consumers, so domestic population growth has a much larger impact on the planet's resources than controlling population growth in developing countries. Criticism of overconsumption in the developed world is related to concerns over global climate change and the disproportionate amount of carbon dioxide U.S. citizens contribute to the atmosphere. For example, the United States has one of the highest rates of energy consumption per person. By curbing excessive energy use and making daily practices more sustainable, U.S. citizens can make a large contribution to the health of the global environment.

Conflicts between population and the environment are sometimes observed when urban areas expand into environmentally sensitive areas or historically agricultural land. This is in part because more and more people are moving to urban areas and because many cities and metropolitan areas are not controlling sprawl (the outward expansion of a city, often in the form of suburbs). In desert cities like Las Vegas and Phoenix, rapid population growth in recent years has led to questions about the high demand for water and energy it takes to supply suburbs in the desert. In Los Angeles, a sprawling freeway system invited automobiles as the metropolitan area expanded over the past several decades and led to the worst air pollution in the country. In response, many diverse measures were taken to reduce traffic congestion (which leads to idling and greater air pollution) and make cars more fuel efficient. The catalytic converter, carpooling, mass transit systems, and other measures have increased air quality in Los Angeles and the surrounding cities. Still, environmental issues in urban areas persist. Some point to sprawl as a large factor because instead of learning to live efficiently within a bounded area of land, many cities and metropolitan areas are still expanding. At the interface of urban areas with agricultural and more natural environments, there continues to be conflicts that bring into view some of the complex interactions between society and environment; interactions that evolve as society changes. One of the frontiers of managing population is not necessarily a matter of numbers, but of managing the complex interactions between humans and their environment.

JENNIFER BJERKE

See also: Population and Family (Health).

References

Christenson, M., T. McDevitt, and K. A. Stanecki. 2004. *Global Population Profile: 2002. International Population Reports.* Washington, DC: U.S. Census Bureau.

Ehrlich, Paul R., and John P. Holdren. 1971. "Impact of Population Growth." *Science* 171: 1212–1217.

Mackun, Paul, and Stevens Wilson. 2011. *Population Distribution and Change: 2000 to 2010.* Washington, DC: U.S. Census Bureau.

Malthus, Thomas R. 1992. *An Essay on the Principle of Population* (selected and introduced by D. Winch). Cambridge: Cambridge University Press.

Wackernagel, Mathis, and William Rees. 1996. *Our Ecological Footprint: Reducing Human Impact on the Earth.* Gabriola Island, BC: New Society Publishers.

PUBLIC PERCEPTIONS AND ACTIONS AROUND CLIMATE CHANGE

As the U.S. environmental movement passes 40 years and enters middle age, the issue of climate change has matured into one of the nation's most polarizing, contested disputes. Debate mounts today over whether climate change is real; if so, whether it is accelerating; and whether it is caused by humans or not. Experts say droughts and wildfires, floods, seasonal anomalies, melting ice, disappearing species, and more intense storms demonstrate the reality that climate change is under way. However, the American public has been increasingly divided on this issue.

Some naysayers claim that fear-mongers and scam artists hawking worthless tonics are looking to profit from an emergent green industry. Far right-wing conservatives suggest that democracy itself is at stake, as they accuse liberal left extremists of using climate change as the ultimate socialist tool to rein in capitalist growth. Those on the far left worry that organized climate change reform could lead to global governance and the emergence of a "new world order" that will threaten national sovereignty. Yet, for the rest—approximately half of all Americans—the symptoms of climate change are real enough for them to make permanent changes in the way they live, in what they consume, and in the actions they take to preserve the planet and to offset, if not counter, the negative impacts of human activity (Jones, 2011).

Such divisiveness raises three key questions: What accounts for these vastly different perceptions across America's cultural, ideological, and political landscape? How strong or debilitating are these cleavages? Finally, amid this contentiousness, what actual progress, if any, has there been to American understanding, preparation, and response to climate change? Exploring these three primary areas of concern reveals a dynamic, complex terrain that shapes a varied landscape of American public perception and response around climate change today.

America's Attitudinal Shifts on Climate Change: Tracing the Boundaries

Paradoxically, from 2000 to 2010, the United States has experienced one of its most acute decades in terms of climate variations and extremes, but overall concern over climate change in 2010 recorded a 20-year low. Some analysts suggest that in the United States, climate concern has been eclipsed by the public's worries over the economy and over finite energy supplies and rising energy costs. Waning focus on climate change may also be due to public irritability (if not exhaustion) from attempts to read between the lines of climate science-speak or terrifying climate "catastrophism," as well as from competing political interests in the climate change debate. While the latter has become increasingly bitter, the dissemination of scientific information has become progressively vague and obtuse.

Blinded by Science—and Politics

Consensus has grown over the past decade among leading scientific experts worldwide on the realities and consequences of climate change (National Research Council, 2010). According to a recent study published in the 2010 National Academy of Sciences Proceedings, approximately 97 percent of the nation's climate researchers believe that climate change is real and is primarily due to anthropogenic (human) causes (Anderegg et al., 2010). Yet this degree of confidence has been waning in recent years for the American public.

Since 2002, when the Intergovernmental Panel on Climate Change (IPCC) issued its report on the potential impacts facing the planet, an often-mistaken assumption and practice by scientists has been that providing more and more information about climate change would lead to better public knowledge on the topic, which in turn would categorically produce greater concern by the masses. Simultaneously, a very vocal, but powerful and industry-funded minority of climate change contrarians has also persistently contested mainstream scientists. These conservative skeptics, often supported by wealthy and powerful fossil fuel interests, receive considerable media coverage and have repeatedly challenged the credibility of independent and objective climate science (Boycoff & Boycoff, 2004; Jaques et al., 2008; Malka et al., 2009; McCright & Dunlap, 2003).

For the American public, the technical complexity of climate science, itself, does not lend well to robust understanding and decision making on this controversial issue (Marquart-Pyatt et al., 2011; Schneider, 2009). The challenges of weighing the costs and benefits from various greenhouse gas emissions that are accumulated over the short term and long term in the atmosphere, recognizing and understanding the signs of climate change versus ambient weather variability, evaluating and assessing scientific models of probability and uncertainty, and considering the varied environmental, social, and economic implications of climate may not be common skill sets for the U.S. vernacular. However, climate scientists have often implicitly assumed that the public makes rational choices and calculated decisions equipped with this complex knowledge and understanding (Moser, 2011; Pidgeon & Fischoff, 2011).

Faced with this daunting science and the purported future of the planet and humanity at stake, Americans more than likely rely on the resources they typically turn to for such profound or complicated decisions. These resources are the veritable wellsprings that consistently nurture Americans' beliefs, values, ideologies, and worldviews (Leiserowitz, 2006; Marquart-Pyatt et al., 2011; Nisbet, 2009). Whether religious, political, or cultural, the overarching doctrines of these resources are capable of aggregating, translating, and framing the issue of climate change on behalf of their followers, according to fundamental sets of standards, norms, and objectives that are familiar to and resound well with their followers.

Recent research also suggests that while there is a positive relationship between education and understanding of climate change for some Americans, for others there is an inverse relationship between these two variables. Specifically, the more U.S. liberals/democrats know and understand climate change, the more likely they are to believe it is real and to be concerned about it. Conversely, the more that U.S. conservatives/republicans know and understand climate change, the less likely they are to believe in it and the less likely they are to support climate change reform (Malka et al., 2009, 38; McCright & Dunlap, 2003, 28). Overall, political ideology appears to be the most significant factor framing American perceptions and actions on climate change.

In fact, a 2011 Gallup poll survey found that while 72 percent of democrats worried about climate change, only 31 percent of republicans expressed this same concern. Moreover, while 62 percent of democrats agreed that climate change was already under way, only 32 percent of republicans believed that to be the case. In terms of what is causing climate change, 71 percent of democrats in 2011 cited human impact on the environment, but only 36 percent of republicans attributed climate change to human causes. A significant gap also existed in 2011 between these two political ideologies and perceptions of media exaggeration of climate change. Though only 22 percent of democrats believed the media was sensationalizing climate change, 67 percent of republicans agreed that the news exaggerated the effects of climate change (Jones, 2011).

Overall, these data, which are part of the Gallup's Annual Social Services Environmental Poll, indicates waning concern by the American public over climate change when compared to years past. Related trends observed in Gallup poll research demonstrate that in general, Americans worry less about the environment when the nation is led by a democratic president than they do when a republican is in charge of the White House (Jones, 2011). While these trends are supported by data from 1987 to 2007, a significant deviation from this norm began in 2007. The nation's economic slowdown, which began in December 2007, may have at least temporarily trumped U.S. concerns over climate change. Gallup poll findings demonstrate as much. In fact, a Gallup poll conducted in 2009 showed that for the first time in 25 years, a majority of Americans surveyed stated that if it came down to a tradeoff, they were willing to sacrifice the environment to some degree in favor of economic growth (Newport, 2009).

Tradeoffs between the Economy and the Environment

Gallup poll researchers began a long-term inquiry into the perceptions of Americans over potential tradeoffs between the economy and the environment in 1984. At that time, six of ten Americans surveyed believed that the environment should be given priority, even if it threatened economic growth (Newport, 2009). As U.S. support of the environment over economic growth grew from 1987 to 1991, the percentage of Americans willing to trade environmental well-being in favor of economic growth dipped to 19 percent during this same period. By 1990–1991, 71 percent of Americans surveyed supported the environment over the economy. Though support for the environment over the economy dropped to 58 percent in 1992, it rebounded to 70 percent in the late 1990s–2000 alongside an economic upswing.

The first persistent decline in Americans' support for the environment can be traced to 2000–2001, when republicans held sway in the White House. By 2003, for the first time since the Gallup survey was conducted, fewer than 50 percent of Americans surveyed favored environmental preservation over economic growth. Economic growth at the expense of the environment dipped again in 2005 but has steadily risen since then, from 37 percent in 2007 to 51 percent in 2009 (Newport, 2009). Today, Americans appear to be more divided over economic versus environmental tradeoffs than they have ever been. For the first time, those willing to sacrifice the environment over the economy represented a solid majority, and under a democratic president no less. These findings suggest that in addition to partisan shifts in political power in the United States, American perceptions and actions on the environment and climate change may be even more profoundly affected by economic pressure and strain.

As a reverberating impact of the U.S. economic recession, unemployment swiftly rose in the United States from 6.6 percent in 2008 to 10 percent of the population in 2010. When the Pew Research Center for People and the Press conducted a poll in 2010 on issue priorities, only 28 percent of Americans designated global warming as a top concern. This marked a 10 percent decline from Pew's 2007 data on American support for climate change reform. Overall, the Pew Report found that not only had the economy, jobs, and terrorism topped the list of Americans' concerns in

2010, but that as these priorities rose, public priority levels simultaneously declined for the environment, illegal immigration, energy, and domestic crime (*Public's Priorities*, 2009). This is not the first time this anomaly has occurred. In 2000, of a list of 13 environmental problems facing the nation, Americans rated global warming as the second least important issue. Moreover, Americans also listed the environment as a whole as 16th on a list of the nation's most pressing problems (Leiserowitz, 2006, 46).

These findings may support previous research on the limits of the American psyche, particularly in terms of how many diverse challenges and degrees of threat the public can simultaneously absorb and manage (Linville & Fisher, 1991; Weber, 2006). In other words, as new stressors emerge or ongoing stressors intensify, Americans are most likely to suppress or table their concerns over other issues, particularly if the latter pose longer-term risks or if uncertainty heightens over how to resolve these concerns (Swim et al., 2009). Alongside rising worries over terrorism after the attacks in 2001, the lingering war in Afghanistan, the tumultuous invasion of Iraq, and the debilitating 2007 economic recession, the amount of attention that Americans focused on climate change diminished. Uncertainty over climate change also intensified in the American public mind in 2009, amid a brouhaha known as "Climate-gate."

"Climate-Gate": A Test of American Trust

A controversy that challenged the integrity and honesty of key climate scientists surfaced in 2009 on the Internet, went viral in the "blogosphere," grabbed the attention of national news, and caused international political reverberations. This scandal, which became known as "Climate-gate," triggered independent investigations by the United Nations, the United Kingdom's Information Commissioner, and the U.S. Senate (Black, 2010; Dunlap & McCright, 2010). Climate-gate stemmed from two massive, unauthorized releases on the Internet in 2009 and 2011 of private e-mails primarily between two key scientists in England and United States who had helped to shape historic and Nobel-renowned global assessments completed by the Intergovernmental Panel on Climate Change (IPCC). These breached communiqués centered on the defensive strategies that these scientists considered and employed to guard their data, preserve their findings, and prevent publication of competing climate change findings they believed originated from well-funded critics' attacks against them.

It is relevant to point out that as a matter of course in the scientific community, new findings—especially those that affect the body of known knowledge—must be vetted by peer review processes prior to publication and acceptance by the overarching scientific community. However, a number of the private e-mails hacked and published online seemed to indicate that in some instances, the climate scientists involved attempted to block access to their data by those they viewed as adversaries and were reluctant to accommodate the publication of other papers critical of their findings (Carrington, 2011, para. 5–6). The IPCC has vehemently denied any role in the suppression of countervailing data or findings.

"Climate-Gate"

The seeds of the Climate-gate controversy were actually sown in 1995, when the Intergovernmental Panel on Climate Change (IPCC) published its second assessment report and ceded that the "balance of evidence suggests a discernable human impact on global climate." Soon thereafter, some of the leading scientists involved in writing that treatise found not only their findings but also their motives and reputations under attack by other researchers and expert consultants for the big oil, automobile, and related industries and their political backers (Pearce, 2010).

The leaked series of e-mails between climate scientists over how to handle these professional assaults had actually persisted for years. Once made public, they caused a storm of controversy over whether climate scientists had exaggerated their findings that Earth was getting hotter and that excess carbon emissions from human activity were largely responsible for this overheating (Pearce, 2010). Though a number of investigations in the United States and United Kingdom validated the integrity of the scientists' data and vindicated their conclusions, these reports raised criticisms over scientists' efforts to block access to their data by skeptics and naysayers.

Regardless, amid the ensuing uproar caused by Climate-gate, the American public, politicians, and even others in the scientific community wondered at the wisdom of allowing such important data to be controlled by an elite group of researchers and began to demand greater transparency. In fact, Climate-gate has been referred to as a "game-changer" that has since compelled climate scientists to be more direct and frank about their own reservations, doubts, and uncertainties (Pearce, 2010, para. 5–8). Some Americans have since questioned the climate science community's integrity, motives, capacity, and willingness to manipulate the public through the selective use of already confounding data. Overall, the fallout from this controversy injured public trust of more Americans over the entire climate change question. A 2010 Gallup poll survey on American perceptions of climate change showed that 13 percent fewer Americans (52 percent) in 2010 than in 2008 (62 percent) believed that most scientists were in agreement that global warming was under way (Newport, 2010).

A robust study on just where Americans place their trust for global warming information conducted by Yale in 2010 found that 26 percent of the American public either strongly or somewhat distrusted scientists. Political orientation and worldview were the strongest predicators of trust and mistrust in the Yale study. Researchers found a close connection between worldview, political orientation, and loss of trust in climate scientists. The Yale study concluded that republican political party affiliation and conservative ideology accounted for 37 percent of the differences in loss of trust by the American public after Climate-gate, while an individualistic (as opposed to egalitarian) worldview accounted for 47 percent of increasing public mistrust (Leiserowitz et al., 2010a).

Speaking Power to Power

The Climate-gate scandal also represented a fortuitous political boost and good timing for libertarian and conservative climate change contrarians, as well as for powerful special interest groups that stood to benefit from casting suspicion on climate change science and the extent of potential human impact as the chief cause of climate change (Dunlap & McCright, 2010; McCright & Dunlap, 2010; Oreskes & Conway, 2010). As a case in point, though climate change advocates and democrats experienced early successes in the Barack Obama administration in 2009 with passage in the U.S. House of Representatives of major federal cap-and-trade climate legislation to limit carbon emissions, this historic measure subsequently died in the U.S. Senate, along with hopes for other stronger domestic climate reform policies.

Amid the storm of Climate-gate and alongside the nation's continuing economic recession, conservative republicans in November 2010 won control of the U.S. House and secured additional seats in the U.S. Senate (Carson & Hellberg, 2010). This political paradigm shift served the interests of well-funded climate contrarians and amplified their long-term crusade against climate change reform platforms. These political groups find powerful support from economic interests in the United States that are heavily connected to fossil fuels industries, including oil, coal, gas, and mining; fossil-fuels-dependent activities, including agriculture, transportation, and electricity production sectors; and the regionally concentrated constituencies that economically rely upon these initiatives.

Collectively, these forces spend considerable dollars to fund climate "debunking" research and to promote negative media press on climate change and climate change reform (Carson & Hellberg, 2010, 2). These efforts have especially resonated among Americans who reside in geographic regions where this interdependent, fossil-fuels infrastructure would be most affected by such climate change reforms as carbon emission–limiting cap-and-trade legislation. In fact, the well-funded launch of the Tea Party as a far right-wing libertarian fringe movement has gained popular momentum and public support by denouncing cap-and-trade legislation and calling climate change a hoax (Carson & Hellberg, 2010).

Especially amid the U.S. economic downturn, the power of the dollar has also played a supporting role in the shaping of American perceptions, priorities, and actions related to climate change. Coal, a significant contributor to global warming, has remained a significant source of energy production and consumption in the United States. In 2009, coal mined and transported across the country produced almost half of the U.S. electricity and more than 20 percent of all U.S. energy in 2009. Moreover, while many outdated production plants and electrical transmission grids have contributed significant pollution from carbon emissions, the cost of coal-produced electricity has also remained fairly inexpensive for consumers who have often been among the least able to pay for energy-efficient improvements (Carson & Hellberg, 2010). The tradeoff between the environment and the economy is much more than perceptual in these instances.

Perceptual Cleavages on Climate Change

Collectively, these events have contributed to waning support and disillusionment by the American public (Newport, 2009). Alongside these scientific, economic, and political divisions and their competing stakeholders, Americans lately have expressed increased uncertainty and confusion about climate change and its causes and effects, compared to American public sentiment in previous years (Chandler, 2011, para. 6–7). In the United States in 2010, there were 11 percent more climate change skeptics than there were in 2008, according to recent Gallup poll surveys. Specifically, in 2010, 49 percent of all Americans believed climate change was under way, compared to 61 percent in 2008. The 2010 figure was just one percentage point higher than the all-time low recorded by Gallup on this issue in 1997.

Opinions over the cause of climate change have also shown increasing cleavage in America; 52 percent of those Gallup surveyed in 2011 blamed human impact on the environment, while 43 percent cited the planet's natural environmental cycles as the main cause of climate change (Jones, 2011). These findings contrast significantly with where perceptions were just three years ago when the spread between those who cited human impact as the cause of climate change was 20 percent higher than those who attributed climate change to natural causes. Forty-three percent of Americans polled by Gallup in 2011 also agreed that the media sensationalizes the impact of global warming, while the remainder were split between believing the media accurately represents the issue or underestimates its impact (Jones, 2011).

With respect to these widening cleavages, a joint study conducted in 2008 and 2010 by the Yale Project on Climate Change and George Mason University concluded that American perceptions were actually fractured between six different clusters of intensity on the issue. The "Six Americas" report identified these groups from highest in intensity to lowest in intensity and labeled these clusters accordingly as "alarmed," "concerned," "cautious," "disengaged," "doubtful," and "dismissive" (Leiserowitz et al., 2010b). Findings demonstrate that while few people were "disengaged," there were almost as many "dismissive" Americans (23 percent) as there were "alarmed" Americans (28 percent). These findings demonstrate a high level of extreme polarization on climate change. In addition, comparisons between the 2008 and 2010 "Six Americas" studies mark significant movement away from concern for climate change. Declines were recorded in the "alarmed" (–8 percent) and "concerned" (–4 percent) clusters while increases were noted in the "cautious" (+8 percent), "doubtful" (+2 percent), and "dismissive" (+9 percent) clusters (Leiserowitz et al., 2010b) of American perceptions on climate change. Moreover, the cluster of Americans who were "dismissive" of climate change represented the largest growth from 2008 to 2010.

Perception of risk from climate change is also on the decline in the minds of Americans. In 2011, approximately 51 percent of all Americans worried a great deal or a fair amount about climate change. While this outcome still represents a majority of the U.S. population that is worried about climate change, it still marks a significant decline compared to Gallup poll data for 2008, when two-thirds (66 percent) of the American public voiced this same concern. The percentage of Americans who doubt whether climate change will ever happen has also risen considerably, from 7 percent in 2001 to 18 percent in 2011 (Jones, 2011). In addition to the contributing factors of political ideology and cultural worldview, perception of risk and denial of climate change reality may be linked to a lack of exposure to nature's furies. Paradoxically, changes in American perceptions of low risk or climate change denial appear to be emerging more often in regions that have been experiencing some of these catastrophes lately.

American Perceptions of Risk from Climate Change: An Experiential Paradox

The weather in the United States has been particularly "noisy" of late, in terms of making the presence of its anomalies and extremes known in certain regions of the nation. When record-setting snows hit the midsection and eastern region of the United States in the winters of 2010 and 2011, global warming skeptics took advantage of the opportunity to mock climate change scientists and to claim instead that, if anything, the climate was cooling. Termed "Snowmageddon," these frigid weather events may very well have temporarily eased Americans' concerns over climate change (Broder, 2010). The record cold and snow in 2010 continued to dominate U.S. climate/weather perceptions. Moisture produced by massive snow melt along with spring and summer rains greatly reduced the size and extent of summer drought. For the second year in a row, the United States also remained hurricane free. Even though record heat hit the southern and eastern United States hard in the summer of 2010 and the northern plains and midwest experienced heavy rains and the sixth busiest summer tornado season in six decades, the general perception of risk from climate change seemed further removed for many Americans (Broder, 2010). These perceptions were not unexpected. After all, the public perception of risk is a complex affair that derives not only from information provided by experts, but also from cultural worldviews, political orientations, trust, and personal experience (Leiserowitz, 2005, 1434). Because of these differences and these different experiences, people are also bound to hold different ideas about what constitutes a "dangerous" climate.

The strident winter and overall "cooling" of U.S. weather experienced by large populations of Americans in 2010 quite possibly contributed to a lower perception of risk and more dismissive attitudes about the prospect of climate change. Psychosocial factors for coping with the stressor of climate change may have played into this scenario as well. Climate change is anticipated to be a long, protracted event spanning the globe and lasting perhaps tens or even hundreds of years. Such an event is difficult to process within one lifetime. Also, researchers point out that because of a lack of current experience or known expectations for climate change, people are more likely to understand climate change and react to it based on the direct, weather-related and environmental impacts they do experience (Swim et al., 2009). Such experiences became much more climate intense in 2011.

In fact, in 2010, climate change scientists had warned that the heating of the planet would be accompanied by more frequent and more intense weather events and not necessarily by warmer temperatures worldwide. Such events would range from more volatile storms and floods, droughts and wildfires, excessive snow or no snow (Rose, 2010). In 2011, 10 significant weather events listed by the National Oceanic and Atmospheric Administration (NOAA) run the gamut of these possibilities.

These included, in order of severity, the tornado super outbreak of April 25–28, 2011; the Southern drought that extended from spring to fall of 2011; massive spring 2011 Mississippi River and Ohio River flooding; Texas and Oklahoma's hottest three-month statewide temperatures on record in the summer of 2011; Hurricane Irene in August 2011; the northern plains and upper midwest flooding in early summer 2011; U.S. wildfires that persisted through the spring and summer of 2011. Tropical Storm Lee in September 2011 and the April 14–16, 2011, tornado outbreak tied for ninth place on NOAA's weather/climate events list (*State of the Climate National Overview*, 2011).

While the intensity of these specific weather events merits NOAA's top 10 list, the varied strengths and types of weather experienced in 2011 have also been differently experienced and mediated across the nation's geographic and cultural landscape. Because of this, the range of American perceptions and actions on climate change are more often taking form today at the regional, state, and local levels.

Conclusions: Where Weather and Climate Hit Home

Despite setbacks at the national level on climate change policy, sagging trust in the climate change science sector, and widening cleavages in worldviews and political ideologies over climate change, Americans are taking actions on their own to reduce greenhouse gas emissions and to shrink the nation's ecological footprint. Substantial progress can be observed at the regional and state levels, as well as in the individual households of Americans themselves. By late 2010, 36 of the nation's 50 states had developed or enacted climate change action plans and 41 states had instituted emission registries for greenhouse gases and data architecture required for tracking (and perhaps in the future, limiting) these emissions. Twenty states have established lower greenhouse gas emission goals (Carson & Hellberg, 2010, 4).

The State of California has taken this one step further. In early 2012, the California Air Resources Board (CARB) was due to finalize operations to put mandatory limits on greenhouse gas emissions and to put the state's mandatory cap-and-trade program into effect. Despite factional opposition from conservative and libertarian partisan groups and fossil fuel interests, a gubernatorial candidate who threatened to suspend the measure, and a proposition to delay implementation until job levels rose for a year, California's Global Warming Solutions Act has managed to stay alive thus far (Carson & Hellberg, 2010, 4). Heavy urban pollution that affects the state's tourism economy and residents' quality of life, alongside extreme drought and wildfires that have plagued Californians since 2007, have likely contributed to this state's aggressive stance on greenhouse gas emissions.

Regional initiatives are also on the rise. One of the most significant actions has included the creation of three regional initiatives in the United States to voluntarily cap greenhouse gas emissions. More than 30 states are taking part in these efforts, coordinated by the Midwestern Greenhouse Gas Reduction Accord, the Regional Greenhouse Gas Initiative, and the Western Climate Initiative. Each of these three regions have experienced a different range of extreme weather and climate events, including flooding, drought, devastating tornado outbreaks, and record snows (*State of the Climate National Overview*, 2011). However, the shared intensity of these unique experiences has produced unprecedented alliances. Though limited in terms of geographic scale and individual emission targets, the collective impact of these three initiatives represents an aggressive and substantial potential target reduction in global greenhouse gas emissions. The tabling of national cap-and-trade legislation has not prevented these three collectives from forging plans to tie their own separate initiatives together and to also synchronize data collection procedures with the federal Environmental Protection Agency's regulations.

Americans as individuals represent the closest proximity of perceptions and actions related to climate change. Though the economy and energy costs take precedence in the minds and pocketbooks of most Americans according to recent polls, these priorities do not necessarily negate behaviors and actions that have a positive impact on the climate. In fact, the U.S. Energy Information Administration reported in 2010 that greenhouse gas emissions fell from 2008 to 2010 (Carson & Hellberg, 2010, 2). Some of this decline can be attributed to the conversion of coal plants to natural gas. However, the economic recession also played a role: Higher electricity and natural gas prices, alongside higher prices for gasoline, have prompted more Americans to adjust their thermostat, to drive less often, and to consume fewer goods.

In fact, according to a March 2011 Gallup poll, most Americans think they need to do what they can on their own to take better care of the environment (O'Driscoll & Weiss, 2011, 1A). Consuming less and making smarter, more energy-efficient decisions in their homes, automobiles, and in the products they buy are how Americans today perceive their environmentally conscious actions. Recent data show that 60 percent of Americans—11 percent more than in 2010—think that climate change is under way, and even more think that climate change will involve turbulent and extreme weather and climate events over the next 50 years (O'Driscoll & Weiss, 2011, 1A).

These findings on regional, state, and individual perceptions and actions illustrate perhaps the best news of all: Regardless of the negative impacts of complex climate science, partisan politics, competing cultural worldviews, loss of trust, or varying levels of perceived risk, the resultant, generalized skepticism produced by these events and conditions is being actively and authentically countered by the perceptions and actions of Americans in their own habitats, where the effects of weather and climate are likely to hit home the most.

KATHLEEN O'HALLERAN

See also: Carbon Footprint (Environment); Global Warming (Environment).

References

Anderegg, William R. L., James W. Prall, Jacob Harold, and Stephen H. Schneider. 2010. "Expert Credibility in Climate Change." *Proceedings of the National Academy of Sciences* 107:27 (June 21): 12107–12109.

Black, Richard. 2010. "Scientists to Review Climate Body." *BBC*, March 10. Available at: http://news.bbc.co.uk/2/hi/8561004.stm.

Boykoff, M. T., and J. M. Boykoff. 2004. "Balance as Bias: Global Warming and the US Prestige Press." *Global Environmental Change* 14: 125–136.

Broder, John M. 2010. "Climate Change Debate Is Heating Up in Deep Freeze." *New York Times*, February 10. Available at: http://www.nytimes.com/2010/02/11/science/earth/11climate.html?hp.

Carrington, Damien. 2011. "Q and A Climategate." *The Guardian*, November 22. Available at: http://www.guardian.co.uk/environment/2010/jul/07/climate-emails-question-answer.

Carson, Marcus, and Joakim Hellberg. 2010. *Washington Descends Deeper into Climate Gridlock: California and the States Creep Forward*. Stockholm: Stockholm Environment Institute. Available at: http://www.sei-international.org/mediamanager/documents/Publications/Climate-mitigation-adaptation/Carson%20-%20US%20PB%20101122c%20web.pdf.

Chandler, Joe. 2011. "Uncertain Science Provides Cold Comfort amid Climate Chaos." *Sydney Morning Herald*, November 22. Available at: http://www.smh.com.au/opinion/society-and-culture/uncertain-science-provides-cold-comfort-amid-climate-chaos-20111121-1nquz.html.

Dempsey, Matt, and David Lungren. 2010. *United States Senate Report "Consensus Exposed": The CRU Controversy*. Washington, DC: U.S. Senate; U.S. Senate Committee on Environment and Public Works Minority Staff. February. Available at: http://epw.senate.gov/public/index.cfm?FuseAction=Files.View&FileStore_id=7db3fbd8-f1b4-4fdf-bd15-12b7df1a0b63.

Dunlap, R. E., and A. M. McCright. 2010. "Climate Change Denial: Sources, Actors and Strategies." In C. Lever-Tracy, ed., *The Routledge International Handbook of Climate Change and Society*. New York: Routledge Press, 240–259.

Jacques, P., R. Dunlap, and M. Freeman. 2008. "The Organization of Denial: Conservative Think Tanks and Environmental Skepticism." *Environmental Politics* 17: 349–385.

Jones, Jeffrey. 2011. "In U.S., Concerns about Global Warming Stable at Lower Levels." *Gallup Politics*, March 11. Available at: http://www.gallup.com/poll/146606/concerns-global-warming-stable-lower-levels.aspx.

Kennedy, Donald. 2004. "Climate Change and Climate Science." *Science* 304:5677 (June 11): 1565.

Leiserowitz, Anthony A. 2005. "American Risk Perceptions: Is Climate Change Dangerous." *Risk Analysis* 25:6: 1433–1442.

Leiserowitz, Anthony A. 2006. "Climate Change Risk Perception and Policy Preferences: The Role of Affect, Imagery, and Values." *Climatic Change* 77: 45–72.

Leiserowitz, A., E. Maibach, and C. Roser-Renouf. 2010a. *Climate Change in the American Mind: Americans' Global Warming Beliefs and Attitudes in January 2010*. New Haven, CT: Yale Project on Climate Change. Available at: http://environment.yale.edu/uploads/AmericansGlobalWarmingBeliefs2010.pdf.

Leiserowitz, A., E. Maibach, and C. Roser-Renouf. 2010b. *Global Warming's Six Americas*. New Haven, CT: Yale Project on Climate Change, Yale University and George Mason University.

Linville, P. W., and G. W. Fischer. 1991. "Preferences for Separating and Combining Events: A Social Application of Prospect Theory and the Mental Accounting Model." *Journal of Personal and Social Psychology* 60: 5–23.

Malka, A., J. A. Krosnick, M. Debell, J. Pasek, and D. Schneider. 2009. "Featuring Skeptics in News Media Stories about Global Warming Reduces Public Beliefs in the Seriousness of Global Warming." Woods Institute for the Environment, Stanford University, Technical Paper. Available at: http://woods.stanford.edu/research/global-warming-skeptics.html.

Marquart-Pyatt, Sandra T., Rachel L. Shwom, Thomas Dietz, Riley E. Dunlap, Stan A. Kaplowitz, Aaron M. McCright, and Sammy Zahran. 2011. "Understanding Public Opinion on Climate Change: A Call for Research." *Environment: Science and Policy for Sustainable Development* 53:4: 38–42.

McCright, A. M., and R. E. Dunlap. 2003. "Defeating Kyoto: The Conservative Movement's Impact on US Climate Change Policy." *Social Problems* 50: 348–373.

McCright, A. M., and R. E. Dunlap. 2010. "Anti-Reflexivity: The American Conservative Movement's Success in Undermining Climate Science and Policy." *Theory, Culture, and Society* 27:2/3: 100–133.

Moser, S. C. 2011. "Communicating Climate Change: History, Challenges, Process, and Future Directions." *Wiley Interdisciplinary Reviews: Climate Change* 1:1: 31–53.

National Research Council. 2010. *Advancing the Science of Climate Change*. Washington, DC: National Academies Press.

Newport, Frank. 2009. "Americans: Economy Takes Precedence over Environment." *Gallup Economy*, March 19. Available at: http://www.gallup.com/poll/116962/Americans-Economy-Takes-Precedence-Environment.aspx.

Newport, Frank. 2010. "Americans' Global Warming Concern Continues to Drop." *Gallup News*, March 11. Available at: http://www.gallup.com/poll/126560/Americans-Global-Warming-Concerns-Continue-Drop.aspx.

Nisbet, M. 2009. "Communicating Climate Change: Why Frames Matter for Public Engagement." *Environment* 51:2: 12–23.

O'Driscoll, Patrick, and Elizabeth Weise. 2011. "Green Living Takes Root, but Habits Die Hard. Doing Right Thing Isn't Easy, Even for Those Who Want to." *USA Today*, March 29, 1A.

Oreskes, N., and E. M. Conway. 2010. *Merchants of Doubt*. New York: Bloomsbury Press.

Pearce, Fred. 2010. "How the 'Climategate' Scandal Is Bogus and Based on Climate Skeptics' Lies." *The Guardian*, February 10. Available at: http://www.guardian.co.uk/environment/2010/feb/09/climategate-bogus-sceptics-lies.

Pidgeon, N., and B. Fischoff. 2011. "The Role of Social and Decision Sciences in Communicating Uncertain Climate Risks." *Nature Climate Change* 1: 35–41.

Public's Priorities for 2010: Economy, Jobs, Terrorism. 2009. Washington, DC: Pew Research Center for the People & the Press. Available at: http://people-press.org/report/584/policy-priorities-2010.

Pooley, E. 2010. *The Climate Wars*. New York: Hyperion.

Rose, Jonathan. 2010. "Global Warming and Weather Psychology." *New York Times*, February 10. Available at: http://roomfordebate.blogs.nytimes.com/2010/02/11/global-warming-and-weather-psychology/.

Schneider, S. H. 2009. *Science as a Contact Sport*. Washington, DC: National Geographic Society.

State of the Climate National Overview: Annual 2011. 2011. National Oceanic and Atmospheric Administration: National Climate Data Center. Available at: http://www.ncdc.noaa.gov/sotc/national/.

Swim, Janet, Susan Clayton, Thomas Doherty, Robert Gifford, George Howard, Joseph Reese, Paul Stern, and Ellen Weber. 2009. "Psychology and Global Climate Change:

Addressing a Multi-faceted Phenomenon and Set of Challenges." American Psychological Association's Task Force on the Interface Between Psychology and Global Climate Change. Available at: http://www.apa.org/science/climate-change.

Weber, E. U. 2006. "Experience-based and Description-based Perceptions of Long-term Risk: Why Global Warming Does Not Scare Us (Yet)." *Climate Change* 77:1/2: 103–120.

RECYCLING

Recycling has become synonymous with going green in America. According to the U.S. Environmental Protection Agency (EPA), recycling is "the recovery of useful materials, such as paper, glass, plastic, and metals, from the trash to use to make new products, reducing the amount of new raw materials needed" (EPA, 2012).

Recycling is only one part of the three-pronged approach to sustainable consumer action: reduce, reuse, recycle. First, we should reduce our consumption: don't buy something unless we truly need it. Second, we should reuse things ourselves or buy at second-hand stores, on Craigslist, at garage sales, or consignment shops. Third, we must recycle materials rather than throw them away, which means sending them to sit in a landfill for hundreds of years. Perhaps most important is "closing the loop" and buying recycled goods. In other words, if you recycle, that only helps the environment if those items are made into something else, thus saving new resources from being used. Trucks could pick up tons of newspaper from our recycle bins, but if consumers do not demand recycled-content paper products, the loop is broken and the newspapers may just end up in a landfill anyway. Going one step further, the concept of zero waste is the "recycling of all materials back into nature or the marketplace in a manner that protects human health and the environment" (Zero Waste America, 2012).

There are several critiques of recycling, from both economic and ecological perspectives. When individual people drive their car several miles to drop off recyclables, they use gasoline and produce carbon dioxide (CO_2). Likewise, if the recycling truck must gather and transport materials some distance to sell them, this requires additional natural resources. Some people note that it is hypocritical to recycle your plastic (petroleum-based) milk jugs while continuing to drive a gas guzzling SUV that only gets 6 miles per gallon. And this criticism has merit, as Americans consider recycling to be their key environmentally friendly duty, yet continue to drive larger vehicles greater distances. Another criticism is the fact that indeed the chemical and plastics industries sponsor recycling events such as the annual America Recycles Day (America Recycles Day, 2012)—rather than initiating the shift toward biodegradable bottles or refillable containers (Reduce, Reuse, Refill! 2012). In terms of the economic efficiency of recycling, we must consider the value of the materials. In some regions there is no market for recycled materials, so they may actually end up in a landfill despite all our good efforts toward recycling. For example, the market for recycled plastics is tricky because there are many different kinds of plastics. We know about plastic number 6 or 1 and such, but there are actually hundreds of types of plastics.

Petroleum and natural gas are the raw materials used to make most plastics. To help with recycling, the industry created the triangle of three "chasing arrows" with the numbers 1 through 7 designated inside. So, there is #1 (PET [PETE], polyethylene terephthalate) and type #2 [HDPE, high-density polyethylene] which are both widely recycled. But this is not always the case. So #5 (PP, polypropylene) which is used in most wide-mouthed (yogurt) containers, is almost never recyclable. Also, #7 designates all "other" types of plastics, which are almost never recycled. It is very difficult to sort all these types of plastics, so it costs extra money to effectively recycle them. In fact, this should be a priority for environmentalists, because no plastic container producers use recycled plastic in their packaging. That means that other types of products must be created from our recycled soft drink bottles, as they will not be used to create a "new" soft drink bottle. In this case, that idea of closing the loop only comes true if the recycled bottle can be used to create another item. Luckily, some businesses have worked on this issue, so we now see carpet, fleece, and a few other items made from recycled plastic.

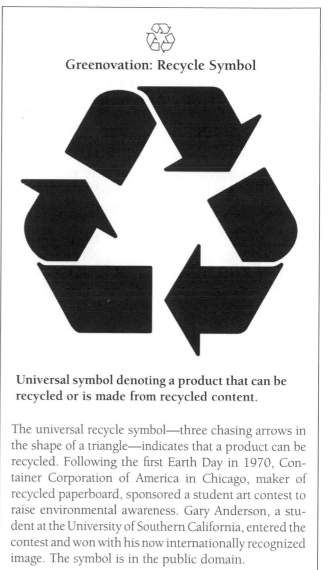

Greenovation: Recycle Symbol

Universal symbol denoting a product that can be recycled or is made from recycled content.

The universal recycle symbol—three chasing arrows in the shape of a triangle—indicates that a product can be recycled. Following the first Earth Day in 1970, Container Corporation of America in Chicago, maker of recycled paperboard, sponsored a student art contest to raise environmental awareness. Gary Anderson, a student at the University of Southern California, entered the contest and won with his now internationally recognized image. The symbol is in the public domain.

KIM KENNEDY WHITE

According to the EPA, Americans do recycle significant amounts of some materials each year, but we still consume and throw away a great deal as well. In 2010, the U.S. per capita waste generation was 4.43 pounds per person per day, giving us a total of 249.9 million tons per day. That year, the recycling rate was 34 percent, meaning that 85 million tons of materials were recycled.

Specifically, the EPA notes that the recycling rates by type of material were as follows: auto batteries: 96.2 percent, newspapers/mechanical papers: 71.6 percent; steel cans: 67.0 percent; yard trimmings: 57.5 percent; aluminum beer and soda cans: 49.6 percent; tires: 35.5 percent; glass containers: 33.4 percent; plastic #2: HDPE natural bottles: 27.5 percent; plastic #1: PET bottles and jars: 21.0 percent.

Even though there are some problems and barriers, recycling is an important aspect of U.S. environmentalism. But to truly go green, we must take action in all areas: reduce our use of resources, reuse what we already have, and recycle what we can. Also, remember to buy recycled goods so that recycled materials are in demand. The ultimate goal must be zero waste.

LESLIE A. DURAM

See also: Brief Comparison of State Laws on Electronics Recycling (documents); Electronic Waste Management, Executive Summary (documents); Electronic Waste Recycling Act, California (documents); Electronic Waste Recycling Act, New Jersey (documents); Model Electronic Recycling Legislation (documents); Reducing Holiday Waste (documents).

References

America Recycles Day. 2012. "Since 1997 . . ." Available at: http://americarecyclesday.org/
    Recycling 101. 2012. "The Recyclo-pedia." Available at: http://earth911.com/recycling/.
"Recycling Is Bullshit: Make Nov. 15 Zero Waste Day, Not America Recycles Day." 2008.
    Available at: http://www.treehugger.com/sustainable-product-design/recycling-is-bull
    shit-make-nov-15-zero-waste-day-not-america-recycles-day.html.
Reduce, Reuse, Refill. 2012. Dedicated to Promoting Refillable Beverage Containers. http://
    refillables.grrn.org/content/home
UN Environment Programme. 2012. "Resource Efficiency." Available at: http://www.unep
    .org/resourceefficiency/.
U.S. Environmental Protection Agency (EPA). 2012. "Waste." Resource Conservation.
    Reduce, Reuse, Recycle. Available at: http://www.epa.gov/osw/conserve/rrr/index.htm.
U.S. Environmental Protection Agency. N.d. "Wastes-Non-Hazardous Waste-Municipal
    Solid Waste. Available at: www.epa.gov/osw/nonhaz/municipal/.
Zero Waste America. 2012. "ZERO WASTE Is the Recycling of All Materials Back into
    Nature." Available at: http://www.zerowasteamerica.org/index.html.

RIVERS AND DAMS

Perceptions and political and public support for dams in the United States have changed significantly in the past 30 years (Graf, 2005). Once symbols of development and societal progress, dams are now concurrently seen as structures that impair natural river functioning. Dams have long been constructed for the myriad benefits they provide: flood control, water storage, ability to reallocate water across the landscape, and hydroelectric power generation. These benefits were used as key selling points for their construction and provided the stimulus for their proliferation across the landscape.

The United States is home to over 79,000 dams (U.S. Army Corps of Engineers, n. d.). In the western United States, only one major river, the Yampa, is undammed over its entire stretch. Most large dams were constructed between the 1920s and the 1960s, a period during which dam construction proposals were advanced on the grounds they provide jobs, water security, and an ability to increase the utility of the landscape. Dams allowed more expansive use of floodplains by providing greater floodwater control and allowed greater utilization of dry lands by providing a mechanism to deliver irrigation water.

In a time that predated in-depth environmental analysis, dams were viewed as highly coveted projects; their environmental costs were either not fully understood or were not adequately weighed in the decision-making process. Today dams are viewed for both their positive attributes, and for their drawbacks in reducing natural stream flows, creating barricades for fish migration, and altering ecosystems by changing water chemistry. These effects can lead to extinction of native aquatic species.

With the passage of the Endangered Species Act (ESA) in 1973, federal agencies were charged with ensuring any action they fund, permit, or carry-out "is not likely to jeopardize the continued existence" of a species listed on the threatened or endangered species lists. With this obligation, management of existing dams has changed. Because of the ESA, dam managers must consult with the U.S. Fish and Wildlife Service or National Oceanic and Atmospheric Administration (NOAA) Fisheries before proceeding with their actions. Dams must now be operated in ways that attempt to protect federally listed threatened or endangered species first. This is a sharp departure from the

Boulder Canyon Project (Hoover Dam)

The Boulder Canyon Project was approved for construction in 1928 with the passage of the Swing-Johnson Act. In addition to the excavation of the All-American Canal, the project called for the construction of a large dam by the U.S. Reclamation Service on the lower Colorado River. It would be used for hydroelectric power, flood control, water storage, and to supply water to farmers and municipalities in a number of different states. Although initial plans called for dam construction in Boulder Canyon, the site was moved to Black Canyon. The new site was eight miles downstream of the original site and was located approximately 30 miles from Las Vegas, Nevada. Deemed geologically inferior to the original site, Black Canyon was selected because it was less expensive to construct the dam there because of its proximity to transportation hubs, and the reservoir behind it promised to hold a greater water capacity. Despite the change in location, the project retained the Boulder Canyon designation. The dam was constructed between 1930 and 1936 and was at the time of completion the highest concrete arch dam in the country. The dam was named in honor of Herbert Hoover, who was serving as president of the United States at the time that dam construction commenced.

The idea of constructing the Boulder Canyon dam arose in the Imperial Valley of California during the early 1900s. Developers envisioned that water from the Colorado River could be used to irrigate the valley, thereby converting an arid region to land suitable for agricultural endeavors. Other western states opposed allowing California to construct a dam because they believed California's true aim was to control all of the Colorado River. It was not until the states of California, Colorado, Nevada, New Mexico, Utah, and Wyoming agreed to the Colorado River Compact in 1922 that plans for the Boulder Dam Project could move forward. Arizona was not a signatory to the compact due to its continued mistrust of California. When it became apparent that the federal government was going to construct the Boulder Canyon dam, Arizona tried to stop through the legal system what it viewed as a project beneficial solely to California. The U.S. Supreme Court ruled against Arizona in 1931.

The U.S. Reclamation Service hired Six Companies, Inc., to construct the dam. The corporation was made up of six of the leading construction companies in the United States. The dam they constructed was 726 feet high and 1,244 feet wide. One of the many engineering feats accomplished during construction was the hardening of the concrete. The amount of concrete used in the dam would have taken up to one century to harden naturally, during which time the dam would have failed due to fractures and fissures. Engineers embedded approximately 592 miles of cooling pipes into the dam structure, through which they passed refrigerated water at a rate of approximately three gallons a minute, in order to harden the concrete quickly (Billington & Jackson, 2006). Once the dam was completed, its reservoir was allowed to fill. The reservoir was named Lake Mead after Elwood Mead, who served as the commissioner of the U.S. Bureau of Reclamation from 1924 to 1936. Encompassing nearly 250 square miles, the lake is the largest human-made reservoir in the United States.

JOHN R. BURCH JR.

"benefits first" approach (i.e., if a dam's primary purpose was to provide irrigation water, that water was delivered to irrigators before the needs of in-stream species were considered) under which many dams were operated prior to the ESA.

The ESA has also reduced the likelihood of new dam construction. Dams change water quality parameters, including water temperature and water nutrient content, fragment available habitat for species, create barriers to migration for fish, and convert freely flowing rivers into a series of deeper still-water reservoirs, and they are likely to have negative impacts on listed species in the river system. These changes have led several notable researchers to pronounce that the era of new dams, at least momentarily, is over.

Dams have and will continue to allow development on floodplains, so removal of structures—even those know to be environmentally destructive—is difficult

Fish ladder at Bonneville Dam in Oregon. (Lori Howard/Dreamstime.com)

because they allow society to develop in areas that naturally are subject to flooding. Most dams either slow the flow of water or impound it at times when flow exceeds downstream demand or when flow reaches a level that would exceed the river's banks. Manipulating stream flow and confining water to the normal river channel prevent flooding and direct the river's kinetic energy into eroding the bottom of the stream channel. This results in the river's height lowering relative to its historic floodplain, which in turn allows utilization of areas of a floodplain that would be difficult to inhabit otherwise because of periodic flooding. At the same time, by reducing or eliminating flood events, dams threaten the long-term productivity of the floodplain in two primary ways: (1) they prevent sediment from the river from being deposited across the floodplain, replenishing nutrients; and (2) flooding allows for infiltration of groundwater in the floodplain, providing a storage of water for utilization by society or for replenishment of river flows during dry periods.

Today, dams are examined more critically than ever before. At the same time their benefit-cost structure is better understood, many dams have reached, or soon will reach, the age of their initial life expectancy. This age threshold may require a reevaluation of these structures, which could provide a catalyst for changing their design or operations to reduce their environmental harm. For example, if a dam must be renovated, fish passages or fish ladders can be added to allow for increased migration of aquatic species. Dam operations are an ongoing management challenge, and recently pilot studies have been done on several river systems, including the Colorado River through the Grand Canyon, to produce controlled flooding. During these events, water is released from upstream dams at a rate that allows for flooding, and the high flow of water can move sediment around the floodplain, reshaping the riparian corridor and restoring some of the natural floodplain processes and nutrient cycling.

Several small dams for which their costs outweighed their benefits have been removed or are slated for removal (e.g., Savage Rapids Dam and Gold Ray Dam on the Rogue River in Oregon, the Elwha River Dam in Washington, San Clemente Dam on the Carmel River in California). These removal projects will become interesting case studies that may help determine whether removal is a realistic option across a broader spectrum.

Dams exemplify the conundrum that is modern society; many dams are known to continually degrade riparian areas, suggesting they are not a sustainable management option. At the same time, the flood control and other benefits dams provide are needed because of the demand for these services, some of which is a direct result of the dam's initial construction.

MICHAEL PEASE

See also: Ocean Restoration and Conservation (Environment); Water and Air Purification (Science); Water Quality and Use (Environment).

References

Billington, David P., and Donald C. Jackson. 2006. *Big Dams of the New Deal Era: A Confluence of Engineering and Politics*. Norman: University of Oklahoma Press.

Boyer, Diane E., and Robert H. Webb. 2007. *Damming Grand Canyon: The 1923 USGS Colorado River Expedition*. Logan: Utah State University Press.

Dunar, Andrew J., and Dennis McBride. 1993. *Building Hoover Dam: An Oral History of the Great Depression*. New York: Twayne Publishers.

Fradkin, Philip L. 1996. *A River No More: The Colorado River and the West*, 2nd ed. Berkeley: University of California Press.

Graf, W. L. 2005. "Geomorphology and American Dams: The Scientific, Social, and Economic Context." *Geomorphology* 71: 3–26.

Kluger, James R. 1992. *Turning on Water with a Shovel: The Career of Elwood Mead*. Albuquerque: University of New Mexico Press.

Pisani, Donald J. 2002. *Water and American Government: The Reclamation Bureau, National Water Policy, and the West, 1902–1935*. Berkeley: University of California Press.

Reisner, Marc. 1986. *Cadillac Desert: The American West and Its Disappearing Water*. New York: Viking.

U.S. Army Corps of Engineers. National Inventory of Dams. Available at: http://geo.usace.army.mil/pgis/f?p=397:1:1203733021104354.

U.S. ENVIRONMENTAL PROTECTION AGENCY

Congress officially brought the U.S. Environmental Protection Agency (EPA) into existence in 1970, but its roots go back as far as 1962. The impetus for the EPA was a best-selling book by Rachel Carson, a bird watcher, titled *Silent Spring*. The carefully researched and wonderfully written work focused on the indiscriminate use of pesticides. Her book was to the environmental movement what Harriet Beecher Stowe's *Uncle Tom's Cabin* was to the abolitionist movement, and it brought together more than 14,000 people who formed a grassroots effort to protect the environment.

From 1962 to 1970, the environmental movement gained strength and support. In a nation disillusioned by the war in Vietnam and civil rights struggles, the environmental movement was something positive for people to concentrate on. Further, the environmental movement has had staying power in the politics and culture of the United States.

In May 1969, President Richard Nixon called for the establishment of a cabinet-level Environmental Quality Council and a Citizens' Advisory Committee on the environment. But he was criticized for the weakness of these agencies, so that December he appointed a White House committee to investigate whether there was a need for a separate environmental agency. In the meantime, Congress had developed a bill called the National Environmental Policy Act (NEPA) sponsored by Senator Gaylord Nelson (D.–Wis.). Nixon signed the act on New Year's Day 1970, establishing the EPA.

The popularity and support for EPA and the success of the first Earth Day celebration in April 1970 (when Americans of all backgrounds took part in activities that improved the environment) helped to strengthen a recommendation from Roy L. Ash, director of the Office of Management and Budget, who argued that the environmental agency must operate independently. Originally reluctant, Nixon eventually accepted the two arguments that if the environmental agency operated under another agency it would remain biased toward that agency and that such a situation would affect objectivity.

Satisfied, Nixon called for "a strong, independent agency." The mission of the EPA included establishing and enforcing environmental protection standards, conducting research, providing assistance to other environmental groups, and helping to develop and recommend new policies. One of the most important charges of the new EPA involved becoming the enforcement arm for federal environmental legislation.

Component parts of the EPA originated in the Department of Health, Education, and Welfare; the Food and Drug Administration; the Atomic Energy Commission; and various other agencies and departments. Nixon named William D. Ruckelshaus as the EPA's first administrator. Ruckelshaus immediately began gaining headlines and publicity for the fledging agency. Only nine days after opening its new offices, the EPA gave the mayors of three cities six months to bring their water supplies into compliance with government standards or come to court. By the end of its first year, the EPA had tackled other problems large and small. It ended the year with the Clean Air Act of 1970, an effort to reduce polluting emissions from U.S. automobiles, among other things. The EPA's mission and its focus of protecting human health and the environment have remained stable and constant throughout its 39-year history. In 2010, the EPA employed about 18,000 people and has

Greenovator: William Ruckelshaus

William Ruckelshaus served in a number of governmental capacities but is best known as the first administrator of the U.S. Environmental Protection Agency (EPA). He was appointed to the position by President Richard Nixon in December 1970 and served until 1973. After a stint in the private sector (1973–1983), he was called back to duty by President Ronald Reagan to try and rescue the fledgling EPA, thus becoming the only person to have been in charge of the agency on more than one occasion.

William Doyle Ruckelshaus was born in Indianapolis, Indiana, on July 24, 1932. Ruckelshaus received his undergraduate degree from Princeton (cum laude) in 1957 and a law degree from Harvard in 1960 (EPA, 2009). An attorney by trade, Ruckelshaus had no experience in environmental matters prior to assuming the position of EPA administrator. He had, however, worked in the Civil Division of the Justice Department under the eye of Attorney General John Mitchell, who recommended him for the job (Switzer, 2004, 74).

Ruckelshaus pushed a "command and control" approach to environmental protection. Setting high standards and aggressively enforcing them seemed to be the right approach for mitigating years of environmental degradation. Among the most celebrated successes of the young agency was the ban on the pesticide DDT (dichloro-diphenyl-trichloroethane; EPA, 2009). During his first term with the EPA, the agency established credibility, and employee morale was high. During his second term, Ruckelshaus introduced the concept of risk management, which has been a driving force within the agency ever since (Andrews, 2006, 215).

In addition to his role with the EPA, Ruckelshaus served with the Justice Department twice (the second time as deputy attorney general, becoming a part of the famous "Saturday Night Massacre" when he refused to comply with Richard Nixon's order to fire Special Prosecutor Archibald Cox) and even headed the Federal Bureau of Investigation. After leaving public office, Ruckelshaus went back into private law in Seattle, Washington. He maintains an active agenda and continues to work on environmental issues, having been appointed to special projects by presidents William Clinton and George W. Bush and Washington governors Gary Locke and Christine Gregoire (EPA, 2009).

JEFFREY ASHLEY AND AARON HACKER

an annual budget of more than $10 billion. As such, it ranks as one of the largest federal agencies, and its regulatory functions are emulated by similar agencies at the state level.

LISA A. ENNIS

See also: Environmental Justice (Activism); Green Movement (Activism); National Environmental Policy Act (documents); National Park Service (Environment); Rachel Carson's *Silent Spring* (Arts); Summary of Recent Federal Agency Environmental Education Projects (documents).

References

Andrews, Richard N. L. 2006. "Risk-Based Decision Making: Policy, Science, and Politics." In Norman J. Vig and Michael E. Kraft, eds., *Environmental Policy: New Directions for the Twenty-First Century*, Washington, DC: CQ Press.

Switzer, Jacqueline Vaughn. 2004. *Environmental Politics: Domestic and Global Dimensions*. Belmont, CA: Thomson.

U.S. Environmental Protection Agency (EPA). 2009. "Agency Administrators." Available at: http://www.epa.gov/history/admin/agency.

WATER QUALITY AND USE

Water use and water quality exhibit a symbiotic relationship. As human populations and per capita demands for water have increased, so too have strains on freshwater supplies (Vitousek et al., 1997). These strains increasingly threaten the overall health of ecosystems, with pronounced and localized impacts on specific resources, particularly aquatic species. Along with the increased strain on supplies is an increase in threats as a result of degraded water quality.

Water quality issues are directly linked to water quantity issues. A quaint, half-joking saying in the water resources field sums up this linkage nicely, "dilution is the solution to pollution." This saying is overly simplistic and a dangerous philosophy, but dilution is key for ameliorating many water quality impairments. As such, threats to overall water quality can be lumped into overly broad categories, issues with discharge of pollutants, and issues with water allocation. Substantial overlap occurs because water use will frequently impact water quality in both manners.

The Clean Water Act breaks water pollution into two broad categories: point-source and non-point-source pollution. Point-source pollutants are those that enter watercourses from a discrete point, a pipe for example. These are frequently the result of industrial or municipal uses—water reentering a river from a factory. Congress, in passing the 1977 amendments to the Clean Water Act, called for an abolishment of discharging pollutants into "waters of the United States" by 1985. This congressional mandate has been ignored because it simply was not attainable—some deposition of pollutants into watercourses is necessary for industrial processes. Instead of an outright ban, the United States regulates these uses via a permit system. Through this permit process the types, quantities, and concentrations of

Dredging equipment lines the river above Ft. Edward, New York, during PCB cleanup of the Hudson River in 2009. General Electric plants in Fort Edward and neighboring Hudson Falls discharged wastewater containing PCBs for decades before the popular lubricant was banned in 1977. (Dennis Donohue/ Shutterstock.com)

pollutants are regulated by the U.S. Environmental Protection Agency (EPA). As a result of this permitting, point-source pollution management has been broadly labeled a success; while point-source pollutants still represent a concerning impact on river systems, the permitting process has improved water quality over pre-Clean Water Act levels, despite the increased populations that use, live along, and rely on these waters.

Non-point-source pollution is any pollution without a determined place of origin. These pollutants are more varied in source and more difficult to manage. This pollution can be of both natural and human sources. For example, exposed soil can runoff during a thunderstorm and enter a watercourse, increasing water turbidity and salinity. These water impairments can threaten aquatic species if allowed to reach high levels. But treatment or management of non-point-source pollutants is difficult because of their disparate sources. To combat non-point-source pollution, the EPA established a program developing maximum allowable levels for individual water impairments—if streams come near these levels, it indicates a need to treat the cause of the pollution.

Since the source may not be clear and may involve numerous locations, treatment options for non-point-source pollution can be complex. Numerous local watershed organizations have begun organizing community-based projects to combat

Greenovator: John D. Dingell Jr.

Democratic Congressman and Chairman of the Committee on Energy and Commerce John D. Dingell Jr. of Michigan has historically functioned as a key advocate for energy conservation and environmental protection legislation.

Dingell's proactive role in the Clean Water Act of 1972 aimed to legally cease practices of the emission and disposal of pollutants into the navigable waters. Nevertheless, the Clean Water Act continues to face resistance due to its ambiguity in defining the parameters of navigable waters and the interests of inversely affected industries.

As the drafter of the 1972 Clean Air Act, Dingell established the foundation for progressive environmental laws expanding beyond the traditions of common-law nuisance from health-threatening industrial activities. By-products of the legislation include nationalizing standards for maximum levels of pollutants such as ozone, lead, and carbon monoxide (Bagley & Savage, 2006). Preserving the visibility in major national parks and requiring the EPA to raise gas emission standards also derived from the enacted law.

During his 50-plus years of service, the 2009 economic crisis involving Ford, General Motors, and Chrysler, all headquartered in Michigan, produced the greatest political strain for Dingell, despite an overall politically successful career. He has a record of balancing environmental goals with protecting the automotive industry. Dingell's work in the House of Representatives has produced a record that has pleased neither the auto industry nor the environmental community.

MICHAEL D. ROYSTER

non-point-source pollution. Many successful projects simultaneously combat non-point-source pollution and improve overall watershed conditions. For example, installing erosion-control structures on steep hills reduces erosion and improves groundwater recharge. Reseeding nonvegetated lands with native grasses and plants can increase soil stability while providing habitat, and planting native plants such as willows in riparian corridors can reduce flooding, reduce water temperature, provide habitat, and reduce erosion.

As non-point-source pollution is studied with greater intensity, agriculture is frequently critiqued for its contributions to water quality degradation. Farmers apply nitrogen and phosphorus-based fertilizers on their lands and crops in order to increase yields. In addition, fungicides, pesticides, and herbicides are added to treat or protect these crops. Precipitation and wind move these substances from agricultural fields to watercourses, where they lead to water impairment. For example, nitrogen-based fertilizers that make it into a watercourse can lead to algal blooms and a subsequent decrease in water quality. In the midwestern United States, this problem is so severe it has lead to a "dead zone" in the Gulf of Mexico where no aquatic life can live during the summer months because of a reduction in dissolved oxygen levels.

In addition to pollution issues, total water use is a concern for most regions of the United States. Once an issue thought to be confined to the western United States, the 2006–2007 drought in the southeastern United States showed that even previously adequate water supplies may periodically be insufficient because of increased population and increased drought severity and frequency. The problem may be compounded because supply-side options may not be available to deal with these shortages. Vitousek et al. (1997) noted that over half of the world's "accessible surface fresh water" is put to use by humans, so any additional withdrawals of water for municipal or agricultural uses will likely impact riparian ecosystems.

Aggressive water conservation programs funded by states and municipalities have led to a decrease in per-capita water use. Many western municipalities offer rebates and other economic incentives for installation of low-flow toilets, high-efficiency washing machines, and converting grass lawns to xeriscaped (dry-land) landscaping. Through these types of efforts, the city of Albuquerque, New Mexico, reports a reduction of use from 249 gallons per person per day in 1990 to 193 gallons per person per day in 2003. This shows substantial progress. Even so, per-capita water use can be reduced further. Santa Fe, New Mexico, has more aggressive water conservation programs and economic programs and claims per-capita water use levels under 100 gallons per day. The city's water conservation page also purports a reduction in per-capita water use of approximately 40 percent between 1995 and 2009.

Like issues related to our energy use, public outreach related to water resource issues, including education about water conservation techniques, is a key component of demand management (Dziegielewski, 2006). More informed and more efficient water use may ultimately be the keys to protecting ecosystems from issues related to water pollution and water use.

MICHAEL PEASE

See also: Bottled Drinking Water Standards (documents); Bottled Water Report Summary from the Government Accountability Office (documents); Natural Resources Conservation Service Watershed and Easement Program (documents); Ocean Restoration and Conservation (Environment); Water and Air Purification (Science); Water Quality and Use (Environment).

References

Bagley, Constance E., and Diane W. Savage. 2006. *Managers and the Legal Environment: Strategies for the 21st Century*. Mason, OH: South-Western College.

Biographical Directory of the U.S. Congress. "Congressman Dingell's Work Protecting and Preserving the Environment." Available at: http://www.house.gov/dingell/issue_environment.shtml.

Broder, John M., and Micheline Maynard. 2009. "As Political Winds Shift Detroit Charts New Course." *New York Times*, May 19; revised May 27, 2009.

Dziegielewski, B. 2003. "Strategies for Managing Water Demand." *Water Resources Update* 126: 29–39.

Sangre de Cristo Water Division, Water Conservation Office. Available at: http://www.water2conserve.com/.

Vitousek, P. M., H. A. Mooney, J. Lubchenco, and J. M. Melillo. 1997. "Human Domination of Earth's Ecosystems." *Science* 277: 494–499.

WILDLIFE, CONSERVATION AND PRESERVATION ORGANIZATIONS

Wildlife conservation and preservation organizations are groups devoted to the protection, management, or restoration of wild animal and plant populations. Although the term *wildlife* includes both flora and fauna, it is most commonly used to refer to wild animal species. In the United States and throughout the world, both governmental agencies and nongovernmental organizations (NGOs) have been instrumental in increasing public awareness of threats to wildlife and protecting wildlife through legislation and treaties such as the Endangered Species Act (ESA; 1973) and the Convention on International Trade in Endangered Species of Wild Fauna and Flora (CITES; 1975). Key U.S. federal agencies for wildlife conservation and management include the Fish and Wildlife Service (FWS), the National Parks Service (NPS), the U.S. Forest Service (USFS), and the Bureau of Land Management (BLM). While wildlife is the central focus of only the FWS, all of these agencies are involved with managing public lands, including the plants and animals that use these lands for habitat. Fish and wildlife in the United States are held in the public trust, to be used by all citizens for noncommercial purposes. Thus, the role of government agencies is to protect wildlife to maintain a range of population levels in perpetuity. Some citizens have found federal protection and management to be insufficient or flawed, and thus many NGOs have formed to lobby for legislation, support wildlife conservation and preservation on lands under private ownership, and educate the public about threats to wildlife populations.

Although conservation and preservation organizations both endeavor to maintain wildlife populations and habitats for future generations, there is a key difference between the terms. *Conservation* generally refers to the management or wise use of nature, while *preservation* emphasizes the protection of wild nature from human use or impact. For example, Ducks Unlimited, an organization founded by duck hunters to conserve waterfowl habitat, exemplifies the conservation approach, while the Sierra Club, founded by John Muir to protect wildness, demonstrates the legacy of preservation in its efforts to set aside land as "wilderness." Among government agencies, conservation is most commonly associated with the USFS and the management of national forest lands for multiple uses (timber extraction, recreation, wildlife habitat, etc.). Most state fish and wildlife agencies are also relatively conservation oriented. Conversely, the NPS reflects the legacy of preservation and the idea that it is possible and desirable to set aside land with minimal or no human influence.

In the United States, the wildlife conservation and preservation movement began in the later half of the 19th century and was heavily influenced by the romantic movement in art and literature, including Henry David Thoreau's writings and Albert Bierstadt's paintings of western landscapes. Sportsmen were essential to early conservation and preservation organizations, as they were among the first to notice declines in fish and game populations and sought to protect wildlife and their habitats. Groups pressed state governments to address the issue of wildlife conservation, and toward the end of the 19th century, many states had established hunting and fishing regulations, though they were not always enforced (Knight &

Bates, 1995). One example of a sportsmen's conservation group is the Boone and Crockett Club, founded by Theodore Roosevelt in 1887 to promote ethical hunting and the establishment of wildlife reserves. While hunting in the American West, Roosevelt witnessed firsthand the growing scarcity of game such as bison. This experience shaped his views on wildlife conservation, and he went on to become one of the most conservation-minded presidents in history (Nash, 1982).

In the late 1800s, the wildlife conservation movement was motivated in large part by the slaughter of birds for their feathers, which were commonly used in women's fashion. The Audubon Society, founded by George Bird Grinnell in 1886, was one of the first groups that sought to protect wild birds and their eggs. Women were particularly influential in the formation and growth of the Audubon Society. Two prominent Bostonians, Harriet Hemenway and Minna Hall, founded the Massachusetts Audubon Society and encouraged local women to boycott hats and other accessories made with feathers. The Audubon Society was instrumental in the passage of federal and state bird protection legislation, including the Lacey Act (1900), which outlawed the interstate transport of game that was killed in violation of any state law, and the New York State Audubon Plumage Law (1910), which prohibited the sale of feathers from threatened species. Two other early successes include the establishment of the first federal wildlife refuge on Florida's Pelican Island by President Theodore Roosevelt in 1903 and the 1916 Migratory Bird Treaty signed by the United States and Canada. These accomplishments set a precedent for federal involvement in the conservation and preservation of wildlife and natural resources and represent the development and expansion of an environmental lobby in the United States in the early 20th century (Graham & Buchheister, 1992).

Numerous other wildlife organizations were formed in the first half of the 20th century. Many were dedicated to protecting or managing wildlife, while others, like the Ecological Society of America (founded in 1915), the National Wildlife Federation (founded in 1936), and the New York Zoological Society (founded in 1895), aimed to promote the study of wildlife and increase public interest in ecological concerns. Due to these efforts, the American public, particularly the upper classes, became increasingly aware of threats to wild animal species during this time. Several prominent New Yorkers, including Theodore Roosevelt, founded the New York Zoological Society, which is now the Wildlife Conservation Society (WCS), and the group managed the New York Zoological Park, which is now the Bronx Zoo. William Temple Hornaday, director of the society in the early 1990s, published several noteworthy books on wildlife, including *Our Vanishing Wild Life: Its Extermination and Preservation* (1913). Through these publications, Hornaday and fellow society members made the endangerment and extinction of wild animal species common knowledge. In 1905, Hornaday and Roosevelt again collaborated to form the American Bison Society, with the goal to reintroduce bison, which were on the brink of extinction, to the Great Plains and American West. The efforts of the American Bison Society were tremendously successful, and due to the reintroductions, the species was no longer in danger of extinction by the 1930s. Now, nearly a century later, there are stable populations of wild bison in the American West, but they are also commonly raised as livestock. Interestingly, the WCS recently relaunched the American Bison Society to protect and restore populations of wild bison in the wake of new threats like urban growth and management as livestock.

Despite the growing awareness and attention to wildlife conservation and preservation, wildlife habitat continued to decline as the western United States was settled and urban centers of the east and midwest expanded in the early to mid-1900s. Still, at the urging of wildlife groups like the Audubon Society, the federal government passed more laws designed to protect or conserve wildlife and habitat and established more federal wildlife refuges. In 1940, the FWS was formed by joining two previous agencies, the U.S. Biological Survey and the Bureau of Fisheries, to manage the burgeoning National Wildlife Refuge System. While the main objective of the FWS was and remains to protect and conserve wildlife, their management directives are often varied and vague. In practice, the FWS not only protects wildlife for its own intrinsic value, but also manages populations for hunting and provides recreational sites for citizens (Knight & Bates, 1995). In this way, FWS and partner organizations such as the Partners for Fish and Wildlife, Sport Fishing and Boating Partnership Council, Trout Unlimited, and Ducks Unlimited reflect the continued influence of sportsmen and sportswomen on conservation policy and practices.

During the environmentalist movement of the 1960s and 1970s, many new wildlife conservation and preservation NGOs were created, while mainstream groups like the Audubon Society expanded to address broader environmental issues. Unlike the conservation movement led by sportsmen and other relatively wealthy citizens around the turn of the century, this movement was more broad based and had concerns beyond wildlife and species extinctions (Kline, 2011). Wildlife habitat remained significant, but organizations were frequently concerned about new threats to wildlife such as pesticides and other environmental toxins. Around this time, several prominent wildlife organizations formed and expanded, including the Defenders of Wildlife and World Wildlife Fund (WWF).

Founded in 1947, Defenders of Wildlife was originally titled the Defenders of Furbearers and sought to protect fur-bearing species such as coyotes from traps and hunting. Over time, the Defenders of Wildlife grew to include all wildlife, with a focus on mammalian predators such as wolves and bears. In the 1990s, the organization was instrumental in the grey wolf reintroduction in the northern Rockies of Wyoming, Montana, and Idaho. They helped to raise the funds to support wolf reintroduction, and the organization's staff assisted with efforts in the field. The success of wolf reintroduction has, in fact, been so successful that the grey wolf was removed from the endangered species list in 2011. As of 2008, the wolf population of the greater Yellowstone area included over 1,000 animals. Despite this success, Defenders of Wildlife has continued to press for wolves to remain legally protected, much to the chagrin of landowners and ranchers who suffer economic losses when wolves prey upon livestock. To generate greater support for wolves, Defenders of Wildlife has provided compensation to some ranchers who experienced predation. Although conflicts between ranchers and environmentalists over wolf reintroduction have at times been heated, Defenders of Wildlife states that ranchers and ranchlands actually help to protect the wolves by providing habitat, and thus it is

Rami, a gray wolf from Mission Wolf, stands on a table during a news conference as handler Kent Weber talks about the animal during a news conference in Broomfield, Colorado in 2000, staged by the Defenders of Wildlife. (AP Photo/David Zalubowski)

beneficial to ensure that ranchers keep ranching rather than develop their land. Despite this seemingly pro-ranching perspective, many consider Defenders of Wildlife a radical environmental organization. The organization has taken a multi-pronged approach to wolf reintroduction and conservation, by working with and compensating ranchers, lobbying the government for greater legislation, educating the public about the ecological benefits of wolves, and collaborating with other NGOs and governmental agencies such as FWS and state conservation agencies. As of 2011, Defenders of Wildlife reports that it has close to 1 million members, reflecting the rise of environmental consciousness and interest in wildlife in the nation over the past century.

Like Defenders of Wildlife, WWF was founded in the post–World War II era. In 1961, a group of prominent European businessmen and scientists convened to raise funds for global conservation projects. Though initially a European organization, it quickly grew to include the United States, and the U.S. part of the WWF now operates as an independent organization. In its early years, WWF raised funds for numerous individual wildlife conservation and preservation projects. In the 1970s, however, it began to focus its attention on broader-scale projects that aimed to conserve biodiversity across regions or even biomes. Instead of emphasizing local, single-species projects, WWF proposed transformative changes in the way organizations and governments approach wildlife conservation and preservation. Like

Defenders of Wildlife, WWF rapidly developed into a powerful political entity that lobbies governments, collaborates with international organizations such as the United Nations, and raises billions of dollars for environmental projects each year. Both WWF and Defenders of Wildlife represent the growth of a powerful environmental lobby in the United States that has become increasingly associated with the preservation of wilderness and distinct from the earlier hunting and fishing emphasis of conservation. They also reflect the increasing emphasis on international-, national-, or regional-scale conservation practices rather than local projects. WWF and other global conservation groups have been criticized, however, for excluding locals from conservation preserves and failing to address the rights of indigenous peoples (Dowie, 2009).

Indeed, as many large organizations began to focus on broad-scale wildlife projects and became more policy oriented in the past few decades of the 20th century, other organizations arose to address more specific concerns that deal with particular locations or single species. Similarly, as the environmental movement became increasingly associated with preservation of wilderness, smaller organizations that merged conservation and hunting or fishing began to reappear. Examples of organizations with relatively specific foci include the National Wild Turkey Federation, Trout Unlimited, Quail Unlimited, the Rocky Mountain Elk Foundation, the Appalachian Bear Rescue Organization, Friends of Great Smoky Mountains National Park, and the United Anglers of Casa Grande High School. Although these groups generally deal with fairly specific wildlife concerns, the scale and scope of their projects vary greatly. While groups like Trout Unlimited deal with cold freshwater fisheries throughout the United States and Canada, other groups, such as Friends of Great Smoky Mountains National Park and the United Anglers of Casa Grande High School, are more limited in their geographic foci.

The story of the United Anglers of Casa Grande High School exemplifies the important role of local grassroots organizations in protecting wildlife and restoring habitats. In 1983, a group of high school students in Petaluma, California, organized the group to improve the habitat of degraded Adobe Creek and save its native steelhead trout population. With the help of a teacher, students removed waste from the river, planted trees to improve riparian habitat, rescued fish from poor habitats, and even created their own fish hatchery. In 2003, 20 years after the formation of the group, 60 steelhead trout returned to Adobe Creek to breed (United Anglers of Casa Grande High School, 2011). Although the focus of the group is relatively narrow, it has been successful in both improving Adobe Creek's fish habitat and raising awareness of stream pollution largely through the efforts of high school student volunteers. Groups such as the United Anglers of Casa Grande High School demonstrate the continued importance of grassroots organizations that focus on improving their local wildlife habitats and environments. They also reflect growing interest among young people in conservation of wildlife and other eco-friendly practices.

Although many of the largest wildlife conservation and preservation organizations such as WWF and Defenders of Wildlife do not extol the benefits of hunting, there are a number of somewhat smaller organizations that view hunting and conservation as, if not synonymous with, at least compatible. The National Wild

Turkey Federation (NWTF), for example, was founded in 1973 with two main foci: conservation and hunting. NWTF seeks to maintain hunting heritage, while also partnering with state and federal agencies to improve turkey habitat on both public and private lands. Partnerships with government wildlife agencies or with other conservation groups have become standard for many conservation and preservation groups, in part because partnerships can provide cash-strapped agencies with resources to plan and carry out conservation projects, while wildlife agencies provide organizations with public land, knowledgeable staff, and the opportunity to influence management practices and policies. Groups like NWTF rely heavily on volunteers to carry out conservation projects and educate the public about the wild turkey and its habitat. According to the organization, the turkey population in North America has flourished from about 1 million to over 7 million birds since the group was founded. NWTF has also been instrumental in encouraging women to participate in hunting and conservation. By linking conservation and recreation, NWTF and like-minded organizations attract a segment of the U.S. population that may not associate themselves with the broader environmental movement. Because some Americans consider groups such as WWF and Defenders of Wildlife radical or leftist, these groups often fail to attract politically moderate or conservative citizens. Based in the southern United States and emphasizing the nation's hunting heritage, NWTF disentangles conservation from politics and suggests that wildlife conservation is compatible with forms of recreation such as hunting.

CHRISTINE BIERMANN

See also: Wildlife, Impact of Eco-Friendly Practices (Environment).

References

Dowie, Mark. 2009. *Conservation Refugees: The Hundred-Year Conflict Between Global Conservation and Native Peoples*. Cambridge, MA: Massachusetts Institute of Technology Press.

Graham, Frank, and Carl W. Buchheister. 1992. *The Audubon Ark: A History of the National Audubon Society*. Austin: University of Texas Press.

Hornaday, William Temple. 1913. *Our Vanishing Wild Life: Its Extermination and Preservation*. New York: Clark and Fritts.

Kline, Benjamin. 2011. *First Along the River: A Brief History of the U.S. Environmental Movement*. New York: Rowman & Littlefield.

Knight, Richard L., and Sarah F. Bates, eds. 1995. *A New Century of Natural Resources Management*. Washington, DC: Island Press.

Nash, Roderick. 1982. *Wilderness and the American Mind*. New Haven: Yale University Press.

United Anglers of Casa Grande High School. 2011. Available at: http://uacg.org.

WILDLIFE, IMPACT OF ECO-FRIENDLY PRACTICES AND AWARENESS

Over the past century, the American public has become increasingly aware of the loss of wildlife habitat and other threats to wild animal and plant species. Awareness has increased in part through the efforts of conservation and preservation organizations such as the Sierra Club and the Audubon Society. The rise of ecology and conservation biology as integrative academic disciplines has also been instrumental in increasing knowledge of biodiversity loss and taking steps to protect wildlife from threats such as habitat loss, pollution, and overhunting. As awareness has increased, many individuals and institutions have adopted eco-friendly practices and policies, which in turn have led to wildlife conservation successes. At the same time, advances in engineering have helped spur new eco-friendly technologies. Despite these new eco-friendly practices and conservation success stories, biodiversity loss has not been completely reversed or mitigated. Indeed, human activity continues to threaten wildlife habitat and populations, though many Americans are working to halt these threats. This overview outlines several areas in which eco-friendly practices and awareness have impacted wildlife in the United States: hunting, fishing, dam removal and engineering, invasive species management, agriculture, outdoor recreation, cultural events, household products, and land management.

Outdoor sports such as hunting and fishing were one of the first areas in which Americans adopted conservation-oriented practices. State regulations on fish and game were established in many states around the turn of the 20th century. During this time, the first wildlife or hunting reserves were created as well, and groups such as the Boone and Crockett Club advocated for ethical and fair sportsmanship. Later, as the 20th century progressed, the disciplines of ecology and conservation biology influenced new fishing and hunting regulations, including the creation of bag limits based on population size and carrying capacity, hunting and fishing seasons, and sex- and size-selective harvesting. An example of this is the establishment of different hunting seasons for male and female specimens of the same species to allow reproduction to occur.

The freshwater fisheries of the United States have also benefited from new eco-friendly regulations and practices, coupled with direct efforts by landowners and volunteer organizations such as Trout Unlimited to restore or improve fish habitat. Specific examples include the removal of dams, the creation of fish ladders to help migrating fish swim past barriers such as dams or culverts, the increasing popularity of catch-and-release fishing, the use of barbless hooks, and the discontinuation of felt-sole wading boots. Many of these factors have already had tremendous effects on ecosystems and wildlife. In Maine's Kennebec River, for example, the removal of Edwards Dam caused alewives, Atlantic salmon, shortnosed sturgeon, and several other fish species to return to the river (Hart et al., 2002). The construction of fish ladders and spillways represents another success for aquatic ecosystems, as ladders allow migrating fish such as salmon to swim upstream to spawn. In the Columbia River's Bonneville Dam, for example, the U.S. Army Corps of Engineers constructed a fish ladder and spillways to allow salmon and steelhead trout to move upstream. Although these efforts are necessary to maintain wild fish populations, it is worth noting that fish ladders and spillways are not always an ultimate solution, as fish are impacted by numerous other factors, such as disease, habitat alteration, and climate change.

Eco-friendly practices among anglers have also impacted fish and aquatic ecosystems. For example, catch-and-release fishing with barbless hooks has grown in popularity in recent years, particularly in regions with highly esteemed trout fisheries, such as Montana and Wyoming. Yellowstone National Park mandates the use of barbless hooks to reduce injuries and fatalities to fish. Although this represents a top-down strategy in which law dictates individuals' behaviors, many anglers choose to practice catch-and-release fishing with barbless hooks regardless of regulations. Practices such as these have been effective in protecting fish populations from recreational fishing, though overfishing is still an issue for many commercial fisheries.

Both aquatic and terrestrial systems have also been the target of interventions to protect native species and eradicate invasive nonnative or introduced species. As globalization has progressed, numerous plant and animal species have ended up far from their native ranges. Invasive species have thus become a primary focus for many scientists, land managers, and citizens. In many cases where introduced species have no native competitors and are able to outcompete native species, management agencies, conservation organizations, and volunteers have made concerted efforts to eradicate nonnative invasives. The National Park Service (NPS), for example, has poisoned several streams in Great Smoky Mountains National Park with piscicides, chemicals that are toxic to fish. Their goal is to kill both nonnative rainbow trout and native brook trout in these streams in order to allow brook trout to later repopulate the area. Similarly, in Yellowstone National Park, the NPS is attempting to eradicate the nonnative lake trout, which has outcompeted the native Yellowstone cutthroat trout and caused its population to dwindle. Fishing regulations in the area now mandate that lake trout caught by anglers are *not* released back into the waterways. The NPS has also implanted some of the nonnative lake trout with radio transmitters so that scientists can determine the location of spawning beds in order to kill large quantities of eggs before they hatch (Johnson, 2011). The lake trout has not only outcompeted the Yellowstone cutthroat, but it has also negatively impacted numerous other species of wildlife (e.g., bears, eagles, egrets) that depend on the Yellowstone cutthroat trout as a food source. These examples from two national parks demonstrate the growing awareness of invasive species and desire to eradicate them using whatever means possible. Further, though, these cases illustrate that eco-friendly practices are not always as straightforward as they seem. Practices or policies designed to improve wildlife habitats or populations at times rely on chemicals and other technologies that harm some species while benefiting others.

Eco-friendly agricultural practices have also benefited wildlife. With the rising demand for organically grown produce, some farmers have turned to techniques such as crop rotation, composting, no-till farming, and biological pest control rather than using synthetic pesticides and fertilizers. These techniques and the elimination of pesticides and fertilizers have been found to lead to greater biodiversity on organic farmland than conventional farmland. Perhaps the best example of the way agricultural practices have impacted wildlife is the case of DDT (dichloro-diphenyl-trichloroethane). In the 1940s and 1950s, DDT was commonly used as an agricultural insecticide. In 1962, however, Rachel Carson's *Silent Spring* began to raise serious questions about the potential hazards of DDT to wildlife and human health. A decade later, the U.S. Environmental Protection Agency (EPA) banned the use of DDT as an insecticide. The effects of this have been tremendous for wildlife. DDT was not only directly toxic to numerous insects and aquatic species, but it also caused many avian species to develop thinner eggshells that could not support growing birds. Because of this, the widespread use of DDT led to enormous declines in bird populations, including the bald eagle, brown pelican, and peregrine falcon, among others. Since DDT was banned, populations have recovered with the help of the Endangered Species Act (1973) and reintroduction efforts. Bald eagles, for example, have been removed from both the endangered and threatened species lists, and the bald eagle population in the lower 48 states has rebounded from less than 500 breeding pairs in 1963 to approximately 10,000 breeding pairs in 2007.

The rise of a "Leave No Trace" wilderness ethic in American culture has also impacted wildlife. "Leave No Trace" originated in the 1960s and 1970s as a set of principles and practices designed to reduce the impact of outdoor recreationists on natural systems. The U.S. Forest Service in particular emphasized minimal impact practices in response to the growing interest in backcountry camping and wilderness recreation during the 1970s and 1980s. The burgeoning wilderness recreation industry as well as organizations such as the Boy Scouts of America and the National Outdoor Leadership School have helped to increase awareness of "Leave No Trace" principles among the general public. Since then, the idea of a "Leave No Trace" wilderness ethic has come to include practices such as packing out all garbage, keeping distance from wildlife, choosing not to build campfires, minimizing camping site alterations, staying on trails to curtail erosion, and burying excrement. Although there are few data on the impacts of these specific practices on wildlife, it is generally accepted that such practices reduce human-wildlife encounters. This is key to the management of many species, particularly large predators such as bears. When bears or other species become habituated to humans or human food, the likelihood of human-wildlife encounters increases and wildlife are also more likely to be injured or killed by vehicles or euthanized by wildlife managers due to habituation to humans (Gunther & Wyman, 2008). Although the "Leave No Trace" ethic has practical value for maintaining the integrity of wildlife populations, it also relies on a wilderness ideal that may be impractical for most landscapes in today's human-dominated world (Turner, 2003).

Although the most publicized eco-friendly practices for wildlife tend to be broad and policy based, many households and businesses are making relatively small changes that collectively have far-reaching impacts for wildlife. Such changes relate to the proper disposal of households goods and the adoption of more eco-friendly cultural traditions. Several states and municipalities, for example, have established used oil recycling programs to encourage the safe disposal of used motor oils. When oil is disposed of improperly, it can pollute waterways and seep into the groundwater supply. Because motor oil contains high concentrations of toxic heavy metals, it is very dangerous to wildlife, particularly aquatic species. Latex rubber balloons are another household product whose effects on wildlife are becoming common knowledge. When helium balloons are released into the atmosphere, they often find their way to the oceans, where they suffocate, choke, and kill marine animals. In particular, balloons are often mistaken for jellyfish by predators such as sea turtles and fish. The strings or ribbons on balloons also pose a risk for wildlife, as they can entangle and trap birds and other species. In response to the increasing awareness of the risks associated with balloons, many states have banned mass launches of balloons, and people are increasingly choosing more eco-friendly ways of celebrating or commemorating occasions, such as planting trees. Weddings are another cultural event in which Americans have adopted eco-friendly practices. Throwing rice at the newlywed couple used to be common practice at weddings, but in recent years concerns have been expressed about rice posing a danger to wildlife, particularly birds. Some claim that uncooked rice harms the stomachs of birds and can ultimately kill them. Interestingly, ornithologists dispute this, claiming that many birds eat wild rice crops with no ill effects. This case demonstrates both the desire of many Americans to adopt eco-friendly practices and the confusion and misinformation surrounding the protection of wildlife.

Another way that citizens have attempted to protect or conserve wildlife is through land ownership and management practices. Many individual landowners attempt to improve wildlife habitat on their land, often in order to attract animals for viewing or hunting. While in the past land was often considered solely in terms of the value of resources such as timber, woodland owners today frequently manage for multiple uses, including timber, recreation, and wildlife. In addition, many state conservation agencies, universities, and local organizations offer educational opportunities for landowners to gain management skills that they can apply to their own land. In the State of Ohio, for example, family forest owners own 73 percent of all forested land, which means that private owners' decision-making and land management practices are essential to maintain large tracts of wildlife habitat. Specific practices employed by private forest owners to improve wildlife habitat include the planting of nut trees to provide food for wildlife, the reclamation of mined land, the removal of invasive species, and selective harvesting to maintain forest openings. In addition, some landowners put their land into a land trust or conservation easement to ensure that the landscape and associated habitat is preserved in years to come.

The rivers and streams of Montana provide another example of landowners intentionally working to improve wildlife habitat on their property. On Mitchell Slough in southwestern Montana, property owners have worked together to turn a degraded streambed used primarily as an irrigation ditch into a seminatural wild trout stream. They dredged the slough, planted vegetation on the banks, and constructed meanders. Over time, fish populations increased, largely due to the improved habitat. Although the examples from Ohio and Montana show that private landowners often protect wildlife and create habitat, such protection can at times have negative effects on ecosystems and wildlife management more broadly. In Montana, private landowners have made it increasingly difficult for state and federal wildlife agencies to manage elk populations. There has been a transition in land ownership over the past few decades in western Montana, as ranchlands are bought up by new owners who discourage hunting and encourage wildlife populations. Although many new owners are ostensibly acting in an eco-friendly manner by discouraging hunting, their actions caused elk populations to balloon rapidly in some areas in the early 2000s. This is particularly problematic because elk are migratory animals, and although there may be sufficient food and habitat on private ranchland, there may not be enough food and habitat elsewhere. Thus, the eco-friendly practices of ranchland owners actually created a challenge for those in charge of managing the wild elk population (Haggerty & Travis, 2006).

In sum, the adoption of eco-friendly practices and increasing awareness of environmental issues has benefited many types of wildlife, including the bald eagle, brown pelican, grizzly bear, and species of fish. Eco-friendly practices have been encouraged through government regulations such as the EPA's ban of DDT in 1972, the efforts of nonprofit organizations to educate the public about ways to protect and conserve our nation's wildlife, and the actions of individual landowners who view the environment and wildlife as intrinsically valuable. Despite these successes, however, negative human impacts on wildlife still persist. Habitat loss remains a significant problem for biodiversity conservation in the United States. Climate change also poses a risk to wildlife, and some studies indicate that animal ranges have already begun to shift due to the changing climate (Chen et al., 2011). In addition, some purportedly eco-friendly practices and policies do not always have clear positive or negative environmental effects. A certain practice may benefit some species of wildlife while harming others. Efforts to eradicate invasive species by poisoning streams or killing large populations of fish demonstrate that wildlife management and conservation practices may be considered beneficial by some and dangerous or wasteful by others. Finally, it is also worth noting that despite the adoption of many eco-friendly practices in the United States, our consumption habits continue to contribute to habitat loss and threaten wildlife elsewhere in the world.

CHRISTINE BIERMANN

See also: Wildlife, Conservation and Preservation Organizations (Environment); Rachel Carson's *Silent Spring* (Arts).

References

Chen, I-Ching, Jane K. Hill, R. Ohlemüller, David B. Roy, and Chris D. Thomas. 2011. "Rapid Range Shifts of Species Associated with High Levels of Climate Warming." *Science* 333:6045: 1024–1026.

Gunther, Kerry A., and Travis Wyman. 2008. "Human Habituated Bears: The Next Challenge in Bear Management in Yellowstone National Park." *Yellowstone Science* 16:2: 35–41.

Haggerty, Julia H., and William R. Travis. 2006. "Out of Administrative Control: Absentee Owners, Resident Elk, and the Shifting Nature of Wildlife Management in Southwestern Montana." *Geoforum* 37: 816–830.

Hart, David D., Thomas E. Johnson, Karen L. Bushaw-Newton, Richard J. Horwitz, Angela T. Benarek, Donald F. Charles, Daniel A. Kreeger, and David J. Velinsky. 2002. "Dam Removal: Challenges and Opportunities for Ecological Research and River Restoration." *Bioscience* 52:8: 669–682.

Johnson, Kirk. 2011. "In Yellowstone, Killing One Kind of Trout to Save Another." *New York Times*, August 11.

Turner, James M. 2003. "From Woodcraft to 'Leave No Trace': Wilderness, Consumerism, and Environmentalism in Twentieth-Century America." *Environmental History* 7:3: 462–484.

Food and Drink

BREWING, ECO-FRIENDLY

Beer occupies a rich and unique role in the American experience. Its identity is intertwined with its makers and resources used to make it; however, those natural inputs, such as grains and water, manufacturing, and distribution all come with environmental costs. The majority of U.S. brewers, small and large, have engaged in some form of eco-friendly or sustainable practice over the past decades. The rise of craft brewing since the 1980s has brought with it a consistent trend of minimizing and offsetting some of the negative environmental impacts of brewing, such as energy and water consumption and waste generation, while at the same time granting Americans more variety in beer choices than they have ever had before. Even as the most well-known industrial brewers green their image and operations, craft brewers represent the leading edge of sustainable brewing business. The story of the U.S. beer industry begins in local taverns, travels across the globe, and returns once more to neighborhood pubs.

The Rise of the Beer Industry

Before the invention of pasteurization and refrigerated transportation, beer had a short life before spoiling. Larger brewers located in the midwest, in America's hinterlands, and along its largest lakes and rivers to ensure an abundant supply of water and grain. Once limited to a tavern and town-based fulfillment, beer became institutionalized by German immigrants and was marketed and sold to people around the world. Three brewers—Anheuser-Busch, Coors, and Miller—came to dominate the market with American-style lagers (*Empires of Industry—Brewed in America*, 1997). Between 2008 and 2009, the Belgian company InBev purchased Anheuser-Busch, and Coors and Miller merged. The industry amassed $101 billion in sales in 2010, of that, craft brewers sold an estimated $7.6 billion ("Brewers Association Reports," 2011).

The Rise of Craft Beer

In 1978, President Jimmy Carter signed into law a bill allowing each state to regulate the limited production of homemade beer and wine, actualizing craft brewing and the diversification of the beer market (H.R. 1337, 95th Congress). In 1991, New Belgium Brewing Co. started in the basement of owners Jeff Lebech and Kim Jordan before growing into a 850,000-barrel operation out of Fort Collins, Colorado (Cioletti, 2007). By 2011, some 1,927 craft brewers were in operation according to the Brewer's Association. In 2010, "craft brewers produced 9,951,956 barrels," though this production only constituted 5 percent of the total volume of U.S. beer sales (Brewer's Association, 2011).

Craft brewers use product variety and environmentally sound practices to appeal to those beer drinkers who are uninterested in another American-style lager or mass manufactured products. Classical economics could not have anticipated the entry of so many successful small brewers into a market dominated by large firms with the advantages of "economies of scale in production, marketing and distribution" (Porter, 1980, 9). In contrast with their multimillion-dollar counterparts, craft brewers are described "as small production organizations that refused to cut corners in their quest for quality, care about their customers and communities, employ traditional methods and ingredients, and appeal to the most discerning consumers" (Carroll & Swaminathan, 2000, 730).

Eco-Friendly Practices in Action

Sustainability presents a framework that incorporates not only environmental or "eco-" principles but also includes two other E's: equity and economy. "Sustainability is an economic state where the demands placed upon the environment by people and commerce can be met without reducing the capacity of the environment to provide for future generations (Hawken, 1994, 139). To illustrate, it is eco-friendly for New Belgium to use wind power over consuming fossil fuels; the brewery's equity lies in its use of an employee-ownership model (Cioletti, 2007); its continued growth since its basement upstart speaks to its economic strength. New Belgium provides a sustainable success story that U.S. brewers and beer drinkers can raise a glass to.

Examples of Craft and Eco-Friendly Brewers in the United States

Following is a list of the eco-friendly brewers in the United States as of 2012:

Sierra Nevada, Chico, California
New Belgium, Fort Collins, Colorado
Boulevard Brewing Company, Kansas City, Missouri
Peak Organic, Portland, Maine
Great Lakes Brewing, Cleveland, Ohio
Squatter's brewpub, Salt Lake City, Utah
Long Trail Brewing, Bridgewater Corners, Vermont

Sierra Nevada Brewing Company reports, "In the beginning, practicing environmental sustainability was an economic necessity. Reducing utility costs through energy and water conservation, recycling and reusing packaging materials, and reducing waste in every area of the company were essential since capital was limited. Over the years, the culture of resource conservation has grown alongside the company" (Sierra Nevada Brewing Company, 2010 "Sustainability," 5). In 2008,

Sierra Nevada Brewing Company completed a 10,000-cell solar panel array, powering nearly its entire operations facility, which remains one of the nation's largest (Sierra Nevada Brewing Company, 2010 "Sustainability," 10). Values that are shared between the environmental and microbrewing movements have created the foundation upon which the brewing industry's most sustainable companies have been built.

In Vermont, Long Trail Brewing Company, like many other eco-friendly brewers, distributes its spent grain to local farmers and also "uses one-third the amount of water as the industry standard brewing process by employing a heat recovery system that converts steam into water for re-use. This process saves 1,100 gallons of propane per month and eliminates the release of smoky water vapor from the facility" (Hasse, 2011). Boulevard Brewing Company is the largest craft brewer in the midwest and continues the craft-brewing trend of ecologically responsible practices, including treating its own wastewater, converting its distribution trucks to hybrid vehicles, and partnering with local Kansas City area companies to form Ripple Glass Recycling as a means of diverting glass from area landfills. This service proved highly necessary: in 2009, Kansas City Metro residents threw away a shocking 150 million pounds of glass (Ripple Glass). Other examples include Great Lakes Brewing Company's fleet of trucks running on vegetable oil and Peak Organic Brewing Company's use of organic grain from local fields (Brown, n.d.). Squatter's Brewpub in Salt Lake City, Utah, follows a triple bottom line business model, focusing on people, planet, and profit.

Local and craft brewers are intrinsically linked to the natural environment, which is the source of their diverse inputs and the methods used to create equally diverse tastes, which in turn provide for their maker's livelihood. Consumers by and large still spend their money on big-name beers; yet, even as overall production of beer suffered in 2010, craft brewers reported a 12 percent sales increase (Brewers Association, 2011). Even in slower economic times more than a few consumers are thirsty for eco-friendly variety.

BRYAN DYKMAN AND LYDIA GIBSON

See also: BioPreferred Program (documents); ChooseMyPlate.gov (documents); Diet, Vegetarian and Vegan (Food); Dietary Guidelines for Americans (documents); Food and Diet (Food); Food and Entertaining (Food); Food, Drink, and Media (Food); Organic Labeling and Marketing Information (documents); Organic and Natural Foods (Food).

References

Brewer's Association. 2011. "Craft Brewing Statistics." Available at: http://www.brewers association.org/pages/business-tools/craft-brewing-statistics/facts.

"Brewers Association Reports 11 Percent Volume Growth for U.S. Craft Brewers in 2010." 2011. Business Wire, March 21.

Boulevard Brewing Co. "Sustainability." Available at: http://www.boulevard.com/brewery/sustainability/.

Brown, Emily. N.d. "Organic Beer and Beyond:10 Eco-Friendly Breweries." Available at: http://www.thedailygreen.com/healthy-eating/latest/organic-brewery-0625.

Carroll, Glenn R., and Anand Swaminathan. 2000. "Why the Microbrewery Movement? Organization Dynamics of Resource Partitioning in the US Brewing Industry." *American Journal of Sociology* 106: 715–762.

Cioletti, Jeff. 2007. "Earth's Brewer." *Beverage World* (October 15): 22–27.

Empires of Industry—Brewed in America. 1997. DVD. Written by Tom Robertson. National Geographic.

Haase, Patrick. 2011. "Part 1 of 2: TOP 4 Sustainable Breweries in Celebration of American Craft Beer Week." Available at: http://www.opportunitygreen.com/green-business-blog/2011/05/16/part-1-of-2-celebrate-american-craft-beer-week-with-sustainable-brews.

Hawken, Paul. 1994. *The Ecology of Commerce.* New York: Harper Business.

Porter, M. E. 1980. *Competitive Strategy.* New York: Free Press.

Ripple Glass. "About Us." Available at: http://rippleglass.com/about-us.php.

Sierra Nevada Brewing Co. "2010 Sustainability Report." Available at: http://www.sierranevada.com/environment/images/2010SierraNevadaSustainabilityReport.pdf.

CORPORATE FOOD SERVICE AND FARM TO TABLE SUSTAINABILITY

Requests for sustainable, organic, local, and ecologically sound food sourcing are soaring on campuses from California to New York. In an era of multiple complex influences, such as climate change, obesity, and soil degradation, demanding food gourmands are pressuring colleges and universities to focus on carbon footprints, biodiversity, and environmental pollution through developing sustainability initiatives. In addition, much attention is placed on farmers, fair trade, and farm workers' rights. J. K. Gibson-Graham (2006, 299) stated: "Academic engagements with sustainability and food have led the way on some campuses, and community gardens and farmers markets add experiential learning about sustainable food to college and university life. Food can be a strong locus for campus sustainability efforts because of its economic clout, corporate connections, and emotional resonance with family traditions, place and identity."

Emerging visions of an alternative agrifood system are marking college dining halls across the country, requiring corporate food service providers to adapt their procurement methods to meet their sustainability goals. As food service providers rise to meet paradigm shifts in college cuisines, corporations are increasing their efforts to develop corporate social responsibility (CSR) initiatives. For some institutions, the sustainable dining hall is an effective marketing strategy and is used as a way to entice the eco-friendly student. After all, "Food is a highly visible symbol of a college's amenities and priorities" (Carlson, 2008, 14).

Similar to other aspects of the food movement, the sustainable dining service is struggling to gain strength in a system dominated by a few large firms. Technological advances and developments in marketing have encouraged the emergence of corporate service providers. As a result, a few mammoth-sized companies serve up countless meals to the future leaders of America. A simultaneous but unrelated movement is "corporate social responsibility," which first gained attention at the end of the Cold War era when large corporations emerged in nearly all food and industrial sectors. The general public grew wary of their intentions, "convinced that big business is at best amoral and at worst greedy," in the words of visionary pollster Elmo Roper (1949). Business leaders were encouraged to mix business responsibility with a hint of social consciousness, which ultimately led to the creation of corporate social responsibility. Until recently, these two movements operated independently, with the set of firms adopting CSR practices that differed from the large corporations prevalent in the business landscape.

Even as large companies compete for long-term contracts with colleges and universities, CSR and the "do well by doing good" spirit of social responsibility has gained momentum. At Emory University, fed by Sodexho, a large provider of food services, the sustainability director assisted Sodexho with increasing the procurement of local foods. For large, national companies, this type of localized help can expand the possibilities for using sustainable food. Indeed, "reputation is a stakeholder's expectation of value vis-à-vis an organization's peers and competitors." Trust is the foundation for a successful client-business relationship, and this is critical in the world of CSR and food service. "And—in the long run, over time, with repeated practice—a firm that consistently does the "right thing" is a firm that is operating on a sustainable basis" (Guest Author, 2011).

In another model, institutions pursue their own vision of who, what, where, why, and how food comes from the farm to their plates. An example of this is at Yale University, where the bar for sustainable practices in dining is set high. In lieu of a contract with a large food service provider, Yale has opted to run a self-administered dining program. The Yale Sustainable Food Project was established to offer students the opportunity to engage with agriculture, connect through learning, share food grown on their campus farm, and work together to address sustainability concerns at the local and global levels. Students helped to draft sustainable purchasing guidelines to be used when making food procurement choices. Taken into consideration were the impediments common in institutional food purchasing that include both conventional food and transportation impacts.

SUSTAINABLE FOOD PURCHASING GUIDE
· ·• FIRST EDITION

Cover of a guide to creating sustainable dining programs, published by the Yale Sustainable Food Project. (Yale Sustainable Food Project)

In the end, certain compromises were simply unavoidable. "Because we buy a large volume of food, and we need a reasonably varied menu, we must regularly make compromises, but we see those compromises as temporary measures as we move toward a more sustainable system" (Yale Sustainable Food Project).

This type of realism has led to increased purchasing of local, organic, and sustainable foods at campuses around the United States. With the explosion of sustainable initiatives within CSR and institutions of higher education, the challenge of marrying corporate food service providers to local priorities emerged. However, real conundrums exist, due to the limits of large-scale food purchasing within our food system. The large companies are able to provide food for low prices by purchasing large quantities under contract. The use of long-term contracts also provides insurance against liabilities like food-borne illnesses, by specifying specific production and handling practices. The reliance on long-term contracts is part of the struggle for institutionalizing sustainable change and developing trust between the food service provider and the client (Carlson, 2008).

Although there is widespread interest in adopting sustainable food practices on college and university campuses, there are significant barriers to establishing a truly sustainable supply chain between producer and consumer. Making serious headway into changing existing procurement practices will likely require input from more than a few committed corporate leaders, students, and faculty. There is a clear need for trust-based relationships between corporate food service providers and their institutions. Most likely, colleges and universities will need to write contracts with food service providers that specify that the food served on campus meets their sustainability goals, including a willingness to pay a higher price for these attributes.

Despite the major strides made so far, an extraordinary amount of work still remains in order to encourage food service providers to fulfill their corporate social responsibility goals and establish meaningful partnerships among clients, distributors, and farmers of various scopes and scales. Although the vision for sustainable dining is growing, it might just take every person who has ever eaten on a college campus to make sure the necessary changes do actually happen.

LAUREL GREYSON AND CAROLYN DIMITRI

See also: BioPreferred Program (documents); Brewing, Eco-Friendly (Food); Choose MyPlate.gov (documents); Dietary Guidelines for Americans (documents); Food and Diet (Food); Food and Entertaining (Food); Food, Drink, and Media (Food); Organic and Natural Foods (Food); Organic Labeling and Marketing Information (documents); Restaurants (Food).

References

Carlson, Scott. 2008. "Colleges Chew on Local-Food Phenomenon." *Chronicle of Higher Education* 55:5: 14.

Gibson-Graham, J. K. 2006. "The End of Capitalism (As We Knew It): A Feminist Critique of Political Economy with New Introduction." Minneapolis: University of Minnesota Press.

Guest Author. 2011. "Experts Weigh in on the Relationship Between Reputation, Trust and Sustainable Business." Available at: http://www.triplepundit.com/2011/07/relationship-between-reputation-trust-sustainable-business/.

Roper, Elmo. 1949. "The Public Looks at Business." *Harvard Business Review* 27: 165–175.

Yale Sustainable Food Project. Available at: http://www.yale.edu/sustainablefood/about _faq.html.

DIET, VEGETARIAN AND VEGAN

A vegetarian diet is one in which meat is excluded, including fowl or seafood or products made from these foods. There are generally three types of vegetarian diets. The vegan diet excludes all animal products such as meat, poultry, fish, eggs, milk, cheese, and other dairy products. Lactovegetarians have a diet that excludes meat, poultry, fish, and eggs, but includes dairy products. A lacto-ovo-vegetarian's diet excludes meat, poultry, and fish, but includes eggs and dairy products. Some vegetarians and vegans also eschew nonfood products (such as leather) that are made from animals.

One main reason for adopting a vegetarian diet is health. The American Dietetic Association's position (2009) on a vegetarian diet is that "appropriately planned vegetarian diets . . . are healthful, nutritionally adequate, and may provide health benefits in the prevention and treatment of certain diseases." Associated benefits can include lower blood cholesterol levels, lower risk of heart disease, lower blood pressure, and lower risk of hypertension and type 2 diabetes, as well as lower body mass index (BMI) and cancer rates.

The reasons vegetarians and vegans adopt these diets are diverse, including concern for the environment, animal rights, religious, ethical concerns, among others. Worldwide statistics on vegetarian diets are not available; the data that do exist are generally from informal sources. In the United States, a 2009 national poll showed that approximately 3 percent of the U.S. population reported they were vegetarians (1 percent of this 3 percent follow a vegan diet) (Vegetarian Resource Group, 2009). Most European countries generally have higher vegetarian rates than this, up to 9 percent in Germany and Switzerland (European Vegetarian Union). Other parts of the world, most notably India, have a much higher proportion of the population following vegetarian diets. A number of factors influence a society's consumption of meat products, including, among others, per capita income, urbanization,

Early Use of the Term Vegetarian

According to the International Vegetarian Union, "the term *vegetarian* was first used around 1840 by the community closely associated with Alcott House School, near London. It was first formally used on September 30th of 1847 at Northwood Villa in Kent, England with the inaugural meeting of The Vegetarian Society. Prior to 1847, the most commonly used equivalent term was 'vegetable diet'. Some referred to themselves as 'Pythagoreans' or adherents of the 'Pythagorean System', after the ancient Greek Pythagoras" (International Vegetarian Union, http://www.ivu.org/).

Greenovation: Ethical Veganism

Ethical vegans entirely reject the commodification of animals. There is disagreement among groups about the extent to which all animal products, particularly products from insects (such as honey or silk), must be avoided. Ethical vegans avoid the use of animal products for clothing, toiletries, or any other reason and will try to avoid ingredients that have been tested on animals.

Greenovation: Economic Vegetarianism

An economic vegetarian is someone who chooses to be a vegetarian either out of necessity or because of a conscious simple living strategy. Such a person may base this belief on a philosophical viewpoint, such as the belief that the consumption of meat is economically unsound or that vegetarianism will help improve public health and curb starvation. (See a related economic analysis of vegetarian diets: Lusk, J. L., and Norwood, F. B. 2009. "Some Economic Benefits and Costs of Vegetarianism." *Agricultural and Resource Economics Review* 38: 109–124.)

social and cultural norms, and access to natural resources. Demand for meat in many countries, especially in developing countries, is rising dramatically as per-capita income and urbanization increase (Steinfeld et al., 2006). Regardless of these statistics, it is clear that the vast majority of the U.S. population relies on a meat-based diet, and the United States has one of the highest per-capita meat consumption in the world.

For many, the adoption of the vegetarian diet addresses numerous environmental issues related specifically to intensive and industrialized livestock production, most notably energy use, effects on greenhouse gases, water pollution, and water use. Other concerns related to livestock production are deforestation and land degradation. Worldwide, livestock production currently accounts for 70 percent of all agricultural and 30 percent of the planet's land. Although many livestock production systems are still extensive in nature, there is an increasing trend toward intensification of livestock production worldwide, especially in poultry and pig production systems.

Energy use is an important concern in livestock production. Agricultural systems overall can be an energy-intensive sector, as we see in the United States (Shoemaker et al., 2006). Direct energy consumption includes the use of gas, diesel, liquid petroleum, natural gas, and electricity. Indirect energy use involves agricultural inputs, such as nitrogen fertilizer, which consume the most energy among production inputs. Of the commodities, feed grain and wheat producers are particularly high-energy consumption commodities. Although hogs, dairy, and cow-calf operations generally have relatively low direct energy costs, indirectly livestock production is energy intensive given that feed grains are a major input for the sector.

Agricultural production also affects greenhouse gases, such as carbon dioxide, nitrous oxide, and methane, and the cumulative effect of these gases are viewed in terms of net global warming potential. Although U.S. agriculture accounts for a relatively small share of total greenhouse gas emissions, it is a major source for two greenhouse gases, methane and nitrous oxide. Livestock production demands large amounts of fossil-fuel–based grain production and results in high levels of methane. In the often-cited study from the UN Food and Agriculture Organization (FAO), Steinfeld and colleagues (2006) estimate that 18 percent of annual worldwide greenhouse gas emissions are attributable to cattle, buffalo, sheep, goats, camels, horses, pigs, and poultry. Further, they estimate that livestock production makes up 37 percent of methane caused by human use, most of that from enteric fermentation by ruminants, 65 percent of nitrous oxide, mostly from manure. Finally, the sector accounts for two-thirds of ammonia emissions, which contribute significantly to acid rain and acidification of ecosystems.

Water, both its use and pollution of, is another key concern as it relates to livestock agriculture. In the United States, water is a resource that is both heavily used by agriculture and energy intensive. Irrigated agriculture accounts for 80 percent of consumptive water used, with over 90 percent in some western states (USDA ERS, 2004). The FAO (Steinfeld et al., 2006) reports that the livestock sector is a key player in increasing water use, currently comprising 8 percent of global human water use. Most of this is for the irrigation of feed crops. Pimentel and Pimentel (1996) report that it requires about 100 times more water to produce 1 kg of animal protein than grain protein; again much of the water used stems from the need for forage and grain inputs in livestock production systems.

Pollution of water bodies is also a key environmental issue, and a number of studies have indicated that animal operations are a significant contributor to water quality impairments in several regions of the United States (Ribaudo & Gollehon, 2006). The FAO report (Steinfeld et al., 2006) notes that the major sources of pollution are from animal wastes, antibiotics and hormones, chemicals from tanneries, fertilizers and pesticides used for feed crops, and sediments from eroded pastures. In the United States, livestock are responsible for an estimated 55 percent of erosion and sediment, 37 percent of pesticide use, 50 percent of antibiotic use, and a third of the loads of nitrogen and phosphorus into freshwater resources (Steinfeld et al., 2006). Individual studies show the impact in the United States (see Ribaudo & Gollehon, 2006 for a fuller list). For example, the U.S. Environmental Protection Agency (EPA) in 1996 reported that "animal operations (feedlots, animal feeding operations, and animal holding areas) were a major factor in 5 percent of impaired rivers and streams, and a contributing source in 20 percent of rivers and streams reported as being impaired" (Ribaudo & Gollehon, 2006, 129). In the Mississippi Basin, animal manure was estimated to contribute 15 percent of the nitrogen (the suspected cause of a large zone of hypoxic waters) load entering the Gulf of Mexico.

Deforestation and land degradation due to livestock production are other issues taken into account for those adopting a vegetarian diet for environmental reasons. This is especially true in areas such as Latin America, where 70 percent of previous forested land in the Amazon region is occupied by pastures (Steinfeld et al., 2006). About 20 percent of the world's pastures and rangelands (almost 75 percent of rangelands in dry areas) have experienced compaction and erosion created mainly by overgrazing.

Loss of biodiversity, which is linked to deforestation in many cases, is greatly impacted by agricultural production methods. The diversity of species in agricultural landscapes is particularly important, as about one-third of the Earth's surface is cropland and pasture, but so too is the reduction in biodiversity due to land use changes to livestock production. A second consideration in biodiversity lies within the agricultural system itself: the genetic diversity of crops produced or animals raised.

Some studies have tried to quantify the environmental benefits of a vegetarian versus meat-based diet, and the research shows that the issues are complex. Within the livestock category alone, there is wide variation of the impact of dietary decisions (Pimentel, 2006; Pimentel & Pimentel, 2003). For example 1 kg of beef requires 13 kg of grain and 30 kg of forage (40 kcal fossil fuel energy); while 1 kg of broiler chicken requires only 2.3 kg of grain. Organic pasture-fed beef, on the other hand, requires only 20 kcal of energy, half that of conventional beef. The ratio of energy input to protein output for major U.S. livestock range from 40:1 kcal for beef cattle, 39:1 for eggs, 14:1 for swine and dairy, to 10:1 for turkeys, and 4:1 for broilers.

When looking at a meat diet in relation to a vegetarian diet, some research has shown that the latter or equal caloric intake requires one-third less fossil fuel than a meat diet (Pimentel & Pimentel, 1996). According to one study, changing to a vegetarian diet has a greater impact on lowering greenhouse gas emissions than buying foods from local sources (Weber & Matthews, 2008). Other studies, however, stress exceptions when looking at the environmental effects. Although the environmental burden of vegetarian foods is usually relatively low when production and processing are considered, if for instance, long-distance air transport, deep-freezing, and some horticultural practices (such as heated greenhouse use) are added into the mixture of the vegetarian diet, the environmental burdens of these foods could exceed those for locally produced organic meat (Reijnders & Soret, 2003).

This research demonstrates that the analysis of environmental costs of vegetarian versus meat-based diets is complex and worthy of further examination. The geographic aspects of livestock production worldwide are complex and often different for developing and developed countries, creating varying environmental costs for consumers in different parts of the world (Duram & Oberholtzer, 2010).

LYDIA OBERHOLTZER

See also: BioPreferred Program (documents); Brewing, Eco-Friendly (Food); Childhood Obesity Facts (documents); ChooseMyPlate.gov (documents); Dietary Guidelines for Americans (documents); Food and Diet (Food); Food and Entertaining (Food); Food, Drink, and Media (Food); Organic and Natural Foods (Food); Organic Labeling and Marketing Information (documents).

References

American Dietetic Association. 2009. "Position of the American Dietetic Association: Vegetarian Diets." *Journal of the American Dietetic Association* 109:7: 1266–1282.

Duram, L., and L. Oberholtzer. 2010. "A Geographic Approach to Examining Place and Natural Resource Use in Local Food Systems." *Renewable Agriculture and Food Systems* 25:2: 99–108.

European Vegetarian Union. Available at: http://www.euroveg.eu/lang/en/info/howmany.php.

Pimentel, D. 2006. "Impacts of Organic Farming on the Efficiency of Energy Use in Agriculture: State of Science Report." Organic Center, Boulder, CO.

Pimentel, D., and M. Pimentel. 1996. *Food, Energy and Society*. Niwot: Colorado University Press.

Pimentel, D., and M. Pimentel. 2003. "Sustainability of Meat-Based and Plant-Based Diets and the Environment." *American Journal of Clinical Nutrition* 78(Suppl.): 660S–663S.

Reijnders, L., and S. Soret. 2003. "Quantification of the Environmental Impact of Different Dietary Protein Choices." *American Journal of Clinical Nutrition* 78:3: 664S–668S.

Ribaudo, M., and N. Gollehon. 2006. "Animal Agriculture and the Environment, Agricultural Resources and Environmental Indicators," edited by Keith Wiebe and Noel Gollehon. Economic Information Bulletin No. (EIB-16). USDA, Economic Research Service, Washington, DC. Available at: http://www.ers.usda.gov/publications/arei/eib16/Chapter4/4.5/.

Shoemaker, R., D. McGranahan, and B. McBride. 2006. "Agriculture and Rural Communities Are Resilient to High Energy Costs: Rising Energy Prices May Prompt Farmers and Rural Residents to Make Tradeoffs in Their Production Practices and Daily Lives." *Amber Waves* 4:2: 18–21.

Steinfeld, H., P. Gerber, T. Wassenaar, V. Castel, M. Rosales, and C. de Haan. 2006. "Livestock's Long Showdown: Environmental Issues and Options." United Nation's Food and Agriculture Organization, Rome, Italy. Available at: ftp://ftp.fao.org/docrep/fao/010/a0701e/A0701E00.pdf.

U.S. Department of Agriculture. 2004. "Briefing Rooms: Irrigation and Water Use." Economic Research Service, Washington, DC. Available at: http://www.ers.usda.gov/Briefing/WaterUse/.

Vegetarian Resource Group. 2009. "How Many Vegetarians Are There . . . ?" Available at: http://www.vrg.org/press/2009poll.htm.

Weber, C. L., and S. H. Matthews. 2008. "Food-Miles and the Relative Climate Impacts of Food Choices in the United States." *Environmental Science and Technology* 42:10: 3508–3513.

FOOD AND DIET

Eating green takes on many forms. Those with an interest in eating ecologically take a number of approaches to doing so, each of which carries with it benefits, including reduced resource use, chemical exposure, chronic disease rates, and waste.

A low-carbon diet refers to the approach of making dietary choices based on the carbon footprint associated with food. These practices aim to reduce the emission of greenhouse gases associated with food production, including carbon dioxide, methane, nitrous oxide, and chlorofluorocarbons (CFCs). Carbon dioxide is produced by any vehicles that burn fossil fuels. Methane is emitted by livestock operations and landfills. Nitrogen oxides are released by industrial agriculture operations that overtill and overirrigate. CFCs are produced by refrigerators used in food shipment and storage.

Environmental Working Group List

This is the Environmental Working Group's (2011) list of most and least pesticide-contaminated fruits and vegetables.

Top 12 Most Pesticide-Contaminated Fruits and Vegetables:

Apples   Grapes
Celery   Sweet bell peppers
Strawberries   Potatoes
Peaches   Blueberries
Spinach   Lettuce
Nectarines   Kale/collard greens

Top 12 Least Pesticide-Contaminated Fruits and Vegetables:

Watermelon   Sweet peas
Cabbage   Asparagus
Kiwi   Avocado
Cantaloupe   Pineapples
Eggplant   Sweet corn
Mangoes   Onions

Source: Environmental Working Group. 2011. "2011 Shopper's Guide to Pesticides in Produce." Available at: http://www.ewg.org/foodnews/list/.

A low-carbon diet consists of primarily plant-based foods, which require a small fraction of the resources for growth compared to animal foods (National Geographic, 2011). Plant agriculture is also associated with far fewer greenhouse gas emissions compared to livestock. A recent report by the UN Food and Agriculture Organization found that livestock is the leading industry in generating global warming greenhouse gases (more than transportation) and is also a major source of land and water degradation. The livestock sector accounts for 9 percent of carbon dioxide, 65 percent of nitrous oxide (most of this comes from manure), 37 percent of methane (from the digestive system of ruminants), and 64 percent of all human-induced ammonia (Steinfeld et al., 2006). Nitrous oxide has 296 times the global warming potential of carbon dioxide and methane has 23 times the global warming potential as carbon dioxide; ammonia contributes significantly to acid rain.

Livestock operations also use confined animal feeding operations (CAFOs), which are especially damaging to the environment. Feed used for CAFOs consists of corn and soy, which comes from industrial operations that use chemical fertilizer, pesticides, and genetically engineered organisms. The soy industry is responsible for the destruction of forests and loss of wildlife habitat in Brazil, Paraguay, and Argentina.

Low-carbon diets depend on organic food that is minimally processed. Organic food is not genetically engineered and is grown without the use of chemical pesticides and fertilizers—petroleum products that increase the carbon footprint of a food. Additional farming practices that are important to reduce carbon footprint of food are less tilling and irrigation, which release nitrous oxides. The processing, packaging, transportation, and distribution of food also require petroleum resources. Processing food is highly water intensive, and packaging relies on petroleum-based plastic. Once packaged, food often travels hundreds of miles between farm and plate. Thus, a low-carbon diet aims to source fresh food locally from local farms, farmers' markets, and gardens. This reduces the amount of water, plastic, and fuel needed, thereby reducing the amount of carbon emitted in the process.

In addition to lower resources use, eating low on the food chain (i.e., a plant-based diet) offers the benefit of lower exposure to environmental toxins. In addition to reducing exposure to agricultural chemicals, such as pesticides and growth hormones, eating low on the food chain results in lower exposure to persistent organic pollutants such as dioxins, metals, flame retardants, and banned pesticides such as DDT (dichloro-diphenyl-trichloroethane). Organophosphate and organochlorine pesticides, commonly used in industrial agriculture, have reproductive, developmental, and neurological impacts on humans and wildlife. Growth hormones found in meat and dairy result in elevated insulin-like growth factor-1 (IGF-1) levels in humans, which are associated cancer. Persistent organic pollutants (POPs) are characterized as being persistent in the environment, bioaccumulative in human tissue, and toxic. POPs affect health by disrupting the endocrine, reproductive, and immune systems and have been linked to cancer and diabetes (Lee et al., 2006).

In addition to lower environmental contaminant exposure, a plant-based diet is inherently more healthful than the standard American diet. A plant-based diet is nutrient rich with plentiful vitamins, minerals, complex carbohydrates, and unsaturated fats. Better health outcomes are seen among plant-eaters, who have lower rates of chronic disease, including cardiovascular disease, cancer, obesity, and diabetes.

The U.S. population comprises a diverse group, and their eating habits are no less diverse. Most Americans would consider themselves omnivores. Vegetarians are herbivores, with a diet that may include some animal products in the form of diary and eggs but no flesh foods of meat and poultry. Pescatarians eat fish but not other flesh foods. Vegans eat no flesh foods. More recent dietary categories emerging include flexitarians—those who may aim to eat vegetarian but are flexible depending on food availability and the situation. Freegans similarly may aim to eat according to certain standards but prioritize eating food that is freely available. Freegans practices gleaning, which is a way of recapturing food that would be otherwise wasted (i.e., through dumpster diving).

While a variety of dietary practices exist in the United States, there are many ways to positively impact the food system. Cooking in a solar oven offers the benefit of no fossil fuels or electricity and does not contaminate air with smoke or greenhouse gases. Another growing movement is that of the raw food diet—that is cooking food only up to the temperature of 104–115°F. Eating food cooked at high temperatures has been shown to induce an inflammatory immune reaction and shorten the lifespan (Vlassara, 2002). Low cooking temperatures preserve the nutrients in food, especially enzymes, vitamins, and proteins, up to 50 percent of which are lost in higher heat cooking.

One of the most promising aspects of the food system today is the revival and growth of farmers markets. Industrialized agriculture has dominated the food

Greenovation: Food Security Act of 1985

The 1985 Farm Bill (officially the Food Security Act of 1985) was one of the periodic acts passed by the U.S. Congress since the Agricultural Adjustment Act of 1933 to deal with issues of farm income, farm productivity, food safety and security, rural life, and resource use. Unlike previous agricultural acts, a conservation section was added to establish policies that would reduce the environmental impact of agriculture in the United States. The "sodbuster" and "swampbuster" provisions specified that any farmer who initiated farming on highly erodible lands or wetlands would be prohibited from participating in any federal farm programs, effectively cutting off subsidies to farmers who engage in farming on such marginal and environmentally sensitive lands. Moreover, the bill included what is now known as the Conservation Reserve Program (CRP).

Through financial incentives, the CRP encouraged the removal of highly erodible lands from cultivation and had a goal of removing between 40 and 45 million acres of such land from agricultural production by 1990. Finally, the conservation provisions of the bill extended the Soil and Water Conservation Act of 1977 and required the U.S. Department of Agriculture (USDA) to evaluate the quality and extent of soil and water resources in 1995 and in 2005 (Glaser, 1985). Given these provisions, the 1985 Farm Bill established the role of the USDA to ensure the environmental sustainability of agriculture and laid the groundwork for further expansion of this role in all subsequent farm bills.

PARKER WHEATLEY

system since World War II, and with it came a host of human and environmental problems. Many communities have responded with an interest in supporting small, family-run, local farms through markets and Community Supported Agriculture (CSAs) services, a weekly subscription service in which households receive a box of farm produce each week. Farmers' markets and CSAs are valuable methods of reconnecting with seasonal, local, and fresh food production.

RAINBOW VOGT

See also: BioPreferred Program (documents); Brewing, Eco-Friendly (Food); ChooseMyPlate .gov (documents); Dietary Guidelines for Americans (documents); Food and Diet (Food); Food and Entertaining (Food); Food, Drink, and Media (Food); Organic and Natural Foods (Food); Organic Labeling and Marketing Information (documents).

References

Glaser, L. K. 1985. "Provisions of the Food Security Act of 1985." Agricultural Information Bulletin, No. 498. Economic Research Service, U.S. Department of Agriculture.

Hayden, F. 1990. "Wetlands Provisions in 1985 and 1990." *Journal of Economic Issues* 24: 575–587.

Lee, D. H., I. K. Lee, K. Song, M. Steffes, W. Toscano, B. A. Baker, and D. R. Jacobs. 2006. "A Strong Dose-Response Relation Between Serum Concentrations of Persistent Organic Pollutants and Diabetes." *Diabetes Care* 29: 1638–1644.

Luzar, E. J. 1988. "Natural Resource Management in Agriculture: An Institutional Analysis of the 1985 Farm Bill." *Journal of Economic Issues* 22: 563–570.

National Geographic. 2011. "The Hidden Water We Use." Available at: http://environ ment.nationalgeographic.com/environment/freshwater/embedded-water/.

Ogg, C. 1992. "Addressing Environmental Needs in Farm Programs." *Agricultural History* 66: 273–278.

Reichelderfer, K. 1988. "Policy Issues Arising from Implementation of the 1985 Farm Bill Conservation Programs. Increasing Understanding of Public Problems and Understanding Paper Series." Farm Foundation. Available at: http://purl.umn.edu/17657.

Steinfeld, Henning, Pierre Gerber, Tom Wassenaar, Vincent Caste, Rosales Mauricio, and Cees de Haan. 2006. "Livestock's Long Shadow–Environmental Issues and Options." Food and Agriculture Organization. Available at: http://www.fao.org/docrep/010/a0701e/a0701e00.htm.

Taff, S., and C. F. Runge. 1986. "Supply Control, Conservation, and Budget Restraint: Conflicting Instruments in the 1985 Farm Bill." Staff Paper No. P86-33. Department of Agricultural and Applied Economics, University of Minnesota.

Vlassara, H., W. Cai, J. Crandall, T. Goldberg, R. Oberstein, V. Dardaine, M. Peppa, and E. Rayfield. 2002. "Inflammatory Mediators Are Induced by Dietary Glycotoxins, a Major Risk Factor for Diabetic Angiopathy." *Proceeding of the National Academy of Science* 99:24: 15596–15601.

FOOD AND ENTERTAINING

According to recent research, 6 in 10 consumers say they are concerned about the sustainability of the foods they eat (Fitzpatrick, 2011). This interest is reflected within all areas of consumerism; not only in the groceries Americans are buying at the store, but in the ways they are entertaining, traveling, and using media. In recent years, the trend of green dining and cooking has permeated into pop culture, progressing beyond a smaller niche issue into a mainstream one. Green cuisine, as it exists in America today, encompasses foods that are produced locally, are grown organically or sustainably, are raised humanely, and incorporate nutrition and ecological integrity.

Catering

Since sustainability has become mainstream, it's now considered popular to display your concern for the environment. Green catering and entertaining is a means for consumers to integrate sustainability into weddings, parties, and dining affairs. The practice is no longer reserved for conservationists; celebrities, media personalities, and everyday consumers are interested in putting on green affairs. From décor to food, green catering covers all aspects of an event; however, when it comes to green considerations, food still takes the cake. Making a menu local, sustainable, organic, or vegetarian friendly are common questions to consider.

The desire for green catering services has grown so large that in 2008, the Sustainable Catering Association was created to meet this need. Operating as a trade association for members within the catering and service industries, the organization aims to teach and train professionals about the benefits of sustainable practices. Caterers may work in direct contact with local farmers and ranchers to create a farm-to-table event as an attempt to minimize waste and energy expenditures.

Green weddings are currently one of the most rapidly growing areas in wedding trends, and planners are incorporating sustainable food options into the actual setting of the wedding. In fact, 48 percent of couples today say that they are committed to incorporating green practices into their weddings (Wedding Planning Institute, 2010). In the popular theme of a farm-to-table wedding, the food is not only brought in from local farms, but the reception itself is hosted on a farm. One such wedding reception may take place on the land where the food for the menu was grown, and in many cases the farmers may be present to talk with guests about the food. The menus are created in accordance with the farm, the season, and the dietary consideration of the guests, with gluten-free and meatless options now becoming part of the norm.

Green Culinary Tourism

Eating green as a trend extends beyond the home kitchen or catered affair and into the greater realm of travel and leisure. Americans are hungry to get a taste of the culture of the places they visit, and they are showing this by engaging in activities that support local businesses and green food producers.

Food tours are a popular hands-on activity that gives travelers a chance to experience their vacation spots at the most local—and thus sustainable—level. Central Coast Food Tours of San Luis Obispo, California, is a prime example of such burgeoning companies. This walking tour takes travelers through the historic downtown of San Luis Obispo, with an emphasis on artisanal food shops and cafés serving up sustainable, seasonal cuisine. Similar food tours exist in several cities—rural and urban alike—throughout America.

While food tours are one aspect of green culinary tourism, classes and workshops are another popular way for consumers to learn about sustainable foods. In the city of Ashville, North Carolina, for example, the Chamber of Commerce devotes an entire section if its operations to "Culinary Adventures." Featured classes include vegetarian foods, farm-to-table cuisine, farmers' markets, and local foods. Similar classes exist throughout America, each offering both tourists and locals the chance to learn about green eating while taking part in a recreational activity.

Of course, the most prevalent way that green entertaining has shown its face in America is in restaurants. Chefs and restaurateurs have taken notice of consumers' interest in sustainable foods, and they've begun offering an exclusive dining experience for such individuals: farm-to-table dining. The trend of farm-to-table brings local and sustainable foods directly from the source—a farm, ranch, or production facility—to the restaurant table, without the usual middle man. This puts consumers one step closer to understanding where their food comes from, and it gives legitimacy and transparency to any foods sold as "sustainable." Several Web sites, such as the American Farm to Table Restaurant Guide, exist solely as a resource to put consumers in touch with such restaurants.

And taking the farm-to-table concept to the next level is the notion of the supper club, a recent phenomenon that connects urban and suburban consumers in dining experiences set in rural environments. Also coined as farm-to-fork experiences, these are themed catered events, typically taking place on the farm where the food is raised. Diners come for a prix fixe menu that teaches them about the foods, the land, and the culture of that space.

Green Foodie Media

Americans are paying attention to green cuisine even when they aren't eating. They've embraced the topic as a popular choice of entertainment on television and in the media. According to *Media Market Journal*, Food Network ranked seventh among ad-supported cable networks in 2011, up four spots from the year before (Rosz, 2011). And as recent book sales in total declined by 4 percent, overall cookbook sales rose 5 percent (Hale, 2010).

This increased interest in food media encompasses all things culinary, from cakes and caterers to personal chefs and celebrity chefs. Among the most prominent celebrity chefs today are those focusing on green cuisine and nutrition. Jamie Oliver, a British chef personality with an emphasis on garden-fresh foods, recently took America by storm with his efforts to reform school lunches. Oliver emphasizes the need for fruits, vegetables, and healthier alternatives in school lunches, and his television shows today revolve around greener foods for kids. His most recent television show, *Jamie Oliver's Food Revolution*, won an Emmy in 2010 for Outstanding Reality Program. Oliver stands alongside other celebrity chefs like Rachel Ray, Emeril Lagasse, and Paula Deen in efforts to make green cuisine a mainstream cause.

Complications and Questions

The complications surrounding green cuisine and entertaining relate back to the greater concerns of sustainable food as a whole. Caterers, chefs, and restaurateurs are constantly torn between choices of a greener product versus a better price for their customers. A menu featuring exclusively local and organic foods may be a better choice for the environment, but will the markup in prices chase consumers away? The value of such offerings must be expressed via education for the consumer. In teaching them the worth of sustainable foods, and in showing them the legitimacy of such labeled products, food operators are able to guide greener choices while educating the community.

For consumers, similar questions must be answered. Finding sustainable food options for an event, while staying within a budget, may seem unreasonable to inexperienced consumers. Again, the role of education comes into play, as does the role of organizations that supply resources for connecting consumers with local food purveyors. The media are doing their fair share in creating learning opportunities for the consumer, but critics are concerned that as long as advertising dollars drive media content, there will always be an industry slant toward consumerism—which may be inherently at odds with green living and sustainability.

The trend of green cuisine continues in America, and it's apparent that all players are interested in doing their parts. Chefs, consumers, government, and media are united in making green cuisine an issue to address from the dinner table into the community and every step along the way.

KIMBERLEY STAKAL

See also: BioPreferred Program (documents); Brewing, Eco-Friendly (Food); ChooseMy Plate.gov (documents); Dietary Guidelines for Americans (documents); Food and Diet (Food); Food, Drink, and Media (Food); Organic and Natural Foods (Food); Organic Labeling and Marketing Information (documents).

References

American Farm to Table. Available at: http://www.americanfarmtotable.com/.

Central Coast Food Tours. Available at http://www.centralcoastfoodtours.com/san-luis-obispo-tour

City Provisions. "Supper Club & Farm Dinners." http://www.cityprovisions.com/supper-club-farm-dinners.htm (cited December 26, 2011).

Explore Asheville. Available at http://www.exploreasheville.com/restaurants/culinary-adventures/

Fitzpatrick, Tara. 2011. "Green Catering." *Food Management*, August 1. Available at: http://food-management.com/business_topics/management/green-catering0811/.

Hale, Todd. 2010. "Food: The Social Network of the Ages." *Nielsen Wire*, November 22. Available at: http://blog.nielsen.com/nielsenwire/consumer/food-the-social-network-of-the-ages/.

MSNBC. "Celeb Chefs Spread Healthy Eating Habits," April 5, 2010. Accessed December 26, 2011. http://today.msnbc.msn.com/id/36180724/ns/today-food/t/celeb-chefs-spread-healthy-eats-ethic/#.TvkDv_JPiSo

Rosz, Jeff. 2011. "Food Network Announces Stellar August 2011 Ratings." *Media Market Journal,* August 30. Available at: http://www.mediamarketjournal.com/2011/08/food-network-announces-stellar-august-2011-ratings/.

Wedding Planning Institute. 2010. "Eco-Friendly Weddings." October 4. Available at: http://www.weddingplanninginstitute.com/blog/category/wedding-industry/wedding-statistics-wedding-industry/.

FOOD, DRINK, AND MEDIA

Americans have a complex relationship with food. The agrarian roots of our country's foundation are still well alive in many traditions; harvest-time holidays such as Thanksgiving are inarguably focused on the rituals of food preparation and enjoyment of family gatherings. But the fast pace of everyday modern society has exacted a high cost: far too many people do not regularly take the time to cook healthy, wholesome meals. A shocking number of young people do not understand the very basic origins of their food, and otherwise very intelligent adults can be wholly ignorant of the ramifications of their daily bread. The unhealthiness of a typical American diet is symptomatic of a food system that for several decades has been sacrificing long-term balance for short-term profit. But the happy news is that trends are changing, and in so many ways the importance of healthy food is being brought back to the forefront of culture. Here we will explore some of the ways U.S. media has gone green with respect to food and drink.

Books and Magazines

Frances Moore-Lappe's best-selling book *Diet for a Small Planet* was first published in 1971 and was groundbreaking in its demonstration of the ill effects of a meat-based diet. Since that time, a vast array of books and magazines has been published extolling the virtues of vegetarian and vegan diets, lauding the benefits of organic food, warning about the dangers of genetically modified organisms, and generally encouraging people to eat more naturally. Here, "natural" may be interpreted to include a variety of components: food produced without synthetic chemicals or hormones added, livestock raised and harvested in humane conditions, a diet that emphasizes seasonal and locally available food (thereby shrinking the carbon footprint of transportation), or even emphasis on raw foods. Such subjects are more frequently entering mainstream publications as well, such as the 2007 cover story of *Time*, which discussed the organic-versus-local debate (Cloud, 2007).

The volume of printed works increases tremendously if we include the intrinsically connected topics of farming and gardening. Books and magazines devoted to urban homesteading, food preservation, and eco-entrepreneurship abound. Further, if we are to understand food's importance in our lives and environment, it is also helpful to know the politics and policy that led to where we are today. Some not-to-miss selections are Eric Schlosser's *Fast Food Nation*, Marion Nestle's *Food Politics*, and Michael Pollan's dual masterpieces *Omnivore's Dilemma* and *In Defense of Food*. For the photography connoisseur, also see *American Farmer: The Heart of Our Country* by Katrina Fried and Paul Mobley.

> ### Greenovators: Men on a Mission—Michael Pollan and Jamie Oliver
>
> Michael Pollan is a journalist, author, and professor who has become a champion for re-creating our agriculture policies and food system for healthier bodies, economies, and environment. He points out that food is at the nexus of three enormous challenges facing our country: health care, energy independence, and climate change. Jamie Oliver is a British chef and restaurateur, mostly known in America for the television show *Jamie Oliver's Food Revolution*, in which he attempts to reform school lunch programs first in Huntington, West Virginia, and then in Los Angeles. Both of these men have made tremendous strides to advance the mission of healthier food for people and planet.

Television

America has enjoyed a buffet of culinary viewing options, dating back to *I Love to Eat*, which ran in 1946–1947 and is credited as the first network cooking show, and explained by author Kathleen Collins, who wrote *Watching What We Eat:*

Celebrity chef, Emeril Lagasse, shares his philosophy for fresh, top quality food on his Planet Green television program, *Emeril Green*. (PRNewsFoto/ Discovery Communications)

The Evolution of Television Cooking Shows. Homemaking maven Martha Stewart made her debut in 1986, and the Food Network launched in 1993. Since that time celebrity chefdom has exploded, and viewers can now devour a variety of competitive cooking programs, food travel journals, and restaurant makeover shows. Most have given a nod to environmental themes, but there are definitely standouts. Nathan Lyon hosts *A Lyon in the Kitchen* on Discovery Health channel, which greatly emphasizes fresh seasonal foods, often visiting farms and farmers' markets as part of the show. In 2008, Emeril Lagasse joined the new Discovery Channel's Planet Green for *Emeril Green*, which partnered with Whole Foods Market to emphasize organic and sustainable cuisine. And for a full-flavored combination of food science, appliance advice, cultural anthropology, and tongue-in-cheek entertainment, it would be tough to top the do-it-yourself genius of Alton Brown's *Good Eats*.

Movies

While there are many theatrical features with food-centric plotlines (*Big Night*, *Soul Food*, *Ratatouille*, *Julie & Julia*), the real feast of this category is to be found in documentaries. In 2003, Morgan Spurlock undertook a grand experiment in *Super Size Me*, existing only on McDonald's food for 30 days. His venture grossed nearly $30 million worldwide and caused him to gain 25 pounds and earn an Academy Award nomination. *King Corn* (2007) depicts two college friends who spend a season in Iowa growing a single acre of corn, navigating farm policy, and following where their corn goes (beef feedlots, high fructose corn syrup). *Food, Inc.* (2008) covered many issues of an industrialized food system: consolidation of the meat industry and vulnerability to bacterial contamination, cheap unhealthy calories owing to counterproductive subsidies, immigrant labor and anti-immigration politics, seed patenting, and much more. Two more excellent selections are *Dive!* (2010) and *Forks Over Knives* (2011). *Dive!* tackles the topic of hunger in a country that wastes fully half of the food it produces, while *Forks Over Knives* examines whether degenerative disease can be controlled or cured by switching to a more plant-based, less processed-foods diet. Online viewing services and instant streaming features such as Netflix make documentaries readily available opportunities for good green edutainment.

Internet

In addition to the above more traditional media, the Internet has thrown open access to many worlds of information. Nearly every book, program, and person named herein is certain to have their own Web site, and a bevy of search engines (one of which—GoodSearch—actually raises money for nonprofits) is ready to help the inquisitive find out how to do just about anything. Web sites, blogs, and social networking platforms galore all provide fantastic opportunities to enhance eco-consciousness of food and drink choices. A couple of recommendations would be TheDailyGreen.com and the Daily Kos group for environmental foodies.

Greenovation: There's an App for that

Beyond even the expanded information universe offered by the Internet, the widespread use of smartphones has led to Americans' fond embrace of portable applications: "apps." For the hungry yet eco-conscious consumer on the go, there are many apps to help make informed choices. Whether you want to locate a vegetarian restaurant or remember which types of produce are best to buy organic, there is indeed an app for that. An app called HarvestMark Food Traceability allows the user to follow their food back to the farm to learn where, when, and how it was grown.

To detour slightly from the media blitz and momentarily mention person-to-person interactive trends, let us consider the "Slow Food" movement and "Green Drinks" environmental networking, both of which are well served by their respective Web sites. The former is an international grassroots movement dedicated to enjoying healthy food in your community and taking care of the environment, which provides the nourishment. It was founded by Carlo Petrini in 1986 and has hundreds of thousands of members in over 150 countries. The latter is an informal means of gathering like-minded environmentalists (usually once a month) for conversation and connectivity. Green Drinks began in 1989, and their Web site currently indicates active chapters in 813 cities worldwide. Slow Food and Green Drinks both cater to the natural human need for satiety and society while also serving to restore health to our ecosystem.

This entry briefly explores some examples of the movement to a greener American diet, as demonstrated by media. There are countless more efforts to build healthy and prosperous local food economies, many of which rely on unsung volunteer heroes. But these trends show that food is becoming important in America once again; valued as the basis of life that it is, rather than being viewed merely as a

Greenovation: To Your Health!

Moderate wine consumption has proven health benefits, and now there is growing interest in organic and biodynamic varieties that also protect environmental health. While organic wines are those made from certified organically grown grapes, biodynamic practices encompass further measures like crop rotation, composting, and others that treat the vineyard as a living organism. Sales of organic and biodynamic wine so far represent a very small percentage of overall wine sales (interesting perspectives on this are available via the Gray Report at http://bit.ly/z5VTzk). Organic beer sales in the United States have enjoyed greater success, more than quadrupling from $9 million in 2003 to $41 million in 2009. In 2005, organic beer tied with organic coffee as the beverage with the fastest-growing sales, according to the Organic Trade Association.

commodity. When First Lady Michelle Obama planted an organic garden at the White House, it set a wonderful example for all as to what might be accomplished. Agriculture and the businesses of food distribution and preparation have impacts on our natural world, which would be hard to overstate, so let's hope that America continues to go green regarding food and drink.

KRIS SCHACHEL

See also: BioPreferred Program (documents); Brewing, Eco-Friendly (Food); Diet, Vegetarian and Vegan (Food); ChooseMyPlate.gov (documents); Dietary Guidelines for Americans (documents); Food and Diet (Food); Food and Entertaining (Food); Organic and Natural Foods (Food); Organic Labeling and Marketing (documents).

References

Cloud, J. 2007. "Eating Better Than Organic." *Time*, March 12.

Collins, K. 2010. *Watching What We Eat: The Evolution of Television Cooking Shows*. New York: Continuum.

Moore-Lappe, F., and A. Moore. 2003. *Hope's Edge: The Next Diet for a Small Planet*. New York: Tarcher.

Petrini, C. 2001. *Slow Food: Collected Thoughts on Taste, Tradition, and the Honest Pleasures of Food*. Chelsea Green.

Pollan, M. 2008. "Farmer in Chief." *New York Times*, October 9.

Stone, M. K., and Z. Barlow, eds. 2005. *Ecological Literacy: Educating Our Children for a Sustainable World*. Sierra Club Books.

GENETICALLY MODIFIED ORGANISMS

Genetic modification of agricultural crops is a process by which genes are transferred from one organism to another to confer certain growth benefits onto a given crop. Unlike traditional forms of plant breeding, genetic modification mixes genes from different species in a laboratory setting in ways that would never occur in nature. Genetic modification uses bacteria to introduce foreign material into host organisms, and thus new genes as well as new bacteria are introduced into organisms that would never occur there otherwise. One example of genetic modification is

Ears of genetically modified corn, produced by Monsanto. Monsanto and other biotechnology companies produce a wide array of genetically modified crops, touting the potential for high yields possible with disease-resistant strains of corn. But critics of bioengineering, including influential nations of the European Union, are worried about the unknown long-term impacts on human health and the environment. (Monsanto U.K.)

bacterially inserting genes from the arctic flounder into strawberries, attempting to make them frost resistant. Another example is putting a human gene into corn so that the corn antibodies can be used as a spermicidal contraceptive gel.

The most common genetically modified (GM) crops in the United States are corn, soy, cotton, and canola. Currently, the majority of these crops are grown using genetically modified seed. Corn is genetically modified to confer pest resistance by inserting genes that produce the bacteria *Bacillus thuringiensis* (Bt) in the corn. This Bt bacterium produces insecticidal toxins and thus increases susceptibility to infection among corn pests. Corn can also be GM to be resistant to Roundup, a glyphosate herbicide produced by Monsanto. This allows GM corn fields to be sprayed with Roundup so that it kills the undesirable plants without killing the corn.

Some of the destructive consequences of GM crops on the ecosystem have been documented in the scientific literature, but much of the investigation into GM crops has been stifled for political reasons. John Losey, a Cornell entomologist, and his colleagues (1999) reported that nearly half of the monarch butterfly caterpillars eating leaves dusted with Bt maize pollen died after four days, compared with none exposed to non-GM pollen. Following publication of this and other papers investigating the impact of GM crops, the methodologies used were called into question and publications were retracted in some cases (after peer review had already been conducted) due to the influence of the industry.

The health impacts of consuming genetically modified organisms (GMOs) are likewise only partially understood. Most research has been conducted in laboratory animals because the U.S. Food and Drug Administration (FDA) did not require extensive human testing of GMOs before release to the public under the category of "generally recognized as safe." The FDA does not require labeling of GM ingredients in food, making it difficult to trace any side effects associated with GMO consumption. This is despite the fact that GM foods have potentially high levels of plant toxicants, pesticides, allergens, and other compounds that disrupt organ function. Australian researchers found that a GM pea caused lung inflammation and other adverse effects in mice (Vanessa et al., 2005). Researchers from France compared organ system and blood data among rats fed GM corn to those who were fed non-GM corn. The side effects linked with GM maize consumption included damage to the kidney and liver (the dietary detoxifying organs), heart, adrenal glands, spleen, and hematopoietic system (de Vendômois et al., 2009).

In addition to ecological and human health complications, GM crops pose threats to the livelihood of farmers. Ignacio Chapela, a biologist at the University of California–Berkeley, published that GM corn has contaminated native maize varieties in Mexico. Maize has been under cultivation for thousands of years in Mexico, where they grow over 3,000 specialized varieties of corn. Monsanto, the company primarily responsible for the cultivation of GM crops in the United States, routinely sues farmers whose crops have been unintentionally contaminated with GM crops through spread of pollen in the wind. Many farmers have lost their farms due to the court expenses incurred while defending themselves. A film called *The Future of Food* documents stories of Monsanto's litigations against farmers.

In late 2011, Boulder County, Colorado, joined other communities in the United States and 30 other countries worldwide in banning GM crops. Efforts to ban GM crops are in support of ethical and sustainable farming practices, wildlife protection, and a safe, local, and chemical-free food supply.

RAINBOW VOGT

See also: BioPreferred Program (documents); Brewing, Eco-Friendly (Food); ChooseMy Plate.gov (documents); Dietary Guidelines (documents); Food and Entertaining (Food); Food and Diet (Food); Food, Drink, and Media (Food); Organic Labeling and Marketing Information (documents); Organic and Natural Foods (Food).

References

de Vendômois, J. S., F. Roullier, D. Cellier, and G. E. Séralini. 2009. "A Comparison of the Effects of Three GM Corn Varieties on Mammalian Health." *International Journal Biological Science* 5: 706–726.

Losey, J., L. S. Rayor, and M. E. Carter. 1999. "Transgenic Pollen Harms Monarch Larvae." *Nature* 399:6733: 214.

Vanessa, E., P. M. Prescott, A. M. Campbell, M. Joerg, E. Marc, P. S. Rothenberg, T. Foster, V. Higgins, and S. P. Hogan. 2005. "Transgenic Expression of Bean-Amylase Inhibitor in Peas Results in Altered Structure and Immunogenicity." *Journal of Agricultural and Food Chemistry* 53:23: 9023–9030.

GROCERS, GREEN

While historically the term *green grocers* referred to retailers of fresh produce, the terminology has shifted in the 21st century. In particular in the United States, the green grocers are typically the food retailers that focus on selling natural, sustainably produced, environmentally friendly, and organic food products. The interest in green or natural grocers started with the back-to-the-earth or the back-to-the-land movement of the 1970s and was part of a broader interest in environmental issues and whole food. Although interest in these grocers lagged in the 1980s, the numbers of green grocers saw rapid growth in the 1990s and into the 21st century. There is no broadly accepted definition of a green grocer, and it is therefore difficult to estimate the number of green grocers in the United States. However, in 2009, the U.S. Department of Agriculture (USDA) estimated that there were approximately 20,000 natural food stores that were selling organic products.

Green grocers are seen to have a positive impact on the environment largely because they carry products that are seen to be made in a fashion that is more sustainable and products that can be disposed of in an environmentally friendly manner. Many food products are organically certified and have been produced using

The Reading Terminal Market, shown here in 2009, offers produce fresh from the field to the people of Philadelphia, Pennsylvania. (U.S. Department of Agriculture)

few synthetic inputs. Local foods, when carried by green grocers, benefit the environment since they require fewer fossil fuels for transportation. It is common to find bulk food items that require few resources in terms of packaging as well as products such as cleaning supplies that are biodegradable and nontoxic. Although many of the products available from green grocers likely have a positive impact on the environment, some critiques have suggested that the environment would be better served if people consumed less rather than simply relying more on green products. Furthermore, the environmental impact of products, such as organic food shipped from China, may be mixed when the impact of transportation is factored into the environmental benefits of organic farming.

The green grocers of today fall into three different categories: chain retailers, independent retailers, and direct marketers. Both chain and independent retailers operate as conventional grocery stores and simply specialize in natural and organic products. Although food is probably the largest part of most green grocers, most carry a wide variety of products such as nutritional supplements, health care products, cleaning supplies, and other items. Direct marketing arrangements are typically not organized as "stores" to the same extent as chain and independent green grocers; however, they still represent a significant and growing location through which consumers are accessing green food. All three categories of green grocers have benefited from growing consumer interest in natural and organic food and have grown in the 21st century.

The expansion of national or regional chain green grocers is perhaps one of the most significant shifts in the green culture of America in the 21st century. In many cases, these retailers may have had roots as small, natural food stores from the middle of the 20th century who grew and consolidated in a pattern similar to conventional food retailers. These retailers are often very large and carry a diverse set of products, sometimes ranging up to 40,000 or more different items. The most notable green grocer in this category is Whole Foods Market, which in 2011 was the largest and fastest growing natural foods retailer in the United States. Whole Foods Market started in 1980 in Austin, Texas, and by 2011 had expanded to nearly 300 locations and 54,000 employees (Whole Food Market, 2011). Of course, Whole Foods Market is not the only green grocer to benefit from growing consumer interest in natural and organic products. Trader Joe's, which first opened in the 1960s and by 2011 had grown to well over 300 locations throughout the United States (Trader Joe's, n.d.). Although Trader Joe's started in California and is still largely concentrated in the western part of the United States, they do operate stores throughout the east coast and midwest.

One of the most significant critiques of green grocers is related to the cost of their products. Organic food is often more expensive than conventional food, and many of the specialty products that fill the shelves of green grocers carry a significant price premium. Critiques suggest that this price premium is problematic from a social justice perspective since it effectively excludes large sectors of the population from shopping there. Although Whole Foods Market has marketed itself as a retailer that sells high-quality natural and organic products, it has also gained the nickname of "Whole Paycheck" as a result of the cost of shopping there. Green grocers, both of the chain and independent variety, defend their prices, noting that the quality of the products is often higher than conventional products and the specialty nature of the products requires higher prices. Their goal is to provide a particular type of product to a growing niche market, not to create universally available food. Furthermore, many green grocers stock locally produced foods, and this is seen as beneficial to the local economy since it keeps food dollars in the community. Therefore, while not everyone is able to shop at these stores, they are still of benefit to the surrounding community by helping support local farmers.

Independent food retailers are similar to chain retailers in that they also specialize in natural and organic food. In contrast, these green grocers typically involve only one, or in some cases a few, retail locations. Although there are exceptions, these are typically much smaller stores than chain retailers and they offer a smaller variety of items. In some cases these retailers may operate as conventional for-profit businesses, while in other cases they may operate as cooperatives that are customer owned and, in some cases, customer operated. The Puget Consumers Cooperate Natural Market in Seattle, Washington, is an example of one of the largest cooperatives in the United States, although there are hundreds located throughout the country. There are likely thousands more small, natural food stores operating as conventional businesses throughout the United States.

The third category of green grocers, direct marketers, is the smallest of the three categories in terms of number of locations as well as sales volume. Nonetheless, it represents the most interesting cultural shift in terms of the structure of food retailing. As opposed to the previous two categories, these green grocers do not operate as retailers, but rather provide venues for the direct sale of products from farmers to consumers. Farmers' markets are the largest and most easily tracked form of these green grocers. Farmers' markets provide a venue for farmers to directly sell their fresh produce to consumers in either open-air or enclosed market places. Typically, farmers pay a fee to the market to support the infrastructure and other costs associated with organizing the market itself. According to the USDA, there were 6,132 farmers markets operating in 2010 (USDA, 2010). The number of markets had grown 349 percent since 1994. In all likelihood, the USDA figures are low estimates since there are many small farmers markets that operate in conjunction with

Farmers' Markets

On a global scale, the idea of the public marketplace as a venue to obtain food and wares has been around since antiquity. Ancient Greece provided for its citizens in municipal marketplaces, the Senate of Ancient Rome guarded a right for it to establish public markets, and during the feudal period in the Middle Ages, markets continued to flourish under the discretion of the papal canon.

Today, food production, food distribution, and food consumption systems in the United States are overwhelmingly organized through global corporations. Prior to refrigeration and trucking systems, early farmers' markets in the United States provided critical markets area for farmers and area residents alike. Local governments took charge of providing a safe and fair marketplace for both vendors and consumers, and the public market system was critical throughout the 19th century in the

United States, despite the growing number of private food stores (Tangires, 2003).

Although farmers' markets continued to exist throughout the 20th century, there was a noticeable resurgence of farmers' markets across the United States beginning in the 1990s. Urban planners are increasingly taking note of farmers' markets as an important opportunity to address community welfare. As the planning profession grows more interested in the interplay between the built environment and health, some scholars are urging their colleagues to take a more active interest in community food issues (Kaufman & Pothukuchi, 2000). Civic leaders with multiple motives are creating farmers' markets because of their role in the economic, social, and environmental improvements in many cities and towns across the United States. Since 1994, the number of farmers' markets has increased 79 percent to just over 3,700 markets in all 50 states, and the number of participating farmers has more than tripled to 67,000 (Payne, 2002). The number of farmers' markets in the United States continues to grow, and according to the U.S. Department of Agriculture, there were 4,685 in August 2008. The 2007 Census of Agriculture reported a remarkable $1.2 billion in food sold directly from farmers to consumers. This is a 17 percent increase over the previous five years. In October 2009, the U.S. Department of Agriculture reported 5,274 farmers markets operating in the United States. This represents an 84 percent increase over the past 10 years. Fifteen percent of these markets operate in winter months, extending their seasons to generate more reliable income for small-scale family farmers and build sustainable local economies (USDA, 2009).

Farmers' markets are largely regulated by state agriculture agencies as well as local and county food safety agencies and local zoning boards. The federal government supports market development through USDA grants, research, and promotion. If the national concern for locally produced food continues, it is expected that the number of farmers' markets will also continue to grow.

MATTHEW LINDSTROM

hospitals, neighborhood centers, churches, and other organizations scattered throughout the country.

Although other direct marketing green grocers are more difficult to track, they nonetheless represent an important set of retailers. Farm side stands, for example, represent a direct operating arrangement where a single farm sells produce directly to consumers. While these stands can be very formally organized with a fully staffed retail building, there are also countless informal stands that involve as a little as a table and a cash box set out along a busy road. In the late 1990s and early 21st century, Community Supported Agriculture (CSA) services also developed as a new way to link consumers with food. In a CSA arrangement, consumers purchase a share of one or more farms produce before the growing season. Throughout the growing season, the farm provides a portion of the farm's produce to each shareholder either at a specified pickup point or directly to the consumer's home. CSA arrangements are meant to benefit farmers by providing them with a reliable and safe market since crop failures due to weather, pests, or other factors will impact all the shareholders rather than just the farmer. Although not a green grocer in the traditional sense, CSA represents a good example of how 21st-century marketing arrangements have shifted in novel directions. According to the U.S. Agricultural Census, there were 12,549 farms marketing through a CSA arrangement in 2007.

Direct market green grocers have, for the most part, escaped the economic critique that has been levered against chain and independent retailers. Since they

Farm Fresh to You owner Thaddeus Barsotti and USDA secretary Tom Vilsack inspect a fresh-pack box of organic produce at the company's warehouse in West Sacramento, California in 2011. An example of Community Supported Agriculture (CSA), Farm Fresh to You is a service that provides regular and direct delivery of organic produce fresh from a local organic farm to residential and business customers in the community. (U.S. Department of Agriculture)

typically involve selling produce directly from farmers to consumers, there is not a middle person to capture the value of the product and, therefore, even organic or natural products can often be found at prices closer to those found in conventional food retailers. On the other hand, direct market green grocers often carry a much more limited selection than traditionally formatted green grocers and may even operate under seasonal limitations. Some markets overcome seasonal limitations by reselling produce that was grown in warmer climates. However, this sometimes creates tension within some markets as some market proponents believe that only locally grown produce should be sold at a market. As a result, some markets have created "producer only" rules that preclude the reselling of produce that was not grown by the seller.

Whether large chain stores such as Whole Foods Market or small, direct sales arrangements like farmers markets, interest in green grocers is growing rapidly in the United States. The recent growth in green grocers can be viewed as part of growing consumer demand for organic and natural food that has been minimally processed or produced with few synthetic inputs. This growing consumer demand for particular types of food has been part of a new wave of "reflexive consumers" who are interested in more than just obtaining inexpensive and convenient food. Rather these reflexive consumers represent a largely affluent middle class who is thinking explicitly about the environmental and social impact of how food is produced and the long-term health consequences of consuming particular types of food. Although 20th-century food was largely about costs and, in the later part of the century, the nutritional quality of the food, the 21st century has been profoundly about how the food itself was produced.

Driven by popular writers such as Michael Pollan (*The Omnivore's Dilemma*) and Eric Schlosser (*Fast Food Nation*) as well as movies such as *Supersize Me* and *Food, Inc.*, consumers of the 21st century have begun to demand changes, not only to food as a product, but also to the process through which it is produced. Changes in the popular media such as the success of the cable television channel Food Network as well as a variety of cooking and food shows on other networks further highlighted America's growing interest in organic and natural food. Consumer interest in how food was produced was further enhanced by growing concerns with food safety. A wide variety of acute food safety problems ranging from H1N1 (swine) and bird flu to *E. coli* poisoning and mad cow disease highlighted the relationship between how food was produced and how safe it was to eat. At the same time, the growing evidence of a link between food consumption and chronic diseases such as cancer and heart disease further provided pressure on grocery stores to provide organic and natural foods to meet this growing demand.

It seems very likely that green grocers will see significant growth going into the early part of the 21st century. However, competition is coming most significantly from conventional food retailers who have expanded their selection of products to include more natural and organic products. In 2006, Walmart announced that it would double its organic offerings in its stores. Many other large food retailers have followed suit in order to take advantage of this growing market. As conventional food retailers increasingly enter into the market previously dominated by specialty stores, green grocers are likely to feel the squeeze.

It also seems very likely that the products that are available in green grocers are likely to see some changes in the future. Both changes will relate directly to the place where products are grown or made. First, locally made or locally grown products will become increasingly important to green grocers. The early roots of green grocers in the middle of the 20th century focused on natural food, and growth through the 1990s was heavily influenced by organic food and, perhaps to a lesser degree, interest in nutritional supplements. As the United States entered the 21st century, local food became the new buzzword, and grocers who were not already engaged in locally sourcing their products have begun to seek, and advertise, products that were produced in the vicinity surrounding their retail establishments. In this thread we see direct market green grocers as having a growing influence on more conventionally formatted green grocers.

Ironically, the second change influencing green grocers will come in the form of globalization. Globalization is likely to influence green grocers in a variety of ways.

It has helped green grocers diversify their product selection by making available a wide variety of ethnically diverse food. It has also created new areas for green grocers to source organic and naturally made products for their stores. Whole Foods Market, for example, sources many organic products from China. Globalization will also create new opportunities for global expansion as markets in the United States become increasingly saturated. The growing middle class in rapidly developing countries, such as China and India, represents significant consumer markets, in particular for the large chain green grocers that are looking to expand.

BRIAN J. THOMAS

See also: BioPreferred Program (documents); Brewing, Eco-Friendly (Food); Diet, Vegetarian and Vegan (Food); ChooseMyPlate.gov (documents); Dietary Guidelines for Americans (documents); Food and Diet (Food); Food and Entertaining (Food); Food, Drink, and Media (Food); Organic and Natural Foods (Food); Organic Labeling and Marketing (documents).

Food Deserts

Food deserts represent areas, often in an inner city, where access to healthy food by a resource-limited population is limited due to the lack of a grocery store or supermarket. The specific distances used to define food deserts ranges from half a mile to a few miles; however, they are typically identified by examining how far supermarkets are from a resource-limited neighborhood. Both neighborhood demographics and distance are important components because many people can easily drive from their homes to a grocery store. On the other hand, in neighborhoods where many residents do not have an automobile or are unable to drive, having a grocery store even one or two miles away can make accessing healthy food difficult. Consequently, food deserts are particularly problematic for low-income and elderly populations as well as for people with disabilities. Food deserts have emerged in many inner cities as large supermarkets have opened in suburban locations to access more affluent consumers and take advantage of open tracts of land where large stores can easily be situated. Small grocers have been unable to compete with the large suburban supermarkets and left many neighborhoods without a nearby food retailer.

References

Farmers' Market Coalition. "'Markets Are Up' Campaigns." Available at: http://farmersmar ketcoalition.org/membership/markets-are-up-campaign/.

Kaufman, Jerome, and Kemeshwari Pothukuchi. 2000. "The Food System: A Stranger to the Planning Field." *Journal of the American Planning Association* 66:2: 113, 119.

Payne, Tim. 2002. "U.S. Farmers' Markets 2000: A Study of Emerging Trends." USDA, May 2002. Available at: http://ageconsearch.umn.edu/bitstream/27625/1/33010173.pdfhttp://webharvest.gov/peth04/20041108033659/http://www.ams.usda.gov/directmarketing/FarmMark.pdf.

Tangires, Helen. 2003. *Public Markets and Civic Culture in the Nineteenth-Century America.* Baltimore: Johns Hopkins University Press.

Trader Joe's. n.d. "Where in the Dickens Can You Find a Trader Joe's." Available at: http://www.traderjoes.com/pdf/locations/all-llocations.pdf.

U.S. Department of Agriculture. 2009. "Organic Agriculture: Organic Market Overview." September 1. Available at: http://www.ers.usda.gov/briefing/organic/demand.htm.

U.S. Department of Agriculture. 2010. "Farmers Market Growth: 1994–2010." Available at: / www.ams.usda.gov/AMSv1.0/ams.fetchTemplateData.do?template=TemplateS&left Nav=WholesaleandFarmersMarkets&page=WFMFarmersMarketGrowth&description= Farmers%20Market%20Growth&acct=frmrdirmkt.

Whole Foods Market, Inc. 2011. "Annual Stakeholders' Report 2010." Available at: http://www.wholefoodsmarket.com/company/pdfs/ar10.pdf.

LOCAL AND SUSTAINABLE FOOD

Over the past few decades, many scholars have examined relocalizing food systems and the development of local food systems (Feenstra, 1997; Hinrichs, 2002; Kloppenburg et al., 1996; Murdoch et al., 2000). These local food systems are often offered as alternatives to the increasing globalization and concentration of the agricultural system. At the same time, local food systems have gained increased media and political attention as President Barack Obama's administration has provided a prominent place for sustainable agriculture at the federal level—from organic gardens cultivated in the White House garden and on U.S. Department of Agriculture (USDA) grounds, to the farmers' market opened just outside the White

First Lady Michelle Obama and White House chef Sam Kass show students from Bancroft Elementary how to plant a garden in 2009. (White House)

House grounds, to the new federal agency work and policies focused on local food systems.

There is no clear geographic definition of what constitutes local. Research has shown that consumers and farmers/businesses have varying ideas of how local can be measured and interpreted, although for many it is an area smaller than state boundaries, such as within a county or "within 100 miles" (Duram & Oberholtzer, 2010; King et al., 2010; Martinez et al., 2010). The 2008 Farm Bill considers a product to be a locally or regionally produced agricultural food product if it is produced and transported less than 400 miles from its origin, or within the state in which it is produced. King and colleagues (2010) further define local food as a product that has been raised, produced, and processed within the locality or region where the product is marketed.

Measuring the extent of local foods systems is also difficult because of the wide array of practices that it encompasses, from direct to consumer marketing at the very smallest scale (such as Community Supported Agriculture—CSA—or local foods served in gourmet restaurants), to local agricultural products available through large food retailers, such as Walmart. In addition, there are limited statistics on the production and distribution of food marketed locally. For example, the Census of Agriculture provides few statistics on local food systems other than direct-to-consumer sales. Regardless, there are real signs that the supply and sales of local foods are increasing, including a surge in consumer interest in these products and a significant rise in the number of farmers' markets, local foods in schools (farm to school), and other direct-to-consumer forms of food marketing over the past decade (Martinez et al., 2010).

Researchers generally estimate that the food system uses between 12 and 20 percent of all energy consumption in the United States (Hendrickson, 1996). They also estimate that fresh produce travels an average of 1,500 miles from farm to table, seemingly resulting in increased energy consumption (Hendrickson, 1996). Advocates of local food systems often cite environmental benefits, such as reducing energy inputs and greenhouse gas emissions, of buying local (Allen & Hinrichs, 2007; Peters et al., 2008). However, quantifying the impact of local food systems on resource use is a complex undertaking, and, thus far, the research has been contradictory and, at times, narrowly focused and inconclusive (Duram & Oberholtzer, 2010).

There are a number of tools that are increasingly being used, most often in the European Union, to study agricultural commodities and systems to determine the environmental impact of local food. The concept of food miles, or measuring the distance and impact of food between where it is grown and consumed, is one measure that has gained popularity in analyzing environmental impacts. Lifecycle assessment is recognized as one way to include energy flows within all stages of the food chain, encompassing all aspects of the production system from beginning to end (Edwards-Jones et al., 2008). The means-ends assessment, on the other hand, includes more subjective considerations about seasonality and locally appropriate crops (Jones, 2002). These tools have been used for a number of commodities over the past decade, with varying results.

In one study, a fruit grown closer to home has reduced energy consumption and carbon dioxide emissions than one from farther away (Jones, 2002). However, seasonality and local conditions in the location of production must also be taken into account when studying local versus nonlocal foods. For example, fruit (such as apples) that is available in the autumn in the northern hemisphere would need to be held in cold storage for consumption the following spring to be available when southern hemisphere fruit is in season. Still, a study of apples consumed in Germany in the springtime, which had been refrigerated for 5 months, found that locally produced German apples require 27 percent less energy than apples shipped in from New Zealand (Blanke & Burdick, 2005). On the other hand, another study found that importation of Spanish field-grown lettuce into the United Kingdom during winter produced fewer greenhouse gas emissions than lettuce produced in UK-protected systems at that time (Hospido et al., 2009). Similar results were found for New Zealand dairy, lamb, and apples imported to the United Kingdom (Wilson, 2007).

Other aspects of the entire system must also be taken into account, such as consumer shopping patterns and transportation systems. Two studies found that consumers driving more than a certain distance (7.4 km and 2 km, respectively) to a local shop are likely to emit more carbon emissions than consumers using home delivery options (Coley et al., 2009; Jones, 2002). Using a bicycle or walking to purchase food or using a bus or getting home delivery instead of using a car to shop can decrease the external environmental costs of the weekly UK food basket significantly (Pretty et al., 2005). In addition, locally produced (within 20 km) food transported to retail outlets, as well as food produced nationally but transported primarily through a rail system, decrease environmental costs (Pretty et al., 2005).

Scale of the food business is also important. In one study on fruit juices and lamb meat (Schlich & Fleissner, 2005), efficiency of production and operations was the most important variable in energy use. In both cases, the imported product (lamb imported from New Zealand and fruit juices from Brazil) required less energy than the same product from regional companies and farms, whose smaller size impacted their ability to invest in energy-saving technologies, resulting in less efficient transportation systems and farming practices. Scale is also raised in a recent study by the USDA as important to energy efficiency in local food systems (King et al., 2010).

Production methods must also be accounted for in any assessment. One recent study showed that greenhouse gas emissions from agriculture were concentrated in the production phase (83 percent), with transportation accounting for only 11 percent of greenhouse gas emissions and final delivery from producer to retailer representing just 4 percent of the total (Weber & Matthews, 2008). Several studies indicated that organic production methods require significantly lower energy inputs than conventional production (Hill, 2009; Pimentel, 2006; Reganold et al., 2001), although often additional inputs in labor hours are needed in the organic system.

Finally, dietary choices and their interplay with local food can significantly impact the environment. According to one study, changing to a vegetarian diet has a greater impact on lowering greenhouse gas emissions than buying local (Weber & Matthews, 2008). However, there are exceptions. While the environmental impact of vegetarian foods is usually relatively low, in some cases, if variables such as long-distance air transport, deep freezing, and some horticultural practices (such as heated greenhouse use) are included in the vegetarian food purchased, the environmental burdens of these foods could exceed those for locally produced organic meat (Reijnders & Soret, 2003).

Regardless of the tools used to assess the impact of eating local versus nonlocal food, as can be seen by the above discussion, the effort is complex. As the demand for local foods increases, many researchers are also grappling with whether regions or localities, especially northern areas and those with arid conditions, have the capacity to provide local food year round and in substantial quantities. Many of these studies take into account land use, which will be of interest to researchers examining the environmental impact of local foods. In addition, other important reasons consumers may purchase local foods (e.g., social, community, economic) are usually not factored into studies focused on the environmental impact of local food systems, although they have been studied in depth (Duram & Oberholtzer, 2010).

LYDIA OBERHOLTZER AND LESLIE A. DURAM

See also: BioPreferred Program (documents); Diet, Vegetarian and Vegan (Food); Choose MyPlate.gov (documents); Dietary Guidelines for Americans (documents); Food and Diet (Food); Food and Entertaining (Food); Food, Drink, and Media (Food); Organic and Natural Foods (Food); Organic Labeling and Marketing (documents).

References

Allen, P., and C. Hinrichs. 2007. "Buying into 'Buy Local': Engagement of United States Local Food Initiatives." In D. Maye, L. Holloway, and M. Kneafsey, eds., *Alternative Food Geographies: Representation and Practice*. Oxford, UK: Elsevier.

Blanke, M. M., and B. Burdick. 2005. "Food (Miles) for Thought: Energy Balance for Locally-Grown versus Imported Apple Fruit." *Environmental Science and Pollution Resource* 12: 125–127.

Coley, D., M. Howard, and M. Winters. 2009. "Local Food, Food Miles and Carbon Emissions: A Comparison of Farm Shop and Mass Distribution Approaches." *Food Policy* 34: 150–155.

Duram, L., and L. Oberholtzer. 2010. "A Geographic Approach to Examining Place and Natural Resource Use in Local Food Systems." *Renewable Agriculture and Food Systems* 25:2: 99–108.

Edwards-Jones, G., L. Mila'i Canals, N. Hounsome, M. Truninger, G. Koerber, B. Hounsome, P. Cross, E. H. York, A. Hospido, K. Plassmann, I. M. Harris, R. T. Edwards, G. A. S. Day, A. Deri Tomos, S. J. Cowell, and D. L. Jones. 2008. "Testing the Assertion that 'Local Food Is Best': The Challenges of an Evidence-Based Approach." *Trends in Food Science and Technology* 19: 265–274.

Feenstra, G. 1997. "Local Food Systems and Sustainable Communities." *American Journal of Alternative Agriculture* 12:1: 28–36.

Hendrickson, J. 1996. "Energy Use in the U.S. Food System: A Summary of Existing Research and Analysis." Center for Integrated Agriculture Systems, University of Wisconsin–Madison. Available at: http://www.cias.wisc.edu/wpcontent/uploads/2009/07/energy use.pdf.

Hill, H. 2009. "Comparing Energy Use in Conventional and Organic Cropping Systems." ATTRA. National Sustainable Agriculture Information Service. Available at: http://www.attra.ncat.org/attra-pub/PDF/croppingsystems.pdf.

Hinrichs, C. C. 2002. "The Practice and Politics of Food System Localization." *Journal of Rural Studies* 19:1: 33–45.

Hospido, A., L. Canals, S. MacLaren, M. Truninger, G. Edwards-Jones, and R. Clift. 2009. "The Role of Seasonality in Lettuce Consumption: A Case Study of Environmental and Social Aspects." *International Journal of Life Cycle Assessment* 14: 381–391.

Jones, A. 2002. "An Environmental Assessment of Food Supply Chains: A Case Study on Dessert Apples." *Environmental Assessment* 30: 560–576.

King, R., M. Hand, G. DiGiacomo, K. Clancy, M. Gómez, S. Hardesty, L. Lev, and E. McLaughlin. 2010. "Comparing the Structure, Size, and Performance of Local and Mainstream Food Supply Chains." U.S. Department of Agriculture, Economic Research Service, Economic Research Report No. 99. Available at: http://www.ers.usda.gov/Publications/ERR99/ERR99.pdf.

Kloppenburg, J., J. Hendrickson, and G. W. Stevenson. 1996. "Coming into the Foodshed." *Agriculture and Human Values* 13:3: 33–42.

Martinez, S., M. Hand, M. Da Pra, S. Pollack, K. Ralston, T. Smith, S. Vogel, S. Clark, L. Lohr, S. Low, and C. Newman. 2010. "Local Food Systems: Concepts, Impacts and Issues." U.S. Department of Agriculture, Economic Research Service. Economic Research Report No. 97. Available at: http://www.ers.usda.gov/Publications/ERR97/ERR97.pdf.

Murdoch, J., T. Marsden, and J. Banks. 2000. "Quality, Nature, and Embeddedness: Some Theoretical Considerations in the Context of the Food Sector." *Economic Geography* 76:2: 107–125.

Peters, C. J., N. L. Bills, J. L. Wilkins, and G. W. Fick. 2008. "Foodshed Analysis and Its Relevance to Sustainability." *Renewable Agriculture and Food Systems* 24: 1–7.

Pimentel, D. 2006. "Impacts of Organic Farming on the Efficiency of Energy Use in Agriculture: State of Science Report." Organic Center, Boulder, Colorado.

Pretty, J. N., A. S. Ball, T. Lang, and J. I. L. Morison. 2005. "Farm Costs and Food Miles: An Assessment of the Full Cost of the UK Weekly Food Basket." *Food Policy* 30: 1–19.

Reganold, J. P., J. D. Glover, P. K. Andrews, and H. R. Hinman. 2001. "Sustainability of Three Apple Production Systems." *Nature* 410: 929–930.

Reijnders, L., and S. Soret. 2003. "Quantification of the Environmental Impact of Different Dietary Protein Choices." *American Journal of Clinical Nutrition* 78:3: 664S–668S.

Schlich, E. H., and U. Fleissner. 2005. "The Ecology of Scale: Assessment of Regional Energy Turnover and Comparison with Global Food." *International Journal of Life Cycle Assessment* 10:3: 219–223.

Weber, C. L., and S. H. Matthews. 2008. "Food-Miles and the Relative Climate Impacts of Food Choices in the United States." *Environmental Science and Technology* 42:10: 3508–3513.

Wilson, T. 2007. "The 'Food Miles' Fallacy." Institute of Public Affairs, Australia. Available at: http://www.ipa.org.au.

ORGANIC AND NATURAL FOODS

Sales of organic and natural foods have increased greatly over the past 20 years (Dimitri & Oberholtzer, 2009). Organic foods, which garnered under $4 billion in sales in 1997, have increased to almost $27 billion by 2011 or approximately

4 percent of overall food sales (Dimitri & Oberholtzer, 2009; OTA, 2011). At the same time, total sales of organic and natural foods combined were estimated at $39 billion for 2010 (Packaged Facts, 2011).

The growth in organic sales has fueled changes at the retail level as well (Dimitri & Oberholtzer, 2009). In the late 1990s, the natural-products channel (independent and small-chain natural product stores, food cooperatives, and large natural-food-product retailers such as Whole Foods Market) was the primary sales outlet for organic food. By 2006, approximately equal shares of organic food were sold in the conventional channel, which includes stores such as Safeway, Walmart, and Sam's Club, as in the natural-products channel. The types of organic products purchased by consumers have also shifted from the majority of sales focused on organic fruits and vegetables in the late 1990s to consumers purchasing a wider range of other products. For instance, in 2008,

Smucker's Natural Peanut Butter (U.S. Food and Drug Administration)

organic dairy, beverages, packaged and prepared foods, and bread and grains accounted for 63 percent of total organic sales.

At its very core, organic farming is a method of food production that considers the farm as an entire system that is connected to the ecosystem and all other aspects of the farm. Formally, organic production is a system that is managed in accordance with the Organic Foods Production Act (OFPA) of 1990 and regulations in Title 7, Part 205 of the Code of Federal Regulations to respond to site-specific conditions by integrating cultural, biological, and mechanical practices that foster cycling of resources, promote ecological balance, and conserve biodiversity (USDA, NOP, 2011).

Congress passed the Organic Foods Production Act of 1990 to establish national standards for organically produced commodities, and the USDA implemented the standards in October 2002 (see USDA NOP, 2008, for more background information). The national organic standards require that organic growers and handlers (including food processors, manufacturers, and some distributors) be certified by state or private agencies or organizations under the uniform standards developed by USDA, unless the farmers and handlers sell less than $5,000 a year in organic agricultural products. Imported agricultural products may be sold in the United States; these products must meet the National Organic Program (NOP) standards, either through foreign certifying agents accredited by the USDA or through recognition agreements. In 2009, the United States entered an equivalency agreement with Canada, allowing products that are produced and certified according to one country's organic standards to be sold and represented as organic in the other country. To gain organic certification, a farmer in the United States (of cropland, pastureland, or livestock) pays a certifier, accredited by the USDA's NOP, to inspect the farm annually and review the farm's organic system plan.

The national organic standards address the methods, practices, and substances used in producing and handling crops, livestock, and processed agricultural products. Although specific practices and materials used by organic operations may vary, the standards require every aspect of organic production and handling to comply with the provisions of the Organic Foods Production Act. The NOP regulations prohibit the use of genetic engineering, ionizing radiation, and sewage sludge in organic production and handling. These standards include a national list of approved synthetic, and prohibited nonsynthetic, substances for use in organic production and handling. Organic crops are raised without using most conventional pesticides and petroleum-based fertilizers. Animals raised on an organic operation must be fed organic feed and given access to the outdoors. They are given no antibiotics or growth hormones.

The labeling requirements under the national standards apply to raw, fresh, and processed products that contain organic ingredients and are based on the percentage of organic ingredients in a product. Agricultural products labeled "100-percent organic" must contain (excluding water and salt) only organically produced ingredients. Products labeled "organic" must consist of at least 95 percent organically produced ingredients. Products labeled "made with organic ingredients" must contain at least 70 percent organic ingredients. Products with less than 70 percent organic ingredients cannot use the term *organic* anywhere on the principal display panel but may identify the specific ingredients that are organically produced in the ingredients statement on the information panel. The USDA organic seal—the words "USDA organic" inside a circle—may be used on agricultural products that are "100 percent organic" or "organic."

The term *natural* often competes with organic foods at the retail level, and the labels for natural can be confusing for consumers. The term *natural* is not regulated, except for meat and poultry. In 1989, the U.S. Food and Drug Administration issued a definition of natural that applies broadly to foods that are minimally processed and free of synthetic preservatives; artificial sweeteners, colors, flavors and other artificial additives; hydrogenated oils; stabilizers; and emulsifiers. Most foods labeled natural are not subject to government controls beyond the regulations and

USDA organic label (U.S. Department of Agriculture)

health codes that apply to all foods. As such, many products labeled "natural" contain things many consumers would not consider natural.

For meat and poultry (Oberholtzer et al., 2006), the USDA Food Safety and Inspection Service (FSIS) requires natural meat and poultry to be free of artificial colors, flavors, sweeteners, preservatives, and ingredients. These products must be minimally processed in a method that does not fundamentally change them. The label must also explain the use of the term *natural* (such as no artificial ingredients or no added colorings). Labeling meat and poultry products natural under FSIS definition does not refer to how the sources of those foods were raised, merely the processing of the product. Unlike the organic label, the natural label does not have to meet requirements for feed, antibiotic use, or pasture. The label does not require third-party certification, as does the use of the organic label.

In an attempt to address the production process of natural meats, in 2009, the USDA's Agricultural Marketing Service (AMS) released the Standards for the Naturally Raised Claim for Livestock and the Meat and Meat Products Derived from Such Livestock. The standard states that in order to sell animal products as "naturally raised," animals must be raised entirely without the growth promotants and antibiotics (except for those listed below) and never have been fed animal (mammalian, avian, or aquatic) by-products derived from the slaughter/harvest process, including manure and litter. All products labeled with a naturally raised marketing claim must incorporate information explicitly stating that animals have been raised in a manner that meets the conditions.

No statistics are kept on lands being used to raise "natural" agricultural products. Statistics on organic lands, on the other hand, have been collected over the years by the USDA's Economic Research Service (ERS) and recently by the 2007 Census of Agriculture. Not surprisingly given the increase in sales, both the quantity of farmland and the number of farms under organic management have expanded over the past 15 years. U.S. organic farmland increased from 1.3 million acres in 1997 to a little over 4.8 million acres in 2008, or 0.6 percent of all agricultural lands in 2008 (Dimitri & Oberholtzer, 2009; USDA, ERS, 2010).

Of this total, 2.7 million acres were in cropland and 2.1 million acres in rangeland and pasture (USDA, ERS, 2010). California is the leading state in certified organic cropland, followed by Wisconsin, North Dakota, Minnesota, and Montana. Livestock numbers have similarly increased from approximately 108,000 in 2002 to over 475,000 in 2008; milk cows account for the majority of these (USDA, ERS, 2010). Poultry numbers, during the same period, increased from 6.3 million to 15.5 million.

Growth in organic farmland in the United States were relatively slow in the 1990s (with annual average increases of 9 percent from 1992 to 1997) but started to increase in the late 1990s and, except for 2002, the year in which the national organic standards were implemented, continued to increase with an average annual growth rate of 15 percent from 2002 to 2008 (Oberholtzer & Dimitri, 2009; USDA, ERS, 2010). At the same time, the number of U.S. organic farms expanded from 5,021 to 12,941 by 2008.

Further supporting these numbers, as a follow-on to the 2007 Census of Agriculture, the USDA's National Agricultural Statistics Service (NASS) conducted the first in-depth national survey of organic farming (USDA, NASS, 2010). The 2008 Organic Production Survey counted 14,540 organic farms (including farms in transition) and ranches in the United States, comprising 4.1 million acres of land.

Consumers choose organic products for a variety of reasons, and the environmental impact of organic versus conventional production methods is an important issue. In terms of this aspect on the farm, the farmers' organic management plan attends to all aspects of the farm over time, which includes soil, water, wetlands, woodlands, wildlife, and food production. Buffer zones are established between organic farmland and adjacent sources of potential water, chemical, or genetic drift to prevent the organic field from being contaminated by actions taken on nearby farms. Natural resources, including soil, water, wetlands, woodlands and wildlife, must be maintained or improved. Soil organic matter (carbon storage) must be maintained or improved along with the physical, chemical, and biological condition of the soil. Erosion must be minimized and biodiversity must be enhanced. Contamination of crops, soil, or water from nutrient management is prohibited.

Certain animal welfare practices such as year-round outdoor access must be implemented. Exactly how these goals are to be achieved is not specified in rules, but they are guided by practice standards relative to the site, the production system, the farmer's plans, and the certifier's approval.

Research is still ongoing to examine the impact of organic versus conventional systems. Two reviews of literature (Pimental et al., 2005; Shepherd et al., 2003) demonstrate many environmental benefits from organic farming, although for some environmental indicators, no difference has been found. Among others, some of the benefits found in these studies include that (1) soil organic matter and nitrogen are higher in the organic farming systems, allowing for more carbon to be sequestered in organic soils (of importance to climate change); (2) high levels of soil organic matter help conserve soil and water resources; (3) fossil energy inputs for organic crop

Greenovations: Organic Lands and Markets Worldwide

Worldwide, 37.2 million hectares of land are in organic production. According to Willer and Kilcher (2011), "the regions with the largest areas of organic agricultural land are Oceania (12.2 million hectares), Europe (9.3 million hectares), and Latin America (8.6 million hectares). The countries with the most organic agricultural land are Australia, Argentina, and the United States. Overall, 0.9 percent of the world's agricultural land is organic." In 2009, there were 1.8 million organic producers worldwide, an increase of 31 percent since 2008. The countries with the most producers are India, Uganda, and Mexico.

Furthermore, "almost two-thirds of the organic agricultural land of 37.2 million hectares in 2009 was grassland/grazing areas (23 million hectares). With a total of at least 5.5 million hectares, arable land constitutes 15 percent of the organic agricultural land" (Willer & Kilcher, 2011). Most of this category of land is used for cereals, including rice, green fodder from arable land, and vegetables. Permanent crops account for approximately 6 percent of the organic agricultural land, the most important being coffee, followed by olives, cocoa, nuts, and grapes.

In 2009, organic food and drink sales were $54.9 billion, with the largest markets in the United States, Germany, and France.

production are about 30 percent lower in organic versus conventionally produced corn; (4) crop rotations and cover cropping typical of organic agriculture reduce soil erosion, pest problems, and pesticide use; (5) abundant biomass both above and below the ground increases biodiversity, which helps in the biological control of pests and increases crop pollination by insects; (6) on average, there is a positive benefit to wildlife conservation on organic farms; (7) many organic systems operate at a lower level of nitrogen intensity than conventional systems; and (8) pesticide pollution from organic farming will be far less common than from conventional agriculture with less damage to drinking water.

LYDIA OBERHOLTZER

See also: BioPreferred Program (documents); Brewing, Eco-Friendly (Food); Choose MyPlate.gov (documents); Diet, Vegetarian and Vegan (Food); Dietary Guidelines for Americans (documents); Food and Diet (Food); Food and Entertaining (Food); Food, Drink, and Media (Food); Organic Labeling and Marketing (documents).

References

Dimitri, C., and L. Oberholtzer. 2009. "Marketing U.S. Organic Foods: Recent Trends from Farms to Consumers." U.S. Department of Agriculture, Economic Research Service.

Oberholtzer, L., C. Greene, and E. Lopez. 2006. "Organic Poultry and Eggs Capture High Price Premiums and Growing Share of Specialty Markets." Outlook Report (LDPM15001). December. Washington, DC: U.S. Department of Agriculture, Economic Research Service.

Organic Trade Association (OTA). 2011. "Industry Statistics and Projected Growth." Available at: http://www.ota.com/organic/mt/business.html.

Packaged Facts. 2011. Press Release: "Natural and Organic Food and Beverage Market to Double by 2015." Available at: http://www.packagedfacts.com/about/release .asp?id=2179.

Pimentel, D., P. Hepperly, J. Hanson, D. Douds, and R. Seidel. 2005. "Environmental, Energetic, and Economic Comparisons of Organic and Conventional Farming Systems." *Bioscience* 55:7: 573–582.

Shepherd, M., B. Pearce, B. Cormack, L. Philipps, S. Cuttle, A. Bhogal, P. Costigan, and R. Unwin. 2003. "An Assessment of the Environmental Impacts of Organic Farming." Department for Environment Food and Rural Affairs (DEFRA). Available at: http:// archive.defra.gov.uk/foodfarm/growing/organic/policy/research/pdf/env-impacts2.pdf.

U.S. Department of Agriculture (USDA), Economic Research Service (ERS). 2010. "Data Sets: Organic Production." Available at: http://www.ers.usda.gov/Data/Organic/.

U.S. Department of Agriculture (USDA), National Organic Program (NOP). 2008. "National Organic Program Background Information." Available at: http://www.ams.usda.gov/ AMSv1.0/getfile?dDocName=STELDEV3004443&acct=nopgeninfo.

U.S. Department of Agriculture (USDA). 2011. "What Is Organic?" Available at: http:// www.ams.usda.gov/AMSv1.0/nop.

U.S. Department of Agriculture (USDA), National Agricultural Statistics Service (NASS). 2010. "2007 Census of Agriculture: 2008 Organic Production Survey Fact Sheet." Available at: http://www.agcensus.usda.gov/.

Willer, H., and Kilcher, L., eds. 2011. "The World of Organic Agriculture. Statistics and Emerging Trends 2011." IFOAM, Bonn, and FiBL, Frick. Available at: http://www .organic-world.net/yearbook-2011.html.

RESTAURANTS

According to a recent survey, 75 percent of Americans eat out at least once a week in a restaurant, and an astounding 99 percent eat out once every two weeks, illustrating in the most poignant terms that Americans love eating someplace other than home, be it fast food or full service. In fact, just under 50 percent of U.S. food dollars (a market of over $1 trillion) are spent on eating out in restaurants, an increase from 34 percent in 1974.

And yet, just as eating out is a firmly embedded cultural practice, as America has "gone green," so too has the practice of eating out itself become a greener, more ecologically attenuated activity. No better sign of this shift is the increasing frequency with which trade publications cover environmental developments in the food service industry. In magazines like *Nation's Restaurant News, Restaurant &*

Institutions, *Restaurant Report*, and *QSR*, where 10 years ago such coverage would be a serious anomaly, now each describes and evaluates various innovations aimed at making the food service industry more sustainable. Variously a product of complex interactions between consumer demand, corporate outreach, supply-chain economics, and environmentalist pressure, the greening of America's restaurants has had a host of effects, both economic and ethical—all of which provide for a kind of optimism in one of the most common, yet often most wasteful, daily consumer experiences.

Broadly construed, an understanding of environmental restaurateurism is concerned with inputs and outputs. Those inputs (what is brought into kitchen and service spaces in order to prepare dishes and the dining experience) and outputs (what is sent away from the restaurant as the result of the preparation, delivery, and eating of foods) fall into four key categories: raw food material, energy use, disposables and waste materials, and external financial support for green causes. Widely divergent, though often interconnected, each area of a restaurant's business has the potential to be greened in one way or another.

The most immediate and notable aspect of restaurants invested in producing environmental change is the sourcing of ecologically sound raw food materials. Indeed, if the purpose of a restaurant is to feed customers prepared food in exchange for money, a green restaurant's purpose is to feed people environmentally conscious food in that same exchange. In this regard green restaurants usually subscribe to one or more facet of the SOLE movement, an acronym that encapsulates its guiding principles: sustainable, organic, local, and ethical. Taken together these ideals suggest a mode of operation that tends toward sourcing food from purveyors who can obtain and distribute food products that are grown, harvested, and disseminated in more just and environmental ways. Some restaurants, like Alice Waters's world-famous Chez Panisse, cut out the middleman almost entirely by negotiating relationships one-to-one with growers in their immediate surroundings of the San Francisco Bay area who support ethical and sustainable practices. By buying direct from local organic farmers, Chez Panisse, as well as all restaurants that prioritize local and organic produce in their preparation, minimize their ecological footprints by reducing resources used in shipping, growing, and processing foods. In other ethical realms, the small national chain Loving Hut focuses almost exclusively on ameliorating climate change through abstaining from animal agriculture, based on the rationale expressed by the UN Food and Agriculture Organization (2006) report "Livestock's Long Shadow" as well as other climate science finding. Run under the auspices of the enigmatic, quasi-religious figurehead of the supreme master Ching Hai, these outlets overwhelm the diner with messages shown over a global television network in each store, pamphlets, and an 800-page treatise (available online) about veganism as both a healthy and compassionate alternative, but especially as the single most important step to take in order to affect global warming. Not just the domain of single restaurants or small chains, national brands also manage to engage in environmental food sourcing. For example, the fast-casual chain Chipotle (2011) is celebrated for their use of Niman Ranch's sustainably raised pork—as well as their use of largely free-range chicken and beef, and organic ingredients where available—ably illustrating the connection between sustainable food practice and consumer health desires, work they deem "food with integrity."

Once this food has been brought into a place, a second area of environmental concern, energy use, becomes relevant in the cooking and serving of that food. To be sure, some ethically sourced restaurants, like raw and macrobiotic, use little to no energy save for that which is required for lighting spaces and cleaning utensils and facilities. However, most small startups and franchisees have little choice or influence in the building or remodeling of their restaurant spaces, given that the majority of businesses use ready-built locations on lease rather than starting from scratch. Still, many find creative ways to reduce their environmental impact in terms of energy use. When leases, remodeling, or initial construction costs allow for changes in design, many common strategies should already be familiar as they are identical to those that can be used by the residential homeowner, including efficient insulated construction materials; using double- and triple-paned windows, as well as multipaned skylights to admit natural (i.e., carbon-free) illumination; insulated wraps for hot water heaters; placement of large window banks facing north or south to avoid direct exposure to the sun and, therefore, radiant heat, while still getting energy-free light during the day; purchasing and using Energy Star–rated appliances, at least where the scale of the restaurant makes them feasible; and rooftop installation of solar collectors for hot water and photovoltaic cells for electricity generation. Beyond this, a number of restaurants—as well as commercial food service purveyors—have taken pains to purchase carbon offsets for their diners as part of their mission (like Florida-based Pizza Fusion), while other businesses opt to purchase offset credits or buy into alternative or renewable power through their utility company. Others, like the recently opened Otarian in Manhattan, build their entire menu around reducing carbon dioxide emissions, and in so doing pass the nominal charge along to their customers, who can then track their carbon savings on a specially designed club card. In each case, the effectiveness of a carbon-reduction policy is tied to that policy's visibility.

While the dining experience itself illustrates the most immediate ways that diners can affect planetary ecological health, restaurants—particularly those in the quick-service/take-out segment—are a key source of tremendous amounts of waste, both in terms of food, intermediary products like paper goods, and disposable packaging. Green waste options abound as composting of food matter is currently becoming more common and as cities like San Francisco are making composting legally obligatory and issuing fines when restaurants refuse to do so. In areas where composting is still a matter of custom rather than law, numerous composting pick-up companies—like the New York Composting Company—arrive in trucks to remove food scraps for a fee; still other restaurants choose affordable on-site composting machines to process food waste on their own. Relatedly, though costs are somewhat higher than conventional plastics items, a number of Earth-conscious restaurants choose compostable takeout containers—like ECO Products and Green Wave, which are made mostly of petroleum-alternative materials like sugarcane—that can then be fed into a composting system. When restaurants do not offer compostable takeout containers, many are still offering biodegradable options (that is, utensils and packaging that decompose in minimal time, but do not release the bound up nutrients of compostable matter) that reduce long-term waste in landfills. Restaurants with high outputs of used cooking oil are in many areas able to give away or even sell their used vegetable oil to companies that convert it into viable petroleum-alternative products that can be used for fuel in cars or even, compellingly, the restaurants themselves. Massachusetts-based Vegawatt, for example, sells in-store converters to restaurants, and uses electricity—which is cheaper than natural gas or conventional fuel oil—to convert cooking oil into alternative heating oil for restaurant appliances such as water heaters, making the switch not only green, but economical after the initial costs have been earned back (Owl, 2011).

While taking care of waste products by turning them into something else on site remains an admirable policy, much of what restaurants have to dispose of as packaging—especially those selling prepackaged goods, like bottled or canned beverages—can be diverted from the landfill by means of recycling programs. However, recycling, usually a straight-forward process at home utilizing either curbside pick-up or transportation of smaller amounts of waste to a central drop-off point, at restaurants becomes a difficult problem given the volume of recyclable waste generated. Although many restaurants desire to recycle all they can, some commercial outfits simply are not able to connect with local recycling agencies in order obtain pick-up—a common reason given by Starbucks as to why there is no corporation-wide requirement to recycle—leaving recycling to those either lucky enough to be part of a pick-up route or energetic enough to sort and haul their own. At the same time, many progressive restaurateurs have adopted a number of strategies to take up the other half of recycling and make use of recycled goods in their stores. Paper goods—at least marginally biodegradable if kept wet and in direct sunlight—come in a variety of options, from napkins to to-go containers, the most progressive of which are not only recycled but also unbleached (noticeable by their brown color), thus limiting the amount of chemicals used in the remanufacturing process. Notable here is Starbucks's decision in 1997 to introduce the recycled paper cup sleeve (though it would take nearly 10 more years for the cup itself to contain recycled paper content—only 10 percent). Other retailers opt for nonwood paper goods, like those made of bamboo or other cellulose, as with the brand Bambu's product line. Recycled goods also find their way into the very construction of the restaurant, as when retailers build or remodel their spaces with reclaimed building materials and furnishings made of recycled materials like plastic bottles, a strategy that has been employed at McDonald's since the early 1990s, in part as a publicity campaign as they phased-out their decidedly ungreen polystyrene burger boxes (Holusha, 1990). For the majority of takeout products that are made of plastics now, however, there is an easily identifiable numeric recycling code on the package for consumers to reference when deciding between the trash or the recycling bin in restaurants, at home, or at work.

Finally, some restaurants, while not committing materially to greening the planet, do make the effort to share a portion of their proceeds with environmental organizations. Many of the largest commercial chains in the United States have some sort of environmental donation built in to their yearly expenditures in what some would argue are public-relations maneuvers meant to make the company look like a responsible corporate citizen. For other, usually smaller businesses, it is simply a matter of necessity that they can part with only a small portion of their income. This choice comes from a number of places, most often the bottom line. Given that restaurants are notoriously operating on the margin, many cannot make systemic changes to their restaurants in terms of sourcing or processing waste, but, wanting to help in some small way, can spare only a little of their profit to environmental funds. Others take a serious lead role, like the California-based chain Native Foods, and commit a portion of their proceeds to animal and environmental organizations in addition to their own use of SOLE foods and responsible packaging.

In each case, the support of green initiatives remains for the time being a some-what costly choice for restaurants, and for many—especially in the small scale—such choices can cause substantial shifts in pricing. However, as many of these changes to green alternatives are often used as the centerpiece of a given restaurant's cachet, many consumers are willing to pay for the increase knowing that it will mean that a portion of their food dollar will support green activities, either explicitly or implicitly, in much the same way that consumers are more likely buy goods emblazoned with the U.S. Olympic team's or Susan G. Komen for the Cure's logo. The green restaurant does well by posting appropriate signage that explains how the uptick in price is connected to a specific environmental purpose. And, until environmentally positive practices become the norm rather than the exception, the need to foreground these moderate price increases will be absolutely essential; without such explanations, the increase in price will seem excessive and unwarranted. For businesses interested in making these sorts of changes to their restaurants, support can be found with the Green Restaurant Association, a nonprofit trade organization that since 1990 has disseminated helpful information to assist restaurants go green, offering as they do not just information but also certification in green food service practices that can then be shown to eaters as a commitment to green practices.

Although Americans do enjoy eating out, it is nonetheless the case that not eating at home remains for many a luxury. Because of this, the choices consumers make at mealtime pose a special sort of challenge to restaurateurs, as the purchases one makes—as well as those one does not—send strong messages to retailers about what a given consumer wants to eat and what a given consumer values. After all, a hungry person can just as well wait to eat until she gets home as she can stop at a drive-through if the array of choices simply do not meet her ethical and gastronomical criteria. By buying what matters as well as what tastes good, so long as consumers keep pressure on restaurateurs to become more environmentally friendly by voting with their dollars, it is likely that the greening of restaurants will continue into the foreseeable future and provide a meaningful site of environmental activism.

TOM HERTWECK

See also: BioPreferred Program (documents); Brewing, Eco-Friendly (Food); ChooseMy Plate.gov (documents); Corporate Food Service (Food); Diet, Vegetarian and Vegan (Food);

Dietary Guidelines for Americans (documents); Food and Entertaining (Food); Food, Drink, and Media (Food); Organic and Natural Foods (Food); Organic Labeling and Marketing (documents).

References

Chipotle. 2011. "Food with Integrity." Available at: http://www.chipotle.com/en-US/fwi/fwi.aspx.

Green Restaurant Association. "Welcome to the Green Restaurant Association." Available at: http://www.dinegreen.com/.

Holusha, John. 1990. "Packaging and Public Image: McDonald's Fills a Big Order." *New York Times*, November 2. Available at: http://www.nytimes.com/1990/11/02/business/packaging-and-public-image-mcdonald-s-fills-a-big-order.html.

Loving Hut. "About Us." Available at: http://lovinghut.us/about.html.

Owl Power Company. 2011. "Vegawatt." Available at: http://www.vegawatt.com/.

Starbucks. "Recycling and Reducing Waste." Available at: http://www.starbucks.com/responsibility/environment/recycling/.

UN Food and Agriculture Organization. "Livestock's Long Shadow." Available at: http://www.fao.org/docrep/010/a0701e/a0701e00.HTM.

URBAN AGRICULTURE

Urban agriculture (UA) is the practice of growing and distributing food in and around cities and is one of the more effective activities urban residents are undertaking in an effort to take control of food security, social injustices, and environmental degradation in their communities. It has provided food, jobs, environmental enhancement, education, beautification, inspiration, and hope. The convergence of many factors such as high unemployment, increased food prices, elimination of food subsidies, the devaluation and systematic elimination of other social safety nets, combined with increased interest in food security and healthy eating habits has resulted in many local UA movements across the United States and other parts of the world (Mougeot, 1999; Turner, 2010).

Benefits of Urban Agriculture

Socioeconomic Impacts of Urban Agriculture

The socioeconomic benefits of UA are the most documented. UA can help alleviate urban poverty and hunger and increase the level of food security by controlling food production at a household level because the food is usually of better quality, lower cost, and more consistently accessible than otherwise purchased food. Studies of UA have shown encouraging data on the benefits that self-produced food can offer the urban poor (EPA, 2009). These benefits are financial as well as physical and include the reduction of household expenses and the nutritional advantages associated with consuming fresh, wholesome food. In addition, the beautification of neglected or vacant land by virtue of UA can lead citizens to extend their proprietary feelings for a garden plot to caring for the health and aesthetics of the larger community (EPA, 2009). Cultivation of urban green spaces can offer facilities otherwise unavailable to the inner cities and also can reduce maintenance costs of parks. UA also provides benefits that are less tangible, such as increased social capital and community building (Bourque, 1999).

Environmental Impacts of Urban Agriculture

The environmental impacts of UA are varied. Responsible UA can be a nonpolluting land use and can efficiently use and reuse scarce land and water resources, reduce transportation energy needs, and packaging waste (Quon, 1999). Both the reintegration of the waste stream with agricultural production and the ability of cities to feed themselves have been recognized as necessary foundations for environmentally sustainable urban communities (Turner, 2010). In addition, UA can contribute to environmental restoration through revegetation, the reestablishment of hydrologic regimes, and the conservation of topsoil. When advocating the benefits of environmental protection and restoration, it is important to educate community residents about the results to avoid backlash and resistance.

General Obstacles to Urban Agriculture

For all of its acknowledged benefits, the practice of UA contains certain fundamental obstacles whether it is for-market or not-for-market purposes (Mougeot, 1999). Obstacles to the general practice of UA fall into four broad categories:

1. Site-related
2. Government-related
3. Procedure-related, and
4. Perception-related.

Site-Related Obstacles

Just as rural agriculture is affected by the physical attributes of the land on which it is practiced, so too is UA. In addition, the physical and political contexts of project sites themselves can present obstacles to establishing and operating successful ventures. Common site-related obstacles include, but are not limited to, site contamination, security and vandalism, and lack of long-term site tenure.

Site Contamination
UA is commonly located on sites that may have been contaminated from past use. The toxicity of an urban site can be a significant obstacle to those forms of UA where food is grown in the existing soil. The underlying concern stems from the question of whether food produced on such land is safe to eat. The amount and type of contamination is unique to specific sites. Although contamination levels may not be

high enough to formally designate the property as a brownfield[1], knowledge of previous land uses can help urban farmers determine whether or not there are any potential health threats.

Security and Vandalism

Vandalism is an unfortunate reality that interferes with UA efforts. Because many sites are community oriented, requiring accessibility for a variety of individuals, and are fully visible, the opportunity for vandalism always exists, especially during the night. Common forms of vandalism include pilfering vegetables, trampling on plants, damaging or stealing signs identifying the project, and using the site to dispose of garbage, drug paraphernalia, and empty alcohol containers.

Lack of Long-Term Site Tenure

A third site-related obstacle to UA is the difficulty of securing tenure over property not owned outright. This is an especially common concern throughout the community gardening world. The core of the tenure issue is that land used for urban food production is frequently owned by private entities or public agencies that view such land usage as temporary. In some cases, advantageous leasing arrangements (such as rent payments of $1 per year) are in place until arrangements are made to utilize these parcels more profitably, typically through development for other uses.

Government-Related Obstacles

The social and political complexities of the urban environment mean that UA is affected by government control and regulation in different ways than conventional rural farming. Governmental obstacles to UA activities are concentrated at the local level, with less direct obstacles presented by state and federal governments (Quon, 1999). A general disinterest in UA is a characteristic of all levels of government.

Local Government

Local government obstacles center around issues of policy and practicality (UA being a nontraditional land use) and attitude and ideology (whether UA represents the "highest and best" use of city land). Efforts by nonprofits to assume ownership or formal access to vacant city-owned parcels for UA represent those situations where this obstacle is likely to be evident.

UA projects can be complicated by conflicts among the different objectives of various municipal agencies having some control over the use and dispensation of vacant land. For example, representatives from multiple departments and agencies commonly influence the designation of vacant properties in many cities. An application to use a vacant land parcel for open space or community gardening may be considered appropriate by one agency and inappropriate by another. Additionally, nonprofits seeking title to city-owned surplus property could face numerous additional points of contact regarding the application. Even after an application is approved, property transfers can take years to complete. Such inefficient management of vacant land in cities with high inventories of unused properties, along with the lack of a comprehensive vision of vacant land reuse, can present very real obstacles to UA.

The general lack of support within city government represents another political obstacle for UA. This could be the result of a narrow understanding of UA and its benefits, the perception of a limited constituency for UA, or simply a focus on other civic priorities. UA is typically disregarded when city officials are searching for viable economic opportunities, leading to a widespread and less-favorable attitude among city government officials about food production as an appropriate use of potentially valuable land. Fortunately, such attitudes toward UA are not always consistent throughout local government. Support often exists within city agencies that provide social services or promote environmental objectives or even among legislators who are environmentally conscious or concerned with food security issues.

Federal and State Government

A similar lack of support for UA exists within higher levels of government. These views often reflect a negative or uninformed perception of UA based on the attitude that agriculture is solely a rural activity. In some states, there are signs of decreased investment in programs supportive of UA, and municipal budget cutbacks have severely limited the role of county extension agencies. Budget reductions have also limited the support that academic institutions are able to offer UA programs.

Procedure-Related Obstacles

UA operations are difficult to initiate and maintain once established. A number of procedural obstacles exist for UA practitioners (Mougeot, 1999). Most of these obstacles apply to all forms of UA, while others apply only to the extension of UA into for-profit endeavors. Specific procedural obstacles will differ among projects, depending on context and circumstance.

Inadequate Financial Resources

Many procedural obstacles reflect the lack of financial resources for UA. In fact, the lack of a steady and consistent stream of outside funding may be the single biggest procedural obstacle to the continued advancement of UA. It is a common characteristic of these activities to run on very limited budgets. Although a community garden can be successful on a shoestring budget with help from volunteers and in-kind material donations, a limited budget can be an obvious deterrent to a market-based operation with greater expenses and less expectation of covering these costs through product sales.

Many UA projects have successfully utilized grant funding. The most frequent source of grants is local government (through federal Community Development Block grants, for example) with the federal government also being a common funder (through the USDA Community Food Projects program and the Job Training Partnership Act, among other sources) (Turner, 2010). Grants from local foundations, small donations from individuals, and fundraising events are also common sources of outside support.

Few sources of public funding specifically designed to include UA are available. Those that do exist, such as the USDA Community Food Projects program, are not focused solely on UA. The increasing popularity and occurrence of UA, however, suggests that there will be greater financial support from the federal government in the future.

The Need to Recruit and Retain Qualified Staff

A critical need of UA organizations is to find and retain qualified staff to manage the time- and labor-intensive projects. Moreover, staff members need to communicate and work effectively with residents at very basic levels of training and supervision. Such positions require specialized knowledge and experience; however, those willing to work UA projects are typically low paid and often young with little previous growing experience. Although they may make up for this lack of experience with energy and enthusiasm, they are susceptible to the pressures of community-based work, including long hours, multiple responsibilities, and the stresses of fundraising.

Inadequate Time

Better performance in UA ideally comes with experience. The timeframe of a startup grant or the course of a fixed-term arrangement for the use of a particular parcel often restricts a project manager's ability to get the operation under way. Consequently, projects involving staff and neighborhood workers with little experience can undergo unsteady beginnings.

Small-Scale Projects

Managing projects at a scale large enough to justify the investment in time and expense is often a concern. UA is often located on small, residential-sized plots in the inner city. Although benefits can be attained in small garden patches, making for-market UA ventures successful will require a size and scale for which there are no commonly accepted standards. Land availability in targeted neighborhoods can also be challenging.

Coordinating a Project across Scattered Sites

There is a potential problem in residential neighborhoods where vacant parcels form a "missing teeth" pattern, characterized by a mixture of noncontiguous buildings and vacant lots within the same block (Mougeot, 1999). A UA operation in such an area will be forced to split itself across multiple sites. Even if the total area is adequate for the project's intentions, fragmenting a UA project could result in managing each site separately. This can lead to certain inefficiencies, such as having to transport equipment from site to site versus duplicating equipment, arranging separate water provisions, or spending work time commuting from site to site.

Conflicts among Partners

Organizations undertaking UA sometimes find it necessary to partner with other groups to access land and obtain technical and financial support. Regardless of the context of the particular UA project, all partnerships are uncertain in the long run because the agendas and objectives of the different partners may differ and are subject to change.

Lack of Sound Business Planning

Both nonmarket and for-market UA projects require strategic planning. Anticipating future events and establishing appropriate contingencies can be especially challenging. Entrepreneurial UA ventures, in particular, are small businesses, and like any other, they require a sound business plan. These demands require special skills that not all project managers will have.

High Startup Costs

Initial operating costs can present difficulties for practitioners of UA, especially individual urban farmers and nonprofit organizations that have scarce resources. Significant startup investments may be needed for such activities as site preparation and environmental remediation, greenhouse construction, and acquiring and installing kitchen and other processing equipment.

Losing Touch with Project Objectives

The investment in time, money, and effort of UA requires a focus on certain clearly defined objectives. It also means that, on occasion, the challenges of pursuing one objective may compromise the achievement of another. Social agendas can be compromised by competing financial objectives.

Perception-Related Obstacles

It is clear that many of the obstacles described so far are based on uninformed or negative perceptions of UA. Although community gardens are not new to cities, the basic idea of city farming by for-profit or nonprofit organizations is a novel one when compared to more conventional land uses. In addition, the image of working the soil is, for better or worse, loaded with cultural meaning (Bourque, 1999; Mougeot, 1999). This, in turn, affects people's perceptions of the validity and worth of UA.

A significant group of obstacles involve negative perceptions toward cultivating food within cities. Concerns for the safety of produce grown on previously developed and vacant lots are often expressed. Perceived low economic payback of urban food production relative to the costs involved is another common argument against UA (Turner, 2010).

A more widespread negative perception is simply that agriculture does not belong in the city. Food production is seen principally as a rural activity, not an urban concern (Bourque, 1999; Mougeot, 1999; Quon, 1999). This was mentioned previously as a significant reason for the lack of governmental support for UA.

Some who favor programs to grow more food locally and regionally advocate for more supportive governmental action to create stronger and more direct linkages between farmers and urban consumers. These proponents challenge the perception that farming is an inappropriate use of city land.

ALLISON H. TURNER

See also: Agriculture (Economics); Local and Sustainable (Food); Organic Labeling and Marketing Information (documents).

Note

1. Brownfields are real property, the expansion, redevelopment, or reuse of which may be complicated by the presence or potential presence of a hazardous substance, pollutant, or contaminant. Cleaning up and reinvesting in these properties protects the environment, reduces blight, and takes development pressures off green spaces and working lands (EPA, 2010).

References

Bourque, M. 1999. Thematic Paper 5: "Policy Options for Urban Agriculture." Growing Cities Growing Food Conference, October.

Environmental Protection Agency (EPA). 2009. "Building Vibrant Communities: Community Benefits of Land Revitalization." Available at: http://www.epa.gov.brownfields/policy/comben.pdf.

Mougeot, L. 1999. Thematic Paper 1: "Urban Agriculture: Definition, Presence, Potentials and Risks." Growing Cities Growing Food Conference, October.

Quon, S. 1999. *Planning for Urban Agriculture: A Review of Tools and Strategies for Urban Planners*. Cities Feeding People Series: Report 28. Ottawa, ON, Canada: International Development Research Centre.

Turner, A. H. 2010. *Establishing Urban Agriculture in Your Community: What You Need to Know before You Get Your Hands Dirty*. Practice Guide No.27. Louisville, KY: Center for Environmental Policy & Management.

Health, Home, and Garden

ANIMAL COMPANIONS

As Americans continue to try to become more environmentally conscious for reasons ranging from economic benefit to social responsibility, certain industries stand out as being easy candidates for becoming greener. The auto industry and the utilities industry are two that quickly come to mind. However, the quest to continually go green does not have to end with these more industrialized sectors. Smaller industries such as the pet industry, for example, stand out as areas where savvy consumers can easily make choices that will benefit the environment in the short and long term. Although businesses like this may not seem to have the greatest impact on the environment at first blush, once one digs a bit deeper it becomes clear that they can have just as large an impact on the effort to go green as a larger business. Additionally, the pet industry is one that many consumers are closely connected to. It can be difficult to see how one's own actions can directly influence environmental impact, but the pet industry is one where such an impact is unavoidable due to the types of choices owners make on a daily basis.

Larry Wright, the president of The Green Pet Shop in Northbrook, Illinois, heads up a company that specializes in the manufacturing of environmentally friendly pet products. The company has only been fully operational for less than two years, but Wright sees a bright future for an operation offering these types of eco-friendly options to consumers. The Green Pet Shop does not have a brick and mortar presence, instead it functions as a manufacturer and distributor to pet stores, and Wright feels that green pet products have come a long way in recent years. He acknowledges that there have been widespread initiatives across the board to go green recently, and the pet industry is no exception.

However, he does assert that there are still some challenges facing his niche of the industry. "Durability of the products is key, as the initial releases of these [environmentally friendly] products were not all that durable," he notes. He also explained that there can typically be a perception that green products tend to be more expensive, so one of the company's major initiatives is to attempt to craft a pricing model that allows their environmentally friendly products to be offered at the same price points as their competitors. By creating a product that costs the same as a more well-known competitor's and ensuring that it offers the same degree of durability, Wright makes it easier for the environmentally conscious pet owner to make a choice that has a more positive impact on the Earth.

In fact, Wright maintains that one of the largest issues facing the green pet industry is the lack of awareness that these types of socially conscious alternatives even exist, and he asserts that "the industry conventions that you go to indicate a growing number of booths and products that are eco-friendly." This type growth of the industry sector seems to predict that green pet products will only grow in popularity, as more and more companies seek to stay competitive by claiming a share of this growing market. Wright contends that consumers are currently focused more on simply purchasing the cheapest product available on the market, but once they realize that environmentally friendly alternatives exist at a similar price, they will be more apt to allow social consciousness to play a role in their decision making.

The American Society for the Prevention of Cruelty to Animals (ASPCA) also offers a variety of tips that overlap with the type of products offered by companies such as Wright's. For example, the ASPCA recommends on their Web site that dog owners "scoop dog poop with biodegradable bags instead of plastic bags from the grocery store." This type of product was one that Wright specifically mentioned during our interview, as he spoke about how those types of bags, which his company manufactures, were ones that consumers have traditionally been wary of due to concerns over the durability of green products. It is a product that simply must work, or consumers will suffer a consequence that could potentially prevent them from buying environmentally friendly poop bags ever again! As was previously mentioned, however, Wright emphasizes that his company has made tremendous strides in dispelling these types of concerns over the perceived lack of durability of green pet products.

Even larger pet chains like Petsmart are willing to explore going green in an age where consumers are so much more conscious of how their purchasing decisions can affect the world as a whole. On Petsmart's Web site, they advertise how owners of all pets can make a difference by actively seeking out an organic alternative to their current pet food. These would be foods made with ingredients that are grown without the aid of pesticides or other fertilizes that can prove to be potentially devastating to the world at large. Additionally, Petsmart advocates the making of one's own dog treats or growing catnip as a further way to both save money and avoid supporting the type of large-scale and potentially destructive industrialized farming that can often can go hand-in-hand with producing mass quantities of all types of food, including pet food.

As consumers become more conscious of the importance of going green, their awareness of what constitutes being environmentally friendly changes as well. When one starts to explore the various options that exist for pet owners who are seeking to become more socially conscious, it's easy to see how many of the same principles can be applied. In some instances, such as with organic foods, there will seemingly always be a premium to pay on these types of products, but the option is indeed there for pet owners who wish to both provide their furry and feathered friends with more nutritious food while simultaneously supporting farming methods that do not take such a toll on the environment. These are just some of the small ways that pet owners in America can continue to go green, and both the proliferation of companies like The Green Pet Shop, as well as the support of the green movement by larger corporations as Petsmart, proves that there is significant interest among pet owners who wish to have greener options in pet products and food.

JACK PITTENGER

See also: Animal Enterprise Protection Act (documents); Animal Enterprise Terrorism Act (documents).

References

American Society for the Prevention of Cruelty to Animals. "Go Green for Pets." Available at: http://www.aspca.org/pet-care/pet-care-tips/go-green-for-pets.aspx.

Petsmart. "Green Paw Print Tip #3: Consider Switching to Natural or Organic Pet Foods." Available at: http://www.mypetsmart.com/petcare/articles/green-paw-print-tip-3-consider-switching-to-natural-or-organic-pet-foods.

Wright, Larry. Interview by author. Tempe, AZ, December 8, 2011.

BEAUTY, COSMETICS, AND MAKEUP

Women wear up to 25 beauty products daily that contain an average of 515 ingredients, according to a 2009 British study conducted by a company called Bionsen. These ingredients include metals, additives, synthetic dyes, fragrances, and parabens. Though these chemicals are classified as carcinogens, endocrine disruptors, and reproductive toxins, their presence in cosmetics has not been tested. An Environmental Working Group (2004) study found that less than 1 percent of all cosmetic products are made from ingredients that have all undergone safety assessments. In the European Union, no chemicals classified as carcinogens, mutagens, or reproductive toxins are legally permitted in personal care products. In the United States, there is no such legislation.

Cosmetics applied directly to the skin have a very high rate of absorption. Rather than being processed through the digestive system, as is the case with food consumption, chemicals applied to the skin are absorbed directly into the bloodstream where many accumulate in tissue and have a wide range of health effects. Two ingredients commonly found in eye makeup are propylene glycol and methylparaben. Propylene glycol, used to aid in absorption of products, is a primary skin irritant as well as a broad systemic toxin that causes kidney, liver, and central nervous system damage in humans, domestic animals, and wildlife. Propylene glycol has the potential to cause acute ocular and respiratory effects (Wieslander et al., 2001). The U.S. Food and Drug Administration (FDA) categorizes propylene glycol as "generally recognized as safe" and allows addition of it to cosmetics and food storage containers.

Parabens are another common ingredient in personal care products, such as cosmetics, lotions, and shampoos. Parabens are used as preservatives and are linked to health effects, including endocrine disruption, breast cancer, and male infertility. Parabens refer to a chemical group of esters, including methylparaben, ethylparaben, propylparaben, isopropylparaben, butylparaben, isobutylparaben, and benzylparaben. This chemical group is unregulated by the FDA, which currently permits their addition to cosmetics, foods, and pharmaceuticals.

Phthalates are plasticizers commonly added to personal care products, household, and electronic products. Despite being regulated as hazardous waste and pollutants to air and water, phthalates, such as dibutyl phthalate (DBP), are common ingredients found in fragranced items, hair spray, and nail polish. DBP has been found to have reproductive and developmental effects, including birth defects in lab animals, primarily to male offspring, including testicular atrophy, reduced sperm count, and structural defects (CERHR, 2000). In 2000, the Centers for Disease Control and Prevention (CDC) scientists announced that levels of some phthalates in women of childbearing age, including DBP and di(2-ethylhexyl) phthalate (DEHP), exceed the government's safe levels set to protect against birth defects. For more than 3 million heavily exposed women of childbearing age, exposures to DBP may be 20 times greater than the average exposures in the rest of the population (Kohn et al., 2000).

A growing interest in green living underlies an interest in protecting the environment and preventing exposure to harmful ingredients in personal care products. However, this interest may be easier to act on in the European Union compared to the United States. According to the seventh amendment of the EU Cosmetics Directive, all ingredients in personal care products must be tested for safety, and no products are permitted to include chemicals classified as carcinogens, reproductive toxins, or mutagens. In contrast, the United States has an antiquated approach of allowing companies to use chemicals they have used historically and categorizing them as "generally recognized as safe." To monitor the safety of new chemicals, there is a voluntary industry-based group that decides which chemicals need to be tested. This has resulted in the FDA banning only 8 of over 12,000 chemicals since 1938. Chemicals are often approved for use based on estimated exposure levels; however, that system fails to account for varying levels of exposure,

Greenovation: Coming Clean Campaign

Consumers might find it surprising that the U.S. government does not regulate the contents of cosmetics or personal care products for health and environmental impacts or safety. The U.S. Department of Agriculture (USDA) allows cosmetics to be labeled as certified organic but does not require it. Consumers can avoid harmful personal care products by using cosmetics that are labeled with the USDA certified organic seal. This label means that the product is certified by the USDA's National Organic Program and includes more than 95 percent organic ingredients. Since 2004, the Organic Consumers Association's Coming Clean Campaign has worked to "Boycott Fake 'Organic' Brands." The campaign seeks not only to provide information about what products are organic according to USDA certifications, but also to encourage consumers to avoid purchasing products that claim to be organic but do not have enough USDA certified organic ingredients to be considered as such. For more information, visit the Organic Consumers Association (http://www.organicconsumers.org) and see the video *The Story of Cosmetics*. Released in July 2010, the video explores the use of toxic chemicals in cosmetics and personal care products.

KIM KENNEDY WHITE

sensitivity to exposure, and increasing exposure levels over time. Product labels may use words such as "natural," "herbal," and "organic" regardless of the product toxicity and are not required to list all ingredients present. Companies are allowed to keep chemicals off labels including nanomaterials, contaminants, by-products of industrial processing, and fragrances. Fragrances alone account for over 3,000 chemicals, none of which are required to be listed on labels.

The difference in regulatory approach can be explained by the use of the Precautionary Principle in the European Union versus the laissez-faire approach in the United States, also called the wait-and-see approach by some critics. Whereas the Precautionary Principle directs policy makers to prioritize public health protection over unknown health effects of PCPs (phencyclidine), the wait-and-see approach favors the freedom of industry to sell products as cheaply as possible. The U.S. approach relies on the market to regulate itself and on litigation to resolve any injustices (i.e., toxic exposure, cancer, reproductive toxicity, and other permanent and life-threatening conditions). The weakness in this approach can be explained by *information asymmetry*, a term used by economist Joseph Stiglitz to describe the inequality of

"On Size and Scapegoating"

Do fat people[1] harm the environment? Some scholars argue that they do. According to researchers Ian Roberts and Phil Edwards, fat people overconsume food, effectively wasting it. They also use excessive fuel for transportation. In fact, it has been claimed that such overconsumption of food and fuel could yield 250 million tons of additional greenhouse gases per year, making a significant contribution to climate change.

However, not all experts are in agreement. In fact, the proportion of food some attribute to overconsumption is dwarfed by the immense amount of food that is simply thrown out each year. Estimates suggest that such outright waste accounts for a staggering one-fourth of food produced in the United States.

Perhaps even more importantly, other scholars suggest that concerns about the "Obesity Epidemic" are overblown and amount to a "moral panic" that only amplifies the stigma against people whose weight or body size exceeds the limits of societal acceptance. Moreover, any particular individual's weight may be attributable to a combination of factors unrelated to levels of food consumption, including genetics. Fat people are likely to maintain their weight, even when they forgo fossil-fuel guzzling modes of transportation in favor of biking or walking; research indicates that permanent weight loss is attainable for only a tiny fraction of people.

So, *do* fat people harm the environment? Yes, they do. But so do people of all sizes, and in a variety of ways ranging from consumptive practices to supporting public policies that undermine the well-being of our planet. And one thing is clear: scapegoating particular groups of people may increase social stigma, but it does little to alleviate global warming.

TRACY ROYCE

---

[1]Here I use the term *fat* in the same way that many body diversity and fat pride scholars and activists do—as matter-of-fact descriptor of large bodies—departing from the stigma attached to terms like *overweight* and *obese*.

knowledge between consumers and producers. Information asymmetry is a central flaw in market capitalism because absence of even minimal toxicity data, as is the case with cosmetics ingredients, works to insulate the industry from the normal supply-demand dynamics of the market, putting into place a dangerous status quo.

The Campaign for Safe Cosmetics is a nongovernmental organization that advocates for protecting the U.S. public through regulating toxic chemicals in personal care products. Skin Deep is a cosmetics database by the Environmental Working Group that provides information and ingredients on over 69,000 personal care products. With such resources, awareness of cosmetics toxicity is growing and U.S. consumers are becoming empowered to choose safe products. As a whole though, the U.S. population remains under threat from a wide range of reproductive and developmental health effects due to the presence of chemicals in everyday household and cosmetic products.

RAINBOW VOGT

See also: Home Furnishings and Interior Design (Health); Local and Sustainable Foods (Food); Pesticides (Environment); Textiles for Furniture and Fashion (Health).

References

Campaign for Safe Cosmetics. "The Story of Cosmetics." Available at: http://safecosmetics .org/.

Campos, Paul, Abigail Saguy, Paul Ernsberger, Eric Oliver, and Glen Gaesser. 2006. "The Epidemiology of Overweight and Obesity: Public Health Crisis or Moral Panic?" *International Journal of Epidemiology* 35:1: 55–60. Available at: http://ije.oxfordjournals.org/content/35/1/55.full.

Center for the Evaluation of Risks to Human Reproduction (CERHR). 2000. "NTP-CERHR Expert Panel Report on Di n Butyl Phthalate." National Toxicology Program. U.S. Department of Health and Human Services.

Childs, Dan. "Do Obese People Aggravate Global Warming?" Available at: http://abcnews .go.com/Health/Diet/story?id=4865889&page=1#.Trh3CWC0x9M.

Environmental Health Association of Nova Scotia. "Guide to Less Toxic Products." Available at: http://lesstoxicguide.ca/index.asp?fetch=personal#lipgl.

Environmental Working Group. 2000. "Dibutyl phthalate." Available at: http://www.health-report.co.uk/phthalates.html (cited on November 1, 2011).

Environmental Working Group. 2004. "Skin Deep: A Safety Assessment of Ingredients in Personal Care Products." Available at: http://www.cosmeticdatabase.com (cited on November 1, 2011).

Kohn, M. C., F. Parham, S. A. Masten, C. J. Portier, M. D. Shelby, J. W. Brock, and L. L. Needham. 2000. "Human Exposure Estimates for Phthalates." *Environmental Health Perspectives* 108:10: A440–A442.

Mylchreest, E., R. C. Cattley, and P. M. Foster. 1998. "Male Reproductive Tract Malformations in Rats Following Gestational and Lactational Exposure to Di(n-butyl) Phthalate: An Antiandrogenic Mechanism?" *Toxicological Sciences* 43:1: 47–60.

Roberts, Ian, and Phil Edwards. 2010. *The Energy Glut: The Politics of Fatness in an Overheating World.* London: Zed Books.

Thomas, Pat. 2008. *Skin Deep: The Essential Guide to What's in the Toiletries and Cosmetics You Use.* Emmaus, PA: Rodale Press.

Wieslander G., D. Norback, and T. Lindgren. 2001. "Experimental Exposure to Propylene Glycol Mist in Aviation Emergency Training: Acute Ocular and Respiratory Effects." *Occupational and Environmental Medicine* 58: 649–655.

COMPLEMENTARY AND ALTERNATIVE MEDICINE

Complementary and alternative medicine (CAM) encompasses an array of healing practices and medical systems developed independently of conventional medicine. Americans turn to complementary treatments while continuing to use conventional medicine and use alternative treatments in place of conventional medicine (NCCAM, 2011b). Some of these practices and systems were established over the past two to three centuries, while others come to us from "ancient and indigenous societies" (Micozzi, 2006, xiii). CAM includes healing practices developed in North America, such as polarity therapy and Native American sweat lodges; in Europe, such as homeopathy; and in India and China, such as Ayurveda and traditional Chinese medicine, respectively (Micozzi, 2006). CAM is distinguished from conventional medicine, also called Western or allopathic medicine (Cassidy, 2006; NCCAM, 2011b). CAM has been variously dubbed "unconventional, nontraditional, integral, [and] holistic" (Micozzi, 2006, xiii). Allopathic medicine is practiced by people who hold the degree of doctor of medicine (M.D.) or doctor of osteopathic medicine (D.O.), whereas CAM practitioners receive training and licensing outside mainstream medical schools through dedicated institutes, schools, and associations. Allopathic doctors may also incorporate CAM therapies into their practices, and some U.S. health insurance companies have added coverage for a few CAM treatments, primarily chiropractic and acupuncture.

Jars containing herbs used in traditional Chinese medicine in Chinatown, San Francisco, California. (iStockPhoto.com)

The usage of CAM has become commonplace in the United States. The 2007 National Health Interview Survey revealed that 38 percent of adult Americans used some form of CAM treatment (NCCAM, 2011b). These treatments may be sorted into a few broad categories: (1) herbal medicine and dietary supplements; (2) mind-body medicine; (3) energy therapies; (4) hands-on therapies; and (5) traditional medical systems (Bauer, 2007; Freeman & Lawlis, 2001; Micozzi, 2006). Many of these therapies require trained health-care professionals for proper application, while others may be done in the privacy of one's home, sometimes after initial training by a professional.

Conventional medicine has a different conception of the human body from the perspectives found among the various CAM practices. While conventional medicine largely treats the physical aspect of the human body, CAM therapies treat the physical and *nonphysical* aspects of the human being. In broad terms conventional medicine perceives the site and treatment of disease as the material, physical body, whereas CAM conceives of a unity between mind and body and therefore employs a holistic approach, considering not just material manifestations of disease but also nonmaterial imbalances of energy (Cassidy, 2006). These contrasting perspectives arise from "numerous cogent models of reality" that form the basis for different social and cultural interpretations of the origins of disease and their treatments and cures (Cassidy, 2006, 29). These models of reality "guide the logic of health care delivery" (Cassidy, 2006, 37).

Critics of allopathic medicine have accused it of being grounded in materialism and reductionism, concentrating "its attention on the [diseased] organ, ignoring the body as a whole" (Haller, 2009, 45). The allopathic concept of the human body directs medical attention to the "physical body, specifically the structure of its tissues and the movement and transformation of chemicals within cells" (Cassidy, 2006, 37). Most forms of CAM, in contrast, share the belief that the human body has not only a material nature but also an energetic nature (Micozzi, 2006). This energetic nature has been described variously as a *vital force* by practitioners of homeopathy (Bauer, 2007; Haller, 2009), *prana* by adherents of Ayurveda (Morrison, 1995), and *chi* or *qi* by practitioners of traditional Chinese medicine (Bauer, 2007). Alternative medical practices aim not only to direct this energy to heal a person's disease state or injury but also to bring this energy into balance to promote well-being and prevent disease. In CAM, the word *disease* may be rejected in favor of the concept of *imbalance*, with the therapeutic goal of bringing the person back into balance (Cassidy, 2006). For example, whereas an allopathic doctor might diagnose an individual with hepatitis, a practitioner of traditional Chinese medicine might describe the condition as "rising Liver fire" (Cassidy, 2006, 40). From the perspective of CAM, then, disease may arise from "nonmaterial determinants" (Haller, 2009, 3), such as spiritual and psychological factors or energy imbalances.

Holistic health care systems seek to overcome medical practices based on the Cartesian presumption of a split between mind and body that characterizes most conventional medical practices (Bix, 2004, 166) by considering the whole person, including his or her physical, spiritual, psychosocial, and energetic dimensions (Cassidy, 2006). Whereas conventional therapy targets the physical symptom or symptoms, holistic therapies target imbalances of energy and expect physical, psychosocial, and spiritual healing responses in the patient. Conventional psychotherapy's acknowledgment, however, of "mind and emotions" (Cassidy, 2006, 39) shows that the allopathic paradigm is not wholly materialistic and at least considers the nonmaterial psyche of a human being.

Long before the term CAM was coined, alternative health care practices flourished in 1800s America. Homeopathy, a holistic system of medicine founded by Samuel Hahnemann in Germany in 1796 with the publication of the book *Organon* (Davidovitch, 2004; Kirschmann, 2004), was introduced to America in 1835 by one of Hahnemann's students who established the first U.S. homeopathic medical school in Allentown, Pennsylvania (Freeman, 2001). Hahnemann coined the word *homeopathy* from the Greek roots *omoios* for "similar" and *pathos* for "feeling" (Carlston, 2006, 96) or "suffering" (Freeman, 2001, 347). He also gave us the word *allopathy* from the Greek word *alloios* for "other" to distinguish between homeopathic and orthodox medicine, which aimed to cure disease by counteracting or suppressing physical symptoms (Carlston, 2006, 96). Homeopathy, however, utilizing tiny doses of highly diluted substances called remedies (Bauer, 2007), operates on a set of principles distinct from those of conventional medicine.

Homeopathy's three fundamental principles or laws are the Principle of Similars, the Principle of Infinitesimal Dose, and the Principle of Specificity of the Individual (Freeman, 2001, 349). The Principle of Similars can also be stated as "like cures like" (Bauer, 2007, 128; Freeman, 2001, 349), an idea articulated in the writings of ancient Greek physician Hippocrates and Renaissance physician Paracelsus (Carlston, 2006): Large doses of a plant, animal, or mineral substance will produce disease symptoms in a healthy person; but when administered in small doses to people already sick with those symptoms, they cure the disease (Bauer, 2007; Freeman, 2001). These remedies are considered "vital" because the power of nature interacts with the vital force of the person to whom the remedy is given to produce the desired effect (Haller, 2009). In other words, homeopathy is based on the "natural healing capacity" of the patient (Carlston, 2006, 97). The Principle of Infinitesimal Dose rests on Hahnemann's observations that the more a substance was diluted the more potent it became (Freeman, 2001). More than 2,000 dilute remedies, derived from plant, mineral, or animal origins, are available today through the homeopathic pharmacopeia and are sold in liquid, pellet, and tablet forms (Bauer, 2007; Carlston, 2006; Freeman, 2001). The Principle of Specificity of the Individual means that remedies are selected to treat the person and his or her unique manifestation of symptoms. For example, not all headaches are alike: Homeopathy has a separate remedy for each of the more than 200 types of headache. Considerations of where in the head the pain resides as well as what types of movements make it worse or better combine with observations of a person's body and personality type to construct a "profile" of the patient so that the specific remedy may be prescribed (Freeman, 2001).

Other nonmainstream therapeutic practices were developed in the United States and remain popular today. In the 1890s American midwest, Daniel David Palmer established the system of *chiropractic* treatment and Andrew Taylor Still founded

Homeopathy in America

In the 1800s homeopathy thrived in the United States and took on a distinctly American character. It incorporated into its pharmacopeia herbs that had been traditionally used in Native American medicine as well as herbs employed by locally based healers such as midwives and herbalists (Carlston, 2006, 102). When life-threatening epidemics hit the American public in the 19th century, homeopathic treatments were reported to be more effective than the toxic treatments prescribed by conventional medicine (Carlston, 2006, 102). An entire academic and medical infrastructure was built up to develop and support the application of homeopathy to public health issues. In 1911, at the height of this first phase of American homeopathy, this alternative medical system boasted numerous local, state, regional, and national societies, clubs, and associations; between 60 and 100 hospitals; 1,000 pharmacies; 13 colleges; and 20 journals (Freeman, 2001; Haller, 2009). In addition, 38 hospitals practiced both homeopathy and orthodox medicine. Opposition from the American Medical Association in the mid-20th century, as well as divisions and conflicts among different groups of homeopaths, caused the homeopathic movement to decline after the 1920s, resulting in the closing of many of its schools and the shuttering of many of its journals. In the latter third of the 20th century, however, homeopathy experienced a resurgence. Professional associations that organize and advocate for standards of homeopathic care include the American Institute of Homeopathy, established in 1844, and the North American Society of Homeopaths, established in 1990. For Americans who complement conventional medicine with alternative treatments, homeopathy is popular in the 21st century. According to the 2007 National Health Interview Survey, an estimated 3.9 million adults and 900,000 children had used homeopathy in the previous year (NCCAM, 2011a). Although controversy remains in scientific circles as to whether the effectiveness of homeopathic treatments can be proved or not according to the scientific method, some "individual observational studies" have shown some positive effects of homeopathy (NCCAM, 2011a), and orthodox science has recorded homeopathic benefits for the treatment of acute childhood diarrhea, allergies, influenza, pain, and vertigo (Bauer, 2007, 128).

osteopathy (Micozzi, 2006). Both of these men deemed themselves "energy" healers and rejected the use of drugs being promoted by conventional medical practitioners (Micozzi, 2006, 13). Homeopathic practitioners were divided on the use of vaccines, which the conventional medical establishment began developing for a whole host of ailments, nearly eight decades after the advent of the first vaccine, which was for smallpox. Conventional medicine, strengthened by the increasingly accepted idea of germ theory in the 1870s and 1880s, was being met with more and more resistance from people who turned to alternative therapies. Women were especially involved in alternative health care practices in the late 1800s and early 1900s and were accepted as members of the American Institute of Homeopathy beginning in 1869, 46 years before they were allowed to join the American Medical Association (Bix, 2004).

As conventional medicine surged at the dawn of the 20th century, many Americans turned to alternative therapies while also opposing orthodox medical practices promoted by the medical establishment. "Radical criticism of regular medicine and public health measures at the turn of the twentieth century was quite often embedded in a network of dissent against the hegemonic Establishment, whether in politics or medicine" (Davidovitch, 2004, 26). Dissenting voices called for medical freedom not only for health care practitioners but also for citizens so that they could take health care matters into their own hands without state interference. Among homeopaths in the early 1900s, a minority vigorously opposed compulsory vaccinations for children, while others accepted their application, considering "vaccination as proof of the homeopathic law of similars" (Davidovitch, 2004, 13). Vaccinations, however, were controversial and seen by some political groups as an intrusion of the state into citizens' private lives (Davidovitch, 2004, 20). Anti-vaccinationism, then, has threaded through American culture for more than 100 years.

The link between ill health in the U.S. population and health of the environment was beginning to register among physicians and dentists in the 1930s (Ackerman, 2004). In that decade the U.S. government laid the foundation for a new agriculture paradigm that resulted in wide-scale environmental damage and sweeping dietary changes for the U.S. population (Goodman & Redclift, 1991). State agricultural subsidies that supported processes of intensification, mechanization, and specialization (Woods, 2005) led to farmland consolidation, and multinational agribusiness firms replaced small-scale production of fruits, vegetables, and animals with large-scale production of globally traded commodities, in particular corn, soybeans, and wheat (Goodman & Redclift, 1991). The Agricultural Adjustment Acts of 1933 and 1938 launched a policy of state market intervention that primarily benefited large commercial growers (Goodman & Redclift, 1991). The resulting production of surpluses in the major commodity crops led to dietary changes for the U.S. population. Agribusinesses gained control of all aspects of food production, including cultivation, processing, packaging, marketing, and distribution, and, partially to absorb the now massive stream of commodity crops, invented highly processed, low-nutrient "foods," such as breakfast cereals. Corporations created a demand for these mass-produced foods through advertising (Goodman & Redclift, 1991; Pollan, 2006). U.S. physicians and dentists, however, began to notice the poor nutritional quality of processed foods and blamed much of Americans' ill health on poor diets (Ackerman, 2004). The American Academy of Applied Nutrition was founded in 1936 by a group of California dentists. In the early 1950s, a group of physicians and laypeople organized to create Natural Foods Associates (now Wisconsin Natural Foods Associates) to sound the alarm about rising rates of chronic health problems in the U.S. population, such as heart disease and cancer, and the relationship between nutritionally deficient foods and nutrient-poor soil (Ackerman, 2004; Hoeting, 2005). Sellers of dietary supplements urged consumption of their products to compensate for nutritionally inadequate diets (Ackerman, 2004, 55). J. I. Rodale, an organic farmer in Pennsylvania, founded the Soil and Health Institute in 1947, the precursor to the Rodale Institute (Rodale Institute, 2011). Rodale published widely on organic farming practices and the connection between healthy soil, healthy food, and healthy people. His publishing company, Rodale Inc., continues to publish many titles on organic farming and human health.

The health foods movement that was born in the 1930s grew and matured in the next three decades (Ackerman, 2004). Health foodists believed that educating the public about nutritionally deficient food would persuade people to demand alternatives. They also called attention to the presence of dangerous chemicals in food and advocated for organic farming years before the environmental movement took off in the 1960s. Promoting environmental protection, health foodists exhorted "farmers to preserve and restore the fertility of their soil by . . . following the conservation practices recommended by the U.S. Soil Conservation Service" (Ackerman, 2004, 63). Their beliefs were validated by Rachel Carson's 1962 book, *Silent Spring*, in which the harmful effects of agricultural chemicals in the environment were highlighted. Citizens seeking alternatives to conventional medicine also sought alternative, healthier sources of food, a trend still apparent today. The organic foods sector, for example, has grown at a rate of 20 percent per year over the past several years, with 4.1 million acres of U.S. farmland in organic production (Laux, 2011).

During the social foment of the 1960s and early 1970s, feminists began to protest conventional medicine, which had given them "the twin disasters of diethylstilbestrol (DES) treatment and the Dalkon Shield" (Bix, 2004, 153). DES had resulted in birth defects in newborns, while the Dalkon Shield had caused serious gynecological injuries (Kolata, 1987). Women claimed that the medical establishment had an inadequate understanding of women's health concerns, needs, and experiences. "Women's health activists explicitly defined holism as superior to allopathic medicine, not only medically, but also politically and socially, in its sensitivity to gender, race, class, and environmental concerns" (Bix, 2004, 153). American women in the countercultural movements increasingly turned to alternative therapies for medical treatment, appreciating "shamanism for its exotic mystery, Chinese medicine for its non-Western emphasis on balance, and herbalism for its harmony with nature" (Bix, 2004, 156). Herbalism, in particular, surged in popularity in the 1990s, and herbalist teachers reminded students that for thousands of years women had been gathering herbs, learning their therapeutic benefits, and administering them to self and loved ones. Herbalists made an explicit connection "between environmentalism and holistic medicine," sometimes calling their therapeutic practices "ecological healing" (Bix, 2004, 169).

Out of a 1969 feminist conference near Boston grew the Boston Women's Health Book Collective, which politicized women's health issues (Bix, 2004) and resulted in the 1973 publication of the trend-setting book *Our Bodies, Ourselves*. The book presented women-centered medical information that women could not find elsewhere and sparked self-education programs. Its subsequent editions featured expanded coverage of holistic medicine. Support for alternative medicine represented an indictment of modernity, whose capitalist, industrialist, and political systems had sickened the Earth and its life forms. Environmentalists and ecofeminists drew parallels between the "gentleness and balance" of holistic medicine and feminine qualities, and they rejected the pathologizing of natural cycles in women's lives, such as menstruation and menopause (Bix, 2004, 164). Critics of the male-dominated medical community called for more funding for breast-cancer research and focused attention on toxins in the environment and the toxic effects of cancer treatments. Women also demanded more mainstream medical research be conducted on women, since much medical knowledge was based on male-only research samples that ignored the important physiological differences between the sexes

(Bix, 2004, 160). Such activism resulted in the 15-year federal Women's Health Initiative (WHI), which enrolled more than 160,000 postmenopausal women in a series of clinical trials and observational study (Bix, 2004). Together with its follow-up Extension Study, the WHI has provided much valuable knowledge on heart disease, breast and colorectal cancer, and osteoporotic fractures in postmenopausal women (WHI, n.d.).

The pursuit of alternatives to conventional medicine has led the mainstream medical establishment to take notice of CAM and to include the concerns of marginalized groups, such as women and people of color. Web sites of such conventional medical establishments as the National Institutes of Health, Mayo Clinic, and Centers for Disease Control and Prevention have large sections dedicated to various CAM therapies. While conventional medicine continues to be largely based on the Cartesian split between "matter and spirit," CAM promotes an integration of mind, body, and spirit (Bix, 2004, 166). Wholeness within the person and unity between people and the environment will promote health for both society and nature.

GINA K. THORNBURG

See also: Eco-Therapy (Health).

References

Ackerman, Michael. 2004. "Science and the Shadow of Ideology in the American Health Foods Movement, 1930s–1960s." In Robert D. Johnston, ed., *The Politics of Healing: Histories of Alternative Medicine in Twentieth-Century North America*. New York and London: Routledge, 56–67.

Bauer, Brent, ed. 2007. *Mayo Clinic Book of Alternative Medicine*. New York: Time.

Bix, Amy Sue. 2004. "Engendering Alternatives: Women's Health Care Choices and Feminist Medical Rebellions." In Robert D. Johnston, ed., *The Politics of Healing: Histories of Alternative Medicine in Twentieth-Century North America*. New York and London: Routledge, 153–180.

Carlston, Michael. 2006. "Homeopathy." In *Fundamentals of Complementary and Integrative Medicine*, 3rd ed. St. Louis, MO: Saunders Elsevier.

Cassidy, Claire M. 2006. "Social and Cultural Factors." In *Fundamentals of Complementary and Integrative Medicine,* 3rd ed. St. Louis, MO: Saunders Elsevier.

Davidovitch, Nadav. 2004. "Negotiating Dissent: Homeopathy and Anti-vaccinationism at the Turn of the Twentieth Century." In Robert D. Johnston, ed., *The Politics of Healing: Histories of Alternative Medicine in Twentieth-Century North America*. New York and London: Routledge, 11–28.

Freeman, Lyn W. 2001. "Homeopathy: Like Cures Like." In *Mosby's Complementary and Alternative Medicine: A Research-Based Approach*. St. Louis, MO: Mosby.

Freeman, Lyn W., and G. Frank Lawlis. 2001. *Mosby's Complementary and Alternative Medicine: A Research-Based Approach*. St. Louis, MO: Mosby.

Goodman, David, and Michael Redclift. 1991. *Refashioning Nature: Food, Ecology and Culture*. London: Routledge.

Haller, John S. 2009. *The History of American Homeopathy: From Rational Medicine to Holistic Health Care*. New Brunswick, NJ: Rutgers University Press.

Hoeting, John. 2005. "The 45-Year Saga of WNFA." *Quarterly Magazine*. Available at: http://www.wisconsinnaturalfoods.org/05w45yearsaga.html.

Kirschmann, Anne T. 2004. "Making Friends for 'Pure' Homeopathy: Hahnemannians and the Twentieth-Century Preservation and Transformation of Homeopathy." In Robert D. Johnston, ed., *The Politics of Healing: Histories of Alternative Medicine in Twentieth-Century North America*. New York and London: Routledge, 29–42.

Kolata, Gina. 1987. "The Sad Legacy of the Dalkon Shield." *New York Times*, December 6. Available at: http://www.nytimes.com/1987/12/06/magazine/the-sad-legacy-of-the-dalkon-shield.html?src=pm.

Laux, Marsha. 2011. "Organic Foods Trends Profile." Agricultural Marketing Resource Center. Available at: http://www.agmrc.org/markets_industries/food/organic_food_trends_profile.cfm.

Micozzi, Marc S., ed. 2006. *Fundamentals of Complementary and Integrative Medicine*, 3rd ed. St. Louis, MO: Saunders Elsevier.

Morrison, Judith H. 1995. *The Book of Ayurveda: A Holistic Approach to Health and Longevity*. New York: Fireside.

National Center for Complementary and Alternative Medicine (NCCAM). 2011a. "Homeopathy: An Introduction." Available at: http://nccam.nih.gov/health/homeopathy/.

National Center for Complementary and Alternative Medicine (NCCAM). 2011b. "What Is Complementary and Alternative Medicine?" Available at: http://nccam.nih.gov/health/whatiscam/.

Pollan, Michael. 2006. *The Omnivore's Dilemma: A Natural History of Four Meals*. New York: Penguin.

Rodale Institute. 2011. "The History of Rodale Institute." Available at: http://rodaleinstitute.org/about_us.

Women's Health Initiative (WHI). n.d. Available at: http://www.whiscience.org/.

Woods, Michael. 2005. *Rural Geography*. London: Sage.

COMPOSTING AND VERICOMPOSTING

Composting is an aerobic decomposition process by which biodegradable materials (such as yard trimmings and vegetable peelings) are broken down over time and transformed into matter suitable for enriching soil and fertilizing plants. Considered a form of recycling, composting is more environmentally sound than disposing of biodegradable materials in the garbage, given that such materials usually end up in landfills, or alternately, incinerated. Unlike compost bins and piles, landfills provide an anaerobic environment for decomposition, which produces significant amounts of methane, a greenhouse gas. In California alone, it is estimated that more than 12 million tons of organic, compostable materials find their way into landfills each year.

Composting is relatively easy and can be practiced in urban, as well as rural, environments. Its success hinges in part on knowing what to compost and what to exclude from the compost bin. Some people also practice "vericomposting," or "vermicomposting" using worms to facilitate the decomposition of organic materials. In the United States, numerous organizations promote composting, providing education, incentives, and a variety of programs for those who wish to adopt this environmental practice. Going beyond mere advocacy, the city of San Francisco has distinguished itself by becoming the first U.S. city to legally require its residents to separate their compostable materials from garbage.

Composting Basics

The aim of composting is simply to facilitate and hasten the naturally occurring decomposition process, thereby transforming biodegradable materials into compost to amend and enrich soil. The process is aerobic, requiring oxygen, as well as moisture, nitrogen, and carbon. Invisible microbial bacteria, along with macrobial decomposers (such as nematodes, redworms, and grubs), decompose the organic, compostable material that is added to a compost pile or bin. Regularly turning one's compost pile aerates the material and speeds up the process.

Successful composting also relies on the composter's ability to include optimal materials in the composting bin or pile, excluding noncompostable or harmful items. Selecting proper materials for composting is also key to reducing the amount of otherwise compostable waste that ends up in landfills. Although experts and advocates don't speak in complete unison about what should and shouldn't be composted or the precise ratios in which such materials should be included, the following basic guidelines are agreed upon by most.

What to Compost

Former chairperson of the UK's Community Composting Network Nicky Scott suggests that "greens" and "browns" belong in the compost bin. "Greens" (which are nitrogen-rich) include grass clippings, houseplants, peelings from uncooked fruits and vegetables, and fresh leaves. "Browns" (which are carbonaceous) may include woody garden prunings, dried leaves, and cardboard tubes from toilet paper and paper towel rolls. Greens and browns can be added in alternating four-inch layers or simply commingled.

According to the Environmental Protection Agency (EPA), other items that can be composted include hair and fur, clean paper, coffee grounds and filters, eggshells, nut shells, hay and straw, sawdust, teabags, dryer lint, clean paper, wood chips, and cotton or wool rags. Some animal manures are also beneficial additions to the compost pile or bin. Herbivore manure, such as that collected from rabbits, cows, goats, llamas, and horses, is ideal (but, as noted below, the feces of carnivores such as cats and dog should be excluded).

What to Exclude from the Composting Bin

Although reducing the amount of waste that goes to landfills is a laudable goal, some items simply should not be composted because they can harm people or plants. As stated previously, although herbivores' manure is beneficial, most pet wastes (notably excluding rabbit excrement, which is particularly high in nitrogen) such as cat and dog feces and soiled cat litter are inappropriate for composting. Such carnivore wastes can contain pathogens, parasites, bacteria, and other elements that

Greenovation: What to Compost

The IN List

- Animal manure
- Cardboard rolls
- Clean paper
- Coffee grounds and filters
- Cotton rags
- Dryer and vacuum cleaner lint
- Eggshells
- Fireplace ashes
- Fruits and vegetables
- Grass clippings
- Hair and fur
- Hay and straw
- Houseplants
- Leaves
- Nut shells
- Sawdust
- Shredded newspaper
- Tea bags
- Wood chips
- Wool rags
- Yard trimmings

The OUT List

Leave Out/Reason Why

- Black walnut tree leaves or twigs
  - Releases substances that might be harmful to plants

- Coal or charcoal ash
  - Might contain substances harmful to plants

- Dairy products (e.g., butter, milk, sour cream, yogurt) and eggs
  - Create odor problems and attract pests such as rodents and flies
  - Diseased or insect-ridden plants
  - Diseases or insects might survive and be transferred back to other plants

- Fats, grease, lard, or oils
  - Create odor problems and attract pests such as rodents and flies

are detrimental to humans. Similarly, plants can be damaged if compost contains clippings from black walnut trees, coal, or charcoal ash. Compost derived from plants that are diseased or have suffered insect damage may also reinfect healthy plants. Grass clippings or other yard trimmings that have been exposed to chemical pesticides can eradicate the beneficial organisms that are essential to composting's success.

Although vegetable and fruit peelings are ideal for composting, many other table scraps are not appropriate because they can attract flies or rodents, as well as causing odor problems. Therefore, dairy products, meat and fish scraps, lard, fats, oils, and grease should not go in the compost bin. In addition to causing the aforementioned problems, meat and fish bones can take an excessively long time to decompose and, if they are sharp, can injure gardeners. Although the above recommendations are relatively uncontroversial for adoption by beginners, some experienced composters have developed special methods for composting particular items such as pet feces.

Additionally, nonbiodegradable materials such as glass, rubber and most plastics, as well as disposable baby diapers don't compost.

Vericomposting

Vericomposting, or the use of earthworms to facilitate the

decomposition of organic materials, can be a good indoor means of composting for apartment dwellers or others who lack access to outdoor spaces. It can also serve as a terrific supplement to traditional composting. Worm farms and vericomposting kits are commercially available and produce nutrient-rich "vermicast" or worm castings (essentially, worm manure). Worms suitable for vericomposting include red wigglers, tiger worms,

- Meat or fish bones and scraps
  - Create odor problems and attract pests such as rodents and flies
- Pet wastes (e.g., dog or cat feces, soiled cat litter)
  - Might contain parasites, bacteria, germs, pathogens, and viruses harmful to humans
- Yard trimmings treated with chemical pesticides
  - Might kill beneficial composting organisms

Source: U.S. Environmental Protection Agency. Available at: http://www.epa.gov/osw/conserve/rrr/composting/basic.htm.

and dendras. Worms should be fed frequently, with small amounts of items such as vegetable peelings, coffee grounds, and rabbit feces, and their food should be covered with moist, shredded newspaper so as not to attract flies. Although some adults may feel uncomfortable with worms, children often love them. A particular benefit of vericomposting is that it can serve as an effective means of boosting children's interest in taking positive action on behalf of the environment.

Advocacy, Composting, and Public Policy

In the United States, composting is encouraged or facilitated by a variety of local, state, and national organizations such as the Environmental Protection Agency, the U.S Composting Council, and the Agricultural Stabilization and Conservation Service (ASCS), which has encouraged the use of compost on farms. Government programs promoting composting vary by state and region and provide a host of benefits, including education, outreach, school programming, grant opportunities, technical assistance, and workshops.

In 2009, as part of an organized effort to divert recyclable waste from landfills and achieve a goal of zero waste by 2020, San Francisco Mayor Gavin Newsom signed into effect the nation's first mandatory composting law. San Francisco business owners and residents are now required by law to sort their compostable materials into a separate green bin; failure to comply can result in warnings and, eventually, fines. Although some residents have expressed worries about the invasion of privacy implied by city inspections of their trash, many others have lauded the law as landmark environmental legislation for a nation that has become better known for its consumption than its conservation.

TRACY ROYCE

See also: Landscaping and Xeriscaping (Health); Recycling (Environment); Waste Management (Science).

References

Bradley, Fern Marshall. 2007. *Rodale's Vegetable Garden Problem Solver: The Best and Latest Advice for Beating Pests, Diseases, and Weeds and Staying a Step Ahead of Trouble in the Garden.* New York: Rodale.

Californians Against Waste. "Composting: A Greenhouse Gas Mitigation Measure." Available at: http://www.cawrecycles.org/issues/ghg/compost.

Campbell, Stu. 1998. *Let It Rot!: The Gardener's Guide to Composting.* North Adams, MA: Storey Publishing.

Cote, John. "S.F. OKs Toughest Recycling Law in U.S.: S.F. Supes OK Mayor's Proposal—Fines for Violators." Available at: http://articles.sfgate.com/2009-06-10/news/17207992_1_bins-fines-composting.

Coyne, Kelly, and Eric Knutzen. 2008. *The Urban Homestead: Your Guide to Self-Sufficient Living in the Heart of the City.* Port Townsend, WA: Process Media.

Davies, Stephanie. 2011. *Composting Inside and Out: 14 Methods to Fit Your Lifestyle.* Cincinnati, OH: Betterway Books.

Environmental Protection Agency. "Wastes—Resource Conservation—Reduce, Reuse, Recycle—Composting." Available at: http://www.epa.gov/osw/conserve/rrr/composting/ (cited on August 14, 2011).

Lowenfels, Jeff, and Wayne Lewis. 2010. *Teaming with Microbes: The Organic Gardener's Guide to the Soil Food Web*, rev. ed. Portland, OR: Timer Press.

McBay, Aric. 2006. *Peak Oil Survival: Preparation for Life After Gridcrash.* Guilford, CT: Lyons Press.

McLaughlin, Chris. 2010. *The Complete Idiot's Guide to Composting.* New York: Alpha Books.

Pleasant, Barbara, and Deborah L. Martin. 2008. *The Complete Compost Gardening Guide.* North Adams, MA: Storey Publishing.

Scott, Nicky. 2005. *Composting: An Easy Household Guide.* White River Junction, VT: Chelsea Green.

Scott, Nicky. 2009. *How to Make and Use Compost: The Ultimate Guide.* Devon, UK: Green Books.

ECO-THERAPY

Eco-therapy engages in the therapeutic identification and relative nature concerning the human condition and our ecosystem. Eco-therapy is essentially a composite of two field disciplines: "eco-psychology," the connection between individual and natural environment; and "psychotherapy," the therapeutic interaction or treatment of assisting individuals to understand and increase their psychological sense of well-being. Thus, through holistic principles, eco-therapy centers on the relationships an individual maintains with the natural environment in order to feel fully integrated in and throughout life.

The concept of ecotherapy first emerged from Theodore Roszak's book *Voice of the Earth* (1992), which called for a need of new methodologies to examine and understand how an individual's level of perception, connection, separation, or dominance over the natural environment largely affects the individual's mental health, views of self-identity, and treatment of both others and the natural environment. Additionally, Warwick Fox's *Toward a Transpersonal Ecology* (1995) further develops the concept of eco-psychology into a philosophy concentrated on connecting to nature and spirituality; such connection to ecology and the human condition is also a spiritual experience to be utilized toward self-realization. Crucially, these writings greatly influenced and provided the foundations of therapeutic methodologies concerning ecotherapy (Chalquist, n.d.).

Eco-therapy can involve a variety of methodologies that heal and restore an individual's mental and emotional balance. Such methodologies are based on the systematic yet holistic analysis of the environment and individuals as well as all species. These methods and modes of study provide an important foundation for thought concerning human spirituality and psychology. Proponents of ecotherapy as well as deep ecologists believe that the lack of recognizing intrinsic value of the biosphere leads to overuse in natural resources, disrespect and destruction of natural landscapes and biological communities, and deterioration of cultures and traditions, which are tightly interwoven with thriving local biodiversity, anxiety, depression, obesity, as well as many other human illnesses. Certain methodologies include shamanic counseling; eastern medicine such as Reiki, acupuncture, or acupressure; wilderness therapies such as vision quests or survival training; and "green acts" such as of gardening, nature meditation, or walking outdoors.

At present, the World Health Organization predicts depression will be the second greatest cause of ill health globally by 2020; one in four individuals will directly experience mental health problems; studies have also linked depression, anxiety and high levels of stress to the amount of nature in social environments. Moreover, 93 percent of medical general practitioners report prescribing antidepressants against their better judgment due to a lack of alternatives (Mind for Better Mental Health, n.d.).

Alternatively, research has also suggested that access to green space (a "natural living environment"; or synthesized "ecological units" such as vegetation, water, soil, rocks, microorganisms and atmosphere that comprise a "natural system") can greatly reduce mental as well as physical distress and improve an individual's overall well-being. In areas where 90 percent of the environment around the home is green, only 10 percent of the residents feel unhealthy, as compared with areas in which 10 percent of the environment is green, where 16 percent of the residents feel unhealthy (Maas et al., 2006). Additionally, research has also indicated that when subjects with mental health problems were sent to exercise either in the woodlands and grasslands or in an indoor mall, 71 percent of those exposed to "green space" experienced decreased levels of depression and 90 percent reported increased levels of self-esteem; while 22 percent of those indoors experienced levels of depression and 44 percent reported decreased levels of self-esteem. Although the causes of this effect remain unknown, the relation between exposure to green environments and individual well-being remains consistent as well as scientifically evident (Sauls, 2011).

Applicatively, national initiatives such as "Walk with a Doc," established in 13 states (Arkansas, California, Colorado, Connecticut, Florida, Hawaii, Indiana, Iowa, Michigan, New York, North Carolina, Ohio, and Pennsylvania as well as North-western Ontario Canada) provide a healthy alternative and viable promotion of green exercise. The project's undertaking is to encourage green exercise and healthy activity for people of all ages, reverse sedentary lifestyles, and prevent heart disease, obesity, anxiety, depression, as well as other unhealthy conditions. In addition to green exercise, the program also provides free blood pressure checks, pedometers, as well as dietary information to its participants.

The "No Child Left Inside" (NCLI) initiative centers on environmental education as a critical function to the success of a student's education; as such, this initiative promotes and develops a sense of stewardship among its participants concerning the environment and its natural resources. This initiative also provides funding to states that initiate or expand environmental education in public schools and provides "outdoor instruction" about the environment in state parks. Successfully, NCLI initiatives have already been adopted in many states throughout the United States.

"Youth and Leaders Living Actively" (YALLA) is a holistic program that addresses the specific needs of refugee youth and their families. The Green Access Ecotherapy program enables YALLA to impact the wider refugee community by healing from the trauma of war through nature and outdoor activities, such as gardening, hiking, camping, and beach outings, for youth diagnosed with posttraumatic stress disorder; promoting environmental stewardship through leadership opportunities and activities that endorse the benefits and value of their environment; and assisting in the acclimation of refugee youth and families to a new culture, home, school, and neighborhood through access to nature and ecotherapeutic practices (YALLA San Diego, n.d.).

In sum, ecotherapy is emerging as a clinically valid treatment option for mental distress and the promotion of balanced mental health and well-being. Although its scholarship is more grounded in contemporary study, the evidence base is growing stronger, and our concern about the environment is also increasing. Thus, ecotherapy grows out of the necessity for a new paradigm in Western psychological analysis; it addresses and recognizes the limits of technocratic solutions that examine the human condition through a skewed frame of empirically abstract analysis. Pragmatically, ecotherapy also supports initiatives in sustainable development, such as building codes and green certification requirements, increased access to green spaces, and increased atmospheric quality in communities and buildings such as hospitals, schools, and offices. Therefore, as the green movement gathers followers and continues, the effects of ecotherapy become definite in its relation to the benefits of mental health (such as lowering stress and boosting self-esteem); the improvement of physical health (such as lowering blood pressure and helping to tackle obesity), as well as providing a source of therapeutic purpose for individuals. Simultaneously, such conscientiousness of health and well-being also fosters a conscientiousness of our ecological environments and biodiversity, inward reflection, and the potential for transformation as we become mindful of our interconnectivity with the world around us.

KAI KAULULAAU

See also: Complementary and Alternative Medicine (Health).

References

Chalquist, Craig. n.d. "The Environmental Crisis Is a Crisis of Consciousness." Available at: http://www.terrapsych.com/crisis.html.

Maas, Jolanda, Robert A. Verheij, Peter P. Groenewegen, Sjerp de Vries, and Peter Spreeuwenberg. 2006. "Green Space, Urbanity, and Health: How Strong Is the Relation?" *Journal of Epidemiology Community Health* 60: 587–592.

Mind for Better Mental Health. n.d. Available at: http://www.mind.org.uk/campaigns_and_issues/report_and_resources/835_ecotherapy.

Sauls, Tiffany. 2011. "Using Nature to Improve Children's Health." Available at: http://www.childrenandnature.org/downloads/GG2011/UsingNature_TiffanySauls.pdf.

YALLA San Diego. n.d. "Eco Therapy Program." Available at: http://www.yallasd.com/eco-therapy.php.

GARDEN, HOME

Home organic gardening is a form of small-scale agriculture that employs techniques such as crop rotation, green manure, and composting to sustain productive soils. Organic gardening should not be confused with chemists' use of the term organic, indicating the presence of carbon. Manufactured fertilizers, pesticides, and

Mallory McDevitt of Wapakoneta, Ohio in her one-acre organic garden. (U.S. Department of Agriculture)

genetically modified organisms are shunned by organic farming practitioners. Organic gardening practices recognize the principles of nature that have sustained life for millions of years without synthetic chemicals (Hamilton, 2004). Over the past several decades, there has been tremendous growth in organic agriculture in the United States, both commercially and in home gardens. In a sense, agriculture has truly come full circle; small-scale organic farming was the earliest form of the world's agriculture. It was not until the past century that nonorganic, chemically intensive gardening methods were even possible as synthetic fertilizers and pesticides were developed and made commercially available (Standage, 2009).

Overall, the resurgence of organic home gardening practices in the United States has occurred in tandem with the rise of do-it-yourself (DIY) culture. Reasons for the increased popularity of organic gardening include achieving greater self-sufficiency, its inherent joy, environmental sustainability, cost savings, health concerns, and community and family aspects (Stonebrook, 2010). In particular, recent concerns about food contamination and distrust of commercial growers have prompted many to plant home organic gardens. When she turned the White House's south lawn into an organic vegetable garden, First Lady Michelle Obama proved to be a boon to organic gardening, raising awareness about organic practices and increasing its popularity nationally (Burros, 2009). Obama herself has cited the health benefits of organic gardens and views them as one way to fight against childhood obesity in America.

The benefits of maintaining an organic vegetable garden are many. For one, organic gardening is generally more cost effective than purchasing produce or using nonorganic inputs such as pesticides and herbicides. Indeed, expenditures for fertilizer and energy using organic methods are estimated to be only 50 percent of the cost of chemical intensive methods. Furthermore, 97 percent fewer pesticides are used in organic methods compared to conventional plant cultivation. Additionally, by growing fruits and vegetables at home, one does not have to pay grocery store prices, which factor in the costs of transportation, handling, and branding in the final retail price tag.

Unlike the abundance of inputs in conventional, chemical intensive agriculture, organic methods are based on closed nutrient cycles, where nutrients are recycled and regenerated. This stands in stark contrast to chemical-reliant methods, which use an abundance of synthetic fertilizers, a large percentage of which are washed into surrounding waterways. The larger-scale effect of this is eutrophication, the introduction of large amounts of fertilizer that can cause extensive algae blooms downstream of the source. The "dead zone" in the Gulf of Mexico is the most obvious example of this detrimental environmental process. Organic gardening and farming, by contrast, do not release large amounts of fertilizers that negatively affect the environment because nutrients are recycled. Organic gardeners' concerns about environmental sustainability tend to dissuade them from engaging in potentially harmful practices that can lead to widespread environmental degradation.

Another environmental benefit for gardening by organic methods is the emphasis placed on long-term soil management (Gillman, 2008). Organic gardeners focus on long-term sustainability by ensuring that nutrients naturally remain in soils from year to year, instead of relying on chemicals to make up for nutrient loss by runoff and plant uptake. In many home organic gardens, gardeners practice no-till methods in which soils are not turned over in between planting seasons. Because tilling actually releases large amounts of carbon gas stored in soils into the atmosphere, organic gardening helps to sequester carbon and mitigate climate change.

Concerns over food miles—the distance a particular food travels from its production location to the end consumer—have become increasingly important to consumers in recent years (Engelhaupt, 2008). At the same time, food miles have increased, as food is produced farther and farther from where it is consumed. As of 2007, the average distance a food travels had increased by 25 percent from 1980. Consumers have expressed concern over this for various reasons, including the energy consumption and carbon emissions from transporting foods long distances, the lack of benefit on the local economy, and the lack of information about where, how, and by whom food is grown. In response to these issues, many consumers have turned to home organic gardening.

Anxieties over a decrease in agrobiodiversity due to the homogenization and genetic modification of agriculture provides another impetus for the practice of home organic gardening. Seed Savers Exchange, a nonprofit organization in Iowa, is one of the largest repositories of rare heirloom seed varieties in America, and part of its mission is to encourage seed diversity by distributing its specialty, untreated, non-genetically modified organism seeds to home gardeners throughout the country.

Because of its growing popularity in America, the green practice of organic gardening has become much more accessible to the general public through organizations such as Seed Savers Exchange. Due to higher demand for organic gardening products (composting bins, seeds, and organic insecticides, for example), their availability has increased greatly, making it much easier to start an organic garden at home. Along with increasing availability of supplies and products, publications about organic gardening have become more common over the past decade. Magazines such as *Mother Earth News* and *Organic Gardening* have gained readership as many other magazines are struggling to remain in print.

Tensions within the realm of organic gardening and farming, however, are present, primarily on the issue of official organic certification. As the market for organic produce has blossomed, the process of becoming certified as an organic producer has become increasingly politicized. The costs of receiving official certification are high, creating difficulties for small organic producers. Furthermore, lobbying groups have pushed to alter the U.S. Department of Agriculture (USDA) regulations to permit some synthetic chemicals in products stamped with the USDA's organic seal of approval (Kindy & Layton, 2009). As a result, many proponents of small-scale organic agriculture are among the most vocal critics of official organic certification. For most small-scale, home organic gardeners, the idea of gardening with organic principles is determined by the actual practices involved in cultivation, not in the label attached to it.

JAMES BAGINSKI

See also: Agriculture (Economics); Composting and Vericomposting (Health); Farming, Conventional (Economics); Farming, Organic (Economics); Landscaping and Xeriscaping (Health).

References

Burros, Marian. 2009. "Obamas to Plant Vegetable Garden at White House." *New York Times*, March 19. Available at: http://www.nytimes.com/2009/03/20/dining/20garden.html.

Engelhaupt, Erika. 2008. "Do Food Miles Matter?" *Environmental Science and Technology* 42: 3482.

Gillman, Jeff. 2008. *The Truth About Organic Gardening*. Portland: Timber Press.

Hamilton, Geoff. 2004. *Organic Gardening*. London: Dorling Kindersley.

Kindy, Kimberly, and Lyndsey Layton. 2009. "Purity of Federal 'Organic' Label Is Questioned." *Washington Post*, July 3. Available at: http://www.washingtonpost.com/wp-dyn/content/article/2009/07/02/AR2009070203365.html.

Mäder, Paul, Andreas Fliessbach, David Dubois, Lucie Gunst, Padruot Fried, and Urs Niggli. 2002. "Soil Fertility and Biodiversity in Organic Farming." *Science* 296: 1694–1697.

Standage, Tom. 2009. *An Edible History of Humanity*. New York: Walker.

Stonebrook, Shelley. 2010. "Good Reasons to Garden." *Mother Earth News*, October 18. Available at: http://www.motherearthnews.com/grow-it/reasons-to-garden-zb0z10zsto.aspx.

Willer, Helga, and Lukas Klicher. 2011. *The World of Organic Agriculture: Statistics and Emerging Trends 2009*. London: IFOAM & FiBL. Available at: http://www.organic-world.net/fileadmin/documents/yearbook/2011/world-of-organic-agriculture-2011-page-1-34.pdf.

GREEN FUNERALS

Green funerals, or "eco-funerals," seek to minimize the environmental impact of the entire funeral process so that the burial sites remain as natural as possible. Traditional funerals require vast amounts of resources and energy. Each year in the United States, the funeral industry uses 827,060 gallons of embalming fluid, 90,000 tons of steel, and 30 million feet of hardwood (maple, cherry, and walnut) for caskets, over 5 million pounds of copper to line the caskets, 136,000 tons of reinforced concrete, and 14,000 tons of steel for vaults. Two products typically sold by U.S. funeral directors illustrate the use of ecologically harmful materials: the "Summerfield" line of caskets is lined with plush velvet and is not biodegradable; the "Lydian" burial vault provides a suitable receptacle for the Summerfield and is made of special concrete designed to resist 5,000 pounds of pressure per square inch. The Lydian is bonded to reinforced plastic and copper and contains an inner liner of fiber-reinforced acrylonitrile butadiene styrene (the same material used in National Football League helmets). The unit has a butyl seal that resists penetration by soil, air, water, or anything else that might contaminate the body. By the same token, modern cemeteries upset the natural landscape with their overuse of valuable open space. Huge expanses of grass are kept alive through the use of fertilizers, herbicides, and frequent watering. Expensive cement vaults, leak-proof caskets, mausoleums, polished granite tombstone markers, and even plastic flowers deplete resources and degrade the landscape. Green burial sites, on the other hand, use indigenous vegetation and are designed to eliminate the use of water, pesticides, or other unnatural materials.

Biodegradable caskets, like this wicker coffin, are part of the new "green burial" movement. (Shutterstock.com)

Embalming

In the United States, embalming became popular during the Civil War and remains a significant source of groundwater pollution. In the modern practice, the blood is drained from the corpse and replaced by Formalin (formaldehyde in water). Some estimates state that 1 million gallons of formaldehyde is buried each year in embalmed human bodies. Embalming is mandatory when bodies are transported by common carriers. Embalming is required by funeral homes when the body will be viewed by the public in an open casket. Eco-options include embalming with formaldehyde-free fluids such as iodine or natural plant extracts and the use of dry ice before a viewing. At present, no state in the United States requires routine embalming of human corpses. The Funeral Rule (15 U.S.C. 57a(a); 15 U.S.C. 46(g); para. 5 U.S.C. 552) enforced by the Federal Trade Commission, states that it is a misrepresentation for funeral homes to fail to disclose that embalming "is not required by law except in certain special cases, if any."

Cremation

Cremation has a significant impact on the environment. The process of cremation entails placing the corpse in a combustible container, placing the container in an

1,800-degree oven for two and one-half hours, and cooling the remains for four to six hours. Cremation has a significant impact on the environment, releasing nitrogen oxides, carbon monoxide, sulfur dioxide, mercury, hydrofluoric acid, hydrochloric acid and persistent organic pollutants (POPs) into the atmosphere. Approximately 40 percent of deceased Americans were cremated in 2010. In some states (Alaska, Arizona, Hawaii, Montana, Nevada, Oregon and Washington) there were more cremations than burials.

The trend toward green funerals began in Great Britain in 1991 and quickly moved to the United States. A green funeral service uses recycled paper for programs and hymn sheets, obtains flowers from local organic gardeners, provides car pools between the funeral home and grave, and serves organic refreshments. Further, green funerals use biodegradable coffins (one made of bamboo jute, for instance), inter the bodies in a green burial ground, and employ a living marker in place of a headstone. Over 300 funeral homes provide eco-friendly burials, up from 30 three years ago. In a recent poll, 43 percent of respondents aged 50 or older would consider a green funeral (up from 21 percent four years ago). Individuals interested in a green funeral should seek good advice by consulting with a green funeral director and stating their intentions ahead of time. Green burial specialists can help plan a green funeral and provide literature on eco-friendly funerals. People wanting a green funeral should put these wishes into writing and give a copy to family members (however, the federal government advises against putting funeral instructions into wills because wills are often not read until after the funeral).

WENDELL G. JOHNSON

Greenovations: Green Practices around the World

A U.S. company, Eternal Reefs, places the remains of the deceased in a module that mimics a coral reef. The artificial reef is dropped into the ocean off the coast of Florida and provides a marine habitat for 500 years. In Sweden, corpses are dipped in liquid nitrogen, become brittle, and then turn to dust. The remains are placed in a shallow grave and decompose, providing nourishment to the soil. By 2012, half of the crematoria in Britain will have filters that reduce mercury (used in dental fillings) emissions given off by cremations. Green funerals are compatible with the practices of the major religious traditions. Judaism and Islam traditionally call for shrouds or simple wooden caskets and no embalming. Hinduism and Buddhism permit cremation, while Catholicism, Judaism, and Islam do not.

See also: Innovation and Invention Competitions (Science); Technology and Impact on Green (Science).

References

Mitford, Jessica. 1963. *The American Way of Death*. New York: Simon and Schuster.

Priesnitz, Wendy. 2008. "Natural Burial—The Ultimate in Recycling." *Natural Life*, May 28. Available at: http://www.naturalburial.coop/2008/05/28/natural-burial-the-ultimate-in-recycling-2/.

Smith, N. 2003. "Greener Ways to the Great Beyond." *Mother Earth News* 197: 56–60.

Stowe, J. P., E. Schmidt, and D. Green. 2001. "Toxic Burials: The Final Insult." *Conservation Biology* 15:6: 1817–1819.

HOME FURNISHINGS AND INTERIOR DESIGN

The future of ecological equilibrium is significantly connected with the harmony of nature and the design of built environments. Interior design practice in the United States is about the responsible and "well-informed process of creating aesthetically pleasing, safe and comfortable residential or commercial environments that respect the earth and its resources" (CIDA, 2011). The design of interiors not only adheres to various sustainable guidelines and principles, but also holistically addresses the user's needs, health and well-being, safety, and welfare through the appropriate selection of materials, furniture, furnishings, and equipment. Various prescriptive and performative codes and standards are reviewed and created by many organizations such as the International Green Construction Code (IGCC), which informs designers on appropriate and innovative solutions. Manifold examples include the intelligent use of materials that support passive to minimum energy systems; natural ventilation, winter solar heat gain, and summer shading; low water requirements; and effective lighting distribution, which impact the sustainability of the interior space (Harmon & Kennon, 2011, 490). Designers also take seriously the inclusive attributes of each product for interiors, since not all of them are manufactured and rated equal in terms of sustainable standards.

Since the ecological revolution in the early 1960s, rules, practices, and discourses have been developed to meet challenges in natural resource management and to continuously promote sustainable awareness (Edwards, 2005). It can be construed that many design initiatives in the evolving invention of materials, development of home furnishings, and the planning of built environments are framed within lifecycle assessments (LCA). The LCA identifies various environmental impacts of furnishings and materials for "all product stages: extraction, transportation, use, and final disposition or reuse" (SFC, 2011). Oftentimes, designers are responsible for the manifold decisions that cause many of the harmful impacts, including global warming, acidification, ozone depletion, photochemical smog, human health, ecological toxicity, fossil fuel depletion, habitat alteration, air pollutants, water pollution, and solid and hazardous waste (*Green Guide*, 2007; Kopec, 2009; Winchip, 2007).

In 2009, the top 100 interior design companies registered an income of $2.7 billion in annual design fees, with 30 percent or about $810 million appropriated to green products (Interior Design Magazine). Multiple initiatives are manifested in design projects that show a good percentile of specified green products, which doubled from 22 to 44 percent from 2006 to 2009. Likewise, the types of clients who are receptive to green design have tremendously increased, making ecological efforts no longer a marginal concern and peripheral effort, but rather a crucial part of the urban social fabric (Slatin, 2008). The growth in the number of companies that have taken pioneering efforts in designing and building interior spaces, recycling waste, and specifying eco-friendly materials, as well as shipping products the green way, have also increased.

With the extent of dialogues in professional interior design practices, all stakeholders (designers, engineers, builders, contractors, and suppliers) in the discipline are becoming more conscious of their contributions to achieve an environmental equilibrium, from sustainable principles and frameworks adapted at various aspects of the design process to methodologies in building systems and the required operational costs. Moreover, stakeholders are expected to participate in the formulation and application of effective environmental performance strategies as embodied in the Environmental Product Declarations (*Green Guide*, 2007, 24). The International Standard Organization (ISO) further develops and publishes materials communicating the environmental management system requirements as highlighted in the ISO 14001 shared by a network of standard institutes located in over 161 countries (Bonda, 2009, G6).

The challenge of fitting an interior space with the specific needs of humanity, based on the designer's sensitivity toward the health, welfare, and safety, goes with every selective choice of home furnishings, building products, and construction materials. Home furnishings used in interiors include furniture, architectural casework (architectural components such as doors, windows, columns, and built-in cabinets), bedding, linens, carpets and rugs, paints and wall coverings, lighting fixtures, and tableware (Elsasser, 2004). In a brief review ranking green products specified by designers, carpet ranks first with 97 percent; hardwood flooring, furniture, and paint are at a triple tie for 94 percent; followed by fabric with 92 percent, lighting and building products equal at 90 percent, and 89 percent for wall coverings (Interior Design, 2009).

There are four major classifications in furniture, including case goods, upholstered, occasional, and bedding (Elsasser, 2004, 222). Designers have become proactive with choices related to furniture design and development for both residential and commercial interior environments. With this wide plethora of goods, one coalition of industry manufacturers formed in 2006, known as the Sustainable Furnishings Council (SFC), calls for the "industry to achieve sustainable development goals that respond to performance improvements in ecological integrity" (SFC, 2011). Some of the objectives of the coalition are focused on raising consumer awareness on green issues; supporting companies that adapt environmentally friendly manufacturing practices (e.g., reduction of carbon emissions and pollutants, use of nonrenewable resources, and nonrecyclable content); and the conduct of LCA, resulting into sustainable products' certification. Another agency, the National Science Foundation (NSF) International, which is involved with various aspects of standards development, collaborated with the American National Standards Institute for the creation of specific regulations, such as NSF 336 for Sustainable Textile Standard and NSF-ANSI 140 for Sustainable Carpet Assessment. The NSF and the Business and Institutional Furniture Manufacturer's Association (BIFMA) also agreed on sustainable product standards to address human and ecosystem health, energy, and material costs and they encourage companies to embrace social responsibility in all stages of production and distribution (*Green*

Guide, 2007). The BIFMA and the Sustainable Forestry Initiative (SFI) also monitor the use and specification of wood for architectural casework and built-in millwork by setting the criteria on acceptable composite woods and agrifiber products. The latter is commonly known in the market as particle board, wheatboard, strawboard, or medium density fiberboard, which should be free from formaldehyde (Harmon & Kennon, 2011, 423). Formaldehyde is classified as a harmful chemical and a probable human carcinogen (Bonda, 2009; Winchip, 2007). Designers should use finishes like stains, coatings, and sealants; and adhesives for veneer, laminates, and wallpaper should carry low volatile organic compound (VOC) levels. They should conscientiously review their Green Label certifications prior to material specification.

Studies in 2007 indicate that the average lifespan of interior finishes is about 50 years, and the chances of being refurbished and retrofitted are between 5 to 10 times (*Green Guide*, 2007, 19). Architecture, engineering, construction, and interior design practitioners take advantage of the Building Information Modelling (BIM), which apparently has shifted the creative thought process in digitally addressing sustainable standards. We see innovative outcomes in the context of generating and managing data related to spatial planning, minimizing errors in the construction phase by establishing drawing consistency in design development, presenting virtual attributes of finishes prior to final specification of materials, and parametrically identifying the relationships of objects with multiple architectural features and elements to be built.

A large percentage of home furnishings have soft components in the product family of bedding and linens. Elsasser (2004) classified bedding to include mattresses, mattress support systems, pads and covers, bed pillows, and other alternative bedding such as foam blocks and futons. He further noted that linens come in many forms that include bedroom-related linens such as sheets, pillowcases, blankets and throws, comforters and bedspreads; towels and bathroom textile–related products; tablecloths, placemats, and napkins; slipcovers; and soft window treatments and curtains. With the current supply chain from the manufacturer, traders, or retailers to users, all textiles are evaluated and tested for toxic substances with the internationally implemented Oeko-Tex Standard 100 certification (Bonda, 2009). Another product family in home furnishings is the soft-floor covering, which has classifications in broadloom, carpet, carpet modules or tiles, and rug (Elsasser, 2004, 316). Broadloom is constructed on a wide loom used for wall-to-wall carpeting and cut-sized rugs. All these materials have textiles components and use adhesives that should also be measured for low chemical emissions to safeguard public health.

One last home furnishing category used in interior environments is the lighting fixtures, which can be categorized as structural or architectural luminaires or portable luminaires, such as drop lights and table lamps. Designers must constantly balance their creative intentions with ecological standards by evaluating the information on product manufacturing and energy use, its long-term value and lifecycle, the harmful substances therein, and what happens when they are eventually disposed.

Interior designers use several criteria for the assessment and specification of home furnishings and materials. Driven by the criteria that encompass ecological design principles and supported by the body of knowledge in renewable/sustainable dichotomy, recycled/recyclable dualism, durability, adaptability, low-embodied energy and locally sourced products, sustainably maintained, and low toxicity levels (Godsey, 2008, 33), the American interior designer is inspiritingly committed to intelligent choices in transforming our built environments as healthy and sustainable spaces.

THELMA LAZO-FLORES

See also: Green Your Holiday Scene (documents); Ten Tips for Hiring a Heating and Cooling Contractor (documents); Textiles for Furniture and Fashion (Health).

References

Bonda, Penny. 2009. "Green Alphabet Soup." In *Green Pages: Neocon World's Trade Fair 2009 Catalogue*. Chicago: Neocon.

Council of Interior Design Accreditation (CIDA). 2011. Available at: http://accredit-id.org/.

Edwards, Andres R. 2005. *The Sustainability Revolution*. Gabriola, BC: New Society Publishers.

Elsasser, Virginia Hencken. 2004. *Know Your Home Furnishings*. New York: Fairchild Books.

Fuad-luke, Alastair. 2002. *Eco-Design: The Sourcebook*. London: Thames and Hudson.

Gale, Frances, and Norman R. Weiss. 2009. "Update on Building Materials Research." *Association for Preservation Technology Bulletin* 40:3/4: 59–65.

Godsey, Lisa. 2008. *Interior Design Materials and Specifications*. New York: Fairchild Books.

Green Guide to NeoCon. 2007. Cedar Rapids, IA: Interiors and Sources.

Harmon, Sharon K., and Katherine E. Kennon. 2011. *The Codes Guidebook for Interiors*. Hoboken, NJ: Wiley.

Interior Design Magazine. 2009. "Lean and Green." *Reed Business Information* (June): 32–34.

Interiors and Sources. 2007. "Product Certification Criteria." *Interiors and Sources* 38–40.

Kopec, Dak. 2009. *Health, Sustainability and the Built Environment*. New York: Fairchild Books.

McDonough, William, and Michael Braungart. 2000. "A World of Abundance." *Interface* 30: 55–65.

National Science Foundation International. 2007. "Working to Develop Industry Standards." In *Green Guide to NeoCon*. Cedar Rapids, IA: Interiors and Sources, 32–34.

Slatin, Peter. 2008. "How Green Design Answers Corporate Demands." In *NeoCon Green Guide*. Cedar Rapids, IA: Interior Design.

Sustainable Furnishings Council (SFC). 2011. "Sustainability: More than a Slogan." Available at: http://www.sustainablefurnishings.org/.

Winchip, Susan. 2007. *Sustainable Design for Interior Environments*. New York: Fairchild.

HOSPITAL AND HEALTH CARE

Sustainability strategies undertaken in most built environments designed for health care positively impact the well-being of human society. Satisfaction is evidently seen in spaces for healing and human recovery process of patients, and areas that support higher productivity rates and better performance of health care professionals and staff. In the United States, hospitals and health care facilities are noted as the second most energy intensive building type due to the continuous 24-hour operation, which creates the significant amount of waste and demand for enormous use of energy, resulting from complex programmatic operations on a daily basis (Gallagher-Rogers, 2011; Samet, 2011). In 2011, over 120 health care facilities have received Leadership in Energy and Environmental Design (LEED) for health care green building certification after it was implemented in 2010. LEED is under the U.S. Green Building flagship. It oversees the certification of green building design and construction of hospitals, the facilities for assisted living and long-term care, centers for education and research, as well as medical offices.

The certification or rating system for sustainable health care looks into many aspects of the physical facility, such as the quality of artificial lighting and increase of daylight within the structure, energy resources for building performance and exterior landscape, better indoor air quality brought by the reduction of chemicals and pollutants, green cleaning and biomedical waste assessment, and recycling practices among many others. From a low 1 percent of sustainable involvement by hospitals as measured in a 2008 study (Carpenter, 2008), there are now over 400 registered projects seeking certification in 2011 (Gallagher-Rogers, 2011).

Green strategies in health care encompass several areas such health care efficiency through green construction, LEED program approaches, LEED ratings and certification, hospital operations that integrated health information management (HMI), PPA rate (utility), and the innovative use of green information technology. It is imperative for environmental sustainability to be the focus of health care operations since the latter correlates with statistics that significantly matter to the entire industry. Health care represents 16 percent of the gross domestic product, 4.1 million employed personnel, an annual energy expense that amounts to $8.3 billion, 2 million pounds of waste per year, and the largest water consumption in any community (Kinney, 2010).

Apart from the U.S. Green Building Council and LEED, various measures of environmental stewardship are long initiated by multiple agencies, which include Green Guide for Health Care (GGCH); American Hospital Association; Coalition for Environmentally Responsible Economies (CERES); Energy Star; Energy Smart Hospitals; American Society of Heating, Refrigerating and Air-Conditioning Engineers (ASHRAE); American Nurses Association, which founded the Hospitals for a Healthy Environment (H2E) and was later named Practice Greenhealth; and many others (Carpenter, 2008, 18; "Who's Who," 2008, 26). Further, the 2008 Green Design and Operations Survey reveals that Energy Star's program is widely used and observed by most hospitals, while GGCH is the least observed. However, in a 2009 survey initiated by Practice Greenhealth, both LEED and GGCH programs are popularly used by facilities for renovation, building, and operations (Johnson, 2010, 79).

As environmental policies and standards change, the list of leaders in the health care sustainability movement also expands (Vernon, 2009) with the presence of American Society for Healthcare Engineering; Global Health and Safety Initiative; Health Care Without Harm (HCWH); Global Health and Safety Initiative (GHSI);

U.S. Environmental Protection Agency (EPA), and the U.S. Department of Energy. In support of the LEED Program Approaches (Kinney, 2010, 26), other agencies also share the same models of sustainable operations that focus on alternative forms of transportation; creation of livable environments through soft-scapes planning; minimize operation costs while providing a comfortable patient experience; conservation of electricity with the use of occupancy sensors and flexible sunshades; reduction in the use of materials outside the local resources; use of sustainable materials and supplies for daily operations, and improvement of hospital air quality.

The link of health care and the environment also faces three dilemmas that need ethical practices. Sustainable health care and ethical responsibilities should operate with three ideals: practices should provide no harm to the human society and the natural world, sustainable measures should be equitably reinforced with goals for social justice, and responsibilities should balance good public health care with environmental sensitivity and awareness (Jameton & Pierce, 2001). Health problems have also evolved in the past six decades, with many of them clearly associated with the compromised standards in the natural ecosystem services such as water purification and waste decomposition; climate stabilization and solar radiation; seed dispersal and pollination; pest control and soil renewal; and biodiversity (Jameton & Pierce, 2001, 365).

As environmental standards are continuously being evaluated and monitored, greening initiatives at hospitals and health care facilities are equally increasing. Nevertheless, a 2008 survey states that the percentage of hospitals that have specified products following LEED standards, sustainable criteria, or representing energy-efficient attributes were not highly significant in the 18 categories of building materials. The top four categories were lighting (65 percent), heating, ventilation, and air conditioning systems (45 percent), mechanical systems 44 percent), and appliances (42 percent) (Carpenter, 2008, 17). Further, percentages of hospitals with installed systems that conserve energy are perceived in three areas: the use of high-efficiency building controls, lighting sensors, and chiller plant optimization (Carpenter, 2008).

In a highly regulated industry, the green practices in U.S. hospitals are not only focused in renovations, building construction, and operations. Other sustainable practices extend to the use of environmental purchasing programs, disposal program of medical waste, water reduction program, and the generation of onsite energy (Johnson, 2010, 79). Supported by an EPA grant, a group of 20 hospitals in various parts of the United States formed a project to develop strategies and initiatives that were implemented under the Green Team in 2009. The initiatives highlighted were recycling of paper and plastic; recycling of bottles and cans; recycling of batteries, fluorescent bulbs, and other equipment; regulation of medical waste; destruction of equipment and computers with zero residual waste; minimal use of printers and copy machines; observance of energy-efficient measures for mechanical and electrical systems; composting of food waste and biodiesel fuel conversion from excess cooking oil; use of green chemicals by services staff; encouraging alternative transportation such as bikes; increasing the awareness levels of hospital personnel along with implementing them with strict compliance efforts (Johnson, 2010, 80).

On another account, the American Society of Healthcare Food Service Administrators share common ground in their sustainability efforts. One sustainable measure on top of everyone's list is buying local food products from accredited farmers and businesses within the community while adhering to quality standards of produce. Other measures include managing costs through the control of fuel surcharges built in to food costs; control of leftovers and the review of portions and demands; periodical evaluation of patient menus and cafeteria menus; exploration of pod assembly and the tray passing process as opposed to room service; balanced use of cook-chill and cook-serve approaches; hiring of culinary trained chefs and nutrition care assistants; and use of computer systems management among many others ("Healthcare," 2008).

Indeed, initiatives undertaken by the health care industry are getting greener each year with the common intentions on cost savings, quality of indoor environment, long-term benefits on sustainability, and in support of the hospital mission. A survey of 6,879 hospitals, with a response rate of 14.2 percent, presented new realities in 2010, putting energy management, water management, and waste management as top priorities. Some noteworthy points are: (1) 50 percent of health care facilities conduct energy audits, and 80 percent find value in preventive maintenance plans; (2) 55 percent will install flow control fixtures on faucets, toilets, and urinals to conserve water; and (3) over 90 percent are engaged in the recycling of cardboard and paper, while nearly 60 percent are tracking their waste volume.

Moreover, nearly 80 percent are active in green cleaning initiatives, which are exemplified in the use of microfiber mops and cloths to reduce water and chemical consumption, and the use of cleaning chemicals that do not negatively harm indoor air quality (Carpenter, 2010). Sustainable health care strategies also comprise new measures, such as the supply of certified green cleaning products (Williamson, 2010); review of policies on prediluted disinfectants for workers' safety; modifications toward preferable cleaning policies of floor, walls, furniture, and equipment; and limiting personnel's exposure to hazardous chemicals, biological products, and contaminants (Carpenter, 2010). The EPA has already cautioned the public as early as 1987 on the environmental effects of the health care industry in terms of waste (Messelbeck & Sutherland, 2000). In fact, even the research and development of medical products and pharmaceutical companies has responded with global health care management (HMI) systems to expand the health care system's performance (Seror, 2001).

With the statistics that every bed in the hospital equates to 25 to 30 pounds of waste, every effort toward efficiency and sustainability matters, which extends to measures by biomedical research facilities. Over 4,500 facility managers and professionals embody the Association of Higher Education Facilities Officers (APPA) in North America, a group that has structured programs at the local, regional, and national levels to conduct education and information efforts in sustainability. The group echoes similar environmental paradigms in purchasing and administrative services; water consumption; campus grounds and land use;

transportation; new campus planning, design and construction; and responsible business practices (Malcolm, 2007; Medlin & Grupenhoff, 2000).

Beyond the larger focus on balancing high performance building and human health, the health care industry is nonetheless making its contribution to the sustainability movement.

THELMA LAZO-FLORES

See also: Community Economic Development and Substantive Participation (Activism); Complementary and Alternative Medicine (Health).

References

Carpenter, Dave. 2008. "Greening Up." *Health Facilities Management* 21:7: 15–21.

Carpenter, Dave. 2010. "Green + Greener." *Health Facilities Management* 23:7: 15–21.

Gallagher-Rogers, Mellisa. 2011. "LEED for Healthcare." *Environmental Design & Construction* 14:4: 30.

"Healthcare Leaders Speak Out." 2008. *Foodservice Director* 21:8: 20–22.

Jameton, Andrew, and Jessica Pierce. 2001. "Environment and Health: Sustainable Health Care and Emerging Ethical Responsibilities." *Canadian Medical Association* 164:3: 365–369.

Johnson, Sherryl. 2010. "Summarizing Green Practices in U.S. Hospitals." *Hospital Topics* 88:3: 75–81.

Kinney, L. M. 2010. "Environmental Sustainability in Healthcare." *Journal for Quality & Participation* 33:2: 23–26.

Malcolm, Christine. 2007. "High-Performance Building and Human Health." *Environmental Design & Construction* 10:8: 48–50.

Medlin, E. L., and John T. Grupenhoff. 2000. "Environmental Practices for Biomedical Research Facilities." *Environmental Health Perspectives* 108:6: 945–948.

Messelbeck, James, and Lare Sutherland. 2000. "Applying Environmental Product Design to Biomedical Products Research." *Environmental Health Perspectives* 108:6: 997–1002.

Samet, Kenneth, A. 2011. "Healthier Hospitals Initiative." *Healthcare Executive* 26:4: 60–63.

Seror, Ann. 2001. "The Internet, Global Healthcare Management Systems, and Sustainable Development: Future Scenarios." *Electronic Journal on Information Systems in Developing Countries* 5:1: 1–18.

"Sustainability in Healthcare Food and Nutrition Services." 2011. *Food Management* 46:7: 9.

Vernon, Walter N. 2009. "Helping Hands: Leaders in the Healthcare Sustainability Movement." *Journal of Healthcare Management* 54:4: 227–230.

"Who's Who in Health Care Sustainability." 2008. *H&HN: Hospitals & Health Networks* 82:8: 26.

Williamson, Julie E. 2010. "Hospitals, Vendors Take Colorful Approaches to Green Cleaning." *Healthcare Purchasing News* 34:4: 36–43.

Wood, John. R. 2008. "Building a Green Future." *Health Facilities Management* 21:4: 38.

LANDSCAPING AND XERISCAPING

Although landscaping can facilitate people's connection to plant life, local wildlife, and the natural world in general, so-called traditional landscaping can also be detrimental to the environment in a number of ways. Paramount among environmentalists' concerns about traditional landscaping is that its upkeep requires a tremendous amount of water. The maintenance of traditional turf lawns and exotic plants (which originated in climates different from the ones is which they are currently planted) accounts for over 50 percent of residential water use in an era when unpolluted water is becoming increasingly scarce and precious (Rubin, 2002, 11, 13). Given that the planet's water supply is finite and that one-sixth of the world's population lacks access to clean, safe drinking water (Bennett, 2005, 12; Rubin, 2002, 11; World Water Council, n.d.), responsible gardening practices that conserve water make a positive contribution to the long-term health of the planet. Xeriscaping, from the Greek *xeros* (dry) and landscaping (Ellefson et al., 1992, 3), serves as an environmentally conscientious alternative to traditional landscaping.

Xeriscaping

Xeriscaping goes by a number of alternative names, including xerogardening, dry-land gardening, drought-tolerant landscaping, and smart scaping. Regardless of the terminology used, xeriscaping constitutes a form of ecologically harmonious garden design and maintenance that conserves water by greatly reducing (or in some instances even eliminating) the need for irrigation. This is achieved in part through the use of native plants, those that are native to the area in which they are to be planted. In the United States, xeriscaping is employed primarily in arid and semiarid regions, as well as in areas in which water is in short supply relative to the demands

An elaborate, yet water-saving xeriscape design that features 20 different species of plants and 12,000 square feet of synthetic turf has been installed at the Navy Exchange (Hawaii) Mall and Commissary at Pearl Harbor in 2010. (U.S. Navy)

of the growing local population. Most sources agree that xeriscaping should be guided by some version of the following seven landscaping principles: planning and design, making soil improvements, efficient irrigation, selecting appropriate plants, mulching the soil, using turf alternatives, and appropriate maintenance (Denver Water, 2011; Ellefson et al., 1992, 9; Weinstein, 1999, viii–ix). Although xeriscaping can radically reduce water consumption, roadblocks to the widespread adoption of xeriscaping remain, including public misperceptions about its aesthetic potential.

The Seven Principles of Xeriscaping

Planning and Design: A plan drawn to scale will facilitate water conservation if it includes not only existing structures such as walls and fences and existing plants, but also areas of shade, slopes, spigots, and low areas where water naturally collects.

Making Soil Improvements: Although soil amendments may not be necessary when planting only native plants, aerating or loosening the soil, as well as adding organic material (compost or manure), can help the soil both retain water and permit it to drain.

Efficient Irrigation: Efficient irrigation entails protecting water from evaporation (by not watering between 10:00 A.M. and 6:00 P.M.) and from waste (by installing and using a rain delay or rain sensor for automatic systems). Irrigation methods should be selected for the specific needs of particular plants (trees, turf, flowerbeds). Deep, infrequent watering promotes the growth of deep roots.

Selecting Appropriate Plants: Plants should be selected for water efficiency and grouped together in zones according to similar needs for water and exposure to sun. No one plant or subset of plants is deemed universally "best" for landscapers and home gardeners to use, but rather landscapers are advised to select plants for compatibility with their particular region and each other. Color and variety are both possible and desirable.

Mulching the Soil: Mulches provide a host of benefits, including cooling plant roots and minimizing evaporation. Mulches can be organic (wood grindings, bark chips) or inorganic (gravel, rocks). Inorganic mulches should be used with care as they can radiate heat.

Using Turf Alternatives: A great deal of water can be conserved by replacing traditional lawns with native grasses or other ground cover with minimal water needs.

Appropriate Maintenance: Even xeriscaped gardens require some degree of ongoing maintenance in the form of pruning, watering, fertilizing, and control of pests.

Benefits and Challenges of Xeriscaping

Xeriscaping can greatly reduce the amount of water used to irrigate residential landscapes, but xeriscaping has benefits beyond water conservation. During droughts and other times of water stress, xeriscape plants are more likely to thrive and remain colorful than exotic plants would under the same conditions (Cooke, 2008, 10). Designing a garden with native plants and improving the quality of one's soil reduces maintenance and reduces or eliminates reliance on chemicals such as fertilizers and pesticides. Native plants also create a natural habitat that is likely to attract local wildlife. Additionally, since gas lawn mowers are no longer needed when turf alternatives replace lawns, xeriscaping has the potential to conserve fossil fuel and reduce pollution (Eartheasy, 2011).

Despite its many benefits, xeriscaping is underutilized in the United States. Even though the maintenance of many nonnative plants and grass lawns is expensive and time consuming, many Americans are reluctant to switch to more sustainable landscaping methods (Rubin, 2002, 23–24). In our current era of water scarcity, explanations for Americans' adherence to the lush lawn aesthetic range from the evolutionary (humans are genetically encoded to prefer short grass), to the cultural (lawns are a form of conspicuous consumption connoting wealth and social class), to the historical and economic (chemical and munitions industries shifted to fertilizer and pesticide production and promotion in the post–World War II era) (Wasowski, 2000, 9–16). Even homeowners who consider themselves to be environmentally conscious may be swayed by misconceptions that xeriscaping necessarily entails a stark, colorless, rock garden punctuated only with cacti (Xeriscape Landscaping Organization, 2011; Wasowski, 2000, 21). In fact, some environmentalists object to the use of the term zero-scaping (as a synonym for xeriscaping) for this very reason: they believe that it fosters public misperceptions about the aesthetic potential of xeriscaped gardens and yards. Environmentalists seeking to promote xeriscaping as a means of conserving water and other resources might do well to emphasize that xeriscaped gardens can include a large variety of colorful, native plants.

How Much Conservation is Enough?

Finally, a debate among proponents of xeriscaping centers on whether some exotic plants may accompany native plants or whether solely native plants are desirable as a means of restoring natural habitats (Rubin, 2002, 27). Part of what is at stake is the issue of whether the ultimate goal of xeriscaping is to minimize watering or to eradicate irrigation altogether once plants are established. Environmentalists of good conscience disagree about whether exotic plants have any place in a "natural" garden, and whether incremental steps toward conservation are sufficient, given the world population's increasing needs for clean drinking water. Ellefson et al. (1992, 73) suggest that xeriscaping principles can be adapted to the goals of the gardener, and that any plant can find a place in the xeriscaped garden if its needs match the climate of the region in which it is to be planted.

TRACY ROYCE

See also: Composting and Vermicomposting (Health); Garden, Home (Health); Water Quality and Use (Environment).

References

Bennett, Jennifer. 2005. *Dryland Gardening: Plants that Survive and Thrive in Tough Conditions*. Buffalo, NY: Firefly Books.

Cooke, Ian. 2008. *Waterwise Gardening: Water, Plants, and Climate: A Practical Guide*. London: New Holland Publishers.

Denver Water. 2011. "Xeriscape Plans." Available at: http://www.denverwater.org/Conservation/Xeriscape/XeriscapePlans/.

Eartheasy. 2011. "Solutions for Sustainable Living, Xeriscape." Available at: http://eartheasy.com/grow_xeriscape.htm.

Ellefson, Connie L., Thomas L. Stephens, and Douglas F. Welsh. 1992. *Xeriscape Gardening: Water Conservation for the American Landscape*. New York: Macmillan.

Filippi, Olivier. 2008. *The Dry Gardening Handbook: Plants and Practices for a Changing Climate*. London: Thames and Hudson.

Rubin, Carole. 2002. *How to Get Your Lawn Off Grass: A North American Guide to Turning Off the Water Tap and Going Native*. Madeira Park, Canada: Harbour Publishing.

Wasowski, Andy, with Sally Wasowski. 2000. *The Landscaping Revolution: Garden With Mother Nature, Not Against Her*. Chicago: Contemporary Books.

Weinstein, Gayle. 1999. *Xeriscape Handbook: A How-To Guide to Natural, Resource-Wise Gardening*. Golden, CO: Fulcrum Publishing.

World Water Council. n.d. "Water Crisis." Available at: http://www.worldwatercouncil.org/index.php?id=25.

Xeriscape Landscaping Organization. 2011. "Myths." Available at: http://xeriscapelandscaping.org/Myths.html.

LIGHTING DESIGN, SUSTAINABLE

Sustainable lighting design is associated with two major components: "waste prevention by reducing weight, toxicity, and energy use; and better material management through manufacturing, recycling, composting, and energy recovery" (Winchip, 2005, 295). A study on human activity patterns by the U.S. Environmental Protection Agency in 1994 indicated that the average American spends 87 percent of their time indoors, 69 percent in residences, and 18 percent at work and other indoor locations (IED, 2011). Under this premise, the dependency of man on two types of indoor lighting becomes evident: natural and artificial. Lighting in both interior and exterior spaces has four important effects on the user: creates a desired ambience, directs a visual focus and attention, controls shading and shadow, and provides or modifies a spatial perception (Pile, 2007, 332).

In the discussion of green issues in lighting design and use of electricity, we can focus on the involvement of five different groups: the self-users; design group (designers, architects, and builders); lighting industry group (fixture designers, engineers, and manufacturers); professional associations and organizations; and government agencies and offices. All of them address sustainability in multiple ways.

First, the individual or self-user depends on light to complete everyday tasks. Consequently, the self-user needs to be conscious of sustainable lighting in the context of what is cost effective, protective of the environment, and conserves energy. Good lighting decisions in the space are also associated with light levels, control of brightness, contrast and glare, control contrast and diffusion, and the economic issues (Pile, 2007). Experts note that the self-user takes more initiative in making energy-efficient lighting choices than the commercial building owner or investor. A consumer shows initiative in the use of light-emitting diode (LED) technology and LED luminaires (Lightlife, 2010). LED is considered by many as the new era in lighting technology, with its revolutionary improvement in the mid-1990s. It was originally introduced in the 1950s as the "first solid-state electronic light source for lighting" (Winchip, 2005, 96). Multiple reviews indicate the many advantages of LED lamps, such as their compact dimensions; durability; controllability; consumption of minimal electrical power; use of less electrical materials; ability to change color temperature; zero-emission of ultraviolet and infrared radiation; directional source; long service life; minimal maintenance; energy-saving potentials; and their eco-friendly technology ("LED," 2010; Winchip, 2005).

Compact fluorescent lightbulbs cost about 75 percent less to operate than incandescent bulbs and last about 10 times longer. (Picstudio/Dreamstime.com)

Second, the design group (designer, architect, and building contractor) addresses every project with energy-efficient methods and conscientious adherence to lighting performance standards, codes, and regulations at the national and local levels. They follow multiple methods and consider many levels of efficiency as they integrate both artificial lighting and day lighting into a building envelope. Designers consider daylight not only an attractive form of illumination in any room, but it is also the only completely low carbon, sustainable light source (Lynch, 2010). The amount of illumination from a regular three-by-five-foot window is similar to about 60- to 100-watt incandescent lamps (Winchip, 2005, 288). The design group treats every space as an opportunity for the assessment of lighting quantity and quality. Quantity of light is associated with the level of illuminance and is measured in footcandles, while lighting quality is the appropriate amount of light for the space (Benya &

Greenovations: Tips for Energy Efficiency

Energy Saving Tips: Lighting

The following energy-saving tips for lighting comes from the U.S. Small Business Administration:

- Turn off lights (and other equipment) when not in use. High utility costs often include paying for energy that is completely wasted.
- Replace incandescent lightbulbs with ENERGY STAR qualified compact fluorescent lamps (CFLs) (http://www.energystar.gov/index.cfm? fuseaction=find_a_product.showProductGroup &pgw_code=LB), wherever appropriate. CFLs cost about 75 percent less to operate and last about 10 times longer.
- Install switch plate occupancy sensors in proper locations to automatically turn off lighting when no one is present and back on when people return. Even good equipment can be installed wrong, so don't install the sensor behind a coat rack, door, bookcase, etc. It must be able to "see" an approaching person's motion to turn on the light before or as they enter an unlit area.
- Adjust lighting to your actual needs; use free "daylight" during the day.
- To prevent glare, eyestrain and headaches, do not "over-light." Too much light can be as bad for visual quality as too little light—and it costs a lot more.
- Install ENERGY STAR qualified exit signs (http://www.energystar.gov/index.cfm?c=exit_ signs.pr_exit_signs). These exit signs can dramatically reduce maintenance by eliminating lamp replacement, and can save up to $10 dollars per sign annually in electricity costs while preventing up to 500 pounds of greenhouse gas emissions.
- Consider upgrading to T8 (1" diameter) fluorescent lamp tubes with solid-state electronic ballasts that are more efficient than older T12 (1.5" diameter) tubes with magnetic ballasts.

KIM KENNEDY WHITE

Source: Tips for Energy Efficiency. U.S. Small Business Administration. Available at: http://www.sba.gov/ content/energy-efficiency.

Leban, 2011, 205). Footcandle is defined as "the amount of light that falls on a surface in a one-foot radius of the source" (Winchip, 2005, 700). In a lighting energy audit for indoors, one basic evaluative model is to assess its quality lighting input using the Q and L equation. The Q represents the goal to achieve the optimum benefits, and the L represents the minimum negative load on the environment (Novitsky, 2010).

Lighting specialists also examine the current electrical power available in a building structure, since "major reductions in energy saving must also emanate from the refurbishment of existing buildings" (Lynch, 2010, 80). A lighting retrofit assessment is the solution to spaces that are underlighted or overlighted. A retrofitting task should be referenced to the Illumination Engineering Society (IES) handbook, where illumination levels are broadly categorized into the seven clusters of activities in a space, required footcandle associated to the activity, and typology of space (e.g., quiet room, corridor, lobby, etc.) (Benya & Leban, 2011, 206–207).

The third group is composed of lighting fixture designers, technical engineers, and manufacturers who represent the lighting industry. These experts are committed to sustainable practices as indicated in the dynamic research and development of technology and energy-efficient systems, such as the creation and production of lighting devices and fixtures and the distribution and waste disposal of products and electrical materials. In architectural lighting alone, over 200 innovative lighting products and systems are introduced each year, such as decorative; industrial; lamps, ballasts, and controls; LEDs and drivers; outdoor and landscape; and specialty (Moffat, 2010, 23). The emphasis in product development is in green models and energy-efficient technology. Further, the National Electrical Manufacturers Association (NEMA) and the Lightfair International also promote environmentalism and ethical behavior in business practices. Through their initiatives, it is much easier now than decades ago to find innovative fixtures that comply with green certification processes and provide carbon footprint analyses and information on energy consumption levels (Casey, 2008).

Fourth, there are various professional organizations, research laboratories, and trade associations that support the legislation of guidelines and standards, facilitate certification programs, plan for educational seminars and workshops for the promotion of green awareness, and provide scholarships for lighting design and engineering. Some professional programs committed to environmentalism include the Illumination Engineering Society of North America (IESNA), American Lighting Association (ALA), The National Council on Qualifications for the Lighting Profession (NCQLP), National Science Foundation (NSF), Lighting Systems Research Group, Energy Star Program, and International Association of Energy Efficient Light (IAEEL). They also disseminate information on research and development of emerging luminaires and lighting systems that support the health, welfare, and safety of end users. Both ALA and NCQLP facilitate certification programs for designers, architects, and contractors (Asay & Patton, 2010). The most popular of the agencies is the U.S. Green Building Council's Leadership in Energy and Environmental Design (LEED), which oversees sustainable lighting design practices through waste prevention and better material choices.

The last group is composed of various government agencies, such as the U.S. Department of Energy, U.S. Environmental Protection Agency, National Fenestration Rating Council (NFRC), and the Office of Energy Efficiency and Renewable Energy (EERE), which create policies and evaluative procedures to protect our ecological equilibrium; use of nonrenewable resources; minimize light, air, water, and soil pollution; and eliminate use of toxic substances (Winchip, 2005, 297). The government also creates tools for building rating systems, lighting assessment in residential and commercial places, designating eco-labels on products, and raising consumer awareness.

THELMA LAZO-FLORES

See also: Home Furnishings and Interior Design (Health); LED Lighting (Science).

References

Asay, Nancy, and Marciann Patton. 2010. *Careers in Interior Design*. New York: Fairchild.

Benya, James R., and Donna J. Leban. 2011. *Lighting Retrofit and Relighting*. Hoboken, NJ: Wiley.

Casey, Megan. 2008. "Going Green: Lighting Manufacturers Tackle Sustainable Business Practices." *Architectural Lighting* (June): 23–24.

Indoor Environment Department (IED). 2011. Staff of the Environmental Energy Technologies Division. "*Commercial Building Ventilation and Indoor Environmental Quality—Indoor VOCs.*" Available at: http://eetd.lbl.gov/ie/viaq/v_voc_1.html.

"LED—The Age of Lighting." 2010. *Lightlife* 4.

Lynch, Henrietta. 2010."Sustainable Society." *Mondo* 56 (August/September): 80.

Moffat, Sallie. 2010. "2010 Product Guide." *Architectural Lighting* (April/May): 23.

Novitsky, B. J. 2010. "It Isn't Easy Grading Green." *Greensource* (May/June): 53.

Pile, John F. 2007. *Interior Design.* Upper Saddle River, NJ: Pearson.

Winchip, Susan. 2005. *Designing a Quality Lighting Environment.* New York: Fairchild.

POPULATION AND FAMILY

Human population growth is the primary cause of greenhouse gas production and deforestation. The U.S. population of approximately 300 million ranks third worldwide after India and China. Among all industrialized nations, the United States has the highest fertility rate, with an annual growth rate of 3.3 million (SUSPS). The disproportionate use of resources by the U.S. population compared to other nations is a driving factor in environmental degradation worldwide. Natural resource and energy use in the United States contributes to deforestation of tropical forests, which accounts for an annual rise of 5.9 billion tons carbon dioxide (CO_2) in the atmosphere (Trees for Travel). This continued trend will result in an added 282 billion tons of CO_2 in the next 50 years.

To avoid causing irreversible environmental damage, the transition from fossil fuels like coal and oil to sustainable sources of energy (solar, wind, water) needs to occur within decades, according to organizations involved in efforts to address the anthropogenic contribution to greenhouse gases. In the meantime, mitigating population growth

New suburban homes replace farmland on the west side of Des Moines, Iowa. (U.S. Department of Agriculture)

would vastly reduce the environmental impact that humans have on the environment.

Concern over population control varies greatly among Americans and is somewhat of a cultural taboo. The topic of overpopulation is often ignored even by environmental groups because it can lead to disinterest in the environmental movement. The notion of population control is offensive to many because it relates to the sensitive topics of race/ethnicity, religion, immigration, women's rights, civil liberties, and industrial development, among others.

Though population control remains controversial, shifting the discussion to focus on how women's education relates to population holds the potential to advance the environmental movement. The relationship between women's education and parity is a clear indicator of the solution to the population problem. Namely, for each year of education a woman receives, she has fewer children (Population Reference Bureau). Upon further investigation, it has been demonstrated that this relationship holds true across cultures, although it is dependent on the type of education received. Women must have reproductive health and family planning education in addition to contraceptive access to realize the benefits of their education in the context of making reproductive decisions.

Increasing the opportunities for reproductive and environmental health education has the potential to reduce unwanted pregnancies and improve health among those who choose to reproduce. The estimated number of unplanned pregnancies in the United States is 400,000, which can be indirectly attributed to political influences restricting access to reproductive education and health services. Despite the seeming ease with which Americans are intentionally or nonintentionally reproducing, biological fertility rates have actually declined over the past 50 years (Carlsen et al., 1992). Declining fertility is likely related to environmental toxic exposure to chemicals, such as endocrine disruptors in the form of petroleum-based compounds and persistent pollutants. As a result, assisted reproductive technology (ART) is used widely. In addition, the costs associated with ART medical procedures such as in vitro fertilization (IVF) and hospital costs due to multiple births resulting from IVF are high, at an estimated $640 million per year in the United States (Van Voorhis, 2007). Reducing exposure to chemical pollutants through environmental health education has the potential of improving the health among those reproducing and perhaps decreasing the need for expensive ART procedures.

Despite the continued desire of Americans to reproduce, social scientists have failed to find an association between having children and happiness (Powdthavee, 2008). On the contrary U.S. and European scholars have reported that parents often report statistically significantly lower levels of happiness (Alesinaa et al., 2004), life satisfaction (Di Tella et al., 2001), marital satisfaction (Twenge et al., 2003), and mental well-being (Oswald & Clark, 2002) compared with nonparents. These findings were found to extend beyond the time when children are dependent on their parents; in other words, "parenting brings challenges that last a lifetime" (Glenn & McLanahan, 1981).

A number of groups have emerged representing those who choose not to have children of their own. Childfree, Childless by Choice, No Kidding!, the

International Social Club for Childfree Couples and Singles, Green Inclined, No Kids, and the Voluntary Human Extinction Movement are some examples. These groups represent a shift toward greater consciousness about the decision to reproduce and perhaps the realization that there are many opportunities to positively impact children's lives regardless of biological parenthood. Conscientious decision making about family composition supports an expanded view of what constitutes an American family, the definition of which now extends to reach a wide group of individuals that includes multiple cultures, multiple generations, single parents, step-parents, same-sex couples, adopted children, and biological children.

RAINBOW VOGT

See also: Population (Environment).

References

Alesinaa, Alberto, Rafael Di Tellab, and Robert MacCulloch. 2004. "Inequality and Happiness: Are Europeans and Americans Different?" *Journal of Public Economics* 88: 2009–2042.

Carlsen, E., A. Giwercman, N. Keiding, and N. Skakkebaek. 1992. "Evidence for Decreasing Quality of Semen During Past 50 Years." *British Medical Journal* 305: 609–613.

Di Tella, Rafael, Robert J. MacCulloch, and Andrew J. Oswald. 2001. "The Macroeconomics of Happiness." Available at: http://www2.warwick.ac.uk/fac/soc/economics/staff/academic/oswald/macrohappinessoct2001.pdf.

Glenn, Norval D., and Sara McLanahan. 1981. "The Effects of Offspring on the Psychological Well-Being of Older Adults." *Journal of Marriage and Family* 43:2: 409–421.

Oswald, Andrew J., and Andrew E. Clark. 2002. "Well-Being in Panels." Department of Economics, University of Warwick, UK. Available at: http://www2.warwick.ac.uk/fac/soc/economics/staff/academic/oswald/revwellbeinginpanelsclarkosdec2002.pdf.

Population Reference Bureau. "Demographic and Health Surveys, 2003–2006." Available at: http://www.prb.org/Educators/TeachersGuides/HumanPopulation/Women.aspx.

Powdthavee, N. 2008. "Putting a Price Tag on Friends, Relatives, and Neighbours: Using Surveys of Life Satisfaction to Value Social Relationships." *Journal of Socio-Economics* 37:4: 1459–1480.

SUSPS (Support U.S. Population Stabilization). "U.S. Birth Rates and Population Growth." Available at: http://www.susps.org/overview/birthrates.html.

Trees for Travel. Available at: http://www.treesfortravel.info/consumer/faqs.html.

Twenge, Jean M, W. Keith Campbell, and Craig A. Foster. 2003. "Parenthood and Marital Satisfaction: A Meta-Analytic Review 2003. *Journal of Marriage and Family* 65:3: 574–583.

Van Voorhis, Bradley J. 2007. "In Vitro Fertilization." *New England Journal of Medicine* 356: 379–382.

TEXTILES FOR FURNITURE AND FASHION

The textile industry plays a vital role in the U.S. and world economy (Asay & Patton, 2010). Textile or fiber component, be it natural, manufactured, or synthetic, is significantly present in clothing and fashion-related products as well as furniture and furnishings. Approximately 12 million tons of textile waste is generated each year in North America, which equates to about 68 pounds of waste per household each year (Desbarats, 2010). The significant amount of materials that fashion and furniture design industries consume compels us to address sustainability and disseminate accurate information on the source and chemical content of textiles, its use and application, and the hazards posed to our health, welfare, and safety.

Differences of opinions on green issues of textiles exist among experts. Some state the quantity of textiles we consume has a minor to moderate impact on sustainable issues in comparison to other materials. Others claim that the "textile industry is one the world's largest contributor to pollution with the amount of chemicals and water" (Oecotextiles, 2011) it requires at any stage of its processing. Nonetheless, it is important to be cognizant of the green issues embracing the procurement, production, use, and disposal of textiles for fashion and furniture. Sustainability in textiles covers a wide spectrum of research: fiber, yarn, or textile production, testing and designing, textile components and finish materials, textile certification and standardization, packaging and transporting, marketing and merchandising, and its total material lifecycle (Asay & Patton, 2010; Pile, 2007; Slotkis, 2006).

In an inclusive examination of textiles for apparel, furniture, and interiors, evaluation criteria were adapted from the assessment of interior materials and specifications (Godsey, 2008, 33). The criteria included aspects such as renewable and sustainable dichotomy, recycled and recyclable dualism, durability, adaptability, embodied energy in materials, sustainable maintenance, and toxicity levels. Embodied energy is the total amount of energy stored in products or materials, such as energy in gathering the raw material, transporting to production and distribution sites, and in manufacturing (Fuad-Luke, 2002, 340). Issues and practices for each criterion are reviewed in the paragraphs that follow.

First, the raw materials in textiles, which are considered renewable, are not always sustainable when the whole product lifecycle is examined (e.g., toxic additives in the manufacturing process reduce the sustainability of natural fiber). For example, cotton is widely perceived as environmentally friendly fiber, but it is also considered the world's second most damaging agricultural crop, with 25 percent of the globally used pesticides being applied to the plants (Oecotextiles, 2011). Interests in renewable biofibers are increasing, such as those derived from bamboo, soy, algae, maize, agricultural waste, and nettle (Bocken et al., 2006). One good material is Bella-Dura, "a branded olefin which is a leading environmentally responsible fabric" (Laing, 2010, 1). This fiber is the only one on the market "that begins as a by-product of post-industrial waste from petroleum refining and ends its life as a fully recyclable product" (Laing, 2010, 1). It uses less embody energy in the manufacturing process and emits zero industrial waste.

A second criterion is the recycled or recyclable properties in textiles. Many textile designers are integrating concepts of upcycling and downcycling in material innovation. The Cradle to Cradle (C2C) certification is one example of the upcycling method for textiles. Downcycling is a process of creating a new material from the waste stream, which results in the lost of its virgin properties (Fuad-Luke, 2002). The purchase of a 250-gram cotton shirt implies using 1,700 grams of fossil fuel, depositing 450 grams of waste into the landfill, and emitting 4 kilograms of carbon dioxide (CO_2) into the atmosphere. However, cotton fabric produced from recovered cotton during the spinning, weaving, or cutting process is another example of upcycling. Yarns derived from postconsumer and postindustrial polyester waste are given a new life in textile production. Postconsumer polyester is made from consumer-discarded polyester, while postindustrial polyester is derived from industrial overruns and obsolete inventories. Recycled polyester reduces oil dependency and waste and contributes less pollution (Laing, 2010, 7). The use of lyocell, a material that is derived from wood pulp, is increasing since the chemicals used for its production are less hazardous to the environment than those used for the production of viscose rayon. The solvent is also recycled efficiently and the wood is harvested from fast-growing eucalyptus trees, making lyocell more environmentally friendly than rayon and acetate (Kadolph, 2010).

The third green criterion is to assess the additives present in textile for durability properties. Researchers have developed nontoxic substances to raise the durability of textiles, resist abrasion and staining, and reduce reaction to natural light. One example is the shear-thickening fluid (STF) added in smart impact protection textiles for apparel and furniture, which increases the rate of shear. The use of reclaimed fibers of olefin, another by-product of petroleum refining, can be added to upholstery materials to increase stain resistance (Brownell, 2008, 172).

Fourth, production value on the adaptability of textiles has also been evaluated as evidenced in the flexibility of finish measurements for widths and lengths, design patterns, and weave construction.

A fifth green consideration of textiles is the presence of low-embodied energy in production and being locally sourced. Linen has been found to be a lower embodied energy fabric than wool since it undergoes fewer layers of production stages. Specification and utilization of textiles from local sources equate to savings in transportation energy for purchase and distribution. In reducing the environmental impacts of textile production, attempts are being made to develop alternative fibers from renewable materials.

The sixth criterion is the quality of textiles to be sustainably maintained. Polyester fibers were found to be more environmentally friendly compared to cotton, since they require less energy for maintenance, including washing, drying, and ironing. Bamboo is known for its fast growth with sufficient rainfall, and it does not depend on fertilizers or pesticides and requires little irrigation (Laing, 2010).

Research on nontoxic additives in textiles is the last green criterion that affects the well-being of users. Many conventional fabrics have multiple carcinogens in them (e.g., chemicals like formaldehyde causes headaches, while glass and metallic fibers cause some chest pains, fatigue, and impaired vision).

Research and development continue to advance the use of textiles that are not only useful in fashion and furniture, but also in other items such as fabric-based architectural structures called Airtecture; electro-luminescent window coverings; energy-harvesting curtains; programmable fabric-light emitting diode (FabriLED);

bi-elastic textiles for large commercial interior installations, and as postindustrial building insulation materials (Brownell 2006, 2008).

THELMA LAZO-FLORES AND JINHEE NAM

See also: Beauty, Cosmetics, and Makeup (Health); Green Your Holiday Scene (documents); Home Furnishings and Interior Design (Health).

References

Asay, Nancy, and Marciann Patton. 2010. *Careers in Interior Design.* New York: Fairchild Books.

Bocken, Nancy, Soren E. Laursen, and Cecilia M. De Rodriguez. 2006. *Well Dressed?: The Present and Future Sustainability of Clothing and Textiles in the United Kingdom.* Cambridge: University of Cambridge Institute for Manufacturing.

Brownell, Blaine. 2006. *Transmaterial.* New York: Princeton Architectural Press.

Brownell, Blaine. 2008. *Transmaterial 2.* New York: Princeton Architectural Press.

Desbarats, A. 2010. "Let's Keep Our Clothing Out of Our Landfills." Available at: http://eartheasy.com/blog/2010/05/lets-keep-clothing-out-of-our-landfills/.

Fuad-Luke, Alastair. 2002. *Eco-Design: The Sourcebook.* San Francisco: Chronicle Books.

Godsey, Lisa. 2008. *Interior Design Materials and Specifications.* New York: Fairchild Books.

Kadolph, S. 2010. *Textiles.* Upper Saddle River, NJ: Prentice-Hall.

Laing, Dayle. 2010. "Glossary of Textile Terms." Available at: http://daylelaing.com.

Oecotextiles. 2011. "Textile Industry Poses Environmental Hazards." Available at: www.Oecotextiles.com.

Rodie, J. 2008. "Greenshield™: Nanoscale Multitasking." *Textile World.* Available at: http://www.textileworld.com/Articles/2008/August_2008/Departments/QFOMAugust.Html.

Slotkis, Susan J. 2006. *Foundations of Interior Design.* New York: Fairchild Books.

"Textiles: Fashion That Doesn't Cost the Earth." 2011. Available at: http://www.scribd.com/doc/8071319/Textiles.

TOYS AND COLLECTIBLES

Toys are a major part of American culture. Birthdays, holidays, and other special events are all occasions for gifting toys. Toys become obsolete to people as they age and are replaced by new ones. Plastics are ubiquitous in our world and are a major component of many toys today. Look down any toy aisle in a store and you will find few products containing no plastic parts. That is potentially hundreds of millions of toys entering the environment each year, in the United States alone. As populations grow, more and more plastics are produced, and more and more toys are purchased.

Plastic Toy Production

An overview of how plastic toys are made will help us understand the environmental implications of this cycle. Plastics begin as petroleum pumped from within the earth. This crude oil is transported to settling tanks and separators to remove undesirable materials such as sand and water. It is then separated into a variety of products in a steel tank using heat. A range of products, including gasoline, asphalt, lubricating and fuel oils, synthetic rubber, plastics, and others, are produced as the heated petroleum condenses at different heights within the tank.

The plastic component resulting from this process is called naphtha. This gas is further heated and then rapidly cooled to create ethylene. When mixed with a solvent and a catalyst, a chemical reaction ensues, producing polymer chains of polyethylene. This is machined into plastic resin pellets, which are used to make a wide range of goods, including toys.

At the manufacturing plant, injection molding is most likely used to create plastic toys and parts. Plastic pellets are funneled into a tube and forced past a heating unit where they melt and get injected into a prefabricated mold. The toy is then cooled and removed from the mold. Imperfections are sanded off and paint may be applied to add detail. This process is repeated for the mass production of toys that will be sold around the world.

Environmental Implications

Degradation begins when the well is drilled to extract the crude oil from the earth. At this stage, soil and water might become polluted from spillage. This is also a possibility when the oil is stored and refined. Air pollution is another potential degradation that can occur during the processing. Once refined, the petroleum-derived products are shipped far and wide. This requires additional energy input and is a potential cause of air, water, and land degradation. Finally, all of the infrastructure required to extract and process the petroleum disturbs the local ecology and contributes to habitat fragmentation.

Environmental degradation might also occur during the manufacturing process. Here too, all of the potential problems associated with chemical spills are relevant, and additional transportation is required. If the product requires painting or sealing, the potential for chemical pollution rises. Once the finished toys are ready, energy is required to ship them to retailers.

Of the hundreds of millions of toys potentially purchased, some break or wear out. These often end up in landfills. Plastics have a long life, and some may never completely degrade. This means that more land is needed for landfill expansion. Further, some of the dyes and paints used to make toys are leached into the environment. When multiplied, these can be toxic when ingested by some forms of life.

While there are several potential causes of environmental degradation in this cycle, it should be noted that various local, state, national, and international institutions govern these at some point in the process. When compared to the rest of the world, the United States has invested significant resources in environmental quality. Further, plastics replace products made from metal and wood, thus reducing environmental degradation caused by mining and logging. In the end, there are tradeoffs, and creating a sustainable ecological footprint requires cutting our demand for new products that end up in landfills.

Reduce, Reuse, Recycle

Buying long-lasting plastics and throwing them away does not contribute to a sustainable society. Reducing demand for new plastic toys is one approach to living more sustainably. Because plastics are long lasting, those that do not break can be used by multiple children. Many of these toys can be found for resale at garage sales, flea markets, and on online retailers and auctions. This practice is especially useful for babies and young children who are not as guided by marketing. An added benefit is that some vintage toys are collectible, even in gently used condition. If a vintage toy is still usable when you are finished using it, selling it becomes easier. If it is not, the cost is often similar to a comparable new product. Switching to used toys ultimately reduces demand for and extraction of crude oil, therefore reducing the amount of potential environmental degradation in the early stages of plastic toy production. Even substituting some new toys with used or vintage toys can have a positive effect, especially when the practice is used across a population.

Although the goal is to reduce the amount of plastic entering landfills, when buying new plastic toys, look for those made of recyclable or recycled plastics. Check with your municipality or sanitation provider to see which types are recycled in your area. This way, if a toy is not usable when you are finished with it, you can recycle it and reduce the plastic content of your local landfill. Further, when consumers demand certain types of products, suppliers produce what is desired.

Plastic is an important part of our society and will continue to be so for a very long time. If we want to enjoy its benefits, we need to make the plastic cycle more sustainable. Though a small action for a household, selecting used or vintage toys, when possible, can have a large collective impact. Every time a used toy is chosen over a comparable new one, the demand for oil is lessened slightly and the potential for environmental degradation is also lessened. Over time, the entire plastic toy cycle could be optimized to minimize environmental degradation.

NATHAN EIDEM

See also: Home Furnishings and Interior Design (Health); Population and Family (Health).

References

Bryce, Douglas M. 1996. *Plastic Injection Molding: Manufacturing Process Fundamentals*. SME.

eBay. "Vintage Plastic Toys." Available at: http://www.ebay.com/sch/items/vintage%20plastic%20toys?_dmd=2&_sop=12.

Oshima, K. "Plastic Bottles Light Up Lives." CNN. Available at: http://www.cnn.com/2011/WORLD/asiapcf/08/30/eco.philippines.bottle/.

Schapiro, M. 2007. *Exposed: The Toxic Chemistry of Everyday Products and What's at Stake for American Power*. White River Junction, VT.

Slavin, B. 2005. *Transformed: How Everyday Things Are Made*. Tonawanda, NY: Kids Can Press.

Tolinski, M. 2011. *Plastics and Sustainability*. Hoboken, NJ: Wiley-Scrivener.

U.S. EPA. "Industrial Stormwater Fact Sheet Series Sector Y: Rubber, Miscellaneous Plastic Products, and Miscellaneous Manufacturing Industries," http://nepis.epa.gov/ (accessed July 25, 2011).

U.S. EPA. "Profile of the Rubber and Plastics Industry, 2nd Edition," EPA Office of Compliance Sector Notebook Project., http://www.epa.gov/compliance/resources/publications/assistance/sectors/notebooks/rubplasn.pdf (accessed July 25, 2011).

U.S. EPA. "Marine Debris Timeline," http://www.epa.gov/gmpo/edresources/debris_t.html (accessed July 25, 2011).

TRAVEL

International travel is at an all-time high, with approximately 9.8 billion outbound flights taken in 2010, representing a 5% increase in growth from 2009. International travel set a new record of 935 million trips in 2010, representing an increase in the number of international travelers by approximately 7 percent. Asia, South American, and the Middle East are experiencing the most growth in international flight, including South Korea, China, Germany, Croatia, and Mexico (ITB, 2011). The number of nights stayed during travel increased by 5 percent and spending during travel increased by 7 percent in 2010 (ITB, 2011). These figures indicate a recovery of the travel industry from the impact of the global economic recession in 2009.

The travel market to and from China is expected to lead the world within this decade, and the travel market throughout Asia, including China, South Korea Malaysia, Taiwan, Japan, Singapore, and India, is growing at double-digit rates. Japan is currently the largest Asian travel market, with 17.5 million trips in 2009, followed by China with 13.1 million trips. China is forecast to grow from 130 million international arrivals in 2009 to nearly 188 million in 2015, representing a 50 percent share of the inbound market to Asia Pacific (ITB, 2011).

The United States has more than 60 million international travelers annually, the majority (56 percent) of whom came from Canada and Mexico. In 2008, 18.9 million Canadians and 13.7 million Mexicans visited the United States, and combined they spent more than $22 billion on travel in the United States. The top five overseas markets for travelers to the United States in 2008 were the United Kingdom with 4.5 million arrivals, Japan with 3.2 million arrivals, Germany with 1.8 million arrivals, France with 1.2 million arrivals, and Italy with 780 thousand arrivals (ITB, 2011).

A combination of economic and convenience-based factors appear to drive increased awareness in the United States of the environmental impact of travel. The U.S. population travels by car and airplane, though more often by car, perhaps due to convenience factors. Leisure travelers used a car 76 percent of the time for travel between 2008 and 2009. By comparison, about 42 percent of U.S. adults reported traveling by air for leisure trips taken in 2008 to 2009. A June 2008 study by the U.S. Travel Association estimated 41 million trips were avoided over the past 12 months at a cost of more than $26 billion to the U.S. economy because of inconvenience encountered during air travel (U.S. Travel Association, 2011).

Less than one-fifth of Americans identify themselves as green, explaining why economic factors likely drive most behaviors that can be interpreted as green, but, fortunately, the environment derives benefits from any behaviors that result in less spending. A Harris Pole comparison between the 2010 and 2009 surveys of U.S. adults found that they are now more likely to describe themselves as conservationist (20 percent in 2010 versus 17 percent in 2009), green (18 percent in 2010 versus 13 percent in 2009), and environmentalist (16 percent in 2010 versus 13 percent in 2009) than they were previously. The same survey, however, found that fewer Americans are now going green, based on reporting behaviors such as likelihood of purchasing a hybrid or more fuel-efficient car (13 percent in 2009 versus 8 percent in 2010) (Steinberg, 2011). Although there may not be great interest in purchasing new cars during an economic recession, there is a growing number who rely on bicycles for transportation and practice "hypermiling" when driving a car. Hypermiling is a method of driving that increases gas mileage by making skillful changes in driving practices. Automobile dependence is aided further by public transportation and city car share programs.

Programs that are designed to offset the environmental impact of air travel include sustainable development and forestry. Trees for Travel is one example of a foundation that invests in people and nature in developing countries to neutralize the greenhouse gas emissions caused by the usage of fossil fuels released during flying and driving. Forestry projects in Malaysia, the Philippines, and Bolivia are supported by the Trees for Travel program in which native species are planted that are best suited to the local environmental conditions. Though sustainable forestry is only one part of the solution to climate change, protection of forests can reduce our carbon dioxide (CO_2) emissions by 25 percent.

The number of trees required to offset the CO_2 emissions that result from a person's travel can be calculated with an emissions calculator. Using emissions levels from an average car, someone driving 1,000 miles per year in a car will have to annually offset approximately 3 tons of CO_2. Since the average person drives for 40 years, a total of 120 tons of carbon dioxide will be produced. With an absorption capacity of 1.2 tons per acre per year, 1.25 acres of forest are required to absorb these emissions (Trees for Travel, 2011). For air travel, the calculation depends on the length of the flight. CO_2 emissions in air travel vary by the length of flight, ranging from 0.9 to 1.3 pounds of CO_2 per passenger mile. By comparison, the commuter rail and subway trains emit 0.35 pounds of CO_2 per passenger mile, and long distance trains emit 0.42 pounds of CO_2 on average. Inner-city commuting buses emit 0.66 pounds of CO_2 per passenger mile and long-distance bus trips emit 0.18 pounds of CO_2 per passenger mile (Carbon Fund, 2011).

In addition to calculations of CO_2 among environmentally savvy travelers, an entire industry called eco-tourism has emerged for those who wish to travel to "natural areas that conserve the environment and sustain the well-being of local people" (Wall, 1997). Ecotourism is one of the fastest growing industries, with annual growth rates of 10–15 percent. However, ecotourism has been criticized for its potential to endanger fragile biodiverse regions for the sake of profit. In her essay titled "Final-Commodifying of the Rainforest: The Pros and Cons of Ecotourism in Costa Rica," Khara Scott-Bey explains that "these areas have also evolved a very complex ecosystem that has been maintained for a long time and is sensitive to change, so in a sense eco-patrons are destroying that which they revere." The article goes on to explain that tourists cause disturbance when travel season interferes with the natural process of an ecosystem, such as breeding and feeding. Even in the case that on-site impact is minimized, the off-site impact still includes hotels and restaurants and other consumer industries that are inherently wasteful.

Travel itself can be considered a wasteful industry, though according to the figures above, our interest in world travel is strong and growing. Although travel necessitates the use of energy and resources, the way in which travel is performed can vastly impact how many resources are used. Ecotourism is based on a well-intended reverence of natural beauty and a genuine interest in protecting areas of biodiverse communities. While it is easy to see the flaw in ecotourism, it is also possible to travel in environmentally responsible ways to destinations of natural beauty. Traveling with an aim to limit resources used and reduce waste generated allows any traveler to be an ecotourist. The art of Chris Jordan encourages travelers to consider every decision with care, especially air travel, which consumed over 20 billion gallons of jet fuel in 2009. Jordan photographically depicts the environmental impact of 1 million plastic cups, the number used on airline flights in the United States every six hours, which do not get recycled. His photo "Packing Peanuts" depicts 166,000 packing peanuts, equal to the number of overnight packages shipped by air in the United States every hour.

RAINBOW VOGT

See also: Questions about Your Community (documents).

References

Carbon Fund. 2011. "Carbon Calculator." Available at: http://www.carbonfund.org/site/pages/carbon_calculators/category/Assumptions.

ITB. 2011. "World Travel Trends Report 2010–2011." Available at: http://www.itb-berlin.de/media/itb/itb_media/itb_pdf/worldttr_2010_2011~1.pdf

Scott-Bey, Khara. "Commodifying the Rainforest: The Pros and Cons of Ecotourism in Costa Rica." May 4, 2002. Available at http://jrscience.wcp.muohio.edu/fieldcourses01/Papers CostaRicaArticles/Final-CommodifyingtheRain.html.

Steinberg, Kathy. 2011. "Fewer Americans Going Green Behaviors since 2009." Harris Poll. Available at: http://www.harrisinteractive.com/NewsRoom/HarrisPolls/tabid/447/ctl/ReadCustom%20Default/mid/1508/ArticleId/667/Default.aspx.

Trees for Travel. 2011. Available at: http://www.treesfortravel.info/consumer/faqs.html.

U.S. Travel Association. 2011. "Travel Facts and Statistics." Available at: http://www.ustravel.org/news/press-kit/travel-facts-and-statistics.

Wall, Geoffrey. 1997. "Is Ecotourism Sustainable?" *Environmental Management* 21:4: 482–491.